ANNUAL REVIEW OF IRISH LAW 1995

Annual Review
of Irish Law 1995

Raymond Byrne
B.C.L., LL.M., Barrister-at-Law
Lecturer in Law, Dublin City University

William Binchy
B.A., B.C.L., LL.M., Barrister-at-Law
Regius Professor of Laws, Trinity College Dublin
Formerly, Research Counsellor, The Law Reform Commission

ROUND HALL SWEET & MAXWELL
DUBLIN

Published in 1997 by
Round Hall Sweet & Maxwell,
Brehon House, 4 Upper Ormond Quay,
Dublin 7.

The typesetting for this book was produced by
Gough Typesetting Services, Dublin.

A catalogue record for this book
is available from the British Library.

ISBN 1-85800-076-9

Printed by
Hartnolls Ltd, Cornwall

Table of Contents

Preface

In this ninth volume in the Annual Review series, our purpose continues to be to provide a review of legal developments, judicial and statutory, that occurred in 1995. In terms of case law, this includes those judgments which were delivered in 1995, regardless of whether they have been (or will be) reported and which were circulated up to the date of the preface. Once again, it is a pleasure to thank those who made the task of completing this volume less onerous.

Mr Justice Brian Walsh (who, as we have mentioned in previous volumes, was the originator of the concept of an Annual Review of Irish Law) continues to be most supportive and we remain very grateful for this. Once again, we are in the debt of a number of people for providing access to library facilities. In particular, Ms Peggy McQuinn, of the Office of the Supreme Court, Ms Margaret Byrne and Ms Mary Gaynor, of the Library of the Incorporated Law Society of Ireland, and Mr Johnathon Armstrong and Ms Therese Broy, of the King's Inns Library, were as helpful as ever with a number of difficult queries from the authors. And once again, Ms Jennifer Aston, Librarian in the Law Library, Four Courts, was also especially helpful in facilitating access to statutory material which is otherwise very difficult to source.

We would also like to express our heartfelt thanks to the staffs of the Dublin City University and Trinity College libraries for their assistance in the research for this volume. This ninth volume in the Annual Review series also marks a departure from previous years. The authors are delighted to have had the benefit of specialist contributions on Company Law, Communications, Contract Law, Equity and Revenue included in the volume. The authors continue to take final responsibility for the overall text as in the past, but are especially grateful for the contributions of David Tomkin and Adam McAuley in Company Law, Eamon Hall in Communications, Eoin O'Dell in Contract Law, Hilary Delany in Equity, Dermot Kelly for Revenue.

Finally, we are very grateful to Round Hall Sweet & Maxwell and Gilbert Gough, whose professionalism ensures the continued production of this series.

Raymond Byrne and William Binchy,
Dublin

November 1996

Table of Cases

Table of Legislation

Table of Statutory Instruments

Table of UK Legislation

International Treaties and Conventions

ANNUAL REVIEW OF IRISH LAW 1995

Administrative Law

GOVERNMENT FUNCTIONS

Appropriation The Appropriations Act 1995 provided as follows. For the year ended 31 December 1995, the amount for supply grants was £10,396,316,000 and for appropriations-in-aid was £963,338,000. A short-fall for the years 1991 and 1993 was also included (see also the 1993 Review, 3). Finally, the Act also established a special account for the payment of *ex gratia* compensation to victims of Anti-D related hepatitis C infection: see also the Health Services chapter, below 339. The 1995 Act came into effect on its signature by the President on December 21, 1995.

Disclosure of interests by public office holders The Ethics in Public Office Act 1995 provides for the disclosure of interests by people holding certain public offices. These include members of the Oireachtas, that is TDs and Senators, An Taoiseach, Ministers, Ministers of State, the Ceann Comhairle and Leas-Cheann Comhairle of Dáil Éireann, the Cathaoirleach and Leas-Cathaoirleach of Seanad Éireann, senior special advisors to public office holders, public and civil servants in designated positions, designated directors of state bodies and senior executives holding designated positions in state bodies. It also provides that gifts worth over £500 to office holders, their spouses and children given by virtue of that office are to be the property of the State and provides that personal appointments by office holders will be temporary and will cease when the office holder leaves office. The Act further establishes an independent Commission and a Select Committee in each House to oversee the provisions of the Act and to establish a register of interests. By virtue of the Ethics in Public Office Act 1995 (Commencement) Order 1995 (SI No.282 of 1995), the Act came into effect on 1 November 1995 insofar as it applies to all relevant office holders other than members of the Houses and the Ceann Comhairle and Leas-Cheann Comhairle of Dáil Éireann, the Cathaoirleach and Leas-Cathaoirleach of Seanad Éireann. The Ethics in Public Office (Designated Positions in Public Bodies) Regulations 1996 (SI No. 57 of 1996) specifies those offices other than those expressly referred to in the 1995 Act which come within its terms. For the categories not within SI No.282 of 1995, a resolution of the both Houses of the Oireachtas was required to bring the Act fully into effect. Such resolutions were made in 1996 and the Act thus became fully operational. We note here merely that the terms of the 1995 Act provoked widespread disagreement within the Oireachtas during its passage, but it may be seen against the background of a commitment made in the relevant programmes of government of the government which took office in 1992 as well as that which took office in December 1994.

Ministers of State: increase   The Ministers and Secretaries (Amendment) Act 1995 amended s. 1 of the Ministers and Secretaries (Amendment) (No. 2) Act 1977 in order to increase from 15 to 17 the number of Ministers of State at Departments of State. The Act came into effect on its signature by the President on January 17, 1995.

JUDICIAL REVIEW

The case law in 1995 concerning the scope of O.84 of the Rules of the Superior Courts is discussed in various chapters in this Review. Readers are advised to refer to the Table of Statutes for reference purposes.

FAIR PROCEDURES

Cross-examination at hearing   The Supreme Court decision in *Gallagher v Revenue Commissioners and Ors (No. 2)* [1995] 1 ILRM 241, in which the Court upheld the right of the applicant to require direct evidence as to the substance of disciplinary charges made against him and to cross-examine the persons making the allegations against him, was discussed in the 1994 Review, 9-10.

ULTRA VIRES

In *Walsh v Irish Red Cross Society*, High Court, 3 February 1995, Geoghegan J held that the expulsion of the applicant from membership of the respondent Society had been *ultra vires* the rules of the Society. The respondent Society had been established pursuant to the powers conferred on the Government by the Red Cross Act 1938. The Irish Red Cross Society Order 1939 (SR & O No. 206 of 1939), made under the 1938 Act, established the Society and set out various provisions governing it. The 1939 Order empowered the Executive Council of the Society to make rules governing a number of matters. The Executive Committee of the Society decided to expel the applicant from its membership on the basis that he had given an interview to a journalist allegedly detrimental to the interests of the Society. The expulsion was confirmed by an order of the Central Council of the Society, following an appeal by the applicant. At the time the applicant had given the interview, there was no express provision in the 1938 Act, the 1939 Order or the Rules of the Society made pursuant to the Order which provided for expulsion. However, subsequent to the interview and before the Executive Committee and the Central Council itself considered and determined the applicant's expulsion, rule 43 of the Society had been amended to permit expulsion.

The applicant sought judicial review, claiming that the amendment to r.43 was *ultra vires* the Central Council; alternatively that if it were *intra vires*, since the interview had occurred before the making of the amended rule, even if the rule could operate retrospectively, the expulsion was invalid for breaches of natural justice and fair procedures. In addition to opposing these arguments by the applicant, the Society argued that judicial review did not lie as the Society was a private body operating its own rules. As already indicated, Geoghegan J granted the relief sought by the applicant.

He rejected the suggestion that any argument could be made based on the terms of the 1939 Order to suggest that a rule of the Society dealing with expulsion would be *ultra vires*. He considered that, since membership of the Society was governed by the 1939 Order, the question of the right to expel was sufficiently a public law issue to enable it to be litigated by way of judicial review. The 1939 Order contemplated that the method by which people became members of the Society would be governed by the rules of the Society and nothing else. He held that the Central Council had thus been empowered to make a rule providing for expulsion, but so long as there was no rule providing for expulsion, there was no power to expel. He went on to conclude that the amended r.43 could not be interpreted to allow removal for conduct which occurred before the rule was made. In any event, he considered that if he was incorrect in that interpretation, he would have held that the amendment itself was *ultra vires* as unfair and unreasonable.

Geoghegan J's judgments also contained some further thoughts on the borderline between matters susceptible of judicial review and those which may only be litigated by means of private law remedies. In the instant case, he held that since the basic provision for membership was contained in the 1939 Order, and since the Order required a rule to be made in relation to any particular aspect of membership, the wrongful expulsion by reason of a retrospective interpretation of the rule was capable of remedy by way of judicial review. However, he also considered that in so far as the dispute between the parties concerned natural justice, this was a matter of private law involving an autonomous private society, albeit created pursuant to a public statute and statutory instrument. In this respect, he opined that if it had been necessary to consider those issues it might have been possible to avail of O.84, r.26(5) of the Rules of the Superior Courts 1986 and allow the matter to proceed as if it were a civil action. However, having regard to the view he had taken on the effect of the amended rule 43, that issue did not arise.

As Geoghegan J acknowledged, this raised the distinction adverted to in recent cases, including *Murphy v The Turf Club* [1989] IR 171 (1989 Review, 14) and *Beirne v Garda Commissioner* [1993] ILRM 1 (1992 Review, 382-3). It would seem that, notwithstanding the substantial case law on this area in recent years, the delicate refinements implicit in cases such as Walsh, in which certain decisions of one body are amenable to judicial review while other are not, are likely to remain for the foreseeable future, thus leaving open the prospect of cases being dismissed for what would appear to be a rather formal distinction lacking real substance. One wonders whether it might be more sensible to incorporate an amendment to O.84 of the 1986 Rules by which such borderline cases could be determined at an early stage, by way of motion, to fall within or without O.84 rather than leaving any doubt to be determined as part of the substantive application for judicial review, by which time limitations may have already run their course.

Agriculture

ANIMAL DISEASES

Animal: extent of definition The Diseases of Animals Act 1966 (First Schedule) (Amendment) (No. 2) Order 1995 (SI No. 97 of 1995), made under the Diseases of Animals Act 1966 extended the definition of 'animal' under the 1966 Act to all animals not already covered by previous such Orders with effect from April 26, 1995.

Bovine spongiform enecphalopathy (BSE) The European Communities (Importation of Cattle from the United Kingdom) Regulations 1995 (SI No. 152 of 1995) are referred to below, 15.

Bovine tuberculosis: movement permits In *Farrell v Minister for Agriculture and Food*, High Court, 11 October 1995, Carroll J held that Article 8 of the Cattle (General Provisions) Order 1980 were *ultra vires* the Diseases of Animals Act 1966, under which the 1980 Order had been made. In this respect, she followed the decision of Murphy J in *Howard v Minister for Agriculture and Food* [1990] 2 IR 260 (1989 Review, 17-18) where Murphy J had held a similar provision in the Bovine Tuberculosis (Attestation of the State and General Provisions) Order 1978 to be *ultra vires* the 1966 Act. In both instances, the Orders were condemned for failing to include a procedure for taking possession of diseased animals by agreement, a matter required by s.20 of the 1966 Act. Carroll J also noted that the defect in the 1980 Order had been cured through the replacement of the 1980 Order by the Cattle (General Provisions) Order 1991 (1991 Review, 20). Similarly, the 1978 Order was replaced by the Bovine Tuberculosis (Attestation of the State and General Provisions) Order 1989 (1989 Review, 17-18). In *Grennan v Minister for Agriculture and Food*, High Court, October 4, 1995, Murphy J had confirmed that the restrictions on movement contained in the 1989 Order were not *ultra vires* the Constitution. He also confirmed the view taken by the Supreme Court in *Rooney v Minister for Agriculture and Food* [1991] 2 IR 539 (1991 Review, 18-19) that the provisions of the 1989 Order did not breach any relevant provisions of the Constitution.

Deer The Diseases of Animals Act 1966 (First Schedule) (Amendment) (No. 2) Order 1995 (SI No. 276 of 1995) inserted epizootic haemorrhagic disease of deer as a Class A disease within the meaning of the 1966 Act with effect from October 20, 1995.

Pigs   The Diseases of Animals Act 1966 (First Schedule) (Amendment) (No. 2) Order 1995 (SI No. 276 of 1995) separated porcine epidemic diarrhoea and porcine corona virus into individual diseases for the purposes of the 1966 Act with effect from October 20, 1995. The Diseases Of Animals (Notification Of Infectious Diseases) Order 1992 (Amendment) Order 1995 (SI No. 275 of 1995) separated porcine epidemic diarrhoea and porcine corona virus into individual diseases for the purposes of notification under the Diseases of Animals Act 1966, also with effect from October 20, 1995. The European Communities (Swine Vesicular Disease) Regulations, 1995 (SI No. 373 of 1995) gave effect to Directive 92/119/EEC and provide for the application of control measures in the event of an outbreak of swine vesicular disease, with effect from December 31, 1995.

Rinderpest and sheep pox   The European Communities (Control Of Infectious Animal Diseases) Regulations 1995 (SI No. 277 of 1995) gave effect to Directive 92/119/EEC and introduced general Community measures for the control of Rinderpest and sheep pox with effect from October 20, 1995. The Diseases Of Animals (Notification Of Infectious Diseases) Order 1995 (SI No. 274 of 1995) made Rinderpest and sheep pox notifiable diseases under the Diseases of Animals Act 1966, also with effect from October 20, 1995.

Poultry   The Diseases Of Animals Act 1966 (First Schedule) (Amendment) Order 1995 (SI No. 46 of 1995), also made under the Diseases of Animals Act 1966 extended the definition of 'poultry' in the 1966 Act to include all birds, with effect from February 27, 1995. The Poultry, Poultry Carcasses, Poultry Eggs and Poultry Products (Restriction On Importation) Order 1971 (Amendment) Order 1995 (SI No. 47 of 1995), also made under the 1966 Act, extended the definition of 'poultry' in the 1971 Order to include all birds, also with effect from February 27, 1995.

ANIMAL WELFARE

Animal pounds: fees   The Pounds (Amendment) Regulations 1995 (SI No. 30 of 1995), made under the Pounds (Provision and Maintenance) Act 1935, increased the pound-keeper's fees prescribed in the Pounds Regulations 1985 with effect from February 13, 1995.

Animal pound: removal of animal by non-owner   In *Flannery v Dean, ISPCA and Meath Branch ISPCA* [1995] 2 ILRM 393, Costello P considered the legal implications of removing an animal from a pound by persons other than its owner. The plaintiff had had made arrangements for the stabling and maintenance of her horses at Killeen Castle, an animal pound within the meaning of the Pounds (Provision and Maintenance) Act 1935. The plaintiff agreed to provide feeding and hay and to pay for the accommodation of the horses. Some time later, the first defendant (acting on behalf of the Meath Branch of the ISPCA), together with a veterinary surgeon and members of the Garda Smochana, arrived at Killeen Castle and found that the horses were in a very poor condition. The first defendant removed the horses from Killeen Castle. A prosecution brought by against the plaintiff under the Protection of Animals Act 1911 was later dismissed. Subsequently, a number of the horses were left with third parties but when the plaintiff failed to collect them or to pay these persons for putting the horses out to grass, they contacted the first defendant, who collected many of the horses from them. The plaintiff instituted the instant proceedings seeking declarations that the horses had been removed from the various premises without title and also seeking damages. Costello P granted the declaratory relief sought against the first and third defendants but refused to award any damages or costs against them. He also dismissed all claims against the ISPCA, the second defendant. Costello P held, not surprisingly, that the horses had been taken without legal title to them from the various places where they were being kept and that the plaintiff was thus entitled to the return of the horses from the possession of the Meath Branch of the ISPCA. However, he also concluded that the plaintiff had failed to establish that she had suffered any damage, so that the claim for damages was unsustainable.

Export welfare certificates: fees   The Diseases Of Animals (Inspection Fees) Order 1995 (SI No. 133 of 1995) revised the level of fees payable in respect of the issue of welfare certificates for animals being exported, as required by the Diseases of Animals Act 1966. The Order came into effect on June 12, 1995.

Intensive farming: calves   The European Communities (Welfare Of Calves) Regulations 1995 (SI No. 90 of 1995) gave effect to Directive 91/629/EEC and laid down standards for the protection of calves kept in intensive or other systems of rearing or fattening. They set out rules for the accommodation of calves and the conditions to be met by the owner or person in charge of the calves to assure their health and safety. The Regulations came into effect on April 25, 1995.

Intensive farming: pigs The European Communities (Welfare Of Pigs) Regulations 1995 (SI No. 91 of 1995) gave effect to Directive 91/630/EEC and laid down standards for the protection of calves kept in intensive or other systems of breeding, rearing or fattening. They set out rules for the accommodation of calves and the conditions to be met by the owner or person in charge of the calves to assure their health and safety. The Regulations came into effect on April 25, 1995.

Slaughter The European Communities (Protection Of Animals At Time Of Slaughter) Regulations 1995 (SI No. 114 of 1995) gave effect to Directive 93/119/EC, and they lay down standards for the protection of animals at the time of slaughter or killing. This includes the rules for the treatment of animals prior to death and for humane methods of slaughtering and killing animals both within the slaughterhouse and at other locations such as farms in order to ensure that animals are spared avoidable pain and suffering. The Regulations are expressly stated to be subject to certain overlapping provisions of the Slaughter of Animals Act 1935 (including certain exemptions for the slaughter of animals in accordance with religious rites, such as the kosher and halal rites) and those of the Abattoirs Act 1988. The Regulations came into effect on June 1, 1995.

Transport The Diseases Of Animals (Protection Of Animals During Transport) Order 1995 (SI No. 98 of 1995), made under the Diseases of Animals Act 1966, gave effect to Directives 91/628/EEC, 92/438/EEC and Decision 94/96/EC and laid down standards for the protection of animals during transport, including rest periods and stipulation for feeding and watering during transport by road, rail, sea or air. The Order also requires that the persons who are entrusted to transport animal. possess the necessary knowledge to care for the animals. The Order came into effect on May 2, 1995.

COMMON AGRICULTURAL POLICY

Milk quotas The European Communities (Milk Quotas) Regulations 1995 (SI No. 266 of 1995) put in place the administrative arrangements necessary for the operation in the State of the milk quota system of the Common Agricultural Policy pursuant to Council Regulations 3950/92 and 2055/93 and Commission Regulations 536/93 and 2562/93. They provide for 'ring-fencing' of milk quotas within disadvantaged areas, the registration of groups of milk purchasers and joint milk purchasers, the extension of time-limits for applications under the listed milk quota Community Regulations and revised application forms. They came into effect on October 4, 1995.

EGGS AND POULTRY

The European Communities (Live Poultry and Hatching Eggs) Regulations 1995 (SI No. 45 of 1995) gave effect to Directive 93/120/EEC on animal health conditions governing intra-Community trade in and imports from third countries of poultry and hatching eggs. The Regulations came into effect on March 1, 1995.

FOOD PROMOTION

Food Promotion Board: composition The An Bord Bia (Amendment) Act 1995 amended s.14 of the An Bord Bia Act 1994 (1994 Review, 15) to provide that the membership of An Bord Bia shall consist of a chairman and 11 ordinary members or any greater number but not more than 13 ordinary members as the Minister for Agriculture shall prescribe. The Act came into effect on July 20, 1995 on its signature by the President. See also The An Bord Bia Acts 1994 and 1995 Order 1995 (SI No. 219 of 1995).

Levy The An Bord Bia Act 1994 (Levy on Slaughtered or Exported Livestock) Order 1995 (SI No. 197 of 1995), made under the An Bord Bia Act 1994 (see the 1994 Review, 15) varied the levy on slaughtered or exported livestock from 1p to 20p with effect from February 6, 1995.

MILK SUPPLY

The Milk (Regulation of Supply) Act 1994 (Section 5) (Commencement) Order 1995 (SI No. 252 of 1995) brought s. 5 of the 1994 Act, which concerns the regulation of milk supply generally in the State (1994 Review, 15) into effect on October 1, 1995. The Milk (Regulation Of Supply) (Levy) Order 1995 (SI No. 253 of 1995) provides for the amount of levy payable under the 1994 Act, with effect from October 1, 1995. The National Milk Agency (Winter Months) Regulations 1995 (SI No. 254 of 1995) specify that October to February shall be winter months for the purposes of the 1994 Act, with effect from September 26, 1995. The National Milk Agency (Members) Regulations 1995 (SI No. 234 of 1995), which came into effect on August 30, 1995, specified the number of members of the Agency's Board representing various interest groups.

PLANT HEALTH

Cereal seed The European Communities (Cereal Seed) (Amendment) Regulations 1995 (SI No. 139 of 1995) amended the European Communities (Cereal Seed) Regulations 1981 to give effect to Directive 95/6/EC and revised the conditions to be satisfied by the crop and the seeds of hybrids of rye with effect from June 9, 1995. The European Communities (Cereal Seed) (Amendment) (No. 2) Regulations 1995 (SI No. 238 of 1995) further amended the 1981 Regulations by revising the fees for cereal crop inspection and certification of cereal seed required under the Regulations with effect from September 5, 1995.

Fertilizers The European Communities (Sampling and Analysis of Fertilizers) Regulations 1995 (SI No. 157 of 1995) amended the European Communities (Sampling and Analysis of Fertilizers) Regulations 1988 in order to implement Directive 95/8/EC concerning the analysis of fertilizers for trace elements of boron, cobalt, copper, iron, manganese, molybdenum and zinc at a concentration greater than 10%. The Regulations came into effect on July 1, 1995.

Fodder plants The European Communities (Seed of Fodder Plants) (Amendment) Regulations 1995 (SI No. 224 of 1995) prescribed new fees for the certification and testing of fodder plant seed in accordance with the Regulations of 1981 to 1993 of the same title, with effect from August 25, 1995.

Oil plant seeds The European Communities (Seed of Oil Plants and Fibre Plants) (Amendment) Regulations 1995 (SI No. 53 of 1995) amended the European Communities (Seed of Oil Plants and Fibre Plants) Regulations 1981 to give effect to Directive 92/107/EEC as to the minimum varietal purity percentage for basic seed and certified seed of Glycine max. The Regulations came into effect on February 28, 1995.

Organisms harmful to plants or plant products The European Communities (Introduction of Organisms Harmful to Plants or Plant Products) (Prohibition) (Amendment) Regulations 1995 (SI No. 50 of 1995), which came into effect on February 24, 1995, implemented Directives 93/103/EC and 94/61/EC and extended the period of provisional recognition of certain protected zones of the Community to July 1, 1995. The European Communities (Introduction of Organisms Harmful to Plants or Plant Products) (Prohibition) (Amendment) (No. 2) Regulations 1995 (SI No. 92 of 1995), which came into effect on April 13, 1995, implemented Directive 95/4/EC.

The European Communities (Introduction of Organisms Harmful to Plants or Plant Products) (Prohibition) (Amendment) (No. 3) Regulations 1995 (SI No. 294 of 1995), which came into effect on November 10, 1995, implemented Directive 95/40/EC and 95/41/EC. The three sets of Regulations involved amendments to the Principal Directive in this area 77/93/EEC. The 1977 Directive was implemented by the European Communities (Introduction of Organisms Harmful to Plants or Plant Products) (Prohibition) 1980.

Pesticide residues   The European Communities (Pesticide Residues) (Cereals) (Amendment) Regulations 1995 (SI No. 164 of 1995) amended the European Communities (Pesticide Residues) (Cereals) Regulations 1988 in order to implement Directive 94/29/EC, which laid down amended maximum pesticide residue limits for a number of chemical substances in cereals. See also SI Nos. 165 and 166 of 1995, below at 15.

Plant protection products: manufacturing controls   The European Communities (Authorization, Placing on the Market, Use and Control of Plant Protection Products) (Amendment) Regulations 1995 (SI No. 200 of 1995) amended the European Communities (Authorization, Placing on the Market, Use and Control of Plant Protection Products) Regulations 1994 (1994 Review, 19) in order to implement Directives 94/37/EC, 94/79/EC and 94/93/EC and also to give effect to certain administrative arrangements necessary to implement Regulations (EC) No. 933/94 and No. 491/95 concerning the standards required in the manufacture of plant protection products.

RETIREMENT OF FARMERS

The European Communities (Retirement of Farmers) Regulations 1995 (SI No. 129 of 1995) amended the European Communities (Retirement Of Farmers) Regulations 1974 by increasing the amount of the annuity payable under the Farmers' Retirement Scheme provided for under Directive 72/160/EEC. The annuity for a single person was increased from £2,340 to £2,399 while that for a married person was increased from £3,504 to £3,592 with effect from May 1, 1995.

TRADE IN ANIMALS, ANIMAL PRODUCTS AND BY-PRODUCTS

Artificial insemination   In *O'Neill v Minister for Agriculture and Food,*

High Court, 5 July 1995, Budd J upheld the regime for the granting of licenses for the provision of artificial insemination (AI) services for agricultural animals pursuant to the Livestock (Artificial Insemination) Act 1947. Budd J considered that the conditions attaching to the licences was not in breach of the Constitution. Nor did he consider that the granting of regional monopolies within the State to certain providers, subject to periodical review, was contrary to Articles 86 or 90 of the EC Treaty. In this respect, he cited with approval the decision of the Court of Justice in *Societe Civile Agricole du Centre d'Insemination de la Crespelle v. Co-operative d'Elevage et d'Insemination Artificielle du Department de la Mayenne*, nyr, October 5, 1994.

Bulls: breeding-permits The Control of Bulls for Breeding (Permits) (Amendment) Regulations 1995 (SI No. 280 of 1995), made under the Control of Bulls for Breeding Act 1986, provided for the continuance of the system of granting permits to persons with small herds to keep unregistered bulls and extend permits already issued until October 31, 1996.

Certificates of specific character The European Communities (Certificates Of Specific Character for Agricultural Products and Foodstuffs) Regulations 1995 (SI No. 149 of 1995) specify enforcement mechanisms, including entry and inspection powers, and create criminal offences and penalties necessary to give full effect to Regulation (EEC) 2082/92. The 1992 Regulation lays down a registration and certification system to indicate that agricultural products and foodstuffs have specific characteristics, including the use of a recognised Community symbol. The 1995 Regulations came into effect on June 7, 1995.

Designation of origin The European Communities (Protection Of Geographical Indications And Designations Of Origin For Agricultural Products And Foodstuffs) Regulations 1995 (SI No. 148 of 1995) specify enforcement mechanisms, including entry and inspection powers, and create criminal offences and penalties necessary to give full effect to Regulation (EEC) 2081/92. The 1992 Regulation lays down a system to indicate the geographical origin and designation of agricultural products and foodstuffs. The 1995 Regulations came into effect on June 7, 1995.

Feedingstuffs The European Communities (Additives in Feedingstuffs) (Amendment) Regulations 1995 (SI No. 9 of 1995), which came into effect on 23 January 1995, amended the European Communities (Additives in Feedingstuffs) Regulations 1989 to give effect to Directives 93/114/EC and 94/40/EC. They introduced provisions governing the authorisation, marketing and labelling of micro-organisms and enzymes intended for use as additives in feedingstuffs, fixed guidelines for the assessment of additives in animal nutrition and established criteria for examining applications for authorisation of micro-organisms and enzymes intended for use as additives in feedingstuffs. The European Communities (Additives in Feedingstuffs) (Amendment) (No. 2) Regulations, 1995 (SI No. 44 of 1995), which came into effect on February 21, 1995, further amended the 1989 Regulations to give effect to Council Directive 94/17/EC on authorised additives in feedingstuffs and their conditions of use. The European Communities (Marketing Of Enzymes, Micro-Organisms and their Preparations in Animal Nutrition) Regulations 1995 (SI No. 237 of 1995), which should be seen against the background of SI No. 9 of 1995, above, and which came into effect on 5 September 1995, gave effect to Directive 93/113/EC. They provide that only those enzymes and micro-organisms set out in the Schedule to the Regulations may be marketed and used in animal feedingstuffs. They also set out the labelling particulars applicable to such products and premixtures and compound feedingstuffs.

Foodstuffs: pesticide residues The European Communities (Pesticide Residues) (Foodstuffs of Animal Origin) (Amendment) Regulations 1995 (SI No. 165 of 1995) amended the European Communities (Pesticide Residues) (Foodstuffs of Animal Origin) Regulations 1988 in order to implement Directive 94/29/EC, which laid down amended maximum pesticide residue limits for a number of chemical substances in foodstuffs. Similarly, the European Communities (Pesticide Residues) (Foodstuffs of Plant Origin Including Fruit and Vegetables) (Amendment) Regulations 1995 (SI No. 166 of 1995) amended the European Communities (Pesticide Residues) (Foodstuffs of Plant Origin Including Fruit and Vegetables) Regulations 1994 (1994 Review, 18) in order to implement Directive 94/30/EC, which laid down amended maximum pesticide residue limits for a number of chemical substances in foodstuffs of plant origin. See also SI No. 164 of 1995, above.

Import of animals and animal products from non-EC States: fees The European Communities (Fees on Import of Products of Animal Origin from Third Countries) Regulations 1995 (SI No. 231 of 1995) implemented Directives 85/73/EEC, 93/118/EC and 94/64/EC concerning charges for veterinary checks on animal products entering the EC from third countries: see the 1994 Review, 21. The Regulations came into force on September 1, 1995.

Import of cattle: United Kingdom The European Communities (Importation of Cattle from the United Kingdom) Regulations 1995 (SI No. 152 of

1995) implemented Decision 94/474/EC and specify the conditions under which cattle may be imported from the United Kingdom. The Regulations were made against the background of the problems associated with bovine spongiform enecphalopathy (BSE). The Regulations came into force on June 26, 1995.

Meat products The European Communities (Meat Products and Other Products of Animal Origin) Regulations 1995 (SI No. 126 of 1995) gave effect to a number of Directives, 77/99/EEC, 92/5/EEC, 92/45/EEC, 92/116/EEC, 92/118/EEC and 92/120/EEC and Decision 94/383/EC. They lay down detailed health requirements for the production (including heating, curing and wrapping) and also the marketing of meat products (including prepared meals) and other products of animal origin intended for human consumption and for the preparation of other foodstuffs. They include detailed standards for manufacturing premises and the operational procedures required for hygienic production, including the affixing of health marks on the meat products. Extensive inspection powers are also conferred on officers of the Department of Agriculture and Food. Of some interest is that Reg. 22 of the 1995 Regulations provide that they are 'applicable in lieu' of ss. 10-13, 21 and 22 of the Pigs and Bacon Act 1935 and ss. 33 and 34 of the Slaughter of Cattle and Sheep Act 1934. This express reference to the provisions of the existing statutory regime is more satisfactory than the vague allusions to such existing provisions which were criticised in the 1993 Review, 35 in relation to similar Regulations in the Agriculture sector. The 1995 Regulations also revoked a number of Regulations and Orders made under certain Acts in this area, while continuing others, all of which are referred to in Regs.22 and 23 of the 1995 Regulations. The Regulations came into effect on May 24, 1995.

Rabbit meat and farmed game The European Communities (Rabbit Meat and Farmed Game Meat) Regulations 1995 (SI No. 278 of 1995) implemented 91/495/EEC. They cover the standards to be met in the hygienic production and marketing of rabbit meat and farmed game meat so as to safeguard public and animal health. In this respect, they contain provisions similar to those in SI No. 126 of 1995, above. They came into effect on November 1, 1995.

Veterinary inspections: fees The European Communities (Fees for Health Inspections and Controls of Fresh Meat) Regulations 1995 (SI No. 34 of 1995) revised with effect from February 13, 1995 the fee payable for veterinary inspection of cattle and introduce charges for inspections of meat plants in accordance with Directive 93/118/EEC.

Wild game   The European Communities (Wild Game) Regulations 1995 (SI No. 298 of 1995) gave effect to Directive 92/45/EEC, as amended by Directive 92/116/EEC. They lay down standards for the hygienic production of wild game meat in approved officially supervised establishments so as to safeguard public and animal health. They came into effect on November 20, 1995. See also SI Nos. 126 and 278 of 1995, above.

WILDLIFE

Delay in prosecution   In *Director of Public Prosecutions v O'Donnell and Ors*, High Court, 10 February 1995 Geoghegan J considered the application of the principles concerning delay in instituting a summary criminal prosecution (as to which see *Director of Public Prosecutions v Byrne* [1994] 2 ILRM 91: 1994 Review, 172) in the context of a prosecution under the Wildlife Act 1976.

Wild birds: special protection areas   The European Communities (Conservation of Wild Birds) (Amendment) Regulations 1995 (SI No. 31 of 1995), the European Communities (Conservation of Wild Birds) (Amendment) (No. 2) Regulations 1995 (SI No. 284 of 1995), the European Communities (Conservation of Wild Birds) (Amendment) (No. 3) Regulations 1995 (SI No. 285 of 1995) and the European Communities (Conservation of Wild Birds) (Amendment) (No. 4) Regulations 1995 (SI No. 286 of 1995) amended the Schedule to the European Communities (Conservation of Wild Birds) Regulations 1985 (which had implemented Directive 79/409/EEC) by adding a number of new areas as special protection areas for wildbirds to the existing list and providing that breach of the Regulations is an offence carrying certain penalties.

Aliens and Immigration

VISA REQUIREMENTS

Additional specified States   The Aliens (Amendment) Order 1995 (SI No. 240 of 1995) amended the Aliens Order 1946 so that a citizen of Somalia requires a transit visa in order to enter the State. The Aliens (Amendment) (No. 2) Order 1995 (SI No. 314 of 1995) further amended the Aliens Order 1946 so that a citizen of the Gambia requires a transit visa in order to enter the State.

Arts and Culture

HERITAGE COUNCIL

The Heritage Act 1995 provided for the establishment of a State body, An Chomhairle Oidhreachta, the Heritage Council. The Council was established on July 10, 1995 pursuant to the Heritage Act 1995 (Establishment Day) order 1995 (SI No. 177 of 1995), thus bringing the Act fully into operation. The functions of the Council are to promote interest in, and public knowledge and appreciation of, the State's physical heritage, to promote co-operation with relevant State, public and private bodies and to increase protection of the State's built heritage. The Heritage Council replaced the non-statutory National Heritage Council.

Commercial Law

ARBITRATION

In *Portsmouth Arms Hotel v Enniscorthy UDC*, High Court, October 14, 1994, O'Hanlon J declined to remit a matter to arbitration pursuant to s. 36 of the Arbitration Act 1954. The plaintiff was the owner of a hotel which had been destroyed by fire. The defendant Council had issued a compulsory purchase order over the site of the hotel, which the plaintiff had not appealed against. The Council then served a notice to treat in 1982 pursuant to the Derelict Sites Act 1961 (since replaced by the Derelict Sites Act 1990: 1990 Review, 410-11), but this was later withdrawn. In February 1983, the Council gave notice to the plaintiff of its intention to enter on and take possession of the site. The question whether the plaintiff was entitled to compensation in the circumstances arising was referred to arbitration. The arbitrator concluded that the withdrawal of the notice to treat had been invalid and he awarded the plaintiff £67,000 in compensation. In the instant proceedings, the plaintiff sought a declaration that the Council had entered on the site and taken possession pursuant to its notice of February 1983, and that it was, therefore, entitled to claim interest on the arbitrator's award from April 1983 to the date of completion of the compulsory acquisition. The Council, in addition to resisting the payment of any interest, sought to have the award remitted back to the arbitrator, on the ground that the arbitrator had been misled into making an excessive award of compensation. The Council also claimed that the plaintiff did not have good title to the site in question. O'Hanlon J in effect refused both parties the relief they claimed.

Rejecting the plaintiff's claim, he held that the Council had only entered the site in pursuance to the notice under the Derelict Sites Act 1961 and not pursuant to the notice of February 1983. Thus, interest on the arbitrator's award only ran from the date of the making of that award.

Refusing to remit the matter back to arbitration, O'Hanlon J considered that the case did not fall into any of the four recognised categories under which an arbitration award could be remitted back to the arbitrator under s. 36 of the Arbitration Act 1956, namely misconduct, error on the face of the award, arbitrator's mistake and fresh evidence. O'Hanlon J pointed out that these four headings had been accepted as correct in the High Court in *Meenaghan v Dublin County Council* [1984] ILRM 616. See also *McStay v Assicurazioni Generali Spa* [1989] IR 248 (HC); [1991] ILRM 237 (SC)

(1991 Review, 27). Forde, *Arbitration Law and Practice* (Round Hall Press, 1994), pp. 125-7, queries whether the power to remit is confined to the four recognised categories. Nonetheless, the approach of O'Hanlon J is consistent with the 'hands off' approach to arbitration evident in other decisions to which he referred, including *Keenan v Shield Insurance Co. Ltd* [1988] IR 89 (1988 Review, 43-6).

In the instant case, O'Hanlon J held that the Council was under a legal obligation to complete the compulsory acquisition and, on good title being shown by the plaintiff, to pay the award of compensation of £67,000.

CASUAL TRADING

Casual Trading Act 1995 The expressed intention of the Casual Trading Act 1995 was to achieve greater decentralisation, efficiency and flexibility in the regulation of casual trading by local authorities than under the regime provided by the Casual Trading Act 1980, which it repealed in full. The principal reforms effected by the 1995 Act were as follows: (a) it devolved the casual trading licensing function from the Minister for Enterprise and Employment to local authorities; (b) it provided for the use of bye-laws by local authorities as the method of regulating and controlling casual trading, thus facilitating greater flexibility and efficiency in regulating casual trading; (c) it limited the list of casual trading activities excluded from the scope of Regulation by comparison with that under the 1980 Act; (d) it effected general improvement in the enforcement of casual trading legislation.

S. 2(1) of the 1995 Act specifies the general trading to which it applies, namely selling goods at a place (including a public road) to which the public have access as of right or at any other place that is a casual trading area. S. 2(2) excludes from the scope of the 1995 Act the following: (a) selling by auction (other than a Dutch auction) by the holder of licence under the Auctioneers and House Agents Acts 1947 to 1973; (b) selling to a person at a place where he or she resides or carries on business; and (c) selling where the seller shows that any profits are for use for charitable purposes or that no remuneration or profit will accrue to the seller or servants or agents of the seller. S. 2(3)· enables the Minister for Enterprise and Employment, by Regulations, to amend (whether by addition, deletion or alteration) such exempted classes of trading, while s. 2(4) enables local authorities to add to the exempted list by way of bye-laws.

S. 3 prohibits casual trading unless carried out by a person who holds a casual trading licence, and contains limitations on such casual trading. S. 4 provides that a local authority shall, subject to certain specified circum-stances, grant a casual trading licence to an applicant who pays the fee (if any) fixed under s. 6 and fulfils certain conditions, including tax clearance. The licensing system will enable a local authority to either issue a general licence without territorial limitation in its own jurisdiction, or to confine it to casual trading areas or special events. The local authority concerned will also be obliged to inform the Minister for Social Welfare when a licence is issued. S. 5 makes provision for the display of a casual trading licence. S. 6 gives general powers and flexibility to a local authority to make bye-laws relating to the control, regulation, supervision and administration of casual trading in its functional area, including bye-laws relating to the designation of casual trading areas, the maximum area to be occupied by a person in a casual trading area, the regulation of access to casual trading areas, the fixing of fees, and enforcement. It also provides for the procedure to be followed by a local authority in the making of bye-laws, and for appeals.

S. 7 replicates s. 8 of the 1980 Act concerning the acquisition and extinguishment of market rights, with the exception that, in addition, it provides that a market or fair remaining unexercised for a period of not less than 10 years after the commencement of the section will be extinguished. S. 8 replicated s. 9 of the 1980 Act, as amended, concerning market rights owned by local authorities and provides: (a) that facilities already provided by a local authority may be taken into consideration in the context of extinguishing a market right; (b) for limitation on an appeal to the District Court to an aggrieved person; and (c) for appeal to the Circuit Court from the District Court. S. 9 replicates s. 10 of the 1980 Act concerning prohibition of false information and alteration of licenses, save for the deletion of the reference to the Minister. S. 10 replicates s. 11 of the 1980 concerning the powers of authorised officers to inspect and examine casual trading area, save for the deletion of the Minister's power under that section to appoint authorised officers and the reference in that section to trading under a permit in a casual trading area, and it also makes an appropriate addition concerning compliance with bye-laws. S. 11 of the 1995 Act replicates s. 12 of the 1980 Act concerning further powers of the Garda Síochána, subject to further expansion of the term 'vehicle' to include a vehicle used for towing. S. 12 replicates s. 13 of the 1980 Act save that it provides for the disposal of goods seized by a Garda Superintendent. S. 13 provides that a local authority shall maintain a register of licences, including as appropriate details kept in electronic form. S. 14 provides for increased maximum penalties for offences by comparison with the 1980 Act. The Act came into effect on dates between May 1, 1995 and October 16, 1995: Casual Trading Act 1995 (Commencement) Order 1995 (SI No. 267 of 1995).

Conditions attaching to licence   In *Shanley v Galway Corporation and Ors* [1995] 1 IR 396, McCracken J dismissed the plaintiff's challenge to certain conditions attached to casual trading by the defendant Corporation under the Casual Trading Act 1980 (since replaced by the Casual Trading Act 1995: see above). The plaintiff, who at all times possessed a casual trading licence, had engaged in casual trading in certain public parts of Galway until 1986, selling pre-cooked food from mobile units. Prior to 1987, the Corporation had not designated any area as a casual trading area under the 1980 Act, but in 1987 it formally designated an area in which the plaintiff had engaged in his business as a casual trading area. The Corporation also determined that any casual trading permit issued in respect of this public area would prohibit trading in food, but this restriction had not been publicly announced. The plaintiff continued to trade without a permit by placing his mobile units on private property, but he was required to cease these activities when the Garda Síochána approached him. The plaintiff instituted the instant proceedings seeking various declaratory relief, arguing, *inter alia*, that the conditions attached to any permit for casual trading in the public area in question were in breach of his constitutional right to earn a livelihood.

The statutory background to the case was that s. 3 of the 1980 Act prohibited a person from engaging in casual trading in a casual trading area without a casual trading licence and permit, or from engaging in casual trading in an area other than a casual trading area without a casual trading licence S. 4 of the 1980 Act provided that the Minister for Enterprise and Employment was empowered to grant a casual trading licence to applicants on payment of a fee (a function since devolved to local authorities by the 1995 Act: see above). S. 5 of the 1980 Act provided that a local authority shall, on payment of a fee, grant a casual trading permit, containing such conditions as the local authority determines, to applicants holding a casual trading licence. S. 7 of the 1980 Act provided that a local authority may designate any land in its functional area to which the public has access as of right, or any land occupied by and in the functional area of the local authority, as a place where casual trading may be carried on. As indicated, McCracken J refused the reliefs sought.

He noted that the 1980 Act had given a very wide discretion to a local authority in designating an area as a casual trading area and in issuing casual trading permits. While he accepted that s. 5 did appear to make the granting of a permit mandatory where an applicant possessed a permit, he pointed out that it also provided that the permit may specify such matters and impose such conditions as the local authority might determine. Having regard to the wide discretion given to a local authority by the 1980 Act, he concluded that the designation of the areas in the defendant Corporation's functional area and the conditions it had imposed were perfectly valid.

He was also satisfied that, had the plaintiff enquired, he would have been informed of the conditions which attached to a casual trading permit. While he thought that it might have been desirable for the Corporation to have set out their policy as to conditions in a pamphlet available to applicants, it was not mandatory for them to do so. And while it was incumbent on the Corporation to take the views of traders into account, there was no obligation on it to negotiate with the plaintiff or other traders.

On the constitutional dimension to the case, McCracken J pointed out that the right to earn a livelihood is not an absolute right. Referring to two leading authorities in this area, *Attorney General v Paperlink Ltd* [1984] ILRM 373 and *Hand v Dublin Corporation* [1991] 1 IR 409; [1991] ILRM 556 (1991 Review, 104-5), he held that the prohibition on casual trading in food in the public area relevant to the plaintiff's livelihood constituted a condition imposed for the common good by the local authority pursuant to an Act of the Oireachtas. On this basis, he concluded that both the delegation by the Oireachtas of powers to impose conditions and the actual exercise of that delegated power in the instant case were not in breach of the plaintiff's constitutional right to earn a livelihood.

The plaintiff had also claimed relief against the other defendants in the case, the Minister for Enterprise and Employment and the State. McCracken J stated that this was based primarily on the assumption that the defendants owed a positive duty of some kind to the plaintiff to ensure that he would be able to earn a livelihood. While McCracken J accepted that Article 40.3 of the Constitution provided that the State shall 'as best it may' protect the plaintiff's right to earn a livelihood it did not impose a positive duty either on the State or on any body such as a local authority to provide a livelihood for the plaintiff. The plaintiff also sought to argue that there was a general obligation on these defendants under Article 40.3.2° to oversee the exercise by the Corporation of its functions under the 1980 Act. McCracken J also rejected this suggestion, holding that Article 40.3.2° relates to an unjust attack on a citizen, and to vindicating the rights of the citizen in the case of injustice done. Since he was satisfied that there had been no unjust attack on the plaintiff's rights and no injustice done to him by the Corporation, the plaintiff's case failed.

CONSUMER CREDIT

Introduction The Consumer Credit Act 1995 involves a much-awaited fundamental alteration to existing legislative regulation on the provision of credit in the State. Many of its provisions owe their origins to the need to implement, belatedly, Directive 87/102/EEC, as amended by Directive 90/88/EEC, concerning consumer credit. However, the Act goes beyond the strict requirements of these Directive by repealing all existing consumer credit legislation and replacing them with a unified legislative framework, incorporating some activities not previously regulated. In this respect, the 1995 Act draws on some elements of the United Kingdoms Consumer Credit Act 1974. Some purely domestic aspects of the 1995 Act are to be found in the provisions replacing and updating the Moneylenders Acts 1900 to 1989; these represent one element of the States response to the difficulties arising in recent years from unlicensed moneylenders and, to some extent, licensed moneylenders. Another significant feature of the 1995 Act in its final form is the transfer from the Central Bank to the Director of Consumer Affairs of the power to monitor customer charges made by most credit institutions. The 1995 Act came into force almost in its entirety (with the sole exception of s. 54(3)) on 1 May 1996: Consumer Credit Act 1995 (Commencement) Order 1996 (SI No. 121 of 1996).

De-regulation As a general comment, we might note that a central feature of the 1995 Act, as its title indicates, is its emphasis on the consumer sector of the market in credit, to the virtual exclusion of what might be described as the business-to-business sector. One consequence is that the 1995 Act involves some 'de-regulation' of existing credit legislation. Thus, the Hire-Purchase Acts 1946 to 1980, which have been repealed and replaced by Part V of the 1995 Act, imposed requirements on all forms of hire-purchase contracts: the provisions of the 1995 Act which are now in place apply to consumer hire-purchase contracts only.

Regulation-making power We note here that the 1995 Act confers wide-ranging Regulation-making powers on the Minister for Enterprise and Employment. This power is not confined to the kind of detailed Regulation-making to be found in many modern Acts. The 1995 Act confers the power to amend by regulation many of the provisions of the 1995 Act itself and, as we shall see, this power has been used extensively in 1996 to amend the terms of the 1995 Act. Some of these involve textual changes to the 1995 Act which would otherwise appear to have required amending legislation. It must be seriously doubted whether the conferral of such an extensive delegated power could withstand the scrutiny of a challenge based on the principles contained in *Cityview Press Ltd v An Chomhairle Oiliúna* [1980] IR 280. The picture is made somewhat more complicated given that the 1995 Act gives effect, at least in part, to Community Directives in this area, but given the 'domestic' nature of many of its provisions, a doubt remains. It is of interest to note that, in the context of textual amendments to ensure compliance with the relevant Directives, the powers conferred by s. 3 of the European Communities Act 1972 have also been employed to amend the 1995 Act. Thus, the European Communities (Consumer Credit Act 1995)

(Amendment) Regulations 1996 (SI No. 277 of 1996) provides for amendments to ss. 2 and 3 of the 1995 Act which, according to the Explanatory Note, were intended to 'bring the Act into line with the aims of Council Directive 87/102/EEC.' It remains to be seen whether this use of the power conferred by s. 3 of the 1972 Act would meet the criteria set down in *Meagher v Minister for Agriculture and Food* [1994] 1 IR 329; [1994] 1 ILRM 1 (1993 Review, 299-304).

General scope   S. 3(1) of the 1995 Act (as amended by SI No. 277 of 1996 referred to above) provides that, subject to the Act itself, the Act applies to:

> all credit agreements, hire-purchase agreements and consumer-hire agreements to which a consumer is a party.

S. 2 of the 1995 Act defines consumer as a 'natural person acting outside his trade, business or profession'.

S. 3(2) provides for certain exceptions to this general provision, and excluded are, *inter alia*, credit agreements granted by a credit union, a loan made by a pawnbroker (regulated by the Pawnbrokers Act 1964 as amended by the 1995 Act) and credit agreements between an employer and employee where the terms are more favourable than those generally offered to the public in the normal course of business. S. 3(3) of the Act that its terms will only apply to housing loans from local authorities if Regulations under the Act are made to this effect. Subject to these exceptions, the 1995 Act is clearly very wide in its scope.

Director of Consumer Affairs   S. 4 of the 1995 Act confers the following powers on the Director of Consumer Affairs: to keep under general review practices or proposed practices affecting any of the obligations imposed by the Act; to investigate any such practices where the public interest so requires or where requested by the Minister for Enterprise and Employment; to institute proceedings seeking to restrain any activities contrary to the Act; to investigate complaints; and to publish Codes of Practice setting out conduct to ensure 'transparency and fairness' in credit agreements covered by the Act. In addition to these general powers, s. 93 of the 1995 Act provides that the Director is responsible for the licensing of moneylenders, s. 116 provides he is responsible for the authorisation of mortgage intermediaries and s. 144 confers similar powers in respect of credit intermediaries. S. 5 of the 1995 Act empowers the Director to require persons to furnish information or records relevant to an investigation or to attend before him for that purpose. The Director may apply to the High Court to commit for contempt a person who obstructs or hinders him in the performance of his functions. S. 6 of the

Act empowers the Director to issue directions regarding the or location size of any statement or notice required under the Act. S. 7 of the 1995 Act empowers the Minister for Enterprise and Employment or the Director to appoint authorised officers for the purposes of enforcing the provisions of the Act and outlines their powers, including what are now commonly-conferred powers of entry and inspection and associated investigative powers. S. 8 of the Act prohibits the disclosure of confidential information obtained by such authorised officers.

Annual percentage rate (APR)   Ss. 9 and 10 of the 1995 Act contain the basic formula for calculating the annual percentage rate or APR, which is the statutory attempt to ensure that a 'true' rate of interest is published by those providing credit under the credit agreements covered by the 1995 Act. S. 9(1) provides that:

> the APR shall be the equivalent, on an annual basis, of the present value of all commitments (loans, repayments and charges), future or existing, agreed by the creditor and the consumer, calculated to the nearest rounded decimal point in accordance with the method of calculation specified in the Fourth Schedule.

While the Fourth Schedule to the 1995 Act contains the detailed method by which the APR is to be calculated, s. 9(2) provides that Regulations may amend the method laid down in the version as passed by the Oireachtas. Of course, any such change must be consistent with the basic elements set out in s. 9(1). S. 10 sets out the criteria for the calculation of APR in respect of credit agreements other than housing loans and in particular provides for the exclusion of certain matters, such as certain charges. The provisions of ss. 9 and 10 replace and update the provisions of the Consumer Information (Consumer Credit) Order 1987, which was revoked by the Consumer Information (Consumer Credit) Order 1987 (Revocation) Order 1996 (SI No. 248 of 1996) with effect from August 8, 1996.

Regulations, offences and penalties   S. 11 provides for the laying of Regulations made before the Houses of the Oireachtas, subject to the negative resolution annulment procedure. S. 12 provides that contravention of various sections of the 1995 Act amount to summary offences only, while for others it is provided that they are indictable. S. 13 provides for penalties, ranging from a maximum fine of £1,500 and/or a maximum of 12 months imprisonment on summary conviction to a maximum fine of £50,000 fine and/or a maximum of 5 years imprisonment on conviction on indictment. S. 14 provides that, in general, offences may be prosecuted summarily by the

Minister for Enterprise and Employment or the Director. However, certain
offences in relation to unlicensed moneylending may only be prosecuted by
a member of the Garda Síochána who may also prosecute any offence in
relation to the moneylending provisions in the Act. S. 15 provides that a
person convicted of an offence shall, unless there are special and substantial
reasons otherwise, be liable for the costs of the Minister or the Director, as
the case may be. S. 16 provides that the Director shall be immune from action
or proceedings in relation to the powers and functions provided for him in
the Act.

Advertising and offering financial accommodation   Part II of the 1995
Act (ss. 20 to 28) deals with the content of advertisements offering financial
accommodation, the intention being to ensure the provision of clear and
accurate information to the consumer. S. 21 outlines the matter which
advertisements must contain in relation to the cost of credit, including a clear
statement of the APR. Save in the case of housing loans, any special
conditions attached to or security required in relation to a loan must be
indicated. S. 22 sets out the essential elements for all advertisements offering
credit in respect of goods and services, except housing loans. They must state
the nature of the financial accommodation, the cash price of the goods or
service, the APR and the total cost of the credit to the consumer, the number,
amount and frequency of repayments and details of any deposit payable. S.
23 provides that advertising for consumer-hire agreements must include a
prominent statement that the goods remain the property of the owner. S. 24
provides that comparative advertising shall contain the terms of each of the
financial accommodation referred to in the advertisement. S. 26 prohibits
advertising of credit as being without charge if it is conditional on further
additional expenditure by the consumer, such as a maintenance or insurance
contract. S. 26 expressly prohibits the display or publication of advertising
which does not comply with Part II of the 1995 Act. S. 149 of the 1995 Act
requires credit institutions to notify the Director within three months of any
charges imposed by them on all customers, whether consumers or otherwise.
The Director is empowered to direct the credit institution to refrain from
imposing such charge in certain circumstances, particularly having regard to
'the promotion of fair competition between . . . credit institutions' and the
commercial justification proffered by the credit institution. S. 28 of the 1995
Act empowers the Minister for Enterprise and Employment to make further
provision by Regulations regarding the form or content of advertisements
relating to the availability or the cost or the provision of credit to consumers
for the purposes of Part II. Thus, the Consumer Credit Act 1995 (Section 28)
Regulations 1996 (SI No. 245 of 1996) involved amendments to ss. 21 and
22 of the 1995 Act. We also note here that the Consumer Credit Act 1995

(Section 2) Regulations 1996 (SI No. 127 of 1996) provides that certain institutions shall be deemed to be credit institutions and mortgage lenders for the purposes of the 1995 Act in addition to those defined in the 1995 Act itself.

Form and content of credit agreements Part III of the 1995 Act (ss. 29 to 39) concerns the form and content of credit agreements other than housing loans, which are dealt with in Part IX of the 1995 Act. S. 30 requires that credit agreements and any contract of guarantee concerning them must be in writing and signed by the consumer and by or on behalf of all other parties involved. The consumer must be given a copy immediately or it must be sent to the consumer within ten days of signature. During this ten day period, the consumer may exercise the right to withdraw from the agreement, that is, s. 30 provides for a ten day 'cooling off' period and a notice to this effect must be included in the agreement. S. 50 of the 1995 Act provides that this rights may be waived by a consumer, but this is subject to certain restrictions. S. 31 of the 1995 Act specifies the other contents of a credit agreement: the amount of the credit lent; the date the credit is to be advanced (if known); the amount and number of the repayments; the rate of interest and APR; the total amount repayable; and the means and cost of termination. A credit card agreement must include: the credit limit, if any, at the commencement of the agreement; the rate of interest and APR; the terms of use and repayment and the means and cost of termination. S. 32 lays down requirements in relation to credit-sale agreements, broadly similar to those in s. 31. S. 35 imposes certain obligations on a credit institution where it agrees to grant an advance on a current account (including an overdraft facility) to a consumer: it must inform the consumer of the credit limit, if any, at the commencement of the facility, the annual rate of interest and the procedure for terminating the facility. The information must be confirmed in writing within ten days. In the case of tacitly agreed overdrafts which extend beyond three months, the information requirements in s. 35 are less onerous. S. 36 provides that a credit agreement other than an overdraft facility, a credit-sale agreement or a moneylending agreement must contain on the front page a notice in the form prescribed in Part I of the Third Schedule to the 1995 Act. As with Part II, s. 37 of the 1995 Act empowers to Minister to prescribe the form and content of credit agreements by Regulations and to amend the relevant provisions of the 1995 Act accordingly. Thus, the Consumer Credit Act 1995 (Section 36) Regulations 1996 (SI No. 128 of 1996) involved amendments to the form prescribed in Part I of the Third Schedule. The Consumer Credit Act 1995 (Section 37) Regulations 1996 (SI No. 129 of 1996) involved amendments to ss. 31 and 35 of the Act. S. 38 expressly prohibits in general the enforcement by a creditor of any credit agreement which does not comply with Part III of the 1995 Act.

Matters arising during currency of agreement   Part IV of the 1995 Act
(ss. 40 to 50) lays down requirements concerning the protection of consumers
during the currency of credit agreements. S. 40 preserves any rights of the
consumer under a credit agreement where the creditor assigns the benefit of
the agreement to a third party. Similarly, s. 41 protects the rights of the
consumer in cases where a bill of exchange or a promissory note is used in
a credit transaction note and expressly provides that the rights conferred by
the 1995 Act take priority over the provisions of the Bills of Exchange Act
1882. Likewise, s. 42 provides that the existence of a credit agreement shall
not affect the rights of a consumer under the Sale of Goods and Supply of
Services Act 1980 and also confers on the consumer a right of action in
certain circumstances against the provider of credit as well as against the
supplier of goods or services. S. 43 imposes a duty on the creditor to supply
documents and information, including the amount paid and outstanding,
where this is requested by a consumer who is party to a credit agreement,
other than a housing loan. S. 44 sets out the criteria for the appropriation of
payments in cases where two or more credit agreements exist between a
consumer and a creditor and the consumer makes a payment which is not
sufficient to discharge the total amount due. S. 45 provides that written
communications from creditors to consumers must be contained in sealed
envelopes addressed and marked as specified and may only be sent in certain
specific circumstances to a consumer's employer or a member of the consumer's family. S. 46 prohibits and restricts visits and telephone calls by the
creditor to the consumer, his employer or the consumer's family. S. 47
provides that a consumer or a person acting on the consumer's behalf may
apply to the Circuit Court for a declaration that the total cost of credit or any
charge provided for in a credit agreement is excessive, and it sets out the
criteria to be used by the Court in making a determination under the section.
Before making any decision, the Court must afford the Director of Consumer
Affairs an opportunity to be heard on the matter. S. 47 does not apply to a
credit agreement relating to credit advanced by a bank or mortgage lender.
S. 48 provides that, where the Circuit Court has decided under s. 47 that the
total cost of credit or any charge is excessive, it may re-open the agreement
so as to do justice between the parties, including setting aside the agreement
in whole or in part. In the case of a moneylending agreement, the Court may
order the Director to revoke, suspend or alter the licence of the holder
concerned. S. 49 of the 1995 Act prohibits demands for payment or making
threats in relation to agreements which are unenforceable under the Act.

Matters arising during termination or on default   Part V of the 1995 Act (ss. 51 to 55) concern the termination of a credit agreement or default by the consumer, other than in the case of a housing loan. S. 52 confers on the consumer a right to terminate a credit agreement other than a housing loan by giving written notice to this effect and the cost of the credit to be charged is to be reduced in accordance with various formulae to be prescribed for different forms of credit. S. 53 entitles the consumer to a reduction in the total cost of credit, calculated in accordance with a formula to be prescribed from time to time, where for any reason the amount owed in a credit agreement, or any sum, becomes payable before the time fixed by the agreement. S. 54 of the 1995 Act limits the rights of the creditor to enforce an agreement and prescribes the steps to be taken by a creditor to enforce provisions of the agreement or recover possession of goods in non-default cases and in the case of breach by the consumer, including the service of notice at least ten days in advance of proposing to take any action. However, on application by the creditor or owner to the relevant court of competent jurisdiction (in many cases, the District Court or Circuit Court), the requirements of notice may be dispensed with where the Court 'is satisfied that it would be just and equitable to do so.' Based on the experience with a similar formula in the (now repealed) Hire-Purchase Acts 1946 to 1980, it is likely that the courts would be reluctant to dispense with these requirements save in limited circumstances. S. 55 empowers the court to ensure that no unjustified enrichment of the creditor ensues from compensation or recovery of goods in any action.

Hire-purchase agreements Part VI of the 1995 Act (ss. 56 to 83) concerns hire-purchase agreements and replaces the Hire-Purchase Acts 1946 to 1980, which have been repealed in full by the 1995 Act. As already indicated, one of the effects of the 1995 Act is that only consumer hire-purchase agreements are now subject to the detailed requirements laid down in the 1995 Act. Nonetheless, the Director retains a general supervisory function in relation to non-consumer hire-purchase agreements. S. 57 provides that, before a hire-purchase agreement is entered into, the owner must state in writing the cash price to the prospective hirer and it sets out the conditions under which this provision is deemed to be complied with, such as where the consumer has inspected the goods and the cash price was attached to them or has seen them is a priced catalogue. S. 65 defines 'hire-purchase price' as the total sum payable by the hirer to complete the purchase of the goods, exclusive of any sum payable by penalty or as compensation for breach of the agreement; it also stipulates that any sum payable by the hirer under a hire purchase agreement by way of a deposit or other initial payment shall form part of the hire purchase price.

Forms of agreement As with other credit agreements, s. 58 of the 1995 Act requires that consumer hire-purchase agreements and any contract of guarantee concerning them must be in writing and signed by the consumer and by or on behalf of all other parties involved. The consumer must be given a copy immediately or it must be sent to the consumer within ten days of signature. During this ten day period, the consumer may exercise the right to withdraw from the agreement, that is, s. 58 provides for a ten day 'cooling off' period and a notice to this effect must be included in the agreement. This right may be waived by a consumer. S. 58 of the 1995 Act also requires that a consumer hire-purchase agreement must contain a statement of: (a) the hire-purchase price, (b) the cash price of the goods to which the agreement relates, (c) the amount of each of the instalments, (d) the date on which they are to be paid, (e) the number of instalments, (f) the names and address of the parties to the agreement and (g) any costs or penalties to which the hirer becomes liable in the event of default. The agreement must also contain a list of the goods which is sufficient to identify them. It must also contain a statement of the hirer's right to terminate the agreement as well as a statement of the restrictions on the rights of the owner or hirer to terminate the contract, as specified in the Fifth Schedule to the 1995 Act. It must also contain a statement to the effect that, pursuant to s. 69, the hirer is obliged to inform the owner of the whereabouts of the goods. Finally, the agreement must contain in a prominent position the words 'Hire-purchase agreement' (which the Act would appear to require be in bold print). As with previous Parts of the 1995 Act, s. 60 empowers to Minister to ensure by Regulations that the content of hire-purchase agreements comply with the 1995 Act and to amend s. 58 and the Fifth Schedule to the 1995 Act accordingly. Thus, the Consumer Credit Act 1995 (Section 60) Regulations 1996 (SI No. 130 of 1996) involved amendments to s. 58 while the Consumer Credit Act 1995 (Section 60) (No. 2) Regulations 1996 (SI No. 246 of 1996) involved amendments to the notice prescribed in the Fifth Schedule.

Compliance with requirements S. 59 reflects the provisions of s. 54 of the 1995 Act concerning credit agreements generally by prohibiting the enforcement of a consumer hire-purchase agreement where ss. 57 and 58 have not been complied with. Similarly, s. 59 provides that, on application by the owner to the relevant court of competent jurisdiction (in many cases, the District Court or Circuit Court), the requirements of ss. 57 and 58 may be dispensed with where the Court 'is satisfied that it would be just and equitable to do so.' As already indicated, based on the experience with a similar formula in the (now repealed) Hire-Purchase Acts 1946 to 1980, it is likely that the courts would be reluctant to dispense with these requirements save in limited circumstances. S. 61 imposes a duty on the owner to ensure that agreements comply with the relevant provisions of the Act, while s. 62 declares void various terms which would purport to exclude the operation of the relevant provisions of the 1995 Act.

Termination of agreement S. 63 of the 1995 Act sets out the hirer's right to terminate the agreement at any time before final payment. In such circumstances, the hirer may do one of two things. First, the hirer may pay the amount, if any, by which one-half of the hire-purchase price exceeds the total of the sums already paid: the '50% formula' provided for under the Hire-Purchase Acts 1946 to 1980. Second, the hirer may purchase the goods using the formula for reduced credit provided for in ss. 52 or 53 of the 1995 Act: this option is new under the 1995 Act. S. 63 also provides that, where the hirer terminates the contract but has failed to take reasonable care of goods, the hirer is liable for such failure Curiously, s. 67 of the 1995 Act repeats this stipulation. S. 64 restricts the rights of the owner to recover possession of goods, let under a hire purchase agreement, from the hirer otherwise than by legal proceedings where one third of the total cost payable under the agreement has been paid: the 'one-third formula' provided for under the 1946 to 1980 Acts. S. 66 empowers the relevant court, pending the hearing and on hearing an action in relation to proceedings taken under section 64, to take certain steps, including delivery of the goods to the owner. Where legal proceedings have commenced the owner is prohibited from enforcing payment other than in those proceedings. S. 68 limits the liability of the guarantor where an owner has recovered possession of goods let under a hire-purchase agreement to the amount which would have been payable by the hirer if he had determined the agreement under s. 63. S. 71 provides that where, before taking legal proceedings to recover goods let under a hire-purchase agreement, the owner made a written request to the hirer to surrender the goods, the hirer's possession of the goods shall be deemed to be adverse to the owner.

Implied terms and exclusion Ss. 74 to 80 replace equivalent provisions in the Hire Purchase Acts 1946 to 1980 concerning implied terms in hire-purchase agreements and their exclusion. While the text of the 1995 Act replicates the earlier provisions, it is important to note that the 1995 Act applies to consumer hire-purchase agreements only, whereas the now-repealed provisions contained some protections for non-consumer hire-purchase agreements. S. 74 concerns the implied terms as to title. S. 75 concerns letting by description. S. 76 concerns undertakings as to quality or fitness, retaining the phrase 'merchantable quality' from s. 14(3) of the Sale of Goods Act 1893. S. 77 concerns hire-purchase agreements by reference to samples. S. 78 restricts the displaying or publication of any statements purporting to restrict the rights of the hirer, while s. 79 prohibits any exclusion of the

implied terms and conditions imposed by ss. 74 to 77. S. 80 of the 1995 Act
imposes liability on persons conducting negotiations antecedent to hire-purchase agreements. S. 81 applies to hire-purchase agreements s. 12 (warranties
for spare parts and servicing) and ss. 15 to 19 (guarantees and undertakings)
of the Sale of Goods and Supply of Services Act 1980. Similarly, s. 82 applies
to the hire-purchase of motor vehicles s. 13 of the 1980 Act, which provides
that the owner and finance provider are jointly answerable for defects.
Finally, s. 83 defines 'antecedent negotiations and representations' for the
purposes of Part VI of the 1995 Act.

Consumer-hire agreements   Part VII of the 1995 Act (ss. 84 to 91) provide
for comprehensive regulation of consumer-hire contracts for the first time.
S. 2 defines such an agreement as one of more than three months duration
for the bailment of goods under which the property in the goods remains with
the owner. As with other credit agreements, s. 84 of the 1995 Act requires
that consumer-hire agreements and any contract of guarantee concerning
them must be in writing and signed by the consumer and by or on behalf of
all other parties involved. The consumer must be given a copy immediately
or it must be sent to the consumer within ten days of signature. During this
ten day period, the consumer may exercise the right to withdraw from the
agreement, that is, s. 84 provides for a ten day 'cooling off' period and a
notice to this effect must be included in the agreement. This right may be
waived by a consumer. S. 84 of the 1995 Act also requires that a consumer-
hire agreement must contain a statement of: (a) the cash price of the goods
to which the agreement relates, (b) the amount of each of the instalments, (c)
the date on which they are to be paid, (d) if the agreement is for a specified
period, the number of instalments, (e) the names and address of the supplier
of the goods (f) any additional costs; (g) cost of early termination, (h) names
and addresses of all the parties; and (i) any costs or penalties to which the
hirer becomes liable in the event of default. It must also contain a list of the
goods which is sufficient to identify them. The agreement must also specify
that the goods remain the property of the owner and a statement of the hirer's
right to withdraw from the agreement during the 'cooling-off' period.
    S. 85 reflects the provisions of s. 54 of the 1995 Act concerning credit
agreements generally by prohibiting the enforcement of a consumer-hire
agreement where s. 84 has not been complied with. Similarly, s. 85 provides
that, on application by the owner to the relevant court of competent jurisdiction (in many cases, the District Court or Circuit Court), the requirements of
s. 84 may be dispensed with where the Court 'is satisfied that it would be
just and equitable to do so.' As already indicated, based on the experience
with a similar formula in the (now repealed) Hire-Purchase Acts 1946 to
1980, it is likely that the courts would be reluctant to dispense with these

requirements save in limited circumstances. S. 86 confers a regulation-making power on the Minister similar to those in other Parts of the 1995 Act. Thus, the Consumer Credit Act 1995 (Section 86) Regulations 1996 (SI No. 131 of 1996) involved amendments to s. 84. S. 87 imposes a duty on the owner to ensure that agreements comply with the relevant provisions of the Act, while s. 88 extends to consumer-hire agreements the provisions of ss. 75 to 83. S. 89 provides for the right of the hirer to terminate a consumer hire agreement by giving notice to the owner. S. 90 provides that the hirer must take reasonable care of the goods and is liable for any failure to do so. S. 91 imposes a duty on the hirer to inform the owner of the whereabouts of the goods if so requested in writing.

Moneylending Part VIII of the 1995 Act (ss. 92 to 114) deals with moneylending and replaces the terms of the Moneylenders Acts 1900 to 1989. As already indicated, Part VIII represents one element of the State's response to the difficulties arising in recent years from unlicensed money-lenders and, to some extent, licensed moneylenders. S. 93 confers on the Director of Consumer Affairs the power to grant a moneylender's licence 'upon such terms and conditions as he sees fit . . .' The minimum criteria to be met by applicants for a licence, the fees involved and the conditions pertaining to the granting of a licence as well as the grounds on which the Director may refuse, suspend, revoke or alter a licence and the process of appeal against his action to the Circuit Court are also specified in s. 93. A moneylender's licence is granted for a period of 12 months. S. 94 requires that a moneylender's licence be displayed at the holder's place of business. S. 95 requires that any moneylending agreement must contain a statement to the effect that is such an agreement. S. 96 prohibits a person from altering or falsifying a moneylender's licence. S. 97 requires the holder of a licence to issue an authorisation to any person acting on his or her behalf where acting away from the moneylender's place of business. S. 98 prohibits persons from engaging in the business of moneylending without a licence and also confers extensive powers on a member of the Garda Síochána to stop, question, search and remove documents from any person whom the member believes is carrying on an unlicensed moneylending business. S. 99 requires that the full credit amount referred to in a moneylending agreement is advanced to the consumer and any deduction in respect of charges, interest or the initial repayment instalment is prohibited. S. 100 requires a moneylender to supply a repayment book to the consumer. The book must contain certain specified information relevant to the agreement, similar to the requirements of other credit agreements regulated by the 1995 Act. S. 101 provides that, for each agreement to which a moneylender is party, a record of that agreement must maintained. This record must be kept for 5 years after the expiry of the agreement and contain detailed information about the agreement and repayments made by the consumer including charges and interest. These records must be treated as confidential and may only be revealed to authorised officers of the Minister or the Director. S. 102 prohibits a moneylender from charging a consumer in respect of expenses relating to the negotiation or granting of the loan. Provision is made that where these charges have been paid by a consumer they are recoverable. S. 103 addresses the question of charges payable under an agreement in respect of repayments made away from the business premises of the moneylender. It must be made clear to the consumer that this charge is being made and that the consumer has the option of avoiding the charge by making repayments at the moneylender's business premises. S. 104 provides that, where any documents found on a person gives rise to a reasonable inference that the person is engaged in moneylending, this creates a presumption that the person was engaged in moneylending. S. 105 confers powers of entry on the Garda Síochána, while s. 108 provides for search warrants of premises to be issued by the District Court. S. 107 prohibits a person from using any document belonging to another person for the purpose of moneylending and provides members of the Garda Síochána with the necessary powers of seizure. S. 108 empowers members of the Garda Síochána to request persons suspected of collecting repayments to produce a moneylender's licence or authorisation. S. 109 provides that persons suspected by a member of the Garda Síochána of being in breach of a moneylending provision may, without warrant, be arrested or may be required to give his name and address. S. 110 prohibits collection of repayments between the hours of 9 pm and 10 am during weekdays or at any time on a Sunday or public holiday. S. 111 prohibits a person who is collecting repayments on a moneylending agreement from selling or offering for sale goods which are to be bought on credit. S. 112 prohibits increased charges or additional charges, other than legal costs in the event of default of payments due under a moneylending agreement. S. 113 provides that a moneylender's licence granted under the (now repealed) Moneylenders Act 1933 which were in force before the enactment of the 1995 Act remained valid; this section is transitional only and ceases to have effect in May 1997 since a moneylender's licence is granted for 12 months. S. 114 empowers the Minister to make Regulations to the effect that a person or class of persons shall not be regarded as engaging in the business of moneylending. A similar power existed under the previous regime: see the 1993 Review, 48.

Housing loans Part IX of the 1995 Act (ss. 115 to 136) applies to a housing loan made by a mortgage lender and sets out an extensive and new regime in this area, drawing in large part on the similar provisions of the United Kingdom's Consumer Credit Act 1974. S. 116 sets out the conditions whereby a person may engage in the business of being a mortgage intermediary, defined in s. 2 of the Act as any person who arranges a mortgage for a commission. The Consumer Credit Act 1995 (Section 120) Regulations 1996 (SI No. 247 of 1996) provide that a 'tied mortgage branch agent' is not to be regarded as a mortgage intermediary for the purposes of the 1995 Act. The Director of Consumer Affairs may determine the form of an application for an authorisation and the fees payable are also set out. An authorisation is valid for 12 months and it must contain specified information and may be refused by the Director on certain specified grounds. The Minister for Enterprise and Employment may, by Regulations, provide that the holder of an authorisation effects a policy of professional indemnity insurance. Persons aggrieved by the granting or refusal to grant an authorisation may appeal to the Circuit Court.

S. 121 provides that a borrower may make early repayment of the whole or part of a housing loan without being liable to pay any redemption fee. The exemption from redemption fees does not apply where the loan agreement provides that the rate of interest is fixed at the time of redemption. The Minister may, by means of Regulations alter the conditions under which a redemption fee is payable. Where a redemption fee is payable this must be stated on information and application forms and other documents pertaining to the loan. Such statement shall also explain the method of calculating the fee. S. 12 details the charges which are excluded in determining the total cost of credit for the purpose of calculating the APR in relation to a housing loan. Charges which the consumer would have to pay whether purchasing by cash or credit as well as charges for non-compliance and certain specified insurance charges are excluded. S. 123 provides that when a mortgage lender notifies an applicant of the approval or refusal of a housing loan, a copy of the valuation report shall be furnished to the applicant. S. 124 provides that insurance which a mortgage lender requires a borrower to effect on property mortgaged to the lender may be effected by the borrower with any insurer. The mortgage lender is prohibited from imposing a requirement which differentiates as between insurance effected through the agency of the mortgage lender and insurance otherwise effected and also from requiring the borrower to pay a fee which the borrower would not pay if the insurance was effected through the agency of the mortgage lender. S. 125 prohibits the mortgage lender from passing on to the borrower costs incurred by the mortgage lender in respect of the legal investigation of title to property offered as security by the borrower, shall be paid by the mortgage lender and shall not be passed on to the borrower. S. 126 imposes the liability on a mortgage lender, except in certain specified cases subject to certain provisions, to arrange a life assurance policy providing, in the event of the death of a borrower before the housing loan is repaid, for payment of a sum equal to the amount outstanding at time of death. S. 127 prohibits a mortgage agent from making or offering a housing loan subject to a condition that any other service, whether or not in connection with the loan, shall be provided by that agent, subsidiary or associated body. S. 128 prescribes the 'health warning' to be used in specified communications referring or relating to a housing loan to the effect that a home is at risk if mortgage payments are not kept up. The requisite wording is 'Warning — Your Home is at risk if you do not keep up payments on a mortgage or any other loan secured on it.' Where the interest rate is variable a notice to the effect that payment rates may be adjusted, must also be included. This must state: 'The payment rates on this housing loan may be adjusted by the lender from time to time.' S. 129 provides that an agreement for a housing loan shall must contain a notice as specified in the Third Schedule to the Act concerning the main terms of the loan, repayments and other connected matters. The content of that notice is now to be found in the Consumer Credit Act 1995 (Section 129) Regulations 1996 (SI No. 132 of 1996). S. 130 requires a mortgage lender to issue, at the time the loan is made, a copy of the mortgage deed, and at specified times after the making of the loan a statement of the total amount outstanding. S. 131 empower the Minister to make Regulations requiring disclosure of other charges. S. 132 requires a mortgage lender to disclose certain charges payable by the borrower. A statement of this fact shall be included in or attached to any communications referring or relating to the loan. S. 133 provides that any communication referring or relating to an endowment loan must contain a 'health warning' to the effect that: 'There is no guarantee that the proceeds of the insurance policy will be sufficient to repay the loan in full when it becomes due for repayment.' Where there is a possibility that during the course of the loan, the borrower may be required to or advised to increase the payments, in order to secure an increase in the proceeds of the policy on maturity, a loan approval document must contain a statement of this possibility. Where the early surrender of the insurance policy in respect of an endowment loan may result in a loss or very little return to the consumer any communication sent to the consumer shall contain a statement of this possibility. Within specified periods an insurer underwriting an insurance policy in respect of an endowment, shall issue to the borrower a statement setting out the value of the policy as estimated by the insurer, at such date. S. 134 requires that any communication in relation to arrears of payments due on a housing loan shall state the amount of the increase in interest and other charges payable in respect of such arrears. Where any communication refers to the possibility of repossession, proceedings being taken under the mortgage shall contain an estimate of the cost to the borrower of such proceedings. S. 135 empowers the Director to give directions to mortgage agents concerning any advertisements in connection with housing loans.

Finally, ss. 136 provides certain protection to the borrower in the event of the winding-up of the lender.

Credit intermediaries Part XI of the 1995 Act (ss. 144 to 148) provide for the authorisation of credit intermediaries on a similar basis to that for mortgage intermediaries and moneylenders.

Registers Part XIII of the 1995 Act (s. 151) requires the Director to establish and maintain registers of moneylenders, credit intermediaries and mortgage intermediaries.

Pawnbrokers Part XV of the 1995 Act (ss. 153 to 155) amends the Pawnbrokers Act 1964 to bring its provisions into line with those contained in the 1995 Act, though it is to be regretted that the 1964 Act was not repealed in its entirety as was done with the Moneylenders Acts.

Miscellaneous Part X of the 1995 Act (ss. 137 to 143) concern a number of miscellaneous matters added to the legislation during its passage through the Oireachtas. S. 137 provides that Regulations may impose obligations on those providing financial accommodation to include display certain information at the place of business. S. 138 prohibits 'inertia selling' provisions in credit agreements, that is, any provisions which require the customer to indicate positively that he or she does not wish to obtain credit, purchase or hire any goods or avail of any service. S. 139 prohibits the sending, knowingly, of any document to a minor (that is, a person under 18 years) inviting the minor to borrow credit or obtain any goods or services on credit. Ss. 140 and 141 confirm that nothing may be done to exclude the provisions of the 1995 Act in any relevant credit agreement or to display any signs to similar effect. S. 142 provides that, where a creditor or owner refuses to enter into a credit agreement the consumer must be informed, on request, of the name and address of any person from whom the creditor or owner sought information concerning the financial standing of the consumer.

S. 143 confers a right on the consumer to correct any information thus obtained if the consumer considers it is inaccurate.

CONSUMER PROTECTION

Consumer credit The Consumer Credit Act 1995 is discussed separately above.

Package holidays The Package Holidays and Travel Trade Act 1995, which gave effect to Directive 90/314/EEC on package holidays, is discussed below, 49-53.

Unfair contract terms The European Communities (Unfair Contract Terms In Consumer Contracts) Regulations 1995 (SI No. 27 of 1995); which gave effect to Directive 93/13/EEC and set out terms which will be deemed to be unfair in contracts between sellers or suppliers and consumers, are discussed in the Contract Law chapter, below, 209.

DRINKS TRADE

Spirit drinks: definition, description and presentation The European Communities (Definition, Description and Presentation of Spirit Drinks) Regulations 1995 (SI No. 300 of 1995) put in place the necessary administrative and enforcement measures required to give full effect to Regulation (EEC) No. 1576/89 and Regulation (EEC) No. 1014/90. They provide penalties for breaches of certain conditions of the two Community Regulations and confer powers of entry to premises upon authorised officers. They came into effect on November 16, 1995.

FINANCIAL SERVICES

Credit institutions: depositor protection scheme The European Communities (Deposit Guarantee Schemes) Regulations 1995 (SI No. 168 of 1995), which gave effect to Directive 94/19/EC, provide for depositors to be compensated for 90% of their deposits up to a specified maximum sum. The Regulations apply to all credit institutions authorised in Ireland, who are required to maintain in the deposit protection account of the Central Bank at least 0.2% of their total deposits. Provision is made for branches of credit institutions authorised elsewhere in the European Union to join the scheme. The Regulations came into effect on July 1, 1995.

Derivative contracts The Netting of Financial Contracts Act 1995 provides for the enforceability of netting between two parties in relation to certain contracts in the financial services sector. Netting involves an agreement between two parties who engage in what are usually described as derivative contracts to set-off their mutual liabilities in order to arrive at a single net amount owing by one party to another. The contracts covered by the 1995 Act include interest-rate, foreign exchange and commodity based contracts. The 1995 Act sets out the terms of what was described in the

Explanatory Memorandum as a master netting agreement and for set-off by those parties of moneys due under the netting agreements and of collateral and guarantees provided in relation to netting agreements. The 1995 Act came into effect on August 1, 1995 on its signature by the President.

Fees: industrial and provident and friendly societies The Industrial And Provident Societies (Fees) Regulations 1995 (SI No. 4 of 1995), made under s. 73 of the Industrial and Provident Societies Act 1893 increased the fees to be paid for matters transacted and inspection of documents under the Industrial and Provident Societies Acts 1893 to 1977. Similarly, the Friendly Societies (Fees) Regulations 1995 (SI No. 6 of 1995), made under s. 96 of the Friendly Societies Act 1896, increased the fees to be paid for matters transacted and inspection of documents under the Friendly Societies Acts 1896 to 1977.

Investment intermediaries The Investment Intermediaries Act 1995 gives effect, *inter alia*, to the Investment Services Directive, 93/22/EEC and the Capital Adequacy Directive, 93/6/EEC. In broad terms, the Act provides that the Minister for Enterprise and Employment is responsible for the authorisation and supervision of investment intermediaries offering investment services other than insurance services, who do not have discretionary control over client funds and who deal only in certain defined investment products. S. 25 of the 1995 Act defines the functions of an investment product intermediary in general terms, but the Explanatory Memorandum to the Act as a Bill explained that, typically, an intermediary will be involved in one or more of the following activities: (i)taking and passing on orders for units in a collective investment scheme, (ii) taking and passing on orders for shares in a company or bonds which are listed on a stock exchange or prize bonds,(iii) acting as a tied agent for a credit institution and taking deposits on its behalf, (iv) acting as a deposit broker, that is, arranging for clients to deposit funds with a credit institution. Under the 1995 Act, the Central Bank is responsible for the supervision of other investment business firms, who are defined in s. 2 of the Act as persons providing investment advice or certain investment business services to third parties on a professional basis. Part II of the Act (ss. 8 to 19) deals with the authorisation of investment business firms. Part III of the 1995 Act (ss. 20 to 24) deals with the regulation and supervision of such firms. Part IV of the Act (ss. 25 to 31) deal with investment product intermediaries. Part V of the Act (ss. 32 to 35) sets out the responsibilities of auditors, including obligations to notify a change in auditor and the power to require a second audit is also provided for. Part VI of the Act (ss. 36 to 54) imposes obligations of probity and competence on employed persons in this sector, provides for the making of codes of conduct and for the award of compensation. It also requires investment intermediaries to enter into bonding arrangements to protect investors. Provision is also made for the acquisition and disposal of significant shareholdings in authorised investment business firms. Part VII of the Act (ss. 55 to 63) involves a self-regulatory structure by which the Central Bank may grant approval to a professional body to operate as an approved professional body for the purposes of the Act. Arising out of certain difficulties which arose in 1996 in connection with this self-regulating aspect of the Act, it would appear that consideration may be given to amending these provisions of the 1995 Act. Part VIII of the Act (ss. 64 to 79) deals with enforcement of the Act, including the appointment of inspectors and provision for offences and associated penalties. Finally, Part IX of the Act (s. 80) amended the Companies Act 1990 so that close-ended investment companies are included in its terms. The Act came into effect on dates between August 1, 1995 and November 1, 1995: Investment Intermediaries Act 1995 (Commencement) Order 1995 (SI No. 207 of 1995).

Stock Exchange   The Stock Exchange Act 1995 enabled the Central Bank to act as the supervisor of the Irish Stock Exchange and of any stock exchange which may he established in the State in the future, thus breaking a long link between the Irish Stock Exchange and the London Stock Exchange. The Bank is now responsible for the authorisation and supervision of the Irish member firms of an approved exchange and will meet obligations in respect of stock exchange member firms arising under the Investment Services Directive, 93/22/EEC and the Capital Adequacy Directive, 93/6/EEC. The Act deals with the approval of stock exchanges, authorisation of member firms and their regulation and further sets out the responsibilities of auditors, the acquisition and disposal of significant shareholdings in approved stock exchanges and their member firms and enforcement provisions which include the appointment of inspectors and offences and penalties. The Act came into effect on dates between August 1, 1995 and September 29, 1995: Stock Exchange Act 1995 (Commencement) Order 1995 (SI No. 206 of 1995) and Stock Exchange Act 1995 (Commencement) (No. 2) Order 1995 (SI No. 255 of 1995).

GUARANTEE

In *McCabe v Bank of Ireland*, Supreme Court, December 19, 1994, the Supreme Court held that, where parties agree verbally that a written guarantee is to be at an end on the occurrence of a specified event, such verbal agreement overrides the contents of the written guarantee. A guarantee, which had been created to deal with a particular transaction which was successfully completed shortly afterwards, had been executed between the plaintiffs and the bank. However, the written terms of the guarantee were to the effect that the guarantee was a continuing security on the plaintiffs as guarantors. The bank subsequently claimed under the guarantee for the balance of a loan on a later and independent transaction. In the High Court, judgment was given for the bank, but on appeal, the Court held in the plaintiffs' favour.

The Court accepted that, on its face, the guarantee clearly created a continuing obligation. However, it was also noted that the parties had clearly agreed verbally, prior to the execution of the guarantee, that once a specific transaction had been completed the guarantee should be at an end. Since this agreement was not qualified in any way and was to subsist irrespective of the contents of the agreement itself, the Court concluded in the plaintiffs' favour. This conclusion is consistent with the case law on exemption clauses by which inconsistent verbal agreements have been held to override the terms of written exemption clauses: see Clark, *Contract Law in Ireland*, 3rd ed. (Sweet & Maxwell, 1993).

INDUSTRIAL DEVELOPMENT

The Industrial Development Act 1995 provided for the establishment and functions of County Enterprise Boards. It also provided for the extension of the powers of Forfas and its agencies (established by the Industrial Development Act 1993: see the 1993 Review, 8-10) to acquire and hold land and other property and to invest in certain bodies. The 1995 Act came into effect between November 27, 1995 and January 1, 1996: Industrial Development Act 1995 (Commencement) Order 1995 (SI No. 308 of 1995).

INSURANCE

Cancellation of contract: no reasons required In *Carna Foods Ltd and Anor v Eagle Star Insurance Co. Ltd* [1995] 2 ILRM 474, McCracken J held that an insurance company was not required to give reasons for cancelling or refusing to renew an insurance contract against the following background. The plaintiffs brought proceedings against the defendant claiming that the defendant had wrongfully failed to disclose the reasons for the cancellation and refusal to renew several policies of insurance, and an order directing the defendant to disclose the reasons for the cancellation and refusal to renew each policy. The plaintiffs also sought a declaration that the defendant was in breach of ss. 4 and 5 of the Competition Act 1991. The plaintiffs had taken out various insurance policies with the defendant in relation to several premises. These policies covered fire, employer's liability and public liability. In June 1993 there had been a fire at a premises owned by the plaintiff and in August 1993 the defendant had notified the plaintiffs that it would not invite the renewal of certain policies which were due to expire in September of that year and that it was also cancelling the remaining policies as of September. The plaintiffs claimed that, because of this and in refusing to disclose their reasons, the plaintiff had been unable to obtain any insurance in substitution for the policies which were cancelled or not renewed. The second plaintiff asserted that he was refused insurance on his private dwelling-house because he disclosed, as he was bound to do, the refusal of the defendant to continue to cover him under the relevant policies. Evidence was given by the plaintiff's broker that he considered the plaintiff to be uninsurable, although he acknowledged that there were insurers who specialised in high-risk insurance. Evidence was also adduced that the plaintiffs would have difficulty in obtaining alternative cover if no reason was given for the cancellation, but that the plaintiff's position would only be marginally improved if reasons had been given. McCracken J refused the relief sought.

He accepted the plaintiff's general contention that statutory powers must be exercised reasonably and that when a decision was taken in the public realm the person affected is entitled to know the reasons for the decision. He referred with approval to the decision in *The State (Daly) v Minister for Agriculture* [1987] IR 165 (1987 Review, 11-12) in this respect. However, turning to the instant case, he noted that there was no procedure or machinery provided for in the contract of insurance dealing with the cancellation of the insurance policy, and that it was thus open to the defendant for any reason or for no reason to refuse the plaintiff's business or to cancel cover.

The plaintiff had relied on the decision in *Glover v BLN Ltd* [1973] IR 388 but McCracken J had no doubt that the decision of an insurance company to cancel or refuse insurance could not be said to be a function of a judicial or quasi-judicial nature, and he could see no reason why the defendant should be obliged to give its reasons and that to decide otherwise would be a serious interference in the contractual position of parties in a commercial contract with very wide ranging consequences. In this respect, he agreed with the views expressed by Keane J on the reach of public law, albeit in a slightly different context, in *Rajah v Royal College of Surgeons in Ireland* [1994] 1 IR 384; [1994] 1 ILRM 233 (1993 Review, 17-18).

McCracken J went on to note that cancellation clauses had been commonplace in insurance policies of this nature for a long time and it had never been suggested that there was any obligation to give reasons for a cancellation. Applying the established tests to determine whether a term should be implied into a contract, citing *The Moorcock* (1889) 14 PD 64 and *Shirlaw v Southern Foundries Ltd* [1939] 2 KB 206, he could not see what business efficacy was to be given to the transaction by giving reasons, nor could it see why the 'officious bystander' should assume there would be any such term. Emphasising that long-standing clauses in policies have the advantage of certainty, he stated that the court should only seek to imply terms into them where the clause had created problems for interpretation.

Finally, with regard to the Competition Act 1991, McCracken J considered that it was necessary for the plaintiffs to establish either, under s. 4, a concerted practice which restricts or distorts trade or, under s. 5, an abuse of a dominant position. He was satisfied that there had been no concerted practice between insurance companies, nor had there been any practice organised by the Insurance Federation of Ireland. The defendant, he held, was clearly not in a dominant position in the market and he was satisfied that there had been no collusion between two or more undertakings to abuse a dominant position.

Fees The Insurance (Fees) Order 1995 (SI No. 128 of 1995), made under the Insurance Act 1989 (1989 Review, 44-7) sets out a revised scale of fees to be paid annually to the Minister of Enterprise and Employment by authorised insurance undertakings. The level of fee is fixed according to the amount of gross premium income in respect of its global business in the case of a head office undertaking and the amount of its gross premium income arising in the State in respect of a branch or agency. The Order came into effect on May 23, 1995.

Non-disclosure of information not amounting to fraud *Superwood Holdings plc and Ors v Sun Alliance Insurance Group, Prudential Assurance Co., Church And General Insurance Co. and Lloyd's Underwriters* [1995] 3 IR 303 was a crucial decision in what had been the longest civil trial in the history of the State. Indeed, we noted in the 1991 Review, 32, that the High Court judgment in the case, delivered by O'Hanlon J after a 115 day hearing, had not been circulated, such was its length. Neither has it been reported in the meantime.

The plaintiffs' claim arose out of a fire at its factory premises, in which the building was destroyed along with materials used in the manufacturing process. The plaintiffs sought to recover compensation under policies of insurance for indemnity for consequential loss. The defendant insurers repudiated the contracts on the grounds of fraud or a claim exaggerated so excessively as to lead to the inference that it could not have been made honestly. The fire had occurred in October 1987. The defendants were notified immediately, and both parties appointed loss-adjusters. During the remainder of 1987 and 1988, the plaintiff sought payments on account on foot of the consequential loss policy. The defendants refused to make such payments and sought more information from the plaintiffs. This was complied with, but it appeared that the relationship between the parties began to deteriorate. In March 1989 the defendants repudiated the policy and refused to refer the matter to arbitration. The plaintiff issued proceedings seeking a sum for consequential loss arising as a direct result of the fire and also damages in respect of breach of contract.

Two conditions of the contract became central to the proceedings. Condition 4 provided that when damage which was to be the subject-matter of a claim occurred, the insurer was to be notified immediately and the insured was to provide at his own expense a statement of his claim along with any documents or records as might reasonably be required by the insurers in their investigation of the claim. This condition also placed an onus on the insured to mitigate his loss, and provided that no claim under the policy would be payable unless the provisions of the condition were complied with. Condition 5 stated that if a claim under the policy should prove to be in any way fraudulent, then all benefit to be obtained under the policy was to be forfeited. The plaintiffs had claimed that the disruption to their business caused by the fire ran for the year of the indemnity whereas the defendants alleged that the business had only been disrupted for three to five weeks. Secondly, the plaintiffs were relying on business projections of the business which had been calculated for a prospectus launched in 1987. The defendants argued that while these projections might honestly have been believed in 1987, that was not the case in November 1988, and it was fraudulent to have them as the basis for the claim at that time. In the High Court, O'Hanlon J held that there had been a deliberate policy of non co-operation adopted by the plaintiffs, including concealing information deliberately, to prevent the defendants from finding out about the plaintiffs' operations. He found that the claim for compensation was far in excess of the real loss sustained by the plaintiffs, that the effort by the plaintiffs to attribute to the fire the downturn which had taken place in sales and profits for the year 1987/1988 was wholly without foundation, and that the projected production for that year could never have been achieved. However, O'Hanlon J also found that the projections in the prospectus for the home market had been valid. However, he concluded that the plaintiff had been in breach of condition 4 of the policy, and by reason of this had disqualified themselves from claiming any payment under the policy. He also found that the amount claimed by the plaintiffs was so exaggerated that this, coupled with the other findings of fact which had been made, entitled him to draw the inference that the claim was fraudulent and therefore in breach of condition 5. The plaintiffs appealed and the Supreme Court upheld the appeal.

Delivering the only reasoned judgment, O'Flaherty J stated that, in cases such as the instant case, where fraud was in issue and the evidence was circumstantial, the role of the appellate court was very specific. While the appellate court should be slow to substitute its own inference of fact for that of the trial judge where such inference depends on oral evidence of recalled facts, this does not apply where the inference is being drawn from circumstantial evidence, as the Court itself had pointed out in *Hay v O'Grady* [1992] 1 IR 210; [1992] ILRM 689 (1992 Review, 470-72).

As to the substance of fraud, the Court referred to the House of Lords decision in *Derry v Peek* (1889) 14 App Cas 337 in stating that to prove fraud it was necessary to prove the required intent. A false statement will be fraudulent unless there was an honest belief in its truth, and one who knowingly alleges that which he knows to be false obviously has no such honest belief. Turning to the corporate context for the instant case, the Court stated that although a company has no mind or will of its own, it can be vicariously liable for fraud through the so-called 'directing mind and will' of the company. Referring to the decisions in *El Ejou v Dollar Land Holdings Ltd* [1994] 2 All ER 685, *Lennards Carrying Co. Ltd v Asiatic Petroleum Co. Ltd* [1915] AC 705 and its own decision in *Taylor v Smith* [1991] IR 142 (1990 Review, 542-5), the Court stated that in order to identify this 'will', it would be necessary to identify the person who had management and control in relation to the particular act or omission which led to the alleged fraud in question.

Citing *Derry v Peek* again, the Court stated that the onus was on the party alleging fraud to prove it. While the Court had held in *Banco Ambrosiano Spa v Ansbacher & Co. Ltd* [1987] ILRM 669 (1987 Review, 274) that in a civil action for fraud the standard of proof remained that of the balance of probabilities, where, as here, proof was largely a matter of inference, the Court noted that it must not be drawn lightly or without due regard to all the circumstances. It also pointed out that there was a presumption that an insured making a claim is acting honestly.

The Court then examined in detail a number of passages in the High Court judgment of O'Hanlon J which the defendants claimed were findings of fact leading inexorably to a finding of fraud. The Court considered, however, that in general these were not relevant to the issue of fraud: findings of haphazard work, optimism and under-estimation were not findings of fraud and, in overall terms, the Court felt that there had been no finding of the necessary intent to prove fraud and it noted that mere exaggeration was not conclusive evidence of fraud. The Court accepted that in some of the extracts relied on by the defendants O'Hanlon J had found that the plaintiffs had deliberately bolstered their turnover, regardless of whether they were making a profit. However the Supreme Court considered that this must be viewed against the background that the plaintiffs were obliged to mitigate their loss. In any event, in the absence of this specific fraud being pleaded, it was not a fact, even if based on credible evidence, from which the inference could be drawn that fraud had occurred.

As to the projections made by the plaintiffs, the Court noted that the witness who could be considered the 'directing mind and will' on this matter had note been cross-examined as to his honest belief in them, nor had O'Hanlon J made a finding to that effect. Again, on this aspect of the case, the Court concluded that there was no credible evidence upon which to make a determination of fraud. The Court noted that O'Hanlon J had found no breaches of condition 5, and concluded that he had erred in making the generalised conclusion that his findings on condition 4 led inexorably to a finding of fraud. The Supreme Court considered that the issues and matters of proof in relation to each condition were entirely different. Thus, the Court allowed the appeal on the issue concerning condition 5 so that the repudiation of the contract was held to be invalid and the contract was thus not void. The Court would also have found in favour of the plaintiff on condition 4 had it been necessary to do so. The case was remitted to the High Court to determine the extent of the losses arising after the fire and what percentage of those losses were attributable to the fire.

Non-life insurance   The European Communities (Non-Life Insurance Accounts) Regulations 1995 (SI No. 202 of 1995) gave further effect to Directives 73/239/EEC, 88/357/EEC, 90/618/EEC and 92/49/EEC. They introduced new statutory returns which are required to be submitted by authorised non-life insurance undertakings whose head office is established in Ireland or outside the European Communities. They came into effect on July 20, 1995.

INTELLECTUAL PROPERTY

Copyright: term of protection   The European Communities (Term of Protection of Copyright) Regulations 1995 (SI No. 158 of 1995) gave effect to Directive 93/98/EEC which sought to harmonise the terms of copyright protection in the Member States. The 1995 Regulations had the effect of extending from 50 to 70 years the copyright protection contained in the Copyright Act 1963 kin relation to literary, dramatic, musical and artistic works and cinematograph films. The existing 50 year protection for sound recordings is repeated in the 1995 Regulations. Similarly, broadcasting rights extend to 50 years after first transmission. The 1995 Regulations introduced a concept new to Irish copyright law, namely economic rights. The 1995

Regulations provide that a new 25 year term of economic rights is granted to a person who publishes for the first time a work in respect of which copyright has expired. Since the effect of the many extensions in the 1993 Directive is to revive some extinguished copyright rights, certain protections where exploitation or preparations for exploitation of a substantial nature of an extinguished work occurred before the adoption of the Directive in 1993 or before its implementation in the Member States were also included in the 1995 Regulations. The 1995 Regulations came into effect on July 1, 1995. In view of the many changes effected to the 1963 Act by recent Regulations implementing Directives, work is advancing on a new Copyright Bill which will include such recent changes. It is to be hoped that such consolidating legislation will be enacted in the near future.

INTERNATIONAL TRADE

Former Yugoslavia The European Communities (Further Discontinuance of Certain Trade with Serb-Controlled Areas of Boznia-Herzegovina) Regulations 1995 (SI No. 163 of 1995) gave full effect to Regulation (EC) No. 2471/94 to provide penalties for trading in breach of the 1994 Regulation, agreed in the context of the continuing war in former Yugoslavia.

PACKAGE HOLIDAYS

The Package Holidays and Travel Trade Act 1995 gave effect to Directive 90/314/EEC concerning package holidays, and the full text of the 1990 Directive is helpfully reproduced as a Schedule to the Act. The 1995 Act also provided for consequential amendments to the Transport (Tour Operators and Travel Trade) Act 1982. The Act is comprehensively analysed by Jonathan Buttimore, (1995) 13 *ILT* 290.

Package holiday defined S. 2 of the 1995 Act defines a package as follows:

> a combination of at least two of the following components pre-arranged by the organiser when sold or offered for sale at an inclusive price and when the service covers a period of more than twenty-four hours or includes overnight accommodation —
>
> (a) transport;
> (b) accommodation;

(c) other tourist services, not ancillary to transport or accommodation, accounting for a significant proportion of the package.

It is clear that this definition covers a brochure-based package holiday. Two additional matters should be mentioned. First, the definition is not confined to packages involving travel abroad, so that the 1995 Act applies to packages arranged within the State. Second, the definition is sufficiently wide to include 'individualised' packages which involve the components referred to in s. 2 of the 1995 Act.

Organiser The organiser is defined in s. 3 of the 1995 Act as a person who, otherwise than occasionally, organises packages and sells or offers them for sale to a consumer, whether directly or through a retailer. Clearly, therefore, travel companies or tour operators licensed by the Department of Transport, Energy and Communications under the 1982 Act come within this definition, but s. 3 is also more wide-ranging in scope. Thus, a travel agent or 'retailer' licensed under the 1982 Act might also come within the terms of 'organiser' where that person puts together a 'package' within the meaning of s. 2 of the Act. The Package Holidays and Travel Trade Act 1995 (Occasional Organisers) Regulations 1995 (SI No. 271 of 1995) specify the classes of persons who may be regarded as organising packages occasionally for the purposes of s. 3 of the 1995 Act.

General obligations of organiser A key provision is s. 20(1) of the 1995 Act, which provides that the organiser of a package holiday:

> shall be liable to the consumer for the proper performance of the contract, irrespective of whether such obligations are to be performed by the organiser, the retailer, or other suppliers of services. . . .

S. 20(2) goes on to provide that, subject to certain defences which we discuss below, the organiser:

> shall be liable to the consumer for any damage caused by the failure to perform the contract or the improper performance of the contract. . . .

These obligations extend considerably the prior responsibilities at common law of a package holiday provider. Thus, where the holidaymaker suffered physical injuries by reason of the negligence or other breach of duty of the proprietor of the hotel where the holiday is spent, for example by reason of the poor maintenance of a pool, responsibility would in general have fallen solely on the hotel proprietor as occupier rather than on the organiser. This was precisely the conclusion arrived at by Judge Smith in *Kavanagh v Falcon Leisure Group (Overseas) Ltd*, Circuit Court, 20 July 1994, comprehensively noted by Nuala Skeffington (1995) 13 *ILT* 211. Indeed, as is noted in that article, the 1995 Act now imposes liability on the operator in precisely those circumstances. Thus, it may be said that the 1995 Act represents another move in the direction of strict liability in connection with certain consumer contracts.

Defences As indicated, however, the 1995 Act provides that this strict liability is subject to certain defences, which are also specified in s. 20(2), namely where the failure or improper performance:

(a) are attributable to the consumer;

(b) are attributable to a third party unconnected with the provision of the service and are unforeseeable or unavoidable; or

(c) are due to force majeure, that is events beyond the control of the organiser and which appear to encompass events that would bring into operation the doctrine of frustration at common law.

Even in the latter two circumstances, s. 20(7) of the 1995 Act provides that it is an implied term of the contract that the organiser 'will give prompt assistance to a consumer in difficulty'. The nature of the assistance is not prescribed.

We should note that s. 22(1) also provides that the provisions of the 1995 Act 'shall not affect' any other remedy or right of action which the organiser may have against other parties involved in the package. Thus, of course, any contractual or tortious remedies remain open to the organiser, including of course any indemnities which may be arranged.

Limitation of liability S. 20(3) of the 1995 Act provides that the organiser may not limit the amount of compensation to be payable for death or personal injury or damage caused to the consumer by the wilful misconduct or 'gross negligence' of the organiser. However, s. 20(5) provides that liability may be limited in accordance with international conventions which provide for limitation of liability. In this connection Jonathan Buttimore draws attention in his article on the 1995 Act to the Warsaw Convention on International Carriage by Air, the International Berne Convention on Carriage by Rail, the Athens Convention on Carriage by Sea and the Paris Convention on the Liability of Innkeepers. In respect of permissible compensation limits, s. 20(4) the 1995 Act provides that the organiser may not limit liability, in the case of an adult, to an amount equal to double the inclusive price of the package and, in the case of a minor, to an amount equal to the inclusive price of the package. Subject to these provisions, s. 20(6) of the 1995 Act provides that the liability imposed by s. 20 'cannot be excluded by any contractual term.' Finally, s. 20(8) provides that s. 20 is without prejudice to the provisions of the Hotel Proprietors Act 1963, a proviso which underlines the 'domestic' aspect of the 1995 Act.

Other duties of organiser   In addition to the central importance of s. 20 of the 1995 Act, we note here the other elements of the Act which impose duties on organisers. S. 10 requires the operator to include in any brochure certain matters, including the destination and means of transport; the type of accommodation; the meal plan; the itinerary; general information concerning passport and visa requirements and health formalities; any deposit required and timetable for payment of balance of price; whether a minimum number of persons is required for the package; any tax or compulsory charge; where the organiser has no place of business in the State, the name and address of a nominated agent; and arrangements in the even of insolvency. S. 11 provides that the organiser is liable for damage caused as a result of reliance on information in a brochure which contains false or misleading information. Ss. 12 to 15 of the 1995 Act also lay down requirements concerning the information to be provided to an intending consumer before conclusion of the contract, the information to be supplied to a consumer before the start of the package, the essential terms of the contract between the organiser and the consumer and that the essential terms of the contract must be made available in writing to the consumer. S. 16 of the 1995 Act allows a consumer who is prevented from proceeding with a package to transfer the booking to another person who satisfies certain conditions specified. S. 17 imposes certain restrictions on price variations by the organiser. S. 18 provides that it is an implied term of the contract that the organiser inform the consumer of any significant change in an essential term before departure (apart from price) and the consumer has the option of withdrawing from the package without penalty. S. 19 of the Act makes provision for organisers who after the commencement of the package are unable to provide a significant portion of the package. S. 22 of the Act sets out security arrangements in the event of insolvency. Ss. 23 to 25 of the Act lay down bonding requirements and insurance provisions. The Approved Bodies (Fees) Regulations 1995 (SI No. 236 of 1995) set out the appropriate fee for bodies which apply to become approved bodies for the purposes of ss. 23 and 24 of the 1995 Act and set the maximum period for which such approval may be granted. They came into effect on 1 September 1995. The Package Holidays and Travel Trade Act 1995 (Bonds) Regulations 1995 (SI No. 270 of 1995)detail the system of bonding for members of approved bodies and came into force on October 1, 1995.

Licensing Ss. 26 to 34 of the 1995 Act amend the provisions of the Transport (Tour Operators and Travel Trade) Act 1982 to take account of the 1995 Act in so far as it concerns the licensing of tour operators and travel agents by the Department of Transport, Energy and Communications. On the 1982 Act, see the 1987 Review, 242.

Commencement The principal provisions of the 1995 Act came into effect on 1 October 1995(s. 5 coming into effect on September 1, 1995): Package Holidays and Travel Trade Act 1995 (Commencement) Order 1995 (SI No. 235 of 1995). We should note here that Article 9 of the 1990 Directive implemented by the 1995 Act provided that Member States were required to bring into force the measures necessary to comply with the Directive before 31 December 1992. In accordance with the views of the Court of Justice in *Francovich v Italy* [1991] ECR I-5357, the failure to implement the Directive within the time limit specified may have implications for the State in respect of package holiday contracts entered into between December 31, 1992 and October 1, 1995.

PERFORMANCE BOND

In *Celtic International Insurance Co. Ltd v Banque Nationale De Paris (Ireland) Ltd* [1995] 2 ILRM 518, the Supreme Court held that a performance bond or guarantee is virtually payable on demand and should be regarded as analogous to a bill of exchange so that a document certifying money to be due under such a bond should be accepted on its face in the absence of exceptional circumstances, such as an allegation of fraud. The background was as follows. A construction company, customers of the defendant bank, had entered into a contract with a Health Board to carry out certain building works. The plaintiff and the building company entered into a contract guarantee bond in favour of the Health Board in respect of the performance of the contract. By a letter of undertaking the defendant undertook to indemnify the plaintiff up to a particular sum against any money which the plaintiff would be required to pay pursuant to the contract guarantee bond. It was a term of this undertaking that the money would be paid when the plaintiff certified it to be due. The defendant in turn obtained counter-indemnification from the building company in respect of the letter of undertaking.

Subsequently, a receiver was appointed to the building company and the building contract was assigned to another company and a deed executed under which the performance of the contract by that company was to be guaranteed by the plaintiff. These deeds were executed with no reference to the defendant. The Health Board later wrote to the plaintiff, calling on the guarantee bond for the sum of £50,445.04 on the basis that the building company, now in receivership, had defaulted in the execution of the contract. The plaintiff then wrote to the defendant certifying that the sum claimed was due. The defendant refused to pay, arguing that the guarantee had been discharged on the date when the building contract had been assigned to another company.

The defendant submitted that the benefit of the counter-cross-indemnity with the original building company was no longer in place and had been removed without its consent. Evidence was given on the plaintiff behalf to the effect that, once the receiver had been appointed to the building company, many sub-contractors had refused to carry out any further work and that, as a consequence, it was unable to carry out the building works for the Health Board and that the Board had threatened to terminate the contract. It was also deposed that if this had happened, the call on the plaintiff's bond would have been substantial, as would the consequential call on the defendant's guarantee, and that therefore the negotiations and subsequent substitution of the second company had been to the benefit of the defendant rather than its detriment.

The High Court had held in the plaintiff's favour and the Supreme Court affirmed. The Court noted that he promise made by the defendant was in respect of default in the execution of the contract, and this was much wider than mere default in the building operations. The Court also noted in passing that the defendant's liability would indeed have been much greater if a different course had been adopted and the building contract had been discharged at the behest of the Health Board.

However, as already indicated, the Supreme Court's main holding was that the certificate on behalf of the Health Board should be accepted on its face in the absence of very exceptional circumstances such as the allegation of fraud. Citing with approval the views expressed in *Edward Owen Engineering Ltd v Barclays Bank International* [1978] 1 All ER 976, *Hamzeh Malas & Sons Ltd v British Imex Industries Ltd* [1958] 2 QB 127 and *Sztejn v J. Henry Schroder Banking Corp*, 31 NY Supp (2d) 631 (1941), the Court concluded that a performance bond or guarantee was virtually a promissory note payable on demand and should be regarded as analogous to a bill of exchange. Finally, we may note that the Court pointed out that, notwithstanding the building company's receivership, it was clear that the counter-indemnity remained in place. However, the Court accepted that this was not, in any event, relevant to the main issue which was that the certificate in question was binding in the absence of any evidence of fraud.

PUBLIC SUPPLY AND WORKS CONTRACTS

Further steps in implementing the EC-based requirement that public service, public supply and public works contracts be open to bids from commercial undertakings in all Member States were given effect in 1995. On previous Regulations, see the 1992 Review, 46, the 1993 Review, 66 and the 1994 Review, 44.

Water, energy, transport and telecommunications   The European Communities (Award Of Contracts by Entities Operating in the Water, Energy, Transport and Telecommunications Sectors) Regulations 1995 (SI No. 51 of 1995), which came into force on February 28, 1995, gave effect to Directive 93/38/EEC. They govern the procedures for the procurement of supplies, works (both building and civil engineering) and services, by certain entities operating in the water, energy, transport and telecommunications sectors where the contract value exceeds the relevant thresholds set out in the 1993 Directive.

TRADE AND TOURISM

Tourist Board   The Tourist Traffic Act 1995 enables Bord Fáilte Éireann, the Irish Tourist Board, to delegate to a contractor the majority of its inspection and associated functions and powers under the Tourist Traffic Acts 1937 to 1987 concerning the registration and grading of tourist accommodation and its functions under the Intoxicating Liquor Act 1988 concerning special restaurant licences. The Act came into effect on July 5, 1995 on its signature by the President.

Communications

Eamonn G. Hall

The European Commission hosted the G7 Conference in Brussels in February 1995. This conference followed the G7 Naples summit of July 1994 when the leaders of the most powerful states in the world decided to hold a conference in Brussels to discuss how to encourage and promote the innovation and development of new technologies including in particular, the implementation of open, competitive and world-wide information infrastructures. The 1995 Conference concentrated on the regulatory framework and competition policies, the implementation of information infrastructures and their accessibility to the public as well as the social and cultural aspects of the information society.

In the course of its deliberations, the G7 Conference emphasised that the regulatory framework should put the user first and meet a variety of complementary societal objectives. It must be designed to allow choice and high quality services at affordable prices. The regulatory framework should be based on an environment that encourages dynamic competition, ensures the separation of operating and regulatory functions as well as promoting interconnectivity and interoperability. Such a regulatory environment would maximise consumer choice by stimulating the creation and flow of information and other content supplied by a wide range of service and content providers.

The G7 Conference considered that open access to networks for services and information suppliers and the enrichment of the citizen through the promotion of diversity, including cultural and linguistic diversity as well as the free expression of ideas, were essential for the creation of the Global Information Society.

The G7 partners expressed a commitment to enable citizens to communicate by virtue of universal service in their respective communications markets. This commitment required consultation and legislation on both the scope and means of providing universal service, especially with regard to its financing, whilst ensuring that the development of networks and the provision of services can be carried out without undue burden on any actors. These themes will be reflected in the review of the law in this chapter.

BROADCASTING

Broadcasting Complaints Commission The sixteenth annual report of the Broadcasting Complaints Commission, (a statutory tribunal established pursuant to the Broadcasting Authority Act 1960 as amended by the Broadcasting Authority (Amendment) Act 1976) was published in 1995. Copies of the Report are laid before both Houses of the Oireachtas and the chairperson of the Commission is Ms Geri Silke, barrister. The Commission is empowered to adjudicate upon complaints in relation to breaches of objectivity, fairness and impartiality and invasion of privacy in the context of news, current affairs programmes, advertising and published matters on both RTE (the national broadcasting service) and other broadcasting services within the State.

In the *Complaint of Gerry Boland* (1995 Annual Report) the complainant argued, amongst other matters, that there had been bias on the part of Gay Byrne, the presenter of the Late Late Show on RTE 1, in relation to the Late Late Show programme broadcast in September 1993. Mr Boland complained that he had been afforded an inequitable amount of time as a guest on the Late Late Show representing an organisation 'The Alliance for Animal Rights' which he co-founded and of which he was a spokesperson. Mr Boland complained that he was told by a researcher on the Late Late Show that he would be the only person on the panel invited to discuss the issue of hare coursing and his campaign which included a call for a picket on Irish Tourist offices abroad. He complained that the RTE Authority failed to be fair to all interests concerned and failed to present the broadcast matter in an objective and impartial manner and without any expression of the Authority's own views thus contravening s. 18(1)(b) of the Broadcasting Authority Act 1960 as amended by the 1976 Act.

In its response to the Commission in the *Boland* case, RTE stated that the Late Late Show focused on the particular tactic of picketing Irish embassies and tourist offices, and the encouragement of foreigners to boycott Ireland, whilst hare coursing remained a legitimate industry or pastime. RTE did not accept the validity of Mr Boland's claim to have been 'set up', 'deceived' and 'deliberately misled' by the Late Late Show production team.

Having considered all the correspondence relating to the complaint, the Commission held that there had been no breach of s. 18(1)(b) of the Broadcasting Authority Act 1960 as amended by the 1976 Act and accordingly dismissed the complaint.

War, violence and their repercussions constituted the subject matter of the *Complaint of Mr Z. Jaksic* (1995 Annual Report). Mr Jaksic complained of the 'Tuesday File' programme broadcast on RTE in February 1994 which reported on the war in Bosnia-Hercegovina. The complaint was made on behalf of the small Serbian community resident in Ireland, disturbed by what Mr Jaksic described as the continuing biased and one-sided reporting of the war in Bosnia-Hercegovina. Mr Jaksic submitted that throughout the programme several references were made that were inaccurate. Mr Jaksic, in effect, stated that RTE had conducted a trial by media, backed by doubtful testimonies, unsubstantiated allegations and innuendoes.

Mr Jaksic submitted that the programme represented 'a demonisation' of the Serbian people and gave the Irish public a totally distorted picture of the Serbs. Mr Jaksic complained that the programme was generally biased against the Serbs in general, that it was based on hearsay and second-hand evidence and that, despite the reporter's repeated statements that RTE possessed evidence of alleged crimes, no such evidence was shown.

In its defence, RTE stated that it did not accept Mr Jaksic' claim that the programme constituted 'a demonisation' of the Serbian people. RTE argued that it was stated during the programme that Serbs too were refugees who had been driven from their homes by Muslim and Croat forces. After a detailed rebuttal of the allegations, RTE concluded that it was satisfied that the television programme followed the highest standards and practice of journalistic investigation and that the broadcast was accurate and fair. The Commission considered the complaint under s. 18(1)(b) of the Broadcasting Authority Act 1960 as amended by the 1976 Act (duties of fairness, objectivity and impartiality) and found that there had been no breach of the provisions of the Act and therefore dismissed the claim.

Many of the complaints to the Broadcasting Complaints Commission do not succeed. Under Article 40.6.1°i of the Constitution, the State guarantees liberty for the exercise, subject to public order and morality, of the right of citizens to express freely their convictions and opinions. In Article 40.6.1°i of the Constitution there is also a particular reference to broadcasting as an organ of public opinion and there is a reference to preserving its rightful liberty of expression, subject to certain restrictions. In that context, it is difficult for a person to prove that a statutory duty of fairness and impartiality had been breached. Accordingly, it is of note that the *Annual Report of the Broadcasting Complaints Commission for 1995* contains a case where the Commission upheld a complaint in relation to the statutory obligations of objectivity and fairness.

In the *Complaint of the Beaumont Hospital Board* (Annual Report, 1995), the board of Beaumont Hospital complained that the current affairs programme, 'Tuesday File' on Baby Michael Walshe, broadcast in March 1993 was presented in a biased manner, was subjective and unfair to many of the interests of persons concerned and very damaging to Beaumont Hospital as an institution and to its staff, medical, nursing and administrative, both personally and collectively. It was argued by Beaumont Hospital that the effect of the broadcast was to damage unfairly the reputation of the hospital and its relationship with patients in the community it served.

The first part of the programme related to the death of baby Michael Walshe who arrived at Beaumont Hospital on Sunday, June 30, 1991 accompanied by a chart from Ardkeen Hospital. Mr O'Laoire, a neurosurgeon, saw the baby the day he arrived and again on July 6, 1991. On the fifth day, Ardkeen Hospital sent a message to Beaumont Hospital with a diagnosis of meningitis and treatment commenced. On the sixth day the baby died. A neuropathologist, Dr Farrell, examined the baby and came to the conclusion that the baby had died from acute prulent meningitis and severe generalised hypoxic ischaemic encephalopathy. The second part of the RTE programme considered the findings of a Ministerial Committee of Inquiry into the conduct of a doctor of the hospital.

In its response to the Commission, RTE submitted that the complainant misrepresented the content, tone and purpose of the programme, unjustifiably attacked the reputation of one of RTE's most senior experienced television producers and falsely accused RTE of a grave breach of its statutory obligations, particularly those of objectivity and impartiality. RTE stated that it was never its intention to criticise Beaumont Hospital or any of its staff. The focus of the programme was stated to be clearly upon Mr O'Laoire's treatment at the hands of a Committee of Inquiry and not upon the conduct of the hospital or its employees.

RTE submitted that the first part of the programme set the conflicting evidence on the immediate cause of the death of baby Michael Walshe in a careful and balanced way. It did suggest that there had been unusual aspects to the death that provoked different responses and which clearly required some explanation. The second part of the programme dealt with the findings of the Ministerial Committee of Inquiry and the question as to whether they were justified 'beyond reasonable doubt'.

In finding for Beaumont Hospital, the Commission held that the RTE Authority was in breach of the statutory duties of objectivity, impartiality and fairness as set out in ss. 18(1)(a) and (b) of the Broadcasting Authority Act 1960, as amended by the 1976 Act. The Commission held that the programme was not fair to the interests of Beaumont Hospital and members of its staff. The Commission was also of the opinion that the programme was presented in such a way as to clearly favour Mr O'Laoire's interests, with the result that it was unfair to the interests of Beaumont Hospital.

The Commission also stated in its decision that the programme was visually presented in such a manner as to be unfair to the interests of Beaumont Hospital and its staff. There were also serious omissions and inaccuracies in the programme. The programme did not leave the viewer with an accurate impression of the issues dealt with by the programme.

In its Annual Report for 1995, in which details of the Beaumont Hospital complaint are outlined, the Commission stated that all decisions made by the Commission had been accepted by the RTE Authority. S. 18C(1) of the Broadcasting Authority Act 1960 as amended by s. 3 of the Broadcasting Authority (Amendment) Act 1976 provides that the Commission must state whether or not the entity complained of, in this instance the RTE Authority, accepted the decision of the Commission.

Competition Rules On April 6, 1995, the Court of Justice of the European Communities delivered its judgment in *RTE & Anor v European Commission* [1995] All ER (EC) 416 known as the *Magill* case. The case commenced in 1986 when Magill TV Guide Ltd. (Magill) attempted to publish a comprehensive television guide containing information on forthcoming programmes of three television broadcasters, whose programmes could be received in most households in Ireland and up to 30% to 40% in Northern Ireland. Magill was prevented from doing so by injunction obtained in the Irish courts by RTE, Independent Television Productions Limited (ITP) (a company established by ITV) and the BBC, publishers of individual guides of their own television programme listings. The Irish High Court so held partly on the ground that Magill publications infringed their copyright in the programme schedules under Irish legislation. See *RTE v Magill TV Guide Ltd* [1988] IR 97.

Magill lodged a complaint with the European Commission alleging that the companies refusal to license the publication of their respective listings was in breach of Article 86 of the EC Treaty which prohibited undertakings which held a dominant position in a specified market from using that position to restrict competition. The Commission held that there had been a breach of Article 86 and ordered the three companies to end that breach by supplying each other and third parties on request with their individual advance weekly programmes and listings. RTE and ITP appealed to the Court of First Instance of the European Communities which upheld the Commission's decision. They then appealed to the Court of Justice.

The Court of Justice dismissed the appeals in *Magill* holding, *inter alia*, that RTE and ITP did occupy a dominant position for the purposes of Article 86 of the Treaty since they enjoyed a de facto monopoly over the information necessary to compile listings for the television programmes received in Ireland and were thus in a position to prevent effective competition in the market in weekly television magazines. On the facts, the companies' refusal, (relying on national copyright provisions), to provide basic information necessary to produce a comprehensive weekly television guide constituted an abuse of a dominant position under Article 86 because it prevented the appearance of a new product which the companies did not offer and for which there was a potential consumer demand.

Accordingly, the appellants had been found to be in breach of Article 86 and it was considered that the imposition of compulsory licensing was the only way to bring an end to that breach. This case will have considerable significance in general for undertakings in relation to copyright.

Re-transmission of Television Programmes   In a significant and comprehensive judgment delivered by Keane J on November 10, 1995, entitled *Carrigaline Community Television Broadcasting Co. Ltd v Minister for Transport, Energy and Communications and Others*, 2 *Irish Current Law Monthly Digest* 4, (High Court, 10 November 1995), the learned judge reviewed aspects of administrative law, constitutional law, competition law and communications law in relation to aspects pertaining to re-transmission of broadcasting programmes and raised issues of considerable significance in relation to broadcasting and the general regulatory policy pursued by the State. The first named plaintiff, Carrigaline Community Television Broadcasting Company Ltd (Carrigaline) had erected an aerial in rural County Cork to re-transmit UK broadcasting programme services to local residents. Carrigaline had applied for a re-transmission licence but had been refused. A year after Carrigaline began re-transmission the Government decided to meet the public demand for the transmission of UK television signals by licensing a system called Microwave Multipoint Distribution System (MMDS) pursuant to the Wireless Telegraphy (Television Programme Re-Transmission) Regulations, 1989 (SI No. 39 of 1989). Carrigaline had not applied for a licence under the 1989 Regulations on the basis that there had been indications from the Minister's Department that he was sympathetic to their position and gave them the impression that they might co-exist with the MMDS system.

In 1988 the Broadcasting and Wireless Telegraphy Act 1988 (No. 19 of 1988) introduced a new and more severe regime for illegal broadcasting activities. However, no prosecutions had been instituted against Carrigaline and any property that had been seized was duly returned. Carrigaline renewed its application for a licence for the re-broadcasting system and received the reply that it was not considered practical to license such a system. Subsequently, Carrigaline issued proceedings against the Minister for Transport, Energy and Communications, the Minister for Arts, Culture and the Gaeltacht, Ireland, the Attorney General and Cork Communications Ltd. Cork Communications Ltd had received the licence for the County Cork region under the MMDS regime. Keane J granted a mandatory injunction directing the Minister for Transport, Energy and Communications to consider Carrigalines application for a re-transmission licence in accordance with law. The court considered that it was obliged to set aside a decision where it was shown to be unlawful because of the manner in which the decision was made, whether because the competent authority failed to consider the matter in a fair and impartial manner or because it took into account factors which it should have excluded or excluded factors which it should have taken into account. Keane J considered that in the case of a licensing regime established under the Wireless Telegraphy Act 1926 (No. 45 of 1926) the Minister while under a duty to consider all applications for licences in a fair and impartial manner, was also entitled to have regard to certain policy considerations.

The court considered, applying *Attorney General v Paperlink Ltd* [1984] ILRM 373, that the right of freedom of expression guaranteed by Article 40.6.1°i was confined to expression of opinion. However, the Court noted that this guarantee was not confined to the expression of one's own opinion but extended to expressing freely the opinions of others. However, the judge held that the relevant provisions sought to be impugned by Carrigaline were neither inconsistent with nor invalid having regard to the relevant articles of the Constitution.

Carrigaline had argued that the Minister could be described as being 'engaged for gain' within the ambit of ss. 4 and 5 of the Competition Act 1991 on the basis that the Minister imposed a charge for the granting of a licence because the annual fee for the licence was based on 5% of the turnover. However, the court held that the Minister was not an undertaking within the meaning of the Competition Act 1991. The court held that there was nothing in the Treaty of Rome which prevented the Minister from conferring on one or more establishments an exclusive right to conduct transmissions. The *ratio* in *Sacchi* [1974] ECR 409 and *E.R.T.* [1991] 1 ECR 2925 was applied.

In the context of the European Convention on Human Rights, the court held that even if it had been possible for Carrigaline to invoke the assistance of Article 10 of the Convention, Keane J was satisfied that the jurisprudence of the Court of Human Rights had no application to the facts of the case.

The Court held that the Minister had rejected Carrigaline's application for a licence without any detailed investigation of the question as to whether it was a feasible method of meeting existing public demand for UK television programme services. The paramount duty of the Minister had been to consider all the proposals before him in a fair and impartial manner. Therefore, the Minister was not entitled to determine in advance that one form of re-transmission alone would be permitted and that franchises would be granted for it to the exclusion of any other system. The court also held that even though Carrigaline in its operations had unarguably been in breach of the law the court should not seek to punish Carrigaline by depriving the plaintiff of its constitutional right. There had been in existence at every stage the machinery by which Carrigaline could have been prosecuted by the Minister.

POSTAL COMMUNICATIONS

In the era of the Global Information Society and the emphasis on the electronic media, insufficient attention may be paid to the postal services. Postal services constitute an essential means of communications and are of vital importance for many social and economical activities throughout the EC Community. Throughout the EC Community postal services employ about 1.8 million workers of which 1.4 million are employed by the public postal operators. An efficient postal sector in Europe is considered to be an important prerequisite for the further development of competitiveness and employment in the European economy.

In a *Proposal for a European Parliament and Council Directive on common rules for the development of Community postal services and the improvement of quality of service* COM (1995) 227 final, the EC Commission considered that it was of 'the utmost importance' to guarantee within the whole Community the maintenance of a good-quality universal service accessible for all users at affordable prices. The EC Commission also noted that the financial viability of such universal service must be ensured. In its 1995 proposal for a European Parliament and Council Directive, the Commission noted that the completion of the internal market for the postal sector requires the further development of the Community postal services and in particular the implementation of the fundamental principles of freedom to provide services and freedom of establishment. It was considered essential that competition would play an important role in this sector of the economy and that there should be 'a level playing field' for all economic actors concerned.

The 1995 Proposal from the Commission above followed on the Commission's *Green Paper on the development of a single market for postal services*, COM (91) 476, final, June 11, 1992 and the subsequent public consultations which led to the European Parliament and the Council inviting the Commission to propose measures necessary for implementing a Community policy on postal services. It was argued that the measures should refer specifically to the definition of universal service, the obligations of the providers of the universal service, the definition of services that may be reserved to the universal service providers, the quality of the universal service, and the required technical standardisation.

In particular, the Council emphasised that the measures proposed should be transparent, simple and easy to manage, to ensure the best possible conditions of monitoring and enforcement. Accordingly, the Commission submitted to the European Parliament, the Council, the Social and Economic Committee and the Committee of the Regions in 1995 a package of measures concerning common rules for the development of Community postal services and the improvement of quality of service and a draft notice on the application of the competition rules to the postal sector and in particular on the assessment of certain State measures relating to postal services. The measures constitute a comprehensive approach for establishing for the first time at Community level a universal postal service and gradual liberalisation and opening up of the postal market to more competition.

Tariffs, Terms and Conditions The Foreign Parcel Post Amendment (No. 30) Scheme, 1995 (SI No. 101 of 1995), made by An Post, in the exercise of the powers conferred on it by section 70 of the Postal and Telecommunications Services Act 1983 authorised increases in fees that may be charged for parcels and certain courier items to destinations outside the State. The scheme also authorised increases in the fees that may be charged for An Post insurance service and customs clearance facility.

In the Inland Post Amendment (No. 52) Scheme, 1995 (SI No. 99 of 1995), An Post was authorised to increase the rates of postage for parcels and to change certain fees charged for the courier service. The Inland Post (Amendment) (No. 53) Scheme, 1995 (SI No. 100 of 1995) reduced the maximum 'trade charge' collectable on certain cash-on-delivery parcels. In its Inland Post Amendment (No. 54) Scheme, 1995 (SI No. 299 of 1995) An Post provided that the sender of a registered item is obliged to value that item when it was being registered. The scheme also limited compensation to the value placed upon the article being transmitted.

TELECOMMUNICATION CARRIER SERVICES

Award of Contracts An example of the implementation of the concept of transparency is illustrated in the European Communities (Award of Contracts by Entities operating in the Water, Energy, Transport and Telecommunications Sectors) Regulations 1995 (SI No. 51 of 1995). The regulations incorporated directly into Irish law EEC Council Directive 93/38 governing the procedures for the procurement for supplies, works (both building and civil engineering) and services by certain utilities including the national telecommunication carrier service. The regulations provide that the appropriate contracting entities including, where applicable, Telecom Éireann, shall comply with the relevant procedures of that Directive.

The procedures apply when certain thresholds are exceeded in terms of value. Contracts are categorised into works contracts including contracts relating to buildings and civil engineering contracts together with the supplies and services necessary to carry them into effect. Where the value of such contracts exceeds ECU 5 million (*c.* IR£3.8 million) the relevant procedures in the Directive apply. Supply and services contracts relating to the supply of goods and services whether financed through purchase, lease, rental or hire purchase and including the supply and installation of plant and equipment, financial advertising and management consultancy services, are subject to the relevant procedures in the Directive where the value of such contracts exceeds ECU 600,000 (*c.* IR£464,000).

Carrier Service Tariffs, Terms and Conditions   Pursuant to section 90 of the Postal and Telecommunications Services Act 1983 (No. 24 of 1983) Telecom Éireann made five schemes in the form of statutory instruments regulating its tariffs, terms and conditions of service during 1995. The Telecommunications (Amendment) Scheme 1995 (SI No. 65 of 1995) provided for changes to certain pricing structures including volume discount schemes. The Telecommunications (Amendment) (No. 2) Scheme 1995 (SI No. 107 of 1995) provided for the reduction of certain telecommunications charges and the extension of the international volume discount scheme. The Telecommunications (Amendment) (No. 3) Scheme 1995 (SI No. 134 of 1995) provided for certain tariffs for the Éircell service. The Telecommunications (Amendment) (No. 4) Scheme 1995 (SI 182 of 1995) provided for a further reduction of certain telecommunications charges, the introduction of certain new services including a data virtual private network facility. The Telecommunications (Amendment) (No. 5) Scheme 1995 (SI No. 315 of 1995) provided for a reduction of specified telecommunications charges, the introduction of a call-answering facility, 1890 calls and the alteration of leased line charges.

Corporate Governance   In August 1995, the Minister for Transport, Energy and Communications, Mr Michael Lowry, TD, announced the establishment of a Task Force to review the efficiency of the existing controls governing the commercial state companies under his aegis. These companies, with a combined turnover of over IR£4 billion in 1994 accounted for half of the commercial State companies then in existence. Telecom Éireann was included in the review that primarily related to an examination of such matters as procurement of goods and services (including capital investment); disposal of assets; internal audit; and corporate governance in general.

The *Report of the Task Force* (October 1995) Stationery Office, (Pn. 1996), chaired by Brendan Tuohy, referred to 'dramatic challenges' facing the commercial State companies 'in an increasingly competitive environment'. The report emphasised the necessity for a balance to be struck between public accountability of these State enterprises and their commercial freedom. The Task Force emphasised the need for increased commerciality among the companies and improved corporate governance. The report noted that an increasingly stringent bureaucratic framework was precisely what must be avoided. It would be difficult for the commercial State companies to operate with the zest of enterprise if they are hampered by rules and procedures that add little by way of effective additional protection or control.

Several recommendations were made in the context of procurement, disposal of assets, internal audit and separately, the issue of what may be described as corporate governance. The Task Force recommended that corporate governance in general needed to be the subject of a separate review. However, in advance of that review, the Review Group made certain proposals. One of these proposals was that persons appointed as chairpersons and directors of boards of the commercial State companies should be appointed solely on the basis of their experience, competence and expertise. The Group concluded that the system of selection, remuneration of directors of their companies should be reviewed.

Premium Rate Telephone Services   A premium rate telephone service is the designation used to describe a telephone service in respect of which part of the telephone charge paid or payable by a telephone customer is shared between a telecommunications network operator and a provider of information or other services over the telephone. This telecommunication service began in Ireland in 1988 when services supplying up-dated weather reports, information on bloodstock and sports results became available over the telephone. Subsequently, several companies specialised in the provision of such information services over the telephone. For example, by June 1995 the Royal College of Surgeons in Ireland provided health information for persons travelling abroad.

Others provided 'adult services' which were recorded and gave rise to some concern. A form of regulation came about by critical reaction. The Telecommunications (Premium Rate Telephone Service) Scheme 1995 (SI No. 194 of 1995) made by Telecom Éireann pursuant to s. 90 of the Postal and Telecommunications Services Act 1983 specified terms and conditions upon which Telecom Éireann provided or assisted in the provision of these telephone services. A regulator of Premium Rate Telephone Services, Judge Mary Kotsonoursis, was appointed in April 1995 together with two lay assessors, Mary Maher, a journalist, and Maurice Hayes, a former Ombudsman for Northern Ireland. They were to be independent of any network service provider and of any provider of any premium rate service.

The 1995 scheme, a statutory instrument, obliged a service provider — meaning a person other than the network telecommunications operator who provided an information service — to comply at all times with any Code of Practice published by the Regulator or any other competent authority. A service provider was obliged in the provision of a service not to use the service for the transmission of any message or other matter which was grossly offensive, or of an indecent, obscene or menacing character, for the transmission of any message or other matter which the service provider, its servants, agents or contractors knew to be false, or for the purpose of causing annoyance, inconvenience or needless anxiety to any person.

Where a service provider is deemed to be in breach of the provisions of the laws laid down in the 1995 statutory instrument, the network service provider is empowered to bar access to some or all of the premium rate telephone services offered until such time as the breach had been remedied or the service provider had given undertakings to the satisfaction of the regulatory authority.

The Regulator of Premium Rate Telephone Services, Judge Mary Kotsonouris, published a Code of Practice in December 1995. The role of the Regulator is to supervise both the content and promotion of premium rate telephone services and enforce the Code of Practice. The premium rate service providers agreed by contract that the Regulator may monitor samples of premium rate telephone services from time to time in order to ascertain whether they complied with codes of practice in respect of their content and promotion. The 1995 Code of Practice specifies that services and promotional material must not contain material indicating 'violence, sadism or cruelty of a repulsive or horrible nature'. Services and promotional literature were also specified not to be of a nature likely to

(i) result in any unreasonable invasion of privacy;
(ii) induce an unacceptable sense of fear or anxiety;
(iii) encourage or incite any person to engage in dangerous practices or to use harmful substances; or
(iv) induce or promote disharmony on the basis of race, religion, gender or sexual orientation.

Services and promotional material must not be of a kind which is likely to cause grave or widespread offence, debase, degrade or demean. Services and promotional literature must not involve the use of 'foul language' and specifically service providers are directed to use all reasonable endeavours 'to ensure that services are not used to promote or facilitate prostitution'. Services and promotional material must not be of a nature which are likely to mislead by inaccuracy, ambiguity, exaggeration, omission or otherwise.

A section of the Code of Practice is devoted to services of a sexual nature. Services of a sexual nature are described as 'services of a sexually suggestive or titillating nature or services where the associated promotional material is of a sexually suggestive or titillating nature.' The service provider is obliged to ensure that premium rate telephone services are not used for the transmission of any message or other matter which is grossly offensive of an indecent or obscene character. Promotions for services of a sexual nature must not appear in publications intended for children or young persons.

Under the heading of 'Childrens' Services', the Code defines a child as a person under 16 years of age. A childrens' service is defined as a telephone service which, in whole or in part, was likely to be attractive to children. Specifically no childrens' service is to cost more than £2 for the total cost of a single telephone call. Promotional material for childrens' services is to state clearly the maximum possible cost of the service and that it would be used only with the agreement of the person responsible for paying the telephone bill. Specifically, promotional material for children is not to promote anything that is likely to result in harm to children or which exploit their credulity, lack of experience or sense of loyalty.

The Regulator is empowered to require 'live services' to be recorded and the recordings are to be made available on demand. Recordings are to be retained by the service provider for a period of not less than 3 months, on a month by month basis.

The Code of Practice also deals with procedures, sanctions and funding. The Regulator is to be funded by a levy on network operators and a levy on service providers.

Radio Paging Service The European Communities (Pan-European Land-based Public Radio Paging Service — ERMES (Regulations), 1995 (SI No. 28 of 1995) gave effect to Council Directive 90/544/EEC. With effect from February 1, 1995 certain radio frequency channels were specifically designated and stated to have priority and to be protected for use by the pan-European land-based public radio paging service (ERMES). The pan-European land-based public radio paging service is a public radio paging service based on a terrestrial infrastructure in the Member States of the European Community conforming to the European Telecommunications Standard (ETS) developed by the European Telecommunications Standards Institute (ETSI) allowing persons wishing to send or receive alert, numeric or alpha-numeric messages anywhere within the coverage of the service.

PUBLICATIONS

Among the articles and commentaries published during 1995 on aspects of communications law in Ireland were the following: C. Baillie, 'The Magill Case and the Berne Convention', 3 *IT Law Today* 3 (1995); Baker and McKenzie, 'ECJ Rules in Magill TV Listings case', *In-House Lawyer*, May 1995, 147; J. Bridgeman, 'Multimedia Products and the Video Recordings

Act 1989 — Blue Movies, Red Tape, White Noise', 2 *Commercial Law Practitioner* 251 (November, 1995); A. Burke, S. Curran, 'Sky Fails to Prevent Sale of Smart Cards', 11 *Computer Law and Practice* 34 (1995); Clifford Chance, 'ECJ Judgment in the Magill Case', 6 *Practical Law for Companies*, 52, (1995); T. Cook 'At Last, the Magill Judgment', *Managing Intellectual Property*, 3, (May 1995); R. Greaves, 'Magill Est Arrive — RTE and ITP v Commission of European Communities', 16 *European Competition Law Review*, 244 (1995); E.G. Hall, 'The Majestic Guarantee: Freedom of Speech — the Non-Renewal of the Section 31 Order', 9 *Dlí* 79, (1995); E.G. Hall, M. Pery Knox-Gore, S. Phelan, D. Kerr, D. McAleese, 'Telecommunications: Legal Issues in the New Competitive Era', *The Irish Centre for European Law*, 1995; G. Hogan, 'The Demise of the Irish Broadcasting Ban', 1 *European Public Law* 67 (1995); C. Keville, 'The Final Word on Magill: the Judgment of the ECJ', 17 *European Intellectual Property Review* 297 (1995); C.G. Miller, 'Magill Case — European Court Final Judgment' 11 *Competition Law and Practice* 62, (1995); F. McCann, 'European Court Rules in Copyright Case of Magill', *In-House Lawyer* 63, (May, 1995); Naborro Nathanson, 'Magill the ECJ Decision', 9 *Corporate Briefing* 6, (1995); and K. Wood, 'Reporting the Courts', 89 *Gazette, Law Society of Ireland* 163, (1995).

Company Law

by Dr David Tomkin and Adam Mc Auley

of the Dublin City University Business School

Company's power to challenge the constitutionality of statutes: *locus standi* **and constitutional rights of companies** *Iarnród Éireann Teo/Irish Rail Ltd v Ireland & Ors.* [1995] 2 ILRM 161. This case concerns a challenge to the constitutionality of s. 12 and 14 of the Civil Liability Act 1961. These sections provide that if liability is apportioned between more than one defendants, and one of the defendants cannot meet its liability, this deficiency must be made up by the other(s).

Irish Rail Ltd (IRL) provides railway and road freight services. One of IRL's trains was involved in an accident. IRL and other defendants were sued in negligence. IRL was held to have been contributorily negligent and liable for 30% of the damages awarded to the plaintiff. The other defendant was liable for the remaining 70% and was impecunious. Therefore, IRL was statutorily obliged to pay 100% of the damages awarded, £16,000. There were approximately 230 other claims arising out of the same accident. IRL therefore estimated that it had a potential liability of over £3.4 million. The only way it could meet this was to reduce services or increase fares or both. After the negligence action, IRL challenged the constitutionality of ss. 12 and 14 of the Civil Liability Act 1961. IRL argued that although it was an artificial legal entity, it nevertheless was entitled to certain constitutional rights. Those rights guaranteed by Articles 40.3.1° and 40.3.2° of the Constitution were violated by the provisions of the 1961 Act.

The defendants argued that artificial legal entities were not entitled to rights under the Constitution and therefore IRL did not have *locus standi* to challenge the legislative provisions.

Although IRL argued that as a corporate entity, it could initiate proceedings in its own name, it nevertheless adopted the frequently used device of joining a shareholder (its company secretary) as a party.

In the High Court, Keane J reviewed the case law on the *locus standi* of artificial legal entities to challenge the constitutionality of statute. Prior to 1969, there had been no judicial determination whether or not artificial legal entities could bring such challenges. In *East Donegal Co-operative Livestock Marts Ltd v Attorney General* [1970] IR 317, O'Keeffe P suggested that artificial persons might not be entitled to rely on constitutional guarantees. He did not have to answer this conclusively. If the artificial person in this case (the company) was not so entitled, then each human plaintiff had *locus standi*. In *East Donegal*, the Supreme Court expressed no view on this particular question.

Keane J then discussed the High Court decision in *Private Motorists Provident Society Ltd v Attorney General* [1983] IR 339. In this case, the company argued that the legislation in question had violated its property rights, guaranteed under Articles 40.3 and 43 of the Constitution. In this case, Carroll J in the High Court first considered Article 43. She looked to *dicta* of Walsh J in *Quinn's Supermarket Ltd v Attorney General* [1972] IR 1. In the *Quinn's Supermarket* case a company attempted to rely on the equality provision contained in Article 40.1. The Article refers to all *human persons* being equal before the law. Walsh J said that this constitutional guarantee of equality was not accorded to a non- human entity such as a limited company. Carroll J said that the provisions of Article 40.1 and 43 were similar in that the guarantees afforded under both articles applied only to human persons. Carroll J merely concluded that the claim under Article 40.3 was unsustainable.

As the company in the *Private Motorists* case had joined one of its shareholders to the proceedings, this enabled the challenge to the Act to be maintained, on the grounds that the shareholder's rights were indirectly affected. Carroll J's judgment was appealed to the Supreme Court. However, the Supreme Court in the *Private Motorists* case did not express any view of the *locus standi* of artificial entities.

Keane J turned to the more recent High Court decision in *Chestvale Properties Ltd v Glackin* [1993] 3 IR 35. This case concerned an attempt by companies to impugn the powers of the inspector under the Companies Acts 1963-1990. The inspector had tried to ascertain the identity of shareholders in the companies under inspection. The companies argued that the powers of the inspector violated their constitutional rights under Article 40.3.

The shareholders in these companies could not claim as plaintiffs that their constitutional rights were being infringed by the inspector's inquiries. To do so, the shareholders in question would have to reveal their identities. This was precisely what the inspector wanted to ascertain, and what the shareholders wished to avoid.

The argument made in *Chestvale*, that the inspector's powers were unconstitutional, could not be made, said Murphy J, unless an individual human person claimed that his or her rights were being infringed. For this purpose, he assumed that the companies had rights under Article 40.3. However, he concluded that the extent to which the inspector's powers interfered with the company's property rights was permissible. It was a means of reconciling the exercise of the company's rights, with the exigencies of the common good, as required by Article 43.

In the light of these decisions, Keane J in *Irish Rail* held that companies *are* possessed of property rights under Article 40.3. Keane J's *ratio* depends on the interpretation given to Article 40.3 and Article 43 in *Blake v Attorney General* [1982] IR 117. In *Blake*, the Supreme Court held that Article 43 did not deal with the citizen's right to own particular items of property. It rather prohibited the abolition of private property as an institution. Article 40.3 on the other hand, protects the individual's right to own particular items of property.

Keane J agreed with Carroll J's reasoning in the *PMPS* case, that Article 40.1 and Article 43 are limited in their application by their wording, to human persons. Keane J found that Article 40.3.2° is not so limited. It refers to the enumerated rights of 'every citizen'. The question was whether the rights guaranteed to citizens are exclusively available to human persons (as opposed to companies).

First, Keane J pointed out that certain rights guaranteed under Article 40.3.2° could only be exercised by human beings, such as the right to life and the right to liberty. Property rights however are in a different category. Companies as well as human persons may invoke the constitutional protection of property rights under Article 40.3.2°. Keane J held that companies should be considered 'citizens' for the purposes of the protection of property rights.

Secondly, if artificial legal entities have rights, these must equally be protected against unjust attack by the laws of the state, in accordance with Article 40.3.2°.

Keane J appreciated that a literal interpretation of the Constitution would not enable the same conclusions to be reached. However, Keane J quoted from Henchy J's decision in *People (DPP) v O'Shea* [1983] ILRM 549, where he said that it may be said of a Constitution, more than of any other legal instrument, that 'the letter killeth, but the spirit giveth life'. Keane J stated that if the framers of the Constitution had wished to confine the property right contained in Article 40.3 exclusively to human persons, they would have done so in the same way as was done in Article 40.1 and Article 43.

Keane J held that it would be a 'spectacular deficiency' if companies were disentitled to constitutional protection. Keane J stated that this deficiency could not be overcome by requiring an individual shareholder to be joined as plaintiff.

Keane J pointed out that the property interest enjoyed by the company is or may be different from that enjoyed by the shareholder. In certain cases such as the *Irish Rail* case, this differing property interest precludes the adoption of the stratagem of joining an individual shareholder as plaintiff. The shareholder may be a bare nominee, or own a single share. In such case, it strains credulity to allege that such a shareholder's property rights have been infringed by the wrong done to the company.

Keane J had to consider the submission made on behalf of the State, that even if corporate bodies have *locus standi*, this did not apply to Irish Rail, because of the way it was incorporated. Keane J held that what was important was not who formed the company, or indeed which legal route led to its incorporation, but rather whether or not the corporate entity possesses the ordinary characteristics such as the power to own property, and the right to sue and be sued. Therefore Irish Rail was entitled to invoke the protection of the Constitution when its property rights were under attack.

Despite the finding that Irish Rail deserved constitutional protection and had *locus standi*, Keane J proceeded to analyse the position, were Irish Rail assumed to have no constitutional protection and no constitutional *locus standi*. Keane J divided the case-law on *locus standi* into two categories.

The first line involved questions of major public or political importance involving changes in the structure or form of government or inter-governmental relations, where it was improbable that a person could be found who could aver some personal disadvantage, were the legislation in question to remain on the statute books. Keane J said that courts had in the past afforded *locus standi* to concerned citizens to facilitate review of constitutionally dubious legislation. Keane J said that this line of authority was unrelated to the dispute in *Irish Rail*.

The second category of cases was that in which a prospective plaintiff was required to establish some entitlement, interest (though not necessarily a right) which had been immediately or potentially affected and for which a remedy was being sought. He instanced as examples *East Donegal Co-Operative Livestock Marts Ltd v Attorney General* [1970] 3 IR 317, *Cahill v Sutton* [1980] IR 261.

Keane J concluded that Irish Rail was a plaintiff entitled under the second category of cases to maintain its claim. Irish Rail's financial interests would be severely affected, were it not entitled to make its claim.

Keane J went on to uphold the constitutionality of ss. 12 and 14 of the Civil Liability Act 1961, thereby allowing the other 223 cases to proceed.

Irish Rail appealed to the Supreme Court (*Iarnród Éireann v Ireland & Others*, 16 July 1996). It was unsuccessful. The Supreme Court did not deal with the question of *locus standi*, nor with companies and their entitlement to constitutional rights.

Keane J's judgment suggests some interesting points.

First, it will be remembered that the *ratio* of Keane J's judgment is that artificial persons are entitled to constitutional rights if they are 'citizens'. Keane J here dealt with a company that was registered, managed, owned, controlled and conducted its business in the State. Which of these criteria is sufficient to establish that the company in question is entitled to claim constitutional rights as a citizen? If a company moves its centre of management from Ireland to some other EU jurisdiction, does it thereby sacrifice its entitlement to constitutional rights?

Second, when a company is registered, managed, owned, controlled and conducted its business in the State and is thereby possessed of constitutional rights, when does it lose them? If the memorandum and articles of the company in question prohibits or precludes possession or ownership of property, does this disentitle the company to claim constitutional rights? Is this dependent on a change to its status (registration and de-registration)? Does the appointment of a liquidator, examiner or receiver mean that the company (as opposed to its creditors) no longer enjoys constitutional rights?

Third, Keane J confined his decision to property rights. As Keane J pointed out, there are certain rights which can only be claimed by human persons, such as the right to life and the right to liberty. There are however other expressed and implied Constitutional rights, which may be asserted by artificial legal entities as citizens. The express right to a good name is but one other example of a right which might apply to companies. The following implied rights could well apply to companies. The right to justice and fair procedures (*In re Haughey* [1971] IR 217, *Balkanbank Ltd v Taher* see below at p. 87); the right of access to the courts (*Macauley v Minister for Posts and Telegraphs* [1966] IR 325); the right to earn a livelihood (*Murphy v Stewart* [1973] IR 97; *Lovett v Grogan* [1995] 3 IR 132).

Fourth, it is unclear what must happen where there is a conflict between the constitutional rights of a human person and a company. Will the courts adopt the principle of interpretation discussed in *Attorney General v X.* [1992] ILRM 401? This is that a court must initially attempt to harmonise rights, but where such an attempt is impossible, to place such rights in a hierarchy of importance. Alternatively, is there some automatic presumption that a 'non-natural' person deserves less protection than a natural person? If the courts were asked to review a constitutional challenge to legislative provision, and there is a balance to be struck between the rights of a company on the one hand, and those of a human being on the other, would the court assume that the balance should be struck in favour of the human person?

Fifth, Keane J did not refer in his judgment to the place of EU treaties in Irish law. EU law provides an existing jurisprudential basis for vesting rights in corporate entities: thus companies enjoy a whole range of economic protections which derive from treaties and are carried through into subordinate legislation.

Sixth, it is not clear how Keane J envisages the relationship between corporate constitutional rights and the rule in *Foss v Harbottle*. Assume that a company has constitutional rights, and these are violated. Where the directors decide not to pursue their remedy, may they rely on the existing principles in *Foss v Harbottle* to prevent the shareholders from usurping the Board's prerogative? Alternatively, given the importance of constitutional rights, may these be vindicated and safeguarded by a shareholder under the head of the fifth exception to *Foss* (whenever the interests of justice so require)?

Does Keane J's judgment suggest that companies are deserving of constitutional protection, or does it suggest that Keane J so held, en route to the decision that s. 12 and 14 of the Civil Liability Act 1961 represented a legislatively created interference with commercial and financial interests which requires redress? If the judgment does suggest the former, it may be one of the clearest signs that the judiciary are moving away from the natural law approach to judicial positivism.

Financial assistance by company to purchase shares in itself *Eccles Hall Ltd v Bank of Nova Scotia*, High Court, February 3, 1995. This case concerned an action in respect of an alleged breach of s. 60 of the 1963 Act.

The company, Eccles Hall Ltd (Eccles) was incorporated in 1983. A husband and wife between them owned the entire issued share capital. The wife was an accountant. Both had experience of property development. Eccles bought Knocklofty House for £275,000. In March 1984 Eccles borrowed £120,000 on the security of a mortgage, to refurbish and improve this property.

In November 1984 the husband entered into an agreement with a new investor, X. This agreement provided that 50% of the equity of Eccles would be sold to X for £180,000. This sum was to be put into what the agreement called a loan account. This loan account was to bear interest at 15% per annum. The agreement stated that the £180,000 or part of it would be used to redeem the mortgage on Knocklofty. X agreed further to advance £156,000 secured by a new mortgage on the property.

In May 1985, a general meeting of Eccles was held. This meeting resolved to increase the share capital of Eccles by the creation of an additional 40,000 ordinary shares of £1 each, and 359,000 10% cumulative redeemable preference shares of £1 each. The meeting further resolved to allot the preference shares half to the husband, half to X.

On June 3, 1986, two mortgage debentures were signed. Eccles, the husband and X, were parties to each. These documents purported to charge to X the repayment of £56,250 and £36,589 respectively.

By the end of 1987, the relationship between X and the husband had deteriorated to the extent that they were no longer on speaking terms. They called in an accountant, Mr Curtin, to negotiate some arrangement whereby X would sell his shareholding and release his charge over Eccles' assets.

Mr Curtin successfully negotiated an agreement. It provided that the husband should pay X £300,000. For this, X would transfer to the husband all his shares in Eccles and release the mortgage. This agreement was completed, but the husband could not come up with the necessary money. Mr Curtin had to find another investor.

Mr Curtin found Y, who was prepared to put up £325,000. Y already had £100,000, but had to borrow the balance from the Bank of Nova Scotia. The bank wanted to take a charge over Eccles's assets, in exchange for the remaining £225,000. The company agreed.

Y set up a company beneficially owned by him. The bank lent Y's company £225,000, charged on the security of the assets of Eccles. Mr X sold his shares in Eccles to Mr Y's company. Subsequently, Eccles went into liquidation.

The liquidator brought a motion contending that the security provided by Eccles to the Bank of Nova Scotia was to enable the acquisition of shares in Eccles, thus contravening s. 60.

In the High Court, Murphy J stated that the agreement to buy Mr X out *appeared* to involve a contravention of s. 60. Murphy J found that there had been a significant diminution in the value of Mr X's shareholding. In November 1984, it had been valued at £180,000. By May 1989 it was valued at £50.

Murphy J held that the £325,000 paid to secure Mr X's withdrawal from the venture was not related to the value of his shares in the company, but to the cost to him of his investment in the enterprise. Murphy J opined that what the cost of Mr X's investment was, and how it was made up was 'unclear'. The documents available were contradictory.

The judge referred to the 1984 transaction. This and the supporting documentation, suggested that it was intended that Mr X should invest by way of shareholding. However, in 1986, two years later, two mortgage debentures were entered into. These suggested that the 1984 transaction was now viewed as a secured loan.

Murphy J considered whether the issue of the two mortgage debentures of 1986 represented consideration for the issue and allotment of preference shares in 1985. Though the company had created preference shares, there was no definitive allotment and issue of these shares. They were however treated as having been issued in the relevant annual accounts.

However when Mr Curtin was negotiating the deal concerning X's withdrawal, he took the view that the shares had not been issued and allotted, and the mortgage debentures were given exclusively as security in respect of loans to the company. In addition, later annual accounts made no reference to redeemable preference shares at all.

Murphy J said that both directors had advanced £643,899 to the company.

£335,319 of this was advanced by Mr X. Murphy J stated that there was no question of any dishonest or artificial scheme of circumventing the provisions of s. 60. The books of account were drawn up long before Mr Y became an investor.

The bank's solicitor's notes in relation to the transaction were tendered in evidence. The solicitor pointed out the potential contravention of s. 60 if the transaction went ahead. The liquidator argued that these notes constituted a warning. For this reason, the transaction appeared to be the repayment of a substantial debt, and the transfer of Eccles' shares for a nominal sum. The solicitor's evidence satisfied Murphy J, that this was not the case. The transaction had always been envisaged as a repayment of money to Mr X.

Murphy J appreciated that the match between the sums owed by the company to Mr X and the sum for which he was willing to sell the shares was so exact as to give rise to suspicion. But Murphy J held that the crucial factor was the state of knowledge of the bank. The company accounts given by the directors, and the replies to requisitions upon title showed that the loans to Eccles Hall Limited amounted to just under £325,000. The £50 was what was paid for the shares. The rest was money owed to the director by the company.

The liquidator argued that the repayment of the debts owed to the company constituted a breach of s. 60 — 'indirectly'.

Murphy J concluded that a defence was provided by s. 60(12). This provides, *inter alia*, that nothing in the section shall be taken to prohibit the discharge of a liability lawfully incurred by it.

The transaction was so obscure, and the accounts and other documentation so ambiguous that it is surprising that Murphy J did not hold the directors culpable. It could be argued that it should at least be *prima facie* up to those directors to exculpate themselves from the presumption that the transaction was an attempt at circumvention of s. 60.

The final point is that as this case turns on the diminution in value of the shares, it might have been helpful to understand how so dramatic a reduction occurred.

Shares *Re Sugar Distributors Ltd* [1996] 1 IRLM 342; [1995] 2 IR 195. S. 89 of the Companies Act 1963 gives the court *inter alia* the power to rectify an invalid issue of shares, where the court is satisfied that it would be just and equitable to do so. This is the first case dealing with an interpretation of s. 89.

There were three companies in a group. Irish Sugar Ltd manufactured and refined sugar. Irish Sugar owned 51% of Sugar Distributors (Holdings) Ltd (SDH). The balance was held by another company, Gladebrook Ltd. SDH owned 100% of a distribution company, called Sugar Distributors Ltd.

In 1988, Irish Sugar and its tax advisers considered the 10% manufacturing relief, available to companies. Under s. 39 of the Finance Act 1980, a company is entitled to be taxed at only 10% in respect of profits from manufacturing. The relief is available to companies in a group, where the manufacturing company holds 90% of the ordinary share capital of the distributing subsidiary company. The section provides that goods sold by the distributing company are deemed to have been manufactured by the distributing company entitled to be charged tax at 10%.

In this case, there were two reasons why the group were disentitled to the relief. First, Irish Sugar only held 51% of the ordinary share capital of SDH. It was necessary therefore to buy out Gladebrook Ltd's interest. This was done. Second, the legislation requires that the holding company must be the parent of the distributing company. Here Irish Sugar was SDL's 'grandchild'.

After Irish Sugar had acquired 100% of SDH's shares, their tax advisers attempted to obtain this relief by way of concession from the Revenue, in order to avoid the trouble and expense of making SDL *de lege* a wholly owned subsidiary of Irish Sugar. The Revenue refused.

Accordingly, the tax advisers suggested that SDL had to become a wholly-owned subsidiary of Irish Sugar, and should therefore issue Irish Sugar with 900,000 redeemable preference shares. This would cause the relationship to fall within s. 39.

The requisite documentation (including draft minutes) were all prepared, but Irish Sugar neglected to effect the relevant transactions and hold the necessary meetings. Instead, the company in its tax returns and companies returns acted as if the necessary steps had been taken. Irish Sugar sought the tax relief in the tax year 1990. The following year, the inspector of taxes pointed out that the company was not entitled to the reliefs claimed, but were instead liable to pay tax.

In 1991, Irish Sugar and Greencore hit the headlines. An inspector was appointed under the Companies Acts 1963-1990. The inspector's report disclosed that the necessary meetings had not been held. Some of the relevant documentation was backdated to a time before the Revenue Commissioners had been approached for the concession which they refused to give Irish Sugar. The inspector stated that this backdating was done with a fraudulent intention. Accordingly, the company took this application under s. 89 in order to rectify the invalid issuing of the redeemable preference shares.

In the High Court, Keane J said that though the words in s. 89 — 'just and equitable' — conveyed a broad discretion on the court, this discretion was not unrestricted. The discretion had to be executed in a judicial manner and according to appropriate criteria. It was necessary to have regard to the *policy* of the section. The policy behind the section was to ensure that those who had innocently purchased shares were not deprived of their property by a flaw in the transfer, and to enable such transfers to be rectified. Keane J referred to an Australian case dealing with a similar but not identical provision, *Millheim v Barewa Oil & Mining NL*. There the judge said that such sections are designed to 'enable the court to make good what was really a defective title of shares in the company. . . .'

Keane J held that Irish Sugar was not attempting to remedy defective title to valueless shares purchased in good faith. The object here was to enable SDL and its associated companies to gain a tax advantage by the retrospective validation of the seriously irregular transactions undertaken. Keane J said that the legislature had not intended that s. 89 would be used in such a way.

The company attempted to argue that there were innocent shareholders who would be prejudiced if the s. 89 application was refused. These shareholders were the shareholders in a parent company, Greencore. Keane J refused to extend the scope of s. 89 to shareholders in another company who, although affected by defective issue and allotments of shares in a group company, were not themselves allottees in the defective issue of shares.

The company also argued that in the alternative, any alleged defect had been cured by the consent of all those who were members of the companies involved. Keane J said that though a court could in certain circumstances make such a declaration, it was not possible to do this here. The aim here was to obtain tax relief for the year under discussion and previous years. This would mean that a court would have to connive with the fiction that meetings had taken place and resolutions passed. The judge refused to accede to this request and dismissed the s. 89 application.

This case shows that the courts will be sympathetic to cases where a transferee/allottee is prejudiced by a flaw in the procedure, but will not allow the section to be used in order to retrospectively introduce a tax avoidance scheme which the applicants had failed to implement properly.

Restriction of directors *Business Communications Ltd v Baxter*, High Court, July 21, 1995. This and the following case, *Re Costello Doors Ltd*, represent the first two judicial analyses of the restriction of directors under the Companies Act 1990.

The legislation attempts to prevent directors of an insolvent company moving on to manage a pre-existing or a new company. S. 149 of the 1990 Act specifically allows a restriction order to be made in two circumstances. First, if at the date of commencement of the winding up of the company, or during the course of the winding up or receivership, it is proved to the court that the company is unable to pay its debts within the meaning of s. 214 of the 1963 Act. Second, a liquidator may certify that a company is unable to pay its debts for the purpose of restricting a director: see *Carway v Attorney General*, High Court, July 3, 1996.

S. 149 catches not just current directors, but those who were removed or resigned or retired at any time up to 12 months' prior to winding up. S. 149 covers shadow directors.

S. 150(1) provides for a five year restriction period. This precludes a disqualified person from involvement in any capacity in company management or promotion, including that of a company secretary.

There are three statutory defences to restriction proceedings. First, s. 150(2)(b) provides that a person may not be restricted if he is a director nominated by a financial institution in connection with the giving of credit facilities to the company, and the company's borrowings have not been guaranteed personally by any director of the company. Second, s. 150(2)(c) provides that a person may not be restricted if he is a director nominated by a joint venture company in connection with the purchase of or subscription of shares in the company. Third, s. 150(2)(a) provides that a person may not be restricted if he can show that he has acted 'honestly and responsibly' in relation to the conduct of the affairs of the company. Obviously, this third defence will be the most frequently used, and therefore its interpretation by the courts is important.

A restricted director may become involved in a new or existing company, but only if such company satisfies certain capital requirements.

In this case, a company was set up with two principal shareholders who were also the only two directors. This company had been engaged in the supply and maintenance of computer hardware, software and electronics. From 1990-1993 it traded successfully. One contract accounted for 80% of its business: that with Philips Electrical Ltd. This was terminated in or about February 1993. The directors maintained that this termination was a breach of contract by Philips. The company thereafter got into difficulties. By June 1993 the financial position of the company was critical. The seriousness of the financial position was not alleviated by the fact that the two directors fell out. The sales director then concentrated on the sales of telecommunications end of the business, whilst the other devoted himself to the financial side.

In June 1993 the directors discussed the position. They agreed in general terms that it would be better to split the business into two. One side would deal with telecommunications. The other would deal with systems solutions. The directors decided that the existing company would cease trading as of 30 June. Thereafter it would transfer its activities to two new companies.

Nothing specific was agreed. The company continued to trade until December 21, 1993. Then two new companies were set up. Both new companies purchased stock from the company. The company was put into voluntary liquidation on February 18, 1994. Between December and February, substantial sums of money were lodged into the company's bank account, thereby reducing the overdraft and consequently the exposure of the directors on foot of their personal guarantees.

At the end of January 1994, the company's lease of its office equipment was terminated. New leases were granted to the two new companies referred to in the previous paragraph.

There was a creditors' meeting held on February 18, 1994. At this meeting a statement of affairs was presented. It stated that the company's assets on realisation would make £219,000. approx. The statement did not include the transactions carried out between the drawing-up of the statement of affairs and the creditors' meeting. Once these transactions were factored in, the liquidator found that the assets would only realise £31,000.

In the High Court, the liquidator brought a motion to have the two directors restricted under Chapter 1 of Part VII of the 1990 Act.

In the High Court, Murphy J in order to interpret the restriction provisions of Chapter 1 of Part VII of the 1990 Act compared those with the disqualification provisions of Chapter 2 of Part VII. Under Chapter 1, Murphy J held that when a court makes a restriction order, it will be for five years unless it is satisfied that the persons concerned fall within the three specific exemptions.

Murphy J states that under Chapter 2, the power and period of disqualification is discretionary. There are two circumstances where these discretionary powers may be exercised. First, where a person has been convicted of an indictable offence of fraud or dishonesty relating to the company. The criminal court convicting and sentencing the director may impose a disqualification period. Second, where in any proceedings or as a result of an application, a court is satisfied that a director is guilty of fraud or breach of duty, or has acted in a manner which makes him unfit to be concerned with the management of a company, the court again may impose a disqualification.

Murphy J said that it followed that the proofs might be difficult to establish under s. 160, since these involve issues of fraud, dishonesty and *mala fides*. Even if it were possible to so make the requisite proofs, it may be that a court will decide to disqualify the director for some period shorter than the five year maximum. Where a court decides under s. 160 to make a disqualification order, it is comprehensive in its effect, *i.e.* there are no exceptions. This is justifiable and credible commercially, on the grounds that those disqualified have been found to have been culpable, whereas persons restricted under s. 150 have failed to act responsibly.

Likewise where a director who has been restricted under s. 150, and now wishes to resume trading through a company, it seems reasonable that such a director may avail again of limited liability only through a company which has satisfied certain requirements as to paid up capital.

The more serious penalty which a s. 150 restriction order imposes is the stigma attached to the making of the order, and the requirement that it should be filed in the companies office. Murphy J said that though the stigma was significant, the penalty was less than in the case of orders made under either s. 160 or s. 33 of the Companies (Amendment) Act 1990 (the reckless and fraudulent trading sections).

Murphy J adverted to the introduction of regulatory control, including the restriction of directors. Pointing out that limited liability is not without cost to society, Murphy J rationalises the introduction of the restriction provisions as part of this cost.

Murphy J then directed his mind to the required standard for exemption sought by the two directors in this case. The directors alleged that they had acted 'honestly and responsibly'. Murphy J made two general points about how such discretion should be judicially exercised. First, there should not be any judicial witch-hunt after every commercial failure; some risk is inevitable. Second, a brand-new business is not expected to satisfy the same standards of administrative and regulatory perfection as a long-established company. Murphy J held that the main requirement for exemption under s. 150 was the exercise of a suitable degree of responsibility. This will be manifested by compliance with the regulatory framework of company law.

The *onus* to show compliance with the regulatory framework of common law was on directors, according to Murphy J. This was a major change in the law, since the other company law provisions required creditors, contributors or liquidators or other claimants to prove that the directors had acted irresponsibly or recklessly. There would be little evidence available to such persons, since the evidence inevitably lay in the hands of the directors. Furthermore such claimants would often be additionally handicapped by virtue of their impoverishment, often because of the depredations of the directors themselves. Murphy J said that this explained why so few of these cases had succeeded under the 1963 Act.

Murphy J said that it was therefore up to the two directors in this case to prove that they had acted 'honestly and responsibly' in relation to the affairs of the company.

Murphy J divided the directors' actions into two periods. The first (June 1993-December 1993) began when the directors had their initial falling-out. During that period, Murphy J found that the conduct of both directors was 'imprudent'. During the second period (December 1993-February 1994) the company had realised its assets and paid sums to its bankers in order to minimise the exposure of the directors. Murphy J referred specifically to the payments made by one director to the company controlled by him. Murphy J said that any person who engaged, permitted or facilitated such actions could not be said to be acting 'responsibly'. Murphy J held that the applications for exemption from disqualification should fail.

The case suggests that though satisfaction of the statutory requirements (including filing of documents) is not of itself a guarantee of good management, failure to demonstrate compliance will make it almost impossible for the directors to satisfy the court that they have acted 'honestly and responsibly'.

The case throws some light on the interpretation of 'honestly and responsibly'. The first is more subjective than objective, the second is more objective than subjective. The judgment clearly supports the time honoured reluctance of the courts to second-guess business decisions, but the authors suggest, it imports a limited requirement of standards of responsibility which are objectively determined, and are not qualified or limited by reference to the director's lack of qualifications or experience.

The most important inference to be taken from this judgment lies in Murphy J's *dictum* that no person could be acquitted of blame if they 'engaged, permitted or facilitated' conduct which was irresponsible. The terms 'permitted or facilitated' are ambiguous. Do they import positive acquiescence in opprobrious conduct? Or, as the authors suggest are the words sufficient to catch a man like the chimeric Marquess of Bute? It is difficult to show how such a person could have acted honestly and responsibly in relation to the affairs of the company.

Murphy J turned to another point. He said that there is a gap in the legislation as to who should institute restriction proceedings. No person is specifically charged with bringing restriction proceedings to court. This gap is partially filled in the case of companies under court liquidation. There, the court can order the liquidator concerned to bring proceedings against the directors. Hence the gap remains in the case of voluntary liquidations (and receiverships).

See Andrew Walker (1995) 'Restriction of Company directors and the provisions of the Companies Acts 1990' *GILSI* Vol. 89, No. 3, p. 121-24; No. 4, p. 168-71; Dr H Linnane (1995) 'Delinquent Directors and others — the Irish approach', *Company Lawyer*, Vol. 16, Part 1, p. 26-7.

Re Costello Doors Ltd (in liquidation), High Court, July 21, 1995. This decision was handed down the same day as the previous case, *Business Communications Ltd v Baxter*.

In this case the company was incorporated in 1986 to supply and install doors principally to the retail market. A husband and wife were the only directors and shareholders. By 1992, the company had a turnover of £2 million. In March 1992, three more directors were appointed to the company. These three were section managers and full-time employees of the company. They resigned as directors in September 1992 as the company had fallen into difficulties and the company had ceased to employ them. However notification of their resignation as directors was never filed with the CRO.

There was a creditors' meeting on the 8 January, at which the directors produced a Statement of Affairs which showed a deficiency of £298,617.

A liquidator was appointed on January 25. He found the deficiency was much greater: £547,000.

In the High Court, Murphy J said that he had to restrict each of the directors from directly or indirectly taking part in company management for five years, unless they could prove that they had acted 'honestly and responsibly' in relation to the affairs of the company.

Murphy J warned that no director will be excused from acting honestly or responsibly because they are a friend, relative or spouse of the 'proprietor' of the company. It is impossible to be nominated as a director and accept the nomination without concomitant involvement.

Murphy J therefore examined the affidavit evidence of the husband. This suggested that the company had traded successfully until 1992. Then the old stock became obsolete and out of fashion and new stock had to be purchased. In order to do this, the company had entered into a contract with another company in order to obtain supplies of doors. This contract was not fulfilled. The supplier had gone into receivership. This was the reason the affidavit gave for the failure of the company.

The husband stated that the accounting books and records were kept properly and in an orderly manner. Two bookkeepers responsible for maintaining the records were named in the affidavit.

The liquidator questioned the husband's claim that proper books of account had been maintained. The liquidator stated that there was insufficient information to complete statutory accounts for the year 1991. Just prior to liquidation, no books and records whatever were maintained.

Murphy J said that the maintenance of proper books and accounts and the employment of appropriate 'experts' (bookkeepers?) would go a long way to discharge the obligation of the directors that they had behaved responsibly. Murphy J found that proper books of account had been maintained up to December 1990. Chartered accountants had so certified. The draft accounts for 1991 were such that the accountants were prepared to issue a similar certificate. The accounts were not perfect. The accountants could not confirm that all sales were properly recorded. They drew attention to defective control systems.

Murphy J pointed out that such a warning should not be ignored. It did not however necessarily involve any condemnation of the management of the company and their practices, nor a want of responsibility. Reviewing the most crucial period of time, the three month period prior to liquidation, proper books of account were not written up. However, primary records were retained.

Murphy J accepted the contention made by the liquidator, that the preservation of basic records is not an adequate compliance with the requirements of the Companies Acts, nor does it provide information in a suitable fashion so as to enable the management to make appropriate decisions, or the auditors to certify the relevant accounts. Murphy J however held that it was not irresponsible to write up the appropriate books for a particular period in circumstances where the book-keeper in question had his employment terminated.

The fact that the husband had invested money in the business was a relevant factor in deciding whether to restrict him or not.

Murphy J, not without some hesitation, felt satisfied that neither the husband nor any other director had acted dishonestly or irresponsibly.

First, it is difficult to see how this case in fact applies the principles set out in *Business Communications Ltd v Baxter*. It will be remembered that the major change in the law provided by s. 150 is the imposition upon directors to prove that in fact they had not acted dishonestly or irresponsibly. To show this, it is important to be able to show that proper records have been kept. In this case, it is clear that proper records were not written up in the pre-liquidation period, and that the auditors could not confirm that sales were properly recorded in respect of the sales for 1990-1991. From these facts, it is hard to see how the directors could have come to any informed decision about the merit or otherwise of any proposed course of action, since they did not know how their company stood financially. It therefore follows that the directors in *Costello Doors* failed Murphy J's own test in *Business Communications*.

Second, we refer to the dictum in *Costello Doors*, that those who take up directorships to facilitate friends, relations or their spouse are not thereby excused from either the discharge of positive functions appropriate to all directors, and the application of s. 150. The question arises as to whether action and inaction are both covered by the dictum in *Costello Doors*. As the authors remark in the discussion of that case, there seems no reason why both would not be covered.

It is interesting that in the *Costello Doors* case, Murphy J appears to have assumed that because the principal director should be exculpated, so, by extension, should the others. But the creditors lost money, and one of the purposes of the requirement that there should be at least two directors to a company, is that the processes of judgment of a single person should be augmented by the input of other(s). The creditors in this case might well wonder how and where the collective judgment of the Board was exercised and if so, how responsibly and honestly.

Directors' directing mind and will   *Superwood Holdings plc v Sun Alliance* [1995] 3 IR 303. One aspect of this case deals with the identification of the directing mind and will of a company. The first stage is to identify who took the decision in question.

This case concerned a fire in company premises. The company sought to recover from their insurers. Their insurers repudiated the contract alleging it to have been a fraudulent claim.

In the High Court, after a 116 day hearing, O'Hanlon J delivered a 423 page judgment holding in favour of the insurers. The company appealed.

In the Supreme Court, Denham J, *inter alia*, stated that in order to avoid a contract on grounds of fraud, it is necessary to specify the allegedly fraudulent acts, and to prove the actor's fraudulent intention. The insurer in this case failed to specify what precise acts were alleged to have been fraudulent. With regard to proof of fraudulent intention, Denham J referred to *Derry v Peek* (1889) 14 App Cas 237. The House of Lords there said that fraud is proved when a false representation is made (1) knowingly (2) without belief in its truth (3) recklessly, careless whether it be true or false.

Having set down the intentional constituent of fraud, Denham J sought to establish how it could be proved that a company possessed the ability to commit it. In *El Ajou v Dollarland Holdings plc & Another* [1994] 2 All ER 685, the Court of Appeal held that the 'directing mind and will' of a company was not necessarily that of a person who is general manager or controller of the company, since the directing mind and will could be found in different persons for different activities. Denham J, relying on this case, said that it was therefore necessary to identify who was responsible for the particular impugned act or omission in the hierarchy of company management.

In this case, Denham J stated that the High Court judge had not properly ascertained who the directing mind and will of the company was. Denham J therefore considered the possible candidates. She included in this list an accountant retained by the company to process the claim. She found as a matter of fact that the insurers had failed to prove fraud against any of these persons, and thus the insurers were liable.

This case is of importance to company lawyers because of the somewhat traditional exposition of liability in terms of 'directing mind and will'. What is novel about this expression of the test is that Denham J clearly leaves open the possibility that a non-employee of the company, such as a professional accountant or solicitor, could well prove to be the directing mind and will of a company, if such a person's advice is uncritically followed.

Directors *Unicorn Investments Ltd v Ewart plc*, High Court, June 29, 1995. This case concerns the authority of a managing director. A company, Ewart plc, entered into an agreement with a financial consultant, Unicorn Investments Ltd, to find an investor for Ewart. The agreement provided that if after such introduction, negotiations were not entered into, no fees were to be paid to Unicorn. However, if such negotiations were entered into, then fees were payable to Unicorn. Further fees were payable if a loan agreement was entered into. If the deal was concluded, and a profit ensued, then Unicorn were entitled to a percentage of that profit.

Unicorn found a German bank. Unicorn arranged a meeting between Ewart and the German bank. This meeting took place in Dublin.

The bank expressed its willingness to take the deal further. Unicorn told Ewart of this. Unicorn looked for its introduction fee. As well, Unicorn sought more information from Ewart for the German bank. Ewart's managing director informed Unicorn that he could not pay, until he had obtained the approval of his Board of Directors.

Unicorn did not receive payment. The entire financial deal broke down. There were inconclusive attempts to re-negotiate the contract between Ewart and Unicorn. Unicorn therefore sought by this action to obtain payment of the fees due to it.

Ewart's defence was that the Board Meeting had decided, following the initial meeting between Ewart and the German bank, not to go ahead with further discussions. Accordingly, no liability arose to Unicorn.

In the High Court, Costello P accepted the evidence adduced by Unicorn as to what happened at the meeting and thereafter. He said that the managing director of Ewart 'unequivocally' agreed to hold further discussions with the German bank for the purpose of arranging for the relevant finance. At no time was Unicorn told either that any decision would have to be taken by the Board of Ewart, nor did the managing director indicate that his authority was circumscribed. Costello P was satisfied that no restrictions were placed on the managing director's ability to commit the company to the contract made between Ewart and Unicorn. Had such restrictions been placed on the managing director, he would have informed Unicorn of this fact. He never did so, and positively affirmed that he could enter into negotiations on Ewart's behalf.

The Board of Ewart had impliedly authorised its managing director and CEO to make the decision as to whether the financial institution was appropriate or not. Having done so, and decided that the German bank was appropriate, Ewart was committed to paying Unicorn the contractually-agreed fee.

Costello P held that Unicorn had made the initial introduction, and that negotiations were to take place and therefore Ewart was obliged to pay Unicorn as agreed.

The order required Ewart to pay not only the fee, but interest.

Derivative action *Balkanbank v Taher*, Supreme Court, January 19, 1995. Two companies (one Irish, one Bulgarian) set up a joint venture company, owned 50-50, in order to trade with Bulgaria. To obtain finance, the Bulgarian partner company transferred £7 million to secure the loans of the joint venture company.

The directors appointed by the Irish partner company to the board of the joint venture company (the Irish directors) drew down the £7 million. The Bulgarian partner company brought an action against these Irish directors for fraud, breach of trust and breach of duty. The Bulgarians said that their consent had never been obtained. They said further that the £7 million had been dissipated.

In the High Court, Blayney J made a finding of fact that the Bulgarians had known about the draw-down. There had been no fraud, breach of trust and breach of duty.

After the close of submissions, the Bulgarians claimed that the directors' use of the money constituted a fraud on the minority. Blayney J, appearing to agree that there was some substance to this claim, allowed the Bulgarians to amend their pleadings, and accorded injunctive orders against the Irish directors prohibiting them from dissipating the remaining £1.2 million. The balance of the £7 million had been lawfully used in company business.

Both sides appealed to the Supreme Court. The Supreme Court said that the plaintiff's action was for breach of trust and duty and for fraud. This action had failed. The trial judge, after delivering judgment, amended the pleadings to permit a derivative action. As a consequence, the defendants had not been afforded the chance of defending this derivative action. It was no minor amendment. It was an amendment which completely changed the nature of the claim.

Hamilton CJ, delivering the judgment of the Supreme Court, held that the requirement of fair procedures meant that the derivative action should have been pleaded at an earlier stage. The defendants could then have questioned whether the Bulgarians were entitled to bring proceedings in the name of the company. Even if the court allowed the Bulgarians to bring the proceedings in the name of the company, the defendants would then have had appropriate time to defend the action. The trial judge had failed to uphold fair procedures. Failure to comply with the obligation entitled the appellant in this case to succeed in the appeal.

In the course of the Supreme Court's judgment, Hamilton CJ discussed the rule and in *Foss v Harbottle* (1843) 2 Hare 461. The rule was concerned with the response to the question, who may sue when a wrong is done to the company? The rule states that the proper plaintiff is the company itself. There are well-established exceptions to the rule. One is where as in this case, there has been fraud on the minority. Hamilton CJ stated that this term does not connote dishonesty or criminality. It is used more in the sense familiar to equitable courts, whereby a person entrusted with powers for one particular purpose uses these powers for another.

Two points require consideration. This case states that fair procedures must be observed in court proceedings. Does this case suggest that a company is entitled to the constitutionally guaranteed right to fair procedures? The authors suggest that it does: see *Irish Rail* above.

Secondly, the authors find the exposition of the rule in *Foss v Harbottle* in this case unhelpful. It is suggested that fraud on the minority is always akin to equitable fraud, to abuse of power. This suggests that a shareholder or director is obliged to use his or her powers not selfishly, but in the interests of the company or a section of it. But this is inaccurate. Certainly *some* examples of fraud on the minority may involve abuse of powers, or may not be criminal or dishonest. But there is no positive duty which compels a company member — or even a director — to avoid all selfish decisions. Thus a director may vote upon contracts in which he is interested, may carry on the company business balancing risk and profit, and a member may cast his vote in complete disregard of everything except his own short term interests, by for example voting in favour of maximum dividends and minimum placing of funds to reserves.

Payment of preferential debts   *Re Manning Furniture Ltd (in receivership)* [1996] 1 ILRM 13. S. 98 of the Companies Act 1963 applies where a receiver is appointed by a holder of a floating charge, and the company is not in liquidation. It obliges the receiver to pay the preferential creditors before paying off his own appointor. What happens where a receiver is appointed pursuant to a charge which is both fixed and floating and the receiver can pay the appointor from the proceeds of the fixed charge? Does such a receiver have to apply the proceeds of the floating charge to discharge the claims of the statutorily preferred creditors? The answer is in the affirmative.

In this case, the company created two chattel mortgages and a floating charge in favour of ICC. Later, it created a fixed charge over its premises in favour of The First National Building Society (FNBS). The FNBS charge was not registered within the prescribed time.

On 9 August 1993 ICC appointed a receiver under their fixed and floating charges. On 11 October, Keane J allowed the FNBS to register its charge late, but with the usual proviso, that others who had acquired rights in priority should not be prejudiced.

The receiver sold all the company's property. The proceeds of sale paid off ICC, and left a surplus. Should the surplus should go to pay off the preferential creditors, or to discharge the debt to FNBS?

In the High Court, McCracken J considered Lardner J's judgment in *Re Eisc Teoranta* [1991] ILRM 760. There a receiver was appointed under a fixed and floating charge. The receiver realised sufficient assets to pay off his appointor. There was a surplus over. A liquidator was then appointed. The question was, should the receiver himself pay off the preferential creditors or should he hand over the surplus to the liquidator?

Lardner J in *Eisc* said that the receiver's statutory duty was to pay off the preferential creditors. McCracken J said that this applied here.

FNBS argued that the facts in *Eisc* and *Manning* were distinguishable. In *Eisc* the liquidator would have had to pay off the statutorily preferred debts, but in *Manning* the second charge holder should be entitled to pay FNBS off ahead of the statutorily preferred creditors.

McCracken J declined to accept this argument. On appointment, s. 98 obliges a receiver to pay off the statutorily preferred debts. The obligation to so do is not altered by the fact that there are other subsequent charge holders. The obligation is not altered by the fact that the receiver can pay off the debenture holder out of the proceeds of the fixed charge, and does not have to touch any of the assets comprised in the floating charges.

McCracken J was pressed with what appears from the judgment to have been a not very convincing argument, that the late registration of the FNBS debenture somehow impacted on the obligation of the ICC receiver to pay off the statutorily preferred creditors. McCracken J unequivocally held that once the ICC receiver had been appointed, the statutorily preferred creditors must be paid. This had to be done prior to any payments to FNBS. It is not easy to see how this conclusion could be resisted. The late registration of the FNBS is surely irrelevant to the clear obligation under s. 98 that the receiver must discharge statutorily preferred debts.

Oppression   *Irish Press plc v Ingersoll Irish Publications Ltd* [1995] 2 ILRM 270; [1995] 2 IR 175. For a full discussion of the facts and the previous judgments in this case, see 1993 Annual Review, p. 60.

The appeal to the Supreme Court related to whether damages could be awarded in respect of a successful application under s. 205. In the Supreme Court, Blayney J, delivering the court's judgment, said that when a court makes an order under s. 205 it must do so 'with a view to bringing to an end the matters complained of'. These words circumscribe the discretion of the court.

Blayney J questioned whether the damages awarded by Barron J in the High Court were given with a view to ending the oppression. This he said was not the object of Barron J's order. The award was to compensate the oppressed companies for the reduction in the value of its shareholding. The order transferring the shares ended the oppression.

Irish Press Publications (IPP) argued that there were s. 205 cases where courts had ordered the sale of shares in the company, and factored into the purchase price some element of compensation. The first of these was *Re*

Greenore Trading Ltd [1980] ILRM 94, where Keane J had directed the oppressor to purchase the shares in the company from the other shareholder, at a premium above the value of the shares. This premium amounted to compensation. The second case, *Scottish Co-operative Wholesale Society v Mayer* [1959] AC 324, was also relevant, although it was an English decision. In that case damages were awarded, and the oppressor was ordered to buy shares at a fair price. This fair price was the value of the shares at the date of the petition as if there had been no oppression. Blayney J said that in these cases, the oppressor had been ordered to buy his victim's shares in the company, to end the oppression. Invariably the consideration was fixed at a 'fair price'. Although there was a compensation element in this fair price, the amount of the consideration was incidental to the main relief. The cases did not establish a general right to compensation.

IPP argued in the alternative that the court's discretion described in s. 205(3) was sufficiently wide, to allow the court to award compensation. Blayney J disagreed for three reasons.

The first reason was that he said that an award of damages would not achieve the object of the section which was to bring the oppression to an end. Secondly, an award of damages was 'purely' [*sic*] a common law remedy for breach of contract or breach of duty. Acts of oppression did not come within this category, said Blayney J. Thirdly, if the Oireachtas had intended to allow for the awarding of damages, it would have done so specifically and clearly.

Ingersoll Publications Ltd cross appealed against the valuation placed on IPP's shares by Barron J. Blayney J accepted Barron J's method of valuation of the shares. However, Barron J's calculation had proceeded on the basis that the company was entitled to £6 million compensation. As Blayney J had held that the company was not so entitled, this sum had to be deducted from the balance sheet, and the effect of such a deduction was to render the shares of nil value.

There are two aspects of Blayney J's judgment which are unsatisfactory.

First, s. 205 accords the court wide discretion as to the orders it may make, once there has been a finding of oppression. The Supreme Court states that an order may only be made if it has the sole purpose of bringing 'to an end the matters complained of'. But the section is not drafted in this way; it specifically states that the order must be made '*with a view* to bringing to an end the matters complained of'. Obviously, the order must relate to the oppression. The section however should not be interpreted as ruling out in every circumstance an award of damages to the oppressed shareholder. Were Blayney J's interpretation correct, a court could not give any remedy in respect of an act of oppression which was not going on whilst the trial was taking place otherwise strictly speaking, the matter complained of would have come to an end.

Second, it seems contradictory to allow 'incidental' damages by way of fixed share price when an oppressor is ordered to purchase the oppressed's shares at a 'fair price', as was done in *Re Greenore*. Such ancillary relief is compensation, and restores to the members the value of the shareholding existing prior to the oppression. The order for the buying of the shares by the oppressor should be done with a view to bringing the matters complained of to an end, without any need for ancillary orders of damages. If this cannot be done without making an order for the sale of shares, then the oppressed person should be allowed to purchase the oppressor's shares. This would have an added benefit of sending a warning to potential and actual oppressors.

Examination of officer of company *Alba Radio Ltd v Haltone (Cork) Ltd* [1995] 2 ILRM 466. This is another illustration of the argument that the Companies Act 1990 is not drafted to cover conduct which occurred prior to its introduction.

In March 1991, the plaintiffs obtained a judgment in the UK for the sum of £40,000 for goods sold to Haltone. This judgment was made enforceable in this jurisdiction by an order of the Master of the High Court in November 1992. Haltone was struck off the Irish register of companies, for failure to make annual returns in 1993. It was restored in February 1995: see *infra*, p. 93.

In this case, the plaintiffs sought to examine a director pursuant to s. 245 of the 1963 Act. This permits the High Court to examine an officer known or suspected to have in his possession any property of the company, or supposed to be indebted to the company. The court can require the officer to answer on oath. These answers may be put down in writing and the director may be required to sign it.

Prior to the 1990 Companies Act, this power could only be exercised where there had been an appointment of a provisional liquidator, or on the making of a winding up order. The 1990 Act extended the scope of this power where it can be proved to the satisfaction of the court that the company is unable to pay its debts and it appears to the court that the reason for the company not being wound up is the insufficiency of the company's assets. The question which the court had to address was whether the section applied retrospectively or not.

In the High Court, Barron J examined the Act's provisions to determine whether or not the section was retrospective. Barron J held that where rights have been acquired or duties imposed in respect of completed transactions prior to the passing of the Act, those rights and duties cannot be affected by the Act unless it is retrospective in its effect. Barron J held that because the law had been changed as to the circumstances in which an application to examine an officer of a company did not mean that the Act had been operated retrospectively. Barron J, making reference to *Dublin Heating Company Ltd v Hefferon Kearns* [1992] ILRM 51, endorsed Murphy J's definition of retrospective legislation.

In *Dublin Heating Company*, Murphy J held that retrospective legislation takes away or impairs any vested right acquired under existing laws, or creates a new obligation, or imposes a new duty or attaches a new disability in respect to transactions already passed. This could be contrasted with the situation which obtained in this case, *Alba Radio Ltd*, where a part of the requirement for action is drawn from a time antecedent to the passing of the statute. Barron J said that there was no right vested in the director not to be examined under s. 245, unless the company was being wound up. The extension of the circumstances under which a director should be examinable does not mean that the section was being operated retrospectively.

Barron J said that were the director to be examined by the court, he might be held liable to some penalty. However, since the director had not been examined, much less penalised, this problem might never arise.

Costs, remuneration and expenses in examinership *Re Coombe Importers Ltd*, High Court, June 22, 1995. Under s. 10 and s. 29 of the Companies (Amendment) Act 1990, an examiner's costs and expenses are accorded priority over all other debts. This matter is extensively reviewed in the 1993 and 1994 Annual Reviews.

In this case, a court had considered an examiner's proposed scheme of arrangement, refused to confirm it, ordered that the company should be wound up, and appointed a liquidator. An application was brought to determine whether or not the examiner should be paid in priority to the liquidator.

In the High Court, Hamilton CJ stated although sufficient funds had been realised to pay both the liquidator and examiner in full, he nevertheless examined the provisions contained in s. 29. This section provides that unless the court order otherwise, the remuneration costs and expenses of the examiner shall be paid out of the revenue of the company or the proceeds of realisation of the company's assets. S. 29(3) provides that the sanctioned remuneration costs and expenses shall be paid before any other claim, whether secured or unsecured, under any compromise, scheme of arrangement, receivership or winding up of the company. By virtue of this section, the examiner ranks ahead of preferential creditors or fixed charge holders.

Hamilton CJ noted that none of the parties advanced any arguments or gave any reasons why the costs of this examinership should not be sanctioned. However Hamilton CJ said that there was an obligation on the court to be vigilant in scrutinising the examiner's application for sanction of payment. This was so particularly in view of the priority accorded payment of such remuneration, costs and expenses.

Reviewing these, Hamilton CJ found that there were two expenditures for goods, and neither was not necessary to keep the company going during the protection period. The judge refused to sanction these.

This case sends warning to suppliers of goods and to examiners.

First, even if the supplier, examiner and all other parties reach a contrary agreement, this does not affect the obligation of the court to review such payments, and disallow those not deemed necessary for the company's survival.

Second, the examiner's costs, remuneration and expenses must all relate exclusively and specifically to keeping the company going during the protection period. The case does not identify how such payments may be characterised. An examiner may form a judgment initially which a court with hindsight might be all too ready to overturn. The effect of the loss of the priority is to send the creditor's claim to the bottom of the list of unsecured creditors. The creditor, not the examiner has to foot the bill. This may also make suppliers less ready to deal with examiners. This may require some legislative attention.

Third, it could be argued that where goods are supplied to an examiner, there is an implied term that payment therefore will only be made subject to court approval? If so, the effect of non-ratification by a court is to make such debts not merely unsecured, but unenforceable. This again needs legislative consideration.

Voluntary liquidation *In re Naiad Ltd*, High Court, February 13, 1995. This case examines the principles applicable in transforming a voluntary liquidation into a winding up by the court. This matter was discussed in the 1994 Annual Review analysis of *In re Gilt Construction Ltd* [1994] 2 ILRM 456. O'Hanlon J pointed out in *In re Gilt* that the court was in general reluctant to take this course.

In *Re Naiad* a creditors' meeting was called. The creditors appointed a liquidator. The petitioner in this case was a major UK-based creditor who was seeking to have the liquidator replaced.

The petitioner's claim that the court should appoint a liquidator in place of the creditor's nominee, was based upon objections to both the notice of meeting and its conduct.

McCracken J in the High Court dealt first with the objection to the notice of the creditor's meeting. The notice was sent out just before Christmas, and the meeting was held on the 3 January. The petitioner did not receive his notice until the day before the meeting. McCracken J held that the company had complied with the provision of s. 266, by posting out the notices ten days prior to the meeting. McCracken J stated that although he was entitled to take into account the timing of the meetings, he was satisfied that there was no breach of the section.

Second, the petitioner claimed that no notice of the meeting was given to the employees who, it was alleged, were creditors. McCracken J dismissed this, as the employees were not creditors. They had been paid until that day. The fact that the chairman of the creditors' meeting had allowed some of the employees to vote (which was an error on his part) did not invalidate the meeting.

Third, it was claimed that the chairman of the creditors' meeting had failed to adjourn the meeting at the request of the SIPTU representative, who spoke for those employees who considered themselves creditors. McCracken J held that the chairman had not contravened any rule or obligation in so refusing to adjourn the meeting. The petitioner had not sought the adjournment. This was sought by the SIPTU representative who did not support the creditor's petition.

Fourth, it was alleged that the company had traded insolvently, and that the creditor-appointed liquidator might not be as prepared to take all possible steps against those responsible as a court ordered liquidator. McCracken J said that whilst there might be some general proposition that creditor-appointed liquidators might be 'director friendly', there was no allegation that this was the case here.

Fifth, the petitioner claimed that the chairman, in taking into account whether a resolution had properly been passed or not by the creditors' meeting, must consider not merely the number of creditors voting for the proposition, but the value of their debt. McCracken J held that a chairman is not under a duty or obligation to seek to ascertain whether the liquidator, supported by the majority in number of the creditors, also has the support in value of those creditors. McCracken J said that were a liquidator placed under such a duty, he would be in an impossible situation. He pointed out that this was not envisaged by the Act. McCracken J in considering this fifth point, examined s. 267 of the 1963 Act. This provides that where the members and the creditors nominate different liquidators, the person nominated by the creditors shall be appointed liquidator. Here the creditors meeting took a vote as to the appointee, and the member's nominee was approved. The petitioner argued that s. 267 should be interpreted as allowing his nominee to act as liquidator. McCracken J rejected this argument. He said that it was an incorrect interpretation of the word 'nominate'. A liquidator had been validly appointed by the member's meeting. The creditors' meeting was faced with a choice between the member's nominee and the petitioner's nominee. It chose the former by vote. Although the petitioner's nominee was nominated by the petitioner who was *a* creditor he was not nominated by *the* creditors.

McCracken J reviewed the authorities on the manner in which the court should transform a creditors' voluntary liquidation into a winding up by the court.

McCracken J first considered *MCH Services Ltd* (1987) BCLC 535. The English court there held that a court should exercise its discretion in changing a voluntary winding up into a court ordered liquidation where the creditors had a 'justifiable sense of grievance'. McCracken J found that although the petition in this case appeared to manifest a sense of grievance, this did not appear justifiable.

McCracken J lastly considered *In re Gilt Construction Ltd* [1994] 2 ILRM 456. In *Re Gilt*, O'Hanlon J held that a court should take into consideration the expense and delay involved in court liquidation, the overall value of assets to be administered, the complexity or otherwise of the task facing the liquidator, and any other relevant factors presented by a petitioner. O'Hanlon J said that a court would look to see if a creditor had an alternative way of having his grievance determined, rather than ordering the transformation of a voluntary winding up into a court winding up. O'Hanlon J pointed out that in every voluntary winding up, it was open to a dissatisfied person to seek court directions under s. 280.

Applying these principles, McCracken J found that the liquidation here was a relatively simple matter. The liquidator had so far carried out all of his functions expeditiously and properly. The only question that remained, concerned the potential personal liability of the directors. There was no justifiable grievance maintainable by the petitioner in this regard, in the light of the previous conduct of the liquidator. He therefore dismissed the petitioner's claim.

This judgment displays the reluctance of courts to change voluntary into court ordered liquidations, just because of a creditor's opinion that a court ordered liquidation might be preferable. There has to be some fundamental flaw with the voluntary liquidation which vitiates its conduct or operation before a court will transform a voluntary winding up into a court liquidation.

The judgment also raises questions about the well-accepted rule that votes at a creditors' meeting are determined by the number of creditors *and* the value of their debt. In most cases it is rare to find any difficulty with this rule. Most practitioners assume that the wording of the rule, being conjunctive, requires that the chairman ensure before declaring a resolution carried, that the proponents of the resolution constitute a majority in number and value.

Forde points out in his *Law of Company Insolvency*, Round Hall Press, Dublin, 1993, pp. 143-144 that this rule does not derive from the Companies Acts 1963-1990, but is contained in O.74, r.62 of the Rules of the Superior Courts 1986. The Companies Acts are silent on the point as to how votes should be taken at creditors meetings.

What happens where the majority in number vote one way, and the majority in value the other? McCracken J suggests that this is a dilemma which can be avoided. He states in this case that the chairman should decide the question on the basis solely of the numerical majority. Having taken a vote on the basis of numbers for or against, the chairman 'is under no obligation' to ascertain whether the proposition is supported by creditors who constitute the majority in value. The reason McCracken J gives, is that if the chairman consults the majority in value and finds that they disagree with the majority in number, (s)he would be in an impossible position. McCracken J says that such a position is one not envisaged by the Act.

The authors point out that this interpretation involves disregarding the express conjunctive wording of O.74, r.26. On the alternative reading, the chairman's function is to take a vote and declare it carried if there is a majority in number *and* value. This would be in accordance with the policy underlying the Act, whereby decisions are taken by the creditors' meeting, by ensuring that creditors who stand to lose the most are paid some special regard. Were any alteration permitted to the underlying policy, the authors would suggest that most regard should be paid to the majority in *value* rather than the numerical majority.

Duty payable by liquidator on money included in accounts *In Re Private Motorists Provident Society Ltd (in liquidation),* High Court, June 23, 1995. This case involves the construction of statutory instruments concerning the duty payable by a liquidator for moneys received during the course of a liquidation.

In 1986 a Statutory Instrument was passed which required duty to be paid on moneys received by the liquidator. In 1989, a new Statutory Instrument altered this to impose the duty to be paid on moneys received by the liquidator *in realisation of the assets of the company.*

In this case, the liquidator was contesting the duty payable on £16.9 million. First, the liquidator argued that as no order had been made under s. 230 of the Companies Act 1963, vesting the goods and property of the society in him, the goods and property in question were still owned by the society. There was no duty therefore payable. Alternatively, the liquidator argued that even if he were obliged to pay some duty, no duty was payable on £10 million. The £10 million was neither an asset of the society nor represented the realisation of an asset of the society.

In the High Court, Murphy J held that there was no substance to the argument that the property never vested in the liquidator. Even if the ownership of the property remained vested in the society, the liquidator had 'realised' the assets and was in charge of the proceeds of sale. Murphy J could

see no argument in law or in logic to support the liquidator's contention. By
so doing, Murphy J had to consider whether some of the moneys represented
the realisation of an asset of the society. This required Murphy J to review
the role and function of a liquidator and interpret the words 'realisation' and
'asset'.

Murphy J held that one of the liquidator's functions is to collect the assets
and apply them in discharge of the company's liabilities. How such assets
are collected depends on their nature and the circumstances of the case. It
may include litigation, sale, or simply taking cash in hand. However so
obtained, the assets must be applied to reduce the company's liabilities, and
all methods by which such assets were obtained and collected or taken in
hand constituted 'realisation', irrespective of whether this was done by sale
or otherwise.

Murphy J drew a distinction between the collection of assets, and
applying the proceeds in discharge of the company's liabilities — 'winding
up' and the situation where a liquidator uses the assets of the company to
continue trading — 'winding down'. Murphy J said that a realisation only
takes place when an asset is liquidated. By its nature therefore, 'realisation'
is a once-off event, usually verifiable by the payment of the proceeds into
the liquidation bank account.

But what of the situation where such moneys earn interest? Murphy J
held that this does not constitute 'realisation' of the assets of the company,
but rather flow from 'post-realisation' activities of the liquidator. Duty is not
payable on these. Murphy J considered thirteen particular transactions in this
liquidation, and divided them into one or other of the above categories. Thus
refunds of VAT received in respect of winding down, or rebates on statutory
redundancy attributable to employment contracts for the winding down
period, or sums erroneously paid out and then refunded (again during the
winding down) are not 'realisations'.

Murphy J dealt with the practical difficulty consequent on his decision.
He acknowledged that a heavy burden would be placed on the High Court
Examiner, as there would be considerable difficulty in categorising particular
payments as 'realisations' or 'non-realisations'.

Murphy J therefore issued a direction which he said was subject to the
approval of the President of the High Court. His direction was that accounts
left by an liquidator with the examiner of the High Court which disclosed
receipts in excess of £100,000 should be accompanied by a statement of how
much if any of such receipts are not liable to duty and upon what grounds.
The examiner may then transmit these to the Revenue Commissioners who
should be then afforded opportunity to make their representations to the
examiner. In default of agreement between the parties, the matter should be
listed for hearing in the High Court. The examiner, Murphy J held, was

constitutionally precluded from assuming any adjudicatory role if the parties could not agree.

Duty payable by liquidator on money included in accounts *In re Hibernian Transport Companies Ltd* [1995] 3 IR 217. Some of the facts about this winding up are detailed in the 1992 Annual Review, p. 94. This application concerned the filing of annual accounts for ten consecutive liquidation years, 1983-1993. The rates payable changed in 1986 from 2% to 2.5%.

In this case, the liquidator had sold all the company's assets. Some of the proceeds had been placed on interest-bearing deposit with banks. Some others, the proceeds had been used to purchase exchequer bills and similar instruments, such that capital accretions took place. The question therefore was whether duty was payable, and at what rate.

In the High Court, Costello P examined the terms of the statutory instrument, and came to the same conclusion as Murphy J in the *PMPS* case above. Costello P held that the High Court examiner must examine the accounts to examine which proceeds are derived from the realisation of the assets of the company and which are not. He decided that where assets were sold, and the proceeds placed on deposit, the ensuing deposit interest was not dutiable. The interest was obtained on foot of the contract between the liquidator and the bank and was an investment and not a realisation. Costello P rejected the argument that the act of crediting the liquidator's account was of itself a realisation of an asset.

Costello P then turned to determine the duty payable on the moneys derived from the realisation of assets. He pointed out that the requirement to lodge an annual liquidation account was a rule more honoured in the breach than in observance. A difficulty arose when there was a change in the rate of duty, and accounts were being filed for years in which the duty was at the old rate.

Two arguments were made to Costello P on behalf of the shareholders of the company.

First, that the relevant rate to be applied was that obtaining at the date of the making of the winding up order, and any changes in the rate subsequent to that date should be ignored. Costello P rejected this. The Minister was vested with power to vary or revise fees chargeable, under the Courts of Justice Act 1936. The liquidator must pay whatever fees are prescribed when liability arises. The law at the date of liquidation is in this context, irrelevant.

Second, the shareholders referred to the accounts for the two liquidation years before the raising of the duty in 1986. They argued that although the accounts for these two years were filed after 1986, duty was payable at the old rate. This raised the question at what date must duty be paid. Costello P held that the fee must be paid when accounts are filed with the examiner, irrespective of the date to which these accounts refer. Liquidators must ensure that they lodge the accounts annually as statute requires. If not, and accounts are filed in a subsequent year, the costs may be greater, as the rate of duty may rise thereby leaving less money for distribution.

Fraudulent trading   *Southern Mineral Oil Ltd & Silk Oil Ireland Ltd v Cooney & Ors.*, High Court, February 10, 1995. This case concerned an application to dismiss fraudulent trading proceedings brought by a liquidator for want of prosecution.

Two companies were established with common directors and shareholders. These companies both became insolvent, and the directors transferred the assets of these companies to a third company, X Ltd.

A liquidator was appointed to the two companies. The liquidator believed that the transfer of the assets of the two companies to X Ltd constituted misfeasance by the directors. The investigation and the institution of the fraudulent trading proceedings was hampered by the lack of assets. In September 1990, the liquidator acquired some funding from the Revenue Commissioners to institute the fraudulent trading proceedings. These were not instituted until August 1994. The reason the liquidator gave was that he was unable to get counsel to draft proceedings. The directors brought a motion to dismiss the proceedings, claiming inordinate and inexcusable delay.

In the High Court, Murphy J pointed out that the court would dismiss proceedings for want of prosecution in two instances. First, where proceedings have been instituted within the limitation period. There, if the court dismisses the action, it may be re-entered, unless its prosecution has been specifically precluded. Second, if a case has been instituted outside the limitation period and the court dismisses it for want of prosecution, the case may not be re-entered. This case fell within the first category.

Murphy J discussed both *Ó Domhnall v Merrick* [1984] IR 151 and *Toal v Duignan (Nos. 1 and 2)* [1991] ILRM 135, 140. The Supreme Court in *Toal* held the court should inquire whether the defendant was in any way responsible for the delay. If the defendant is not responsible, then the court must balance the possible injustice to the plaintiff from being prevented from pursuing his cause of action, against the probable injustice to the defendant in having to defend such a claim.

The directors argued that the principle in *Toal* only applied to civil proceedings, and fraudulent trading proceedings are governed by criminal law principles in relation to delay. Criminal law courts require an accused person to be brought to trial with 'reasonable expedition'.

Murphy J rejected the directors' argument that civil fraudulent trading proceedings had to be brought to trial expeditiously. Murphy J based this rejection upon the decision in *O'Keeffe v Ferris* [1994] 1 ILRM 425. This affirmed that fraudulent trading proceedings are not criminal proceedings. Murphy J however said that the gravity of the matter should be taken into account, when balancing the right of the plaintiff to pursue his claim, against that of the defendant not to have to defend an unreasonable claim. If the gravity of the matter is taken into account, said Murphy J, this would go against the defendant's claim to have the matter dismissed. Murphy J said that the defendant would be unlikely to have forgotten about the matter, or overlooked details of serious consequence.

Murphy J said further, that proceedings such as those in the instant case have to be initiated by leave of the court. No court hearing such an application would allow the proceedings to run, were this to cause injustice to the defendant. A subsequent court could set aside any order made by a previous court, which would allow such proceedings to run, if it decided that to bar the plaintiff would unjustly interfere with his or her constitutional rights.

Murphy J applied these principles. He said that although the winding up of the two companies had been initiated six years before, the delays complained of had only occurred in the last four years. The question was whether the delay in the previous years was such as to make it unjust to allow the proceedings to go ahead against these defendants.

Murphy J examined the relevant facts. One of the directors had died. The illness of a former auditor of Silk was also important. So was the winding up of the transferee company, X Ltd.

Murphy J found that the evidence available to the liquidator would not be less than that available to the defendants. The liquidator's evidence was confined to the documentation he received after his appointment. The evidence of the directors related to conversations which occurred and transactions effected prior to the liquidation. There would be some clear advantage to the liquidator in this respect. On balancing these considerations, it appeared that the proceedings should be allowed to continue. This was so particularly as the liquidator was statutorily bound to protect the interests of creditors.

In *Countyglen plc v Carway* [1995] 1 ILRM 481, the High Court dealt with an application by a company for an interlocutory Mareva injunction against its directors.

An inspector had been appointed on 19 January 1994. The inspector's reports concluded that certain transactions were fraudulent. The inspector said that Carway and other family members were involved in these. These activities resulted in financial loss to the company. The company brought proceedings for fraud, breach of duty and conspiracy against Carway and others, seeking an order whereby Carway and others would pay £1.14 million to the company. Prior to the plenary hearing, interim injunctions were granted on December 5, 1994, prohibiting the respondents reducing their assets below that sum. On December 20, the High Court directed Carway to disclose details of all assets to the examiner of the High Court before December 30. The company then ought an interlocutory Mareva injunction and other relief.

In the High Court, Murphy J stated that the proper test to apply when an interlocutory injunction is sought in these circumstances, is whether there is a substantial question to be tried. Relying upon the Supreme Court decision in *Campus Oil Ltd v Minister for Industry & Energy* [1983] ILRM 541, Murphy J held that an applicant does not have to establish as a matter of probability that his claim will succeed. It would be entirely inappropriate for a court on an interlocutory application, to review such of the evidence as is available to it, and attempt to forecast the outcome of the proceedings as a matter of probability.

Murphy J said that there was substantial evidence to support the allegations of serious fraud and breach of trust against the respondents. Although these were being challenged, it was not the function of the court to ascertain which view was likely to prevail.

Murphy J then turned to the principles applicable to Mareva injunctions. In *Fleming v Ranks (Ireland) Ltd* [1983] ILRM 541, McWilliam J had laid down the test that there had to be a 'real and substantial risk' of the removal or disposal of the respondent's assets with a view to evade any obligation to the plaintiff. The order does not exist to preserve assets in case the plaintiffs claim succeeds, but to prevent an anticipated abuse by a respondent of his legal rights so as to frustrate unjustly the anticipated order of the court.

Murphy J looked to see what assets the Carway family had, and what danger there was of their dissipation or transfer outside the jurisdiction. The only asset that could be identified was Carway's family home. The judge looked at the nature of the Carway business and Carway's lifestyle, and said that it was such as to facilitate the transfer of assets on an international basis. Murphy J examined Carway's affidavits, and found that he had failed to identify what assets he had in the jurisdiction, and deal with the allegation or suspicion that these assets might be dissipated in order to frustrate any court order.

Murphy J was surprised that Carway did not claim that the interlocutory order would cause any difficulty for him. Murphy J rejected the argument that the Mareva injunction impinged on the constitutional property rights of the respondents. He said that as the affidavit did not identify the extent of the property concerned, he could not consider whether or not there was a breach of property rights. Murphy J said that on the inference from the facts before the court, the likelihood was that the respondent would dissipate the assets he had within the jurisdiction in order to defeat the plaintiffs claim. Murphy

J granted the Mareva injunction but restricted its application to assets within the jurisdiction.

Murphy J required the respondent to swear an affidavit of discovery in relation to the assets within the jurisdiction, for the purposes of the Mareva injunction. Murphy J warned that the discovery should only be used for this litigation, and if it were used for any other purpose, this would be in contempt of court.

O'Mahony v Horgan [1996] 1 ILRM 161. This case concerned an application for a Mareva injunction against directors accused of fraudulent trading. The company concerned here was involved in cattle import-export. The company was put into liquidation on November 8, 1991.

The liquidator estimated that as of March 1992, the company was insolvent to the amount of £11.6 million. The liquidator claimed that the company had made loans to the directors of £1.9 million.

On the June 18, 1993, the liquidator sought to make the three directors personally liable for the debts of the company. On June 23, 1993, the liquidator sought an injunction preventing one of the directors from receiving the proceeds of an insurance policy.

Murphy J granted an injunction in the High Court, restraining one of the directors from disposing of or dissipating the proceeds of an insurance policy, amounting to the sum of £71,000 and interest. The director appealed.

In the Supreme Court, Hamilton CJ listed the criteria that Murphy J considered when deciding to grant the Mareva injunction. First, a plaintiff should make full and frank disclosure of all matters in his knowledge which are material for the judge to know. Second, a plaintiff should give particulars of his claims against the defendant, stating the grounds of his claim and the amount thereof and fairly stating the points made against it by the defendant. Three, a plaintiff should give some grounds for believing that the defendant had assets within the jurisdiction. The existence of a bank account is normally sufficient. Four, a plaintiff should give some grounds for asserting that there is a risk that the assets shall be removed or dissipated. Five, a plaintiff must give an undertaking in damages in case his case fails.

Hamilton CJ stated that at common law, a plaintiff was not entitled to claim security to guarantee satisfaction of a judgment which the plaintiff may eventually obtain. Hamilton CJ made reference to the well-known English decisions of *Nippon Yusen Kaishea v Karagerogis* [1975] 1 WLR 1093, and *Mareva Compania Navera SA v International Bulkcarriers SA* [1975] 2 Lloyds' Rep 509, and *Third Chandris Shipping Corporation v Unimarine SA* [1979] QB 645. He also referred to the Irish decision of *Fleming v Ranks* [1983] ILRM 541.

Hamilton CJ said that these cases establish that before a Mareva injunction may be granted, there must be an intention to dispose of assets, in order to evade obligation to the plaintiff and to frustrate the anticipated order of the court. Hamilton CJ said it was not sufficient to show that the defendant might dissipate assets in the ordinary course of business, or in the payment of lawful debts. The question for the Supreme Court was whether the liquidator had shown in the High Court that the director was likely to dissipate the proceeds of the insurance policy with the intention of evading his obligation (if any) to the liquidator.

The Chief Justice considered the liquidator's affidavit. The liquidator was concerned that even if he obtained a court order making the director liable, there would be nothing left to satisfy it, unless a Mareva injunction was granted. Hamilton CJ stated that though this apprehension might be well justified, the liquidator had failed to show the director had the intention to dissipate the assets so as to frustrate any order made by the court against him. The director was entitled to the proceeds of the policy of insurance. He could use such moneys either to make good the damage done, or otherwise. This might well mean that the money would not be available to meet any decree which the liquidator might obtain against the director. However, that fact of itself does not entitle the liquidator to the injunction sought.

A liquidator who suspects that a director may be planning to interfere with disputed assets is not entitled to any greater consideration than any other litigant.

Restoration of company to the register of companies *In re Haltone (Cork) Ltd* High Court, February 7, 1995. This company was incorporated on October 7, 1985. It did not file annual returns. It was struck off on September 25, 1993. The petitioner, a UK creditor, sought the restoration of Haltone to the register, to enforce an English judgment, and to initiate proceedings against the directors of Haltone, in order to make them personally liable for the company's debt.

In the High Court, O'Hanlon J outlined the court's power to order the restoration of a company to the Register in appropriate circumstances. O'Hanlon J said that where the company itself petitions for its restoration, there are no major problems so long as annual and other returns are all filed. However, as in this case, such restoration was evidently not in the directors' interests. They might not necessarily file returns and fulfil the other requisite functions. Thus there was a difficulty in ordering the company's restoration. O'Hanlon J held that the petitioner's application should be acceded to, so that a reasonable opportunity should be afforded to the petitioner to bring proceedings against the company and its officers.

It would be interesting to speculate on whether it might be open to the Registrar to take further proceedings against the company and its directors for failing to file the requisite annual returns consequent on the restoration. There are no policy reasons why this should be so and thus provide yet another deterrent to company officers who fail to comply with filing requirements.

STATUTORY CHANGES

S. 174 of the Finance Act 1995 In 1985, in *Re Keenan Brothers* the Supreme Court held that it was possible to create a fixed charge over book debts. This gave the fixed charge holder priority over other creditors, including the Revenue Commissioners. Accordingly, in order to reverse the effect of this judgment, s. 115 of the Finance Act 1986 provided that where the Revenue are owed outstanding PAYE and VAT, they may call on the holder of a fixed charge over book debts to pay a sum to the Revenue. This sum may be the entire owing on PAYE and VAT. The Revenue may seek payment of the company's debt for PAYE and VAT from the charge holder. The Revenue may seek repayment of all sums received by the charge holder from the company, including sums paid to him in other capacities.

There are two restrictions upon this condition. First, only sums owing since notification are caught. Secondly, only sums received from the company by the charge holder are covered, so that he may not be asked to pay out of his own pocket, as it were.

The effect of this section was that lenders were averse to accepting fixed charges over book debts as security. Therefore, in 1995, s. 174 of the Finance Act was passed. This section amends but does not repeal s. 115 of the Finance Act 1986. It is structured similarly.

S. 174 commences by imposing liability on the holder of a fixed charge over book debts for PAYE and VAT owed by the company which created the charge. The section sets out in what circumstances the holder of the fixed charge will not be liable.

The holder will not be liable unless he has been notified in writing by the Revenue that the company has failed to pay PAYE and VAT debts. There is a possibility that the charge holder on notification by the Revenue may be liable for the past, present and future debts of the company for PAYE and VAT.

In order to escape liability for past PAYE and VAT debts of the company, the charge holder must furnish to the Revenue details of the charge similar to those contained in the form required under s. 99 of the Companies Act 1963. The time limit for furnishing this information is the later of either 21 days after the introduction of s. 174, or 21 days after the creation of the charge.

Another exemption provision allows the charge holder to retain amounts paid over to him by the company before the date on which he has been notified in writing by the Revenue of the sums owing for PAYE and VAT. The relationship between this exemption and the others is unclear. Presumably, a person who has failed to give charge details to the Revenue cannot use this exemption to escape liability for past PAYE and VAT.

The Revenue may seek repayment of all sums received by the charge holder from the company, including sums paid to him in other capacities. In this connection, the Revenue's claims against the charge holder are limited to the amount the charge holder received from the company. Thus, if the sums due and owing exceed what the charge holder has received from the company, the charge holder will not be liable for the shortfall under this section.

The section now allows the Revenue to lift or repeal any notification given to a fixed charge holder by way of notice. However, this notice will not affect any liability which may have been incurred by the charge holder, prior to notice. The notice does not preclude the Revenue re-introducing a further or other notification at a later date.

It must come as a complete surprise to readers to learn that the purported aim of this section is to promote borrowing, by making it possible for companies to give security over book debts. It would be hard to envisage a more uncertain and inefficient way of attempting to achieve such an objective. For a full discussion of the section and its various pitfalls, see T.B. Courtney, *Company Law Review*, Round Hall Sweet & Maxwell, 1995, pp. 33-40.

SI No. 56 of 1995: Land Act 1965 (Additional Categories of Qualified Persons) Regulations 1995 The Land Act 1945 places some restrictions on those who are qualified to own land in Ireland. This instrument adds to the list of those qualified, a body corporate incorporated in a Member State of the European Communities or other European State which us a contracting party to the European Economic Area Agreement. Such a body corporate must be one having its registered office, central administration or principal place of business within the territory of these states.

Conflicts of Law

FOREIGN DIVORCE

In *V. McC. v J. McC.*, Supreme Court, July 28, 1995, a question of domicile arose in the context of a foreign divorce. The appellant husband had been born or married parents in Tyrone in 1945. When he was four his family came to live in the State, where he grew up and later obtained employment. He married the respondent in 1968. The parties separated in 1977. The appellant issued divorce proceedings in England in November 1984. A decree absolute was granted in August 1986. He then married another woman in England.

The respondent's proceedings for maintenance and other relief were ongoing in the Irish courts. The appellant invoked the English divorce as a reason to resist those proceedings.

The crucial question was whether the appellant had acquired an English domicile of choice at the time he instituted the divorce proceedings in 1984. Geoghegan J held that he had not; the Supreme Court dismissed the appeal.

The evidence was to the effect that the appellant had been in employment with one employer for over twenty years when he received a year's leave of absence in January 1983. For six months he spent the time working between Africa and Ireland. He then took up employment in England in the same area of work that he had done in Ireland. He was followed to England by the woman whom he was later to marry there. She obtained work with the same employer. When asked whether or not he had had any fixed intention at that stage as to what his future was or where his future might lie, his reply was:

> Well, I was ambitious and I was excited about the potential for getting into the industry in Britain, in England.

He said that he could not see how he could do much more for himself professionally within an Irish context, adding:

> There was no intention of returning, one could not have seen into the future and seen the dramatically changing fortunes of both countries and economies and certainly if the British economy had remained as they were [*sic*], we would have remained there.

The appellant resigned from his English employment in February 1986. He set up an independent company and worked mainly on a freelance basis until he returned to Dublin early in 1989, where he continued to reside with his new wife and their children.

The appellant sought to rely on his purchase of a house in London in 1984 as persuasive evidence of his intention to reside indefinitely in England. He gave evidence on the matter as follows:

> We decided that was it, we started looking for a property. We bought an apartment and at that time the property market was booming and property prices were increasing and after a year we started to look at a house, because we had paid a certain amount and it had doubled in value — and it was the fashion at the time, people were trading up all the time, it was a booming situation. Ireland was still very flat and recessionary, so there was really no intention of leaving what was a booming economy, a booming job opportunity scenario. I had been promoted and was having an income I never could have had [with my Irish employer] so there was no question of returning to Ireland at that time.

The respondent argued, however, that the purchase of the house could be explained sufficiently on the basis it was a good business deal, to take advantage of what the appellant had called a 'boom' situation, for such period as it might last.

Egan J (O'Flaherty and Blayney JJ concurring) analysed the issues as follows. The appellant's domicile of origin in Northern Ireland had 'only lasted for a very short period as he came to Dublin as a very young child.' The Republic of Ireland was the state of his domicile of choice. In a somewhat obscure passage, Egan J noted that it had been argued that the appellant's domicile of choice:

> has the same status as a domicile of origin in so far as onus of proof necessary to disturb it was concerned. I cannot accept this proposition despite the minimal period which elapsed between the domicile of origin and its displacement by a domicile of choice. I fully accept, however, that the onus of displacing this domicile of choice is a heavy one.

This passage provokes two comments. First, if it suggests that the domicile of origin was replaced by a domicile of choice when the appellant moved from Tyrone to Dublin at the age of four, it is entirely novel, since the traditional approach is to regard minors as having a domicile of dependency during their minority. Secondly, the earlier case law is to the effect that, though the onus of displacing a domicile of choice is heavy, it is lighter than that required to displace the domicile of origin.

Egan J went on to observe that events after the crucial date in November 1984 could be relevant only in so far as they assisted the court in drawing inferences as to what might have been the appellant's actual intention in November 1984. The actual period spent in England was 'short and was consistent, as was all the evidence, with a purely 'career' move.' There was ample evidence to support Geoghegan J's view that the appellant had not acquired an English domicile.

A number of important issues fell for consideration in *P.L. v An tÁrd Chláraitheóir* [1995] 2 ILRM 241. The facts were simple enough. The applicant for judicial review had separated from his wife in 1984. His wife had gone to live in England, taking her children with her. An English court awarded her custody in August 1986. Thirteen months later she obtained a divorce from her husband. In 1993 the applicant gave notice to the Dublin Registrar of Marriages of his intention to marry a second time. The Registrar consulted the Registrar General, who advised that the marriage should not proceed as it did not appear that the applicant and his wife had been domiciled in England at the time of the divorce in 1987. Although the applicant had provided the Registrar with an affidavit from his wife, averring that, when she had moved to England, it was her intention to establish a permanent home there with her children, the Registrar did not change his opinion on the issue of domicile. The applicant sought a declaration that the English divorce should be recognised under Irish law and an order of *mandamus* directing the Registrar General to issue him a licence and certificate of marriage.

The first issue was whether the Register General had any power to investigate and decide upon the validity of foreign divorces under Irish law. The applicant argued that he had not; even if Regulations of 1892 purported to give him that power — and they fell short of clearly doing so — they could not, as delegated legislation, expand powers that had not been given to the Registrar General under the Marriages Acts.

Kinlen J reviewed the statutory provisions in detail. Fortified by English decisions of a similar statutory framework (*R. v Hammersmith Superintendent Registrar of Marriages, ex parte Mir- Anwaruddin* [1917] 1 KB 634; *R. v Brentwood Superintendent Registrar of Marriages, ex parte Arian* [1968] 3 All ER 279), he interpreted s. 16 of the Marriages (Ireland) Act 1844 as entitling the Registrar on his own initiative to determine whether or not there was any lawful impediment to a proposed marriage. Section 23, which allowed a member of the public to intervene in relation to an impediment, should be seen as supplementing, rather than as being the necessary precondition to activating, the Registrar's investigatory power.

Kinlen J had little sympathy for the argument advanced on behalf of the

Registrar General that, as a public office holder, he was under a duty to uphold the Constitution and that this conferred on him the power to investigate the validity of a foreign divorce, independently of any statutory powers he might enjoy. Echoing Walsh J's observations in *Gaffney v Gaffney* [1975] IR 133, at 150, Kinlen J said that it seemed clear that Article 41.3.3° did not necessarily require that domicile represent the only test for recognition of foreign divorces:

> Accordingly, the correct ascertainment of the domicile of the parties to a divorce is not to be regarded as a constitutional imperative, but rather derives from the legislation governing the recognition of foreign judicial decrees of dissolution of marriage, viz. the Domicile and Recognition of Foreign Divorces Act, 1986. The powers of the Registrar derive from the 1844 Act and the 1863 Act, respectively, which entitle him to determine whether or not there is a lawful impediment to a marriage; the existence of a lawful impediment, in this context, depends on whether or not a foreign divorce is recognised under Irish law. The basis for such recognition is itself provided for by the Domicile and Recognition of Foreign Divorces Act, 1986. Reliance on the Constitution directly, therefore, is unnecessary and serves only to confuse the issue.

Perhaps this resolution to the argument does not do it full justice. The prohibition on divorce in Article 41, prior to November 26, 1995, undoubtedly had implications on the treatment of foreign divorces in Ireland. If, for example, a practice had developed whereby large numbers of people who were clearly of Irish domicile were obtaining foreign divorces by assertions that they were domiciled abroad, when these were demonstrably false, the knowing acquiescence of the Registrar General in this practice would have damaged the efficacy of the constitutional prohibition on divorce. It is true that the Oireachtas might have replaced the domiciled-based test for recognition of foreign divorces by another test, such as that of habitual residence (as recommended by the Law Reform Commission, then under the Presidency of Walsh J, in its *Report on the Recognition of Foreign Divorce and Legal Separation* (LRC 10–1985)), but again it is easy to envisage cases of attempted fraudulent evasion of the new test which would subvert the efficacy of the prohibition on divorce.

One has to doubt whether the Oireachtas was *entirely* free to confer recognition on foreign divorces without restriction. At some point a lax statutory criterion for the recognition of foreign divorces would be so subversive of the policy of the prohibition on divorce legislation *within* the State, contained in Article 41.3.2°, as to be impermissible. For example, if the Oireachtas had dispensed with any requirement of domicile, habitual residence or even presence in the foreign state granting the divorce and legislated for the recognition of 'mail order' divorces obtainable by the expenditure of a 52 pence stamp, this would have made a mockery of the public policy underlying Article 41.3.2°.

The next issue in *P.L.* concerned the court's scrutiny of the Registrar General's decision. Kinlen J took the view that this was not a context in which to supply the doctrine that a decision-making tribunal's determination should be upheld unless it was unreasonable or clearly in excess of jurisdiction. The case was not concerned with a situation where an administrative tribunal had been afforded a discretion in an administrative matter; it was one turning on the determination of a legal issue, which was a matter for the court. This conclusion is undoubtedly correct: clearly the court has power to quash a decision of the Registrar General or to make an order of *mandamus* against him, where this is necessary to give effect to the court's determination of the issue whether the foreign divorce decree should be afforded recognition under Irish law.

Turning to the question of the English divorce in the instant case, Kinlen J noted that it would be capable of recognition under s. 5(1) of the Domicile and Recognition of Foreign Divorces Act 1986 if the wife was domiciled in England at the time she obtained the divorce. The question thus reduced itself to one of evidence.

The Register General sought to discount the relevance of the wife's evidence as to her domicile for four reasons: statements of intention made by a party to a cause were entitled to little weight; the wife had been in England for only two years when she commenced proceedings for divorce; she had not established sufficient links in England to give rise to a clear intention at the relevant time to reside *permanently* in England; and she had referred in her evidence to returning to Ireland as 'going home to Ireland'.

As to the first of these reasons, Kinlen J acknowledged that it was true that, in *Gillis v Gillis* (1874) IR 8 Eq 597, at 607, Warren J had said that 'statements of intention made by a party in a case are entitled to little weight', but in *Gillis* the propositus had sought by his assertions to contradict the inference that would otherwise have arisen from his conduct. In the light of this inconsistency, it was not unnatural that the court would attach greater significance to a person's actions than to his words. The later Irish decisions of *In re Sillar* [1956] IR 344, *Moffett v Moffett* [1920] 1 IR 57 and *C.M. v T.M.* [1990] 2 IR 52 supported this view.

In any event, it seemed doubtful that the assumption underlying the supposed rule regarding the weight to be attached to the statements of intentions made by a party in a cause was applicable in the instant case. Geoghegan J, speaking ex tempore, in *M.C. v. M.C.*, High Court, unreported, January 20, 1994, had observed that:

... whereas some weight must be attached to what the person alleging the change of domicile actually says in the witness box was his intention, the court must view such evidence with scepticism. This is because the person alleging the change of domicile, while not telling lies necessarily or in any way trying to mislead the court, may engage in an element of wishful thinking and colouring when the actual intention of that party is an essential element of fact to be proved if he is to succeed in the case. For that reason the courts have traditionally, over the years, primarily paid attention to the surrounding facts and circumstances rather than to what the person actually says in the witness box.

This reasoning did not seem to apply to the applicant's first wife in the instant case since there was no obvious benefit to be gained for her from the outcome of the proceedings.

Kinlen J did not consider that the first wife's period of residence of only two years prior to the instigation of the divorce proceedings should lead him to draw an unfavourable inference as to her domiciliary intention. It was well established that the length of residence was immaterial for the purpose of acquiring a domicile of choice; domicile could be established immediately if there was clear proof of intention. Greater significance, however, could be attached to the fact that the first wife had remained in Britain for a period of over ten years and was still resident there. This subsequent period of residence was of more greater probative value as to her intentions than the fact that she had been resident in England for only two years before commencing the divorce proceedings.

In her affidavit, the first wife had deposed that in the autumn of 1986 she had taken proceedings to obtain sole custody of her children and had instructed her solicitors in England to commence divorce proceedings. She added:

> ... It was my intention to take such proceedings in England to regularise my position. I did not take out similar proceedings in Ireland as I did not wish to return to Ireland and did not see any need to clarify my legal position in that jurisdiction.

Echoing Gannon J in *In re Fleming Deceased* [1987] IRLM 638, at 647 (as to which see the 1987 Review 58-62), Kinlen J considered that, in the absence of contradictory evidence, a court was entitled to presume that a person resident in England for a significant period of time would respect and comply with the relevant legislation there concerning the obtaining of divorces and would not deceive the English court as to her true domicile in order to obtain a divorce under false pretences. Clearly, if evidence of such

fraudulent action were brought to the court's attention, it would not recognise
such a divorce obtained without jurisdiction. This was exactly the situation
that had arisen in *Gaffney v. Gaffney* [1975] IR 133. Cf. W. Binchy, *Irish
Conflicts of Law* (1988), 284-9.

It was also submitted on behalf of the Registrar General that the first wife
had failed to prove by objective evidence that she had established *permanent*
links in England, rather than an intention to remain in England for an
indefinite period. Kinlen J considered that this was based on a misconception
of the High Court decision in *M.(C.) v M.(T.)* [1988] ILRM 456; [1990] 2 IR
52, analysed in the 1988 Review 77-80, it had seemed to Barr J that

> there is an important distinction between setting up home for an indefi-
> nite period in a particular place and setting up permanent home there.

This statement had to be read in light of Barr J's subsequent comments as
follows:

> On the other hand, a home which is established in a particular place for
> an indefinite period may depend upon the continuance of certain cir-
> cumstances which are themselves indefinite as to likely duration. In my
> view a home set up on the latter basis does not have the element of
> permanency as so defined which is an essential indicator of a change of
> domicile. The evidence establishes clearly that the family home and the
> professional base established by the husband in Ireland depended on the
> continuance in substantial measure of the financial advantage which he
> derived from taking up residence in this jurisdiction.

Read in the context of the facts of that particular case, it was clear that
Barr J's reference to an indefinite period should be understood as a reference
to a residence which is contingent on particular events. From the facts of that
case, the husband's residence in Ireland had been contingent on tax concessions. There clearly was no comparison between that case and the circumstances of the instant case.

Finally, Kinlen J considered that 'no great significance' could be attached
to the first wife's reference to 'going home to Ireland'. He did not refer to
earlier decisions, which support his view: cf. *Bell v Kennedy* (1868) LR 1 Sc
& Div 307 (HL, *per* Lord Cairns LC), *Davis v Adair* [1895] 1 IR 379, at 458
(CA, *per* Barry LJ).

Kinlen J, in the light of his analysis on these four issues, accordingly
granted the review sought by the applicant.

In the 1989 Review, 88-90, we analysed *M.(C.) v T.(C.)* [1991] ILRM
268 where Barr J held that a maintenance order made under s. 5(1)(A) of the

Family Law (Maintenance of Spouses and Children) Act 1976 remained valid and enforceable, notwithstanding the fact that the spouse's marriage was subsequently dissolved abroad by a divorce recognised in Irish private international law, unless and until that order was 'varied or rescinded by the court on foot of a further application by either party'. In *In re G.Y., an infant; M.Y. v A.Y.*, High Court, December 11, 1995, Budd J applied *C.M. v T.M.* where the husband, in breach of his undertaking to the High Court in proceedings for judicial separation that he would take no steps to convert an English divorce decree nisi into a decree absolute, had gone ahead and done precisely that.

Budd J observed that:

> [t]his Court should not permit the defendant to derive benefit from his breach of undertaking and contempt of Court and must deal with the matter on the basis of the marital status of the parties when the Court embarked on hearing the case.

It should be noted that Barr J had proceeded on the basis that the continuing vitality of a maintenance order made under s. 5(1)(a) did not depend on the wrongful conduct of the maintenance debtor. Of course, the attitude of a court to an application by a maintenance debtor to vary or discharge the order in the light of an intervening divorce would undoubtedly be coloured by the circumstances that disturbed Budd J.

This aspect of the law has subsequently been addressed by Part III of the Family Law 1995, which we discuss in the Family Law Chapter, below, 317-19.

JURISDICTION

Admiralty Article 22 of the Brussels Convention provides that:

> [w]here related actions are brought in the courts of different contracting states any court other than the court first seized may, while the actions are pending at first instance, stay its proceedings. . . .

In *The MV Turquoise Bleu: Medscope Marine Ltd v MTM Metal Trading and Manufacturing Ltd* [1996] 1 ILRM 406, Barr J was called on to determine the parameters of this provision. The facts were somewhat complicated but may be distilled as follows. The plaintiff owned the cargo vessel, the *Turquoise Bleu*. The defendant was an Austrian company, registered in Ireland for tax purposes, with 'no real connection with Ireland.' The plaintiff

chartered the vessel to Link, a Belgian company, in relation to the transpor-
tation of steel from Europe to the Far East. The defendant concluded a
subcharterparty with Link for the shipment of wire rods from St. Petersburg
to Ho Chi Min City. After the wire rods had been loaded, the vessel proceeded
to Antwerp, where it was intended to load further cargo. During the voyage
she required salvage services in Belgian territorial waters. The salvers
arrested the ship as security for their salvage claim against the plaintiff. The
matter was resolved and the vessel was released from arrest. Link, however,
failed to provide additional cargo and the plaintiff refused to permit the vessel
to leave Antwerp. The plaintiff's claim against Link under the charterparty
was one for freight and demurrage; it was referred to arbitration. The
defendant had paid all freight charges for carriage of its cargo to Vietnam.

The defendant commenced proceedings in the Antwerp Court of First
Instance against the plaintiff for the arrest of the vessel consequent on its
refusal to let it leave the port. The Court made an order on January 21, 1994
directing the arrest of the vehicle as security for the defendant's claim for
damages against the plaintiff. The vessel was duly arrested and the amount
for security for its release was fixed. The defendant brought further proceedings against the plaintiff on May 20, 1994 in the Antwerp Commercial Court
pursuant to the arrest of the ship. An introductory hearing was held by that
court on June 7. The plaintiff brought two applications in those proceedings
for the lifting of the arrest of the vessel. The Court delivered two judgments
on July 14 refusing to release the vessel from arrest.

The plaintiff commenced proceedings against the defendant in the Irish
High Court by plenary summons dated February 9, 1994. It sought relief
under a number of headings. The statement of claim restricted itself to
seeking a declaration that the plaintiff was entitled to a lien over the
defendant's cargo on board the *Turquoise Bleu* by reason of Link's breach
of its charterparty and an order for sale of the cargo pursuant to O.50, r.3 of
the Rules of the Superior Courts 1986.

The defendant sought an order staying the proceedings under Article 22.
In the alternative it sought an order staying the proceedings pursuant to the
inherent jurisdiction of the court.

The plaintiff argued that under Article 22 the Irish High Court was the
court first seized of the matter. It sought to characterise the jurisdiction of
the Antwerp arrest judge as being limited to arrest and attachment measures,
with no power to give a decision on the substantive issues in dispute. It
proferred an affidavit sworn by a Belgian advocate in support of this
contention.

Barr J considered that Article 1489 of the Belgian Procedure Code did
not have such a restrictive meaning; he was fortified in this view by a replying
affidavit sworn by another Belgian advocate. Barr J rejected the differentia-

tion between 'arrest proceedings' and 'substantive proceedings' which the plaintiff sought to establish. Article 22 was designed to avoid the risk of irreconcilable decisions resulting from the litigation of related actions in two or more contracting states. There was 'nothing in Article 22 or elsewhere in the Brussels Convention about . . . 'substantive proceedings'.'

It appeared that there was a great degree of similarity between the functions of the Belgian arrest judge and the Irish Admiralty judge when dealing with an application for the arrest of a vessel:

> In Irish law application for an arrest warrant is commonly the first step taken by a plaintiff in admiralty proceedings against the owner of a ship and it is made *ex parte*. It is not an application which is independent and complete in itself. It is a step taken by the plaintiff to provide for security in respect of his claim against the ship owner. It is incumbent on a plaintiff who applies for a warrant directing the arrest of a ship to furnish this Court by affidavit with details of his claim against the shipowner and other information as specified in O.64, r.6(1) of the Rules of the Superior Courts, including an averment that the plaintiff's claim has not been satisfied. The claim is not investigated by the court at that stage. It can make no order on the merits of the claim on an arrest application as the defendant is not before the court.

> It will be appreciated, therefore, that an application to this Court for the arrest of a vessel is not a self-contained application which stands in isolation, but is a step in larger proceedings concerning the plaintiff's claim against the shipowner. As in Belgian law under article 1489 . . ., the issuing of an arrest warrant does not establish any wrongdoing or breach of contract on the part of the shipowner and does not in any way prejudice the owner's defence to the plaintiff's claim or any counter-claim he may wish to bring in the plaintiff's action.

In *Doran v Power* [1996] 1 ILRM 55, a collision occurred in international waters between a vessel owned by a resident Irish national and a vessel owned by a French company. The Irish national and a crew member of the Irish vessel were drowned. The father of the crew member sued the Irish owner of the vessel and the French company, asserting jurisdiction against the latter under Articles 2 and 6 of the Brussels Convention of 1968.

The Supreme Court held that the plaintiff should have proceeded under the International Convention on Certain Rules Concerning Jurisdiction in Matters of Collision (commonly known as 'the Collision Convention'), which was signed at Brussels in 1952 and implemented into Irish law by the Jurisdiction of Courts (Maritime Conventions) Act 1989: see the 1989

Review 69-73. Article 57 of the Brussels Convention provides that it is

> not to affect any convention to which the contracting states are or will
> be parties and which, in relation to particular matters, govern jurisdic-
> tion or the recognition or enforcement of judgments.

The Collision Convention is one such convention. Under Article 1(1), an action for collisions occurring between seagoing vessels (*inter alia*) can be taken before the courts of the defendant's habitual residence. (The Article also sets out other jurisdictional grounds.) Article 3(3) provides that a national court seized of one action pursuant to that convention may exercise jurisdiction 'under its national laws in further actions arising from the same incident'. It was therefore clear that the French company was properly before the court because jurisdiction arose under the Collision Convention, just as it would have done (albeit by means of a differently traced nexus) under the Brussels Convention of 1968 had it applied. It was necessary to amend the endorsement on the plenary summons but, once this had been done, the action could proceed.

In a second set of proceedings arising from the accident, the family of the owner of the Irish vessel sued a crew member who had been on watch at the time of the collision, as well as the French company. The French company sought unsuccessfully to convince the court that 'an action for collision occurring between seagoing vessels', to which Article 1(1) of the Collision Convention referred, connoted only actions against *owners* of such vessels, rather than crew members. Blayney J considered that the wording in the article was 'extremely general' and sufficiently wide to embrace the action against the crew member which, in the circumstances, he was satisfied was not simply a device for enabling the plaintiffs to include the French company in the proceedings.

Contract In *United Meat Packers (Ballaghaderreen) Ltd v Nordstern Allegmeine Versicherungs AG* [1996] 2 ILRM 260, Carroll J emphasised the requirement of proceeding strictly in accordance with the rules relating to suing defendants out of the jurisdiction. The plaintiff had obtained leave from Geoghegan J to serve notice of the proceedings against certain of the defendants in Switzerland, on the basis of O.11, s. 1(e)(ii) of the Rules of the Superior Courts 1986, claiming that the contract had been made within the jurisdiction by the agent of these defendants. They entered an appearance under protest and brought a motion to have the proceedings against them struck out on the ground that the contract had not in fact been made within the jurisdiction, or alternatively, because at the date of the issue of the summons, the Lugano Convention, to which Switzerland is a party, applied and the plaintiff could equally well have issued a summons under that convention.

Carroll J held that the defendants were entitled to succeed in their application. She distinguished *Doran v Power* [1996] 1 ILRM 55 (noted above, 115) on the basis that in the instant case the summons had been issued under O. 11 with leave of the court and it was not a case of its being issued under Lugano Convention, where no leave was necessary. The two were 'mutually exclusive'. O.11, r.1 had been amended by SI No. 14 of 1989, by inserting the words 'provided that an originating summons is not a summons to which O.11.9(A) applies' before the words 'service out of the jurisdiction of an originating summons'. O.4, r.1(A), as inserted by article 1 of SI No. 14 of 1989, required an endorsement under the Brussels Convention. In *Doran v Power*, no particular form of endorsement had been necessary under the Collision Convention.

The Jurisdiction of Courts and Enforcement of Judgments Act 1993 had incorporated the Lugano Convention into Irish law: see the 1993 Review, 118. S. 1 provided that the 1993 Act was to be construed as one with the Jurisdiction of Courts and Enforcement of Jurisdiction (European Communities) Act 1988, which incorporated the Brussels Convention into Irish law. It followed that an endorsement was necessary under the Lugano Convention.

Carroll J commented:

> The defendant chose to apply under O.11 and the ground on which it based that application was untrue. The Swiss defendants were entitled to object and, in my opinion, they are entitled to succeed. If the plaintiff chooses to make another application based on O.11, r.1(e)(iii), so be it, in which case the Swiss defendants can enter an appearance under protest and argue their case on the ground it does not apply. Or if the plaintiff decides to go down the Lugano route, the Swiss defendants are entitled to argue it does not apply by virtue of Articles 12 or 17 of that convention.

Unconditional appearance   Article 18 of the Brussels Convention provides as follows:

> Apart from jurisdiction derived from other provisions of this Convention, a court of a contracting state before whom a defendant enters an appearance shall have jurisdiction. This rule shall not apply where appearance was entered solely to contest the jurisdiction or where another court has exclusive jurisdiction by virtue of Article 16.

In *Murray v Times Newspapers Ltd*, High Court, December 12, 1995, in proceedings for defamation, Barron J held that the defendant was not able to rely on the other provisions of the Convention since Article 16 had no application and the defendant had entered an unconditional appearance. He acknowledged that the decisions of *Campbell International Trading House Ltd v Van Aart* [1992] ILRM 663; [1992] 2 IR 305(noted in the 1992 Review 128-30) and *O'Neill v Ryan* [1993] ILRM 557 were authorities for the proposition that, even where there has been an unconditional appearance, the court may entertain an application to strike out a claim on the basis that it has no jurisdiction under the Convention. It was, however, clear from those decisions that the application could succeed only where there was 'something in the nature of mistake or similar justifying circumstances.' No such situation arose in the instant case, where the application had 'no merits'. A reason for delay had been given which was 'manifestly incorrect'.

On the basis, therefore, that the court had jurisdiction under Article 18, it seemed to Barron J that it could 'not have the jurisdiction to which it would have been entitled by virtue of Article 5(3)', which deals with jurisdiction in tort, but rather that the jurisdiction under Article 18 was 'the ordinary jurisdiction which this Court was entitled to exercise in respect of claims for defamation'. This is the jurisdiction, based on submission by the defendant, that our courts had, under Irish private international law, prior to the 1988 Act and which our courts continue to have with respect to cases falling outside the scope of that Act: see Binchy, *op. cit.*, 129-31.

Barron J was thus not called on to address the rules as to jurisdiction and choice of law in defamation cases which the Court of Justice laid down in *Shevill v Presse Alliance S.A.* [1995] ECR I–415, noted by Forsyth, [1995] Camb LJ 515.

As to the question of jurisdiction, the Court of Justice stated:

> . . . On a proper construction of the expression 'place where the harmful event occurred' in Article 5(3) of the Convention, the victim of a libel by a newspaper article distributed in several contracting States may bring an action for damages against the publisher either before the Courts of the contracting State of the place where the publisher of the defamatory publication is established, which have jurisdiction to award damages for all the harm caused by the defamation, or before the Courts of each contracting State in which the publication was distributed and where the victim claims to have suffered injury to his reputation, which have jurisdiction to rule solely in respect of the harm caused in the State of the Court seised.

In relation to choice of the law to be applied by the courts having jurisdiction, the Court said:

> ... The criteria for assessing whether the event in question is harmful
> and the evidence required of the existence and extent of the harm alleged
> by the victim of the defamation are not governed by the Convention but
> by the substantive law determined by the national conflict of laws rules
> of the Court seised, provided that the effectiveness of the Convention
> is not thereby impaired.

FOREIGN JUDGMENT

Divorce   Earlier in this chapter, above, 107-114, in the section entitled
Foreign Divorce, we analyse Kinlen J's decision in *P.L. v An tÁrd
Chláraitheóir* [1995] 2 ILRM 241.

Protective measures   Article 39 of the Brussels Convention provides that:

> [d]uring the time specified for an appeal pursuant to Article 36 and until
> any such appeal has been determined, no measures of enforcement may
> be taken other than protective measures taken against the property of
> the party against whom enforcement is sought.

> The decision authorising enforcement shall carry with it the powers to
> proceed to any such protective measures.

In *Barnaby (London) Ltd v Mullen* [1996] 2 ILRM 24, the plaintiff,
having obtained a judgment in England for over a quarter of a million pounds
in relation to a debt for goods allegedly sold and delivered to the defendant,
subsequently successfully sought an order from the Master of the High Court
for enforcement of the judgment within the State. The defendant was given
the requisite period of one month for appeal against this order.

Shortly before the Master made the order, the plaintiff issued a plenary
summons in Ireland, seeking the setting aside of a purported conveyance by
the defendant of a house to his wife under the Conveyancing Act (Ireland)
1634, as having been made in contemplation of and for the purposes of
avoiding the liabilities of the defendant to the plaintiff. The plaintiff pleaded
in the statement of claim that it was its intention to register a judgment
mortgage over the property and thereafter, in the event of non-payment of
the judgment, to seek a charging order and order for sale.

The defendant contended that the statement of claim was an effort at
execution, precluded by Article 39. Kinlen J rejected this argument, being of

the view that the proceedings to have the conveyance declared fraudulent was not a measure of enforcement but rather a protective measure taken against the property of the party against whom enforcement was sought. This rendered irrelevant the ruling of the Court of Justice in *De Wolf v Harry Cox BV* (Case 42/76) [1976] ECR 1759 that a party who has obtained a judgment in his or her favour in a contracting state, enforceable under Article 31, may not apply to a court in another contracting state. It is hard to see how the Irish proceedings under the 1634 Act could in any event be regarded as identical in form or substance, to the English proceedings. Kinlen J described litigation under that Act as 'a statutory method to restore the *status quo*'. This is surely correct.

The defendant argued furthermore that he had not been properly served with the Master's enforcement order as he had been living separately from his wife and was not residing at the family home. Kinlen J did not agree. He noted that the Court of Justice, in *Carron v Federal Republic of Germany* (Case 198/85) [1986] ECR 2437, had stated that the consequences of a failure to comply with the rules on the furnishing of an address for service were, by virtue of Article 33 of the Convention, governed by the law of the state in which enforcement was sought, provided that the aims of the convention were respected.

In the particular circumstances of the case, Kinlen J was satisfied that there had been service on the defendant by service of the Master's order on his wife at the family home and possibly also by the service which had been made as a matter of courtesy on the defendant's solicitor.

Procedure   In *Paper Properties Ltd. v Power Corporation plc* [1996] 1 ILRM 475, the defendants raised a number of objections to the enforcement in the State of an English judgment. Among these was the fact that the notice given by the plaintiff to the defendants of the enforcement of the English order, as required by r.10 of O. 42(A) of the Rules of the Superior Courts was defective. R. 10 requires the notice of enforcement to state 'full particulars of the judgment declared to be enforceable and the order for enforcement. . . .' In the instant case, the notice had failed to mention an order that £7,500 security for costs was to be paid out of the plaintiff's solicitors or that leave to present a petition of appeal to the House of Lords from the English Court of Appeal had been refused. The plaintiff replied that it had cited only the parts of the judgment relevant for enforcement. It had not been seeking enforcement of those parts of the judgment concerned with the security for costs and the refusal of leave to appeal.

Carroll J rejected the defendants' argument on this issue. She referred to s. 6 of the Jurisdiction of Courts and Enforcement of Judgments (European Communities) Act 1988, which provides that:

> [s]ubject to s. 8(4) of this Act and to restriction on enforcement contained in article 39(a), a judgment other than maintenance order in respect of which an enforcement order has been made, shall, to the extent to which the enforcement of the judgment is authorised by the enforcement order, be of the same force and effect.

It seemed to Carroll J that 'full particulars of the part of the judgment sought to be enforced is what is required, not a lot of detail which has no relevance.'

One may perhaps wonder whether it is wise to limit the enforcing party's obligation, contrary to the relevant provision of the Rules of the Superior Courts, to giving notice of only that part of a judgment which, for the present, that party is seeking to enforce. It is relatively easy to envisage cases where the failure to give notice of other aspects of the judgment might prejudice a defendant.

The second objection raised by the defendants was that service had not been in accordance with the Master's order, which had provided that a copy of the order together with an enforcement order should be served on the defendants 'by prepaid registered post and prepaid ordinary post addressed to the defendant at its registered office on 58 South Mall, Cork and by facsimile'. The notice had been served by fax, not at the registered office but at the office of the first named defendant in Dublin and notice was not served against the second named defendant.

It seemed to Carroll J that the requirement to serve both defendants had been a typing-error. She adjourned the proceedings on this issue to enable the plaintiff to apply to the Master under the slip rule. (The plaintiff subsequently did so and the order was amended to require service on only the first named defendant.) As to the issue relating to service by fax, Carroll J considered that there was no substance in the first defendant's argument. The fax had been sent to the only fax number shown in the fax directory. The first defendant's registered office was the address of its solicitor.

Carroll J observed that:

> [t]he purpose of service is to make sure that the party to be served gets the notice. This was achieved threefold by ordinary post, registered post and fax. There was no fax address given. The order does not say fax at the registered office. So this argument does not succeed.

In *Voluntary Purchasing Groups Inc v Insurco International Ltd*, High Court, April 3, 1995, McCracken J stated that he would Tpass no judgment' on whether the plaintiff, who had obtained a default judgment against the defendants in Texas, had been entitled to obtain an *ex parte* order in the High Court, pursuant to the provisions of the Foreign Tribunals Evidence Act

1856, so that it could obtain evidence in aid of the execution of the judgment. At the time of the application to the High Court, the default judgment was under appeal and was subsequently set aside. While thus passing no judgment on the substantive question of the plaintiff's entitlement to obtain the order, McCracken J was of the view that, if it chose to seek an order at a time when an appeal was pending, it had to suffer the consequences, so far as costs were concerned, when the appeal was successful.

INTERNATIONAL CHILD ABDUCTION

The Hague Convention In *In re S.A.C. (a minor); D.C. v L.C.*, High Court, January 13, 1995, the parents of the eight-year-old girl whose welfare was in issue were British nationals resident in London. The respondent, accompanied by a young woman, removed the child wrongfully from the jurisdiction of the English courts, contrary to the Hague Convention, breaching the applicant's right of joint custody. There was no question of acquiescence under Article 13(a). The crucial issues were whether the return of the girl would expose her to physical or psychological harm or place her in an otherwise intolerable situation (Article 13(b)) and whether the child was of sufficient maturity to have her wishes taken into account.

Morris J found that both parties had been habitual users of marijuana, but that the respondent had discontinued the habit since he had come to Ireland. When the girl was living with the applicant, the applicant habitually shouted at her and beat her and the child 'reacted in a manner which had the effect to exacerbating the problem with her mother, causing her increased irritation and tension'. The applicant had been advised by her doctor to seek psychiatric help to overcome the irritation that she was experiencing.

Morris J believed that the relationship between the applicant and her daughter, had been 'one of hostility and aggression'. From time to time the applicant had made unguarded comments to the effect that she would do away with the girl if she thought she would get away with it. Whilst there was no validity in these threats, nonetheless they were an indication of the unhappy relationship which the girl had with her mother. Morris J was satisfied that the applicant did not have 'the capacity, demeanour or disposition' to care for children. Her two elder children had been put into care and subsequently adopted and the daughter whose welfare was in question had been in care for a time.

Whatever criticism might be levelled at the respondent, who, after two marriages, was now living with a woman significantly younger than himself, Morris J was satisfied that he was devoted to his daughter and had her welfare as his first priority. He had made appropriate arrangements for her enrollment in a local school, where she was doing well.

Morris J emphatically rejected the suggestion that the respondent had sexually interfered with his daughter. There had been an occasions where the daughter 'was involved with other children in conduct which could broadly be described as sexual interference' but, notwithstanding that the applicant had known of this, she had taken no steps to ensure that it did not recur. This failure to react to such information showed that no child could hope to be properly cared for when in the applicant's care.

Morris J, whilst realising that the association between the young woman, the respondent and his daughter might well be temporary, was satisfied that she was a responsible and satisfactory companion for the child:

> Again, while acknowledging that it is undesirable that [the child]'s father should be residing with a lady other than his wife and there is a danger from this bad example to [the child], nevertheless, in the overall context of the unsatisfactory nature of this case, I believe that it is a factor not to be weighed heavily in the balance.

Morris J, having had the opportunity of hearing the applicant, came to the firm conclusion that to return her daughter to her would be irresponsible. There was a high probability that she would be exposed to physical violence and a certainty that she would be exposed to verbal abuse. Moreover, Morris J did not believe that her material needs would be adequately catered for. Using the language of Article 13(b), he expressed the view that to live with the applicant would expose the child to psychological harm and that life for her would be quite intolerable.

It was therefore out of the question that the court should order the return of the child *to her mother*; but it was necessary to address the possibility of returning her to the *jurisdiction of the English courts* so that appropriate proceedings could be instituted for her care and custody. Morris J came to the conclusion that this option was not practicable. The respondent had not sufficient assets to provide himself with accommodation in England until these proceedings were concluded. The possible alternative of putting the girl into care was, in Morris J's opinion, unacceptable.

Morris J turned to the question of the child's wishes. Applying the test adopted by Eubank J in *S. v. S.* [1992] 2 FLR 492, he held that the exercise of judicial discretion under Article 13 to refuse to return the child to his or her or country of origin if the child objects must arise only where the objection is advanced for 'mature and cogent reasons'. In the instant case the reasons for the child's wishing to remain in Ireland (which Morris J did not disclose in his judgment) were not mature and cogent and accordingly he did not take into account the girl's views when deciding, under Article 13(b), not to order her return to England.

The Luxembourg Convention   In *In re C.E.O.C. (a minor); C. v R.* [1996] 1 ILRM 63, the Supreme Court was called on to interpret s. 34 (1) of the Child Abduction and Enforcement of Custody Orders Act 1991, which provides that:

> where a court in the State makes a decision relating to the custody of a child who has been removed from the State that court may also, on an application made by any person for the purposes of Article 12 of the Luxembourg Convention, make a declaration that the removal of the child from the State was unlawful if it is satisfied that the applicant has an interest in the matter and that the child has been taken from or sent or kept out of the State without the consent of any of the persons having the right to determine the child's place of residence under the law of the State.

Article 12 of the Luxembourg Convention provides as follows:

> Where, at the time of the removal of a child across an international frontier, there is no enforceable decision given in a contracting state relating to his custody, the provisions of this Convention shall apply to any subsequent decision, relating to the custody of that child and declaring the removal to be unlawful, given in a contracting state at the request of any interested person.

In the instant case, the parties had cohabited in Ireland, during which time a baby was born to the mother. The father was named on the birth certificate with his consent. When the baby was two months old the mother took the baby to England, at the invitation of her own mother, who resided there and had sent return tickets to her. The mother did not however, bring the child back. She remained in England; her solicitors asserted on her behalf that she had no intention of returning to Ireland.

The father obtained a custody order under the Guardianship of Infants Act 1964 in the District Court in proceedings in which the mother chose not to participate. The father did not request the District Court to make a declaration of unlawful removal under s. 34 of the 1991 Act because 'it was believed' (*per* Denham J, at 66) that the District Court did not have jurisdiction to do so. The father then brought High Court proceedings seeking, and obtaining, declarations that there had been an unlawful removal and that the mother's failure to return the minor to the jurisdiction of the Irish courts constituted a breach of the father's rights to custody pursuant to the Luxembourg Convention and a continuing breach of the District Court order.

Denham J (Hamilton CJ and Blayney J concurring) noted that the use in s. 34(1) of the words 'that court' and 'may also' clearly established a consequential jurisdiction after an order relating to the custody of the child had been made by that court. Article 12 envisaged a subsequent single decision since it provided that the Convention was to apply 'to any subsequent decision, relating to the custody of that child and declaring the removal to be unlawful. . . .'

Thus s. 34(1) of the 1991 Act was entirely consistent with Article 12 of the Luxembourg Convention. There was no conflict or ambiguity. In view of the fact that a decision relating to custody of a child, especially a baby, as in the instant case, was never final but evolved with the child, retaining in changing times the fundamental concept of the welfare of the child, it was reasonable for the Oireachtas to have prescribed that both the custody issue and the issue as to whether the removal of the child was unlawful should be determined by the same court. It was also in tune with the requirement under the 1991 Act and the Luxembourg Convention to conduct the proceedings with expedition. There was no need to delve into a complex analysis of the 1991 Act and the Luxembourg Convention as the issue was determined on the plain and commonsense meaning of the words which clearly indicated that the two issues should be determined by the same court.

Thus the High Court, as it had made no decision relating to custody in the case, had no jurisdiction pursuant to s. 34(1) of the 1991 Act to make the order of unlawful removal of the minor. Such a decision might be made only, in this instance, by the District Court.

The second declaration made in the High Court related to a breach of the father's right of custody under the Luxembourg Convention and was not a decision relating to custody. Accordingly, it was not a decision relating to custody as referred to in s. 34(1) of the 1991 Act, and not being such it did not give jurisdiction to make an order declaring that the removal of the minor from the State was unlawful.

In conclusion Denham J noted with regret the considerable delay in processing the proceedings. Such delay was contrary to the Luxembourg Convention and the 1991 Act. However, in the circumstances, the legal issue was clear, and the appeal had to be allowed.

SECURITY FOR COSTS

In *Maher v Phelan*, High Court, November 3, 1995, Carroll J, responding to the judgment of the Court of Justice in *Mund and Tester v Hatrex*

International Transport [1994] 2 ECR I–467, which was concerned with seizure of assets, and to Article 7 of the Treaty of Rome, which prohibits discrimination on the basis of nationality, held that security for costs should not be ordered against a plaintiff who was not resident in Ireland but was resident elsewhere in the European Union if such an order would not be made against a plaintiff resident in Ireland. She considered that the judgments to the contrary by the English Court of Appeal in *De Bry v Fitzgerald* [1991] 1 WLR 552 and *Barclay Administration Incorporated v McClelland* [1992] 2 QB 401 had been overtaken by *Mund and Tester*.

Even if these cases did not warrant such a conclusion, Carroll J considered that the same outcome should ensue. Orders for security for costs were based on a perception that it would be difficult to enforce the ultimate orders of the court of trial abroad. This concern had been resolved by the promulgation of the Brussels Judgments Convention. In any event, in the circumstances of the instant case, it was clear that the plaintiff had substantial assets within the jurisdiction, as well as in England, and was not arranging his affairs to make himself judgment-proof.

SOVEREIGN IMMUNITY

In the 1994 Review, 107, we discussed Costello J's judgment in *McElhinney v Williams* [1994] 2 ILRM 115, upholding the British Secretary of State for Defence's invocation of sovereign immunity for proceedings alleging an assault in County Donegal on an Irish plaintiff by a British corporal. The Supreme Court rejected the plaintiff's appeal: [1996] 1 ILRM 276.

Hamilton CJ (O'Flaherty and Blayney JJ concurring) rejected the plaintiff's claim that public international law recognised as an exception to the immunity principle the liability of a foreign state in relation to tortious acts of its agents resulting in personal injuries, where those acts were committed in the forum state. It was true that legislation in Britain, the United States of America, Canada and Australia, as well as the European Convention on State Immunity of 1972, so provided, but in the Chief Justice's view:

[a d]istinction must be drawn between the provisions of legislation in a number of states and provisions of public international law and the principles set forth in individual state legislation cannot be regarded as establishing principles of public international law.

The provisions of statutes cannot be used as evidence of what international law is: statutes are evidence of the domestic law in the individual states and not evidence of international law generally.

Whilst it is of course true that a statute is a creature of domestic law, it is surely too absolute a stance to exclude from consideration the transnational phenomenon of the enactment on a very wide-ranging scale of statutes which address issues of public international law when one is attempting to discern the present status of a particular international law principle. The weight that should be attached to this element is, of course, a separate matter.

Article 11 of the European Convention on State Immunity provides that immunity may not be claimed in proceedings for personal injury or property damage within the territory of the forum state where the author of the injury or damage was present in that territory at the relevant time. Hamilton CJ considered that he did not have to decide whether the terms of the Convention were part of Irish domestic law because the plaintiff's claim would in any event be defeated by Article 31, which retains sovereign immunity in respect of the conduct of one contracting state's armed forces when on the territory of another contracting state. The contrast between international law and Irish domestic law in this context is poignant. The Irish army is liable, to civilians and its own soldiers alike, for acts of negligence: *Ryan v Ireland* [1989] IR IR 177 analysed in the 1989 Review 410-8, but a foreign state is not liable to Irish citizens for any torts, intentional or negligent, committed by members of its armed forces within the State.

Hamilton CJ was satisfied that, in spite of the 'herculean efforts' of the plaintiff's legal advisers, it was not a principle of public international law that the immunity granted to sovereign states should be restricted by making them liable in respect of tortious acts committed their servants or agents causing personal injuries where these acts were committed *jure imperii*. He placed much reliance on an article by Dr Helmut Steinberger in the 1984 Encyclopedia of Public International Law which was in accord with this conclusion.

The Chief Justice rejected the plaintiff's alternative argument that, even if sovereign immunity applied generally to acts of the kind alleged in his claim, the principle of reciprocity should render it ineffective, since under s. 5 of the British State Immunity Act 1978 such immunity would not be granted to Ireland in respect of similar acts committed in Britain. The Chief Justice invoked a statement of Lord Porter in *United States of America v Dolfus Mieg et Compagnie SA* [1952] 1 All ER 572, at 586 as well as O'Connell's telling observation in *International Law* (2nd ed., 1970), 847, that the objections to reciprocity of this kind are that 'it introduces relativity into the law and involves counsel in complex investigation of foreign law; and that it nega-tives any standard for international law.'

Hamilton CJ rejected in one conclusory sentence the plaintiff's argument that sovereign immunity would interfere with his constitutional right to bodily integrity. The Chief Justice contented himself to observe that he was 'satisfied that the principle of sovereign immunity does not contravene any constitutional rights of the [plaintiff]'. This conclusion was scarcely surprising. Having in *Meskell v Corás Iompair Éireann* [1973] IR invented (or, perhaps more diplomatically, recognised) the notion that a citizen's constitutional rights may be vindicated by an award of damages in the event of violation by persons or institutions other than the State, the courts have shown themselves unwilling to embark in any serious analysis of the juridical implications of this bold transformation of Irish constitutional law.

It is a pity that the Supreme Court was not exercised by the intellectual challenge of examining why the doctrine of sovereign immunity should be assumed automatically to apply to violations of constitutional rights. Undoubtedly the pragmatic solution is to hold that, if sovereign immunity is good enough to defeat claims under a State's domestic common law, it should not have to give way to claims framed in terms of violations of constitutional rights. But that pragmatic, unreflective, response betrays a reluctance to recognise the radical departure from conventional constitutional theory which *Meskell* represents. *Meskell* may have been wrongly decided and Irish constitutional law may yet return to the 'State action' limitation of the constitutional theory of United States of America but, if it is the case that an Irish citizen's constitutional rights may be vindicated against any person or other legal entity guilty of infringing them, then the Supreme Court must offer an explanation as to why these constitutional rights may not be vindicated against a foreign state or the servants of that State.

Perhaps the answer is that the public international law doctrine of sovereign immunity is sturdy enough to defeat whatever legal entitlements may be generated by a particular state's domestic law, but to this two responses may be made. First, it is not clear that, from the standpoint of public international law, sovereign immunity should necessarily prevail against a claim rooted in the constitutional law of a particular state. A *Meskell*-type claim under constitutional law theory is rare, though not unique. The Supreme Court ought to have seriously addressed the question whether, under public international law principles, claims grounded in constitutional law as opposed to civil law should necessarily be assumed without question to be defeated by the concept of sovereign immunity.

Secondly, from the standpoint of Irish constitutional law, public international law principles have an important, but not superior status. The virulent positivism evident in the Supreme Court's decision in *In re the Regulation of Information (Services Outside the State for Termination of Pregnancies) Bill 1995* [1995] 2 ILRM 81 should have made it plain that the inherent worth of a particular normative legal order has no claim to the attention of the Supreme Court save to the extent that it defers to the norms, for the time being, incorporated in the Irish Constitution. It may well be that, having

examined the concept of sovereign immunity in the context of the constitutional norms of 1995, the Supreme Court could have come to the conclusion
that the claim for an alleged assault on an Irish citizen by a member of a
foreign army in County Donegal should be dismissed *in limine*, but the issue
seems worthy of more than one sentence.

Constitutional Law

ACCESS TO COURTS

Fiat of Attorney General In *Scarff v Commissioners of Public Works in Ireland and Ors*, High Court, March 15, 1995, Flood J queried whether proceedings could be maintained on behalf of an unincorporated association in the absence of either an application for a representative order or the fiat of the Attorney General. Whether the requirement of such fiat is consistent with the right of access to the courts was not considered.

General In *Colmey and Ors v Pinewood Developments Ltd* [1995] 1 ILRM 331 (see the 1994 Review, 12), the right of access to the courts was raised in the context of ejectment proceedings.

Law library for lay litigants In *MacGairbhith v Attorney General* [1991] 2 IR 412; Supreme Court, March 29, 1995, the Court affirmed the view of O'Hanlon J in the High Court (1991 Review, 98-9) that the State was not obliged to provide a law library for lay litigants such as the plaintiff to facilitate the right of access to the courts under Article 40.3. The Court accepted that the ordinary lay man who was unable or unwilling to engage a lawyer to represent him in the courts must, under the Constitution, be allowed full and free access to the courts in his personal capacity to assert and defend his legal rights. Normally such person was given as much assistance as was reasonable by judges and court staff in the presentation of his case. However, the Court held that the further obligation to provide a law library for the use and enlightenment of such persons did not arise as a result of one of the unspecified rights which might arise by inference in the interpretation of the Constitution. The Court stated that while it might well be desirable that a law library be available in certain centres of population so that the citizens could consult there and read about their rights, this was aside from the question of going to court, and was not something that was requisite under the Constitution. It is notable that the issue of court fees, addressed by O'Hanlon J in the High Court (1991 Review, 98-99) did not arise in the Supreme Court.

ADMINISTRATION OF JUSTICE

Professional body: discipline In *Geoghegan v Institute of Chartered Accountants in Ireland* [1995] 3 IR 86, the Supreme Court affirmed the conclusion of Murphy J in the High Court (1993 Review, 141-7) in which he rejected two arguments challenging the constitutional validity of the mechanism by which the Institute of Chartered Accountants in Ireland conducts a disciplinary hearing into alleged professional misconduct by the applicant, a chartered accountant and member of the Institute. The first point argued concerned the Institute's establishment by Royal Charter. The second was that, in conducting a disciplinary hearing, the Institute was engaged in the exercise of the judicial power under Article 34 of the Constitution. As in the 1993 Review, for ease of discussion, we examine both these arguments together.

We also outlined the general background to the case in the 1993 Review. Briefly, to recapitulate, the circumstances were as follows. The Institute had been incorporated by Royal Charter on May 14, 1888. Under the Charter, the Institute was given power to sue and be sued in its own name and was also given power to make by-laws regulating its affairs, but that such by-laws would not have any effect unless and until they had been submitted to and allowed by the Privy Council in Ireland. A private Act of the Oireachtas, the Institute of Chartered Accountants in Ireland (Charter Amendment) Act 1966, amended the 1888 Charter by providing inter alia that any by-laws made by the Institute would not have any effect 'unless and until they have been submitted to and allowed by the Government.' The Act also provided that: '[s]ave as hereby amended the Charter shall be and remain in full force and effect.' On April 18, 1989, the Institute amended its existing by-laws and these were allowed by the Government by an instrument under seal of September 12, 1989.

The amended by-laws provided that if a member was guilty of misconduct in carrying out his or her professional duties they would be liable to disciplinary action. This would take the form of a preliminary investigation by an Investigating Committee, with the possibility of penalties being imposed by means of a decision of a Disciplinary Committee constituted under the by-laws. Penalties envisaged in the by-laws ranged from admonishment to exclusion from membership of the Institute.

As Murphy J pointed out in his judgment in the High Court, although neither the 1888 Charter or the 1966 Act granted members of the Institute a monopoly in the practice of the profession of accountancy, the Institute was one of the bodies recognised along with a limited number of others for the purposes of auditing of companies under the Companies Acts 1963 to 1990. Murphy J commented that suspension or expulsion from the Institute thus involved not only loss of the auditing recognition but also 'would be likely to have a devastating effect on the professional practice of any of its members.'

In April 1992, the Institute informed the applicant that it had received a complaint concerning auditing procedures for which he was alleged to be responsible. On September 2, 1992, the Institute informed him that the Investigating Committee had formed the opinion that a *prima facie* case of professional misconduct had been established and that a Disciplinary Committee would conduct a hearing into the matter on September 14, 1992. The applicant then sought, by way of judicial review, an order of *certiorari* quashing the convening of the Disciplinary Committee and an order of prohibition restraining the continuation of the disciplinary proceedings. As already indicated, the basis of the applicant's claim was that the Committee would be involved in the unconstitutional exercise of the judicial power which was, under Article 34, exclusively a matter for the courts. As also already indicated, Murphy J rejected this claim and this was affirmed by the Supreme Court.

The Supreme Court noted that a key issue was whether a body which was validly incorporated in the 19th Century, under a Charter granted in accordance with the royal prerogative, withered away or ceased to have the right to exercise the powers conferred on it by the charter on the coming into operation of either the 1922 or 1937 Constitution. On this point, the existing jurisprudence of the Court, namely *Byrne v Ireland* [1972] IR 241, *Webb v Ireland* [1988] IR 353 (1987 Review, 104-7) and *Howard v Commissioners of Public Works in Ireland* [1994] 1 IR 101; [1993] ILRM 665 (1993 Review, 430-2), apparently involved the complete demise of the royal prerogative. Notwithstanding these authorities, however, the Supreme Court agreed with Murphy J that there was no reason why the Institute and all comparable bodies, whether formed under public or private legislation or incorporated by royal charter as part of the royal prerogative or residual legislative power, should not continue to have a valid and effective existence on the formation of the independent Irish State. The Court also added, as had Murphy J, that s. 7 of the 1966 Act had specifically provided that the charter 'shall be and remain in full force and effect', thus creating the additional bulwark of the presumption of constitutionality for the Charter.

Turning to the Institute's disciplinary powers, the Court also accepted distinction drawn by Murphy J between the position of the Institute and that of the Law Society of Ireland, whose powers to strike of the roll of solicitors had been declared invalid as an administration of justice in *In re the Solicitors Act 1954* [1960] IR 239. The Court noted that, in the Institute's case, the relationship with its members was based on contract, whereas that of the Law Society was based on an Act of the Oireachtas. The members of the Institute had come together by a form of contract, they had agreed to be bound by the charter and bye-laws and there was no question, the Court held, of the Oireachtas giving powers to a body to perform judicial functions.

The Supreme Court did, however, add that the Institute's Committee was bound to act judicially and it noted that the bye-laws contemplated that that should be so. Thus, proceedings before the Committee and Appeal Tribunal had to be conducted in accordance with natural and constitutional justice and similar principles applied to whatever findings they arrived at.

The other principal issue dealt with by the Court was the form of proceedings appropriate to challenge a decision alleged to be in breach of fair procedures. In this respect, the Court was deeply divided, reflecting an inability in recent years to declare the limits of public and private law in this respect (see the 1990 Review, 12-14). O'Flaherty and Blayney JJ were of the view that judicial review did not lie under O.84 of the Rules of the Superior Courts 1986. However, Denham and Egan JJ held that judicial review would lie. Hamilton CJ stated that, since this matter was not necessary for the resolution of the case, he would reserve his final view for a case where it was necessary for determination.

We do not reiterate here the comments made in the 1993 Review concerning our doubts about the High Court decision; these apply equally to the conclusions in the Supreme Court. We recognise the pragmatic benefits of the Supreme Court conclusion, but doubt whether it is fully consistent with the authorities on the royal prerogative. Similar doubts are expressed in Hogan and Whyte, *Kelly's The Irish Constitution*, 3rd ed. (Butterworths, 1994) pp. 343-4.

Remission of fines   In *Brennan v Minister for Justice and Ors* [1995] 1 IR 612, Geoghegan J rejected the applicant's argument that the Minister's power to remit sentences under s. 23 of the Criminal Justice Act 1951 was in conflict with Article 34.1, but he made some important comments on the mode of operating the power which imposed new restrictions on what until the *Brennan* case had been an apparently unfettered power.

The applicant was, at the date of the hearing, a District Court judge. He sought judicial review of a number of decisions made by the respondent Minister is exercise of her powers under s. 23 of the Criminal Justice Act 1951 in which she had reduced or remitting fines which he had imposed in criminal proceedings. Article 13.6 of the Constitution provides that the power of remission and commutation is vested in the President but could be conferred by law on other authorities. S.23 of the 1951 Act provides that the government could remit, in whole or in part, any fine or disqualification imposed by a court exercising criminal jurisdiction and that this power could be delegated by the government to the Minister for Justice.

Evidence was given of the system that had been adopted by the Minister when dealing with petitions to reduce fines and the circumstances surrounding the reduction of each of the fines in question were explored. Under the system in operation when a petition was opened on behalf of a person who had been fined, the local Gardaí were asked to report on the situation. A senior civil servant would then consider the Garda report and his comments would go to the Assistant Principal Officer in the Department of Justice who would then advise the Minister. Evidence was adduced that the Minister had decided to remit fines because they would cause financial hardship to the petitioners, even where the Gardaí and her civil servants had advised against remission. The applicant relied on these instances to demonstrate that the Minister had wrongfully interfered with his judicial decisions and had herself been purporting to administer justice contrary to Article 34.1 of the Constitution. As indicated, Geoghegan J refused the orders of *certiorari* seeking to quash the remittals made by the Minister, but he granted the declaration sought that the Minister had misapplied her powers.

He held that the power to determine an appropriate sentence and the power to remit or to reduce a sentence on grounds of mercy were different kinds of power and it did not follow that because one constituted the judicial power the other also constituted the judicial power. He held that the power to commute or remit under Article 13.6 of the Constitution was the executive administration of mercy rather than the judicial administration of justice. He considered that Article 13.6 of the Constitution must be read and interpreted in the light of the prerogative powers of mercy which existed in Ireland at least until 1922. It had never been a feature of the exercise of that power that it should involve some kind of hearing in public. Nor did he consider that there should be an absolute obligation on the person considering whether or not to exercise a power of remission to consult the trial judge. Indeed, he felt that, having regard to the separation of powers, such a practice could be regarded as dubious.

He did, however, accept a key submission by the applicant, namely that the power to commute or remit under Article 13.6 must have been intended to be exercised sparingly. This was reinforced by the fact that the power was, by the Constitution itself, vested only in the President. He noted that there was no evidence in the examples before the court that the Minister had found any unusual or exceptional circumstances to justify her modifying the applicant's orders. Indeed, the evidence showed that the kind of points which had been put forward in the petitions to the Minister were all points which either were or could have been put before the applicant when he was considering sentence. Geoghegan J noted that a District Court judge's order could be appealed to the Circuit Court, where the court had to embark on a complete rehearing. Therefore it was only in the rarest of circumstances that the Minister could modify a District Court judge's order imposing a fine, on the basis that she thought the decision was wrong. In this respect, he concluded that the power of remission had not been properly exercised by the Minister in that she appeared to have exercised a kind of parallel system of justice and to have purported to administer justice. He considered that there was clear evidence to indicate that the entire system which was in use was *ultra vires* both the 1951 Act and the Constitution.

He went on to hold that, although the power of remission need not be exercised in public, it was constitutionally necessary that all the evidence and information leading up to and the reasons for the exercise of the power be recorded. This was a consequence of the special nature of the power and was necessary to ensure the accountability of those exercising the power in question. Once the power in question was exercised within the limits he had referred to, s. 23 of the 1951 Act remained valid having regard to the provisions of Articles 34 and 40.3 of the Constitution. As to the instant cases, Geoghegan J concluded that, while Minister had exercised her powers incorrectly, it would have been unfair of the court to remove the benefits already obtained by those whose fines were reduced. Therefore the orders of certiorari sought in respect of each of those cases were refused, but he granted a declaration that, in each of the cases, the Minister had not properly exercised her power of remission. The consequences of the Brennan case would appear to be that procedural steps necessary to ensure an intra vires exercise of the power conferred by s. 23 of the 1951 Act would need to be in place. In addition, in order to meet the test of 'sparing use' the future operation of the s. 23 power must be monitored to prevent excessive remittals of decisions.

Reporting restrictions In *The People v W.M.* [1995] 1 IR 226, Carney J held that s. 5 of the Punishment of Incest Act 1908 precluded the press from attending or adverting to any proceedings under the 1908 Act. S.5 of the 1908 Act has since been replaced by s. 6 of the Criminal Law (Incest Proceedings) Act 1995. The *W.M.* case and the 1995 Act are discussed in the Criminal Law chapter, 251, below.

DIVORCE

Reintroduction of divorce 1995 was the year when divorce was reintroduced into Irish law, by way of referendum, after an absence of seventy years. On November 24, 1995, by a vote of 818, 842 to 809, 728, the Fifteenth Amendment to the Constitution replaced Article 41.3.2° which had prohibited the enactment of a law providing for the grant of a dissolution of marriage, by a provision as follows:

A Court designated by law may grant a dissolution of marriage where, but only where, it is satisfied that:

i at the date of the institution of the proceedings, the spouses have lived apart from one another for a period of, or periods amounting to, at least four years during the previous five years,

ii there is no reasonable prospect of a reconciliation between the spouses,

iii such provision as the Court considers proper having regard to the circumstances exists, or will be made, for the spouses, any children of either or both of them and any other person prescribed by law, and

iv any further conditions prescribed by law are complied with.

The social arguments Before examining the scope of this provision, it may be useful to rehearse briefly the principal social arguments made by proponents and opponents of the measure. (It should be mentioned that the first author of this *Review* was an opponent of the measure.)

In favour of the introduction of divorce, it was argued that there is no social interest in the preservation of the empty shell of marriages that have broken down: a decree of divorce records the death of the marriage rather than acting as its executioner. It was contended that people should not be punished for the mistake of marrying unwisely and that, especially where there has been violence or desertion, they should not be prevented from the chance of finding happiness in a second relationship. It was argued that the prohibition on divorce had led to legal anomalies, that it offended against the principles of pluralism and that it was inimical to reconciliation with the majority in the North. The doubling in the rate of marriage breakdown over the previous decade was also highlighted as indicating the need for divorce.

Those who opposed the introduction of divorce argued that people who wished to make a permanent irrevocable commitment to each other were entitled to social and legal support; making every marriage subject to a legal regime providing for divorce would be damaging since it would reward those who deserted their partners. International experience over the past couple of decades made it plain that divorce results in severe economic hardship, especially for divorced women and the children of the first family. Opponents of divorce also argued that divorce was on balance damaging to the psychological welfare of children by adding new sources of difficulty (such as step-relationships) to children already suffering from the effects of marriage breakdown. As to the incidence of marital breakdown, opponents of divorce suggested that at less than 4% of all marriages, the figure was strikingly low by international standards; divorce would be likely to contribute to an increase in marital instability.

The referendum challenge A challenge to the validity of the referendum was made by Des Hanafin, Chairman of the Anti-Divorce Campaign. He argued that the Government had acted unconstitutionally in spending several hundreds of thousands of pounds of public funds on an advertising campaign designed to yield a vote in favour of divorce and that as a result had materially affected the outcome of the referendum. In *McKenna v An Taoiseach (No. 2)* [1996] 1 ILRM 81; [1995] 2 IR 10, the Supreme Court had held that the Government's action in thus diverting public funds infringed at least three constitutional rights: the right of equality, the right of freedom of expression and the right of a fair democratic process in referenda. Mr. Hanafin failed to convince the High Court or the Supreme Court that the expenditure of this sum altered the opinion of 4,558 voters in a poll of 1,628,570: *Hanafin v Minister for the Environment* [1996] 2 ILRM 161.

The wider constitutional framework It may be useful to place the divorce measure in a wider constitutional framework. It will be recalled that Article 41.1.1° involves the recognition by the State of the family as:

> the natural primary and fundamental unit group of Society, and as a moral institution possessing inalienable and imprescriptible rights, antecedent and superior to all positive law.

This understanding of the family is embedded in the natural law, which regards irrevocable commitment as within the capacity of most people and which considers lifelong marriage as worthy of legal support as one of the deepest manifestations of human freedom and autonomy. This is a bold and confident perception of human beings. It is directly contrary to the philosophy that underlies divorce, which regards permanent marriage as too much for society to expect. Yet curiously Article 41.1.1° has been left unamended by the introduction of divorce. It is hard to believe that any thoughtful proponent of divorce would regard the family based on *impermanent* comment as 'a moral institution possessing inalienable and imprescriptible rights, antecedent and superior to all positive law.' Certainly no such claim has ever been recorded as having been made by any advocate of divorce, in Ireland or elsewhere.

Prior to divorce it was clear that the family which Article 41 recognised was the family based on marriage. The Supreme Court so held in *The State (Nicolaou) v Attorney General* [1966] IR 567, a conclusion that was scarcely surprising in view of Article 41.3.1° (still part of Article 41), whereunder the

State pledges itself 'to guard with special care the institution of Marriage, on which the Family is founded, and to protect it against attack.'

The institution of marriage clearly merits special care by the State if marriage involves a lifelong irrevocable commitment. If marriage is redefined so as to remove the element that distinguishes it from impermanent, entirely revocable, commitment, then the question has to arise as to why it should be afforded special care by the State. It might perhaps be considered that there is some benefit in formalising interpersonal sexual relationships, even where nothing by way of real commitment is required: but, when one looks closely at what this benefit may be, it proves somewhat illusory. Proponents of no-fault divorce used to argue that it would reduce the social and legal problems associated with the status of illegitimacy which the law ascribed to the children of second unions; today it is clear that reform is better achieved by abolition of the status of illegitimacy and that a liberal divorce facility leads to an increase of cohabitation, rather than remarriage, after separation.

The family, marriage and divorce   In the light of the divorce amendment, the Supreme Court will inevitably be called on to revisit the identification of 'the Family' with the family based on marriage. Two principal approaches are likely to be advocated. The first is to hold that the Family, for the purpose of Article 41, means the family based on marriage, as the concept of marriage has now been redefined. This approach could plausibly be supported by a formalistic, literal interpretation of the words of Article 41, partially recast by the divorce amendment, but at the price of withdrawing from any substantive examination of the issues of principle involved. If the Court were to examine these issues, it would be hard pressed to articulate convincing reasons for discrimination at a constitutional level between unformalised cohabitation, without the requirement of permanent commitment, and formalised cohabitation, similarly without the requirement of permanent commitment.

It has to be said that the strong likelihood is that the Court will favour the first approach. It demonstrated a virulent positivism in the abortion information case, which we discuss below, 145. It showed little understanding of the nature of permanent commitment in *T.F. v Ireland* [1995] 2 ILRM 321, where the Court failed to distinguish between an inability to live with one's spouse and the free choice not to do so: see the Family Law Chapter, below, 286.

If 'the Family', for the purposes of Article 41, is the family based on marriage, where does that leave the first family after divorce? Is the second family to be given constitutional recognition to the exclusion of the first? Or does Article 41 continue to protect the first family *as well as* the second?

There is no easy answer to these questions. The Attorney General, Mr.

Gleeson, has argued that, '[j]ust as a woman with children whose husband dies continues to be a member of a family based on marriage, so does a woman with children who is divorced': letter to Mr. Mervyn Taylor TD, Minister for Equality and Law Reform, November 21, 1995. If the suggestion is that the divorced mother and children represent a constitutionally protected family unit, the implications for divorced fathers are alarming.

It can hardly be the case that the constitutional protection under Article 41 should depend on which parent has custody of the children. If that were the test, then 'the Family' receiving the constitutional protection could oscillate, depending on custody arrangements from time to time.

If *both* divorced parents, together with their children, continue to form a constitutionally protected family, and the divorced husband remarries, then two unit groups compete for constitutional protection. The jurisprudence on Article 41, prior to the introduction of divorce, indicated that Article 41 was concerned to afford 'protection of the family from external forces' (*L. v L.* [1992] ILRM 115, at 121 (Supreme Court, per Finlay CJ)) rather than 'to create any particular right within the family, or to grant to any individual member of the family rights, whether of property or otherwise, against other members of the family' (*id.*). In similar terms, Costello J, in *Murray v Ireland* [1985] IR 532 observed that:

> the rights in Article 41.1.1° are those which can properly be said to belong to the institution itself as distinct from the personal rights, which each individual member might enjoy by virtue of membership of the family. No doubt if the rights of the unit group were threatened or infringed, any member of the family could move the court to uphold them, but the cause of action would then be the threat to the rights granted to the unit, and not to those of its individual members.

If Article 41 protects 'the Family' (as opposed to 'families') and if members of the first family and the second family form two groups that fall within the genus described as 'the Family', then it would appear that legislation distinguishing between the respective entitlements of members of the first family and members of the second family would not offend against Article 41 since this would be legislation affecting the entitlements of individual members of 'the Family' rather than protecting the family 'from external forces'. Thus, on this interpretation of the Family, there would be no constitutional objection under Article 41 to legislation giving preference to the second family to the detriment of the first.

If the Court rejects such an interpretation and holds that the first family is to be afforded protection by Article 41 separate from the protection afforded to the second family, how should the court determine situations of inevitable conflict between these two families? What principles should apply and what is their provenance? Does each family represent an 'external force' relative to the other?

The answer to these questions must be found in the concept of the right to divorce inhering in the right to marry. Since November 24, 1995, Article 41 gives constitutional recognition to impermanent commitment. It does not seek to investigate who is responsible for the divorce or to afford any explicit protection to the first family *after* divorce. Once the Court has granted a divorce, it has done its work and is given no further function by the amendment.

In this context it is significant that the amendment gives to the Oireachtas an untrammeled power to require the Court, before granting a divorce, to ensure that 'proper' provision exists, or will be made, for any person (as well as the spouses and any children of either or both of them) whom the Oireachtas specifies. Thus, the Oireachtas has a constitutional mandate to require, for example, that a person with whom a divorcing spouse is already cohabiting should be such a designated beneficiary and the Court has a corresponding constitutional obligation, in such circumstances, to respect that legislative diminution of the entitlements of the other spouse and the children of the first family.

The second possible interpretation of the meaning of 'the Family', for the purpose of Article 41, is that, in view of the fundamental redefinition of marriage, with the removal of any element of permanent commitment, a family based on marriage is different from a non-marital family only in a formal sense and that accordingly Article 41 should be interpreted as recognising not only marital families but also other interpersonal relationships which can fairly be describe as having the basic elements of a family. There are some difficulties with this approach. As the Constitution Review Group observed at pages 321-2 of its Report, published in May 1996,

> [t]he first and obvious difficulty is that once one goes beyond the family based on marriage definition becomes very difficult. Thus the multiplicity of differing units which may be capable of being considered as families include:
>
> a cohabiting heterosexual couple with no children;
>
> a cohabiting heterosexual couple looking after the children of either or both (of the) parents;
>
> a cohabiting heterosexual couple either of whom is already married, whose children (all or some of them) are being looked after elsewhere;

homosexual and lesbian couples.

Questions will also arise as to what duration of cohabitation (one month? six months? one year? five years?) would qualify for treatment as a family. Furthermore, certain persons living together either with or without children may be deliberately choosing to do so, without being married, that is, choosing deliberately not to have a legal basis for their relationship. Would it be an interference with their personal rights to accord in effect a legal status to their family unit?

It should be noted that the Review Group was addressing the question whether Article 41 should be *amended* to extend recognition to families not based on marriage. It was not seeking to *interpret* Article 41 in the light of the divorce amendment, since at the time it submitted its Report for publication, the validity of the referendum was still in doubt. For our purposes, the point of difference is of no great importance: the difficulties in determining the scope of protection to non-marital families are formidable.

When one attempts to integrate the new divorce regime with Article 42, the difficulties become insurmountable. Article 42 is clearly based on the identity between 'the Family' and lifelong marriage. Article 42.1 provides as follows:

The State acknowledges that the primary and natural educator of the child is the Family and guarantees to respect the inalienable right and duty of parents to provide, according to their means, for the religious and moral, intellectual, physical and social education of their children.

If Article 41 is to embrace second families within the compass of 'the Family', what is the position where a man, having abandoned his family and divorced his wife, remarries? Legislation reducing the entitlement to financial support of the divorced wife and children of the first family would not offend against Article 41, either because the first family is no longer constitutionally protected after divorce or because the individual members of the first and second families all form parts of the constitutional genus, 'the Family', recognised by Article 41, and discrimination between these individuals is not prohibited by that Article. In contrast, 'the Family' for the purposes of Article 42, has to be composed of parents and child (or children) even where those parents have divorced and married other partners; legislation restricting the entitlements of one of these parents, qua parent, relative to the entitlements of the other parent (who may have established a second family, receiving constitutional protection under Article 41) would not be constitutional by virtue of Article 42.

Irrevocable commitment, the Constitution and public policy It is interesting to consider the position of a man and a woman who wish to commit
themselves to each other irrevocably for life. Each of them seeks to make the
free choice to exclude the possibility of seeking a divorce. Are they able to
do so in a legally enforceable way, such as by contract, deed or application
to the court for a declaration?

The question can be answered only addressing the deeper principles
involved. Before doing so, it may be noted that, at a contemporary cultural
level, one encounters a concatenation of competing values: a strong emphasis
on individual autonomy; a concern for the present rather than for the long
term; a view of the State as an unwelcome and inefficient moral policeman;
a suspicion about 'parental rights' and an emphasis on children's welfare
(and, increasingly, autonomy); philosophical doubts about the possibility of
free will; and disdain for religiously-based inspiration or acceptance of life's
contingencies and inevitable pains. These values are not always articulated
in the context of the issue of divorce, but they are there nonetheless. If human
beings lack free will, if their existence is inherently meaningless, and if the
notion that the moral claims of others can restrict one's autonomy is misconceived, then the very idea of lifelong irrevocable interpersonal commitment
will seem threatening, restrictive and subversive of autonomy. If, on the other
hand, human beings are indeed free and if their existence gains meaning and
significance from moral choices that are integral to that freedom, then the
idea of embracing an entirely uncertain future, for richer, for poorer, in
sickness and in health, will not seem as frightening as it clearly does to
proponents of divorce.

The man and woman who seek legal support for their choice will argue
that their exclusion of the option of divorce, far from being contrary to public
policy, is both an attribute of human autonomy and a socially beneficial
decision. Society has a strong interest in encouraging, rather than subverting,
irrevocable interpersonal commitment in the family context. The empirical
studies make it plain that the most beneficial relationship between parents,
so far as children are concerned, is one where the parents are committed to
each other for life.

What argument can be marshalled against the entitlement of a man and
a woman to have legal support for their choice to exclude the option of
divorce? The most obvious one is that, if the People by way of constitutional
amendment, albeit by a very small majority, redefined marriage so as to
introduce the quality of dissolubility, that decision must have been premised
on the view that it is wrong that any marriage should lack this quality. One
may, however, wonder whether such a clear assumption necessarily underlay
that decision. Prior to the constitutional amendment, there was only one
model of marriage, which was that which excluded the possibility of divorce.

In deciding to introduce a model of marriage that includes the option of divorce can it really be said that the people necessarily chose to exclude the option (for those who want it) of lifelong marriage? From the standpoint of pluralism, cultural and religious, a ruthless denial of legal recognition to lifelong marriage is hard to explain or justify.

The divorce legislation of 1996   In the 1996 Review, we shall analyse in detail the provisions of the Family Law (Divorce) Act 1996. Here we need merely note that the Act has no use for the explicit concept of desertion when determining the entitlement to ancillary financial orders and that it requires the court, when determining this entitlement, to have regard, among other things, to the 'financial needs, obligations and responsibilities which each of the spouses has or is likely to have in the foreseeable future (whether in the case of the remarriage of the spouse of otherwise)': s. 20(2)(b). When marriage was for life, it was not constitutionally permissible to divert the resources of the financially stronger spouse (usually the husband) to a third party with whom that spouse was living, to the detriment of the other spouse (usually the wife) and the children of the first family. It should be noted that paragraph *iii* of the divorce amendment gives specific constitutional protection to this legislative reduction in the rights of the divorced wife and children.

EQUALITY

In *Mackie v Wilde and Longin* [1995] 1 ILRM 468, Morris J considered the guarantee of equality in Article 40.1 of the Constitution in the context of the appropriate evidential standing to give different versions of events: see the discussion in the Solicitors chapter, 465, below.

LIBERTY

Civil commitment: mental health   In *R.T. v Director of the Central Mental Hospital* [1995] 2 ILRM 354, Costello J held that s. 207 of the Mental Treatment Act 1945 was invalid having regard to the Constitution.

In 1977 the applicant, had been admitted to a psychiatric hospital as a 'temporary chargeable patient' under the 1945 Act. While in hospital, the applicant was charged with causing actual bodily harm to a fellow patient. At the trial in the District Court, the District Court judge certified, pursuant to s. 207(1) of the 1945 Act, that there was *prima facie* evidence that the applicant had committed the offence alleged and that if placed on trial he would be unfit to plead. The applicant was certified as suitable for transfer to the Central Mental Hospital and was so transferred in August 1978. The applicant's condition later improved and he was of a stable disposition from April 1992. It was recommended that he was a suitable candidate for supervised hostel accommodation, but no action was taken by the authorities to transfer him. In 1994, the applicant sought an inquiry into the legality of his detention pursuant to Article 40.4 of the Constitution and, pursuant to Article 40.4.3°, an order that if the detention in the Central Mental Hospital was or continued to be in accordance with law that such law was invalid, having regard to the provisions of the Constitution. As indicated, Costello J granted the relief sought.

Costello J noted that the provisions of s. 207(2)(d) of the Mental Treatment Act 1945 rendered the applicant's detention lawful. Rather more controversially, he also took the view that a lawful imprisonment could not be rendered unlawful by reason of the conditions of detention, distinguishing in this respect two English authorities, *Middleweek v Chief Constable of Merseyside* [1990] 3 All ER 662 and *R. v Deputy of Parkhurst Prison, ex p. Hague; Weldon v Home Office* [1991] 3 All ER 733. It is to be regretted that Costello J did not refer in more depth to his own excellent contribution to the case law in this area, *Murray v Ireland* [1985] IR 532 (HC); [1985] ILRM 542(HC); [1991] ILRM 465 (SC) (see 1991 Review, 101-4). Had he done so, he might have been prepared to accept that, in certain limited circumstances, conditions of confinement may be of such a nature as to constitute the deprivation of liberty otherwise than 'in accordance with law'.

However, moving on to the central issue in *R.T.*, Costello J was of the view that the defects in s. 207 of the 1945 Act were such that there were no adequate safeguards against abuse or error in the making of a transfer order and in the continuance of indefinite detention which the section permitted. He held that the defects in the procedures under s. 207 directly impinged on the constitutional right to liberty of temporary patients and that s. 207 fell far short of internationally accepted standards. He concluded that the defects rendered s. 207 unconstitutional because the State had failed adequately to protect the right to liberty of temporary patients. For further consideration of the *R.T.* decision, see Cooney and O'Neill, *Civil Commitment* (Baikonur, 1996).

LIFE OF UNBORN

Abortion Information In the 1992 Review, 195-208, we analysed the constitutional referenda of that year in relation to abortion. It will be recalled that the proposal on the substantive issue of abortion was rejected by the voters but the 'travel' and 'information' amendments were approved.

Article 40.3.3°, thus amended, provides as follows:

The State acknowledges the right to life of the unborn and, with due regard to the equal right to life of the mother, guarantees in its laws to respect, and, as far as practicable, by its laws to defend and vindicate that right.

This subsection shall not limit freedom to travel between the State and another state.

This subsection shall not limit freedom to obtain or make available, in the State, subject to such conditions as may be laid down by law, information relating to services lawfully available in another state.

The Minister for Health, Mr. Michael Noonan, introduced a measure, the Regulation of Information (Services Outside the State for Termination of Pregnancies) Bill 1995, which in due course was passed by the Dáil and the Seanad. The President referred the Bill to the Supreme Court under Article 26.

The Bill rendered lawful the publication within the State, subject to certain limitations, of information relating to abortion services lawfully available outside the state. Advocacy or promotion of abortion continued to be unlawful.

Counsel appointed to argue against the constitutional validity of the Bill from the standpoint of the unborn put forward three principal arguments. The first, and most ambitious, was that, since abortion, whether within the State or abroad, offends against the right to life of the unborn and thus violates a humanitarian principle that is at the heart of natural law, legislation which purports to validate acts that assist in the destruction of unborn life is not true law, regardless of its compliance with the requirements of due promulgation under positive law. The second argument was that, since our Constitution encapsulates the principles of natural law, it is subject to an implicit limitation on amendment to the extent that those principles would be violated or rendered philosophically incoherent. The third argument was essentially based on the principle of harmonious interpretation: it was to the effect that the 'travel' and 'information' amendments to the Constitution should be interpreted in a manner that most easily harmonised with the principles of natural law which had been incorporated in, and remained part of, the Constitution.

The first argument invited the judges of the Supreme Court to take a stand on a matter of jurisprudence that is far from academic. This concerns the nature and purpose of law and the position of judges, legal practitioners, administrators and members of the wider community who have a role that involves the application or implementation of particular laws at any particular time. If the laws, although duly promulgated under positive law, violate natural law, for example by violating the right of innocent members of society, what should the person called on to give effect to the particular law do?

The answer *within* the particular legal order is perfectly clear: that the function of the judge, practitioner or administrator is not to question but to implement. (Whether that is the answer of the Irish constitutional order was addressed in the second argument put forward by counsel challenging the validity of the Bill.) From the standpoint of jurisprudential theory, the question arises as to whether the true obligation rests on the judge, practitioner or administrator to articulate just principles of law, faithful to fundamental human rights, or to apply without demur whatever norms may have been incorporated in accordance with positivist criteria, regardless the violation of human rights which they involve.

The *second* argument put forward by counsel for the unborn did not require the judges to adopt any jurisprudential or moral position. Instead, it was to the effect that, prescinding from the merits or otherwise of natural law philosophy, the Constitution, properly interpreted, involves an encapsulation of the principles of natural law at its core and that therefore any purported amendment to the Constitution which violates, or compromises, these principles cannot be effective. There is such a phenomenon as philosophical incoherence: acceptance of the right to life of human beings, born and unborn, is a coherent position, rendered incoherent by a law which would deny that right on Thursdays, for example, or where the violation takes place outside the State, as the Bill provided. No one could speak of a coherent human rights philosophy which makes an exception for Tamils or Travellers; our Constitution, having embraced a human rights philosophy, cannot later embrace principles which render that philosophy incoherent or which go further and violate the principles of that philosophy. It is perfectly possible for the Irish people to engage in a new constitutional start by embracing a new Constitution with new norms, but, according to this second argument, if there is to be consistency with the philosophical scaffolding of the present Constitution, there is an implicit limitation on the scope of amendment of the Constitution.

There are some reasons for treating this argument seriously. Courts in a number of countries have accepted the principle of implicit limitation on amendability in the light of basic principles that are rooted in the Constitution. Thus, in *Gandhi v Raj Narain* (1975) ASC 2299, the Indian Supreme Court held that the Indian Constitution, which was, in express terms, capable of easy amendment, was nonetheless subject to the implicit limitation that any such amendment should be in accordance with democratic structure of the State: See Anthony Whelan, 'Constitutional Amendments in Ireland: The Competing Claims of Democracy', ch. 4 of G. Quinn, A. Ingram & S. Livingstone (eds.), *Justice and Legal Theory in Ireland* (1995), at 68-9. In Ireland, Kennedy CJ's dissenting judgment in *The State (Ryan) v Lennon* [1935] IR 170 and Gavan Duffy J's judgment in *The State (Burke) v Lennon* [1940] IR 136 reflect a similar approach; see John Kelly, *The Irish Constitution* (3rd ed., by G. Hogan and G. Whyte, 1994), 673-4. Even if one regarded the principles of natural law as entirely repulsive, one would have to accept that they embrace norms of generality and consistency of application, violated by the geographical restrictions prescribed by the Bill, which renders the right to life of a helpless being contingent on the place where that life is terminated.

Against the second argument, it may be replied that the detail, as well as the open-ended character, of the express powers of amendment contained in Article 46 of the Constitution tell against an interpretation of implicit unamendability. If it had been intended to render natural law principles immune from qualification it would have been easy to have so provided. The experience with the 1922 Constitution had been such as to put the drafters of the 1937 Constitution on their guard against an inappropriately broad power of amendment. Moreover, the inclusion of the transitory Article 51 in the 1937 Constitution suggests that the question of the scope of permissible amendment was thoroughly addressed. Furthermore, if such a principle of implicit qualification to the capacity to amend the Constitution were to be accepted, it would be difficult to apply in practice. There is some debate about which school of natural law theory underlies the Fundamental Rights provisions of the Constitution. Mr Justice Brian Walsh ('The Constitution and Constitutional Rights', in Litton (ed.), *The Constitution of Ireland, 1937–1987* (1988)) and Mr. Justice Declan Costello ('Natural Law, the Constitution and the Courts' in *Essays in Memory of Alexis Fitzgerald* (1988)) have convincingly argued that Thomist Principles are at the heart of these provisions but not all commentators accepts that this is so and Walsh J's observations in *McGee v Attorney General* [1974] IR 284, at 319 have generated particular controversy: see the 1992 Review, 169-71.

A further objection to the second argument is its apparently anti-democratic character. Why should the people be spancelled from amending the Constitution as they wish? To this it may be replied that the people always retain the power and entitlement to establish a new constitutional order by a democratic process similar to that which promulgated the 1937 Constitution itself. There is no question of the people being locked unwillingly in a constitutional order which they wish to reject; but, as long as they wish to adhere to that order, they must respect the limitation that it presribes in respect of amendment.

That riposte may, however, be considered to devalue the claims of democracy: a new constitutional start is not something that should be treated so casually. Moreover, the democratic values that permeate the 1937 Constitution are themselves of sufficient potency to support, and probably sustain, the argument against implicit restriction on amendability on account of the natural law dimension to the Constitution. See Whelan op. cit., *passim*.

The third argument put forward by counsel for the unborn was that the principle of harmonious interpretation of the provisions of the Constitution led to the conclusion that the 'information' amendment, in referring to 'freedom to obtain or make available information relating to services lawfully available in another state', connoted information of a general nature concerning abortion rather than specific information as to the identity and locality of abortion clinics which the Supreme Court in *Attorney General (Society for the Protection of Unborn Children (Ireland) Ltd v Open Door Counselling Ltd* [1988] ILRM 19; [1988] IR 593 had characterised as unconstitutional assistance in the ultimate destruction of the life of the unborn. For consideration of the strengths and weaknesses of this argument, see the 1992 Review, 206-7.

The Supreme Court judgment, rejecting these arguments and upholding the constitutional validity of the Bill, betrays a failure to understand the crucial distinction between the first and second arguments. As we have seen, the first argument did not propose an interpretation of any positive legal order but rather advanced a legal thesis deriving from a particular jurisprudential theory as to the relationship between fundamental human rights and positive legal processes. The second argument was exclusively based on interpretation of the positive provisions of the Constitution; it did not invite the members of the Court to hold that the Constitution was, as it were, 'trumped' by natural law. The essence of the second argument was that since the Constitution has manifestly incorporated natural law principles into the heart of the Fundamental Rights provisions, these principles had to be respected, not because they were *superior* to the other positive provisions of the Constitution, but simply because they had thus been incorporated as an integral part of the Constitutional structure.

There was, perhaps, danger that the Supreme Court would misunderstand the second argument, since counsel express it in terms of the 'superiority' of the natural law over the Constitution. In doing so, he was not inviting the Court to reject its own legal order. On the contrary, he was making an argument from *within* that legal order. If we assume that it is correct to describe the Irish Constitution as founded on the acceptance of natural law theory, then the Constitution is based on the premise that certain human rights are indeed anterior to all positive law, including the Constitution itself.

Commentators on the Constitution, speaking 'outside' it, are perfectly entitled to criticise that premise on the basis that it involves poor, or retrograde, philosophy. The fact that the Irish Constitution is premised on a particular premise does not make that premise true or desirable. But if one is a judge acting within the Irish Constitutional order, then, from the standpoint of positivist legal theory, he or she is obliged to act in harmony with that premise, which is integral to the constitutional structure. A judge appointed under the Irish constitution has to accept that the Constitution, properly interpreted, concedes the anterior, 'superior', quality of natural law. This genuflection is a constitutional mandate, yet the Court interpreted it as a challenge to the Constitution's legal pre-eminence.

Hamilton CJ, delivering the judgment of the Court, expended much energy and space in establishing 'the supremacy of the Constitution' and the fact that all organs of the state, including the judiciary, are subject to the Constitution.

After reviewing judicial utterances in *McGee v Attorney General* [1974] IR 284, *Ryan v Attorney General* [1965] IR 294, *The State (Healy) v Donoghue* [1976] IR 325 and *Attorney General v X* [1992] 1 IR 1, the Chief Justice observed that:

> [F]rom a consideration of all the cases which recognised the existence of a personal right which was not specifically enumerated in the Constitution, it is manifest that the court in each such case had satisfied itself that such a personal right was one guaranteed by the provisions of the Constitution, interpreted in accordance with its ideas of prudence, justice and charity.

> The courts, as they were and are bound to, recognised the Constitution as the fundamental law of the State to which the organs of the State were subject and at no stage recognised the provisions of the natural law as superior to the Constitution.

The people were entitled to amend the Constitution in accordance with Article 46 of the Constitution, thus amended, was 'the fundamental and supreme law of the State representing as it does the will of the people'.

In a penetrating analysis of the decision ('Natural Law and the Constitution' (1996) 14 *ILT (ns)* 8, at 11, (footnote citation omitted), Gerry Whyte concludes that the manner in which the Supreme Court rejected the argument by counsel for the unborn on the supremacy of natural law was unsatisfactory in a number of respects:

> Essential premises are not properly established; judicial precedents and

constitutional provisions which appear to endorse natural law theory are not properly engaged (and, indeed, in the case of Mr. Justice Walsh's remarks [in *McGee v Attorney General* [1974] IR 284], are perversely cited in support of a positivist understanding of the Constitution which he would never endorse); and there is a failure to address obvious questions raised by the judgment, such as whether there is any residual role for natural law theory under the Constitution and if so, for which variants of that theory. Ultimately, it must be said, the Supreme Court's reasoning is somewhat simplistic and lacking in sophistication.

The Court's judgment on the validity of the Bill addressed a number of other important issues. Counsel for the unborn sought to encourage the Court to revisit its judgment in *Attorney General v X* [1992] 1 IR 1, on the basis that no argument had been addressed to the Court on the question of the natural law, the Attorney General had wrongly conceded that the provisions of the Eighth Amendment envisaged a lawful abortion taking place in the State and no medical evidence had been adduced with regard to the question of the medical necessity for an abortion.

In one sentence the Court rejected these several criticisms of its analysis in *X*:

> Having regard to the judgment and decision of this Court, which recognises and emphasises the supremacy of the Constitution, this Court is satisfied that in the consideration of the issues raised in that case and the conflicting constitutional rights involved, the proper principles were applied to the interpretation of the relevant provisions of the Constitution and in the determination of the issues raised therein and rejects this submission.

This sentence is conclusory rather than analytical and answers none of the issues raised by counsel, save perhaps to suggest that, although the unborn's right to life may have been violated under natural law principles, the Constitution gave no protection against that violation.

It will be recalled that *Attorney General at the Relation of the Society for the Protection of Unborn Children (Ireland) Ltd v Open Door Counselling Ltd* [1994] 1 ILRM 256, which we analysed in the 1993 Review, 160-5, Denham J appeared to derive from the 'travel' amendment what amounted to the establishment of a right to have an abortion abroad, untrammeled by any of the criteria prescribed by the Supreme Court in *X*. The only requirement would be that the abortion service was provided in accordance with the law of the foreign country where it took place. In practice, this would mean that there would be an entitlement to have a foreign abortion on demand; no one has seriously argued that the English Abortion Act 1967 has any other effect. Denham J also considered that the provision of information as to the identity and location of places where abortion takes place was justified by the 'travel' amendment.

In the abortion information reference under Article 26 little was said about the 'travel' amendment, but one passage of the Court's judgment may have particular significance:

> The provisions of the Thirteenth Amendment relate to travel, the Fourteenth Amendment relate to information and the Bill prescribes the conditions subject to which the information may be given to individual women or the general public.

> The provisions of the Thirteenth Amendment or of the Fourteenth Amendment or of the Bill do not give aright to abortion or termination of pregnancy where none existed prior to their enactment.

This would appear to suggest that the Court rejected the notion that the 'travel' (or 'information') amendment, in exposing the life of the unborn to enhanced danger of destruction by removing the legal protection that had formerly existed, thereby establishing a *right* to terminate that life abroad.

Courts throughout the world in recent years have addressed the question of possible the legal interest the father of an unborn child or the parents of a minor daughter who is pregnant to prevent the abortion. See, e.g., *Paton v United Kingdom* (1980) 3 EHRR 408; *Tremblay v Daigle* (1989) 62 DLR (4th) 634; *Re F.* [1988] Fam 122.

In the abortion information reference, Counsel for the unborn challenged the validity of the Bill on the basis that it permitted the giving of information as to the identity and location of abortion clinics without informing the husband or the parents of the fact that the information had been sought and given. Counsel agreed that this accounted to a failure by the Oireachtas to respect and, so far as practicable, to defend the constitutional rights of these other parties.

The Court's somewhat laconic response is of some interest. It noted that the constitutional rights and obligations of parents with regard to the care and control of their children and the rights of the husband as a member of a family, remained 'unaffected by the provisions of the Fourteenth Amendment and of the Bill'. Invoking the principles laid down in *East Donegal Co-operative Livestock Mart Ltd v Attorney General* [1970] IR 317, the Court noted that a person giving abortion information under s. 5 of the Bill was required also to give information to all the courses of action open to the pregnant person in relation to her particular circumstances and was obliged not to advocate or promote the termination of pregnancy. It had to be presumed that,

> in the giving of such information, counselling and advice, the person giving same will have regard to and give advice in accordance with the principles of constitutional justice and if there is any departure from these principles, such departure would be restrained and corrected by the courts.

> Constitutional justice requires that in the giving of such information, counselling and advice regard be had to the rights of persons likely to be affected by such information, counselling and advice.

In these circumstances, the failure of the Bill to include a notification provision did not render it unconstitutional.

This elliptical analysis, makes it clear that neither the 'information' amendment nor the Bill has reduced in any way the constitutional rights of parents or husband, but it appears that the Court envisaged that these rights be protected effectively from infringement by the manner in which the information provider discharges his or her statutory obligations under s. 5 when communicating *with the person who is pregnant*. It is hard to see how anything that might thus be communicated could afford that protection. A woman contemplating abortion without informing the father is hardly likely to change her mind on being told of the father's constitutional entitlements or even being encouraged to heed them. The same difficulties apply, though perhaps with somewhat less force, to a pregnant minor who is reminded of her parent's rights and obligations. Incidentally, one may wonder how an information provider would be able to give any confident description of the nature of the constitutional rights of the father (or, as the case may be the parents of a pregnant minor) when the Court chose to give no guidance as to their provenance and contours.

It does not appear that the Court considered that an information provider would be under any duty of disclosure to the parents or husband. No express language of the judgment would suggest that the Court envisaged such an obligation. Nevertheless, in view of the fact that in many cases it would be impossible to protect the constitutional entitlements of parents or husband without informing them of the prospect of an abortion taking place, which has been enhanced by the disclosure of the identity and location of abortion clinics, a future court may hold that a duty of disclosure can arise.

It should be noted that the 'travel' and 'information' amendments, while not limited by the first paragraph of Article 40.3.3°, have to be read in conjunction with all the other provisions of the Constitution, notably Articles

40.1, 40.3.1° and 20, 41 and 42. The Court offered no guidance as to the relevance of these provisions. Obvious questions arise. For example, are there any circumstances in which would be entitled, or required, under Article 42 to seek to deter their minor daughter from having an abortion? Has a father, married or unmarried, any right to be consulted before his unborn child is aborted?

We can only speculate as to the answers to these questions. Whatever they may be the outcome of the Supreme Court's decisions is that the unborn have no entitlement to be protected by anyone from the provision of lethal information which the Supreme Court, in *Attorney General (Society for the Protection of Unborn Children (Ireland) Ltd) v Open Door Counselling Ltd* [1988] ILRM 19; [1988] IR 593, recognised as having 'the direct consequence of destroying the expressly guaranteed constitutional right to life of the unborn'.

LIVELIHOOD

In *Shanley v Galway Corporation and Ors* [1995] 1 IR 396, McCracken J considered the limits to the right to earn a livelihood in the context of the legislation concerning casual trading: see the Commercial Law chapter, 22, above.

LOCUS STANDI

Attorney General　The standing of the Attorney General to enforce public rights was considered in *Incorporated Law Society of Ireland v Carroll* [1995] 3 IR 145 (HC), 165 (SC): see the discussion in the Solicitors chapter, 467, below.

OIREACHTAS

Dáil Éireann constituency revisions　The Electoral (Amendment) Act 1995 gave effect to the constituency boundary revisions for the constituencies to elect members at the next General Election to Dáil Éireann recommended by the 1995 Report of the Constituency Revision Commission. The total number of members to be elected will remain unchanged at 166, but a number of important changes to the constituencies set by the Electoral (Amendment) Act 1990 (1990 Review, 176) are effected. While the 1995 Act formally became law on 20 July 1995, the boundary changes will not come into operation until the next dissolution of Dáil Éireann, that is, until the calling of the next General Election.

Internal affairs of Oireachtas not reviewable In *O'Malley v Ceann Comhairle, Minister for Enterprise and Employment and Ors*, High Court, July 28, 1995, Barron J declined to allow judicial review proceedings to be launched to challenge a ruling of the Ceann Comhairle refusing the applicant to put certain questions to a Minister in Dáil Éireann.

The applicant, a Dáil Deputy, had sought liberty to seek judicial review of the first respondent's decision not to allow in full a Dáil question asked by him to be answered by the Minister on May 24, 1989. The question was one of a series relating to the beef industry to which the applicant had sought replies since April 1989. On May 25, 1989 a general election was announced, the Dáil was dissolved and A was not re-elected. The applicant had sought to raise the matters involved in his question during a submission to the Tribunal of Inquiry into the Beef Processing Industry (1993 Review, 11-12) and took the matter up with the first respondent again following the Beef Tribunal's report in August 1994. As indicated, Barron J refused the relief sought.

Referring to the doctrine of the separation of powers, he considered that the judicial arm of government had no authority to interfere with the internal affairs of Dáil Éireann.

He added that Article 15.10 of the Constitution, which provided that each House of the Oireachtas is empowered to make its own rules and standing orders, to attach penalties for their infringement, to ensure freedom of debate, to protect its official documents and its members' private papers, and to protect itself and its members against interference, molestation or attempts to corrupt its members in the exercise of their duties, reinforced the doctrine of the separation of powers. Barron J also referred to Article 28.4, which provides that the Government is responsible to Dáil Éireann. In his view, there was nothing which ceased to make the Government responsible to the Dáil merely because the first respondent had exercised his jurisdiction. The exercise of this function was an internal matter for the Dáil itself. Barron J noted that the first respondent could be challenged by any member of the Dáil in accordance with standing orders. Once the Dáil had been dissolved, that right ceased as the affairs of that Dáil had been terminated. Such matters would no longer be capable of internal review by the then members nor could they be reviewed by the members of any succeeding Dáil. Barron J concluded that, having regard to the report of the Tribunal of Inquiry into the Beef Industry and the submission of the applicant to that body, there was no justification for reopening these matters after the delay between the original question in 1989 and the hearing of the application.

Members' allowances: Oireachtas Committee chairs   The Oireachtas (Allowances To Members) (Amendment) Act 1994 (Section 2) Order 1995 (SI No. 78 of 1995), made under the Oireachtas (Allowances to Members) (Amendment) Act 1994 (1994 Review, 117) provided for the payment of allowances to the chairpersons of certain Oireachtas Committees, with effect from 23 March 1995.

PROPERTY RIGHTS

The decision in *Iarnród Éireann-Irish Rail v Ireland* [1995] 2 ILRM 161 is discussed in the Torts chapter, 544, below.

REFERENDUM

Forms   The Referendum (Forms) Regulations 1995 (SI No.246 of 1995), made under the Referendum Act 1994 (1994 Review, 122), prescribe the forms to be used as Provisional Referendum Certificates at constitutional referenda and ordinary referenda. As they came into effect on September 21, 1995, they were applicable to the referendum to amend Article 41, discussed above 138.

RIGHT TO LIFE

In *In re a Ward of Court* [1995] 2 ILRM 401, the Supreme Court grappled with issues relating to the right to life of the disabled and the circumstances in which it might be proper to authorise the withdrawal of food from a person who is receiving nutrition through a tube. The decision provoked a flood of commentary, including Whyte, 'The Right to Die Under the Irish Constitution' [1997] *European Public Law* (forthcoming), O'Carroll, 'The Right to Die: A Critique of Supreme Court Judgment in "the Ward" Case' (1995) 84 *Studies* 375, Feenan, 'Death, Dying and the Law' (1996) 14 *ILT (ns)* 90, Hanafin, 'Last Rites or Rights at Last: The Development of a Right to Die in Irish Constitutional Law', (1996) 18 *J of Social Welfare & Family L* 429, Tomkin & McAuley, 'Re A Ward of Court: Legal Analysis', (1995) 2 *Medico-Legal J of Ireland* 45, Iglesias, 'Ethics, Brain-Death, and the Medical Concept of the Human Being', *id.*, 51, especially at 56-7, Rev. Kenneth Kearon, '*Re A Ward of Court*: Ethical Comment', *id.*, 58, Mason & Laurie, 'The Management of the Persistent Vegetative State in the British Isles' [1996] *Juridical Rev* 263, especially at 270-2. Much of the commentary, even by some of those sympathetic to the outcome in the case, is critical of the Court's analysis. Dr. John Keown, writing in the Cambridge Law Journal, has observed that, '[i]f this is the sort of reasoning a written Constitution produces, long may we remain without one': 'Life and Death in Dublin' [1996] *Camb LJ* 6, at 8.

The case concerned a woman who in 1972, at the age of twenty-two, had undergone a minor operation under general anaesthetic. During the procedure she suffered three cardiac arrests resulting in anoxic brain damage of a very serious nature. For the first five or six months after the operation, there were minimal signs of recovery but they did not continue and 'if anything faded with the passing years' *per* Lynch J. For twenty years she was fed through a nasogastric tube but, especially in the later years, she seemed to find this distressing and it was replaced by a gastrostomy tube in 1992. This became detached in December 1993. A new tube was inserted which came out the next day and had to be reinserted under general anaesthetic.

The woman had been made a ward of court in 1974. Her father, who was appointed as committee to her person and estate, died in 1988. Her sister was then appointed as her committee. She retired in 1994 and her mother was appointed as committee in her place.

On March 7, 1995, the committee and family of the ward sought an order that all artificial nutrition and hydration of the ward should cease. Lynch J described her condition as being 'nearly, but not quite, what in modern times has become known as persistent or permanent vegetative state (PVS).' He went on to describe her condition in greater detail:

> In the present case, the ward's heart and lungs function normally. Assuming that she is adequately furnished with nutrition and hydration (nourishment), her digestive system operates normally as do her bodily functions, although bowel movements require some assistance, but as she cannot swallow and as her teeth are spasticaly clenched together, she cannot receive nourishment in the normal way and as already stated, is and has had to be tube fed since the catastrophe. Assuming that she continues to be nourished by tube, she could live for many years but of course she might also die in the short term if she developed some infection such as pneumonia, unless it were treated aggressively with antibiotics.

The ward has no capacity for speech or for communicating. A speech therapist failed to elicit any means of communication. She has a minimal capacity to recognise, for example, the long established nursing staff and to react to strangers by showing distress. She also follows or tracks people with her eyes and reacts to noise, although the latter is mainly, if not indeed, wholly reflex from the brain stem and a large element of reflex eye tracking is also present in the former which, however, also has some minimal purposive content.

> ... I am satisfied that, although the ward is not fully PVS, she is very nearly so and such cognitive capacity as she possesses is extremely minimal. A fully PVS person cannot feel pain and has no capacity for pleasure or displeasure even though they may groan or grimace or cry, especially in response to painful stimuli, nor have they any realisation whatever of their tragic situation. This is probably the ward's state but if such minimal cognition as she has includes an inkling of her catastrophic condition, then I am satisfied that that would be a terrible torment to her and her situation would be worse than if she were fully PVS. There is no prospect whatsoever of any improvement in the condition of the ward.

Lynch J, applying the 'best interest' test articulated by the House of Lords in *Airedale NHS Trust v Bland* [1993] AC 789, authorised the removal of the gastrostomy tube.

The Attorney General, the institution where the ward had been receiving care for many years and the guardian *ad litem* all appealed to the Supreme Court, which, by a four to one majority, Egan J dissenting, upheld Lynch J.

Several themes exercised the judges. We shall examine each of them in turn.

Autonomy and equality   The first was the relevance of an autonomy-based entitlement to refuse life-saving medical treatment. Counsel on behalf of all the appellants argued that, since the ward, by virtue of her mental capacity, was unable to exercise that entitlement, it was not open to anyone else to exercise that right on her behalf.

The majority rejected their contention. Hamilton CJ reasoned as follows:

> If such submissions were to be correct, the ward, by virtue of her incapacity, would be deprived of the opportunity to exercise, or have exercised on her behalf, a right enjoyed by other citizens of the State.

Article 40.1 of the Constitution provides that:

> All citizens shall, as human persons, be equal before the law. This shall not be held to mean that the State shall not in its enactments have due regard to differences of capacity, physical and moral, and of social function.

> The loss by an individual of his or her mental capacity does not result in any diminution of his or her personal rights recognised by the Constitution, including the right to life, the right to bodily integrity, the right to privacy, including self-determination, and the right to refuse medical care or treatment.

> The ward is entitled to have all these rights respected, defended, vindicated and protected from unjust attack and they are in no way lessened or diminished by reason of her incapacity.

It must be said that this analysis is less than convincing. If the very existence of a particular right depends on certain conditions being fulfilled, then no question of unconstitutional inequality of treatment can arise if a person in respect of whom those conditions are not fulfilled is not permitted to exercise that right. This is precisely what the proviso to Article 40.1 recognises. Thus, there is no unconstitutional discrimination if, for example, an eight year old child is denied the entitlement to exercise the right to marry. Whether one says that the child has not such a right which in the circumstances may not at this time be exercised is a matter of indifference.

Debate may of course take place about whether the range of application of a particular right has been properly defined: thus, legitimate controversy can arise about the extent to which autonomy-based rights may be exercised by eight year old children. In the instant case, Hamilton CJ was not entering into a debate of that kind. He was of the view that some injustice would be done to a non-autonomous person by denying to him or her the right to exercise an autonomy-based choice to forego treatment in circumstances where, by reason of that person's mental incapacity, he or she lacks autonomy. Apart from the fact that no injustice is involved, in the case of this particular right the absence of an entitlement to exercise it coincides with the practical inability to do so. A non-autonomous person, by definition, cannot exercise the right to autonomy even if the law, as the Chief Justice would wish, were to ascribe such a right to that person.

One should of course be careful to analyse closely the values that underlie the verbal articulation of any particular right to ensure that one reaches the heart of that right. So, for example, freedom of expression goes far deeper than a 'surface' entitlement to communicate by word, pen or keyboard. In the context of autonomy-based rights, there can be legitimate argument about the possibility of extending the underlying values to people who are not at a particular time capable of making autonomous choices. Thus, for example, there might be considered to be merit in the notion of ascribing to a person who has become non-autonomous the choice as to a particular course of action which he or she would be likely to have made had he or she maintained an autonomous capacity. In relation to the issue that arose in the instant case, the Court might have sought to determine how the ward would have been likely to have chosen on the question whether she should continue to be fed through the tube. The point to note here is that, in deciding whether to adopt this strategy, the Court would not be attempting the impossible task of applying the principles of equality of treatment in an inappropriate context but rather would be seeking to give to the values that underlie the rights associated with autonomy their appropriate remit.

Why should the majority have proceeded down the cul de sac of an autonomy-based equality principle? The answer appears to be that it believed that, unless it could base its entitlement to authorise removal of the tube on an autonomous person's 'right to die', it would, in Blayney J's words, be 'powerless'.

It should be noted that Hamilton CJ identified rights *other* than merely the right of self-determination as inhering in a non-autonomous person. He referred to the right to life, the right to bodily integrity and the right to privacy which extended beyond the right to self-determination. He was entirely correct in this respect. A non-autonomous patient has an inherent human dignity and rights of bodily integrity and privacy which require particularly zealous protection in view of his or her situation of dependency.

The several judgments of the majority throw little light on the source or scope of autonomy-based rights, especially in the context of the choice to embark on a course of action or omissions which is likely, or certain, to result in one's death. Hamilton CJ, deriving support from Costello P's article, 'The Terminally Ill: The Law's Concern' (1986) 21 *Ir Jur (ns)* 35, considered that '[a] competent adult if terminally ill has the right to forego or discontinue life-saving treatment.' Costello P's argument hardly assisted the Chief of Justice In the instant case the ward was not *terminally* ill: she was *chronically* ill. For those who saw her life as lacking meaning or dignity, the problem was not that she was dying but rather that, if she continued to be fed, she might live for a further twenty years.

O'Flaherty J expressed the view that 'there is an absolute right in a competent person to refuse medical treatment even if it leads to death.' He considered that 'it would be correct to describe the right in our law as founded both on the common law as well as the constitutional rights to bodily integrity and privacy.'

Denham J went somewhat further than either the Chief Justice or O'Flaherty J. She analysed the issue as follows:

> Medical treatment may not be given to an adult person of full capacity without his or her consent. There are a few rare exceptions to this, e.g., in regard to contagious diseases; in a medical emergency where the

patient is unable to communicate. This right arises out of civil, criminal and constitutional law. If medical treatment is given without consent it may be a trespass against the person in civil law, a battery in criminal law, and a breach of the individual's constitutional rights. The consent which is given by an adult of full capacity is a matter of choice. It is not necessarily a decision based on medical considerations. Thus, medical treatment may be refused for other than medical reasons, or reasons most citizens would regard as rational, but the person of full age and capacity may make the decision for their own reasons.

Denham J's analysis brings into the open the larger issues that underlie the question of the right of a competent person to forego medical treatment. What is the basis of that right and what are its contours?

A right to commit suicide? It is beyond serious controversy that a person faced with the hard choice between a painful and complicated, high risk treatment, on the one hand, and the prospect of the risk of early death, on the other, is not obliged to take the former option. But it is not so clear that a differently weighted choice between a simple, painless medical treatment and early or immediate death necessarily involves a positive entitlement to choose to kill oneself by rejecting the simple treatment. Denham J would appear to regard the latter choice in such a case as within the entitlement of the individual concerned. She is clear that the motivation in making the choice need have nothing to do with medical considerations. Thus a man with a heart condition who wished to commit suicide for reasons entirely uncon-nected with his health would, on this analysis, have the right to do so by failing to take his tablets on the onset of an attack of angina when he knows that the tablets will prevent a heart attack which otherwise will occur.

If a person has the substantive entitlement to commit suicide by refusing medical treatment, it is hard to see what principle would deny the entitlement to commit suicide by other means. Let us take the position of two men who are disposed to commit suicide. The first is the man with the heart condition to whom we have already referred. The second is a man with no similar heart condition. Both of them wish to commit suicide for reasons unconnected to their health. On Denham J's analysis, the first man has the entitlement to choose *not to take* the tablets. What principle would deny the second man the entitlement to die by *taking* the tablets in sufficient numbers?

Why should the contingent fact that suicide may be accomplished in some cases by the refusal of medical treatment render such a process lawful even where the motivation for suicide is unconnected with a medical treatment? The answer cannot be that suicide by refusal of medical treatment is an omission rather than a positive act, unless we are to understand from Denham

J's analysis that she would countenance suicide by omission in all circumstances where there is no question of medical treatment being involved. Such an entitlement would embrace death by self-induced starvation but it could also range more broadly to cover cases where a person, with a suicidal intent, declines to accept assistance, or to take positive steps, necessary to ensure his or her continued existence.

The notion of a right to commit suicide, whether by refusal of medical treatment or otherwise, requires some further clarification. The law could draw the line at any of several points. It could provide that, in respect of a person with such a disposition, no *obligation* to intervene preventively rests on other persons (such as relations or doctors) or on agencies of the State (such as the Gardaí or the Attorney General). It could go further and provide that none of these other persons or agencies has any entitlement to intervene, prospectively or retrospectively. Thus, the Criminal Law (Suicide) Act 1993 removes the criminal sanction from the offence of attempting suicide (whilst retaining the prohibition on aiding, abetting, counselling or procuring another's suicide or attempted suicide): See the 1993 Review, 271. It could go further still and provide that a person with such a suicidal disposition has a substantive constitutional right to die, which must be respected, so far as practicable, by the State, through its laws and the actions of its agencies and by all the citizens of the State in their conduct directed (at least intentionally) towards that person: cf. *P.H. v Murphy & Sons* [1987] IR 621. Such a broadly defined right would raise precisely the kind of issue as to the entitlement of an incapacitated person to receive physical assistance to accomplish the goal of suicide as has come before courts and legislatures in other jurisdictions in recent years.

It is perhaps significant that, whereas Hamilton CJ considered it 'important to emphasise that the court can never sanction steps to terminate life' and that '[n]o person has the right to terminate or have terminated his or her life or to accelerate or have accelerated his or her death' and O'Flaherty J stated that '[t]his case is not about euthanasia' which, he observed related to 'the termination of life by a positive act', there is no similar limitation in Denham J's judgment. Indeed, the following passage seems consistent only with the notion that there is a right to commit suicide in certain circumstances.

> The right to life is the pre-eminent personal right. The State has guaranteed in its laws to respect this right. The respect is absolute. This right refers to all lives: all lives are respected for the benefit of the individual and for the common good. The State's respect for the life of the individual encompasses the right of the individual to, for example, refuse a blood transfusion for religious reasons. In the recognition of the individual's autonomy life is respected.

The requirement to defend and vindicate the life is a requirement 'as far as practicable', it is not an absolute. Life itself is not an absolute.

The State stands firmly committed to protect personal rights. These are the rights personal to the individual. . . .

In this case, the right to life is in issue. The State, under the Constitution, must protect 'as best it may' that life from unjust attack. Thus, it also is not an absolute right, it is qualified.

The emphasis here is on autonomy and the non-absolute quality of the requirement to defend and vindicate a person's life. It is hard to read this passage as closing the door completely to a right to suicide, with a correlative obligation on the part of the State and other persons to respect that right.

Adoption of the 'best interests' test Having held that a non-autonomous person should not be deprived of an entitlement that applied to an autonomous person, the majority had the difficult task of articulating how precisely the exercise of autonomy can be translated into a context where no autonomy is possible. The majority was divided on the merits of trying to second-guess what the ward would herself have chosen. O'Flaherty J considered that such an approach would be appropriate 'only where the person has had the foresight to provide for future eventualities. That must be unusual (if it ever happens) at the present time; with increased publicity in regard to these type of cases it may get more common'. In contrast, Denham J regarded the person's previously expressed views as one factor (among several) that merited consideration. It should be noted that in the High Court, Lynch J held that, while the best interests of the ward was 'the acid test', he took into account what the ward's own wishes would have been had she been granted a momentary lucid period. In the Supreme Court, the majority, while not expressly rejecting this aspect of Lynch J's judgment, preferred to identify the criterion as in the best interests of the ward. It is clear that Hamilton CJ, O'Flaherty J and Blayney J adopted this approach; whether Denham J's judgment can properly be so characterised we shall examine presently.

In *Airedale NHS Trust v Bland* [1993] AC 789, the House of Lords applied a 'best interests' test in relation to a person who was in a condition of complete PVS. The judges in that case made it clear, at least at a formal level, that the test was whether there was any benefit to be derived from continuing the feeding through the tube and not whether it was better than the person should be dead than alive. Lord Goff observed that 'the question is not whether it is in the best interests of the patient that he should die. The question is whether it is in the best interests of the patient that his life should be prolonged by the continuance of this form of medical treatment or care.' The question posed thus concentrated on the benefit (or otherwise) of continued medical treatment. The fact that death would be a consequence of a decision in favour of withdrawing the treatment was not a factor, formally at least, that affected the court in coming to its decision.

In the Irish case, there was a tendency both in the High Court and the Supreme Court to address the existential issue more openly in terms of whether it was in the ward's best interests 'that her life should be prolonged by continuance of the particular medical treatment which she was receiving' (*per* Lynch J, approved by Hamilton J as 'the proper test') The emphasis on the constitutional rights of privacy and bodily integrity took the analysis outside the scope of a narrow medical decision.

Egan J's dissent was based on the fact that the ward retained some element of cognitive function. Any effort to measure its value 'would be dangerous' and should not be undertaken by the Court.

Denham J's version of the 'best interests' test appears to be considerably wider than that of her colleagues in the majority. It extended to the best interests of the ward, 'within constitutional parameters', taking into account fifteen specific factors, set out in her judgment with no indication as to their respective weights:

(1) The ward's condition.

(2) The current medical treatment and care of the ward.

(3) The degree of bodily invasion of the ward the medical treatment requires.

(4) The legal and constitutional process to be carried through in order that medical treatment be given and received.

(5) The ward's life history, including whether there has been adequate time to achieve an accurate diagnosis.

(6) The prognosis on medical treatment.

(7) Any previous views that were expressed by the ward that are relevant, and proved as a matter of fact on the balance of probabilities.

(8) The family's view.

(9) The medical options.

(10) The view of any relevant carer.

(11) The spiritual aspect.

(12) The ward's constitutional right to:

(a) Life.

(b) Privacy.

(c) Bodily Integrity.

(d) Autonomy.

(e) Dignity in life.

(f) Dignity in death.

(13) The constitutional requirement that the ward's life be (a) respected, (b) vindicated, and (c) protected.

(14) The constitutional requirement that life be protected for the common good. The case commences with a constitutional presumption that the ward's life be protected.

(15) The burden of proof is on the applicants to establish their application on the balance of probabilities, taking into consideration that this Court will not draw its conclusions lightly or without due regard to all the relevant circumstances.

In qualifying the 'best interests' test by these several constitutional factors, Denham J has made it abundantly plain that the Court's decision is not a medical, but a philosophical, one, addressing the significance of existence and the question whether the State, through its judicial organ, is entitled to insist upon one particular ontological perspective. We return to this theme later in our analysis of the decision.

A further aspect of Denham J's approach is that it involves the Court, when applying the 'best interests' test, to taking into account the totality of the ward's constitutional rights, including autonomy-based rights. In the instant case the ward was not autonomous and had not expressed clear wishes on the question of her treatment prior to losing her autonomy. One can envisage cases, however, where a ward may have a high degree of autonomy, such as where the ward is a minor aged seventeen. How can autonomy and the 'best interests' of the minor be reconciled? If the minor 'has everything to live for' but wishes nonetheless to die, what is the Court to do? Later in our analysis, we return to this question.

Letting nature take its course   There was much emphasis in the several judgments of the majority on the need to let nature take its course. Hamilton CJ observed that,

> [a]s the process of dying is part, and an ultimate consequence, of life, the right to life necessarily implies the right to have nature take its course and die a natural death and, unless the individual concerned so wishes, not to have life artificially maintained by the provision of nourishment by abnormal artificial means, which have no curative effect and which are intended merely to prolong life.

This right, as so defined, does not include the right to have life terminated or death accelerated and is confined to the natural process of dying. No person has the right to terminate his or her life or to accelerate or have accelerated his or her death.

In somewhat similar terms, O'Flaherty J observed that the case was:

not about terminating a life but only to allow nature to take its course which would have happened even a short number of years ago and still does in places where medical technology has not advanced as far as it has in this country, for example. But now the advance of medical science may result in rendering a patient a prisoner in a ward from which there may be no release for many years without any enjoyment or quality of life: indeed without life in any acceptable meaning of that concept except in the sense that by means of various mechanisms life is kept in the body.

Denham J, echoing Brennan J in his dissenting judgment in *Cruzan v Director, Missouri Department of Health* (1990) 497 US 261, asked whether the ward was a 'passive prisoner of medical technology.' She added:

If that be so, is it in keeping with her right as a human person to dignity?

The notion of letting nature take its course has strong intuitive attraction, but it scarcely means that technology should necessarily be regarded as the enemy of nature. There never has been a golden age in which human beings disdained technology. The idea that some principled distinction can be drawn in this context between unsullied nature and artificial technology is quite mistaken. Of course the recent advances in medical science and technology have greatly enhanced the capacity to keep people alive when they have little or no cognitive awareness. There are undoubtedly circumstances where continued resort to this technology would be futile; but nothing is gained by attempting to characterise technology, as such, as the enemy of nature.

Feeding and medical treatment The propensity of the majority to draw a distinction between 'nature' (which must have its way) and 'artificial' processes (which should be withdrawn from the patient) was apparent on the question of the provision of food. As has been mentioned, the ward was receiving her food through a gastrostomy tube. Feeding is generally regarded as a supportive act of solidarity to another human being. Parents feed their child, not because the child is ill but because the child is hungry. If the parents neglect that obligation, the child will die from hunger. The idea that a patient with very significantly restricted cognitive capacity should be starved to death may seem abhorrent to many people.

Starving someone is wrong because it is a lethal denial of humanitarian support to a person who depends on others for that support. Dependency is not something to be ashamed of: the human endeavour is founded of our embracing our interdependence.

The majority gave no indication that it would countenance starving someone to death, even where that person's life is, to quote O'Flaherty J, one 'without purpose, meaning or dignity.' But, in authorising the removal of the means whereby the ward was being fed, was it not authorising an act that would inevitably result in death by starvation? No, said the majority, reasoning as follows: feeding through a gastrostomy tube constitutes medical treatment; the cessation of medical treatment is permissible where this is in the ward's best interests; after the feeding apparatus is removed, '[t]he true cause of the ward's death will not be the withdrawal of such nourishment but the injuries [the ward] sustained [in] 1972': *per* Hamilton CJ.

It appears that the majority considered that the fact that the feeding process constituted medical treatment was crucial: Blayney J observed that '[n]ormal food and drink could never be categorised as medical treatment.' It is not clear, however, why the mere fact that a process may be characterised as medical treatment should have such centrality in deciding whether a ward is to continue to live. If in wardship proceedings 'the best interests of the ward' represents the appropriate test to apply in all cases, why should it not be applied in cases where a particular course of action which does not constitute medical treatment is not in the best interests of the ward? Why should the Court have to shelter behind the characterisation of the process as medical treatment?

Perhaps the answer is that it is far more comfortable to address troubling issues of value relating to life and death as though they were essentially medical questions. Medicine has the aura of scientific objectivity, of empirical predictions, of clinical judgments and a tradition of altruistic concern for the patient's welfare. In truth, the Court was being called on to decide whether continuing to keep the ward alive was desirable. The fact that the ward was being fed through a gastrostomy tube was not the problem.

Ian Kennedy and Andrew Grubb, in *Medical Law: Text with Materials* (2nd ed., 1994), 1230, grasp the nettle. They address the question of the provision of food where the patient can swallow and is spoon-fed:

> Is this a form of medical treatment and thus may be discontinued or withheld? Or is it a separate regime of care which the doctor is obliged to continue even though the patient's condition is hopeless and further medical treatment is agreed to be futile? In our view, the solution to the problem does not lie in the process of labelling the intervention as

'treatment' or 'care' or indeed anything else. Instead, the solution lies
in reminding ourselves that the doctor's obligation is to act in the 'best
interests' of the patient. . . . Continuing to spoon-feed the patient would
frustrate this end and thus would not be in the patient's 'best interests'.
Of course, the validity of this analysis must be set against the quite
natural repugnance some might feel at the idea of denying a patient what
look like the basic requirements of life. Indeed, this repugnance may
persuade a court to accept that there is a difference between artificial
feeding and spoon-feeding. . . . While understandable, we think this is
wrong. This is not to say that we argue that the patient should suffer
before he dies. Rather, we revert to the doctor's general duty to comfort
which would entitle the doctor to administer whatever medicine necessary to alleviate any distress which may be caused to the patient.

This argument is surely a more honest one than a rationale based on a medical
characterisation. It leads inevitably to some further questions. If it is lawful
to starve a person to death where that person is a physically ill patient in a
hospital, why should it not be similarly lawful to starve a mentally ill patient
to death where the patient's 'best interests' so ordain? If death by starvation
is permissible, why not death by swifter, more humane and 'dignified'
means?

It should be borne in mind that the majority position on autonomy-based
entitlements seems capable of embracing the entitlement to starve oneself to
death. It would be hard to read Denham J's judgment differently and the logic
of Hamilton CJ and O'Flaherty J's judgments would suggest a similar
conclusion. Blayney J's analysis is expressed more narrowly and would have
to be developed before it could go so far. At all events, if the law concedes
to an autonomous person the right to refuse to be given food by ordinary
means, such as by a spoon, then the principle of equality between the
autonomous and the non-autonomous which the majority mistakenly sought
to apply would mean that, where the best interests of a non-autonomous
person are that his or her life should not continue, then that person should be
starved to death.

Causation and 'lawful killing'   The majority's ascription of the cause of
the death to the ward which would undoubtedly follow from the withdrawal
of food is worthy of consideration. According to the majority, the cause of
death would not be starvation but rather the injuries which she had sustained
twenty three years previously. There is an element of intellectual self-deceit
here. cf. Biggs, 'Euthanasia and Death with Dignity: Still Poised on the
Fulcrum of Homicide' [1996] *Crim L Rev* 878, at 882-3. A death certificate
would be likely to record the absence of nutrition as the cause of death if the

doctor providing the certificate was unaware of the court proceedings that preceded the withdrawal of the feeding regime through the gastostomy tube. Egan J, dissenting, faced that reality:

> The removal of the tube would . . . result in death within a short period of time. It matters not how euphemistically it is worded. The inevitable result of removal would be to kill the human being.

J.K. Mason and G.T. Laurie ('The Management of the Persistent Vegetative State in the British Isles' [1996] *Juridical Rev* 263 at 271) are of similar view:

> It was common ground that the ward would live for several years provided she was treated. She could not, therefore, be regarded as other than chronically ill at the time the application to the court was made. The only way in which she could become terminally ill was to terminate treatment, of which that of most immediate concern was artificial feeding.

The authors go on to observe that, while the characterisation of the ward's original injuries in 1972 as the true cause of her death 'was, of course, essential to the Chief Justice's constitutional argument,' this was

> scarcely tenable on the grounds of logic and [was] also unsatisfactory for practical reasons. It is true to say that the ultimate cause of her death was her original injury. The proximate cause must, however, be the results of starvation because, otherwise, there was nothing to cause her death. In practice, it seems desirable that the mortality statistics should be maintained correctly — if for no other reason than that it would be useful to be able to discover how often such decisions are made. There would be no difficulty in certifying death as being due to inanition due to *lawful* removal of support due to severe brain damage due to cerebral hypoxia. . . . (*Id.*, at 280.)

Dermot Feenan also considers the characterisation of the earlier injuries as the cause of the ward's death to be wrong:

> In the present case it was clear that withdrawal of nutrition and hydration would inevitably lead to the ward's death within weeks. Hamilton CJ cloaks the precision of the language on murder and manslaughter with disavowal in legally imprecise terms that the case is not about 'putting down the old and infirm, the mentally defective or the physically infirm'. He adds that the court can never 'sanction steps to terminate

life.' Yet it is the step of withdrawing feeding that effectively ends the ward's life.

O'Flaherty J states that what is involved is not termination of life by a positive act but letting nature take its course. This, too, is unconvincing. Whether withdrawal of feeding by a carer is treated as an act or omission does not affect the basic actus reus of homicide — to cause death.

The Supreme Court could have dealt with this issue, and therefore clarified the remaining murkiness, by holding that the killing was not, pursuant to s. 4(1) of the Criminal Justice Act 1964, an *unlawful* killing in so far as the doctor was not legally required — in the view of the ward's prolonged and irreversibly vegetative condition, the intrusiveness and probable painfulness of treatment, and her rights to a natural death, privacy, and bodily integrity — to provide treatment which had no curative effect and was intended merely to prolong life. 'Death, Dying and the Law' (1996) 14 *Ir L T (ns)* 90, at 93 (footnote reference omitted).

It should be noted that, if the withdrawal of feeding is characterised as causative of the death, then there is no way that the principle of double effect, recognised by Devlin J in *R. v Adams (Bodkin)* [1957] Crim LR 365, (cf. Charleton & Bolger, 'The Law at Life's End', Part I (1995) *Incorporated L Soc of Ireland Gazette* 29, at 30) could justify the action, since the measure could not be regarded as 'incidentally shorten[ing] life. . . .' The *causal nexus* is a good deal more intimate and direct.

The slippery slope   O'Flaherty J was of the view that the Court, in authorising the cessation of feeding, was 'not thereby going down any slippery slope or stepping into an abyss.' The commentators on the decision are not so confident. Dr. John Keown has observed ([1996] Camb LJ, at 8) that the Law Lords in *Bland* took one step on the slippery slope:

the Irish Supreme Court has taken the next, and on the basis of reasoning which could easily justify further steps.

O'Flaherty J's analysis, far from giving assurance, is the source of serious concern:

The ward may be alive but she has no life at all. Lynch J finds as fact that, although the ward is not fully PVS, she is very nearly so and such cognitive capacity as she possesses is extremely minimal. . . .

Thus the circumstances of the current case are clearly distinguishable from the position as regards, for example, a seriously mentally handicapped person. A mentally handicapped person is conscious of his or her situation and is capable of obtaining pleasure and enjoyment from life. It is fanciful to attempt to equate the position of the ward in this case with that of a person whose life has been impaired by handicap. The analogy is both false and misleading; the quality of the ward's life was never in issue; she is not living a life in any meaningful sense. We are concerned here only with allowing nature to take its course and for the ward to die with dignity.

If capacity to obtain 'pleasure and enjoyment from life' is to be the test, where does that leave those who suffer from serious, incurable depression, those in chronic pain, those who suffer from paranoid schizophrenia, those with severe learning difficulties who suffer significant frustrations and newborn infants with serious disabilities? O'Flaherty J's felicific calculus is surely a most dangerous instrument. Cf. David Lamb, *Down the Slippery Slope: Arguing in Applied Ethics* (1988), chapter 7, Yale Kamisar, 'Physician-assisted Suicide: The Last Bridge to Active Voluntary Euthanasia', chapter 15 of J. Keown ed., *Euthanasia Examined: Ethical, Clinical and Legal Perspectives* (1995), at 244-5, O'Carroll, *op. cit.*, at 379.

Once the Supreme Court is willing to authorise the withdrawal of feeding from a person with some 'minimal' capacity to recognise long established nursing staff, to react to strangers by showing distress and to track people with her eyes with 'some minimal purposive content', there can be no principled objection to ranging further. Lynch J himself adopted reasoning which could be called in aid of an argument in favour of withdrawing nutrition by means of a tube from those with a higher level of awareness. If the ward's cognitive capacity included an inkling of her catastrophic condition, 'that would be a terrible torment to her and her situation would be worse that if she were fully PVS.'

Bodily integrity and privacy A striking feature of the several judgments of the majority is the ease with which the concepts of bodily integrity and privacy are invoked in support of the decision to withdraw feeding from the ward, coupled with the absence of any substantial analysis of what these concepts involve. It seems that the majority preferred to rely on their emotive potency rather than to examine, and test the contours of, the values that underlie them.

Hamilton CJ noted that providing nutrition to the ward through the tube was a treatment that 'is intrusive [and] constitutes an interference with the integrity of her body. . . .' O'Flaherty J identified the right of a person to refuse medical treatment as being 'founded on the on the common law as well as the constitutional rights of bodily integrity and privacy'. Blayney J did not address these aspects of the case. In contrast, Denham J had much to say in relation to them. Having stated that an adult person of full capacity may refuse to consent to medical treatment for any reason, which need not be based on medical considerations, she observed that the requirement of consent to medical treatment 'is an aspect of a person's right to bodily integrity under Article 40.3 of the Constitution. . . .' She went on to state that:

> [p]art of the right to privacy is the giving or refusing of consent to medical treatment. Merely because medical treatment becomes necessary to sustain life does not mean that the right to privacy is lost, neither is the right lost by a person becoming insentient. Nor is the right lost if the person becomes insentient and needs medical treatment to sustain life and is cared for by people who can and wish to continue taking care of the person. Simply it means that the right may be exercised by a different process. The individual retains their personal rights.

> The right to privacy is not absolute. It has to be balanced against the State's duty to protect and vindicate life. However, 'the individual's right to privacy grows as the degree of bodily invasion increases'. See *In re Quinlan* (1976) 70 NJ 10, at p. 41.

> The increasing personal right to privacy is such a situation is consistent with the defence and vindication of life being 'as far as practicable': Article 40.3.1°, and the protection being 'as best it may': Article 40.3.2°.

> A constituent of the right of privacy is the right to die naturally, with dignity and with minimum suffering. This right is not lost to a person if they become incapacitated or insentient.

It will be seen from these several quotations from the judgments of Hamilton CJ, O'Flaherty and Denham JJ that they involve a radical revision of how the rights to bodily integrity and privacy had previously been articulated by the courts. Yet there is no indication of any awareness on the part of these judges that they were fundamentally reforming these rights.

The three judges invoked Kenny J's articulation of the right to bodily integrity in *Ryan v Attorney General* [1965] IR 294, at 313; Denham J actually quoted what Kenny J had to say:

> In my opinion, one of the personal rights of the citizen protected by the general guarantee [in Article 40.3] is the right to bodily integrity. I

understand the right to bodily integrity to mean that no mutilation of the body or any of its members may be carried out on any citizen under the authority of the law except for the good of the whole body and that no process which is or may, as a matter of probability, be dangerous or harmful to the life or health of the citizens or any of them may be imposed (in the sense of being made compulsory) by an Act of the Oireachtas.

It is hard to read from this definition of the constitutional right to bodily integrity (or, indeed to discern from the intervening case law: cf. J. Kelly, *The Irish Constitution* (3rd ed., 1994, by G. Hogan & G. Whyte), 757-61) any justification for the proposition that feeding a non-autonomous person through a tube, with the purpose of giving her sufficient nutrition to keep her alive, violates her constitutional right to bodily integrity. The majority's attempt to treat a non-autonomous person as though she were autonomous led it to articulate constitutional rights which clearly had no application to the situation.

As regards an autonomous person, it is interesting to note how the Supreme Court in *Ryan* disposed on the question of the right to bodily integrity. The Attorney General had intimated that he was prepared to concede the existence of such a right in the words 'a right to the integrity of the person'. Counsel for the plaintiff contended that Kenny J's definition was too narrow and he argued that *any* interference with bodily constitution was a violation of the right. The Supreme Court was not called on to address this argument as it held against the plaintiff on the evidence. It was therefore

unnecessary to define 'bodily integrity' or the 'right to the integrity of the person' or to consider to what degree and in what circumstances the State might interfere with the right, whether for the benefit of the individual concerned, the common good, or by way of punishment.

There is in these cautious remarks some evidence that the Supreme Court in *Ryan* was aware of the possibility that the right to bodily integrity could protect autonomous decisions, even against paternalistic intervention by the State. It should be recalled that *Ryan* was the first decision in which specificity was conferred on any of the previously unspecified personal rights recognised under Article 40.3.1°. It was not until two decades later that a right to individual (non-marital) privacy was tentatively recognised. Indeed, in *Norris v Attorney General* [1984] IR 36 O'Higgins CJ (for the majority) stated:

There are many acts done in private which the State is entitled to condemn, whether such be done by an individual on his own or with another. The law has always condemned abortion, incest, suicide attempts, suicide pacts, euthanasia or mercy killing. These are prohibited simply because they are morally wrong and regardless of the fact, which may exist in some instances, that no harm or injury to others is involved.

Any attempt in the wardship case to develop a constitutional right to commit suicide should have confronted this hurdle. For the Court to embrace the philosophy of John Stuart Mill with no apparent consciousness of the profound transformation of underlying values that this involves is a sad revelation.

When one examines Henchy J's dissenting judgment in *Norris*, it is possible to find language that could be invoked by a court in support of an autonomy-based entitlement to choose to die. Henchy J regarded privacy as involving:

> a complex of rights, varying in nature, purpose and range, each necessarily a facet of the citizens core of individuality within the constitutional order. . . . [T]hey would all appear to fall within a secluded area of activity or non-activity which may be claimed as necessary for the expression of an individual personality, for purposes not always necessarily moral or commendable, but meriting recognition in circumstances which do not endanger considerations such as State security, public order on morality, or other essential components of the common good.

It is hard to interpret these observations as warranting State intervention resulting in death by starvation of a non-autonomous person. The notion of the *expression* of an individual personally is clearly linked to autonomy.

Dignity, the individual and the significance of existence It is impossible fully to understand legal analysis of issues relating to life, dying, killing and death unless one realises that underlying that analysis is a complex amalgam of metaphysics, ethics and political philosophy. The answer that the majority gave in the wardship case lacks philosophical coherence.

Hamilton CJ observed that:

> [t]he sanctity of human life is recognised in all civilised jurisdictions and is based on the nature of man.

> The Constitution recognises this right and grants to it the protection set forth in the Constitution. The courts have recognised that the right to life springs from the right of every individual to life.

The Chief Justice appears here to have no difficulty with the idea of the Constitution's recognising a right based on natural law. How this can be reconciled with the Court's decision in the abortion information case (cf. *supra* 145 *et seq.*) is not easy to see.

We have already discussed in detail the acceptance by the Chief Justice, O'Flaherty and Denham JJ of the notion that there is a constitutionally-based entitlement to commit suicide by refusal of medical treatment. In Denham J's view, this entitlement embraces cases where the motivation to die is unrelated to the medical treatment; indeed, as we have seen, her judgment would seem consistent with a more wide-ranging entitlement to suicide.

The majority, therefore, has accepted the idea that an individual's conduct based on that individual's perception of the meaning or significance of life should receive constitutional support. Indeed, nothing in these judgments would suggest that this constitutional support should be withdrawn from an individual who, in seeking to commit suicide, is knowingly acting contrary to his or her own value system. The entitlement thus recognised is not merely to act with *integrity* to one's value system but also to act in *violation* of it. How this approach can be reconciled with natural law theory is hard to see.

There is, moreover, a clear indication in the judgments of O'Flaherty and Denham JJ that the right to life does not necessarily embrace a right to life below a certain standard. As O'Flaherty J put it, '[t]he ward may be alive but she has no life at all.' Artificial means should not preserve 'what technically is life but life without purpose, meaning or dignity.' In Denham J's view,

[t]o care for the dying, to love and cherish them, and to free them from suffering rather than simply to postpone death, is to have fundamental respect for the sanctity of life and its end.

What emerges is a very definite philosophical understanding of life, which the majority enforces through the law, resulting in the death of the ward. One should not forget that, in spite of the majority's extensive discussion of autonomy, choice and consent, the ward did not choose to die and the decision does not proceed on the basis that, in authorising her death, the Court was not seeking to her presumed wishes.

It may be useful to mention at this juncture the relevance of religion. Lynch J was willing to accept the (conflicting) evidence of moral theologians for two reasons: first, to show that in proposing the withdrawal of nutrition, the ward's family were not contravening their own ethic and, secondly, because, 'the matter being *res integra*, the views of theologians of various faiths are of assistance in that they endeavour to apply right reason to the problems for decision by the court and analogous problems.' Denham J approved of this approach, whilst asserting that the Supreme Court 'is a court of law, and the Constitution and law are applied; not moral law.' O'Flaherty observed that, '[f]or those of religious belief death is not an end but a beginning.' It is not clear from his judgment what significance he intended to attach to this fact as to belief — content.

Thus, the Court was polite to religion at a surface level, while showing no interest in examining the relationship between religion and philosophy. Let us consider the approaches of three people. The first asserts that God exists, and is the author of life; that we hold our own lives and the lives of others in a sacred trust; and that we are no more entitled to commit suicide than we are entitled intentionally to bring about the direct termination of another innocent life. Cf. Cohen-Almagor, 'Reflections on the Intriguing Issue of the Right to Die In Dignity' (1995) 29 *Israel L Rev* 677, at 687-8. The second asserts that the idea of God is a foolish human construction, designed to immunise us from the terror of the finitude and contingency which mark every life; that existence has no purpose or meaning; and that there comes a point where the proper human response is to choose (for oneself or for those who cannot make that choice) to defeat the indignity of a dependent and futile existence by terminating it. The third person asserts no religious propositions but expresses an understanding of life which embraces to the full its finitude and contingency, understanding these aspects to represent the foundation on which a truly humane ethical system can be built. This person regards the acceptance of contingency as embracing the acceptance of all manifestations of human life. On this approach, the idea that a person's dignity can be compromised by dependency on others is misconceived: one person's dependency generates an entitlement to loving care and support (which were, incidentally, manifest in the medical and nursing care that the ward received over the years).

If these three people were to address the issues raised in the wardship case, their answers would depend on their differing world views, differing understandings of the meaning and significance of existence and differing assessments of the relationship between society and the individual in regard to decisions affecting life and death. Metaphysics, religion, ethics and political philosophy inextricably merge. Dworkin, in *Life's Dominion* (1993), argues that, in the broadest sense, these life-and-death questions inevitably are religious in nature. This is true but not the full story.

Contemporary society believes that it is possible to segment the religious from the normative and thus to divorce the connection between religiously inspired ethics and a secular value system. Ethical positions that derive from religious inspiration are frequently dismissed without consideration on the basis of their 'sectarian' character. Thus, in our hypothetical scenario, the position of the first person will be devalued or ignored whilst the position of the third person will be fully respected by the law, even though their normative content is essentially identical.

Contemporary society fails to heed fully the inexorable connection between ethics and metaphysics. Everyone has a theory of the significance and meaning of existence (even if that theory is profoundly antimetaphysical). Such a metaphysical theory is integrated into one's value system and has direct implications on the content of that value system, impacting on how one understands one's moral obligations to others and to oneself. Much normative debate taking place on issues of life and death professes to relate simply to values (or, even more narrowly, rights) but in truth the issues cannot properly be understood without regard to the metaphysical debate that underlies, and to a large extent influences the adoption of, particular value positions.

What are the implications for the law? Must our Constitution be metaphysically neutral or is it permissible for it to adopt a particular position about the nature and significance of existence? May it do so in relation to the autonomous individual free to make life and death decisions, that affect only himself or herself, according to his or her own metaphysical understanding of existence? Is it right that a parent (or other surrogate decision-maker) should be entitled to have his or her metaphysical perspective applied to life-and-death decisions made about a non-autonomous minor child?

Whatever the proper answers to these questions may be, it is clear that, with respect to a non-autonomous person, the Supreme Court imposed a very definite metaphysical perception of the significance of existence. Whilst invoking the rhetoric of 'the sanctity of life', it evinces a deep existential despair in relation to the lives of defenceless, dependent people, treating their need for human solidarity as manifesting the lack of dignity. If the Court was indeed entitled to adopt a particular metaphysical perception of the significance of existence, it surely should have given effect to the existential perspective of natural law theory, which permeates Article 40 of the Constitution. This failure is a crucial defect of the majority's approach. In the natural law theory which the Constitution has incorporated, life has an inherent value; it is not the product of mere subjective assessment. Society through its laws, including laws developed by the courts, must respect the inherent value and dignity of life. There is no right to suicide or to authorise the termination of the life of anyone with very limited cognitive capacity who depends on nursing care for his or her food and drink. The very concept of 'life without purpose, meaning or dignity' has no place in the natural law theory which our Constitution has embraced.

Some further implications of a 'best interests' test In adopting uncritically the 'best interests' test to determine whether the ward's life should be allowed to continue, the majority failed to address some of the significant

questions that arise. We have already noted that the majority allowed itself
to address the issue of the ward's best interests, not simply in terms of her
medical welfare, but in terms of whether it was for her benefit to *continue to
exist*. That transition means that the Court has established a criterion with
ominous implications for other patients with serious disabilities.

A further problem with the 'best interests' test concerns its integration
with a person's constitutional rights. The whole point about autonomy-based
entitlements is that they should enable a person to choose to do what is not
in his or her best interests. At a formal level a court could argue that the
exercise of autonomy is so pre-eminent an entitlement that giving effect to
it will inevitably in one's best interests, but that solution has an aura of
rationalisation.

If 'best interests' are to be the test, how is the Court to deal with the case
of a seventeen year-old minor ward of court who wishes to kill himself by
refusing medical treatment? The logic of the majority's analysis in that the
Court should let autonomy prevail and permit, or even assist, the minor to a
commit suicide. If this is so, the 'best interests' test is surely supplanted.

The Court's approach to cases where the ward is adult and lacks autonomy is at least clear, however controversial it may be: the 'best interests' test
should be applied. But what is the position where no wardship proceedings
have been taken. Do parents of non-autonomous minor children and do
relatives of adult non-autonomous patients have the entitlement to authorise,
or even order, the withdrawal of feeding by tube, on the basis of a 'best
interest' test?

The difficulty with agreeing that they do springs primarily from the fact
that the Court laid emphasis on its paternalistic jurisdiction being based on
its role under wardship proceedings; in the absence of such justification, what
is the basis of entitlement of any private person to authorise a course of action
leading, and intended to lead, to the death of another?

That matter was not resolved in the instant case. The majority declined
to accept that Article 41 of the Constitution gave to the family the last word
in a case where the patient was a ward of court. Echoing Lynch J's approach,
Hamilton CJ stated:

> The family had invoked the jurisdiction of the court, and the court then
> became responsible for all decisions with regard to the person and estate
> of the ward. . . . In the exercise of [its *parens patrial*] jurisdiction, the
> court will have regard to but not be bound by the wishes of the
> committee and members of the family. The ultimate responsibility for
> making the necessary decision rests of the court.

It will be recalled that in the instant case, the doctors and nurses of the institution were opposed to removing the feeding tube. As to the position where parents or relatives find themselves *in agreement with* the doctors, the Court's decision is not entirely clear. (See the excellent analysis on this point by Tomkin & McAuley (1995) 2 *Medico-Legal J of Ireland* 45, at 48-9.) If the *bona fide* wishes of parents or relatives, which are not opposed by the doctors, can justify the withdrawal of medical treatment, or feeding through a tube, this would result in a radical transformation of previously accepted norms of treatment of the disabled, whether newborn, aged or otherwise.

Why should this be so? The answer is that *bona fide* wishes, based on the particular metaphysical view of the parents or relatives as to the meaning and worth of life in particular circumstances (such as where a recently born child has serious disabilities or where an elderly relative has Alzheimer's disease), could result in the termination of that person's life, through the withdrawal of medical treatment, in circumstances where the Court, *if it had been exercising wardship jurisdiction,* would have come to a different existential perspective or because, while adopting the same existential perspective as the parents and relatives, it regarded the best interests of the person as being served by the continuation of his or her life.

It must be acknowledged that, apart altogether from the particular life-and-death context in which we are considering the entitlement of parents or relatives to authorise particular treatment regime for a child or other person, the general legal issue as to the circumstances in which parent's or relatives' consent is necessary or sufficient is one on which the instant case gives no guidance and in relation to which several uncertainties attack. The (limited) judicial authorities that address the subject have to be read in the light of a rapidly developing constitutional jurisprudence on which the wardship case is part.

Ordinary and extraordinary means of treatment A striking feature of the several judgments of the majority is their failure to give any express approval to the established ethical approach between ordinary and extraordinary means of treatment. Indeed Denham J was clearly liable to this approach, stating that '[it is not pertinent whether the treatment is ordinary or extraordinary treatment.'

Rev. Kenneth Kearon ('*Re a Ward of Court:* Ethical Comment' (1995) 2 *Medico-Legal J of Ireland* 58, at 58-9 explains that:

> [t]his important distinction in ethics is most often used today in the context of life support and life prolonging medical treatments, so it is especially relevant in the judgment under consideration. It can be understood thus:

'Extraordinary means are all medicines, treatments and operations that (i) do not offer a reasonable hope of success or (ii) cannot be obtained or used without excessive hardship — i.e. excessive pain, cost or other inconvenience'.

"Ordinary" means that which does offer a reasonable hope of success, or which can be obtained or used without excessive hardship. It's important here to note the technical meaning of "ordinary" in this context — the word does not mean "routine" or "customary", and carries with it the further implication or moral obligation. While treatment cannot be forced on any person against their wishes, implicit in the ordinary/extraordinary distinction is a moral obligation on carers to offer, and for the patient to accept, ordinary treatment while extraordinary treatment carries no such obligation.

A further aspect of the ordinary/extraordinary distinction is that it is not a way of categorising medical treatments. The judgment as to whether a specific treatment is or is not ordinary can only be made by the patient or from the patient's perspective. Antibiotics may be ordinary treatment for one patient, but extraordinary for another. Further, it is possible for a form of treatment to being as ordinary, but over time to become extraordinary.

Why should there have been such antipathy in the wardship case to this approach? The suspicion must arise that the majority identified it (wrongly) as a distinctively Catholic approach. It is curious that the Court chose to hear the evidence of moral theologians rather than of moral philosophers who could have enlightened the Court on the relevant principles of natural law philosophy which applied to the case.

The aftermath of the decision The Medical Counsel, having considered the Supreme Court decision, issued a statement on August 4, 1995 in which it reiterated what it had stated in its *Guide to Ethical Conduct and Behaviour and to Fitness to Practice*. It there emphasised the obligation resting on doctors to do their best to preserve life an never to act in the detriment of their patient. It stated its view that:

access to nutrition and hydration is one of the basic needs of human beings. This remains so even when, from time to time, this need can only be fulfilled by means of long established methods such nosgastric and gastrostomy tube feeding.

An Bord Altranais issued a statement on 18 August reaffirming the principle laid out in *The Code of Professional Conduct for Each Nurse and Midwife*.

The position has thus been reached that the Supreme Court's decisions on abortion and on the withdrawal of nutrition from patients have not the support of medical ethics as articulated by the relevant medical and nursing bodies. That is in itself a starling fact. Even more a matter of concern is the poverty of the majority's analysis in the wardship case. Whilst in the abortion information case, the Court's hostility to natural law principles is evident to any readers, the wardship case rejects natural law in an equally summary fashion but without any apparent full knowledge of what exactly was at stake in the case.

TRIAL OF OFFENCES

Burden of proof and evidential burden In *O'Leary v Attorney General* [1991] ILRM 454 (HC); [1995] 2 ILRM 259 (SC), the Supreme Court upheld the decision of Costello J in the High Court that s. 24 of the Offences against the State Act 1939 was not repugnant to the Constitution.

The background to the decision was that the plaintiff had been convicted in the Special Criminal Court of membership of an unlawful organisation, namely the Irish Republican Army (IRA), and of possession of incriminating documents, contrary to ss. 21 and 12 of the 1939 Act. At his trial, the plaintiff had accepted that certain posters, containing the words 'IRA calls the shots', were in his possession, but he stated that he possessed them as a member of the political party Sinn Fiin and denied that he was a member of the IRA. The trial court rejected his denial of IRA membership. S.24 of the 1939 Act provides that on the trial of a person charged with being a member of an unlawful organisation, proof to the satisfaction of the court that an incriminating document relating to the organisation was found on that person or in his possession or on lands or premises owned or occupied by him or under his control 'shall, without more, be evidence until the contrary is proved' that such person was a member of the organisation at the time alleged in the charge. The plaintiff's conviction was upheld by the Court of Criminal Appeal: see *The People v O'Leary* (1988) 3 Frewen 163 (1988 Review, 162-4 and 190-1). He then instituted the instant proceedings, seeking a declaration, *inter alia*, that s. 24 of the 1939 Act was unconstitutional. He submitted that the words 'until the contrary is proved' imposed the burden on the accused of proving that he was not a member of an unlawful organisation, which in effect meant that the burden was thrown on him to prove that he was not guilty of the offence. The High Court refused to grant a declaration that the provisions of s. 24 of the 1939 Act were repugnant to the Constitution: 1990

Review, 178-82. As indicated, the Supreme Court upheld this decision.

The Court accepted, citing its decision in *Hardy v Ireland* [1994] 2 IR 550 (1993 Review, 172-4), that the presumption of innocence and the associated burden of proof was a necessary ingredient for a trial in due course of law pursuant to Article 38.1 of the Constitution. However, as Costello J had done in the High Court, the Court drew a distinction between the burden of proof and the evidentiary burden of proof. The Court held that, while the burden of proof may not shift from the prosecution, the evidential burden could change in the course of a criminal trial.

In this respect, the Court noted that s. 24 of the 1939 Act permitted no more than that possession of an incriminating document was to amount to evidence only rather than be taken as proof. Thus, the probative value of the possession of such a document could be shaken in many ways, such as cross-examination, by pointing to the mental capacity of the accused or the circumstances by which he came to be in possession of the document.

The Supreme Court stated that no court should act as an automaton in the assessment of evidence and it should always approach its task in a responsible manner having proper regard to the paramount place that the presumption of innocence occupied in any criminal trial. Despite this warning about the potential for abuse inherent in s. 24 of the 1939 Act, the Court was not prepared to regard it as being in conflict with the essential nature of the criminal trial posited by Article 38.1. Of course, the Court was thus affirming the analysis of Costello J in the High Court, but we note again here our earlier criticisms about the effect of its provisions, in particular in the circumstances of the plaintiff's case: see the 1988 Review, 162-4 and the 1990 Review, 178-82. We note also that the principles in the *O'Leary* case were applied by Murphy J in *Rock v Ireland and Ors*, High Court, November 10, 1995: see the Criminal Law chapter, 243, below.

Contract Law

Eoin O'Dell

School of Law, Trinity College Dublin

Friel, *The Law of Contract* (The Round Hall Press) is a new work on the subject published in 1995.

CONSIDERATION

Introduction The doctrine of consideration is *the* distinctive feature of the law of contract in the common law world, and it was important in two High Court cases this year. In *AIB v Fagan* (High Court, November 10, 1995) Costello P found no benefit and thus no consideration on the facts; and in *Riordan v Carroll* [1996] 2 ILRM 241 Kinlen J *obiter* referred to the rule that a promise to accept part-payment of a debt in satisfaction of that debt, is, without more, unenforceable. Costello P's approach reflects existing orthodoxy; recent developments elsewhere in the common law world seem to pose great difficulty for this orthodoxy in the context both of consideration for renegotiated contracts and of the part-payment rule at issue in Kinlen J's judgment. The analysis here will locate Costello P's decision in *AIB v Fagan* in its orthodox context, consider these recent developments, and, in that light, assess Kinlen J's decision in *Riordan v Carroll*.

Definition The starting point of the modern doctrine of consideration in the law of contract is usually taken as Pollock's definition adopted by the House of Lords in *Dunlop v Selfridge*: 'An act or forbearance of the one party, or the promise thereof, is the price for which the promise of the other is bought, and the promise thus given for value is enforceable'. ([1915] AC 847, 855; cp. *Police Principles of Contract* (8th ed, 1911) p. 175). The essence of this definition is that each party gives and receives something, a bargained-for exchange. In this scenario, it may be said in respect of each party's giving, that the party giving suffers a detriment and the other party gains a corresponding benefit; or, in respect of each party's receipt, that the party receiving gains a benefit and the other party suffers a corresponding detriment. So, in the situation of a sale of goods for a price, there is 'something for something': the seller suffers the detriment of giving over the goods and the buyer gains the benefit of getting them, while the seller gains the benefit of the receipt of the price and the buyer suffers the detriment of paying it.

An analysis of consideration in terms of benefit and detriment figured in the judgment of Costello P in *AIB v Fagan* (High Court, November 10, 1995). One firm of solicitors, T, had formerly acted for Greendale and certain others. T's retainer was discharged, and R thereafter acted for Greendale and those others. T and R had negotiated over the manner in which fees outstanding to T would be discharged in consideration of T's waiver of their common law lien on the files in their possession and the release of these files to R. It was agreed that the waiver and transfer would occur in consideration (*inter alia*) of 'the discharge [of] fees due to T from the proceeds of any settlement or award referred to in the files. . . '. Thereafter, R confirmed that their 'undertaking to discharge [T's] costs to date, in respect of the . . . files, on the conclusion of the said actions, [was] not conditional upon the successful outcome of proceedings'.

Greendale had been wound up, its assets sold, and, by court order, a sum placed in a joint deposit account in the names of both T and R. As to whether T had a claim to a portion of the deposit on foot of R's undertaking, Costello P held not: 'as these actions have not yet concluded T have no claim on foot of this undertaking for their fees on these two actions . . . '.

Upon direction from Greendale, R gave a further undertaking in respect of further files, but some of those files related to work done not for Greendale but for its controllers and other companies controlled by them. As to whether T had a claim to money in the joint deposit account in respect of those files, Costello P held that:

> T had performed professional work for the [the controller and other companies] . . . and these parties (not Greendale) owed the fees the subject of this claim. The common law lien [arising from this work] was not in respect of Greendale's files and Greendale obtained no benefit from the undertaking given by which these files were released to the parties' new solicitors.

Since Greendale had not received anything, it had nothing to pay for. The essence of the bargain theory of consideration, expressed in terms of benefit and detriment, is that there must be 'something for something': here Greendale did not receive a 'something', a benefit, there was no basis upon which to require them to pay a 'something' and incur a detriment.

If the paradigm of a benefit-detriment bargain is 'something for something', then it follows that where a contract seems to provide for 'something for nothing', it does not provide for consideration, and is consequently unenforceable. Thus, where a contract already provides for a given perform-ance for a given price, an agreement merely to perform that same perform-ance for a higher price is unenforceable: given that the performance is already due, the increase in price is 'something for nothing', unsupported by consid-eration, and thus unenforceable. Again, where a contract already provides for a given price for a given performance, an agreement to accept a lesser price for that same performance is likewise unenforceable: given that the price is already due, the reduction in the amount owed is 'something for nothing', unsupported by consideration, and thus unenforceable.

The rule, that if a person is under a contractual obligation to do something, there is no consideration for an increase in the contract price if he merely does what he has contracted to do, is usually taken to have been established in *Stilk v Myrick* ((1809) 2 Camp 317 (170 ER 1168); 6 Esp 129 (170 ER 851), although the reports of the case are not good (see Beale, Bishop and Furmston, *Contract, Cases and Materials* (3rd ed, 1995) p. 106; *cp.* Treitel, *The Law of Contract* (9th ed, 1995) p. 89) and the precise *ratio* of the case is elusive (see Reynolds and Treitel (1965) 7 *Malaya L Rev* 1, 4-9). The rule that part payment of an existing debt does not discharge that debt is usually taken to have been established by *Pinnel's Case* (1602) 5 Co Rep 117a; 77 ER 237 and confirmed by the House of Lords in *Foakes v Beer* (1884) 9 App Cas 605.

The pre-existing duty rule, and the part-payment rule, have long been regarded as inflexible and rigidly technical products of a monolithic bargain view of the doctrine of consideration. However, if, as Prof Atiyah has long argued, the proper basis of the doctrine is instead to be found, not in bargain, but in the protection of a promisee's *reliance* on the promisor's promise, then the objections (above) to refusing to enforce a promise to perform a pre-ex-isting duty or to accept part-payment of an existing debt falls away, and if the promisee has in fact relied on those promises, there would on this view be a good consideration and thus the promises would be enforceable. (See, generally, Atiyah, *Consideration in Contract. A Fundamental Restatement* (Canberra, 1971); Atiyah, *The Rise and Fall of Freedom of Contract* (Oxford, 1979)). Nevertheless, one does not need to seek beyond bargain for a flexible approach to the doctrine of consideration; for example, if A promises to pay B £100 if B renders a service to C, and B in fact does so, then B can enforce A's promise; B has suffered a detriment (he has performed the service) A has not gained a corresponding benefit. A rigid bargain approach to consid-eration expressed in terms of benefit and detriment might be thought to render A's promise unenforceable, but it has been held that it is enough that the promisee suffer a detriment even if the promisor has gained no corresponding benefit, it is enough if the promisee provided consideration even if it did not go to the promisor (see Treitel, p. 77).

Recent developments The decision of the Court of Appeal in England in *Williams v Roffey* [1991] 1 QB 1; [1990] 1 All ER 512 is of enormous significance to the doctrine of consideration; at the very least it evinces a flexible and less technical approach to the doctrine of consideration. The judgments are expressed in terms of benefit and detriment, and if the decision can be rationalised in those terms, then it represents a flexible approach to orthodox bargain principles. If however, the judgments cannot be rationalised in those terms, then either the decision is wrong, or if correct, it represents a paradigm shift in the doctrine of consideration. (See, generally, Adams and Brownsword (1990) 53 *MLR* 536; Coote (1990) 3 *JCL* 23; Halson (1990) 106 *LQR* 183; Hooley [1991] *JBL* 19; E. Noble (1991) 141 *NLJ* 1529; Phang (1991) 107 *LQR* 21).

The headcontractor, A, hired a builder, B to refurbish a block of 27 flats. In the contract between A and B, there were very severe penalty clauses for failure to complete the work on time. In the course of the work, B in turn hired a sub-contractor carpenter, C. C agreed to do the work for £20,000. It turned out that the decline in the building industry upset C's cashflow so that their bid of £20,000 was consequently insufficient; and B's inadequately supervised employees made it difficult for C to carry out its work. Thus, after completing 9 flats, and having done some work on most of the others, C was in danger of non- completion. B (faced with the penalties in the head contract if C failed to complete) therefore called a meeting with C, and agreed to a further £10,300 to be paid at the rate of £575 for each completed flat. C continued the work, but B did not pay the agreed increase. C sued B for the increase, and succeeded: this, in essence, is *Williams v Roffey* (where Williams is C, the carpenter suing B, the builder, Roffey, for the increased price; it is a recent example of the perennial problem of the enforceability of modified contracts: see, generally, Reynolds and Treitel (*supra*); Stoljar (1957) 35 *Can Bar Rev* 485; Aivazan, Treblicock and Penny (1984) 22 *Osgoode Hall LJ* 65; and, in the context of *Williams v Roffey*, Halyk (1991) *Sask L Rev* 393; Halson [1991] *CLP* 111).

Under the rule in *Stilk v Myrick*, there is no consideration in an agreement to perform a pre-existing duty; there, a ship had sailed from London to the Baltic, where two crew-men deserted; the contracts of employment clearly envisaged that the remaining crew would sail the ship to London, but instead they sought and received from the master a promise to divide the wages of the deserters among the remaining crew if they sailed the ship home. In an action to recover the extra wages, Lord Ellenborough held the promise unenforceable for want of consideration. That being so, it should equally have been an answer to Williams' claim against Roffey. However, doubts have been judicially expressed about the pre-existing duty rule (see *e.g.*, *Ward v Byham* [1956] 2 All ER 318, 319; *Williams v Williams* [1957] 1 WLR

148, 151; *McKerring v The Minister for Agriculture* [1989] ILRM 82), and its rationale academically questioned (Carter, Phang and Poole (1995) 8 *JCL* 248). Indeed, in the general case of a renegotiated contract, Lord Hailsham had said that 'I imagine that a modern court would have found no difficulty in discovering consideration for such a promise. Businessmen know their own business best, even when they appear to grant an indulgence . . .' (*Woodhouse v Nigerian Produce Marketing* [1972] AC 741). To the extent, therefore, that *Williams v Roffey* represents this view, then it is an excellent and welcome example of the courts being guided 'less by technical questions of consideration than by questions of fairness, reasonableness and commercial utility' (Adams and Brownsword (1990) 53 *MLR* 536, 537). Clearly, however, to reach the conclusion that the promise for the extra payments for the flats was enforceable, the Court of Appeal still had to find consideration for that promise.

First, in answer to the argument that the rule in *Stilk v Myrick* provided a complete defence, the Court of Appeal, taking a 'pragmatic approach' ([1990] 1 All ER 512, 524 *per* Russell LJ) to the question of consideration, held in favour of C. Thus, in the course of his decision, Russell LJ held that:

> Consideration there must still be but in my judgment the courts nowadays should be more ready to find its existence so as to reflect the intention of the parties to the contract where bargaining powers are not unequal and where the finding of consideration reflects the true intention of the parties. ([1990] 1 All ER 512, 524; Purchas LJ too stressed that he was being guided by the true intention of the parties.)

B had obtained many practical benefits from the continuance of contract, not least of which was the fact that he avoided penalties under his headcontract with A (see *e.g.* [1990] 1 All ER 512, 518 *per* Glidewell LJ, 524 *per* Russell LJ, 527 *per* Purchas LJ). Furthermore, B obtained C's continued performance and a more orderly and efficient performance of the contract, and avoided the trouble and expense of obtaining a substitute. Benefit was thus easily found. Importantly, whilst C performed, the important practical benefits to B came not from the performance *per se* but from the consequences for B *vis-à-vis* A of that performance. Thus, it might be said that if it is enough that the promisee provide consideration even if it did not go to the promisor, then, *Williams v Roffey* supports the converse that it should equally be enough if the promisor receives consideration even if did not come from the promisee.

Second, the Court in *Williams v Roffey* justified its more flexible attitude to the rule in *Stilk v Myrick* by pointing out that, when the case was decided, there was an underdeveloped doctrine of duress at common law, so the defendant who sought to avoid a contract which was entered into at some pressure was forced to rely on doctrines such as consideration to avoid the contract. ([1990] 1 All ER 512, 518, 521-522 *per* Glidewell LJ, 524 *per* Russell LJ, 527 *per* Purchas LJ; *cp. Musumeci v Winadell* (1994) 34 NSWLR 723, 738 *per* Santow J). Now, however, since there is a well developed modern doctrine of duress, it is no longer necessary to distort the doctrine of consideration by requiring it to serve the functions of the defence of duress. Thus, there can be an approach to the doctrine of consideration more flexible than that contemplated in cases like *Stilk v Myrick.*

Lest it be thought that an Irish court may not be inclined to follow this approach, consider that of Murphy J in *In re PMPA Garage (Longmile) Ltd (No. 1)* [1992] 1 IR 315. Between 1977 and 1984, some companies in the Private Motorists Provident Association (PMPA) Group of companies received loans from the Private Motorists Provident Society (the PMPS), a provident society which was a member of the Group. Every company in the Group became party to an agreement to guarantee these loans. The Group collapsed, and the Society sought to be admitted as a creditor of PMPA Garage (Longmile) Ltd, a Group company which had joined in the execution of the guarantee, but did not receive any loan. One of the many issues before the Court was the question whether the guarantee was supported by consideration (on the other issues, see MacCann (1992) *ILT (ns)* 79 and 151, 155-157; O'Dell (1992) 14 *DULJ* (ns) 123; and the 1991 Review pp. 45-51). On this issue, Murphy J held that the evidence disclosed a sufficient consideration:

> it was in the interest and for the benefit of each individual company to ensure and promote the success of the other companies in the group and that in addition to the benefits secured indirectly in that way the individual companies also enjoyed at least the opportunity, and perhaps the reality, of advances from the PMPS which could only have been obtained on the security of the fellow members of the group acting as a whole. An additional benefit accruing to the individual guarantors is the fact, . . . that the subsequent guarantees discharged the earlier ones. ([1992] 1 IR 315, 327).

It is clear that the flexible and pragmatic attitude to benefit and consideration in this case is on all fours with that in *Williams v Roffey.* In both cases, the court was prepared to look beyond form to the factual reality, and to ask whether, in fact, a benefit accrued, which benefit the law could then recognise as consideration (see, *e.g.* Treitel, p. 90).

Nevertheless, the question must be posed: in what precisely did the consideration on the facts of *Williams v Roffey* consist? If C is seeking to enforce B's promise, what consideration did C give and B receive? The Court of Appeal identified many practical benefits which they said sufficed, (C's continued performance, a more orderly and efficient performance of the contract, avoidance of the trouble and expense of obtaining a substitute, and, especially, avoiding the penalty clauses in the headcontract with A) but to the extent that such benefits comprised 'of chance rather than assurance, [they] confer[ed] benefits of an illusory and unenforceable kind' (Chen-Wishart 'Consideration, Practical Benefit and the Emperor's New Clothes' in Beatson and Friedmann (eds.) *Good Faith and Fault in Contract Law* (Oxford, 1995) p. 123, at p. 133; this objection seems especially apt to the benefits found in *PMPA*). For example, it has been argued that the benefit conferred on B was the comfort which they thereby derived 'from their own perception of a greater chance of completion of the project on time' (Hooley [1991] *JBL* 19, 28). But it has been properly objected to this that reassurance is no more than sentimental value, than the ties of love and affection, and equally unenforceable (Chen-Wishart, p. 127). Or, again, the consideration received by B may be an 'objectively better chance of performance' of the contract by C. But again, this is not sufficient: 'we are still essentially talking about the same performance to which the promisor is already entitled under the original contract. The practical benefit consists only of the promisor's hope that he or she will be put in as good a position as if the original contract had been performed. . . . this "provides nothing that is not already the promisor's right".' (Chen-Wishart, p. 128, emphasis in original, citing Coote (1990) 3 *JCL* 23, 28). Consequently, Chen-Wishart argues that to say that a promise to pay more for the same work can count as consideration:

> because it confers a 'practical benefit' on the promisor is a trick no less than that played by the tailor of the emperor's new clothes. It cannot disguise the fact that practical benefit neither confers any enforceable benefit additional to that contained in the original contract, nor buys any enforceable expectation to the reciprocal promise to pay more. Like the emperor's new clothes, the benefit described as 'practical' turns out to be a lot less than presented. The words 'illusory' and 'naked' would not be inapt (*id.*, p. 124).

However, the formulations of benefit so far discussed tell only half the story; their focus is on the simple fact of the promisee ultimately getting what he originally bargained for, and (as Chen-Wishart's objections show) the weakness of such formulations is easily demonstrated. However, on the facts of *Williams v Roffey*, it was not so much that the promisee would ultimately get what he originally bargained for that was important, as the fact that he would get it *in different circumstances*. It is clear that where the background circumstances change, getting something different is good consideration; thus 'the crew of a ship may be justified in refusing to complete a voyage because so many of their fellows have deserted that completion will involve hazards of a kind not originally contemplated. If they are induced to go on by a promise of extra pay, they do something which they were not bound to do, and can recover the extra pay. (Treitel, p. 91; citing *Hartley v Ponsonby* (1857) 7 El&Bl 872; 119 ER 1471). Again, it is clear that where the background circumstances remain the same, getting something different is good consideration: the 'promisee may provide other consideration for the new promise by doing, or promising to do, more than he was bound by the original contract to do' (Treitel, p. 91; *cp.* Clark, *Contract Law in Ireland* (3rd ed, Sweet & Maxwell, London, 1994) p. 58). But if getting something different in the same circumstances is good consideration, then why can it not be that getting the same thing in different circumstances also constitutes good consideration? Given the new circumstances, the contract as originally agreed could not be performed. By negotiating to ensure that in the new circumstances the contract can again be performed, the promisee does receive a new benefit: without the renegotiation he receives nothing; with it, he receives something. Thus, he receives a good consideration. Indeed, in *Williams v Roffey*, B's consideration (C's continued performance, a more orderly and efficient performance of the contract, avoidance of the trouble and expense of obtaining a substitute, and, especially, avoiding the penalty clauses in the headcontract with A) really only makes sense when viewed as that which is received *in the context of the new background market circumstances*; getting C's performance in the new circumstances is 'something different', and is thus good consideration.

That this is at least a plausible reading of *Williams v Roffey* is borne out by its subsequent history. It was soon followed in *Anangel Atlas Compania Naviera SA v Ishikawajima-Harima Heavy Industries Co. (No. 2)* [1990] 2 Lloyd's Rep 526 (Hirst J; see Tolhurst (1991) 4 *JCL* 257; Clarke [1991] *LMCLQ* 305). A purchaser entered into a contract with a ship-builder to purchase a ship's hull. Thereafter, the ship-building industry suffered a serious slump, the ship-builder's business was threatened, and the purchaser became reluctant to take delivery of the hull. The purchaser was the ship-builder's key customer, and fearing the consequences of other customers following the purchaser's lead, the ship-builder agreed to alterations in the contract, promising various concessions so as to give the customer favourable treatment to induce purchase and on time acceptance of delivery. Hirst J found that there were 'practical benefits' and thus consideration for the new agreement. The change in background circumstances meant that delivery in the new market conditions was something different to delivery in the old conditions. (See also *Lee v GEC Plessey Telecommunications* [1993] IRLR

383 (Colman J)). *Williams v Roffey* has also been approved and followed in New South Wales in *Musumeci v Winadell* (1994) 34 NSWLR 723 (Santow J) and in New Zealand in *Newman Tours v Ranier Investments* [1992] 2 NZLR 68, 80 *per* Fisher J: 'Even the agreement to perform existing contractual obligations, followed by actual performance in reliance upon that subsequent agreement, can constitute fresh consideration' citing, *inter alia*, Williams v Roffey.

If the key to *Williams v Roffey* and *Anangel* is the fact that the receipt of the original performance in new circumstances is as much 'something different' as the receipt of something new in the original circumstances, then Chen-Wishart's objections fall away. Her critique is that since the bargain theory of consideration requires something for something, and since on the facts, there was something for nothing (a promise of more for the same), there could not be consideration consistent with the bargain theory, and since the bargain theory underpins many other contract doctrines (*e.g.* the rules relating to gratuitous promises, past consideration, frustration, estoppel, duress, and the calculation of damages) a finding of consideration so radically inconsistent with the bargain theory is incompatible with current notions of contractual enforcement. However, it is submitted here that receiving the same in new circumstances does amount to receiving 'something different', and therefore does amount to consideration. On this reading, Williams v Roffey is entirely consistent with the bargain theory of consideration, though it does represent a nuanced incremental development of pre-existing orthodoxy.

Objections similar to Chen-Wishart's have been voiced in Ireland. Thus, Prof Clark writes that the 'application of such a controversial and difficult proposition not only threatens to further undermine the bargain theory, it also makes the boundary between promissory estoppel and consideration even more difficult to draw. Perhaps a more rational response would have required the Court of Appeal to negative the consideration argument that the plaintiff successfully utilised, and to address the issues from a promissory estoppel perspective.' (Clark, p. 46). Again Friel has pointed to what he sees as the 'fuzzy reasoning' in the decision which 'has done much to damage the concept of consideration', so that if it is correct 'then it is on the basis of promissory estoppel and not a tortured definition of consideration' (p. 105 n 94; *cp.* p. 106, text with n.95; p. 119).

First, the objection that the decision in *Williams v Roffey* undermines the doctrine of consideration have been addressed in the argument above that it is entirely consistent with the bargain theory. Second, an estoppel solution to the facts of *Williams v Roffey* has attracted many commentators (*e.g.* Carter, Phang and Poole (1995) 8 *JCL* 248, 265; Chen-Wishart, p. 149; Halyk (1991) *Sask L Rev* 393, 414; O'Sullivan [1996] CLJ 219, 226; *Musumeci v*

Winadell (1994) 34 NSWLR 723, 750 *per* Santow J). In fact, the Court of
Appeal in *Williams v Roffey* (and Russell LJ in particular) indicated that, had
it not been precluded by the pleadings, it would have welcomed an estoppel
argument; though if consideration was properly found on the facts (as it is
submitted here that it was), then resort to estoppel would not be necessary.
Third, in giving something (consideration) in exchange for a promise, the
promisee *expects* to receive something (consideration) in return, and the
bargain theory of consideration enforces promises in the context of such a
'something for something' exchange (of benefit and detriment) so as to
protect that expectation; whereas estoppel enforces promises because they
have foreseeably been *relied* upon to the detriment of the promisee; since the
protection of expectations and reliance are clearly separate functions, the
boundary between consideration and estoppel is quite clear. Finally, in
PMPA, the consideration for the guarantee given by PMPS was the maintenance in business of its key customers, the PMPA group of companies, in
the new circumstances of the group's market difficulties: in this respect, the
consideration was the receipt of the same in different circumstances, and it
is similar both to *Williams v Roffey* and to *Anangel*. Consequently, it is
submitted that (pace Chen-Wishart, Clark, and Friel), *Williams v Roffey*
represents a sound evolution in the bargain theory of consideration, which
evolution has also been achieved in Ireland in *PMPA*.

***Williams v Roffey* and part payment of a debt**   The denial of consideration
for the performance of a pre-existing duty and for the part payment of a debt
flows from a similar application of the bargain theory of consideration. If
'practical benefit' (or the obtaining of the original performance in new
circumstances) can constitute an exception to the pre-existing duty rule, it
seems difficult to deny that 'practical benefit' could similarly constitute an
exception to the part-payment rule. Thus, Chen-Wishart writes that 'practical
benefits, which support the enforcement of promises of more for the same,
must also logically support the enforcement of promises of the same for less'
(Chen-Wishart, p. 135, referring to Treitel, p. 115, and to Adams and
Brownsword (1990) 53 *MLR* 536, 540). Treitel and Adams and Brownsword
would adopt the premiss, and thus accept the extension. Of course, since
Chen-Wishart would deny the premiss, she would thus also deny the extension; similarly O'Sullivan, 'In Defence of *Foakes v Beer*' [1996] *CLJ* 219,
who argues that '"accepting less" and "paying more" are not straightforward
mirror images of each other' ([1996] *CLJ* 219, 220, emphasis in original)
(see also Friel, pp. 106, 114-117).
       The difficulty in the way of the extension is *Pinnel's Case* (1602) 5 Co
Rep 117a; 77 ER 237 and the decision of the House of Lords in *Foakes v
Beer* (1884) 9 App Cas 605, neither of which was referred to by the Court

of Appeal in *Williams v Roffey*. Nevertheless, in New South Wales, *Williams v Roffey* has been understood as capable of applying to find consideration in the context of a part payment of an existing debt: *Musumeci v Winadell* (1994) 34 NSWLR 723, 747 *per* Santow J. Here, a tenant was held to provide a practical benefit to the landlord as consideration for an agreement to accept a lesser rent.

However, in *Re Selectmove* [1995] 1 WLR 474 (CA) (see Peel (1994) 110 *LQR* 353; Phang [1994] *LMCLQ* 336) a company owed a debt to the Revenue, and sought to agree a repayment schedule. The Court of Appeal held that the schedule had not in fact been agreed, but considered that had it been, although it could have constituted a 'practical benefit' within the *Williams v Roffey* understanding of that notion, the decision of the House of Lords in *Foakes v Beer* rendered it 'impossible' find consideration for what in fact amounted to a part payment of a debt. Similarly in *Re C (a debtor)* (May 11, 1994, CA; discussed in Carter, Phang and Poole (1995) 8 *JCL* 248, 257) the Legal Aid Board had demanded £16,556 but had received only £14,000 accompanied by a note that if this amount was not accepted in full settlement, it was to be returned. The Board accepted it 'on account', and the Court of Appeal found that there was no agreement to settle the debt for the lesser amount. The Board also relied on *Pinnel's Case* and *Foakes v Beer*, and Bingham MR held that there was no additional benefit or detriment on the facts, the effect of which was that even if there had been such an agreement, it would not have been enforceable. In both courts, considerations of precedent (*Foakes v Beer* is a decision of the House of Lords) precluded the application of *Williams v Roffey* is this situation. On the other hand, in New South Wales, Santow J in *Musumeci v Winadell*, believing himself untrammelled by such considerations of precedent, had no difficulty in applying *Williams v Roffey* and finding a practical benefit in the context of a part-payment of a debt.

After *Williams v Roffey*, where the background circumstances have altered, getting the same thing in these different circumstances constitutes good consideration: it is a 'something different'. In the context of a part-payment of an existing debt, an agreement to accept a lesser price for a previously agreed performance is unenforceable: given that the price is already due, the reduction in the amount owed is 'something for nothing', unsupported by consideration, and thus unenforceable. But where the background circumstances remain the same, getting something different is good consideration (*e.g.* Clark, p. 58, giving the examples in this context of payment early, or in a different place, or by some new means; consider also the example of a composition with creditors): again it is a 'something different'. The question of principle posed by *Re Selectmove* and *Re C* is whether, if D owes P a debt, practical benefits accruing to P by virtue of the circumstances of the part-payment can amount to a good consideration for a promise by P to accept part-payment. Very often it will be of practical benefit to a trade creditor to receive a part-payment in satisfaction of the full amount, especially where payment is early, or in a different place, or by some new means, or in a composition with creditors; thus, the recognised exceptions to *Foakes v Beer* can be seen simply as examples of the recognition of practical benefit in the context of part-payment prior to Williams v Roffey. And, if these circumstances constitute practical benefit, it is submitted that it is *a fortiori* where background market conditions have changed for either party or both (in *Robichaud v Caisse Populaire* (1990) 69 DLR (4th) 589 (NBCA) immediate payment and the saving of time, effort and expense were held to constitute consideration, again a 'practical benefit'). In all cases, it is of the essence of the second agreement that the creditor is in fact getting 'something different'. Thus, where part-payment results in the debtor getting 'something for nothing', there is no consideration, *(Foakes v Beer)*, but where the creditor in fact gets a practical benefit (a 'something different') then there is good consideration (*Williams v Roffey*). On this analysis, then the latter case does not amount to the death-knell for the former; it merely rationally explains the existing exceptions to the former. Although in *Re Selectmove* Peter Gibson LJ was of the view that part payment or instalment payments would invariably be of practical benefit to a creditor, and it is relatively easy to see a practical benefit in such circumstances to a trade creditor, who for market reasons may need the money (which, basically, was the landlord's position in *Musumeci v Winadell*), it is much more difficult to see any practical benefit to the Revenue (or, perhaps, to the Legal Aid Board in *Re C*) unembarrassed by such market considerations.

Consequently, then, the notion of 'practical benefit' has an important role to play in the context of consideration for part payment of a debt. Furthermore, adherence to precedent (the rule in *Pinnel's Case* and *Foakes v Beer*) should not preclude its application because the exceptions to that rule are best understood as examples of such a practical benefit.

Although *Pinnel's Case* has been followed in pre-1922 Irish cases (*e.g. Drogheda Corporation v Fairtlough* (1858) 8 Ir CLR 98) and in Northern Ireland (*O'Neill v Murphy* [1936] NI 16), neither Clark (at pp. 57 to 58) nor Friel (at pp. 106, 112-117) provides a post-1963 example of its application in an Irish court. Had matters remained so, then the type of considerations of precedent which constrained the Court of Appeal in *Re Selectmove* and *Re C* would not have prevented an Irish court reaching a result similar to *Musumeci v Winadell* in an appropriate case. However, *Pinnel's Case* and *Foakes v Beer* have been considered by Kinlen J in *Riordan v Carroll* [1996] 2 ILRM 241 in the second of this year's consideration cases.

Here, a lessor had leased premises to the defendant on August 1, 1993, and later waived rents due in February and March 1994. The plaintiffs in this action are assignees from the lessors, and sought the rent from April 1994. It remained unpaid. In July 1994, the plaintiffs sought, and in March 1995, the plaintiffs obtained, in the Circuit Court an order for possession and arrears and damages for breaches of covenant. The defendant appealed. After the commencement of the appeal, the defendant sought to rely on a document, dated November 11, 1993, which came to light on discovery, alleging that it was a collateral agreement between the defendant and an agent of the lessor which was binding without notice upon the plaintiff, by which the lessor waived rent pending determination of a dispute over dampness. There was an issue as to whether the November 11, 1993 document was admissible, it was conditionally admitted under O. 61, r.8 RSC, but ultimately held inadmissible. Nevertheless, Kinlen J purported to consider its effect.

The plaintiff argued that it was unsupported by fresh consideration from the defendant. Kinlen J considered that the 'rule in *Pinnel's Case* affirmed in *Foakes v Beer* is that when a party to a contract gives up a right under the contract, he is not bound by the waiver unless he has given consideration for it' (referring for support to the headnote of *Foakes v Beer*).

He found as a fact the written agreement did not evidence a wavier of the obligation to pay rent, and even on the evidence adduced by her, the defendant was bound to pay it. Further, even if the document did have the effect alleged by the defendant, he was 'quite satisfied from the evidence that there was no consideration for the document . . . '. It was a simple waiver of rent, a reduction of a debt without consideration, and properly held unenforceable (*Pinnel's Case, Foakes v Beer*). There was nothing on the facts to suggest that the lessors or the plaintiff-assignees received any practical benefit from the waiver; in fact, quite the contrary. Thus, there was nothing upon which to ground an argument based upon *Williams v Roffey*, or PMPA; and nothing in the facts or the holding in *Riordan v Carroll* precludes an Irish court applying them to reach a result such as that in *Musumeci v Winadell*, in which the landlord's market circumstances were such that the receipt of a lower rent from the tenant did in fact constitute a practical benefit.

Finally, in *Riordan v Carroll*, Kinlen J noted that counsel on behalf of the defendant 'argued that in view of the *High Trees* case [*Central London Property Trust v High Trees House* [1947] KB 130] there was an equitable estoppel, even though in writing and with no clear consideration. However, in view of the findings of fact which I have just made, I do not think it necessary to deal with this point.' Certainly, where one party makes a promise which is foreseeably relied upon by another to his detriment, the first party will be held to that promise. Consequently, where a landlord promises a reduction in rent, to the extent that the promise has been foreseeably and detrimentally relied upon by a tenant, the landlord will be held to that promise (as in *High Trees* itself; see also *Musumeci v Winadell*). Thus, the doctrine of estoppel often provides an alternative means of enforcing promises which the doctrine of consideration cannot enforce. Nevertheless, since the (in any event inadmissible) document did not contain a promise to waive the rent, no question of estoppel could arise.

DURESS

The law on duress in the common law world has recently undergone something of a seachange. It used to be thought that for the common law to find duress sufficient to avoid a contract (as opposed to equity finding actual undue influence), there had to be 'duress of the person', such as violence or threats of violence to the plaintiff. Anything less, such as 'duress of goods', though sufficient to order restitution of benefits transferred otherwise than by contract (*Astley v Reynolds* (1731) 2 Str 915), was not sufficient to avoid a contract: this was the rule in *Skeate v Beale* (1841) 11 Ad & E 983. (For criticism, see *e.g.* Beatson [1974] *CLJ* 97; 'Duress, Restitution and Contract Renegotiation' Essay 5 in Beatson, *The Use and Abuse of Unjust Enrichment* (Oxford, 1991) p. 95). However, it has now been accepted that the rule in *Skeate v Beale* was bereft of logic and justification and has been abrogated by the rise of the notion of economic duress; thus, in *The Evia Luck*, Lord Goff recently commented that '[i]t was at one time thought that, at common law, the only form of duress which would entitle a party to avoid a contract on that ground was duress of the person. . . . However, that limitation has been discarded; and it is now accepted that economic pressure may be sufficient to amount to duress for this purpose, . . .' (*Dimskal Shipping Co. v ITWF (No. 2)* [1991] 3 WLR 875, 883); in this context, it is submitted that the test for duress which emerges in the economic duress cases is properly to be understood more generally as the test for duress at law (on this test, note the debate in Atiyah (1982) 98 *LQR* 197; Tipaldy (1983) 99 *LQR* 197; Atiyah (1983) 99 *LQR* 353; Phang (1990) 53 *MLR* 107; Birks [1990] *LMCLQ* 342; Phang (1992) 5 *JCL* 147).

No Irish case has yet made this move in the economic context (though *cf.* Clark, p. 262). However, in family law, the courts have in fact rejected the view that the test for duress is confined to duress of the person (*e.g. M.K. (orse M. McC.) v F. McC.* [1982] ILRM 277; *P.W. v A. O'C. (orse W.)* [1993] 1 IR 324); and since this view is informed by the fact that for this purpose the contract of marriage is no different from any other contract, it is submitted that the conclusions in the family context should apply *mutatis* to the contract context.

Although the Supreme Court could have made such a determination in

O'Donnell v O'Donnell (Supreme Court, 31 March 1995) but it seems that the Court was not minded to take the opportunity thereby presented. Here, two brothers ran a solicitors practice, but fell out. They decided to refer their differences to arbitration, and then settled the arbitration by contract. The plaintiff then alleged that the defendant had procured his consent to that contract of settlement by duress arising from the fact that the plaintiff was 'rather strapped financially and was in a bad way' and that the defendant 'must have known of that, and through delay in making payments and so forth had put him under this sort of pressure' (*per* O'Flaherty J at p. 6). In the High Court, after a hearing before Hamilton P (on 11 and 15 November 1988), the plaintiff's claim was dismissed. On appeal to the Supreme Court, for O'Flaherty J, the 'question to be posed is what more can any court have before it be satisfied that the party has been fully freely independently advised and that he had the services of solicitor and counsel when he made the settlement . . .' (at pp. 5-6). Counsel for the defendant/respondent submitted 'that there was not given any evidence of duress in any legal sense of that term or any form of overbearing conduct or pressure or misrepresentation or any of these indicia of duress that one looks for. None of that is in the case. It seems to be centering [*sic*] on the single matter of the plaintiff's financial weakness'. (at p. 7). It seems, therefore, that in the first sentence quoted here, counsel submitted that duress was limited to the sense contemplated in *Skeate v Beale* (above); it is not clear whether in the second and third sentences, O'Flaherty J was expanding upon counsel's submission or agreeing with it. It is submitted that, in the light of the developments sketched above, it should be read as the former. In the event, O'Flaherty J, in an *ex tempore* judgment, emphatically dismissed the appeal.

EXCLUSION CLAUSES

Incorporation It is a common observation that the courts lean against exclusion clauses. Thus, there is a strict requirement that the clause be incorporated into the contract; such rules of incorporation usually turn on the existence of a course of dealing or on notice, and the rules on notice have been expanded to require harsh exclusion clauses to be brought to the attention of the other party. (For example, in *Spurling v Bradshaw* [1956] 2 All ER 121 and *Thornton v Shoe Lane Parking* [1971] 1 All ER 686 Lord Denning MR required that the exclusion clause be 'printed in red ink . . . with a red hand pointing to it'. See also *Interfoto v Stiletto* [1988] 1 All ER 348 (CA)).

Of course, this requires that there first be an exclusion clause to incorporate; an interesting example of a situation where it was held that the exclusion

198 Annual Review of Irish Law 1995

of liability would have required an exclusion clause but that one was absent, is provided by this year's Supreme Court decision in *Staunton v Toyota (Ireland) Ltd and Fieldhill Investments Ltd* [1996] 1 ILRM 171 (Supreme Court, on appeal from High Court, 15 April 1988, Costello J. Staunton, an employee of Toyota, was injured in an accident at Fieldhill's filling station involving a gas dispenser installed by Flogas. The accident could have been prevented had a protective barrier been installed, but despite discussions between Fieldhill and Flogas, it was not installed. *After* the installation, Fieldhill entered into an agreement with Flogas containing a clause by which Fieldhill agreed to indemnify Flogas in respect of claims 'occasioned by the use of the' dispenser. Staunton recovered in part in a negligence action against Toyota and Fieldhill, and Fieldhill sought contribution from Flogas. The contribution claim raised issues under the Civil Liability Act, 1961. Flogas also sought to argue that the indemnity clause operated to exclude their liability to Fieldhill. Costello J held that, since the injury to Staunton had occurred because he had reversed into the dispenser, the injury was not occasioned by its 'use'. Counsel for Flogas argued that the clause in its entirety was capable of application to the facts, and O'Flaherty J seemed to agree that this interpretation would be open. However, Costello J had also held that 'insofar as the case was made that Flogas was negligent in not providing a barrier, . . . this omission predated the contract, and if Flogas wished to exclude liability for such negligence there should have been an express stipulation dealing with it' (as explained by O'Flaherty J: [1996] 1 ILRM 171, 180) and with this holding O'Flaherty J agreed. In the absence of a clear and express exclusion clause, there was no basis upon which to avoid liability in tort.

Contra proferentem If there is an exclusion clause which has been validly incorporated, it is nevertheless subject to a strict *contra proferentem* reading; though on occasion it may be felt that the interpretation strains the language of the clause too much (see the criticism of strained construction by Lord Diplock in *Photo Productions v Securicor* [1980] 1 All ER 556 and Lord Wilberforce in *Ailsa Craig v Malvern Fishing* [1983] 1 All ER 101). *Lynch v Lynch* [1996] 1 ILRM 311 provides a good example of the application of the *contra proferentem* rule.

Mr Lynch owned and insured a van, his daughter borrowed the van to go to work. After she got out, the handbrake failed, the car rolled, and injured Ms Lynch in circumstances for which Mr Lynch was found liable (in tort). Ms Lynch sought to proceed against her father's insurance company, pursuant to the terms of section 76 of the Road Traffic Act, 1961 which allows the injured party to execute judgment against the insured's insurer. Section 76(3) however allows this action if the accident happened in a 'public place'; the accident occurred in the car park of the factory in which Ms Lynch worked; but Costello P held that because the car park was used by employees and customers of, and suppliers and visitors to, customers of, the factory, and also by spectators at matches at the nearby football ground and by farmers going to the nearby mart, when accident occurred, the car park was a public place. The insurance company was thus *prima facie* liable on the insurance policy, but the policy contained an exclusion clause, providing that it would not be liable for death of or injury to 'the person driving or in charge for the purpose of driving' of the van.

Costello P construed the clause as 'intended to except the company from liability to a person making a claim under the policy who was physically driving the vehicle at the time when the accident giving rise to the claim occurred or who was in charge physically of the vehicle for the purposes of driving it when the accident occurred'. Consequently, he did not think that 'the exclusion clause was intended to exclude liability to a person who had suffered injury after she had left the vehicle; such a person was no longer physically in charge of it for the purposes of driving it'. This narrow reading of the exclusion clause — though Costello P did not describe it as such — is an excellent example of a *contra proferentem* reading of such a clause. Indeed, that rule is even more strictly applied in the case of personal injury; and it might be said that such a policy underlies Costello P's decision. A similar policy is to be found in *White v John Warwick* [1953] 2 All ER 1021; the plaintiff hired a bicycle from the defendant, the contract provided that nothing 'shall render the owners liable for any personal injuries'. As the plaintiff rode the bicycle, the saddle tilted, she was thrown from it and injured. The Court of Appeal held that although the term excluded liability in contract, it did not exclude liability in tort, and that the defendants were in breach of their duty to take reasonable care. Nevertheless, a well-drafted exclusion clause will operate to exclude such personal liability, as occurred, for example, in *Regan v RIAC* [1990] 1 IR 278 (see the 1989 Review, pp. 126-7).

Fundamental breach   No term has been more misunderstood in the law of contract than the phrase 'fundamental breach'. It has been deployed in the context of exclusion clauses and in the context of termination for breach, and in each case it has an entirely separate meaning.

Fundamental breach and exclusion clauses   In the context of exclusion clauses, it arises as follows: A is in serious and flagrant breach of his contract with B. B sues. A sets up an exclusion clause as a defence. On one view, if the breach is sufficiently serious, A should never be allowed to set up an exclusion clause. In the language of the cases, if A has committed a *fundamental breach* of his contract, it should be a *rule of law* that he cannot rely on his exclusion clause. On another view, and in reaction against this, it has been argued that it should be a matter of interpretation as to whether the exclusion clause actually covers the breach or not. In the language of the cases, the rule is that if, as a matter of construction (interpretation) it is clear that the exclusion clause covers the breach, then it should be allowed to operate. The former approach is called the 'rule of law' approach, the latter, the 'construction' approach. In England, in *Karsales v Wallis* [1956] 1 WLR 936, London Denning MR unambiguously championed the 'rule of law' approach. In *Suisse Atlantique* [1967] 1 AC 361 the House of Lords sought to abandon it, suggesting in effect that it is a matter of 'construction', though their language was ambiguous. In *Harbutts Plasticine v Wayne Tank* [1970] 1 QB 447 Lord Denning MR tried to resurrect the 'rule of law' approach, taking advantage of the ambiguity in *Suisse Atlantique*: but in *Photo Productions v Securicor* [1980] 1 All ER 556, their Lordships finally buried the 'rule of law' approach, a position they affirmed in *George Mitchell (Chesterhall) v Finney Locke Seeds* [1983] 1 All ER 108 (CA); [1983] 2 All ER 737 (HL).

In Ireland, in *Clayton Love v B&I Transport* (1970) ILTR 157 the Supreme Court embraced the rule of law approach (note, however, that Dr Forde argues that the Supreme Court in here in fact 'obliquely endorsed' the construction view (Forde, *Commercial Law in Ireland* (Dublin, 1990) p. 28)). Nevertheless, Prof Clark writes that *Photo Productions* and some later High Court *dicta*, 'will no doubt cause the Supreme court to reconsider its own approach in Clayton Love' (Clark, p. 149; *cp*. Clark and Clarke, *Contract, Cases and Materials* (Dublin, 1995) p. 357). However, it is submitted that this does not necessarily follow. The actual reasons given by the House of Lords in *Suisse Atlantique*, *Photo Productions*, and *George Mitchell*, for transcending the 'rule of law' approach are important: primarily, their Lordships recognised that the approach had merit, but that subsequently statute had provided a better approach to that issue. Thus, Lord Wilberforce in *Photo Productions* wrote that the 'doctrine of "fundamental breach", despite its imperfections and doubtful parentage, has served a useful purpose. There were a large number of problems, productive of injustice, in which it was worse than unsatisfactory to leave exception clauses to operate. . . . But since then, Parliament has taken a hand: it has passed the Unfair Contract Terms Act 1977' (1980) 1 All ER 556, 561). Similarly, the terms of the Sale of Goods Act, 1979 were in issue in *George Mitchell*. The equivalent Irish statutes, the Sale of Goods Act, 1893 and the Sale of Goods and Supply of Services Act, 1980 simply do not have the same reach or breadth as the

English statutes: the Irish legislation only covers consumer contracts for the sale of goods, a definition which has a large exclusionary effect, whereas the English 1977 Act covers *all* contracts. Thus, in *British Leyland Exports v Brittain Manufacturing*, which was not a consumer contract, the defendant succeeded in relying on its exclusion clause, and O'Hanlon J observed that 'in the absence of legislation similar to the Unfair Contract Terms Act, 1977, the fairness or unfairness of the contract is not a matter with which the Court should concern itself . . . '. ([1981] IR 335, 345). In the absence of such statutory protection, the justification for the abandonment of the 'rule of law' approach disappears. Presumably, now, however, the control of exclusion clauses in the *Unfair Contract Terms Directive* (Council Directive 93/13/EEC of 5 April 1993 would be sufficient to allow the abandonment of the rule of law approach, but this is a matter for final testing in an appropriate case.

Fundamental breach and termination A breach of contract does not of itself have the effect of terminating the contract. If the breach is not of a sufficiently serious term (usually described as a warranty), the contract remains on foot, and the innocent party has the right to recover damages. If the breach is of a sufficiently serious term, the innocent party can choose whether to terminate or to affirm the contract: 'in this context, 'fundamental breach' is used to describe a breach of contract which is sufficiently serious to entitle the injured party to repudiate the contract; this has nothing to do with the vexed question of the applicability of an exception clause after fundamental breach . . .' (Clark, p. 415). A similar conclusion seems to have been reached by Morris J in *Parkarran v M&P Construction* (High Court, 9 November 1995).

The basic question at issue in this case was whether an arbitration clause, in a contract terminated by (repudiatory) breach, was nonetheless enforceable notwithstanding the termination. Morris J held that it was (citing *Heyman v Darwins* [1942] AC 356(HL); on this point see the Repudiation section of this chapter, below pp. 228-32). It seems that in *Parkarran*, it was argued 'that *Clayton Love v B&I Shipping* should be taken as authority to contradict the principles enunciated in *Heyman v Darwins* . . . '. Presumably, this reference to *Clayton Love* can be taken as a reference to the treatment by the Supreme Court of the issue of fundamental breach. If so, it should be remembered that the treatment of fundamental breach in that case was in context of exclusion clauses; and the phrase fundamental breach has a different meaning there than it has in the context of repudiatory breach which was the context of *Parkarran*. Therefore, since they are about different things, there is nothing in *Clayton Love* to contradict *Heyman*. Consequently, Morris J held that he did not accept that Clayton contradicted *Heyman*.

FAILURE OF CONSIDERATION

Where a contract is void (such as by frustration, or *ultra vires*), then any benefits which have been transferred under the contract can be recovered as having been transferred for a consideration which has failed. In the immediately preceding section, it was pointed out that the phrase 'fundamental breach' is used by the common law in at least two senses. Likewise with the phrase 'consideration'. In one sense, it means that which is given and received under a contract: the price of a promise, or the promise itself (see above p. 183). However, as is clear since the decision of the House of Lords in *Fibrosa Spolka Akcynja v Fairbairn Lawson Combe Barbour* [1943] AC 32, in the context of the doctrine of failure of consideration, it has an entirely distinct meaning: 'when one is considering the law of failure of consideration and of the quasi-contractual right to recover money on that ground, it is generally speaking, not the promise which is referred to as the consideration, but the performance of that promise. The money was paid to secure performance, and, if performance fails, the inducement which brought about the payment is not fulfilled.' ([1943] AC 32, 47 *per* Lord Simon). Thus, 'there was no intent to enrich [the defendant] in the events which have happened' . . . The payment was originally conditional. The condition of retaining it is eventual performance. Accordingly, when that condition fails, the right to retain the money must simultaneously fail. ([1943] AC 32, 64-65 *per* Lord Wright). The Supreme Court adopted this approach in *United Dominions Trust v Shannon Caravans* [1976] IR 225: '. . . where a plaintiff has paid money in pursuance of his obligations under a contract and the consideration for which he entered into the contract totally fails, he may bring an action for the return of the money so paid (as money had and received to his use) . . . ' ([1976] IR 225, 231 *per* Griffin J).

Thus, it is clear that the doctrine of consideration is a doctrine of the law of contract, whereas the doctrine of failure of consideration is a doctrine of the law of restitution (cp *Fibrosa, supra, passim*; *Baltic Shipping v Dillon (The Mikhail Lermontov)* (1993) 176 CLR 344, 375-376; *Dublin Corporation v Building and Allied Trade Union* [1996] 2 ILRM 547, 558 *per* Keane J). Indeed, given that the rationale of the latter doctrine is that if a benefit is transferred on a basis which has failed it may be recovered back in the law of restitution, the doctrine has been described as a 'failure of basis' (see *e.g.* Burrows pp. 252), and if this description were adopted as the title for the restitutionary cause of action, it would have the welcome effect of diverting attention away from the unfortunate possible elision of the two separate senses of the word 'consideration'.

The best example of such a failure of basis occurs where a party pays to receive title to property but fails to receive it. The failure to transfer title is a breach of contract sufficiently serious to terminate a contract, and once the contract has been so rescinded, the payor can recover back the purchase price or instalments as having been paid upon a basis (consideration) which has failed. Thus, in *Rowland v Divall* [1923] 2 KB 500, the plaintiff had purchased a stolen car from the defendant, and sued to recover his purchase price; Atkin LJ held that 'the buyer has not received any part of that which he contracted to receive — namely, the property and right to possession — and, that being so, there has been a total failure of consideration.' ([1923] 2 KB 500, 506; see also *Butterworth v Kingsway Motors* [1954] 1 WLR 1286; *United Dominions Trust v Shannon Caravans* [1976] IR 225; and *Chartered Trust v Healy* (High Court, 10 December 1985, Barron J) in all of which the relevant failure of basis was the failure to give title.

An excellent example of such failure of basis is provided by the decision of Barron J in *Woodchester Investments v O'Driscoll* (High Court, July 27, 1995). Here, P had bought a stolen horsebox from D1. Barron J held that, clearly, P 'got nothing for his money. There was total failure of consideration. He is accordingly entitled to recover his money from the person or persons with whom he purported to contract as principal or principals' (at p. 3). He held that D1 was entirely innocent of the fraud and had acted as agent for D4 (who was solely responsible for the scheme), and thus that D4 was liable to P.

As to the liability of D4 and D1's consequent defence, in *Holland v Russell* (1861) 1 B&S 424; *affd* (1863) 4 B&S 14 it was held that when money is paid to an agent in circumstances in which the payor has a cause of action in restitution to recover the money, and the agent, without notice of that claim bona fide pays on to his principal, the liability of the agent ceases and the claim can only be brought against the principal. (On the agent's defence in such circumstances, see *e.g.* Goff and Jones, *The Law of Restitution* (4th ed, Sweet & Maxwell, London, 1993) p. 750). 'Various explanations have traditionally been put forward. It is sometimes said that the receipt of the agent is the receipt of the principal, so that by the receipt the agent is not enriched. Elsewhere it is thought to be an early manifestation of the defence of change of position. Another explanation focuses on the fact that in receiving the benefit from the plaintiff and paying it over to his principal, the agent is merely performing his duty to his principal. A fourth looks to agent's assumption of responsibility and justifies the immunity on the basis that the agent undertakes no liability to anyone other than his principal. . . . [A fifth] reason for the defence is that the plaintiff is in certain circumstances estopped from bringing a claim against an agent who has done no more than follow his (the plaintiff's) instructions and make a payment over to his principal.' (Swadling, 'The Nature of Ministerial Receipt' in Birks (ed.), *Laundering and Tracing* (Oxford, 1995) 243, 243-244). On whatever basis the defence of an agent who has paid over may be justified, it would seem clearly to have been properly applied on the facts of *Woodchester Investments v O'Driscoll.*

However, in this regard, Burrows has pointed out that there are in fact two separate lines of authority on this issue. On one view, 'only the principal can be sued in restitution: it does not matter whether the principal received the money or not, because payment to the agent constitutes payment to the principal' (p. 481). On the other view, the agent may be sued unless he has 'in good faith paid the money over to his principal, or done something equivalent' (*id.*, p. 482), such as spending on the principal's behalf and with his authority, but only where the principal is a disclosed principal. Barron J's treatment does not clearly separate out these issues. On the first view, D1's receipt as agent is sufficient to afford D1 with a defence and make D4 liable. However, on the second view that the agent is personally liable to the plaintiff unless he has paid over to the disclosed principal or done something equivalent, the facts of Woodchester are rather more problematic. Here, after receipt, D1 the agent had applied the proceeds to debts owed by D4 the principal to D1, D3 and D5. Barron J held that they 'received the moneys . . . as creditors of' D4. Such payments constitute the equivalent of payment over to the principal (as in *Holland v Russell* (above)); however, there is little in the judgment from which to discern whether D1 had disclosed that D4 was his principal, indeed there is a dispute as to whether he identified someone else as the principal, and Barron J held that he did not. Thus, Barron J's judgment is consistent with the first of Burrows' views, and is difficult to accommodate within the second. For what it is worth, therefore, it must be regarded as an Irish authority in favour of a broad defence of ministerial receipt.

ILLEGALITY

Illegal and *ultra vires* contracts　　The line between an *ultra vires* contract and an illegal contract is a difficult one to draw, but it is a necessary one. An *ultra vires* contract is one which is beyond the capacity of the contracting party, an illegal contract is one which is contrary to public policy. Although in neither case is such a contract enforceable, there is a range of remedies available in the context of *ultra vires* contracts which may not be available in the context of illegal contracts. Thus, an estoppel may arise on the facts of an *ultra vires* contract, or a party who transferred benefit under such a contract may be able to recover such benefits in the law of restitution (see e.g., *In re PMPA (Longmile) Garage (No. 2)* [1992] 1 IR 332, [1992] ILRM 349, O'Dell, 'Estoppel and *Ultra Vires* Contracts' (1992) 14 *DULJ (ns)* 123; and the 1992 Review, pp. 48-51). Such remedies may and usually will not be available in the context of illegal contracts. Thus, Dodd J in *O'Hehir v Cahill* (1912) 97 ILTR 274, 276 (in a decision expressly affirmed on appeal) observed that:

> The ambiguity in the word illegal has frequently been pointed out. It is not 'illegal' to lend beyond powers, in the sense that it is 'illegal' to enter into a gambling transaction. Out of a transaction that is illegal in the one sense, no action can arise. But out of a transaction that is illegal in the sense of being *ultra vires*, rights both legal and equitable may arise.

The line is relatively easy to draw when a statute or a common law rule is the source of the illegality and a constituent document such as a company's memorandum and articles of association are the reason why an action is *ultra vires*. It is less easy to draw where a statute is the relevant source of *vires*, such as is the case with a statutory corporation.

It is clear that a statutory corporation has only those powers stated in the statute or those necessarily and properly required for carrying into effect the purposes of incorporation. What the statute does not so expressly or impliedly authorise is beyond the corporation's powers. Thus, in *Huntsgrove Developments v Meath Co. Co.* [1994] 2 ILRM 36 (see the 1993 Review, pp. 19, 28, 427-428), Lardner J held, *inter alia*, that the Council did have the power to accept, from a third party not a party to the proceedings, a gift; it 'was not unlawful or *ultra vires* merely because it was received by the planning authority without specific statutory authority' ([1994] 2 ILRM 36, 54). This finding of *vires* seems questionable both as a matter of logic and as a matter of authority (compare *Howard v Commissioners for Public Works* [1994] 1 IR 101 (especially the decision of Costello J in the High Court); see the 1993 Review, pp. 430-434). Nevertheless, the same test for the vires of local authorities as statutory corporations as commended itself to the House of Lords in *Hazell v Hammersmith and Fulham LBC* [1992] 2 AC 1 is applied both by Lardner J in *Huntsgrove* and by Murphy J in *Keane v An Bord Pleanála* (High Court, October 4, 1995, Murphy J), the decision of the Supreme Court on appeal will be discussed in the 1996 Review).

However, if a statute is the source of the capacity of a statutory corporation, action by the corporation *ultra vires* could be represented as an action contrary to the terms of a statute, and on the basis of such a representation, the line between *ultra vires* and illegality becomes more difficult to draw. Precisely this distinction was at the heart of the Supreme Court decision of Egan J (Hamilton CJ, O'Flaherty J concurring) in *Foras Áiseanna Soathair and The Minister for Social Welfare v Abbott and Ryan* (Supreme Court, May 23, 1995). Here, an Appeals Officer determined that Abbot and Ryan would be entitled to social welfare payments if their contracts of employment had been *intra vires* FÁS. This matter was submitted to the High Court, where Lardner J held that their contracts were not *ultra vires*; but that they were in fact illegal, in that they infringed a statutory prohibition against FÁS entering into contracts for the appointment of staff without the consent of the Minister, and that the illegality was such that the Appeals Officer could not regard it 'as competent for the purposes of the Social Welfare legislation'. Abbott and Ryan appealed, and Egan J for the Supreme Court held that the contracts were not illegal. As this was the only matter appealed against, it followed that Lardner J's finding that the contracts were not *ultra vires* meant that the contracts were not void either for illegality or as *ultra vires*; thus the contracts were valid and the Appeals Officer could determine their claim. (Note, however, that as a matter of authority, it is clear (*pace* the High Court in this case) that to do an act that requires ministerial consent without such consent is to act *ultra vires: Hennessy v NAIDA* [1947] IR 159).

On the issue of whether the contract was in fact illegal, Egan J held that it 'would be unusual to find a term rendering contracts illegal nestling amongst provisions dealing with the capacity, functions powers and duties of a . . . statutory corporation. It would seem that if [the section] is to have the effect of avoiding contracts, it must be with respect to the question of capacity of the corporation' rather than with the legality of the contract (at p. 19; Egan J's emphasis). On the line between *ultra vires* and illegality, Egan J was of the opinion that:

> a distinction must be drawn between illegal acts and *ultra vires* acts. This distinction must flow from the discretion the Court enjoys in relation to each. If a contract is expressly or impliedly prohibited by statute, the Court will not enforce the contract. . . . the general principle is that where a contract is found to be illegal, whether by reason of the fact that its object is the committing of an illegal act or that it is expressly or impliedly prohibited by statute, it will not be recognised at law. . . . The situation as regards *ultra vires* acts somewhat more complicated. Although, such acts are clearly void *ab initio* and destitute of all legal effect, it may happen in practice that the validity of the void act may be immune from challenge. (at pp. 8-9)

Thus far, there is little to choose between this decision and the principles set out above. Thus, at private law, if a contract is illegal, it is void, and cannot be enforced, and no other judicial remedy is normally available; whereas, if a contract is simply *ultra vires*, although it is void and cannot be enforced, other judicial remedies such as restitution are normally available. Consequently, these principles apply to actions commenced by summons. A contract *ultra vires* a statutory corporation is of the same quality as a contract *ultra vires* a company, and if a private law action commenced by summons is commenced against such a company, these principles will apply.

At public law, it would seem that the same distinctions between illegal and *ultra vires* contracts can *prima facie* be drawn. However, a plaintiff in a public law action must seek a remedy in judicial review under Order 84 (RSC), such remedies are available in theory as a matter of discretion; and it seems from this judgment that even if a plaintiff would be entitled to an Order 84 remedy consequent upon a determination that a statutory corporation acted *ultra vires*, that remedy may be refused in the exercise of the judge's discretion. Citing the decision of the Supreme Court in *Minister for Education v RTC Letterkenny* [1995] 1 ILRM 438 (see the 1994 Review, 235), Egan J observed that a remedy under Order 84, such as *certiorari*, is discretionary, and continued that, in this public law context, the effect:

> of the discretionary nature of the remedies in respect of an *ultra vires* contract entered into by a statutory corporation forms the basis of a distinction between illegal contracts and *ultra vires* contracts. Although, it may be only rarely that the Court will exercise its discretion to refuse a remedy sought, it is this element of uncertainty which discounts any reliance on the *ultra vires* nature of a contract on the part of the Appeals Officer. It would clearly be anomalous were the Appeals Officer to be in a position to treat as invalid a contract, which the Court in its discretion might refuse to invalidate. It may very well be that a Court would be reluctant to grant the relief sought in such a case as this where the statutory corporation, in effect, is attempting to profit from its action in entering into an allegedly *ultra vires* contract, by denying it was required to make contributions under the Social Welfare Legislation. It would be particularly harsh were an employee to lose his statutory rights through no fault of his own. . . .
>
> Judicial review remedies, such as, for example, prohibition and *mandamus*, might lie in the case of an *ultra vires* contract but might not be available in the context of entering into an illegal contract. (pp. 12-13)

Thus, at public law, since remedies are discretionary, a court might exercise its discretion to refuse a declaration that a contract is *ultra vires* a statutory corporation, or to refuse a remedy of *certiorari*, *mandamus* or prohibition consequent upon a finding that a contract is *ultra vires* a statutory corporation. Importantly, such discretion is relevant only in the public law context; it would be quite wrong to characterise the available remedies at private law for *ultra vires* contracts (referred to above) as similarly discretionary. It would not, however, be inappropriate to say that a measure of discretion is open to a court in the context of illegal contracts at private law; this was one of the issues which was before Costello P in *Shield Life Insurance v Ulster Bank* [1995] 3 IR 225 (immediately below).

Discretion and remedies for illegal contracts If a plaintiff's claim is founded in an illegality or is contrary to public policy, then a defendant can raise this illegality since the court will not lend its aid to such a claim. However, in recent years, to this orthodoxy there has grown up a discretionary exception, by which, if such a defence was relied upon, the court should look beyond the fact of the illegality to the *quality* of the illegality relied upon and the proximity of the illegal conduct to the plaintiff's claim, to determine whether there was an illegality of which the court should take notice, and if there was, whether by affording the plaintiff the relief sought, it would affront the public conscience more than by refusing it. This 'public conscience' test was extensively analysed in the 1993 Review pp. 179-189; here it is sufficient to observe that it seems first to have been articulated by Hutchinson J in the High Court in *Thackwell v Barclays Bank* [1986] 1 All ER 676, where a claim for conversion was dismissed, but only after an enquiry into the substance of the plaintiff's fraud, and not simply on the basis of the plaintiff's implication in the illegality. A similar issue presented itself for resolution by Costello P in *Shield Life Insurance v Ulster Bank* [1995] 3 IR 225.

A fraudulent insurance broker had, without the plaintiff's knowledge, diverted to his accounts with the defendant bank, cheques payable to the plaintiff. The plaintiff claimed that the bank was liable in negligence for breach of its duty to the plaintiff and for the conversion of the cheques; Costello P agreed (on this, see the Tort law chapter, below, pp. 536-7; on conversion of a cheque, *cf.* the contrary view of Lord Templeman in *Lipkin Gorman v Karpnale* [1991] 2 AC 548 (HL) and note the trenchant critique of this view in Watts (1991) 107 *LQR* 521). The defendant bank then claimed that 'even though the plaintiff may have been the payee of the cheque and was deprived of its proceeds by the broker's fraud, and even though it was completely innocent of any wrongdoing, and even though the bank may have been [liable to the plaintiff] . . . the court should refuse the plaintiff's claim on the grounds of public policy, the grounds of public policy being the application of the doctrine *ex turpi causa non oritur actio*' ([1995] 3 IR 225, 236), a claim which Costello P confessed to finding 'most startling' (*id.*) and which the defendants advanced on foot of *Thackwell v Barclays Bank*. Costello P held:

In *Thackwell v Barclays Bank* the court agreed that when the doctrine [of *ex turpi causa non oritur actio*] was invoked its task was firstly (a) to look at the proximity of the illegal conduct relied on by the defendant with the claim maintained by the plaintiff and then (b) 'consider whether there are other considerations which as a matter of public policy ought to effect the plaintiff's right to recover' (at p. 687). The court concluded that the plaintiff was not entitled to recover in conversion against the bank because the cheque alleged to have been converted constituted in reality the very proceeds of the fraudulent conduct established in the case and judge expressed the view that 'by permitting Mr Thackwell recover the proceeds of this cheque from the bank I should, as it seems to me, be indirectly assisting in the commission of a crime' (p. 689) and as a matter of public policy he declared [that the defendant] would not have been entitled to relief. I can find no considerations of public policy in this case which would justify a refusal of the plaintiff's claim should negligence be established. Certainly the court would not be assisting in the commission of a crime by so doing, because it would, by awarding damages, be ordering the return of stolen money. The court's order would in effect compensate the payee of a cheque which had, as a matter of the application of common law principles, been converted by the collecting bank. This defence must therefore fail. ([1995] 3 IR 225, 237)

With respect, this must be right. The defence advanced on behalf of the bank, at least as characterised by Costello P, amounted to the proposition that since there was fraud on the facts, the plaintiff's claim arose *ex turpi causa*. However, here, the plaintiff had been the *victim* of the fraud, not the perpetrator; if the defence had succeeded, it would have amounted to the proposition that since a victim of a fraud is implicated in the fraud, the victim's cause of action in respect of that fraud is tainted in illegality, which would have had the effect of precluding a victim of fraud from suing on foot of the fraud. Since this is a plainly absurd conclusion, the proposition from which it derives must be rejected, as Costello P did.

In the 1993 Review, it was argued that 'there is abundant evidence that there is an evolving flexibility of judicial attitudes to illegality' (p. 188); the decision of Costello P in *Shield Life Insurance v Ulster Bank* surely provides further support to that argument.

IMPLIED TERMS

In *Gilheaney v The Revenue Commissioners* (High Court, October 4, 1995) it was submitted on behalf of the applicant that one of the terms of the alleged contract was implied rather than express, but nothing turned on this as Costello P held that the respondent had made no offer capable of acceptance by the applicant. In *Sepes Establishment v KSK Enterprises* [1993] 2 IR 225; [1993] ILRM 46 O'Hanlon J considered, *inter alia*, the implication of terms to give business efficacy to a contract (see [1993] 2 IR 225, 233-234; 1992 Review pp. 413-414; the decision of the Supreme Court (May 21, 1996) on appeal from O'Hanlon J will be analysed in next year's review). And the *Unfair Contract Terms Directive* (Council Directive 93/13/EEC of 5 April 1993) will take effect as a strengthening of the protection afforded by the Sale of Goods and Supply of Services Act, 1980 — the main thrust of that Act is to imply terms protective of consumers into consumer contracts, the main thrust of the Directive is remove terms inimical to the interests of consumers from consumer contracts. However, in *Carna Foods v Eagle Star Insurance Co.* [1995] 1 IR 526; [1995] 2 ILRM 474 McCracken J rejected the plaintiff's claim that there was implied, in their contract of insurance with the defendant, a term by which the defendant had a duty to give reasons if it chose to cancel certain insurance policies and to gave notice that it would not renew others.

McCracken J acknowledged that, in certain circumstances, there may be a duty to give reasons for administrative decisions subject to judicial review (referring to *State (Daly) v Minister for Agriculture* [1987] IR 165; [1988] ILRM 173), but he held that this duty does not extend to a purely contractual relationship such as that in the present case (referring to *Glover v BLN* [1973] IR 388 and *Rajah v Royal College of Surgeons* [1994] 1 IR 384; [1994] 1 ILRM 233; see the 1993 Review, pp. 12, 17-18, 30). As to whether the alleged duty to give reasons could arise from a term implied into the contract, McCracken J set out both the 'business efficacy' test and the 'officious bystander' test, and observed that the latter 'probably amounts to the same thing' as the former (though cf Clark, p. 116; Treitel, p. 186).

As to the 'business efficacy' test, McCracken J cited the well-known words of Bowen LJ in *The Moorcock* (1889) 14 PD 64, 68 that a term may be implied 'from the presumed intention of the parties with the object of giving the transaction such efficacy as both parties must have intended that at all events it should have' (*cp. Luxor (Eastbourne) v Cooper* [1941] AC 108, 137 *per* Lord Wright). As to the 'officious bystander' test, McCracken J cited the well-known words of MacKinnon LJ in *Shirlaw v Southern Foundries*:

> *Prima facie*, that which in any contract is left to be implied and need not be expressed is something so obvious that it goes without saying; so that, if while the parties making their bargain, an officious bystander were to suggest some express provision for it in the agreement, they would testily suppress him with a common 'Oh, of course'. ([1939] 2 KB 206, 227; *affd* [1940] AC 701).

In so doing, McCracken was following a well-trodden path. In *Tradax v Irish Grain Board*, O'Higgins CJ (Hederman J concurring) set out the passages from *The Moorcock* and *Shirlaw*, and cautioned that the power to imply terms 'must be exercised with care. The Courts have no role in acting as contract makers' ([1984] IR 1, 14). Again, in *Grehan v NEHB* [1989] IR 422 Costello J likewise referred to both tests and counselled caution in the implication of a term. Such terms are implied in fact, to represent the presumed intentions of the parties to the contract. Consequently, give the primacy of the intentions of the parties themselves, a court will not imply a term simply because it is reasonable to do so (*e.g. Trollope & Colls v NW Metropolitan HB* [1973] 1 WLR 601, 609). It 'is not the function of a court to write a contract for parties who have met upon commercially equal terms; if such parties want to enter into unreasonable, unfair, or even disastrous contracts, that is their business, not the business of the courts' (*Tradax v Irish Grain Board* [1984] IR 1, 26 *per* McCarthy J (dissenting on the application of an agreed principle to the facts)).

> fail to see how either test could possibly apply in the present case. Cancellation clauses have been commonplace in insurance policies of this nature for a long time and it has never been suggested that there is any obligation to give reasons for a cancellation. I cannot see what business efficacy is to be given to the transaction by giving reasons. Nor can I see why the bystander should assume that there would be any such terms. Long-standing clauses in policies have the advantage of certainty. To seek to imply terms into them seems to me only to create uncertainty and I would not do so unless the clause had created problems for interpretation, which does not arise here.

Thus, from the perspective of the law of contract, there was no basis upon which to imply as a matter of fact, a term into the insurance contract, that an insurer must give the insured reasons for the exercise of a cancellation clause. Although such a clause may be said to be reasonable, as was pointed out above, a term is implied into a contract, not because it is reasonable, but because it represents the presumed intentions of the parties.

McCracken J also reached a similar conclusion on the basis of ss. 4 and 5 of the Competition Act, 1991, but his conclusions on refusal to supply must now be read in the light of the decision of Carroll J in *A&N v United Drug Wholesalers* [1996] 2 ILRM 42.

OFFER AND ACCEPTANCE

Analysing the process of negotiations   The rules of offer and acceptance, though described as 'a rather technical and schematic doctrine of contract' (*New Zealand Shipping v Satterthwaite (The Eurymedon)* [1975] AC 154 *per* Lord Wilberforce), are the basis of law's analysis of the process of the parties' negotiations. Many recent important cases have turned on this basic point of whether certain negotiations have, on the facts, amounted to a contract (see, for example, *Pernod Ricard v FII Fyffes plc* (High Court, October 21, 1988; Supreme Court, November 11, 1988; see the 1988 Review p. 133) and *Aga Kahn v Firestone* [1992] ILRM 31 (see the 1991 Review, p. 115)). This was the issue in two of this year's cases, the decision of Murphy J in *AIB v ICC and Mech-Con* (High Court, October 4, 1995) and that of Carroll J in *Hanley v Someport-Walon* [1995] 2 IR 132.

In *AIB v ICC and Mech-Con*, as a consequence of dealings between 1985 and 1989, it seemed that Mech-Con had given ICC a charge over certain property (Millstream House) in substitution for a charge over other property (Raffeen), and then gave a charge to AIB over assets including Raffeen. When Mech-Con's business deteriorated, on January 24, 1991, ICC wrote to AIB to 'confirm ICC's agreement to AIB taking security over . . . Raffeen . . . subject to ICC's security retaining priority for a figure up to £100,000 . . . '. On January 30, 1991, ICC wrote to AIB to advise that it was 'not in a position to release the security . . . over . . . Raffeen . . . '. By fax to ICC on February 1, 1991, AIB referred to ICC's letter of January 24 'agreeing to AIB holding security over Mech-Con's . . . property at Raffeen . . . subject to [ICC] retaining priority for a figure of up to £100,000 . . . '.

The basic question in the case seems to have been whether this 1991 correspondence amounted to a contract. Although ICC argued, *inter alia*, that the letter of the 25th was not an offer 'but a mere statement of intent', and that if there was an agreement it was 'made as a result of a common mistake in as much as both parties had acted under the erroneous belief that the Company had provided ICC with the additional security required by it', and despite difficulties of determination, Murphy J held that the letter of January 24 embodied a valid compromise of the rights of ICC and AIB, on the basis that the more probable interpretation of the bargain between the parties was that AIB sought confirmation from the ICC that a charge was available to AIB.

For Murphy J, ICC 'had to know that AIB had been promised a full release of the charge on the Raffeen lands more than two years previously. Not only had that promise been made but all the administrative work necessary to fulfil it had been implemented.' On December 12, 1989, a solicitor for Mech-Con wrote to AIB to confirm that the ICC 'charge . . .

[could] be released subject to the alternative security . . . being put in place';
the solicitor also wrote to the solicitor for AIB that Mech-Con had 'agreed
with the ICC that this charge can now be released'. The release was ultimately
signed on March 14, 1990, but not delivered to the Registrar of Titles.
Furthermore, ICC had 'intended to take other security and had satisfied itself
as to the value therefor. In fact [ICC] was being asked in some form or
another, will ICC do now what is said more than two years ago it would do?
Not only was that the question but in substance the reply was "We will; but
having regard to the changed circumstances we want to retain the first
£100,00 of the proceeds of the lands at Raffeen as part of our security." It
seems to me that the banking executives were effecting a sensible bargain
which would operate as an immediate binding agreement in the commercial
interests of both parties.'

Contracts and Conflicts In *Unidare v Scott* [1991] 2 IR 88 (see the 1991
Review pp. 87-88) the question before the Supreme Court was as to whether
a jurisdiction clause had been incorporated into a contract created by four
telexes passing between the parties. Such questions implicate issues of offer
and acceptance for Contract law (has the clause been offered and accepted?)
as well as issues of jurisdiction for Conflicts. A similar scenario presented
itself to Carroll J in *Hanley v Someport-Walon* [1995] 2 IR 132.

The plaintiffs claimed that they made an agreement with the first defendant on April 22, 1991 in relation to shipping certain cargo from June 3 to
7, 1991. Problems arose on June 5, in respect of which the plaintiff issued a
plenary summons June 24, 1991, claiming that the agreement contained a
clause conferring jurisdiction upon the courts of Ireland. The agreement was
derived from a series of telexes faxes sent by MIT on behalf of the plaintiffs
to the first defendants and back from February 14, 1991 to April 22, 1991
when MIT sent a telex to the first defendant setting out their proposed terms
of a booking form.

The dispute having arisen, on June 13, 1991 MIT on behalf of the plaintiff
faxed to the first defendant 'a *pro forma* booking note dated April 22,
1991 . . . but only the front side of it. . . . The conditions printed on the reverse
side of the first page were not faxed.' And on June 24, 1991, MIT posted to
the first defendant for signature 'an original conline booking note still dated
April 24, 1991. . . with the terms of the carriers' bill of lading included for
the first time . . .' but this was not received by the first defendant until July
1, 1991. From the judgment, it seems that the jurisdiction clause upon which
the plaintiff sought to rely was not mentioned in the terms agreed on April
22, 1991, it was contained on the reverse side of the pro forma booking note
(that part which had not been faxed), and was first brought to the attention
of the first defendant when the original booking note was posted. In these

circumstances, Carroll J held that:

> the plaintiffs have not proved a consensus on the inclusion in the contract of the particular provision conferring jurisdiction. Mr Lenormant [a director of the first defendant] was not aware specifically of clause 3 and in my opinion it cannot be said he ought to have been aware of it. The first defendant did not receive a copy of the fully printed general conditions until 1 July 1991, which was after the issue of the plenary summons [24 June 1991]. Therefore the plaintiffs must fail on this ground. ([1995] 2 IR 132, 140).

It seems that Carroll J held that the jurisdiction clause did not form part of the contract. But if that is so, then it would have been more to the point to have held that the first defendant did not receive a copy of the fully printed general conditions containing the jurisdiction clause until July 1, 1991, which was after the date upon which the plaintiffs alleged that the contract had been made by fax, April 22, 1991. Since the jurisdiction clause was not in the contract as agreed, it could not be relied upon in a dispute arising out of the contract.

As to the fact that the negotiations were conducted by fax and telex, in *Entores v Miles Far East Corp* [1955] 2 QB 327 Denning LJ offered an analysis of negotiations by telex predicated upon the notion that it is a form of instantaneous communication between the parties, and that the rule in such circumstances 'is different from the rule about the post. The contract is only complete when the acceptance is received by the offeror: and the contract is made at the place where the acceptance is received'. This analysis was adopted by the House of Lords in *Brinkibon v Stahag Stahl* [1983] 2 AC 34; and Clark (p. 16, n.43) refers to *Unidare v Scott* as 'a recent Irish case which seems to apply' *Entores*. Presumably, Prof Clark would consider that not only does Carroll J in *Hanley v Someport-Walon* seem to do likewise but she also seems to extend it to apply to communication by fax as well as by telex. Finally, here, note that the postal rule aspects of *Entores* were approved by the Supreme Court in *Kelly v Cruise Catering* [1994] ILRM 394 (SC) (see the 1994 Review, pp. 143-6); and, had anything turned on it here, if the June 24, 1991 letter sent by MIT on behalf of the plaintiffs to the first defendants had been an acceptance, then that postal rule would have deemed that the acceptance was effective from the date of posting (June 24, 1991) not the date of arrival (July 1, 1991).

Intention in offer and acceptance The concept of intention is at the heart of the analysis of whether, on a given set of facts, there is a contract, not only in the context of the doctrine of intention to create legal relations, but also in the context of whether it was intended that a statement which seems to be an offer is in fact an offer, an acceptance is an acceptance, and so forth. A statement in the form of an offer, but which is however not intended to be an offer, is not an offer. This is the lesson of the invitation to treat cases, in which the line between offer and invitation to treat turns on intention.

Thus, in *Boyers v Duke* [1905] 2 IR 617 where the plaintiff wrote to the defendant asking for the lowest quotation for goods and the defendant replied simply stating a price, O'Brien LCJ held that nothing in the quotation of the price contained an intention to sell at the price so that it was thus invitation to treat, not an offer. On the other hand, in *Dooley v Egan* (1938) 72 ILTR 155 the defendant enquired of the plaintiff whether he (the plaintiff) could supply medical instrument cabinets and the plaintiff replied with a detailed 'quotation' letter, including the sentence: '[a]ll quotations are made for immediate acceptance only and are subject to change without notice', Meredith J held that 'this quotation was an offer subject to immediate acceptance . . . I will therefore take this quotation as a definite offer. . . . '. The quotation in the first case was not intended to be an offer, in the second, it was so intended. Thus, in principle, a statement in negotiations cannot be an offer unless it is intended to be an offer. This principle was applied by Costello P in *Gilheaney v The Revenue Commissioners* (High Court, October 4, 1995) to the question whether the applicant's initial appointment was a contract or the exercise of a statutory power by the Minister for Finance, which question arose in the context of whether a subsequent circular amounted to an offer accepted by the applicant.

As to the first question, Costello P held that it could 'best be answered by applying basic principles of the law of contract and to consider whether the minister when making the appointment *intended* enter into contractual relations with the appointee' (at p. 22 (emphasis added); citing *R. v Civil Service Appeal Board* [1998] 3 All ER 686 (this point was not taken on appeal: [1989] 2 All ER 207)). Costello P considered that when 'considering whether a minister intends to enter into a contract when he appoints a civil servant it is relevant to bear in mind the limits which are placed by law on the contractual terms to which he could agree' (*id.*). In this case, many of the provisions of the Civil Service Commissioners Act, 1956 prohibit certain terms and regulate many others. Consequently, Costello P concluded that 'in the absence of evidence of a clear intention to enter into the very restricted type of agreement which the law would permit him to enter into the minister in making the applicant's appointment to the civil service had no intention of entering a contractual relationship, with him; and that the legal basis for his appointment is an administrative act made by the exercise of statutory powers' (at p. 24).

As to the second question, Costello P acknowledged that, in theory, 'a minister could enter into a contract with a serving civil servant who original appointment had been made by the exercise of a statutory power and was not contractual' (at p. 24). Here, the applicant submitted that by circular in October 1993, the Revenue Commissioners had made an offer to members of the staff:

> (a) that from the application for appointment a panel would be established on which candidates names would be placed in order of merit;
> (b) that the post would be offered to the candidates on the panel in the order of merit established and that future vacancies in the post would be filled in a like manner;
> (c) that as the panel was established for an indefinite period future vacancies in the post would be filled from the panel until it was exhausted or 'closed' (ie terminated) by agreement with the staff's union.

The applicant was subsequently notified that he had been placed third on the panel of successful applicants, but was not appointed to a subsequent vacancy. He argued that he had accepted the offer by application for the post and that there had been a breach of this contract by that failure to appoint. Costello P held that 'the determination of this issue must take into account the very restricted nature of a contract permissible under section 17 [of the Civil Service Commissioners Act 1956]. This section empowers a minister to vary and cancel arrangements for the promotion of civil servants, and this discretionary power cannot be fettered by contract. This means that the only *intra vires* contract which could be entered into was one which allowed the respondents to vary or cancel its terms and I can find no evidence of such an unusual contract.' (at p. 25). He thus held that the respondents 'were performing administrative acts under their statutory section 17 powers and were not entering into contractual relations either with the applicant or any other officers who may have applied pursuant to the circular' (at p. 26). This amounts to saying that, in the statutory context, the respondent could not have intended the circular to constitute an offer.

Ultimately, therefore, on the question whether the initial appointment or the subsequent circular were contractual, Costello P applied the basic principle that a statement in negotiations cannot be an offer unless it is intended to be an offer.

Communication of offers and acceptances Logic and principle dictate a general rule that the offer or acceptance must be communicated. As to an offer, in *Tansey v College of Occupational Therapists* [1995] 2 ILRM 603 (August 27, 1986), Murphy J held that '[l]ogical analysis would suggest that

the offer must be communicated to the person for whom it is intended . . . '.
Thus, in *Wilson v Belfast Corporation* (1921) 55 ILTR 205, on August 5,
1914, the Corporation passed a resolution to continue to pay half-wages to
all employees who joined the defence forces in the First World War. A
newspaper, without the authority of the Corporation, published a report of
the resolution. At a later meeting, the Corporation passed a further resolution
limiting the scheme to those already in the service of the council on August
5. Some time thereafter, Mr Wilson joined the Corporation, then joined the
Army, and his dependent-survivors sought his half-pay on the basis of the
August 5 resolution. It was held that since he entered the Corporation's
employment after that date, he did not satisfy the terms of the scheme;
O'Connor LJ continued, *obiter*, that the resolution did not amount to an offer,
(as in the cases discussed above with *Gilheany*), and even it did, it was not
communicated: 'The reporter puts the resolution into the press: its publication is not authorised by the Corporation and could not be prevented by them.
. . . '. Thus, for O'Connor LJ, the resolution could not have constituted an
offer, because it was not validly communicated to the potential offerees.

Similarly, as to an acceptance, in *Carlill v Carbolic Smoke Ball Co.*
[1893] 1 QB 256 Bowen LJ held that 'an acceptance of an offer ought to be
notified to the person who makes the offer, in order that the two minds may
come together'. Whether there was such a communication was an issue which
was addressed by Murphy J in *Kennedy and ors v AIB plc and AIB Finance
Ltd* (High Court, May 18, 1995). The facts in issue occurred against a
background of many transactions between the plaintiff and the defendants,
which had become increasingly tense, especially as to whether there had been
an agreement to extend an overdraft by £100,000. The plaintiffs applied for
a loan of £250,000 from AIB Finance; this amounted to an offer by the
plaintiffs to borrow the £250,000. A committee internal to AIB Finance
ultimately decided make the loan; this amounted to a decision to accept the
offer. Nevertheless, it was established that the application would need the
sanction not only of AIB Finance but also of AIB, and that the agents of AIB
Finance made it clear to the plaintiffs made it clear that further internal
procedures needed to be followed. AIB subsequently refused to sanction the
loan. Murphy J, after detailing the facts, held that essentially, the plaintiff's
claim was laid in contract; they contended that 'on three occasions the
defendants . . . agreed to provide [loan] facilities [the £250,000 and the
£100,00]. . . . On the balance of probabilities, I am not satisfied that [the
agents] made the statements or representations alleged by the plaintiffs.
Accordingly, the claim in contract must fail.' (The plaintiffs' claim in
negligence is considered in the Tort chapter, pp. 519-20, below.

It is clear that the decision of AIB Finance in *Kennedy* to accept the
plaintiffs offer was of the same incohate nature as the decision of Belfast

Corporation in *Wilson* to make an offer to the plaintiffs. Neither was complete; and the claim by the plaintiffs in *Kennedy* that AIB Finance had accepted the offer failed because the defendants' procedures for such acceptances had not been followed.

PRINCIPLES OF INTERPRETATION

In the interpretation of contracts, it is well settled that a court should attempt to give meaning to every provision of the contract; so that, where there is an irreconcilable inconsistency between two terms, a term of the contract should be rejected. This principle formed the basis of the decision of Murphy J in *Lac Minerals v Chevron Mineral Corporation of Ireland and Ivernia* [1995] 1 ILRM 161 (see the 1994 Review pp. 146-7). However, it may be that the inconsistency is too great to be resolved merely by ignoring a term (or terms); in such a case, a court may have to imply a term or terms. In *Montgomery v Shepperton Investment Co.* (High Court, July 11, 1995) Geoghegan J held that the lease was 'full of internal contradictions' (p. 3) which it was 'impossible to reconcile', so that it was therefore 'essential to imply terms into it' (p. 2). Presumably, such terms are implied on the basis of the necessity to give business efficacy to the contract (see pp. 210-12 above).

More generally, in the interpretation of written contracts, a court will usually start from the position that the entire of the contract is embodied in the writing, that the contract is complete on its face. Many consequences flow from this. Take three examples. First, the conduct of the parties subsequent to the making of the contract is inadmissible as a guide to the interpretation of the contract (*In re Wogan's (Drogheda) (No. 1)* [1993] 1 IR 157; see the 1992 Review, pp. 53-56). Second, 'a deed or an agreement in writing is to be construed as a whole to give effect to the intention of the parties and . . . the relevant time to ascertain that intention is the date of the instrument' (*Lillington v Doyles Stores* (Supreme Court, April 14, 1995) *per* O'Flaherty J). Thus, in a lease of premises for use as a supermarket entered into in 1973, since the business of a supermarket did not in 1973 include the sale of newspapers, a covenant which confined a lessee to the business of a supermarket precluded the sale of newspapers. Consequently O'Flaherty J upheld the High Court's grant of an injunction (January 22, 1991, Costello J, *ex tempore*) to restrain the appellant from selling newspapers in its supermarket was upheld. Third, evidence extrinsic to the contract is inadmissible insofar as it is directed to the question of interpretation: 'evidence cannot be admitted . . . to add to, vary or contradict a written instrument. . . . where a contract has been reduced to writing, neither party can rely on extrinsic evidence of terms alleged to have been agreed' (Treitel, p. 176).

This third example is usually referred to as the parol evidence rule, a rule more often honoured in the breach than in the observance. It was at issue in *Bank of Ireland v McCabe* (Supreme Court, December 19, 1994). Flood J in the court below (High Court, March 25, 1993; see the 1993 Review, pp. 189-191, 193-194) had admitted, as descriptive of the circumstances under which a written guarantee came into existence, the evidence of a bank manager extrinsic to the guarantee; and held that since the guarantee was expressed to cover present and future liabilities, it covered both the initial loan in respect of which it was executed and also a subsequent loan to which the bank in the present case sought to apply it.

On appeal, Egan J in the Supreme Court posed the question whether it could be said that the defendants were 'attempting to vary the terms of an agreement in writing which is not ambiguous? On its face it clearly created a continuing obligation' (at pp. 7 to 8). As a consequence, *prima facie*, Egan J was of the view that 'a defence based solely on an alleged variation ought not to succeed' (at p. 8). However, he continued that in his view, the 'real defence seem[ed] . . . to be that the . . . guarantee was entered into to cover a specific transaction but the bank are attempting to use it for another purpose *i.e.* to cover a later transaction'. Therefore, he concluded that 'it has been said over and over again that he law of contract depends upon the agreement of the parties. The parties in this case agreed that once a specific transaction had been completed the guarantee was at an end. They did not qualify this in any way so it meant that there was to be so irrespective of the contents of the agreement itself' (at p. 9) and therefore allowed the appeal and held against the bank.

With respect, however, the learned judge's analysis begs the question. Of course, the law of contract is about agreement, but if the agreement has been reduced to writing, the law of contract (by means of the parol evidence rule) proceeds from the view that such writing is complete, and that oral evidence to contradict it is inadmissible for the purposes of interpretation unless a term is ambiguous. The term was not ambiguous, and thus there would seem to have been no basis upon which to take into account the oral evidence; that being so, the law of contract would say that the contract as agreed and reduced to writing is the agreement which is relevant for its purposes. However, Egan J was of the view that the parties had in fact agreed a matter not properly recorded in the writing; it is submitted that the proper way to deal with such an eventuality is to rectify the writing so as to reflect the actual agreement: thus, a guarantee expressed to apply to present and future liabilities should be rectified to refer simply to present liabilities.

PRIVITY

Introduction It is a truth universally acknowledged, that a doctrine in receipt of much criticism, must be in need of reform. So it is with the doctrine of privity of contract, by which only those who are parties to a contract can sue upon it. To this principle, the law and equity have developed a myriad of exceptions, supplemented liberally by statute. In the context of insurance contracts, *McManus v Cable Management* (High Court, July 8, 1994) Morris J insisted upon the doctrine in all of its vigour; whereas in *O&E Telephones v Alcatel Business Systems Ltd and National Telephones Systems Ltd* (High Court, 17 May 1995) McCracken J applied with alacrity the principle of benefit and burden by way of exception to the doctrine of privity.

Insurance contracts and the doctrine of privity One of the most common statutory exceptions concerns a contract between and insurer and an insured enforceable by the beneficiary named in the contract upon the happening of the insured event (see Clark, pp. 390-393). However, in the absence of an express statutory grant of the right to sue, the common law position would seem to be that in general such a beneficiary is not privy to the contract and cannot sue upon it. Thus, in *McManus v Cable Management*, High Court, July 8, 1994, the plaintiff sued the defendant for negligence, and sought a declaration against the defendant's insurance company compelling it to indemnify the defendant in the event that the plaintiff's action was successful. The insurance company applied to have the application against it struck out on the grounds that the plaintiff was not privy to the contract between the insurer and the insured, but the plaintiff argued that the defendant in entering an employer's insurance policy with the insurance company, acted as trustee for the plaintiff who was the beneficiary under the policy. Citing *Green v Russell* [1959] 2 QB 226; *Prudential Staff Union v Hall* [1947] 1 KB 685, which did not seem to aid the plaintiff's claim to be entitled to sue upon the insurance contract, and *Bradley v Eagle Star Insurance Co.* [1989] 1 All ER 961 in which the House of Lords had held that the beneficiary's right in such circumstances does not arise until the relevant liability is established and the amount ascertained, Morris J held that he was 'satisfied on these authorities that no case can be made out on the plaintiff's behalf to indicate that he had any entitlement to the benefits payable under the policy' and therefore directed that the proceedings against the third party be struck out as disclosing no reasonable cause of action (compare the cases discussed in Price, 'Insurers, Privity and Procedure' (1996) 59 *MLR* 738). In this respect, it is a straightforward application of the doctrine of privity.

However, there are signs elsewhere in the Common Law world that the privity rule is crumbling. (An excellent summary of the issues raised by abrogation of or departure from the rule is to be found in the English Law Commission's Consultation Paper on *Privity of Contract* (Consultation Paper No 121; 1991), and its subsequent Report: *Privity of Contract: Contracts for the Benefit of Third Parties* (Law Com No 242; 1996); see generally Burrows [1996] *LMCLQ* 467). For example, in a context not dissimilar to the facts of *McManus*, the High Court of Australia, in *Trident General Insurance v McNeice Bros* (1988) 165 CLR 107 was faced with a situation in which the insurer had agreed with the insured that if the insured event occurred the insurer would indemnify the insurer and also certain other named beneficiaries. There was no statute which gave such beneficiaries a direct right of action upon the contract between the insured and the insurer to compel the insurer to pay upon the happening of the insured event. Nevertheless, by a majority of 5 to 2, the beneficiary was allowed to sue on foot of the insurance contract. Toohey J mounted a scathing attack on the privity doctrine: it is 'based on shaky foundations and, in its widest form, lacks support in both logic and jurisprudence', and Mason CJ and Wilson J in joint judgment seem also to have been prepared to abrogate the privity doctrine entirely: for them, there 'is much substance in the criticisms directed at the traditional common law rules', found little substance in the defences of those rules, and seemed prepared to countenance a 'simple departure from the traditional rules [which] would lead to third party enforceability of such a contract, . . . '. Deane J held in the beneficiary's favour on the ground that 'there is no reason in principle or in common sense why the party to the contract should not hold the benefit of the insurer's promise to indemnify him on his own behalf and [hold] the benefit of the promise to indemnify others respectively upon trust for those others . . . It is difficult to envisage a class of contract in which the creation of such a trust would be more readily discernible than the type of contract which is involved in the present case, namely, a policy of insurance indemnifying both a party to the contract and others who are designated [in the contract]' but he refused to abandon the privity doctrine altogether. Gaudron J's reasons for holding in favour of the named beneficiaries came from the law of restitution, but she too refused to abandon the privity doctrine; Brennan and Dawson JJ in separate judgments affirmed the privity doctrine (for Brennan J it is 'both settled and fundamental') and held that it precluded the plaintiff's action here. (Thus, on the privity issue, the vote was 4-3 in favour of retention, though the views of the abolitionists are very compelling, and only 2 of the 4 in this majority provided a strong defence of the doctrine).

Taking such sentiments and applying them to the facts of *McManus*: if the position of Toohey J, and of Mason CJ and Wilson J, were adopted then privity would be no bar to the plaintiff's claim; but Deane J's *dictum* would

not seem to reach the facts here, since the promise in *McNeice* was one by
which the insurer promised to indemnify the third party, which promise the
insured was to hold on trust for the third party, whereas here it is a promise
by the insurer to the insured to indemnify the insured (and not a third party),
even Deane J did not seem to contemplate the insured holding that promise
on trust for the third party; Gaudron J's reasons are not applicable on these
facts, and the dissents of Brennan and Dawson JJ support the conclusion that
privity is a bar to the plaintiff's claim. However, even if privity were not a
bar, the plaintiff would still have had to meet the objection that the relevant
right would not accrue until a determination of liability, but it may be that
this objection would not have precluded a declaration that the insurer would
be liable to indemnify its insured if the insured were to be found liable to the
plaintiff in the main action.

The principle of benefit and burden   Under the rule in *Tulk v Moxhay*
(1848) 2 Ph 774; 41 ER 1143, it is a principle of equity that the burden of a
restrictive covenant will run with the land to which it relates so as to bind all
successors in title to the original covenantor (except a *bona fide* purchaser
for value without notice). 'Thus, the restrictive covenant is a means not only
of conferring enforceable rights on a person who is not a party to the contract;
it may also, even more unusually, impose a burden on a person who is not a
party to the contract.' (Downes, *Textbook on Contract* (4th ed, 1995) p. 374).
So much is now uncontroversial.

However, in *De Mattos v Gibson* (1858) 4 DeG&J 276, ten years after
Tulk v Moxhay, in a case involving, not real property but a ship, Knight Bruce
LJ observed that:

> Reason and justice seem to prescribe that, at least as a general rule,
> where a man, by gift or purchase, acquires property from another, with
> knowledge of a previous contract, lawfully and for valuable considera-
> tion made by him with a third person, to use and employ the property
> for a particular purpose in a specified manner, the acquirer shall not, to
> the material damage of the third person, in opposition to the contract
> and inconsistently with it, use and employ the property in a manner not
> allowable to the giver or seller. ((1858) 4 DeG&J 276, 282)

The rule in *Tulk v Moxhay* is now understood as a rule which applies to
real property (Treitel, p. 562; Coughlan, *Property Law in Ireland* (Gill &
Macmillan, Dublin, 1995) p. 270) and which owes 'nothing to the De Mattos
principle' (*Law Debenture Trust Corp v Ural Caspian Oil Corp* [1993] 2 All
ER 355, 361 *per* Hoffmann J (as he then was)). On the other hand, the

principle in *De Mattos v Gibson* has been applied beyond real property, not only in the case itself, but also in the Privy Council case of *Lord Strathcona SS Co. v Dominion Coal Co.* [1926] AC 108 where the then owner of a ship was prevented from using it inconsistently with a charter granted by a previous owner. This principle was doubted by Diplock J (as he then was) in *Port Line Ltd v Ben Line Steamers* [1958] 2 QB 146, but, in various contexts, it has been accepted by Megarry VC in *Tito v Waddell (No. 2)* [1977] Ch 106, 300 (grudgingly), Browne-Wilkinson J in *Swiss Bank v Lloyds Bank* [1979] Ch 548 (*cp.* [1982] AC 584; and note another aspect of this case discussed in the 1993 Review, pp. 183-184) and by Hoffmann J in *Law Debenture Trust Corp v Ural Caspian Oil Corp* [1993] 2 All ER 355 (Tettenborn [1993] *CLJ* 382).

In *Law Debenture Trust*, four Russian companies were in line to receive compensation from the post-Soviet Russian government in respect of Soviet expropriation of their assets. Shell was the controlling shareholder in the companies and Leisure Overseas bid for their shares. Shell, and some other shareholders, agreed to sell on condition that if the companies were to receive compensation, Leisure Overseas would apply that compensation for the benefit of the existing shareholders. Consequently, by four separate agreements (the agreements), each of the Russian companies and Leisure Overseas entered into an agreement with the plaintiff Law Debenture Trust as trustee for the existing shareholders by which Leisure Overseas covenanted that it would seek such compensation from the government, that they would pay it to the existing shareholders (less their expenses), and that if they sold their shares in the companies they would require of the purchasers that they covenant in similar terms with Law Debenture Trust as trustee for the existing shareholders. Leisure Overseas, in breach of the agreements, sold their shares to Hilldon without requiring such a covenant; the companies then received compensation but this was not passed on to the shareholders; and Hilldon then sold the shares to Caspian.

The plaintiff, citing *De Mattos v Gibson*, argued that Hilldon and Caspian were liable to the plaintiff, on the grounds that since they took the benefit of their shares with knowledge of the agreements and of the breach thereof by Leisure Overseas, they also took the burden of performance of the agreements. On an application by Hilldon and Caspian to strike out this aspect of the plaintiff's claim, Hoffmann J characterised the principle as one which 'has had its ups and downs over the past 130 years' (361), clarified that the enforceability of restrictive covenants against the purchaser of land 'owed nothing to the *De Mattos* principle' (*id.*), and pointed to other setbacks, where, for example, the principle 'failed to secure the enforceability of resale price maintenance agreements against retailers who acquired stock with full knowledge of the covenants into which their wholesalers had entered.' (362)

Although he was prepared to accept the doctrine, nevertheless, Hoffmann J felt 'bound to say that neither *Strathcona* nor *Swiss Bank* make it entirely clear when the principle applies and when it does not . . .' (362). However, even assuming that it applied on the facts, the plaintiff faced the difficulty not of 'whether the principle applies but [of] the extent of the remedy which it provides. *One thing is beyond doubt: it does not provide a panacea for outflanking the doctrine of privity.* . . . the *De Mattos* principle permits no more than the grant of a negative injunction to restrain the third party from doing acts which would be inconsistent with performance of the contract by the original contracting party. The terms of the injunction must be such that refraining altogether from action would constitute compliance.' (363; emphasis added.) He justified this characterisation of the principle and remedy by reference to the authorities, and concluded that 'there is not a single case in which the *De Mattos* principle has been used to impose upon a purchaser a positive duty to perform the covenants of his predecessor. It cannot therefore save the claim to performance of the covenants by Hilldon and Caspian from being struck out. The negative injunction granted in *De Mattos* and the *Strathcona* is of no use to the plaintiff. . . .' (364; the Court of Appeal did not disturb these conclusions: [1995] 1 All ER 157)) Thus, the *De Mattos* principle stands as a limited exception to the doctrine of privity of contract.

In the alternative, in *Law Debenture Trust*, the plaintiff relied on the principle, derived from the judgment of Megarry VC in *Tito v Waddell (No. 2)* [1977] Ch 106, that he who takes the benefit of a transaction must also take the burden; provided that the right and burden, though independent of each other, arise under the same instrument ([1977] Ch 106, 290). Thus, an assignee of a benefit created by contract must also take the burden arising in that contract. But, concerned that such a principle, without some limits, would subvert the doctrine of privity of contract, Megarry VC stressed that if 'the circumstances show that the assignee intended to take only the benefit, and that burden was intended to be borne in the same way as it had been borne previously' then the principle does not apply. As Hoffmann J put it in *Law Debenture Trust*, one 'must be able to infer from that transaction [the assignment] that the assignee was intended to assume the burden.' (365) The principle of benefit and burden applied only to rights and burden arising out of the same instrument, but that was not the case in *Law Debenture Trust*, where the shares has been transferred to Leisure Overseas by transfers from some of the registered shareholders, while the covenant was made by Leisure Overseas with the plaintiff as trustee for all shareholders.

This principle of benefit and burden was also at issue in the judgment of McCracken J in *O&E Telephones v Alcatel Business Systems Ltd and National Telephones Systems Ltd* (High Court, May 17, 1995). Pursuant to the terms of a distribution agreement made in December 1986, between O&E

and National Telephones, in 1987 and again in 1990, it was arranged that National would supply certain customers directly with equipment, and pay O&E a commission in respect of each sale. In 1990, Alcatel took over National, and in 1991 Alcatel sought to terminate National's contractual arrangements with O&E on three months notice, so that from then on Alcatel would deal directly and solely with the customers. In 1992, National ceased trading. In these circumstances, it was held by McCracken J that, although Alcatel was not a party to the contract between O&E and National, and there was no evidence of a novation or an assignment from National to Alcatel, Alcatel had the benefit of O&E's work and was still liable to pay the commission to O&E until, as was the case at trial, the equipment became obsolete and was no longer being marketed.

On the novation point, McCracken J adopted the definition in *Scarf v Jardine* (1882) 7 App Cas 345 — 'that there being a contract in existence, some new contract is substituted for it, either between the same parties (for that might be) or between different parties; the consideration mutually being the discharge of the old contract' — and concluded that since novation 'cannot be forced upon a party, and there is no evidence before me that the plaintiff ever released the second defendant from its obligations under the contract in consideration of these obligations being performed by the first defendant', Alcatel did not become liable to O&E under the doctrine of novation.

Nevertheless, Alcatel were in effect allowed to sue on the contract between O&E and Alcatel, and this departure from the doctrine of privity was justified on the basis of the principles stated in the judgment of Megarry VC in *Tito v Waddell (No. 2)* [1977] Ch 106. For McCracken J:

a distinction was made [in *Tito*] between what was called the conditional benefit principle and the pure principle of benefit and burden. It was recognised in that case that situations may arise where a right or benefit under a contract is assigned but the assignment is conditional on certain burdens being assumed by the assignee, and that this condition is an intrinsic part of the right which the assignee takes. In my view, the present case is a good example of this, and as the first defendant [Alcatel] took over or had assigned to it in some form the benefit of the contract, including the benefit of the introduction to the customers by the plaintiff, the obligation to pay a commission was an intrinsic part of that benefit, and the first defendant [Alcatel] must be deemed to have taken the benefit with the burden or obligation to discharge the commission to the plaintiff. Accordingly, I hold that the second defendant [National] is liable to the plaintiff in respect of sales up to 1 January 1992 [when it ceased trading] and the first defendant [Alcatel] is liable to pay commission on sales after that date.' (pp. 14-15).

With respect, McCracken J, having initially kept the conditional and pure principles of benefit and burden distinct, then seems to have proceeded to conflate them. By the conditional principle of benefit and burden, Megarry VC seems to have meant that, upon the true construction of the contract assigning the benefit, assumption of the benefit is made expressly conditional upon the assumption of the burden. This occurs because it reflects the true intentions of the parties to the contract of assignment. On the other hand, by the pure principle of benefit and burden, Megarry VC seems to have meant that, by operation of law, the assumption of the benefit is to be made conditional upon the assumption of the burden (and even then, as we have seen, it appears that this can be excluded if the intention of the parties is to the contrary). If McCracken J is properly to adopt the conditional principle of benefit and burden, he must then seek for the actual intentions of the parties. Instead, since McCracken J held that Alcatel '*must be deemed* to have taken the benefit with the burden' (emphasis supplied), he seems to have been imposing this obligation, not as a matter of the true intention of the parties, but as a matter of law, and must thus be taken to have applied the pure principle.

Alcatel's liability is premised upon the fact that they 'took over or had assigned' the benefit of the contract between O&E and National. However, McCracken J had already held that on the facts there had been no such assignment — there was 'no evidence of any actual assignment by the second defendant to the first defendant of the rights or obligations under the contract with the plaintiff' (p. 13), on the facts, the position was simply that customers which once were serviced by National now went to Alcatel — and the pure principle of benefit and burden in *Tito v Waddell* seems only to apply in respect of assignments or similar direct transfers of the relevant benefit. Thus, strict application of the principle in *Tito* and *Law Debenture Trust* probably would not justify the result arrived at in *O&E v Alcatel*. Consequently, it seems that Irish law now takes a less strict view of the pure principle of benefit and burden than that being taken in the English courts.

If however, it were to be concluded that the more strict view is preferable, the result in *O&E v Alcatel* would require justification on different grounds. In this regard, it may be thought that the rather broad statement of principle in *De Mattos v Gibson* (above) may provide a solution: Alcatel acquired National, with knowledge of a previous contract, lawfully and for valuable consideration made by National with O&E, and should not, therefore, to the material damage of O&E, in opposition to the contract and inconsistently with it, use and employ the property of National in a manner not allowable to National. However, by its own terms, the *De Mattos* principle is confined to property (see, *e.g.* Treitel, pp. 561 *et seq.*): it concerns the position of parties to an original contract relating to property, which property is subsequently dealt with, so that the new purchaser can be bound by terms in the original contract relating to that property. The agreement between O&E and National did not relate to property but to services rendered by O&E to National. Thus, for *De Mattos* to apply here would represent a significant extension of the principle in that case; whereas the trend, even in those cases which accept it, is to confine it to property. Furthermore, as was pointed out in *Law Debenture Trust*, the appropriate remedy is a negative declaration, and on the facts of *O&E v Alcatel*, a declaration that Alcatel should not now supply those clients of National's who had been introduced by O&E would have availed the plaintiffs not a whit.

Nevertheless, an explanation of the result from the law of Restitution may be to hand. In *Allied Discount Card v Bord Fáilte Éireann* [1992] 2 IR 185; [1993] Restitution Law Review 158 the plaintiffs had been hired in 1986 by the defendants to canvass shops willing to provide discounts to tourists, and to design and produce booklets of vouchers which could be given to these tourists to obtain the discounts. The arrangement was not renewed, but the defendant included discount vouchers in its catalogues in 1987 and 1988 advertising campaigns, many of which were based on, or were copies of, the plaintiff's 1986 vouchers. Lynch J held that the defendant had an 'unfair benefit' in 1987 and 1988 from the plaintiff's work in canvassing traders and preparing the booklets were thus 'unjustly enriched at the plaintiff's expense', so that the plaintiffs were entitled to 'restitution for [that] unjust enrichment'. Likewise, in *O&E*, as McCracken J expressly held, Alcatel has the benefit of O&E's earlier work, and can thus be said to have been enriched at O&E's expense. The factor which rendered Alcatel's receipt 'unjust' is most likely the free acceptance by Alcatel of the benefit of O&E's work. In the 1994 Review (p. 139), it was explained that 'the essence of this cause of action has recently been neatly summed up by Aldous J: 'why should a man who receives and uses a service, knowing that it is not being rendered free, not pay for it?'. (*BAGS v Gilbert* [1994] FSR 723, 743). Where a plaintiff confers a benefit upon a defendant, and the defendant, with the opportunity to reject, fails to exercise that opportunity, the defendant comes under a duty to make restitution to the plaintiff in the amount of the benefit so conferred.'

All of the requirements of such a cause of action are made out here: Alcatel had the opportunity to reject the benefit of O&E's service by not pursuing the clients introduced by O&E to National, but they chose to accept it by so pursuing them. In many cases, the defendant will have requested the enrichment (as for example in negotiations for a contract which ultimately fails to materialise, or in the context of an ineffective contract), and it has been argued that in such request-based situations, a cause of action in restitution is more properly to be found in an expanded notion of failure of consideration (Burrows, *The Law of Restitution* (Butterworths, London, 1993) pp. 12, 315-320). However, there are still cases in which there has been a free acceptance by the defendant of a benefit rendered by the plaintiff in circumstances in which there has been no request by the enriched defendant that the plaintiff confer the enrichment, and the best explanation for restitution in such circumstances is still free acceptance (Birks, 'In Defence of Free Acceptance' in Burrows (ed.), *Essays on the Law of Restitution*, 104, pp. 115-120 calls such an acceptance a 'secret acceptance': since the plaintiff is not aware that the defendant has accepted the enrichment, from the perspective of the plaintiff the defendant's acceptance is 'secret'). *O&E v Alcatel* is a paradigm example of such a secret acceptance, a free acceptance where there is no request. (For another example of a cause of action in restitution supplying a remedy when the doctrine of privity precludes reliance upon the contract, see *Trident General Insurance v McNeice Bros.*, 1988) 165 CLR 107, 174-177 *per* Gaudron J, discussed Treitel, pp. 566-567 and Mason and Carter, *Restitution Law in Australia* (Butterworths, Sydney, 1995) pp. 721-724).

REMEDIES FOR BREACH

If a bilateral contract is a relation of reciprocal obligations, then when one party performs his obligations under a contract, then the other will be liable to perform his, and a failure so to perform is a breach of contract. A straightforward application of this principle is to be found in the decision of Costello P in *Unicorn Investments v Ewart* (High Court, June 29, 1995). Here, the essence of the agreement was that if U were to introduce E to a bank interested in arranging finance for a deal which E wished to undertake, and if E decided to hold further discussion with the bank, then E would 'immediately pay a fee of £150,000' to U; but if E were to decide to have no further communications with the bank, then no fee would be payable. Costello P held that such an agreement had been entered into, that U had found such a bank and effected the relevant introduction, and that E had continued negotiations; consequently, Costello P held that U was entitled to the contractual fee.

REPUDIATION

In the discussion of the decision of Morris J in *Parkarran v M&P Construction* (High Court, November 9, 1995), it was pointed out that a breach before performance of a contract does not of itself necessarily have the effect of terminating a contract. Instead, where the breach amounts to or results from a repudiation of the contract, '(1). . . the aggrieved party has an election to accept the repudiation or affirm the contract . . . (2) An act of acceptance requires no particular form; . . . It is sufficient that the communication or conduct clearly and unequivocally conveys to the repudiating party that the aggrieved party is treating the contract as at an end. . . .' (*Vitol SA v Norelf (The Santa Clara)* [1996] AC 800 (HL); [1996] 3 All ER 193, 200 *per* Lord Steyn). Such principles determine whether, as a matter of law, one party has done an action amounting to a repudiatory breach of the contract, and the other has done an action amounting to an acceptance of the repudiatory breach, sufficient to determine the contract as a matter of law. Furthermore, where 'a plaintiff is entitled to, and does, rescind for anticipatory breach, two results follow. First, he is released from future obligations under the contract . . . Secondly, the injured party is no longer bound to perform in order to establish his right of action on the contract; . . .' (Treitel, p. 776). It follows from this that although the contract is brought to an end, it is not void (or, as it often tautologically said, not void *ab initio*). Consequently, clauses such as arbitration clauses can continue to have effect notwithstanding such repudiation.

This situation, where breach by repudiation brings a contract to an end as a matter of law, must be carefully distinguished from a situation in which the contract itself provides for circumstances in which one party may treat the contract as at an end as a consequence of the actions of the other party. In the former situation , the contract is determined by operation of law; in the latter, it is determined because of the intentions of the parties. Although the word 'repudiation' may be used to describe both situations, they are very different. In *Superwood Holdings v Sun Alliance* [1995] 3 IR 303, an insurer purported to rely on clause 5 the insurance contract to repudiate its liability to indemnify the insured in respect of the happening of an insured event (a fire) (see the Insurance section of the Commercial Law chapter, above pp. 45-8); this is quite clearly a repudiation not of the former kind but of the latter. Clause 5 in effect allowed repudiation for fraud. O'Hanlon J in the High Court found that the insured's claim had been fraudulent, and held in favour of the insurer. On appeal, the Supreme Court held that, although the facts disclosed 'a mosaic of optimism, hope, shambles, chaos, [and] growth [but] not deception' (at p. 40 of the judgment of Denham J) on the part of the insured, this did not amount to fraud, and thus allowed the appeal on that ground. Nevertheless, it has been held that an insured's overstatement of losses sustained can constitute a breach of his 'the duty to exercise the utmost good faith . . . [which] continues throughout the relationship up to and including the making of a claim on foot of a policy.' *Fagan v General*

Accident Fire and Life Assurance Corporation (High Court, February 19, 1993; see the 1993 Review, pp. 52-53; 178-179; note that in that context, a sentence which should have read 'it would not be in good faith for the insurance company to require the impossible of the insured' was erroneously printed without the 'not'), and, though it is arguable that the insurer's position in *Superwood* could be justified on this ground stated in *Fagan*, it was not considered by the Supreme Court.

However, the insurer also sought to justify its refusal to indemnify on the grounds that the insured had not complied with the requirements of the policy in the making of such claims as provided for in clause 4 of the policy. Denham J plainly deprecated the late reliance placed by the insurer on this point, especially because it had not initially been pleaded (p. 56) and held:

> I am satisfied that the respondents having elected to repudiate the contract and thus refused to the appellants the benefit of the contract, and further the fact that the of the repudiation was fraud and that this claim in this way denied the appellants the right to arbitration on the issue, it would be, and was, entirely unfair to the appellants to enable the respondents at the same time to rely on the agreement, *i.e.* condition 4. They had a right to elect, and having made the election, and not pleaded otherwise, must stand or fall on the issue of fraud (p. 57).

She concluded that the respondents were therefore 'estopped', as a matter of 'fair procedures — constitutional justice' (at p. 58) from relying on clause 4 of the contract. Nevertheless, she took the point, and concluded that the respondent's claim on clause 4 was not well founded on the facts. One wonders whether it is in fact correct to conflate the doctrine of estoppel and the principles of fair procedures and of natural justice into reflections of the vague idea that it was 'entirely unfair' for the respondents to act in a particular way. Such conflation seems sloppy, especially since the principle which seems to emerge from this conflation is of significant practical importance; in the words of Blayney J, (concurring with Denham J) the principle is that 'where an insurance company avoids a policy of insurance, . . . they cannot at the same time seek to rely on a term contained in that policy' (at pp. 18-19 of his judgment).

Furthermore, the analysis of the learned judges on many issues in their judgments leaves much to be desired. As to the judgment of Denham J, she was of the opinion that a 'void contract may not be enforced' (p. 52), and held, in a passage headed 'void *ab initio*' that the 'effect of repudiation of the contract by the respondents on the grounds of fraud was to render it void. The contract ceased to exist. . . . if fraud was [*sic*] proved, the appellant would have no right under the contract. Having pleaded a void contract, the respondents could not then rely on a clause of the contract which they had repudiated' (pp. 51- 52). With respect, whilst it is accurate to state that a void contract may not be enforced, much of the rest of this passage is flawed. First, the effect of fraud upon a contract is not to render it void but *voidable* and therefore liable to be set aside. Second, the effect of repudiation as a matter of law is not to render the contract void *ab initio*, but instead to allow the innocent party to treat the contract as at an end; it has the effect of determining the primary obligations of performance, but other terms such as arbitration clauses continue (see above).

Third, the passage seems to treat fraud and repudiation independently of the contract, whereas it is clear that they were simply shorthands for the actions of the insured which the insurance company felt allowed it to treat the policy as at an end according to the terms of the policy. And although it may be that the notion of fraud as provided for in the contract is the same as that provided for in *Derry v Peek* (1889) 14 App Cas 337 (approved by Denham J at p. 28), the notions of repudiation by operation of law and according to the terms of the contract must carefully be distinguished (see above); thus, even if (*per impossible*) repudiation by operation of law were to have the effect of rendering a contract void *ab initio*, there is nothing in this to require that the determination of a contract according to the terms of the contract itself should have this effect; indeed, if the contract is to be determined according to its terms, by definition, the contract must have been on foot and cannot logically be void *ab initio*.

The core issue in Blayney J's judgment is little better: he relied on a line of arbitration cases which held that if a contract is void or has otherwise already been determined, then a party to the contract which has been so declared void or avoided cannot rely on a term of that contract, and therefore cannot enforce an arbitration clause in such a contract. The line of authority is *Ballasty v Army, Navy and General Assurance Association* (1916) 50 ILTR 114, *Furey v Eagle Star* (1922) 56 ILTR 23 and *Coen v Employers Liability Assurance Corporation* [1962] IR 315; and it was founded upon the decision of the House of Lords in *Juredini v National British and Irish Insurance Company* [1915] AC 499. But the House of Lords has held that, whilst it may be that an arbitrator cannot usually decide upon the initial existence of the contract (and so cannot usually decide, for example, whether a contract is void for mistake), if the contract has come into existence, and thereafter been terminated (as by breach, repudiation, frustration, or even by the terms of the contract itself) an arbitrator does have jurisdiction, an arbitration clause can be enforced and a dispute referred to arbitration: this is *Heyman v Darwins* [1942] AC 356 (HL): it has been followed recently in Ireland on this point in *Parkarran v M&P Construction* (High Court, 9 November 1995) above; see Forde, *Arbitration Law and Procedure* (The Round Hall Press, Dublin,

1994, pp. 34-35). Indeed, *Heyman* has been expansively applied, so that even where the contract may be infected with illegality, a dispute can nonetheless be referred to arbitration (see *e.g. Harbour Insurance v Kansa General* [1993] QB 701, Forde, p. 36; *Vogelaar v Callaghan* [1996] 2 ILRM 226, 231 *per* Barron J; see Simons (1996) Bar Review 68). Their Lordships in *Heyman* disapproved of *Juredini*, and unless there is some reason other than this point upon which to support it, it must be regarded as wrongly decided (*cf.* Mustill and Boyd, *Commercial Arbitration* (2nd ed, Butterworths, London, 1989) p. 111, n 16). Consequently, it is submitted that *Ballasty* and *Furey* are no longer good law. As to *Coen*, it is submitted that it fundamentally misunderstood the effect of *Heyman*. In *Coen*, Budd J held that the effect of *Heyman* was not only that 'if one party to the contract alleges that it is void *ab initio* . . . the arbitration clause cannot operate' ([1962] IR 315, 334) but also that 'where the dispute involves in fact the repudiation of the existence of that type of contract which one of the parties relies upon, the same principle applies . . .' ([1962] IR 315, 336), whereas on the very facts of *Heyman* itself, the House of Lords held that such a repudiation did not have such an effect. Nevertheless, in *Superwood*, Blayney J approved *Juredini* and the decision of Budd J in *Coen*, and held that since the insurer had repudiated the contract it could not rely upon a clause in it. With respect, this takes an axe to the very trunk of the principle upon which *Heyman* is decided, a principle which is at the heart of the modern law and practice of arbitration (see *e.g.* Forde, pp. 33-36; Mustill and Boyd, pp. 108-113) and which has formed the basis of very many modern Irish decisions (*e.g. Parkarran, Vogelaar (supra)*). Strictly speaking, since Blayney J expressly concurred in the decision of Denham J, and merely presented his judgment as a supplementary reason for the decision, it is *obiter*, and, given its potential effect upon arbitration, it ought not to be followed.

All this is not to say that a principle such as that which seems to emerge from the case, that 'where an insurance company avoids a policy of insurance, . . . they cannot at the same time seek to rely on a term contained in that policy' (at pp. 18-19 of the judgment of Blayney J) is not a justifiable one; it is merely to say that such a principle is not justified by the reasons given in the case.

RISK ALLOCATION BY CONTRACT

There are many matters ancillary to the performance of the contract which the parties can also regulate by the terms of the contract. For example, one party may have the duty to insure; or a party may seek to exclude liability in certain circumstances; the effect of such an exclusion clause is to cast the risk of the occurrence of those circumstances upon the other party. (When an exclusion clause is understood as an expression of the distribution of risks or of an obligation to bear risks, it is often in practice a statement of obligation to insure). Again, the contract may provide that one or other party is to bear the loss if the contract is unenforceable, or would otherwise be void (or voidable) for mistake or frustration; here, the effect is to cast the risk of the unenforceability or voidness upon that party. Or the performance of the contract may itself involve risk of injury; and the terms of the contract may allocate liability in the event of that injury occurring. An interesting example of risk allocation by contract in such circumstances is provided by the judgment of Morris J in *McCann and Cummins v Brinks Allied and Ulster Bank* (High Court, May 12, 1995).

Here, the plaintiffs were security men employed by Brinks Allied, and, during a delivery of cash to the Bank, they were injured in a holdup. They sued both Brinks and the bank for negligence. The plaintiffs' claim against Brinks turned on the method of delivery of the cash at the bank (they had to walk with the cash 47 feet across the bank forecourt rather than deliver it from the van through a chute into the bank); their claim against bank turned on knowledge of the danger on the part of bank, there having been two previous raids. Brinks claimed that the bank had refused to co-operate with Brinks attempts to make the delivery procedure safer, and argued that the Bank must in those circumstances bear the full responsibility for the loss and damage suffered by the plaintiffs. The plaintiffs' claim against Brinks succeeded in full, essentially on the grounds that Brinks, as employers, failed to provide a safe system of work; (Brinks for a 'small cost' could have installed the chute; 'this work should have been carried out by Brinks if they chose to take on the contract of delivering the money to this Bank'; and on the balance of probabilities if the chute had been installed, the injuries would not have occurred. This aspect of the case is analysed in the Tort chapter, below, 487).

As to the plaintiffs' claim against the bank, Morris J noted that the contract between Brinks and the bank was entered into after the two previous raids, and the bank did not want to have the vans travel over the forecourt area of the bank. Consequently, in his view,

> the options open to Brinks at this stage are clear. They can decline to enter into this contract, or alternatively they must devise a method of carrying out the contract which both incorporates the appropriate safety features and meets with the Bank's approval. In my view what they may *not* do is, for commercial and financial reasons, accept the contract encumbered with its unsatisfactory features, of which they were well aware, and at the same time seek to blame the Bank if loss is suffered

by their security men by reason of that problem.

It is clear that at the relevant time, in 1988, Brinks were in close competition with other security companies for the Bank's business. If they chose to accept this business, then I see no reason why they should seek to foist upon the Bank when the damage has been suffered, an onus or a responsibility which the Bank declined to accept when the contract was being negotiated. . . . In my opinion it is not open to Brinks to transfer to the Bank any loss which arises from the occurrence of an incident from a risk recognised as existing during the time the contract was under negotiation.

In other words, the bank could not be made liable since the risk here had been cast upon Brinks by the contract between Brinks and the bank. This is entirely consistent with the current law on exclusion clauses. Take a contract by which A agrees to render a service to B, but, by a validly incorporated exclusion clause, A excludes liability in certain circumstances; A sub-contracts certain aspects of the performance to C. If, during performance of the sub-contract, C incurs a liability to B in circumstances in which if A had incurred that liability A could take advantage of the exclusion clause, the courts will often allow the protection of the exclusion clause to C even though C is not a party to the contract between A and B (*Elder, Dempster v Paterson, Zochonis* [1924] AC 522; *Scruttons v Midland Silicones* [1962] AC 446; *New Zealand Shipping v Satterthwaite (The Eurymedon)* [1975] AC 154; this is by way of an exception both to the doctrine of privity of contract, (above pp. 219-27) and to the hostility with which the law usually views exclusion clauses (above pp. 196-200); and, although there may be certain fact scenarios in which it is possible to find that A was C's agent, so that there is a contract between B and C, the doctrine does not depend on agency but is of general application: *The New York Star* [1980] 3 All ER 257; [1981] 1 WLR 138 (PC); see now *The Pioneer Container* [1994] 2 AC 324, and *The Mahkutai* [1996] 3 All ER 502 (HL); *cp. London Drugs v Kuehne & Nagel International* (1992) 97 DLR (4th) 261 (SCC)). In such cases, the intent of the exclusion clause is to allocate the risk of the happening of certain events to B; and, by allowing C the protection of the exclusion clause, the effect is to ensure that the risk of the happening of those events remains with B (*e.g. The Mahkutai* [1996] 3 All ER 502, 509g *per* Lord Goff). The essence of the position is that the parties' allocation of the risk ought to be respected. Similarly, in *McCann and Cummins v Brinks Allied and Ulster Bank* the parties' allocation of the risk was respected.

UNDUE INFLUENCE

In *Bank of Ireland v Smyth* [1993] 2 IR 102; [1993] ILRM 790 (HC); [1996] 1 ILRM 241 (SC) the defendant sought to defend an unpaid mortgagee's claim for possession of a family home on the basis of s. 3 of the Family Home Protection Act, 1976. The circumstances of the case raise profound structural questions not only for Family Law (see *infra*, 302-7) and Land Law, but also for the law of Contract. We analysed the High Court decision in the 1993 Review, pp. 194-209, 328, 383-388 (note that at p. 209, by typographical error, the Supreme Court decision of *Nestor v Murphy* [1979] IR 326 was misdescribed as *'R. v Murphy'*).

In *Smyth*, the first and second defendants were husband and wife, respectively. The first defendant had charged property (the defendant's house and lands) as security for borrowings advanced by the plaintiff bank. In this action, the plaintiff sought possession of the house and lands pursuant to the terms of the security. Section 3(1) of the Family Home Protection Act 1976 provides that:

> [w]here a spouse, without the prior consent in writing of the other spouse, purports to convey any interest in the family home to any person except the other spouse, then . . . the purported conveyance shall be void.

The second defendant resisted on the grounds that her consent for the purposes of s. 3 of the Act was not a true consent in that she was not advised to obtain independent legal advice and that she did not have a proper understanding of what she was signing. In the High Court, Geoghegan J held that the advice of the bank manager to the second defendant was inadequate, in particular because he did not advise her to obtain independent advice, and, as a consequence, she did not validly consent to her husband's granting of the charge.

The source of Geoghegan J's analysis of the necessity of independent advice was the decision of the Court of Appeal in England in *Barclays Bank v O'Brien* [1993] QB 109. By the time it was decided in the House of Lords ([1994] 1 AC 180), the issue in the case had resolved itself into one of undue influence; consequently, much of the analysis of the decision of Geoghegan J and of s. 3 concentrated on the undue influence. However, as was demonstrated in the 1993 Review, at pp. 202-208, emptying the law on undue influence into s. 3 of the Act is fundamentally misconceived; the notion of undue influence is irrelevant on the facts of *Smyth* and incompatible with s. 3 of the Act. Further, there are many reasons, other than undue influence on one spouse by the other or by the bank manager or by a third party, why a spouse would not have consented to the other spouse's conveyance. Furthermore, it was also argued that the presence of independent advice is at best an unreliable guide. There may be no such advice, and yet the contract could be voluntary; or, there may be independent advice, and yet the undue influence could be so strong that such advice would be ineffective or ignored. In either such case, a search simply for independent advice would reach a different conclusion to an analysis of whether there was in truth a voluntary consent. Thus, independent advice is not some talismanic cure for coercion; it may be an important factor to be taken into account, but it should not be used a proxy for an analysis as whether a spouse's consent was a valid one. [To similar effect, see *Crédit Lyonnais v Burch* (1996) 146 NLJ 1421, 1422 *per* Millett LJ; on the notion of independent advice in English law after *O'Brien*, see *e.g.* A. Chandler, 'Undue Influence and the Function of Independent Advice' (1995) 111 *LQR* 51; for the position in Australia, see Sneddon, 'Lenders and Independent Solicitors' Certificates for Guarantors and Borrowers: Risk Minimisation or Loss Sharing?' (1996) 24 *Aus Business L Rev* 5].

As to undue influence, it was pointed out in the 1993 Review that, in a contract between P and D, which P entered into because of the undue influence exercised upon D by T, there were at least five strategies available to call the validity of the contract between P and D into question. First, since the enforceability of the contract against D is based upon D's consent, the simple fact of T's coercion vitiating D's consent to the contract should be sufficient to allow D to avoid the contract with P (the 'coercion *simpliciter*' strategy). Second, if T were an agent for P, since the acts of the agent are the acts of the principal, if T has coerced D, in law it is as if P had coerced D, and D can avoid the contract (the 'agency' strategy). Third, according to *Barclays Bank v O'Brien* [1994] 1 AC 180, since T's exercise of undue influence is an equitable wrong which gives the party coerced, D, an equity to set aside the contract, if P has notice of T's undue influence, then D can avoid the contract (the 'notice' strategy. For the subsequent treatment of *O'Brien* in the Court of Appeal, see *e.g.* Fehlberg (1996) 59 *MLR* 675). Fourth, a court could simply hold that in all the circumstances of the case, T's coercion made it 'unconscionable' for P to enforce the contract as against D, or the transaction was 'improvident' for D (the 'unconscionability' strategy; though not in fact open on the pleadings, this approach commended itself in principle to the Court of Appeal in *Crédit Lyonnais v Burch* (1996) 146 NLJ 1421, where the 'terms of the mortgage were so harsh and unconscionable as to make it hardly necessary for a court of equity to rely on [*O'Brien*] as a reason for avoiding the transaction . . . Equity's jurisdiction to relieve against such transactions [unconscionable bargains] . . . is at least as venerable as its jurisdiction to relieve against those procured by undue influence' (per Nourse LJ; a similar approach has been canvassed in Ireland in Mee (1994) 16 *DULJ (ns)* 197)). Fifth, if T and D are husband and wife, and if vulnerable wives possess a special equity as against creditors such as P to whom they offer security for debts of their husbands, then D may be able to avoid the contract with P (the 'special equity' strategy).

To this list must now be added at least two more strategies. Thus, sixth, the contract between P and D may be said to be unenforceable because of P's complicity or culpability in T's equitable fraud on D (and the basis of that complicity is P's notice of T's equitable fraud). (Let this be the 'equitable fraud' strategy: see Dixon and Harpum [1994] *Conv* 421 purporting to explain *O'Brien, supra*; for analysis of this view, see *e.g.* Battersby [1995] *LS* 35; Sparkes [1995] *Conv* 250). And, seventh, the contract between P and D may be said to be unenforceable because, and only when, P actually knew of T's undue influence: on this view, it is not enough that P have constructive notice of T's undue influence. This is the position adopted in *Mumford v Bank of Scotland* (1994) SLT 1288 by the Lord President in the Inner House of Session rejecting the constructive notice approach taken by the House of Lords in O'Brien (see McKendrick 'The Undue Influence of English Law?' in McQueen (ed.), *Scots Law into the 21st Century* (Edinburgh, 1996; and McKendrick [1996] *Restitution Law Review* 100). (Let this be the 'actual knowledge' strategy).

The analysis in the 1993 Review concluded in favour of the first, coercion *simpliciter*, strategy on the grounds that it is entirely sound in principle. As to the alternatives: either a court enforces a contract plainly procured by objectionable means, or spuriously finds that T is an agent for P (if using the 'agency' strategy), or that P knew of T's undue influence (if using the 'actual knowledge' strategy), or that P had notice of T's undue influence (if using the 'notice' strategy or the Dixon and Harpum 'equitable fraud' alternative). The unconscionability strategy allows the court to render objectionable contracts unenforceable, but if that result is achieved as a consequence simply of the fact of the (actual or presumed) undue influence, saying that the transaction is thereby unconscionable or improvident adds nothing of sub-stance to the analysis and is not therefore necessary. As to the 'special equity' strategy, it is probably unconstitutional having regard to the emerging constitutional doctrine of spousal equality, and, if not, should anyhow be rejected as adding as little to the analysis as characterising the transaction as unconscionable (*cf.* Williams (1994) 8 *JCL* 67; Aitkin (1996) 70 *ALJ* 808). The agency, actual knowledge, notice, equitable fraud, unconscionability and special equity strategies being unsatisfactory, the law should reject them and adopt the coercion *simpliciter* strategy.

A more sophisticated argument to the same conclusion has been made in Mee, 'An Alternative Approach to Third Party Undue Influence and Misrepresentation' (1995) 46 *NILQ* 147, who argues that in principle undue influence should 'be treated as a vitiating factor in all cases, giving the victim a *prima facie* entitlement to the remedy of recission' (148). Thus, on this view, where D contracts with P because of T's undue influence, the contract between P and D ought to be as liable to be set aside as if D had contracted with P because of P's undue influence. However, in an important suggestion, he points to the practical problems to which this solution in principle gives rise (160), and, as a pragmatic limit on the extent of such potential liability 'to protect the rights of innocent contracting parties' (156), proposes that there may be circumstances in which 'this remedy would be subject to the defence that the person seeking to uphold the contract has acted in reliance on its validity' and without notice of the vitiating factor (148, *cp.* p. 156 *et seq.*): thus, the element of notice is removed from the cause of action and placed in the context of the defence (which seems to be akin to estoppel).

When *Smyth* reached the Supreme Court ([1996] 1 ILRM 241), the approach of Blayney J was fundamentally different to that taken in the High Court. (Sanfey (1996) 3 *CLP* 31; Mee (1996) 14 *ILT (ns)* 188, 209. Eschewing any reliance on notions of undue influence, Blayney J (Hamilton CJ, Egan J concurring) simply focused on the language of s. 3 of the Family Home Protection Act 1976, and conducted an exercise in statutory interpretation on the notion of 'consent' in that section. For him, the 'question of what the requirements are which a consent has to comply with in order to be valid has not as yet been considered by any court. It seems to me that they have to be deduced from the object of the Act itself and from *dicta* of this Court explaining it, and also from authorities setting out what requirements have been laid down for consents which are required in other contexts', such other contexts being marriage and adoption. [One might also consider the Hague Convention on the Civil Aspects of Child Abduction, 1980 incorporated into Irish law by the Child Abduction and Enforcement of Custody Orders Act 1991, Article 13 of which Convention provides that the Court is 'not bound' to order the return of a child where 'the person . . . having the care of the person of the child . . . had *consented* to or subsequently acquiesced in' the child's removal. On this notion of consent, see *In re P.K. and A.K.; N.K. v J.K.* [1994] 3 IR 483, 485-488 *per* Morris J and *In re R.; P. v B.* [1994] 3 IR 507, 518 *per* Denham J. After conducting this exercise, Blayney J concluded that:

> the consequences of a consent given under s. 3 are not as far-reaching as the consequences of a consent to marry or place a child for adoption but one of the elements required for the validity of the consent in each of these cases is in my opinion applicable in the case of a consent under s. 3 also. This the requirement that the consent must be an 'informed

consent'. . . . In my opinion, the consent of the spouse under s. 3 must satisfy this requirement. It must be a fully informed consent. The spouse giving it must know what it is that he or she is consenting to. Since giving one's consent means that one is approving of something, obviously a precondition is that one should have knowledge of what it is that one is approving of.

In the instant case I am satisfied that Mrs Smyth did not know what she was consenting to. She believed that the charge would affect the land only and would not affect the family home. She was not aware that the charge covered the family home as well. Her consent, therefore, was not a fully informed consent and on that ground was in my opinion invalid.

With respect, this is a much more straightforward and satisfactory basis upon which to reach the conclusion that the consent of the second defendant did not satisfy the terms of s. 3 than that articulated by Geoghegan J. Furthermore, Blayney J pointed out that the deficiencies in the bank's procedures for advising the second defendant did not necessarily have the consequences ascribed to them by Geoghegan J: for Blayney J, the Bank did not owe any duty arising from the s. 3 of the Family Home Protection Act, 1976 to explain the charge fully to Mrs Smyth, to enquire as to her state of knowledge or to suggest to her that she should get independent advice. Referring to s. 3 of the Conveyancing Act 1882, Blayney J concluded that if such steps ought to have been taken, it was to protect the bank's own interests 'to ensure that it got good title to the land which was the subject of the charge.'

That there will be problems in practice with these conclusions would seem, however, to be inevitable (see *e.g.* the 1993 Review, pp. 386-388; Mee (1996) 14 *ILT (ns)* 188, 209). Nevertheless, the conclusions of Blayney J have had the effect of removing illegitimate reliance on notions of independent advice and undue influence from the analysis of s. 3 of the 1976 Act and returning the proper focus to the terms of the Act itself. If it is now to prove inadequate to its practical context, then the remedy is to amend it, not to create further difficulties with sophist interpretations of its sections.

Coroners

INQUEST VERDICT

The ban on returning a suicide verdict at an inquest, upheld by O'Hanlon J in *The State (McKeown) v Scully* [1986] IR 524; [1986] ILRM 133, was confirmed by the decision of the Supreme Court in *Green v McLoughlin* [1991] 1 IR 309 (HC); Supreme Court, January 26, 1995. The decision of Johnson J in the instant case, in which he had reached the same conclusion, is discussed in the 1990 Review, 189-90. The respondent Coroner had allowed evidence to be led concerning the deceased's state of mind leading up to his death; the jury's verdict was that death was due to discharge from a rifle in accordance with the medical evidence while the balance of the mind was disturbed.

Delivering the only reasoned judgment in the Supreme Court, O'Flaherty J drew attention to the restrictions on the powers of an inquest jury in s. 30 of the Coroners Act 1962. It is confined to determining 'who, how, when and where', that is, to determine who the deceased person was, as well as how, when and where he or she died. The 1962 Act thus precludes a jury from giving a verdict which would involve the implication of either civil or criminal liability on the part of the deceased. While O'Flaherty J acknowledged that s. 40 of the 1962 Act empowers a jury to make a finding of murder, manslaughter or infanticide, he pointed out that this is confined to third party involvement in the death. Since there was no evidence of such in the instant matter, the Court agreed with the conclusion of Johnson J that the respondent Coroner should not have permitted any evidence to be led as to the mental state of the deceased leading up to his death. While the conclusion of the Court appears to be supported by the text of the 1962 Act, it is to be hoped that amending legislation will be enacted to ensure that relevant information concerning suicide will not be lacking arising from the limitations currently placed on inquests.

Criminal Law

BAIL

In *The People v Connell (No. 2)*, Supreme Court, May 15, 1995, the Supreme Court declined to interfere with a decision of the High Court to refuse bail to the defendant. The defendant had been convicted of murder but this conviction had been quashed by the Court of Criminal Appeal: *The People v Connell* [1995] 1 IR 244, discussed below, 246. The defendant then faced trial on a number of outstanding counts on the indictment that had contained the count of murder; these included charges of attempted murder, arson and assault occasioning actual bodily harm. In the defendant's High Court application for bail, evidence was given by a Garda that if granted bail, the defendant would not stand trial. Other witnesses gave evidence of their fear of intimidation, and the High Court's decision was that there was a likelihood of interference with witnesses. The High Court also accepted Garda evidence that there was a serious danger that the defendant would not turn up for his trial, having regard to his lack of roots in this State.

The Supreme Court noted firstly that where there were primary findings of fact on the credibility of witnesses, the Court was not entitled to interfere with a High Court's finding in that regard, citing its decision in *Hay v O'Grady* [1992] 1 IR 210; [1992] ILRM 689 (1992 Review, 470) in this regard. Since the High Court had made clear findings, had weighed all the matters up and there had not been any error in the mode in which it had approached this case under the principles stated in *The People v O'Callaghan* [1966] IR 501, the Court affirmed the decision to refuse bail.

BINDING TO THE PEACE

In *Clarke v Hogan* [1995] 1 IR 310, Barron J held that a witness who may be bound over to the peace has a right to call witnesses and address the court. At the conclusion of a case involving charges of common assault, the respondent judge of the District Court had bound the defendant in the case to keep the peace and had made similar orders in relation to four witnesses in the case, of which the applicant was one. The respondent had given no indication during the trial that he intended such a course nor had he given the applicant an opportunity to address the court in relation to the order. On judicial review, Barron J quashed the order.

Barron J held that, once the District Court had jurisdiction to hear the matter, jurisdiction to bind to the peace was thereby shown on the face of the order. However, he went on to state that, since s. 43(13) of the Criminal Justice Administration Act 1914 envisaged the right of a defendant to call witnesses and address the court when an order to be bound to the peace is to be made, it followed that a witness was entitled to the same rights. This was especially having regard to the constitutional guarantee of fair procedures in Article 40.3. Finally, he concluded that, for justice to be seen to be done, the respondent should have indicated how he was thinking and to have invited submissions on this.

CASE STATED

Precluded where District Court declines jurisdiction   In *Director of Public Prosecutions (Whelan) v Delaney* [1996] 1 ILRM 70, Lavan J held that an appeal by way of case stated did not lie under s. 52 of the Courts (Supplemental Provisions) Act 1961, which precludes an appeal concerning 'proceedings relating to an indictable offence which is not being dealt with summarily by the court'. In the instant case the District Court judge had formed the view that the offences alleged against the defendant were not minor offences fit to be tried summarily. Lavan J concluded that the wording of s. 52 of the 1961 Act was sufficient to exclude from the case stated procedure a question of law arising from an offence which the district justice had decided to send forward for trial on indictment. The questions of law which were the subject-matter of the case stated were therefore moot, and the Court could not entertain the case stated under s. 52 of the 1961 Act. It would thus appear that an application for judicial review is the only remedy available in such instances.

DELAY

Indictment prosecution   In *McGavigan v Director of Public Prosecutions and Ors*, High Court, February 15, 1995 O'Hanlon J considered the application of the principles concerning delay in instituting a prosecution on indictment, as to which see *Cahalane v Murphy* [1994] 2 IR 262 (1994 Review, 171).

Summary prosecution   In *Director of Public Prosecutions v O'Donnell and Ors* [1995] 2 IR 294 Geoghegan J considered the application of the principles concerning delay in instituting a summary criminal prosecution, as to which see *Director of Public Prosecutions v Byrne* [1994] 2 IR 236; [1994] 2 ILRM 91 (1994 Review, 172).

EVIDENCE

Evidential burden shift In *Rock v Ireland and Ors*, High Court, November 10, 1995, Murphy J upheld the constitutional validity of ss. 18 and 19 of the Criminal Justice Act 1984. S. 18 of the Criminal Justice Act 1984 provides that, where a person has been arrested without a warrant and that person has a mark or object or other matter in their possession which a Garda believes might be attributable to that person's participation in the commission of the offence for which he had been arrested, then in any subsequent proceedings against them, a failure by that person to account for the presence of the object in question may entitle the court to draw inferences from that failure or refusal. S. 18 also provides that the failure or refusal may amount to corroboration of any other material evidence but that a person should not be convicted solely on an inference drawn from such refusal or failure.

S. 19 of the 1984 Act, which relates to inferences which could be drawn from an accused's presence at a particular place, is to similar effect.

When the applicant was arrested he had in his possession a bag containing a quantity of notes which appeared to be US dollars. After his arrest he was conveyed to a Garda station where he was charged with being in possession of forged bank notes while knowing the same to be forged. While at the Garda station, the meaning of ss. 18 and 19 of the 1984 Act was explained to him. The applicant sought a declaration that ss. 18 and 19 of the 1984 Act were repugnant to the Constitution. As indicated, Murphy J refused the relief sought. Central to his judgment was a review of the decision of Costello J in *Heaney v Attorney General* [1994] 3 IR 593 (1994 Review, 128) and of the Supreme Court in *O'Leary v Attorney General* [1995] 2 ILRM 259: see the Constitutional Law chapter, 181, above.

Murphy J accepted that, in general terms it had been accepted in *Heaney* that the right to remain silent was a necessary ingredient of a fair trial. However, he also pointed out that the Supreme Court had accepted in *O'Leary* that where a statute provided that a particular act or event was to constitute some evidence of guilt, the value of which could be challenged by a variety of means, this was not contrary to the Constitution. In the instant case, he concluded that there was no significant difference between the provision in s. 18 of the 1984 Act that inferences might be drawn from the silence of the accused or that such silence might amount to corroboration. In neither event was the accused required to exculpate himself and he could challenge the wisdom or strength of the inferences drawn. Because of this it could not be said that the presumption of innocence had been set to one side or the burden of proof shifted to the accused.

The applicant had also argued that the doctrine of proportionality should not be applied to constitutional rights, as Costello J had done in the *Heaney* case. But Murphy J took the view that this view had been implicitly supported by the Supreme Court in the *O'Leary* case. Indeed, in concluding that Costello J had taken the correct approach in Heaney, Murphy J anticipated the outcome of the Supreme Court decision in *Heaney* in 1996, to which we will return in the 1996 Review.

Finally, Murphy J dealt with the contention that s. 18 of the 1984 Act amounted to converting the common law accusatorial criminal process into an inquisitorial process. He rejected this, holding that s. 18 was merely an evidence-gathering operation which would result in certain circumstances in additional evidence being made available by the prosecution. In his view, that did not in any way set at nought what he described as the adversarial (*recte* accusatorial) system on which the existing process depended. By way of comment, it must be said, however, that s. 18 involves considerable changes in prior evidential rules. The courts have clearly come to the conclusion, as evidenced by the decisions in *O'Leary, Heaney* and *Rock*, that no fundamental shift in the accusatorial nature of the system has occurred. It may be argued, however, that taken in combination a sense of creeping towards the inquisitorial model is at work.

Exclusion for breach of Custody Regulations In *Director of Public Prosecutions v Spratt* [1995] 2 ILRM 117 and *The People v Connell* [1995] 1 IR 244, O'Hanlon J and the Court of Criminal Appeal, respectively, considered the effect of non-compliance with the Criminal Justice Act 1984 (Treatment of Persons in Custody in Garda Síochána Stations) Regulations 1987 (1987 Review, 119-20). S. 7 of the Criminal Justice Act 1984 provides that non-compliance with the 1987 Regulations shall not 'in itself' render inadmissible any evidence subsequently obtained. In *Spratt* and *Connell*, some differences in approach to s. 7 of the 1984 Act may be detected.

In *Director of Public Prosecutions v Spratt* [1995] 2 ILRM 117, the defendant had been charged with the drink-driving offence in s. 49 of the Road Traffic Act 1961, as amended. At his trial in the District Court, the arresting Garda was unable to state whether the defendant had been informed of his rights or furnished with a notice of his rights in accordance with the provisions of the 1987 Regulations, made pursuant to s. 7 of the Criminal Justice Act 1984. S. 7(3) of the 1984 Act provides that failure to observe any such Regulations 'shall not of itself . . . affect the lawfulness of the custody of the detained person or the admissibility in evidence of any statement made by him.' Reg.8 of the 1987 Regulations provides that an arrested person shall be informed without delay of the matter in respect of which he has been arrested and of his entitlement to consult a solicitor together with a notice containing such information. It was submitted on the defendant's behalf that as there was no evidence to establish that the 1987 Regulations had been complied with, his prosecution was invalid. Counsel for the prosecution argued that s. 49 of the 1961 Act, as amended, provided for its own procedural code to be followed when a person was arrested and brought to a Garda station and that the provisions of s. 5 of the 1984 Act and the 1987 Regulations were not applicable to persons arrested under s. 49(6) of the 1961.

O'Hanlon J rejected this latter submission and held that the provisions of the 1984 Act and the 1987 Regulations applied in relation to persons arrested under s. 49(6) of the 1961 Act, except in so far as they were expressly given a restrictive application, as was the case with ss. 4 and 6 of the 1984 Act.

He went on to state that the phrase 'of itself' in s. 7(3) of the 1984 Act meant that non-observance of the 1987 Regulations did not bring about automatically the exclusion from evidence of all that was done and said while the accused was in custody. Rather, it was a matter for the court of trial to adjudicate in every case as to the impact the non-compliance should have on the prosecution's case. Citing with approval the decision in *Walsh v Ó Buachalla* [1991] 1 IR 56 (1990 Review, 150-4), he held that evidence obtained following a deliberate and conscious breach of an accused person's constitutional rights must be excluded only if it had been obtained as a result of that breach. In the absence of a causative link between the breach and the obtaining of the evidence, O'Hanlon J held that such evidence was admissible.

O'Hanlon J went on to state that, if a breach of the defendant's constitutional rights occurred, the correct approach was to determine in what manner the accused had been prejudiced. In the instant case, he noted that the defendant had been in custody awaiting the arrival of the medical practitioner who was to take a sample of blood or urine, which the accused was obliged by law to provide and that access to or advice from a solicitor could not have averted his fate. Since non-compliance with the requirements of the 1987 Regulations or failure to give formal proof of compliance with them did not of itself invalidate the prosecution, it remained a matter for judicial discretion to decide whether the non-compliance or failure to prove compliance was of such character that it should lead to a dismissal of the charge against the accused. In this respect, he stated that the prosecution should lead evidence to show that the constitutional rights of the accused had been respected and vindicated in relation to the matters referred to in the 1984 Act and the 1987

Regulations, but failure to do so should not necessarily lead to a dismissal of the charge against the accused.

In the second case considering the 1987 Regulations, *The People v Connell* [1995] 1 IR 244, a different approach may be discerned. In *Connell*, the context was, moreover, rather different. In December 1991, the defendant had been found guilty of the murder of a woman in July 1982. The had not been charged with the offence until nine years after the murder. He had been arrested on the evening of 20 May 1991 under s. 30 of the Offences Against the State Act 1939 on suspicion of two offences of arson, brought to a Garda station and there detained for 48 hours under the 1939 Act. Following questioning in relation to the arson offences, the interrogation concentrated on the murder in 1982, and on 22 May the defendant signed a statement admitting to the murder. During the defendant's trial, the trial judge had ruled on the *voir dire* that the statement was voluntary and not obtained by anything in the nature of oppression or violence. No application had been made to the trial judge to exclude the statement on the grounds that the defendant had been deprived of his right to a solicitor. During the course of the application to the Court of Criminal Appeal, it was submitted that the defendant had been denied his constitutional right of access to a solicitor at a relevant time, that the statement had been taken in breach of the Criminal Justice Act 1984, and the 1987 Regulations discussed in the *Spratt* case, above. Reg.12(4) of the 1987 Regulations provides that if an interview continued for four hours 'it shall be either terminated or adjourned for a reasonable time.'

The Court of Criminal Appeal quashed the defendant's conviction and declined to direct a new trial, since the admission had been the sole evidence in the trial.

The Court considered that the central question in the appeal was whether the statement was properly admitted. In this regard, the Court noted that the defendant had first been interrogated in the Garda station on May 20 for five hours and 15 minutes, a period exceeding that prescribed by the Custody Regulations 1987, and there was no suggestion or evidence that at any period during that night the defendant had been asleep. The interview on May 21 again exceeded the time limit permitted, as did a later interview that evening, and it was not denied that for the entire period of his detention in the Garda station he did not receive the benefit of any sleep. The interview on May 22, during which the inculpatory statement was taken, again exceeded the permitted time-limit.

The Court noted that, while the Garda evidence was that the defendant, when offered rest after four hours, expressed his wish to continue the interviews, Reg.12(4) of the Custody Regulations 1987 was a mandatory provision which did not provide for any waiver by an accused person. On this basis, the statement had been taken in breach of a statutory prohibition.

Turning to another aspect of the case in which it may be compared with the *Spratt* case, the Court in *Connell* noted that the defendant had not had access to a solicitor prior to making the inculpatory admission. Citing the Supreme Court's decision in *The People v Healy* [1990] 2 IR 73; [1990] ILRM 313 (1989 Review, 137-9) the Court emphasised first that the right of access to a solicitor was a constitutional right which should not be denied. The Court described as 'inexcusable' that a distant relative of the defendant's who also on the fringe of the Garda investigating team, and who had been requested by the defendant to contact the defendant's solicitor, should have received an answer from the Garda station that the defendant had been contacted by his solicitor on the morning of 22 May. The Court commented that this false information had dispensed with any necessity for the relative to continue trying to contact the defendant's solicitor. The Court stated that this was a matter of great importance as the defendant might well have avoided making the inculpatory statement had he received legal advice that morning.

The question then arose as to whether this false information had involved a conscious and deliberate act by a Garda. Without making a conclusive determination on this issue, the Court held that the taking of the statement against this background fell short of the requirements for fairness, the test adumbrated by Griffin J in *The People v. Shaw* [1982] IR 1. In addition, the Court commented that it was 'deplorable' that the Custody Regulations 1987 had in many respects been seriously ignored by the authorities.

The Court then turned to s. 7(3) of the 1984 Act, and it particular the provision stating that non-compliance with the 1987 Regulations would not 'of itself' render a statement inadmissible. The Court accepted that a statement could not be held to be inadmissible by the mere fact that it had been taken in the course of an interview lasting more than four hours. The Court considered that the words 'of itself' suggested that there could be factors other than the passage of time which could render inadmissible the statement. The Court considered that such factors obtained in the instant case. Thus, the defendant's request to his relative to contact his solicitor had effectively been negatived; in addition the defendant had not received the benefit of any sleep during the entire period of his detention. The Court cited its decision in *The People v McNally and Breathnach* (1981) 2 Frewen 43 to support the conclusion that lack of sleep had been recognised as a contributory factor relevant to the admissibility of a statement (the *McNally and Breathnach* case had concerned the Judges' Rules, to which the Custody Regulations 1987 may be compared: see the 1987 Review, 119-20). Having regard to the combination of all these factors, the Court came to the conclusion that statement taken on 22 May should not have been admitted in evidence and that the conviction should be quashed. As already indicated, no order was

made for a new trial as it was conceded that the statement was an essential
ingredient of a conviction.

We have already noted that in *Connell*, the Court of Criminal Appeal
took a different view both of the constitutional nature of the right of access
to a solicitor and the words 'in itself' in s. 7(3) of the Criminal Justice Act
1984 than was apparent by O'Hanlon J in the *Spratt* case. By way of
comment, we should note that in the course of his judgment O'Hanlon J in
Spratt opined that the right to be informed of the right to access to a solicitor
had not been elevated into a constitutional right in this jurisdiction, and he
commented that if it were already recognised as a constitutional right, it
would have been unnecessary to enact the corresponding provisions of the
1984 Act and the 1987 Regulations. O'Hanlon J referred in this context to
Andrew Butler's article on *Walsh v Ó Buachalla*, 'The Right to be Informed
of the Right to a Lawyer' (1993) ICLJ 173. While it might have been accurate
to suggest that, *in 1984*, the state of Irish law was such that the right to be
informed of the right to a lawyer had not been elevated to a constitutional
level, the same could not be said in the wake of the decision of the Supreme
Court in 1990 in *The People v Healy* [1990] 2 IR 73; [1990] ILRM 313 (1989
Review, 137-9). The *Healy* case had established a clear constitutional
dimension to access to a lawyer in police custody and this was clearly
acknowledged by the Court of Criminal Appeal in *Connell*. The approach
taken by O'Hanlon J in *Spratt*, confirming that in the *Walsh* case, suggested
that he had little enthusiasm for the constitutional dimension to this issue.
Although the Court in *Connell* did not expressly go so far as the position
established by the United States Supreme Court in *Miranda v Arizona*, 384
US 436 (1964), it indicates that a strong line may be adopted, at least in cases
where there are cumulative indications of attempts to frustrate access to a
lawyer.

Sworn evidence and unsworn evidence In *Director of Public Prosecutions (Lee) v Colwell*, High Court, November 17, 1994, the reliability of
direct oral evidence in contrast with a written unsworn evidence arose against
the following background. The defendant had been charged with dangerous
driving under the Road Traffic Act 1961 and possession of a controlled drug,
contrary to the Misuse of Drugs Act 1977. At his trial in the District Court,
the arresting Garda gave evidence that he had detained the defendant pursuant
to s. 3 of the Misuse of Drugs Act 1977, that on searching his car he found
cannabis, that he had arrested the defendant pursuant to s. 25 of the 1977 Act,
had cautioned him and had later given him an oral warning of an intention
to prosecute pursuant to the Road Traffic Act 1961. At the request of the
defendant's solicitor, an unsworn statement of another Garda, who was
unable to give oral evidence, was read out in court: this was to the effect that

the Garda had heard the arresting Garda inform the defendant that he was being arrested pursuant to s. 23 of the Misuse of Drugs Act 1977. The trial judge dismissed both charges against the defendant. He considered that the unsworn statement had raised a question that the defendant had been arrested in purported exercise of powers under s. 23 of the 1977 Act; but since no power of arrest existed under s. 23 the charge under the 1977 Act could not stand. Since there was also a doubt whether the defendant had been informed of the charge on which he was being arrested at the time of arrest, he also dismissed the charge under s. 53 of the Road Traffic Act 1961 on the ground that the defendant had been arrested under the 1977 Act.

On appeal by way of case stated, Barr J held that the trial judge had erred and he remitted the prosecution to the District Court. He held that there were insufficient grounds for declining to act on the oral testimony of the arresting officer. In particular, he held that a written, unsworn, statement cannot have the same evidential status as the sworn testimony of a reputable witness. Accordingly, there was insufficient evidence to raise a doubt that the defendant had not been informed that he was being charged with an offence under s. 3 of the 1977 Act. Finally, applying the decision of the Court of Criminal Appeal in *The People v. Kehoe (N.)* [1985] IR 444, Barr J held that there was no obligation on the arresting Garda to release the defendant from his arrest under the Misuse of Drugs Act 1977 before charging him with dangerous driving under the Road Traffic Act 1961.

Video evidence The decision in *White v Ireland* [1995] 2 IR 268, in which Kinlen J upheld the validity of ss. 12 and 13 of the Criminal Evidence Act 1992, will be discussed in the 1996 Review.

EXTRADITION

Constitutional rights: whether in danger The Supreme Court decision in *Larkin v O'Dea* [1994] 2 ILRM 448 (HC); [1995] 2 ILRM 1 (SC) was discussed in the 1994 Review, 181.

Corresponding offences: robbery In *O'Shea v Conroy* [1995] 2 ILRM 527, Flood J held that offences alleged to have been committed by the plaintiff under the British Theft Act 1968 corresponded to similar offences in the Larceny Act 1916, notwithstanding the use of the words 'rob' and 'stole' in the warrants seeking the plaintiff's extradition. He applied the test laid down in *Wyatt v McLoughlin* [1974] IR 378 and *Wilson v Sheehan* [1979] IR 423 that the Court must examine the factual components of the offences alleged. On this basis, he refused to interfere with the order for the plaintiff's extradition. He reached a similar conclusion in his judgment in *Boyhan v*

Conroy, High Court, 26 May 1996, in which he delivered judgment on the same date as that in *O'Shea*.

Unjust, oppressive or invidious   In *Fusco v O'Dea*, High Court, June 28, 1995, Geoghegan J held that, by reason of the lapse of time since the request for extradition had been made, it would be 'unjust, oppressive or invidious' within the meaning of s. 50(2)(bbb) of the Extradition Act 1965, inserted by the Extradition (Amendment) Act 1987 (1987 Review, 132). In this case, the applicant had been convicted in the Northern Ireland Crown Court in 1981 on various charges. The conviction had been made in his absence, as he had escaped from prison in Northern Ireland in 1981 while on remand. He was later arrested in the State in 1982 and charged with the offence of escape from the Northern Ireland prison, in accordance with the Criminal Law (Jurisdiction) Act 1976. He elected to be tried for this offence in the State, and no attempt was made at the time to have him extradited to Northern Ireland in respect of the convictions entered in the Crown Court. The applicant was convicted on the charge of prison escape and was sentenced to a term of imprisonment, which would have expired in December 1991. Shortly before this, the applicant was brought from prison pursuant to a warrant issued in 1991 seeking his extradition to Northern Ireland in respect of the 1981 Crown Court conviction.

In the circumstances which arose, Geoghegan J declined to order extradition and ordered his release. He considered that from the tenor of communications between the Gardaí and the RUC in 1982, it was clear that the Northern Ireland authorities had decided against extradition in relation to the prison escape and opted for the procedure under the Criminal Law (Jurisdiction) Act 1976. It followed, he felt, that a high-level decision had been made at that time not to seek extradition in relation to the original offences for which the applicant had been convicted. He concluded that the Criminal Law (Jurisdiction) Act 1976 had been invoked because of the perceived impossibility at the time of securing his extradition.

Given that the political offence exemption in the 1965 Act had subsequently become more limited, Geoghegan J held that there was nothing 'in theory' to stop the Northern Ireland authorities changing their minds and applying for extradition in respect of the original offences. However, the surrounding circumstances might entitle a person to invoke successfully s. 50(2)(bbb) of the 1965 Act. In the instant case, the relevant offences had been committed in 1980 and the date of conviction was June 1981. There was a long lapse of time which, combined with other exceptional circumstances in this case, would render it 'unjust, oppressive or invidious' to deliver up the applicant under s. 47 of the 1965 Act. In those circumstances, he ordered the release of the applicant.

INCEST PROCEEDINGS

Reporting restrictions   In *The People v W.M.* [1995] 1 IR 226, Carney J held, in two separate rulings, that s. 5 of the Punishment of Incest Act 1908 precluded the press from attending or adverting to any proceedings under the 1908 Act and prevented a trial judge from disseminating any information concerning such trials. S. 5 of the 1908 Act provided: 'All proceedings under this Act are to be held *in camera*.' For many years, the media had considered that they were precluded from attending or reporting on such cases, but in the 1980s some newspapers had begun to report incest trials in a manner similar to that used in other sexual offences cases. The decision of Carney J in the *W.M.* case, in which the defendant had pleaded guilty to certain charges under the 1908 Act, revealed that this practice was in direct conflict with the express terms of the 1908 Act. In a novel departure, Carney J invited representatives of the various media to address the court on the constitutional validity of s. 5 of the 1908 Act. The Court was addressed by counsel for the accused, the Attorney General, the Director of Public Prosecutions, the National Newspapers of Ireland and Radio Telefís Éireann.

Carney J considered the validity of s. 5 of the 1908 Act against the background of Article 34.1 of the Constitution which provides that justice shall be administered in public, 'save in such special and limited cases as may be prescribed by law.' He also applied the principles laid down by Walsh J in *In re R. Ltd* [1989] IR 126. In this context, Carney J held that s. 5 of the 1908 Act could not have survived the enactment of the 1937 Constitution, though the reasons for this were confined to observing that it: 'was in conflict with Article 34 and was not saved as being a special and limited case prescribed by law.' Despite this conclusion, he went on to consider the effect of s. 45(3) of the Courts (Supplemental Provisions) Act 1961, which provides that:

> Any provision contained in any statute of the Parliament of the former United Kingdom or of the Oireachtas of Saorstát Éireann which provided for the administration of justice otherwise than in public and which is not in force solely by reason of its being inconsistent with the provisions of the Constitution of Saorstát Éireann or the Constitution, as the case may be, shall have full force and effect.

Carney J was of the view that, since s. 45(3) of the 1961 Act enjoyed a presumption of constitutionality, and since its validity had not been challenged (and, he added, 'cannot be challenged') in the instant proceedings, it had:

restored s. 5 of the 1908 Act to full force and effect, with the enjoyment after its Lazarus-like resurrection, of a like presumption of constitutionality.

He concluded that s. 5 of the 1908 Act fell into the category of 'mandatory privacy' adverted to by Walsh J in *In re R. Ltd.* Carney J was fully aware of the implications of his decision and, indeed, he noted that 'pending legislative intervention incest trials . . . will have to be held in total secrecy so far as the public is concerned'. He concluded by rejecting the suggestion that a trial judge could 'prepare and circulate a synopsis of the evidence given and sentence imposed.' He considered that this suggestion was 'contrary to the tenor of the judgment' of McCarthy J for the Court of Criminal Appeal in *The People v Barr (No. 3)*, Court of Criminal Appeal, July 21, 1992 (1992 Review, 257-9). In *Barr*, the Court had stated that it was improper for a trial judge to have 'vetted' newspaper reports in advance of their publication. Presumably, Carney J considered that the preparation of synopses by a trial judge was to be equated with this, though they would appear to be rather different in terms.

To underline the extent of the conclusion arrived at, Carney J held, in a second ruling in the *W.M.* case that he was precluded by s. 5 of the 1908 Act from giving a health board any information regarding the conviction and sentence in the instant case. In the immediate aftermath of the first ruling in the case and the sentencing of the defendant, a health board had sought information concerning the defendant, which Carney J accepted it required in order to perform its statutory duties towards children. In this second ruling, Carney J drew attention to the need for legislative intervention, pointing out that s. 5 of the 1908 act had 'tied my hands'. He went so far as to suggest that, if there was swift legislative intervention, he would be prepared to release the required information to the health board were s. 5 of the 1908 Act to be removed from the legislative picture.

The nod in the direction of amending legislation was taken up by the Oireachtas. S. 2 of the Criminal Law (Incest Proceedings) Act 1995 (the other provisions of the 1995 Act are considered below) has replaced s. 5 of the 1908 Act; it provides that in prosecutions for incest, the trial judge is required to exclude the general public, but bona fide representatives of the media as well as court officers and those directly involved in the case can attend the hearing; and while the verdict and sentence (if any) must be pronounced in public, the names of the defendant and the complainant may only be published by the media where the court authorises this. These provisions are similar to those in s. 6 of the Criminal Law (Rape) Act 1981, as amended by s. 11 of the Criminal Law (Rape) (Amendment)Act 1990, to which Carney J had adverted in his judgment in *W.M.* The 1995 Act came into effect on

July 5, 1995 on its signature by the President. The rulings in *W.M.* drew attention to what had been an anomalous situation, and it is to be welcomed that the Oireachtas acted with great speed in response to the decision in the case.

Reporting restrictions and penalties for incest We have already noted that the principal catalyst for the enactment of the Criminal Law (Incest Proceedings) Act 1995 was the decision of Carney J in *The People v W.M.* [1995] 1 IR 226, discussed above. The 1995 Act, as enacted, differs markedly from the original terms of the Criminal Law (Incest Proceedings) (No. 2) Bill 1995 which was the initial response to the *W.M.* case. The 1995 Bill had been introduced in the Seanad and substantial amendments were proposed at Committee Stage by the Opposition; these were largely accepted by the Minister for Justice and the 1995 Act as enacted owes its form to amendments proposed by the Minister and approved in the Seanad at Report Stage: see 143 Seanad Debates cols. 165-206 (27 April 1995).

S. 2 of the 1995 Act replaced the requirement in s. 5 of the Punishment of Incest Act 1908 that incest prosecutions be held *in camera*. The terms of s. 2 have been described above. S. 6 of the 1995 Act formally repealed s. 5 of the 1908 Act. S. 3 of the 1995 Act provides for the continuing anonymity of both the person charged with incest offences under the 1908 Act and also for the person in relation to whom the offence has been committed. This differs in some respect to the comparable provisions in the Criminal Law (Rape) Act 1981, as amended by s. 11 of the Criminal Law (Rape) (Amendment)Act 1990, since the anonymity of a defendant in rape and associated cases is, in general, removed on conviction; the distinction in incest cases reflects the reality that identification of the defendant would lead to identification of the person in relation to whom the offence was committed. S. 4 of the 1995 Act sets out the penalties for publication of either name, these being largely in line with those provided for under the 1981 and 1990 Acts.

Finally, s. 5 of the 1995 Act increased the penalty on conviction for incest under s. 1 of the 1908 Act from the 20 years imprisonment provided for in the Criminal Justice Act 1993 (see the 1993 Review, 256-7) to life imprisonment. This mirrors the maximum penalty provided for under the Criminal Law Amendment Act 1935 in relation to what is sometimes referred to as statutory rape.

MISCARRIAGES OF JUSTICE

We will discuss the decisions of the Court of Criminal Appeal in *The People v Maleady* [1995] 2 IR 517 and *The People v Pringle* [1995] 2 IR 547, which

Annual Review of Irish Law 1995

considered the effect of s. 2 of the Criminal Procedure Act 1993, in the 1997 Review, in light of the Supreme Court decision in these cases, delivered on 4 March 1997.

MISUSE OF DRUGS

Forfeiture order In *Bowes v Devally* [1995] 2 ILRM 148, the applicant successfully applied by way of judicial review for an order of *certiorari* quashing an order of the respondent Circuit Court judge for the forfeiture of a sum of money in purported compliance with s. 30 of the Misuse of Drugs Act 1977. The applicant had been convicted in the District Court of possession of a small quantity of a controlled drug pursuant to s. 3 of the 1977 Act, that is, possession without an indication of an intent to supply. At the time of the applicant's arrest, however, a sum of money was found in the same room in which the drugs were located. A forensic report had established that there were traces of cannabis resin on the money. The applicant claimed she had been looking after the money for her mother and could not account for the traces of resin. In the District Court, the judge was satisfied that this sum of money was related to the offence and ordered that the money be forfeited pursuant to s. 30 of the 1977 Act. This was affirmed by the respondent on appeal from the District Court conviction and forfeiture order. The respondent's order made no express reference to the forfeiture order but had simply confirmed the District Court decision.

The applicant claimed that the forfeiture order was *ultra vires*. It was argued on the respondent's behalf that the traces of cannabis resin on the money constituted a sufficient evidential base on which the respondent could reasonably have been satisfied that the money forfeited related to the offence for which the applicant had been convicted and that, therefore, his order had been made within jurisdiction. However, Geoghegan J did not accept this submission. As indicated, he quashed the forfeiture order and remitted the matter back to the respondent.

Geoghegan J referred with approval to a number of English authorities, including *R. v Morgan* [1977] Crim LR 488, *R. v Cuthbertson* [1981] AC 470, *R. v Ribeyre* (1982) 4 Cr App R (S) 165, *R. v Llewellyn (K.)* (1985) 7 Cr App R (S) 225 and *R. v Cox* (1986) 8 Cr App R(S) 384. He concluded that, since an order of forfeiture is part of the penalty imposed in a prosecution under the 1977 Act, the circumstances in which such an order can be made must therefore be strictly construed. In this context, he noted that s. 30 of the 1977 Act clearly requires that the property to be forfeited must be related to the particular offence in respect of which the defendant has been convicted. As the applicant had been convicted of possession of drugs simpliciter, the money had no relevance to the offence. He opined, obiter, that the position would be different if the applicant had been convicted of possession of drugs with intent to supply. Nonetheless, in the instant case the order made pursuant to s. 30 of the 1977 Act had been made *ultra vires*.

Geoghegan J concluded that it would be impossible to quash the respondent's order only insofar as it affirmed the forfeiture part of the District Court order, as that would constitute an unacceptable form of severance within the meaning of the decision in *The State (Kiernan) v de Burca* [1963] IR 348. In these circumstances, he held that the appropriate remedy was to quash the entire order and remit the matter back to the respondent with a direction to remove the forfeiture order but otherwise to affirm the District Court order, that is, the conviction.

MONEY LAUNDERING

Detailed Regulations were made in 1995 under the Criminal Justice Act 1994 to describe the measures required of financial institutions under the 1994 Act to combat money laundering: see the Criminal Justice Act 1994 (Section 32(10)(a)) Regulations 1995 (SI No. 104 of 1995), the Criminal Justice Act 1994 (Section 32(10)(b)) Regulations 1995 (SI No. 105 of 1995), the Criminal Justice Act 1994 (Section 32(10)(d)) Regulations 1995 (SI No. 106 of 1995) and the Criminal Justice Act 1994 (Section 32(10)(d)) (No. 2) Regulations 1995 (SI No. 324 of 1995). On the 1994 Act, see the 1994 Review, 174-5.

PROCEDURE

Prosecution of summary offences by corporate body In *Kelly v Foyle Fisheries Commission and McMenamin,* High Court, April 24, 1995 (discussed in the Fisheries chapter, 333, below) Morris J held that the respondent Commission had statutory authority to initiate summary proceedings under the Foyle Fisheries Act 1952, distinguishing the circumstances from those in *Cumman Luthchleas Gael Teo v Windle* [1994] 1 IR 525 (1993 Review, 476-9).

Return for trial: additional charges In *King v Neilan* [1996] 1 ILRM 17, the Supreme Court (Hamilton CJ, Egan and Blayney JJ) held that the effect of s. 18 of the Criminal Procedure Act 1967 was that if an accused was sent forward for trial on the charge in respect of which he was originally charged and in respect of which he had waived a preliminary hearing, additional counts could not be entered on any indictment against him. There was, however, nothing in the 1967 Act to prevent the prosecution bringing additional charges even if they arose from the same circumstances as the original charge, provided that the requirements laid down in Part II of the 1967 Act were complied with, that is, that a preliminary examination would be held in the District Court concerning such additional charges. While the Court considered that it would be more desirable for all charges arising out the same incident to be heard at the same time, and that this might not occur in the instant case, it concluded that the applicant was not deprived of the right to a trial in due course of law pursuant to Article 38.1 of the Constitution.

Return for trial: summons involving Garda　In *Finnegan v Clifford* [1996] 1 ILRM 446, Carney J upheld the validity of a return for trial based on a summons issued by the respondent judge of the District Court. The applicant, a member of the Garda Síochána, relied on the requirement in s. 88(3) of the Courts of Justice Act 1924 that a summons issued in such a case required the signature of a District Court judge. Such had been obtained in the instant case, but the applicant argued that, since the summons bore the heading 'Courts (No. 3) Act 1986, it did not comply with the 1924 Act. Carney J concluded, however, that all relevant aspects of the 1924 Act had been complied with. He also pointed out, in accordance with the decision of the Supreme Court in *Attorney General (McDonnell) v Higgins* [1964] IR 374, that a summons does not confer jurisdiction on a court but in merely a process to secure attendance in court. On that basis, any possible defect in the summons would not deprive the District Court or trial court of jurisdiction to enter into the proceedings. Ultimately, he concluded that the applicant had been validly returned for trial.

ROAD TRAFFIC

Blood sample　In *Director of Public Prosecutions v Corcoran* [1996] 1 ILRM 181, Lavan J considered s. 13(1)(b) of the Road Traffic (Amendment) Act 1978, which provides that, where a person is brought to a Garda station under s. 49 of the Road Traffic Act 1961, there is a requirement on the arrested person to permit the taking of a blood sample which may be discharged if the person gives a sample of urine instead. However, Lavan J accepted that where, as here, through no fault of the subject, a blood sample could not be taken, there was nothing in the plain language of s. 13(1)(b) of the 1978 Act to suggest that the optional provisions of a urine sample thereby became obligatory. He accepted that his construction of the statute may be undesirable. However, since the Court, in construing a penal statute, was not entitled to go beyond the plain meaning of the subsection concerned, he considered that he was constrained to reach this conclusion. In this respect, he relied on the principles adumbrated by the Supreme Court in *Howard v Commissioners of Public Works in Ireland* [1994] 1 IR 101; [1993] ILRM 665 (1993 Review, 430-2). In the circumstances, therefore, he concluded that where a person opted to permit a specimen of blood to be taken but, through no fault of his own, the designated doctor was unable to obtain that specimen, then that person was under no legal obligation to furnish a specimen of his urine.

Disqualification In *Glynn v Hussey* [1996] 1 ILRM 235, the Supreme Court upheld a 10 years disqualification from driving imposed by the respondent judge of the District Court made under s. 27(1) of the Road Traffic Act 1961 on foot of a conviction for a number of offences under the 1961 Act, including driving without a licence and giving a false name to a Garda. The respondent judge had taken into account that the applicant had been convicted on a drink-driving charge under s. 49 of the 1961 Act just over 14 months previously. In the circumstances, the Supreme Court accepted that the respondent had not erred in a way that would justify granting judicial review. The Court also noted that the protection of the common good required that the right to drive a motor vehicle cannot be unrestricted and that the constitutional validity of disqualification, as a secondary punishment, had been upheld in *Conroy v Attorney General* [1965] IR 411.

Invocation of statutory basis for providing sample In *Brennan v Director of Public Prosecutions* [1996] 1 ILRM 267, the Supreme Court held that, on foot of an arrest under s. 49 of the Road Traffic Act 1961, it was sufficient for the Gardaí to inform the arrested person that he was obliged to provide a sample of blood or urine and that failure to do so was itself an offence. The Court held that it was necessary for the Gardaí to inform the arrested person of the precise statutory provision, namely s. 13 of the Road Traffic (Amendment) Act 1978, which provided for such offence and penalty.

SENTENCING

Guilty plea In *The People v D.(J.)*, High Court, April 27, 1995, Carney J held that, where an accused had made a full confession and had pleaded guilty to the offence of rape, the imposition of the maximum sentence was precluded and the court was confined to imposing such a determinate sentence as would take full account of all the factors for and against the accused.

The defendant had confessed and pleaded guilty to raping his mother.

The rape involved violence and bondage and led to her hospitalisation. The defendant had previous convictions, including a similar offence and had a background of violent abuse by his father. In imposing a sentence of 15 years' penal servitude from the date of sentencing, but suspending three years having regard to time spent in custody, Carney J stated that the nature of his crime and all factors mitigating both in his favour and against him had to be taken into account. Carney J indicated that he would have sentenced the defendant on the basis that he should not be released until, in the opinion of the appropriate experts, his release was safe from the point of view of society in general and women in particular. However, having regard to the decision of the Court of Criminal Appeal in *The People v Jackson*, Court of Criminal Appeal, April 26, 1993 (1993 Review, 260) and of the Supreme Court in *G. v Director of Public Prosecutions* [1994] 1 IR 374 he accepted that this would amount to a form of preventative detention which was not known to Irish law. Thus, Carney J concluded that the imposition of the maximum sentence was precluded by reason of the accused's plea of guilty and confession.

While Carney J was undoubtedly correct in concluding that a sentence imposed for the avowed purpose of 'protecting society' is impermissible, it is difficult to conclude that the decisions of the Irish courts preclude the imposition of a maximum sentence in the case of a person pleading guilty. In the context of manslaughter, the Supreme Court held in *The People v Conroy* [1989] ILRM 139 (1988 Review, 180) that while a maximum sentence would be 'exceptional', it did not preclude such a sentence in some circumstances. Just as the Court in *The People v Tiernan* [1988] IR 250 (1988 Review, 181) regarded as exceptional the imposition of a non-custodial sentence in a rape case (an example being Carney J's judgment in *The People v W.C.* [1994] 1 ILRM 321 (1993 Review, 261-3), it is to be assumed that in some circumstances the maximum penalty is one which would be regarded as being appropriate both for the offence and the offender, albeit in highly unusual circumstances. Whether the circumstances in the instant case would have merited such a sentence is a moot point; it is merely argued here that such an option cannot be precluded in all cases. However, we should note that Carney J applied the same approach to such cases in *The People v J.R.*, High Court, December 5, 1995, in which he imposed a 15 year sentence in a case in which there had been guilty pleas to 25 representative counts, including rape, unlawful carnal knowledge, indecent assault and sexual assault, including what Carney J described as the rape of a girl of four years of age.'

Defence Forces

REPRESENTATIVE ASSOCIATIONS

In *Dorgan and Ors v Permanent Defence Forces Other Ranks Representative Association (PDFORRA)*, High Court, May 11, 1994, Costello J considered the Standing Orders of the respondent, PDFORRA, which had been established pursuant to the Defence (Amendment) Act 1990 (1990 Review, 266-7).

In 1993, a representative of the southern region on the National Executive of the respondent Association (hereinafter the representative), sought a meeting of the National Executive to consider a vote of no confidence in the Association's General Secretary. Prior to this meeting being held, the southern region held a meeting during which it became clear that it did not support the call for a no confidence vote, and the representative on the National Executive indicated his intention to resign. The meeting then resolved to replace the representative on the National Executive with another person (hereinafter the replacement). The representative wrote to the National Executive to tender his resignation and this was accepted. The replacement attended this meeting pursuant to the resolution of the southern region that he replace the representative. The representative then had what Costello J described as 'second thoughts.' He wrote to the National Executive to withdraw his resignation and the National Executive held a meeting at which they rescinded his resignation. Subsequently, the representative and the General Secretary resigned from the National Executive.

The plaintiffs, the members of the southern region, sought declarations to the effect that the representative had resigned and that the replacement had been validly appointed. Costello J granted the first declaration but refused the second.

As to whether the representative had resigned, he noted that the standing orders of the Association provided that the resolution accepting the representative's resignation could not be rescinded for a period of three months. It was not thus not possible for the National Executive to rescind its acceptance of his resignation, so that his resignation remained effective.

As to the replacement's appointment, Costello J noted that Standing Order 8 of the Association required that an important appointment should not be made otherwise than by secret ballot. He pointed out that the 1993 meeting of the southern region was held in order to obtain an explanation of the representative's proposed No Confidence motion. Once that explanation was obtained, he considered that it was not open to the meeting to appoint a replacement without first circulating an agenda and then holding a secret ballot. Thus, in the circumstances, the replacement's appointment was not valid and he refused to grant the declaration sought.

Education

DUBLIN INSTITUTE OF TECHNOLOGY

Governing body elections   In *Grennan and Keating v Dublin Institute Of Technology and Minister for Education*, High Court, March 16, 1995, Geoghegan J upheld a 'gender balance' direction issued by the Minister for Education concerning the election of the governing body of the Dublin Institute of Technology (the DIT).

The plaintiffs were members of the academic staff of the DIT. The functions, powers, composition of and elections to the DIT's governing body were provided for in the Dublin Institute of Technology Act 1992 (see the 1992 Review, 309). Pursuant to s.6(4)(b) of the 1992 Act, the members of the governing body were to include 'two persons', members of the academic staff and elected by the staff, in accordance with the regulations made by the governing body. In 1994, the Director of Higher Education in the Department of Education wrote to the Director of the DIT, reminding him that the Minister had determined that, as a matter of policy, regulations to be drawn up by colleges' governing bodies were to provide for the election of one woman and one man. The governing body, by regulation, provided for a system of election under which one male and one female member of the academic staff would be elected as the 'two persons' referred to in the 1992 Act and the regulation recited the terms of the Minister's policy direction. The plaintiffs contended that there was no power under the 1992 Act to hold a gender-based election. Alternatively, they argued that even if such power existed, the election was invalid since the governing body had not exercised its own independent judgment in deciding to hold such an election, having considered itself bound to follow the direction given by the Minister. Geoghegan J refused the relief sought.

He held that, as a matter of construction, one man and one woman together constituted 'two persons', so that pursuant to s.6(4)(b) of the 1992 Act the governing body was not precluded from regulating an election in such a way that the two persons must comprise one male and one female. He noted that the Oireachtas had envisaged that there could be various methods of election since s.6(4)(b) of the 1922 Act referred to election by the staff 'in accordance with the regulations made by the governing body'. He accepted that it would have been envisaged that any method adopted would be 'fair and democratic', but he concluded that the particular method adopted in the election regulation was one which would be regarded by reasonable people as fair and democratic and that to prescribe such method was within the governing body's powers, irrespective of whether any policy direction had been given by the Minister.

Finally, he also pointed out that since s.7(1) of the 1992 Act provided that the governing body must exercise its functions 'subject to such policies as may be determined by the Minister from time to time', this empowered the Minister to direct the governing body, as in the instant case, to ensure that the election resulted in one male and one female nominee. In the instant case, Geoghegan J held that the Minister had issued a policy directive which the governing body was obliged to obey, and the effect of which was to direct the governing body to do something it was empowered to do under the Act. On these grounds, as indicated, he refused the relief sought.

The decision of Geoghegan J is of interest since the level of control exercised by the Minister in respect of the DIT is replicated in similar legislation enacted in recent years concerning other third level colleges such as the Regional Technical Colleges Act 1992 (1992 Review, 312). The wide discretion afforded the Minister by Geoghegan J in the *Grennan and Keating* case will also prove of interest in the context of extending such Ministerial discretion to the wider university sector pursuant to the Universities Bill 1996, which will be discussed in a future Review.

VOCATIONAL EDUCATION

The Vocational Education (Grants for Annual Schemes of Committees) Regulations 1995 (SI No.384 of 1995), made under the Vocational Education Act 1930, provided for the additional, supplemental and special grants to Vocational Education Committees for 1996.

Electricity and Energy

GENERAL REGULATION OF ELECTRICITY AND ENERGY

The Energy (Miscellaneous Provisions) Act 1995 incorporates a number of changes to the existing statutory regime concerning the production, supply, sale, transmission, distribution and use of forms of energy. It thus effects considerable changes to the powers and functions of two State bodies, Bord Gáis Éireann (BGE, the Irish Gas Board), the Electricity Supply Board (ESB) and, to a minor extent, Bord na Móna, the Turf Development Board. The main focus of the 1995 Act is on the activities of BGE, amending existing legislation on the operation of gas pipelines and electricity cables offshore, inspection of energy infrastructure facilities, the investigation of accidents involving those facilities and extending and strengthening the Minister for Energy's powers to grant offshore licensing and lease undertakings. In this respect, the 1995 Act involves amendments to the Continental Shelf Act 1968, the Safety, Health and Welfare (Offshore Installations) Act 1987 and the Sea Pollution Act 1991 in so far as offshore exploration activity is concerned. The 1995 Act amends the Fuels (Control of Supplies) Act 1971 and 1982 concerning petroleum production and supplies from offshore installations in emergency situations. The 1995 Act also deals with the control of theft of electricity and gas and recoupment from the ESB of the costs of reviews of the provision and regulation of electricity services carried out by the Minister. The 1995 Act came into effect on 21 December 1995 on its signature by the President, but certain provisions have retrospective effect.

MINERAL EXPLORATION

Applications for licences and fees   The Minerals Development (Application Fees for Certain State Mining Licenses) Regulations 1995 (SI No. 214 of 1994) revised the procedure for applying for prospecting licences and increased the fee therefor. The 1995 Regulations came into effect on August 1, 1995.

Renewal and validation of licences   The Minerals Development Act 1995, which came into effect on July 17, 1995 on its signature by the President, provided for the validation of certain existing minerals prospecting licences and increased penalties for offences under the Minerals Development Act 1940.

PETROLEUM

National minimum stock: National Oil Reserves Agency The European Communities (Minimum Stocks Of Petroleum Oils) Regulations 1995 (SI No.96 of 1995) provided for the establishment by the Minister for Transport Energy and Communications of a National Oil Reserves Agency. The 1995 Regulations give effect in an amended form to the requirements in Directives 68/414/EEC and 72/425/EEC, which require Member States to maintain minimum oil reserves, namely 90 days average oil consumption. These Directives had previously been implemented by the European Communities (Minimum Stocks Of Petroleum Oils) Regulations 1974 to 1977, which had, in effect, placed the burden of complying with the Directives on private oil importers. The 1974 and 1977 Regulations were revoked by the 1995 Regulations. The Regulations provide that the costs incurred by the Agency will be funded by a levy on oil sales to be collected by the Agency from oil companies, the sum to be based on market share to be calculated by the Minister on the basis of information provided under the 1995 Regulations. The Regulations came into effect on June 1, 1995.

Whitegate offtake The Petroleum Oils (Regulation or Control of Acquisition, Supply, Distribution or Marketing) (Continuance) Order 1995 (SI No. 340 of 1995) continued through 1996 the regime outlined in the Fuels (Petroleum Oils) Order 1983, which requires petroleum fuel importers to purchase a proportion of their products from the State-owned Irish National Petroleum Corporation Ltd's refinery in Whitegate, Cork. On the 1983 Order, see the 1994 Review, 246.

Equity

TRUSTS

Resulting trusts Where a joint deposit account is opened in a manner which allows the depositor alone to retain dominion over the money in the account during his lifetime but which displays the intention that the balance should go to the other party should he survive him, the question arises whether the money which remains in the account on the depositor's death should be subject to a resulting trust in favour of his estate or whether it can be paid over to the other party. This question, which has provoked considerable debate in recent years in view of the divergence between established principles in this jurisdiction and elsewhere, appears to have finally been resolved by the Supreme Court in *Lynch v Burke* [1996] 1 ILRM 114. The deceased opened a joint account in the names of herself and the first named defendant, her niece. All lodgments were made by the deceased and the account deposit book was endorsed payable to the deceased only or survivor. The deceased bequeathed all her property to the plaintiff and in the High Court ([1990] 1 IR 1) O'Hanlon J held that a resulting trust arose and that therefore the plaintiff was entitled to the money remaining in the joint account. He stated that as a general principle where money is deposited in a joint account by a person who subsequently dies there is an equitable presumption of a resulting trust against the survivor in favour of the estate of the deceased in respect of the beneficial interest in the monies remaining on deposit at the time of death. Although on the facts, O'Hanlon J held that the deceased had intended that the first named defendant would be entitled by right of survivorship to the beneficial interest in this money and the equitable presumption in favour of the deceased's estate was therefore rebutted, he felt obliged on the authority of the Supreme Court decision in *Owens v Greene* [1932] IR 225 to hold that the transaction was an invalid gift and an unsuccessful attempt to make a testamentary disposition otherwise than by will. Despite this conclusion there were definite signs in O'Hanlon J's judgment that he was unhappy with the reasoning in the earlier Supreme Court decision, which as he pointed out, appeared to conflict with the interpretation of this branch of the law in many other common law Jurisdictions. In particular the approach taken by Dixon and Evatt JJ in the Australian High Court in *Russell v Scott* (1936) 55 CLR 440, which involved regarding both parties upon the opening of the account as being jointly entitled at common law to a chose in action consisting of their contractual right against the bank which would accrue to the survivor, was a plausible alternative and avoided the difficulties inherent in regarding the transaction as a testamentary disposition, namely the need for compliance with the requisite statutory formalities.

Delivering the judgment of the Supreme Court, O'Flaherty J considered the legal effect of opening a deposit account in joint names. He said that by her presence and signature, it was manifest that the first named defendant was a party to the contract from the outset and she must be entitled to claim as a party to the contract under its terms. He quoted with approval from the judgment of Dixon and Evatt JJ in *Russell v Scott* and stated that since historically, the concept of a resulting trust was an invention of equity to defeat the misappropriation of property as a consequence of potentially fraudulent or improvident transactions, it would be paradoxical if the doctrine was allowed to defeat the clear intention of the donor as found by the trial judge. O'Flaherty J pointed out that in *Owens v Greene*, the Supreme Court had been concerned to emphasise the importance of testamentary dispositions being required to comply with statutory requirements. He commented that if the arrangement in the case before him was not testamentary, which in his view it was not, these statutory requirements had no application. O'Flaherty J also stated that *Owens* had given cause for unease on a number of grounds and concluded that it was wrongly decided and should be overruled. He said that at law the defendant had a legal interest in the monies on deposit either by reason of the contractual relationship of the parties or in the alternative as a gift, which admittedly was not a completed gift in the conventional sense but was one which should be upheld as being a gift subject to a contingency namely, the donor's death.

One cannot but agree with O'Flaherty J's conclusion that the result arrived at by the Supreme Court will introduce a measure of consistency into this area of the law, and as he stated 'restore . . . equity to the high ground which it should properly occupy to ameliorate the harshness of common law rules on occasion rather than itself be an instrument of injustice'. While in some respects the manner in which this result was achieved was somewhat convoluted, the Supreme Court judgment should lay rest the rather paradoxical decision of *Owens v Greene* once and for all.

Constructive trusts The potential of the constructive trust as a device which will provide a remedy where 'justice and good conscience' demand it was explored by Barron J in *Murray v Murray*, High Court, December 15, 1995. The defendant was the legal owner of premises in respect of which he had paid the initial deposit; the remainder, approximately three quarters of the price, was paid by way of a mortgage. The plaintiff, his nephew, had lived in the premises with his aunt, the defendant's sister, for many years and it was accepted by Barron J that the defendant had intended to transfer the house to his sister. While she was alive she paid the mortgage instalments and most of the outgoings on the property. After her death the plaintiff claimed a declaration that the entire beneficial ownership in the house was vested in his aunt at the date of her death and the defendant claimed the legal and beneficial ownership himself. The plaintiff claimed that the circumstances were such that it would be unconscionable for the defendant to rely on his legal title and he relied on the decision of *Hussey v Palmer* to support this claim. Barron J stated: 'It is I think quite clear that the law will impose a constructive trust in all circumstances where it would be unjust and unconscionable not to do so.' In his view *Hussey* was authority for the proposition that in certain circumstances where equity so required, 'a debt may be secured by the device of a constructive trust on the property created by the money involved'. He said that in the case before him the equity to create a constructive trust arose from the payment of monies which had resulted in the property being freed from the mortgage and the owner being relieved of other outgoings. He concluded that the aunt was at the date of her death entitled to three quarters of the beneficial interest in the property so, the plaintiff, being her next of kin, was a tenant in common of the premises with the defendant.

The language used by Barron J is reminiscent of that employed by him in *N.A.D. v T.D.* [1985] ILRM 153 in which he made the following statement: 'The constructive trust is imposed by operation of law independently of intention in order to satisfy the demands of justice and good conscience. Its imposition is dependent upon the conduct of the person upon whom the trust is imposed and prevents him from acting in breach of good faith.' That case concerned a claim relating to contributions allegedly made by the plaintiff towards the building of a house on a site bought in her husband's name. Barron J said that the essential prerequisite for the imposition of a constructive trust in such a case was that there must be an element in the conduct of the person upon whom it is imposed which would make it inequitable for him to assert his legal rights. He concluded that there was no evidence of conduct on the part of the husband which would make it inequitable to deny the wife's claim and her claim to a share in the house therefore failed. (See also the judgment of Costello J in *H.K.N. Investment Oy v Incotrade Pvt Ltd* [1993] 3 IR 152).

In view of the fact that any extension of the circumstances in which the purchase money resulting trust can be inferred seems to have been ruled out by the Supreme Court in *L. v L.* [1992] 2 IR 77, the use of a constructive trust as a means of conferring beneficial ownership in property may have further potential for development in this jurisdiction, particularly in the context of co-habitees to whom the provisions of the Judicial Separation and Family

Law Reform Act 1989 do not apply. While the common intention constructive trust developed in England and applied in this context has severe
limitations, principally the fact that the intention underlying the imposition
of such a trust should be founded on express agreement, the type of constructive trust utilised by Barron J in *Murray* would not appear to be so limited.

Voidable trusts   S. 10 of the Conveyancing Act (Ireland) 1634 provides
that any gift, grant or conveyance of property made for the purpose of
delaying, hindering or defrauding creditors is 'void' as against such creditors
and this has been interpreted as meaning 'voidable' — (see *Re Eichholz*
[1959] Ch 708). As Palles CB stated in *Re Moroney* (1887) 21 LR IR 27,
60-61 no actual intention need exist in the mind of the grantor but where the
necessary or probable result of his denuding himself of the property is to
defeat or delay creditors, the intent is as a matter of law assumed from the
necessary or probable consequences of the act done. This approach was
followed recently in *McQuillan v Maguire* [1996] 1 ILRM 395 in which the
plaintiffs were granted a well charging order over 50 per cent of a premises
which belonged to the first named defendant despite the fact that he had
purported to consent to an order declaring that his wife, the second named
defendant, was entitled to the entire beneficial interest in it. A decree in favour
of the plaintiffs against the first named defendant in relation to a building
contract had been converted into a judgment mortgage. A month after the
decree was made the second named defendant instituted proceedings under
the Married Women's Status Act 1957 and subsequently the consent order
was made. The plaintiffs submitted that the order in these proceedings was
obtained by collusion. Costello P referred to *Re Moroney* and said that the
court did not have to find that the agreement had been motivated by actual
fraud in order to set it aside. If it could be shown that the necessary or probable
result of the agreement was to defeat or delay creditors, it could be avoided.
He concluded that the agreement was void as it had the effect both of
hindering and delaying the payment of a debt due by the first named
defendant and he held that the plaintiffs were entitled to a well charging order
over 50 per cent of the premises on the basis that the wife had a 50% beneficial
interest by virtue of contributions she had made to earlier family homes.

Trustee's duties   The extent of the duty imposed on a trustee in relation to
investment of trust property has recently been considered in this jurisdiction
in some detail by Murphy J in *Stacey v Branch* [1995] 2 ILRM 136. The
plaintiff beneficiary brought a claim against the defendant trustee alleging a
breach of trust on the grounds that the latter had not managed a trust property
with the necessary degree of care and claimed specifically that if this house
had been let over a period of 14 years rather than maintained by a caretaker,

it would have yielded a substantial rental income. The trust deed conferred on the defendant the power to deal with this property 'as he in his absolute discretion shall think fit' pending the attainment of 21 years by the plaintiff. Murphy J made it clear that words such as 'absolute discretion' would not necessarily relieve a trustee from his duty to exercise reasonable care and prudence. However, he was satisfied that the defendant's decision to place the caretaker in occupation of the premises was one made *bona fide* in the exercise of his discretion and he dismissed the plaintiff's claim. Murphy J also gave some consideration to the nature of a trustee's duty of investment in general terms. He stated that in carrying out his duties, the trustee must take such care as a reasonably cautious man would take having regard not only to interest of those who are entitled to the income but to the interests of those who will take in the future. In exercising his discretion a trustee must act honestly and diligently and in selecting investments he must take as much care as a prudent man would take in making an investment for the benefit of persons for whom he felt morally obliged to provide.

This statement which requires a trustee in selecting investments to exercise the care which a prudent man would take in making an investment for the benefit of persons for whom he felt morally obliged to provide would seem to impose a relatively stringent standard on trustees. However, in practice losses sustained by a trust tend to be attributable to lack of initiative on the part of a trustee rather than to speculative investment decisions. A recent example of this is the decision of the English Court of Appeal in *Nestle v National Westminster Bank plc* [1993] 1 WLR 1260 in which a beneficiary failed to establish liability on the part of the defendant despite the complete lack of foresight displayed by the bank. Legatt LJ even went so far as to comment that: 'No testator, in the light of this example, would choose this bank for the effective management of his investment.' As Doyle has commented ((1991) 5 *Trust Law International* 138, 142) there is no reported case in which a trustee has been found liable for a breach of trust arising from investment within the ambit of that authorised by the trust instrument or the general law where the trust capital has simply continued to erode as a result and he concludes that 'the burden of proof facing potentially litigious beneficiaries is prohibitively high.' While risk taking on the part of trustees ought not to be encouraged, perhaps the courts in both jurisdictions should re-assess whether decisions such as *Stacey* and *Nestle* are unduly lenient towards the trustee who fails to make effective and informed decisions about the management of trust assets under his control.

EQUITABLE REMEDIES

Interlocutory injunctions   In *B. & S. Ltd v Irish Auto Trader Ltd* [1995] 2 ILRM 152 which concerned allegations of passing off in relation to a magazine, McCracken J applied the now well established test of whether there was a serious issue to be tried and whether, on the balance of convenience, an injunction should be granted. McCracken J referred to the judgment of Lord Diplock in *American Cyanamid Co. v Ethicon Ltd* [1975] AC 396 and said that in his view the entire test in such cases rests on a consideration of where the balance of convenience lies but that the adequacy of damages is a very important element and may often be the decisive element in considering where this balance lies. While McCracken J accepted that the court will normally take whatever steps are necessary to preserve the status quo, he held that in view of the fact, *inter alia*, that the defendant had acted in a *bona fide* manner and that there was unlikely to be any confusion between the parties' magazines the interlocutory injunction sought should be refused. He concluded that this was one of the unusual cases where the balance of convenience lay in favour of refusing an injunction, notwithstanding the fact that this involved altering the status quo. A similar approach to the issue of the need to preserve the status quo in actions involving interlocutory injunctions can be seen in another judgment of McCracken J in *Private Research Ltd v Brosnan* [1996] 1 ILRM 27. This case concerned the plaintiff's application for an interlocutory injunction to restrain alleged breach of copyright and breach of confidence on the defendant's part in relation to a publication. McCracken J considered whether damages would be an adequate remedy for either party and concluded that they would not be and then proceeded to examine the general issue of the balance of convenience. He said that weighing heavily in the plaintiff's favour was 'the general rule that, where possible, the court should strive to maintain the status quo'. However, he stressed that this was only one element which must be assessed in considering where the balance of convenience lies and said that there was no absolute rule that the status quo must be maintained. McCracken J concluded that the inconvenience which would be caused to the defendants if an injunction were granted seemed to him to far outweigh any inconvenience which would be caused to the plaintiff if the injunction were refused and in the circumstances, he decided to decline to grant the interlocutory injunction sought. A further decision concerning an application for an interlocutory injunction is that of the Supreme Court in *Ferris v Ward*, November 7, 1995 in which the court applied the *American Cyanamid* principles and reiterated that it was no part of the court's function at the interlocutory stage to try to resolve conflicts of evidence on affidavit nor difficult questions of law.

Mareva injunctions   The fact that Mareva injunctions may be granted on a worldwide basis was confirmed by Costello J in *Deutsche Bank Atkiengesellchaft v Murtagh* [1995] 1 ILRM 381, which was considered in the 1994 Annual Review. However, some residual doubt remains about this point in the light of the judgment of Murphy J in *Countyglen plc v Carway* [1995] 1 ILRM 481 which was delivered about a month later without reference to the earlier decision. In addition, the *Countyglen* judgment is interesting in that it confirms that where a plaintiff seeks a Mareva injunction, as with any other form of interlocutory injunction, the first hurdle which he must overcome is to satisfy the court that there is a substantial question to be tried and not that he has a *prima facie* case. The applicant company brought proceedings against the respondents seeking various orders including a declaration that they had been guilty of fraud and/or conspiracy to defraud, breach of trust and breach of duty and orders pursuant to s. 12 of the Companies Act 1990 directing the respondents to repay sums which they had allegedly unlawfully and wrongfully removed from the company. The High Court granted an interim Mareva injunction and the issue of whether to grant an interlocutory order and ancillary relief then came before the court. Murphy J stated that he doubted that there was any significant difference between the expressions 'good arguable case' and 'substantial question to be tried', but he said that if such a distinction could be drawn he would prefer the latter formulation. He confirmed that the 'probability test' had been rejected by the Supreme Court in *Campus Oil Ltd v Minister for Industry & Energy (No. 2)* [1983] IR 88 and stated: 'in my view, it would be entirely inappropriate for the court on an interlocutory application to review such of the evidence as is available to it and attempt to forecast the outcome of the proceedings as a matter of probability or likelihood. What can and should be done is to determine that there is a fair and serious question to be tried.' Murphy J said that it was in relation to the risk of the defendant's assets being dissipated in advance of any judgment and also with regard to the general balance of convenience that considerations different from those pertaining in relation to conventional injunctions arose. On the basis of the evidence available to the court, Murphy J concluded that the proper inference to draw was that the defendants did have assets within the jurisdiction, that there was a real risk that these assets would be dissipated and that the defendants were not apprehensive of any real inconvenience to them as a result of a Mareva injunction being granted and he made the order sought.

Murphy J made an order confined to assets within the jurisdiction of the court because this was the form of relief sought by the plaintiff but on the basis of this he directed that an order for discovery made against the defendants should also be confined to assets within the jurisdiction although in this instance the order was sought in wider terms. As the statement that

Mareva injunctions should not extend to extra-territorial assets appears to be based on a restrictive authority (*Allied Arab Bank Ltd v Hajjar* [1988] QB 787) which has not been followed either in England, e.g., *Babanaft International Co. SA v Bassatne* [1990] Ch 13; *Republic of Haiti v Duvalier* [1990] 1 QB 202) or in this jurisdiction (*Deutsche Bank Atkiengesellchaft v Murtagh* [1995] 1 ILRM 381; *Balkanbank v Taher*, High Court, March 29, 1995 — see Courtney (1996) 3 *CLP* 1, 4 n. 17), it is unlikely that the approach taken by Murphy J would be followed if a case arose in which an extra-territorial Mareva injunction was required to avoid the frustration of a subsequent order of the court.

This fact that the rationale behind the grant of what have sometimes been referred to as rather 'draconian' orders is that they should operate 'as a measure against abuse rather than a form of security for the plaintiff' (see Zuckerman 'Mareva and Interlocutory Injunctions Disentangled' (1992) 108 LQR 559, 56 1) was recently reiterated by the Supreme Court in *O'Mahony v Horgan* [1996] 1 ILRM 161. The judgments in this case are important as they echo the point made by Scott LJ in the English Court of Appeal in *Polly Peck International plc v Nadir* [1992] 4 All ER 769 that the reason for granting Mareva injunctions is to prevent a defendant from dissipating his assets with a view to avoiding any subsequent order of the court and that such orders are not merely intended as a form of security for plaintiffs. In *O'Mahony*, the plaintiff had been appointed liquidator of a company of which the respondents were directors. Murphy J granted an interlocutory injunction to restrain the second named respondent from disposing of or dissipating a sum of money payable under an insurance policy. The Supreme Court allowed the appeal by the second named respondent and held that before a plaintiff will be entitled to a Mareva injunction, he must establish that there is a likelihood that the defendant's assets will be dissipated with the intention that they would not be available to meet any decree ultimately made in the proceedings and this intention had not been established in the case before the court. Hamilton CJ stated that a Mareva injunction should only be granted if the plaintiff can establish that he has an arguable case that he will succeed in the action and that the anticipated disposal of the defendant's assets is for the purpose of preventing a plaintiff from recovering damages and not merely for the purpose of carrying on a business or discharging lawful debts. This requirement is an important safeguard and should temper an over eagerness to grant an order which can have catastrophic effects on a defendant's ability to continue carrying on legitimate business. As O'Flaherty J commented: 'it need to be emphasised that the Mareva injunction is a very powerful remedy which if improperly invoked will bring about an injustice, something that it was designed to prevent.'

European Community Law and the European Union

IMPLEMENTATION OF COMMUNITY LAW

Relevant European Community law matters are discussed in the individual chapters of this Review. In addition, readers are referred to the Table of European Communities Legislation Implemented by Statutory Instrument in Irish Current Law Monthly Digest for a comprehensive listing of Community law implemented during 1995.

SUPERVISION OF SECONDARY LEGISLATION

The European Communities (Amendment) Act 1995 amended s. 4 of the European Communities Act 1972 to provide that the reference therein to the 'Joint Committee on Foreign Affairs' (inserted by the European Communities (Amendment) Act 1994) be replaced by the 'Joint Committee on European Affairs'. This reflected the decision to establish the Joint Committee on European Affairs which now exercises the statutory functions conferred in relation to the supervision of the secondary legislation of the European Communities. The 1995 Act came into effect on May 23, 1995.

Family Law

ADOPTION

Parental failure   In *Western Health Board v An Bord Uchtála* [1996] 1 ILRM 434, the Supreme Court failed to take the opportunity to develop the jurisprudence on parental abandonment in relation to compulsory adoption. It will be recalled that the Adoption Act 1988 permits the compulsory adoption of any child, regardless of the marital status of his or her parents, on the basis of parental 'failure', where that failure constitutes an abandonment on the part of the parents of their parental rights. It may be useful to quote in full what must be shown to the satisfaction of the court under s. 3(1) of the 1988 Act:

> I(A) for a continuous period of not less than twelve months immediately preceding the time of the making of the application, the parents of the child to whom the declaration under s. 2(1) relates, for physical or moral reasons, have failed in their duty towards the child,
> (B) it is likely that such failure will continue without interruption until the child attains the age of eighteen years,
> (C) such failure constitutes an abandonment on the part of the parents of all parental rights, whether under the Constitution or otherwise, with respect of the child, and
> (D) by reason of such failure the State, as guardian of the common good, should supply the place of parents,
>
> II that the child:
> (A) at the time of the making of the application, is in the custody of and has a home with the applicants,
> (B) for a continuous period of not less than twelve months immediately preceding that time has been in the custody of, and has had a home with, the applicants, and
>
> III that the adoption of the child by the applicants is an appropriate means by which to supply the place of the parents.

When the Supreme Court addressed the constitutional validity of the measure in the Article 26 reference of *In re Adoption (No. 2) Bill 1987* [1989]

ILRM 266; [1989] IR 656, Finlay CJ made it plain that, in s. 3, the provisions of the sub-clauses I(A) to II(B) inclusive provided a series of matters which had to be established *seriatim* to the satisfaction of the court:

> They are not merely matters to be taken into consideration by the court in exercising a general discretion but are framed in the much more stringent form of being absolutely essential proofs requiring separately to be established. Failure in any one of these proofs absolutely prohibits the making of the authorising order, no matter how strong might be the evidence available of its desirability from the point of view of the child.

The Chief Justice addressed the requirement of parental abandonment as follows:

> The concept of abandonment of parental rights falls to be considered after it has been established that a failure of parental duty for physical or moral reasons has continued for more than twelve months and is likely to continue until the child attains eighteen years of age. The sub-clause clearly envisages that there might be cases where such failure was established but an abandonment of rights was not proved. An abandonment could be established by evidence of the conduct of the parent or parents concerned which would in certain cases include statements made by them and/or the nature and type of the failure in duty which had been established. A mere statement by a parent or parents that they wished to abandon a child would not necessarily constitute proof in any particular case of the fact of abandonment but may do so. Failure of parental duty established under sub-clause I(A) and (B) is not of itself evidence of abandonment. The necessity for the proof of abandonment indicates a special regard for the constitutionally protected parental rights.

In *Western Health Board v An Bord Uchtála*, the child's parents had married in 1983. The father left the mother in 1987, when the spouses already had three children, because she was having an affair with another man. He returned to the family home on one occasion in February 1988, when the child whose adoption was in issue was conceived as a result of the father's 'forcing himself on [the mother] and having sexual intercourse with her without her consent.'

When the child, a girl, was born in November 1988, the mother, believing the man with whom she was having the affair was the father, placed the child for adoption. When she took this step it was discovered that she had given her husband's name as the father for the birth certificate. The social worker who was concerned with the matter sought to obtain a signed declaration from him that he was not the father. He was by now living in England. The father refused to sign the declaration as he believed himself to be the child's father. He agreed to undergo a DNA test but failed to keep the appointment. He returned to Ireland in September 1990 and eventually had the test in May 1991. It showed that he was the father. In November 1991, he met the social worker, said that he would like to see his daughter and indicated that he wished to have her return from the couple to whom she had been given. The social worker advised the necessity for care in such course and discussed with him the options that existed with regard to the care of the child if she were returned to him. Following this, the Western Health Board set in train the application for an order under s. 3 of the 1988 Act. The father sought custody of his daughter in July 1992. His solicitor had on his behalf sought her return the previous December. Part of the delay in the institution of the proceedings was attributable to the father's delay in obtaining legal aid.

Having considered these facts and the evidence of the father's conduct, his delay and procrastination, his expressed reluctance to give up his daughter, his expressed claim to recover her and his explanation of this in evidence, Lardner J was unable to conclude that the proper inference to be drawn from the evidence was that the father's failure to perform his duty as a parent amounted to a total and final abandonment of his rights within s. 3(1)I(C) of the Act. (The mother did not contest that her failure amounted to such abandonment on her part.)

Lardner J quoted in full the passage on parental abandonment from Finlay CJ's judgment in the Article 26 reference which we have set out above. It seemed to Lardner J that:

> conversely to what the Chief Justice says there, statements of a parent maybe evidence of a wish or an intention not to abandon their child. They may not be decisive evidence but they may be evidence to consider in a particular case. Having considered the evidence of [the father]'s conduct from 1988 to 1992, to which I have already referred, . . . I am unable to conclude that the proper inference is that all the conduct constituting failure by [the father] to perform his duty as a parent amounts to a total and final abandonment of his rights as a parent within s. 3(1)(I)(C). It seems to me that, considering all the evidence, it falls short of supporting such an interference.

Accordingly Lardner J declined to make an order under s. 3.

On appeal to the Supreme Court, counsel for the appellants argued that Lardner J had misdirected himself in law in holding that the statement of a parent 'may be evidence of a wish or an intention not to abandon [a] child'.

Hamilton CJ (O'Flaherty, Egan, Blayney and Denham JJ concurring) rejected this contention. He referred to Finlay CJ's statement that the necessity for the proof of abandonment 'indicates a special regard for the constitutionally protected parental rights' and observed that Lardner J had been 'obliged to have regard to such rights, particularly the natural father's rights, and to consider all the evidence in the case, including the evidence with regard to the failure of the father in the fulfillment of his duty to the child and his actions and statements relevant to the question whether or not the failure to fulfill his duty towards the child constituted an abandonment of such rights'. Lardner had not been entitled to, and did not, regard the failure of parental duty as being of itself evidence of abandonment by the father of his rights as a parent.

Applying the test laid down in *Hay v O'Grady* [1992] ILRM 689; [1992] 1 IR 210 (which we analyse in the 1992 Review 470-3), Hamilton CJ considered that there was 'ample evidence' supporting Lardner J's finding: the father's failure to sign the declaration that he was not the girl's father, his expressed desire to see her and have her returned from the proposed adoptive parents, his objection to the proposed adoption and his issue of a summons claiming custody of his daughter. While it was open to an appellate court to substitute its own inference of fact, it 'should be slow to do so where such depends upon oral evidence or recollection of fact and a different inference has been drawn by the trial judge.'

The Supreme Court judgment throws little light on the important conceptual issues surrounding the notion of abandonment of parental rights and its relationship to conduct and, specifically, statements by a parent. Some of the questions that the Court might have addressed are the following. Is the requirement of proof of abandonment of parental rights in the empirical or normative order? Is it something entirely separate from parental failure? If not, what is the basis of an inference of abandonment from conduct? Is abandonment of parental rights premised on a free act of will by a parent? Must a parent be conscious of the legal quality and implications of his or her act and intend to alter his or her legal position or is it sufficient that the parent intend to achieve certain factual rather than legal goals? The answer to these questions must surely affect the resolution of the question of how the court should regard what parents say (or do not say).

In *Southern Health Board v An Bord Uchtála* [1995] 2 ILRM 369, Costello J gave some important guidance on key provisions of the Adoption Act 1988. The facts of the case were tragic. The child whose welfare was in issue was born in 1986. He was a member of a family of travellers, who came from a very deprived background. He was taken into care when he was fourteen months old after he was found unattended in a caravan, with a string around his waist attached to a window, tied in such a way that he could not lie down. He lived with foster parents until August 1989, when, as a result of a court order, he was returned to his parents. Some months later, it became clear that, after his return, he had been subjected to very serious assaults by one or other or both of his parents, causing fractures and bruises which were left untreated. Costello J's judgment graphically describes these acts of cruelty and neglect.

The child was again taken into care in December 1989 and went to live again with his foster parents. He recovered quickly from his injuries at a physical level but was left with serious psychological disturbance amounting to a post-traumatic stress disorder. A consultant psychiatrist advised against any parental access in 1990 and in 1994 he confirmed this advice. He was of opinion that the child 'should not be exposed to his natural parents until his late teens or perhaps early twenties and only if he then expressed a wish to see them': *per* Costello J. The psychiatrist was of the view that the child would continue to suffer from a post-traumatic stress disorder until that time.

In September 1991, the foster parents applied to adopt the child. After unsuccessfully trying on several occasions to hold a hearing at which his parents would be present, An Bord Uchtála made a declaration under s. 2 of the 1988 Act that, if the court made an order under s. 3(1), it would, subject to s. 2(2), make the adoption order.

Costello J was satisfied that the requirements of s. 3(1)(I)(A) had been fulfilled. For the previous twelve months, the child's parents had failed in their duty towards him:

> Their duty was to act as his guardians and as loving parents to further his welfare. They showed themselves unfit to discharge that duty and by their own actions made necessary the application of the law which disables them from fulfilling it because they have lawfully been deprived of his custody. Thus, since prior to December 1989 and up to the present time and there has been a failure to fulfill their duty to [their child].

As regards the crucial requirements contained in s. 3(1)(I)(B), Costello J held that the parents' failure to fulfill their duties towards the child would continue until he attained the age of eighteen. Costello J reasoned as follows:

> In the light of the evidence, no court will in the future allow [the child] return to the custody of his parents and so they have disabled themselves by their conduct from fulfilling their duty into the future. I am aware, of course, that when [the child] reaches the age of sixteen the Fit Persons Order will expire. But in cases such as this where a young person does not wish to leave his foster parents and where, having reached the age

of sixteen, the welfare of the young person would not be served by allowing the natural parents to exercise a right to custody, the court will take the young person into wardship and direct that he remain in the custody of the foster parents until the age of eighteen. It is reasonable to assume that this would happen in this case should [the] parents seek his return when he reaches the age of sixteen. Thus the legal disability (stemming from the [parents]' conduct) will continue until [the child] reaches the age of eighteen.

One may question whether the requirement that 'it is likely that such [parental] failure will continue without interruption until the child attains the age of eighteen years' can be equiperated with a likelihood that the *consequences of earlier parental failure* will last until that time. That the consequences of earlier failure are not the same as the continuance of earlier failure can be seen if we consider the case of an abusive or neglectful parent, clearly guilty of parental failure, who dies when the child is aged ten. The evidence may well establish that the consequences of that parental failure will continue, after the death of the parent, throughout the child's minority but manifestly there will be ongoing parental failure during those eight years.

Perhaps Costello J was arguing that the parent's earlier failure was so serious as to render them unable to discharge their duty in future years to their child. One should look closely at this approach. An inability to fulfill one's duty in the future as a result of one's prior failure need not necessarily involve a failure (or a likelihood of such failure) of one's duty in the future. A parent who has not been guilty of any failure may for one of a number of reasons not be likely to be able to fulfill his or her duty in the future. For example, the child may have been taken from the jurisdiction to a foreign country from which, as a matter of practical certainty, the child will not return. Cf. *Cosgrove v Ireland* [1982] ILRM 48. The parent whose parental rights have thus been infringed will be unable to fulfill his or her duty to the child but that does not imply any future failure of duty on his or her part. The fact that an inability to fulfil one's parental duty in the future may be attributable to past *failure of duty* does not, as a matter of principle, transform that inability into future failure.

It might be thought that Costello J was seeking to recognise a concept akin to estoppel, whereby parents may disable themselves by their conduct from denying that it is likely that their failure will continue until the child is eighteen. The language quoted above does not, however, seem consistent with this interpretation; nor would s. 3 appear to warrant the introduction of estoppel in this way.

On the requirement under s.3(1)(I)(C) that the parental failure should constitute 'an abandonment on the part of the parents of all parental rights, whether under the Constitution or otherwise, with respect to the child,' Costello J accepted that an order under s. 3 would not be appropriate in every case where a child was given into the care of foster parents as a result of a Fit Person Order. Each case depended on its own facts; the conduct of the parents had to be examined to see whether it constituted 'abandonment' of their parental rights. In the instant case, Costello J was of opinion that the parents' conduct had been:

> so egregious and so reprehensible that it constituted an abandonment by them of their rights. The law will not permit parents who acted in the way [the child]'s parents acted towards him to exercise rights over him. By so conducting themselves they must be regarded as having abandoned such rights.

Costello J thus considered that the concept of abandonment by conduct is one in the moral domain. Bad parents are denied their parental rights by being deemed to have abandoned them. There is, however, an important distinction between forfeiture and abandonment. There may be good policy arguments that bad parents should on account of their badness be required to forfeit their parental rights but the 1988 Act, as interpreted in *In re Adoption (No. 2) Bill 1987* [1989] ILRM 266; [1989] IR 656, does not equate badness with abandonment. On the contrary, the Supreme Court's acceptance that the question whether there has been an abandonment of parental rights can depend in part on what the parents say makes it plain that the concept can have a 'no fault' dimension. Nevertheless, there appears in the judgment of Walsh J in *G. v An Bord Uchtála* [1980] IR 37, at 79 to be a recognition that there is indeed the possibility of inferring abandonment from the particular moral quality of the parental conduct:

> A parent may for physical or moral reasons decide to abandon his position as a parent or he or she may be deemed to have abandoned that position; a failure in parental duty may itself be evidence of such an abandonment.

The other requirements of s. 3(1) were easily complied with in the instant case. Accordingly, Costello J made the order under that provision.

Consent issues In *M. O'C. v Sacred Heart Adoption Society and An Bord Uchtála* [1996] 1 ILRM 297, the Supreme Court was called on to address important issues of constitutional law relating to adoption. The facts of the case can be stated briefly. The plaintiff, the mother of a child born outside marriage, placed her child for adoption, having consulted with a social worker of the defendant Society. She later sought the return of her child; the couple with whom the child had been placed for adoption sought an order under s. 3 of the Adoption Act 1974 dispensing with the plaintiff's consent to the making of an adoption order by An Bord Uchtála and an order granting them custody of the child in the meantime. Morris J held in favour of the couple and made an order under s. 3 dispensing with the mother's consent: [1995] 1 ILRM 229. By the time the case came on appeal to the Supreme Court, the mother was no longer seeking the return of her child but she was still resisting the dispensation with her consent to the child's adoption, wishing to assert her rights of visitation.

Counsel for the mother laid great stress on the constitutional dimensions of her right to protect, care for and have custody of her child. He contended that she had not given her informed agreement to the placement of her child for adoption. To satisfy the requirement of being such an informed agreement it would have been necessary for her to be aware of the nature of the right she was surrendering at least to the extent that she was aware that this was a right that could not be taken away from her but rather had to be voluntarily given up by her. Counsel placed considerable emphasis on the test that Walsh J set out in *G. v An Bord Uchtála* [1980] IR 32, at 80.

O'Flaherty J summarised counsel for the plaintiff's submissions in this context as follows:

> [W]hile the plaintiff was told that the effect of the adoption order would be that she would lose her rights in law something entirely different was occurring. By *placing* her child for adoption she was surrendering or abandoning her rights both constitutional and legal. Not only was the plaintiff not informed of what was occurring but she was told that the effect of the adoption order would be that she would lose her rights but this is entirely inconsistent with the concept that she was already surrendering or abandoning those rights by the placement of the child for adoption. It necessarily followed from telling her that the effect of the adoption order would be that she would lose those rights, that she was left with the impression that she would continue to enjoy those rights if she decided to refuse to consent to the making of the adoption order and if the prospective adopters, as a result of such refusal, applied to the High Court to dispense with her consent.

O'Flaherty J (Hamilton CJ, Egan, Blayney and Denham JJ concurring) said that he believed these submissions were fundamentally misconceived and based on giving characteristics to the decision to place a child for adoption which were not justified in law. He endorsed Henchy J's description of the adoption process in *G. v An Bord Uchtála* [1980] IR 32, at 86, which emphasised that consent to placement for adoption can never in itself, amount to an extinguishment of the mother's rights, but rather puts them 'in temporary abeyance'. O'Flaherty J agreed with Walsh J that these rights were constitutional in nature; support for that view was forthcoming in the judgment of the Supreme Court in the Article 26 reference, *Adoption (No. 2) Bill 1987* [1989] ILRM 266; [1989] IR 656. See the 1988 Review 246-52. O'Flaherty J did not, however, think that the question whether the mother's rights were constitutional or simply legal involved an important distinction in the working of the adoption code.

There was no doubt that the placement for an adoption was 'a giant step' which might lead to the High Court's later dispensing with the mother's consent to the adoption. Therefore, the consequences of placement had to be explained very clearly to the mother. The Supreme Court in *In re D.G., An Infant; O.G. v An Bord Uchtála* [1991] ILRM 514, at 539-540 (*per* Finlay CJ, speaking for the Court) had emphasised this requirement. Cf. the 1991 Review, 287-91.

In an important passage, O'Flaherty J stated:

> The correct approach is to regard the mother's constitutional rights as subsisting right up to the time that an adoption order is made by the Adoption Board. It is clear, of course, that those constitutional rights will have undergone a modification by virtue of the fact that she has placed the child for adoption and, as Finlay CJ points out [in '.G.], the possible consequences that may flow from that decision must be made very clear to her. But fact that she has placed the child for adoption is by no means the end of the process. The High Court judge in deciding whether an order should be made dispensing with the consent must, of course, bring all his for her experience and powers of intellect, as well as of heart, to bear on what will often be excruciatingly difficult decision. In doing that the judge must always put at the forefront of all considerations what the best interests of the child require having regard to the terms of s. 3 of the 1974 Act. The best interests of the child will be served, not by placing to one side in any respect the mother's situation but, on the contrary, having full regard to her and whatever may be advanced on her behalf in the matter. That was essentially the situation in the G case, though I appreciate that Walsh J attached critical importance to the decision made at the placement for adoption stage.
>
> Of course, the judge's function is not anything as crude as to resolve a contest between parties: rather the judge must engage in an *inquiry* to decide what is in the best interests of the child. The judge will have regard, too, to the situation of the adopters, always keeping in a central

position what the best interests of the child require.

In O'Flaherty J's view, Morris J had complied with the purpose and policy of the adoption code as thus set forth. Even if he had had the belief, based on a reading of the judgments of O'Higgins CJ, Walsh and Parke JJ in *G. v. An Bord Uchtála*, that the plaintiff had abandoned all constitutional rights by the very act of placement, nonetheless he had applied the correct test as enunciated by Finlay CJ in the *O.G.* case, on the requirement of obtaining the mother's fully informed agreement to the placement. In a significant passage, O'Flaherty J commented:

> That is what is really important rather than to engage in a categorisation of rights. 'Parental rights' (the words used in the legislation) are sufficiently wide to cover all categories of rights and, as I have said, can only be extinguished when the adoption order is made.

Counsel for the plaintiff pointed out that Morris J appeared to have considered the child's welfare under s. 2 rather than s. 3(2) of the 1974 Act, when the case squarely fell under s. 3(2). S. 2 requires the court to regard the welfare of the child as 'the first and paramount consideration'. Under s. 3 the court must have regard to the 'best interests' of the child. O'Flaherty J considered that this was not a matter of significance. Whilst the Oireachtas where it used different words in the two provisions had to be taken to intend 'a different shade of meaning at least', nonetheless, Morris J had 'duly embarked on the form of inquiry and arrived at a decision that clearly satisfied the "best interests" requirements of s. 3'. It was even possible that the reference in Morris J's judgment to s. 2 was a clerical error; in any event, no complaint had been made about his actual adjudication in dealing with the child's interests or his consideration of the evidence of all the parties.

Finally, O'Flaherty J noted that, after an order had been made under s. 3 of the 1974 Act, An Bord Uchtála would not have power to make a final order for the adoption of the child while custody proceedings were pending: cf. the Adoption Act 1952, s. 16(4).

In a brief concurring judgment, Hamilton CJ observed that proceedings of the kind before the court 'usually arise because the decision by the natural mother to place her child for adoption is made a time when [she] is vulnerable and concerned for the future of her child and subsequently changes her mind. . . .' The mother's decision to place her child for adoption had not been 'an abandonment of her child', but rather 'a decision made by her in what she conceived, in her circumstances at the time, to be the best interests of her child.' Her actions in seeking a good home for the child and in meeting the proposed adopters were those 'of a loving and concerned mother motivated by her concern to ensure the best interest of her child.' The decision of the court was based on these interests and not in any way on her lack of fitness.

In *A.C. v St. Patrick's Guild Adoption Society and T.H. and P.H. v An Bord Uchtála*, High Court, July 31, 1995, a mother who gave birth to a child in 1992, when she was aged thirty, was not initially sure what she should do. She hoped that the father, a married man with whom she was living, would agree to rear the child with her and his two daughters. She left the child in the care of an adoption society for six weeks. During this time she ceased to reside with the father and went back to a mobile home where she had formerly lived. After the six week period, she agreed to place her child for adoption. A year later, she changed her mind and sought the return of the child. The couple with whom the child had been living sought an order pursuant to s. 3 of the Adoption Act 1974 granting them custody and dispensing with the mother's consent to the child's adoption.

Flood J dismissed the mother's claim. He was satisfied that, in placing her child for adoption, she had acted freely. The social worker who had been involved with the placing of the child for adoption had acted with realism and great prudence in giving the mother time to explore the options. She had not placed her under any pressure. On the contrary, her conduct had at all relevant times been 'more consistent with acknowledging and respecting the maternal and constitutional right of the mother to the care and custody of her child.'

Flood J was of the view that the mother had been 'fully appraised of, and thus understood the consequences of, her decision to proceed with placement for adoption.' He observed:

> In the course of each individual's life, decisions are made in which existing personal circumstances and opportunities are reflected. There is virtually no individual who would not acknowledge, in relation to some major decision, that if ideal circumstances or indeed specifically different circumstances existed their decision would have been different. Their actual decision is not to be considered as non-voluntary or lacking in assent or otherwise vitiated by the absence of an ideal scenario. We live in a real world where choices have to be made. If that choice is predicted by the non-existence of desired circumstances and is made in the light of such non-existence or some non-existent circumstance the choices and consequences that flow cannot be annulled or declared void simply because, on mature reflection, at some time post the date of decision, when we are pregnant with the wisdom of hindsight we recognise the error of our decision and want to change it.

On the s. 3 application, Flood J, without enlarging upon the evidence, had no hesitation in dispensing with the mother's consent to the adoption of her child.

Rules of evidence The Irish courts have been zealous to ensure that access of litigants to evidence in the hands of servants of the State will not be defeated by the unregulated invocation of executive privilege. In *Murphy v Dublin Corporation* [1972] IR 215 the Supreme Court made it plain that it rested with the judiciary, and not the executive, to decide whether the public interest required disclosure: see J. Kelly, *The Irish Constitution* (3rd ed., by G. Hogan and G. Whyte, 1994), 376-9. S. 8 of the Adoption Act 1976 requires the court to decline to make orders for (inter alia) the discovery of documents of An Bord Uchtála unless 'it is satisfied that it is in the best interest of any child concerned not to do so'. Thus, the public interest has in this context given way to the best interest of the child.

Costello J applied this focus in *B. (P.) v L. (A.) (Adoption Board) (Privilege)* [1996] IFLR 121 (High Court, 1995), in holding, on a consultative case stated, that in guardianship proceedings taken by an unmarried father, the District Judge had been incorrect in dismissing An Bord Uchtála's application to set aside a *subpoena duces tecum* served on the Registrar by the mother of the child seeking documents and correspondence between it and the father.

Costello J referred to the principles articulated in Murphy and to the provision of s. 8. He commented:

> Where . . . the Oireachtas has by statute established statutory principles relating to documentary privilege and, in effect, has established public policy in the matter, it seems to me that the court should apply the statutory, and not the common law, principles. That is the position in this case.

Costello J went on to note that, if the court made an order under s. 8, An Bord Uchtála would be required to disclose and allow inspection and copying of the document referred to in the order. This did not, however, necessarily mean that the document would be admissible in evidence. The rules of evidence would apply; thus, for example, the rule against hearsay might render the document inadmissible.

DIVORCE

In the Constitutional Law Chapter, above, 138, we examine the fundamental change in Irish family law brought about by the re-introduction of a divorce jurisdiction, following the passage of the amendment to the Constitution on November 24, 1995.

Part III of the Family Law Act 1995 contains important provisions enabling Irish courts to make finanacial orders, such as property periodical payment orders and lump sum orders, in relation to spouses divorced abroad. We examine Part III later in the Chapter, below, 317-9.

JUDICIAL SEPARATION

Constitutional validity of 1989 legislation   *T.F. v Ireland* [1995] 2 ILRM 321; [1995] 1 IR 321, the Supreme Court, affirming Murphy J's judgment in the High Court ([1994] 2 ILRM 401, upheld the constitutional validity of ss. 2(1)(f), 3(1) and (2), 16(a) and 19 of the Judicial Separation and Family Law Reform Act 1989. The outcome had been scarcely in doubt but the Court's analysis is disappointingly narrow.

The plaintiff had two principal criticisms of the legislation. The first, and stronger, criticism was that ground (f) of s. 2(1), which required the court to grant a decree of judicial separation where a normal marital relationship had not existed between the spouses for at least a year, constituted an attack on the institution of marriage and the plaintiff's individual rights within the marriage because it rewarded a spouse who was at fault and penalised an innocent spouse, who did not want to be judicially separated. Under the former law, only the victim of matrimonial wrongdoing was entitled to a divorce *a mensa et thoro*.

The response of Murphy J and of the Supreme Court was in essence that this ground was merely a response to the factual reality of a breakdown of marriage, regardless of the question of who was responsible and that, since this did not break 'the bond' of marriage, it did not offend against Article 41 of the Constitution. Thus, Hamilton CJ, delivering the decision of the Supreme Court (pursuant to Article 34.4.5°) stated:

> Is the provision of entitlement to a decree of judicial separation in such a situation a failure to guard with special care the institution of marriage and to protect it from attack or is it an attempt by the Oireachtas to deal with the unfortunate situation created by the breakdown of a marriage and the inability of one or other of the spouses to cohabit with the other?

> It is the view of this Court that it is the latter and having regard to the numerous safeguards of people's rights contained in the Act as a whole . . ., does not constitute an attack on the institution of marriage or a failure to guard it with special care or an unjust attack on the personal

rights of the plaintiff/appellant.

Neither does it constitute an attack on the family, which is the foundation of the institution of Marriage.

The casual acceptance of the 'no-fault' philosophy and the presumption that a decision by a spouse not to cohabit is based on an *inability* to do so cannot be reconciled with the philosophy, on which Article 41 is founded, which regards marital commitment as a manifestation of human freedom. Choosing to live with one's spouse or to leave the home is at the heart of that freedom. If it can truly be said of a spouse that he or she deserted the other spouse — and ground (c) of s. 2(1) accepts that it can — then it is not possible to treat the decision to abandon one's spouse as manifesting an inability to cohabit.

The plaintiff's second principal attack was on ss. 16(A) and 19 of the Act, which gave the court, on (or after) granting a decree of judicial separation, power to grant an order conferring on one of the spouses the right to occupy the family home to the exclusion of the other spouse. The plaintiff contended that these provisions infringed his property rights guaranteed under Article 43 of the Constitution. The Supreme Court rejected the argument on the basis that the plaintiff's rights of ownership had not been affected; moreover, the provisions, which could be varied subsequently, should be seen as part of the overall scheme, of Part II of the Act, which was designed to ensure as far as practicable that provision be made in the interests of the family as a whole.

Agreement not to pursue judicial separation proceedings In *F. v F.,* Supreme Court, November 30, 1995, some important issues of principle arose, but were scarcely touched on by the Court. The matter came before the Supreme Court by way of consultative case stated from the Circuit Court. The wife had in 1986 sought a decree of divorce *a mensa et thoro* against her husband, a barring order and alimony. The judgments do not state the ground or grounds on which she sought the decree. It must have been adultery, cruelty or 'unnatural practices', the only grounds that existed under that regime. The proceedings, actively defended, were stayed by consent in 1987. In the consent agreement, the husband agreed to remain out of the family home and to pay maintenance. The wife was given custody of their two dependent children, with reasonable access for the husband. Liberty to apply was reserved.

In 1992 the wife sought a judicial separation under the Judicial Separation and Family Law Reform Act 1989, together with a number of ancillary orders. She sought an order deeming the 1987 consent order to be an order for judicial separation pursuant to ground (f) of s. 2(1) of the 1989 Act.

The Circuit Court judge submitted the following question to the Supreme Court:

> Is the applicant entitled to effectively disregard the earlier proceedings and liberty to apply therein and bring the second set of proceedings seeking the relief claimed?

The Supreme Court, by a four-to-one majority, answered the question in the negative. Blayney J (O'Flaherty and Egan JJ concurring) reasoned as follows. It was clear from the terms of s. 8(1) and (2) of the 1989 Act that the effect of a decree for judicial separation was 'exactly the same' as the effect of the former decree of divorce *a mensa et thoro*:

> There is no difference between the two. They are the same form of proceedings giving the same relief. The only effect of the 1989 Act was to alter the title of the proceedings and to widen the grounds on which the relief could be obtained.

The 1987 consent had recited that 'the parties hereto have agreed to stay and settle the proceedings herein on the following terms' and contained a term whereby they agreed 'not to molest or interfere with each other wheresoever.' In *Courtney v Courtney* [1923] 2 IR 31 the Court of Appeal had held that an agreement to separate was a bar to bringing subsequent proceedings for a divorce *a mensa et thoro*. MacKenzie J, in *K. v K.* [1988] IR 161 (noted in the 1988 Review, 243-4) had followed *Courtney v Courtney*. If the 1989 Act had not been passed, and for some reason the applicant had become dissatisfied with the terms of the consent, she would 'clearly' not have been entitled to issue new proceedings for a divorce *a mensa et thoro*. Since there was no difference between an action for divorce *a mensa et thoro* and an action for a judicial separation, the same principle should apply.

Counsel for the applicant argued that the effect of the consent entered into by the parties was to contract out of the 1989 Act and that this was not permissible; it followed that the consent entered into by the applicant did not preclude her from bringing her new proceedings under the 1989 Act. There was, however, no useful analogy to be drawn between the Supreme Court decision of *H.D. v P.D.*, May 8, 1978 and the instant case. In *H.D. v P.D.*, the Court had held that a wife who had settled a divorce *a mensa et thoro* petition on terms whereunder she agreed to accept a sum of money 'in full satisfaction of all claims in the petition' was nonetheless entitled to apply for an order for maintenance against her husband under s. 5 of the Family Law (Maintenance of Spouses and Children) Act. The position in the instant case was very different:

> The issue is not whether a term in the consent entered into by the applicant is preventing her from issuing proceedings under the 1989 Act. What the Court has to consider is the whole effect of the consent, not simply the effect of one term. And the whole effect of the consent entered into in the proceedings in 1987 was to satisfy and discharge the applicant's claim for a divorce *a mensa et thoro* so that she was barred thereafter from bringing such a claim. And this continued to be the position after the 1989 Act became law as it did not introduce any new cause of action but altered the title of the procedure to judicial separation.

There was an additional reason why the wife should not be entitled to continue her proceedings under the 1989 Act. In Blayney J's view, she did not need a judicial separation. She had been lawfully separated from her husband for the previous seven years. The proceedings she had instituted were not for the purpose of obtaining a judicial separation but were an attempt on her part obtain an order so that she could ask the Court to make various ancillary orders in her favour:

> So she is asking the Court to give her relief she does not need with a view to being in a position to obtain other orders that she would like to have. It seems to me that this is not a form of proceeding to which the Court should lend its support.

Finally, the maxim *nemo debet bis vexari pro eadem causa* applied. The respondent had already had to face one application for a divorce *a mensa et thoro*. Having settled that, he should not be obliged to face a second action seeking 'exactly the same relief albeit under a different name.'

Denham J's judgment, with which O'Flaherty J concurred, might on first perusal appear to be based on the same reasoning as that of Blayney J. She noted that:

> the essence of this judgment is that the two actions (divorce *a mensa et thoro* and judicial separation) are the same cause of action subject to law, especially the 1989 Act.

Yet earlier in her judgment she observed that the 1989 Act did not explicitly deem an action for divorce *a mensa et thoro* to be an action for judicial separation and that such an inference 'could not be drawn from the Act.'

Denham J under the heading *'Res Judicata'*, expressed the view that the wife, having taken proceedings against her husband for divorce *a mensa et thoro*, which 'were for the same cause of action as the proceedings under the 1989 Act', and having obtained a court order on the matter, could not proceed against him in the same cause. The initial cause of action was 'now merged in the court order.'

Denham J stressed the virtues of certainty and finality of litigation. The care of dependents was one area where there could be no finality, but in other areas the general norm regarding certainty should apply 'unless excluded by law or justice'. In the instant case, the wife had received many benefits from the 1987 consent. Denham J pointed out that, for the future, she had the benefit of the law in existence at the commencement of her proceedings for divorce *a mensa et thoro*; 'of specific importance' was s. 27 of the Family Law (Maintenance of Spouses and Children) Act 1976, which effectively overrides a provision in an agreement seeking to exclude the right of a party, subsequent to the agreement, to apply to the court for a maintenance order under s. 5.

Hamilton CJ dissented. Noting that he was the single dissentient and that the sole purpose of a consultative case stated was to have determined by the Supreme Court the point of law referred to it by the Circuit Court judge, the Chief Justice did not give the reasons for his dissent 'as no useful purpose would be served' by his so doing since the point of law was determined by the judgments of his colleagues. This is unfortunate. Many aspects of the majority's holding could have been critically analysed, to the benefit of future cases.

The primary weakness in the majority's holding is the identification of proceedings for divorce *a mensa et thoro* with proceedings for judicial separation. Is there *really* 'no difference between the two'? At a formal level there is, of course, no difference: s. 8(1) of the 1989 Act has a curiously traditional aura in providing that, where the court grants a decree of judicial separation, 'it shall no longer be obligatory for the spouses who were the parties to such proceedings to cohabit.' Yet if we allow the light of reality to shine through, the machinery for judicial separation is strikingly different from divorce *a mensa et thoro*. The purpose of divorce *a mensa et thoro* was to protect the victims of matrimonial misconduct and to penalise those who had engaged in that misconduct. Spouses had a genuine obligation to cohabit, backed by the financial sanctions of divorce *a mensa et thoro* and the more robust sanction of committal to prison under the action for restitution of conjugal rights (abolished in 1988: see the 1988 Review, 244-5). The grant of a decree for divorce *a mensa et thoro*, therefore, relieving the petitioner of the obligation to cohabit, was a matter of some moment.

S. 8(1) uses the same language but in an entirely hollow way. Under the

1989 Act, the obligation to cohabit prior to obtaining a decree for judicial separation has lost all of its force. The very process of not cohabiting with one's spouse generates an entitlement to a decree for judicial separation and consequent relief from the obligation of cohabitation.

The 1989 Act has at its core a philosophy closer to that of divorce based on breakdown of marriage than to that which underlay the remedy of divorce *a mensa et thoro*. It retains a formal similarity to the former remedy, as well as some fault-based grounds identical or similar to their predecessors but it fosters values which, whatever their merits, have no counterpart in the former remedy of divorce *a mensa et thoro*.

Having said this, it must be acknowledged that the Supreme Court in *F. v Ireland*, above, upheld the constitutional validity of the 1989 legislation. In doing so, it endorsed this shift in values, apparently on the narrow basis that the 'bond' of marriage remained unbroken. It is also true that it is impossible to regard the transformation from divorce *a mensa et thoro* in isolation from the developments in family law that had been taking place over the previous fifteen years. The Family Law (Maintenance of Spouses and Children) Act 1976 made entitlement to a maintenance order depend simply on the failure by the respondent spouse to provide proper maintenance for the family rather than on breach of the obligation to cohabit. As has been mentioned, the action for restitution of conjugal rights (which had previously fallen into desuetude) was abolished in 1988. The courts, even before the 1989 Act, had placed considerably less emphasis on matrimonial fault than formerly. (See, for example, *N.(C.) v N.(R.)*, [1996] IFLR 1 (Dublin Circuit Family Court, 1995), where Judge McGuinness used s. 15(1)(c) of the Act to override a *dum casta* provision in a separation agreement).

It is also true, of course, that the 1989 Act improved the position in many important ways. It removed sex discrimination and greatly extended the range and utility of ancillary orders, especially in relation to financial matters.

It was for this latter reason, as Blayney J observed, that the wife *F. v F.* was seeking a decree for judicial separation. She wished to avail herself of these wide-ranging ancillary remedies. If one regards the process established by the 1989 Act, with its new grounds for a decree and a wide array of ancillary orders, it seems highly formalistic to perceive the action for judicial separation as no different from the former proceedings for divorce *a mensa et thoro*.

F. v F. may with benefit be read in conjunction with *H.(J.) v H.(R.)* [1996] IFLR 23 (High Court, Barr J, 1995), which we discuss below, 308-12.

Ancillary orders in proceedings for judicial separation   Part II of the Family Law Act 1995 re-enacts, with some modifications, Part II of the Judicial Separation and Family Law Reform Act 1989. We examine this most important statutory reform later in the chapter, in our analysis of the entire Act of 1995: see below 313-30.

Sale of the family home   In *S.B. v R.B.* [1996] Ir Law Log Weekly 379 (Circuit Court (Dublin), Judge McGuinness, May 10, 1995), the parties had married in 1975. The husband was a divorced person. Their daughter was born in 1977. The husband left the family home in 1986 and 'went to reside with [another woman] with whom he had been, previously having an adulterous relationship.' The family home was in the spouses' joint names.

The wife sought, and with no difficulty, obtained a decree of judicial separation on the basis of ground (e). The contention centred, not on the grounds, but on the ancillary orders that the court might make.

The house was worth £110,000. About £13,000 was outstanding in mortgage repayments which were £119 *per* month. The husband had 'in general paid maintenance to his wife on a regular basis' since he had left the house although there had 'been some difficulties'. He had failed to pay the £150 per week ordered by a District Justice in 1987 and an attachment order had had to be made. In the context of the judicial separation proceedings, the same amount of maintenance had been ordered.

The wife sought an order under s. 15 of the 1989 Act for the transfer of the home and contents into her name. The husband had a different proposal: to sell the house and divide the proceeds so that he would secure one third and his wife two thirds. He was living in a house, with the woman for whom he had left his wife, which they had bought in 1990 for £75,000 subject to a stabilizer mortgage of £58,000, with monthly payments of nearly £800. He argued that, if the family home were disposed of, he and the woman would be able to obtain an endowment mortgage which would reduce the monthly payments to £500.

Judge McGuinness ordered the sale of the family home. Of the projected nett proceeds of £94,000, the wife should receive £85,000. Judge McGuinness acknowledged that the wife and her daughter would not wish to move from their home, where they had lived for a considerable number of years, but she felt that this would be outweighed by the advantage to the wife of having a secure family home in her own name free from any mortgage. Judge McGuinness ordered the husband to continue paying £150 support per week to his wife and children. She extinguished each party's succession rights against the other.

The report of the judgment is an extended summary, rather than a direct quotation, of what Judge McGuinness said. One should therefore be cautious about venturing any criticism. Nonetheless, on the basis of the report, it seems arguable that the better solution would have been to preserve the family home so that the wife and her daughter were not put to the distress of having to buy another considerably less expensive residence. The amount owing on the mortgage was relatively modest: only £13,000 on a house worth £110,000. The husband had been neither a model maintenance debtor nor a model taxpayer since he owed money to the Revenue Commissioners; he had, moreover, chosen to buy a home by means of expensive financing of £800 a month when his stated earnings (about which Judge McGuinness evinced some slight scepticism) were only £18,000 *per* annum and those of the woman with whom he was living were £6,000. The judgment contains no assessment of the value of the house in 1995 but it seems reasonable to suppose that it might have increased from the value of £75,000 five years previously.

The husband also had purchased a 'moderately expensive car' for which he was providing 'most of the funding'. Judge McGuinness stated that she had to find that his way of life took little account of his wife's needs.

From a distance, the outcome seems harsh on the wife and nineteen year old daughter and lenient to the husband. The whole purpose of the Judicial Separation and Family Reform Act 1989 was meant to be to improve and extend the range of ancillary orders that might be made on granting a decree of judicial separation; yet the outcome in this case is one from which the wife would have been protected under the former law.

Ancillary order affecting foreign trust   In *F.(R.) v F.(J.)* [1996] IFLR 12 (Dublin Circuit Family Court, 1995), it appeared that the husband, in proceedings for judicial separation, had transferred some of his assets to a trust in Alderney which was subject to the Law of Guernsey. No evidence was adduced as to the law of Guernsey and no submission were made as to the effectiveness of any order that might be made by the Circuit Court. Instead, as Judge McGuinness noted, the applicant's case seemed to have 'sailed happily along, confident that an order of the Dublin Circuit Court would be binding on the Alderney dominated trustees of a trust, governed by the law of Guernsey. Judge McGuinness was 'far from sure' that this was so and considered that it would be improper for her to make an order on the Guernsey trustees, in the absence of evidence of service.

Judge McGuinness nonetheless considered that she had power to make orders under s. 15 of the 1989 Act directing the husband to pay £25,000 to his wife from the trust funds in Guernsey. From a practical standpoint, that order would have teeth: the husband, if he continued to maintain any presence in Ireland, could not avoid his obligation, and no court in Ireland would defer to an argument based on private international law in the face of the manifest needs of the wife.

NULLITY OF MARRIAGE

Grounds

Prior existing marriage In *B. v R.*, High Court, January 24, 1995, Costello J grappled with a conundrum that had never previously come before the Irish courts: if parties validly marry abroad in circumstances where the marriage is recognised under Irish private international law and then subsequently, during the subsistence of that marriage, go through a ceremony of marriage with each other for a second time, in Ireland, what is the status of the *second* marriage?

In *B. v R.*, the plaintiff was Irish, the defendant, a citizen of the United States of America. After a whirlwind romance, they had married in a civil ceremony in the United States. They later returned to Ireland for a full religious ceremony according to the rites of the Catholic church, without telling the plaintiff's family or the priest of the earlier civil ceremony. Inaccurate particulars were apparently contained in the entry to the Marriage Register Book, required under s. 11 of the Registration of Marriages (Ireland) Act 1863.

The couple continued to live in the United States for some time but eventually, when difficulties arose in the marriage, the plaintiff left the defendant and returned to Ireland. The defendant divorced her in the United States on the ground of her desertion.

The plaintiff sought a declaration that the Irish ceremony of marriage was void; she did not petition for a decree of nullity in its regard. The defendant, who was represented, informed the court that he had no objection to the plaintiff's claim.

Costello J analysed the issue as follows. It was clear that the American marriage was valid in Irish law. It was equally clear that no crime of bigamy had occurred since s. 57 of the Offences Against the Person Act 1861 required proof of a marriage 'to any other person' during the lifetime of one's spouse. The civil law relating to legal incapacity to marry was 'an expression of the same principle on which the criminal law proceeds'. Irish and English textbooks were in accord that the law rendered invalid the remarriage to a third party but not the remarriage of spouses of an existing marriage to *each other*.

Counsel has been unable to cite any authority which would suggest that the principle recorded in the textbooks was incorrect. Costello J stated:

> A moment's reflection will show why this is so. The reason for the legal incapacity referred to arises from the nature of marriage as recognised both by the common law and by the ecclesiastical law formerly admin-

istered in the Ecclesiastical Courts. Marriage was and is regarded as the voluntary and permanent union of one man and one woman to the exclusion of all others for life. It follows that each spouse to a valid marriage is not capable of marrying another whilst the marriage subsists. The nature of marriage, however, does not call for the imposition of a similar disability should the spouses decide (for whatever reason) to go through another ceremony of marriage with each other. Such a second marriage was not rendered void therefore by virtue of their first marriage. And so, if the parties to a marriage which (a) has been entered into outside the jurisdiction and which (b) is recognised as valid inside the jurisdiction by the operation of the applicable rules of private international law enter into (for whatever reason) a second marriage to each other in this jurisdiction, there is no principle of our marriage laws which renders the Irish marriage null and void and neither spouse is entitled to a decree of nullity by reason of the subsistence of the foreign marriage at the time the Irish marriage was celebrated.

Nor was the second marriage rendered invalid by statute. Although it was virtually certain that the formalities required by s. 11 of the Registration of Marriages (Ireland) Act 1863 had not been properly complied with, this would not invalidate the marriage ceremony itself, and counsel for the plaintiff had accepted that this is so.

Costello J therefore concluded that the plaintiff had failed to establish that the Irish marriage was invalid under Irish law. In the light of this conclusion, he saw no need to express a view on whether the court could have made a declaratory order in the proceedings.

The conclusion that the second marriage was not void raises the interesting question as to whether spouses are in any sense capable of being simultaneously married to each other more than once. Of course a couple whose marriage has been annulled, dissolved or declared void are capable of marrying each other subsequently but surely it makes no sense to speak of a valid marriage taking place between spouses who are already validly married to each other? It is obvious that, viewed from two different legal orders, spouses who have validly married each other according to one order but not the other may, by subsequently marrying validly according to the other order, acquire the status of being validly married in accordance with both orders; but in such case each order recognises the validity of only one of the marriages. Thus, for example, in the circumstances of the present case, the Catholic Church would not recognise the validity of the first civil marriage. Conversely, in the famous 'Lourdes marriages' cases, parties who had married in accordance with the rites of the Catholic Church in ceremonies at Lourdes, without having gone through a ceremony of civil marriage according to the requirements of French law entered into invalid marriages under French law and in turn under the rules of Irish private international law since the *lex loci contractus* governs formalities of marriage. (That is why s. 2 of the Marriages Act 1972 was considered necessary to confer retrospective validation upon those marriages: Cf. W. Binchy, *Irish Conflicts of Law* (1988), 233-7).

To return to the conundrum in the instant case, it seems clear beyond argument that the Irish marriage was not valid. There is no way that a couple can make a true matrimonial commitment to one another more than once during the subsistence of the marriage. Of course spouses can renew their commitment by ceremony or by internal orientation of will but such a process is in truth a *reinforcement* of the original commitment rather than some entirely new and separate commitment.

If the Irish marriage was not valid should it have been declared void (or been the subject of a decree of nullity had the plaintiff sought one)? Common law jurisprudence on this area of the law is less sophisticated than its civil law counterpart. French law, for example, has the concept of *mariages inexistants*, which lack even such putative capacity for validity as to be capable of being declared void.

Duress In *A.C. v P.J.* [1995] 2 IR 253, the petitioner sought a decree of nullity on the grounds that, in the circumstances which existed at the date of her marriage, she had not given a real consent to the marriage. The proceedings were defended.

The petitioner was born in 1952. Her father was a small farmer and part-time postman. Her mother managed the home, which Barron J described as 'very strict, religious and pious'. The parents had a strong wish to see their children succeed in life and were prepared to make sacrifices so that they might have the necessary education. The knowledge of this desire inhibited the petitioner. She felt under stress at exam time and resorted to anti-depressant tablets. She failed to get into a teacher training college and failed her first year examination in Arts at a university. She felt by so doing she had let her parents down.

After leaving college the petitioner obtained jobs in the Dublin area. While working in a hospital in September, 1972, she met the respondent, who was doing similar work. They started going out together. Her relationship with her parents, based on her belief that she had let them down, inhibited her from telling them that she had a boyfriend and from going home that autumn. When she went home at Christmas she did not tell her parents that she was going out with a boy. She became engaged in January, 1973. She met the respondent's parents, who came from a different part of the country, but she still did not tell her parents.

In February, 1973, she wanted to break off her engagement but the respondent forced her to continue. At the end of the St. Patrick's Day week-end, at his persuasion, she went down with him to her parent's home. The petitioner was sure that her parents would not approve and

> the whole manner in which she acted made such disapproval more likely. As Barron J noted in his judgment, 'the visit was not a success'. They then returned to Dublin and on the same evening had sexual intercourse for the first time.

The following month the petitioner found that she was pregnant. Barron J's judgment records that the petitioner:

> was devastated. Her circumstances were such that she had no one to turn to. She knew her parents would be equally devastated and was totally unable to tell them. Her only solution was to agree to get married. This agreement was dependent solely upon the existence of her pregnancy. She made efforts to abort which were unsuccessful. She ultimately went to a general practitioner who had her admitted to a psychiatric hospital.

The consultant psychiatrist under whose care she came said that she was suffering from acute anxiety. Barron J was satisfied from her evidence that the petitioner saw marriage as the only means of escape from the situation in which she found herself. She remained afraid that she might take steps to end her pregnancy and asked the hospital staff to deprive her of anything which she could use to this end.

No one was told of her pregnancy save the respondent and the medical staff. She left all the arrangements for her wedding to her mother. She was discharged from hospital the day before the wedding and travelled down with the respondent to her home that night. Her father described the petitioner on her wedding day before the ceremony as shaking all over, trembling and chain-smoking. He said that she did not seem happy.

Barron J had no doubt that the petitioner's feelings on that day sprang from two main factors: *First*, her fear of how her parents would react if they realised that she was pregnant; and *secondly*, her wish not to marry the respondent because she felt dominated by him. In his view the petitioner had been motivated solely to bring her unhappy situation to an end.

The petitioner's fear of her parents was 'genuine and justifiable'. This was later borne out by their reaction, after she was married, to the news given to them the following month that she was pregnant and in their failure to come to see her for some eighteen months after her marriage. In her mind, there was no way she could have continued to term without getting married. Barron J was satisfied also that she had tried to break off her relationship with the respondent before her pregnancy and that, if it had terminated, she would not have gone through a ceremony of marriage with him.

The subsequent history of the relationship between the petitioner and the respondent was 'fairly predictable'. The respondent had no true understanding of her feelings at any time.

The first child to the parties was born in December 1973. They had five children in all, whose ages ranged at the time of the judgment from twenty-one to ten.

The question that Barron J had to consider was whether the petitioner's consent to the marriage had been a full and free exercise of an independent will. Barron J was quite satisfied that the circumstances surrounding her pregnancy and the attitude which her parents would have adopted to such pregnancy was of a character which the petitioner had been constitutionally unable to withstand and which had led her inexorably to her marriage.

Much the same circumstances had arisen in *N. (orse. K.) v K.* [1985] IR 733. In that case it was found that the shock of discovering that she was pregnant had put the petitioner into a state where she could not think clearly and where the only outcome which she contemplated was that of marriage. There, as in the instant case, the petitioner had received no advice on alternative options. Even closer to the facts of the instant case were those in *D.B. (orse. O'R.) v O'R.* [1991] ILRM 160; [1991] 1 IR 289, noted in the 1990 Review, 297-301. In that case also the duress had arisen from the circumstances themselves which the petitioner was not able to withstand, as a result of which her apparent consent to the marriage was not a true consent.

Barron J was satisfied that the petitioner's case came within the principles enunciated in these cases and that her apparent connect to be married was not such as was required by the law. Accordingly he granted a decree of nullity upon this ground.

Intoxication If a party was so intoxicated at the time of going through a ceremony of marriage as to be incapable of knowing what is happening, this can be a ground for annulment. In *R. McG. v N.K. (otherwise known as N. McG.)*, High Court, May 23, 1995, the petitioner, who suffered from alcoholism, gave graphic evidence of having woken up in bed with the respondent, to be told by her that they had just become married. He claimed that he remembered nothing of the wedding day. Morris J rejected this account. He was 'perfectly satisfied' from the respondent's evidence that it had been the petitioner's wish to marry her and that he had co-operated 'in a half-hearted and in an unsatisfactory way' in making preparations for the marriage, by buying clothes and rings, by having his bungalow decorated and by going to a mental hospital for a week before the wedding to cure his alcoholism.

Morris J was of the view that the petitioner lacked relational capacity (see below 300) but he nonetheless dismissed the petition on the ground of approbation: see below 301.

Relational incapacity In the 1992 Review 341-2, we analysed *P.K. v M.B.N. (otherwise K.)*, High Court, November 27, 1992, where Costello J granted an annulment on the basis that the respondent was suffering from a paranoid psychosis which made it impossible for her to sustain a normal marital relationship or to form and sustain a lasting marital relationship. The Supreme Court affirmed on April 3, 1995. Hamilton CJ (Egan and Blayney JJ concurring) was content to recite elements of Costello J's judgment and to observe that, if his findings were supported by credible evidence, the Supreme Court was bound by them. The Chief Justice went on to observe that '[t]estimony with regard to mental illness must of necessity relate to facts and inferences drawn from such facts.' Costello J, having satisfied himself with regard to the qualifications and experience of a chief psychiatrist of a large psychiatric hospital, had been entitled to accept and rely on his evidence.

This deference to psychiatric evidence is perhaps excessive. The courts — including the Supreme Court itself — have made it plain that, while naturally psychiatric evidence is crucial to the determination of whether the ground of mental illness or relational incapacity has been established, in the last analysis it is the function of the court, and not the psychiatrist, to make this determination.

In this regard, *P.K. v M.B.N. (otherwise K.)* may be contrasted with *K.T. v D.T.*, Supreme Court, October 12, 1995, affirming Murphy J's judgment in the High Court on March 18, 1992, which we analyse in the 1992 Review, 342-5. Two eminent psychiatrists were in agreement that the marriage had been doomed from the beginning on account of the parties' lack of capacity for emotional closeness. Murphy J had dismissed the petition, being of the view that their inadequacy of emotional response was not sufficiently serious to justify granting a decree. He had come to this conclusion with some difficulty, but in the last analysis considered that it would not be proper for him to abdicate his own function in the case by yielding simply to the views of the psychiatrists. In dismissing the appeal, Egan J (Hamilton CJ and O'Flaherty J concurring) stated that Murphy J had been 'of course, quite correct in this.'

Egan J added:

What, in any event, I ask myself is a 'normal' marriage relationship? There must surely be a great number of marriages which were entered into with little or no objective hope of survival due to mental or emotional instability, violent disposition, alcoholism and other causes of an intimate or sexual nature.

In the present case despite differing attitudes towards sexual activity there must have been a fair amount of full sexual intercourse. There was no suggestion of any disposition towards violence or outward manifestation of serious psychiatric problems at the actual time of the marriage. We may have opinions but we have not proof.

This passage is of interest for number of reasons. It is not unlike what Keane J said in *F. (Otherwise H.C.) v C.* [1991] 1 ILRM 65, which found no support in the Supreme Court: see the 1990 Review, 291-7. It betrays a certain scepticism about the fundamental conceptual coherence of the ground first recognised in *R.S.J. v J.S.J.* [1982] ILRM 263. In contrast, however, to Keane J, Egan J's emphasis on the quantum of sexual intercourse in the marriage, with the lack of emphasis on the relational quality, may seem to some to reflect an attitude of some bygone times. Keane J's rejection of *R.S.J.* was based on a clearly articulated view that divorce rather than nullity of marriage was the appropriate response to human frailty.

In *R. McG v N.K. (otherwise known as N. McG.)*, High Court, May 23, 1995, Morris J held that the petitioner, who had gone through a ceremony of marriage at the age of fifty in 1981, was incapable of entering into and sustaining a normal marriage relationship with the respondent. The petitioner had a long history of alcoholism. One of the psychiatrists who gave evidence expressed the opinion that the petitioner lacked the capacity of 'high order thinking' in regard to such matters as a relationship with a future wife, his own future and the commitment that marriage involves. Two other psychiatrists were also of the view that the petitioner lacked the requisite matrimonial capacity.

Morris J was of opinion that he would be 'flying in the face of the evidence' to reach the conclusion that the petitioner's appreciation of the contract of marriage was 'anything approaching normal'. He dismissed the petition on the ground of approbation, however. We consider this aspect of the case below, 301.

In the 1993 Review 317, we analysed *A.B. v E.B.*, High Court, October 14, 1993, where Budd J dismissed proceedings for nullity of marriage. The kernel of the petitioner's case was that the respondent's experiences as a child had so scarred her personality that at the time of the marriage in 1973 she was unable to enter into or sustain a normal marital relationship 'having special regard to the sexual relationship and in particular to a reasonable degree of frequency of sexual intimacy and intercourse.' Budd J rejected this contention. The evidence indicated that the sexual abuse suffered by the respondent as a child had not had a serious or lasting effect upon her. The respondent's inhibitions were 'probably no greater than the inhibitions of many happy married women in this country. . . . It was the petitioner's infidelity that had caused a deep loss of trust and a deep cause of hurt to the respondent which had exacerbated her lack of appetite to respond to his sexual demands.'

The petitioner appealed unsuccessfully to the Supreme Court. In a judgment delivered on July 31, 1995. Denham J (Egan and Blayney JJ concurring), applying the test laid down in the *Hay v O'Grady* [1992] IR 210, held that the findings of fact made by Budd J were supported by credible evidence and his holdings of law were correct.

Nonage Later in the Chapter, below 321-2 we examine ss. 31 and 33 of the Family Law Act 1995, which raise the minimum age for marriage from sixteen to eighteen years, retaining the possibility of judicial exemption for serious reasons where this is in the interests of the parties to the intended marriage.

Formalities S. 32 of the Family Law Act 1995 introduces a requirement of prior notification to the Registrar of an intended marriage three months before the intended date. S. 33 provides for judicial exemption in limited circumstances. We discuss these provisions later in the Chapter, in our overall examination of the 1995 Act, below, 313-30.

Bars to a decree In *R. McG v N.K. (otherwise known as N. McG.)*, High Court, May 23, 1995, Morris J dismissed a petition on the ground of approbation where the petitioner had established that he lacked the capacity to enter and sustain a normal marriage relationship: see above 300. The parties had gone through a ceremony of marriage in 1981. Six years later the respondent had issued maintenance proceedings against the petitioner, which he had sought (unsuccessfully) to defeat on the ground of her desertion. He defaulted on the maintenance order and a warrant was issued in 1988 and again in 1990. The petitioner then sought a variation of the maintenance order. It was only later in 1990 that the petitioner sought to challenge the validity of the marriage, on the advice of a solicitor.

Morris J considered that two factors were 'of prime importance'. The first was that, on two occasions, the petitioner had sought protection from family law legislation which would not be available to someone who was not married. The second was that throughout all this time the petitioner had been in receipt of advices from solicitors 'who, it must be assumed, advised him fully in relation to his marital status and the methods available to him to avoid making maintenance payments.' Accordingly, it appeared to Morris J that, 'with full knowledge of his rights, the petitioner sought to rely upon his marital status as conferring on him rights under Family Law legislation and this at a time when he had full knowledge of his rights and he accordingly approbated the marriage by so doing.'

One may question whether it should necessarily be assumed, apparently on an irrebuttable basis, that solicitors who are consulted by clients with specific family law problems, such as being sued for maintenance, will, or should, automatically address the question of petitioning for nullity of marriage as a strategy for avoiding making maintenance payments. It all depends on what the client presents to his or her solicitor as 'the problem' and what facts he or she discloses. There have been several instances where solicitors have not in fact addressed the question of petitioning for nullity when consulted on other family law issues. See, *e.g., P.W. v A.O.C. (otherwise W.)* [1992] ILRM 536, which we noted in the 1992 Review, 208.

Jurisdiction   S. 39 of the Family Law Act 1995 prescribes new jurisdictional rules for proceedings for nullity of marriage. We examine s. 39 later in the Chapter, below, 324.

THE FAMILY HOME

Scope of legislative protection   In *Allied Irish Banks v O'Neill*, High Court, December 13, 1995, Laffoy J was called on to answer a question which had been asked many times previously about the scope of protection afforded by the Family Home Protection Act 1976 but which curiously had not been definitively resolved over a period of nineteen years. This was whether s. 3(1) of the Act, which renders void a conveyance of the family home without the consent of the non-owning spouse, renders void the conveyance to the extent that it purports to convey *other property in conjunction with the family home.*

Previous judicial utterances suggested that severance was not possible. In the Supreme Court decision of *Hamilton v Hamilton* [1982] IR 466, at 490 Costello J had rejected such a contention as unsustainable and in *Bank of Ireland v Smyth* [1996] 1 ILRM 241, Blayney J, while reserving his position on the issue, had intimated that his inclination would be to agree with Costello J.

In *Allied Irish Banks v O'Neill*, the wife had made an equitable mortgage to the plaintiff bank to secure her indebtedness, by depositing the land certificate of the family home and lands, consisting of over sixty-three acres. The bank later sought a declaration that the sum of £5,000 stood well charged on her interest in the lands and an order that payment of this sum be enforced by sale or by the appointment of a receiver.

The deposit had been made without the husband's prior consent, as required by the 1976 Act. The essential issue, therefore, was whether the entire conveyance was void or whether severance of that portion of the property conveyed which did not constitute a family home should be permitted.

Laffoy J held that severance was indeed permissible. She reasoned as follows. In defining the expression 'family home' and in defining the extent of the property to which the protection of the Act should apply, the Oireachtas had clearly recognised that the family home might be part of a larger holding. Moreover, in defining the expressions 'family home' and 'dwelling', the Oireachtas had itself theoretically severed such a larger holding and theoretically created two new holdings: the family home as defined in the legislation, and the balance of the holding. Had the Oireachtas intended that an instrument designed to effect a disposition of a family home, thus defined, and other property would be wholly and entirely void for non-compliance with s. 3 and indivisible, such theoretical severance would have been unnecessary (This is not perhaps the strongest point in Laffoy J's analysis. Clearly the 1976 Act had to contain a definition of the expression of 'family home'. Its inclusion does not necessarily imply any view on the party of the Oireachtas on the question of severance.)

Laffoy J went on to stress that the Oireachtas had chosen in s.3(1) to render void a purported conveyance of 'any interest in the family home' without the necessary consent of the other spouse. On a literal interpretation of this provision, by reference to the definition in the Act, the Oireachtas could have intended to render void the purported conveyance or disposition only insofar as it affected the family home:

> To interpret subsection (1) as rendering void not only the conveyance or disposition insofar as it affects the family home portion but also insofar as it affects other property included in the conveyance or disposition, is to ignore the fact that what the legislature by the words it has used has rendered void is a purported conveyance of an interest in the 'family home', to which expression the legislature has ascribed a specific meaning. Therefore, in my view, when subsection (1) is literally interpreted giving the words and expressions 'convey', 'interest', 'family home' and 'conveyance' the meanings ascribed to them by the legislature, the inescapable conclusion is that the intention of the legislature was that the effect of non-compliance with the prior consent requirement of subsection (1) in relation to a conveyance which purports to convey an interest in the family home, as defined, and other property

is to render void only the conveyance of the interest in the family home.

A purposive approach towards statutory construction would yield the same result. A construction of s. 3(1) that permitted severance was 'entirely consistent with the legislative scheme as expressed in the Act of 1976 as a whole. . . .'

Laffoy J acknowledged that the construction she favoured undoubtedly created difficulties between the disponer and the disponee but these were no less capable of resolution than the difficulties that would flow from an interpretation of s. 3(1) as extending the invalidity to the entire transaction. The courts were familiar with handling the case of a disposition where the disponer had a disposing power over part only of the property that was the subject of the disposition.

> To hold that the equitable mortgage only effectively charged part of the lands registered on the folio is not to alter the scope and intention of the transaction or to rewrite the bargain between the parties: it is merely to recognise that the parties only partially effectively implemented their bargain, as would have been the case if, say, the [wife] had lost title to part of the lands registered on the folio prior to deposit of the land certificate by operation of the Statute of Limitations 1957 against her.

Whatever the merits of Laffoy J's analysis, one suspects that the Supreme Court, if called on to determine the issue, will favour the view adopted *obiter* in *Hamilton v Hamilton* and *Bank of Ireland v Smyth*. As a matter of practicality this view has more to commend it.

In *McQuillan v Maguire* [1996] 1 ILRM 394, Costello J applied the test set out by Henchy J in *M.C. v M.C.* [1986] ILRM 1, at 2 relating to spousal shares in the family home:

> . . . [w]here the . . . home has been purchased in the name of the husband, and the wife has, either directly or indirectly, made contribution towards the purchase price or towards the discharge of mortgage instalments, the husband will be held to be a trustee for the wife of a share in the house roughly corresponding with the proportion of the purchase money represented by the wife's total contribution. Such a trust will be inferred when the wife's contribution is of such a size and kind as will justify the conclusion that the acquisition of the house was achieved by the joint efforts of the spouses.

In the instant case, the plaintiffs, in a building dispute, had obtained a consent decree against the first defendant for £45,000. Shortly afterwards his wife, the second defendant, took proceedings under the Married Women's Status Act 1957 against him, which resulted in an order by consent declaring that she was entitled to the entire beneficial interest in the premises over which the plaintiffs had obtained a judgment mortgage.

On the basis of the evidence in the case, Costello J found that the second defendant had contributed about half of the total cost of the site and the erection of a dwelling in which she and the first defendant had lived and accordingly had a 50% equitable interest in it. This house was in due course sold and the house which was the subject matter of the litigation was purchased with its proceeds. Costello J held that the second defendant had a 50% interest in the house. As the agreement between the two defendants in the proceedings under the Married Women's Status Act 1957 had had the effect of 'hindering and delaying the payment of debt' due to the plaintiffs, Costello J declared it void. Accordingly the plaintiffs were entitled to a well-charging order against the first defendant's 50% interest in the house.

Later in the Chapter, below, 328-30, we examine s. 54 of the Family Law Act 1995, which restricts the scope of protection under the Family Home Protection Act 1976, in particular by narrowing the definition of 'dwelling' under s. 2(2) of the 1976 Act and introducing what is in effect a six-year limitation period subject to certain conditions.

Consent to conveyance of the family home   In *Bank of Ireland v Smyth* [1996] 1 ILRM 241, the Supreme Court, affirming Geoghegan J in the High Court [1993] ILRM 790; [1993] 2 IR 102, held that a consent by the non-owning spouse under s. 3 of the Family Home Protection Act 1976 to a conveyance of an interest in the family home by the owner spouse must be a 'fully informed' one. Blayney J (Hamilton CJ and Egan J concurring) stated that the spouse giving the consent

> must know what it is that he or she is consenting to. Since giving one's consent means that one is approving of something, obviously a precondition is that one should have knowledge of what it is that one is approving of.

The Court rejected, in formal terms at least, the contention that the bank in whose favour a charge is made has a duty to explain fully to the non-owning spouse the nature of the charge and to suggest to her (or him) that she (or he) obtain independent legal advice. Such steps should indeed be taken, but in the bank's interest to ensure that the consent is a fully informed one rather than in discharge of some duty owed to the non-owning spouse. Thus, recent developments in England will have no direct relevance. It is, however, hard to believe that they did not influence the outcome in this case indirectly.

Bankruptcy and the family home   In *Rubotham as Official Assignee in Bankruptcy in the Estate of Young, a Bankrupt v Young*, High Court, May 23, 1995, the difficult question of how to do justice as between creditors and the family of a bankrupt fell for decision. The defendant's husband had been adjudicated bankrupt in 1988. There were admitted liabilities in the bankruptcy of about £140,000, with disputed claims for a further £84,000. The official assignee sought an order for the sale of the family home, which was variously valued at £135,000 and £190,000. S. 61 of the Bankruptcy Act 1988 provides in part as follows:

> (4) Notwithstanding any provision to the contrary contained in subsection (3), no disposition of property of a bankrupt, arranging debtor or person dying insolvent, which comprises a family home within the meaning of the Family Home Protection Act, 1976 shall be made without the prior sanction of the Court, and any disposition made without such sanction shall be void.

> (5) On an application by the Official Assignee under this section for an order for the sale of a family home, the Court, notwithstanding anything contained in this or any other enactment, shall have the power to order postponement of the sale of the family home having regard to the interests of the creditors and of the spouse and dependents of the bankrupt as well as to all the circumstances of the case.

The defendant sought a postponement of sale pending the satisfactory resolution of queries that her accountant had made in regard to partnership accounts which were relevant to the bankruptcy. McCracken J declined to grant a postponement on this basis (though he deferred the sale for four months to allow the family a reasonable opportunity of acquiring a new house with the defendant's share of the proceeds of sale).

McCracken J observed that he had been referred to a number of English decisions under the Law of Property Act 1925, s. 30, the Matrimonial Homes Act 1967 and the Matrimonial Causes Act 1973; while these cases might be of some assistance, they had been decided under different legislation, but they all emphasised that, if discretion was to be exercised in favour of a bankrupt's family, 'this must only be done under exceptional circumstances.' One may perhaps wonder whether any general principle articulated in English decisions in the context of the disposition of the family home should be given even tentative weight in the context of pre-divorce Irish law on the subject. It is quite clear that the policy underlying the Family Home Protection Act 1976 was formulated in full knowledge of English experience under the Matrimonial Homes Act 1967 and with the specific intention of departing from the approach adopted by the 1967 Act. The speech of the Minister for Justice, Mr Cooney, on Second Reading in the Dáil leaves no doubt on this. It is, however, also true that the social policy underlying the 1976 Act was designed to frustrate vindictive or selfish husbands rather than to provide a bulwark to wives to protect them from their husbands' creditors.

McCracken J noted that s. 61(5) of the 1988 Act required him to have regard to the competing interests of the creditors' and the bankrupt's family. As far as the creditors were concerned, the bankrupt had been adjudicated almost seven years previously; they had been paid nothing and would receive nothing unless and until the family home was sold. Even then they would not be paid in full and there would be no funds for any claim that they might have to interest. On the other hand, the spouse and five children had for these years lived in the house, 'in reality at the expense of the creditors.' While at the time of the adjudication some of the children had been minors, they had all reached full age, although two were unemployed. McCracken J saw little merit in the accounting point.

Accordingly McCracken J saw 'no real grounds' for postponing the sale any longer. The defendant and her family had 'in effect had a postponement of seven years.' Subject to the deferral of four months, he made the order under s. 61(4).

Sale of the family home in judicial separation proceedings Earlier in the Chapter, above, 292-3, we analyse Judge McGuinness's decision in *S.B. v R.B.* [1996] Ir Law Log Weekly 379, where she ordered the sale of a family home, in which the wife and children resided, on making an order for judicial separation at the application of the wife.

SUPPORT OBLIGATIONS

Clearing arrears In the 1993 Review 317, we analysed *M.M. v C.M.*, High Court, July 26, 1993, where O'Hanlon J granted a degree of judicial separation under ground (f) of s. 2(1) of the Judicial Separation and Family Law Reform Act 1989. The case returned to the High Court two years later. Morris J delivered judgment on July 26, 1995. The husband had fallen into serious arrears in respect of maintenance and payment of the mortgage on the family home. The wife had been obliged to obtain loans from her family and friends and, on occasions, to obtain food vouchers from the St. Vincent de Paul Society. The solution adopted by Morris J, with consent of both parties, was to make an order under s. 15(1) of the 1989 Act, transferring the husband's share in the family home to his wife, in lieu of the arrears. This share was valued in excess of what was owing. (S. 17 of the Family Law Act 1995, which we note below, 316, gives the court power to direct the amount due retrospectively under a maintenance order to be paid in one sum,with credit given for any sums paid to the creditor spouse in the intervening period.)

Morris J adjourned the wife's application to have her husband committed for contempt, with liberty to re-enter. He took into account the fact that the husband had been 'extremely upset by the circumstances of this case' (which involved an affair between his wife and a priest) and that this might have 'led him to behave in a manner which was inappropriate.' He pointed out that, if the husband was of opinion that he was unable to make the payments which he had earlier undertaken, it was open to him to apply to the court to have them reviewed. Pending such a successful application, the original order should stand.

Finally Morris J, on the wife's application, terminated the husband's access to the family home for the purpose of carrying out business at his office there. Since the husband practised mainly from the apartment where he resided and did 'a significant amount of his work in public houses' and treated his car 'to a large extent as an office', he had no need to return to his former home. His continued attendance there had been a source of upset for the children in that it brought him into contact with their mother, 'with disturbing results.'

Paternalism versus autonomy   In *H. (J.) v H. (R.)* [1996] ILFR 23 (High Court, Barr J, 1995), an opportunity arose to determine, for once and for all, the fundamental issues of policy relating to the conflict between paternalism and spousal autonomy. On one view, spouses should be free to come to any agreement they wish as to financial matters without legal restraint, provided there is no duress or undue influence. Indeed, that is the basis on which the Supreme Court struck down the Matrimonial Home Bill 1993: [1994] 1 ILRM 241; [1994] 1 IR 305. See our comments in the 1994 Review 320. On another view, there is a need to protect spouses from signing away their right to apply to the court at some time in the future for proper maintenance from their spouses. On this approach, it should always be possible to apply to the court; whether or not that application should succeed would be a matter for the court to decide in the light of all the circumstances, including the fact that the applicant has agreed with the other spouse not to have later recourse to the courts. This view is an amalgam of several perceptions: that it is hard to predict the future; that people are notoriously shortsighted in the face of what seems like a large lump sum; and that wives and children need distinct protection by the courts from husbands who often have greater economic resources and better access to legal advice.

At all events, s. 27 of the Family Law (Maintenance of Spouses and Children) Act 1976 renders void an agreement in so far as it would have the effect of excluding or limiting the operation of provisions in the Act including

s. 5, which enables a spouse to apply to the court for a maintenance order where the other spouse has failed to provide such maintenance for the family 'as is proper in the circumstances'. In *H.D. v P.D.*, Supreme Court, May 8, 1978, the Court, without express reference to s. 27, interpreted the policy of the 1976 Act as a whole as being so strong and universal in its application as to defeat any attempt to oust its jurisdiction by private agreement.

We have in earlier years noted how the courts have proved incapable of dealing with the differing implications for husbands and wives of a policy that prevents a final determination by private agreement of the parties' maintenance entitlements. (At a formal level, the distinction is not based on gender but, as a matter of economic and sociological reality, it is.) Whereas a wife may come back to court after having ostensibly resolved finally by private agreement her maintenance entitlements relative to her husband, a husband has been held disentitled to apply for a variation downwards of his maintenance obligations as prescribed in the agreement (in the absence, of course, of a clause permitting this) or for a maintenance order in his favour under s. 5 of the 1976 Act.

In *H. (J.) v H. (R.)*, the husband was very rich. The parties entered into a consent agreement in the context of judicial proceedings in 1992. This included the payment of maintenance to the wife and children (with a built-in cost-of-living increase), a lump sum payment by the husband to the wife of £70,000, the transfer to the wife of the husband's interest in the family home and the discharge by him of forthcoming mortgage payments. The agreement also provided (in clause 11) that:

> [i]n the event of a fundamental change in the financial circumstance [*sic*] of either the husband or the wife, the wife shall be entitled to serve notice upon the husband informing him of her need for a greater sum of maintenance in excess of that provided herein. The husband may serve notice upon the wife informing her of his intention to reduce the sum of maintenance that he is paying to her in accordance with the provisions herein. . . .

In the absence of agreement to the proposed revised maintenance, there was a provision for arbitration or reference to the court. Clause 29 provided that the parties agreed that the separation agreement constituted a full and final separation of all matters outstanding between them, including any claim which the wife might have under the Judicial Separation and Family Law Reform Act 1989 or any amending legislation.

In 1994 the husband was made redundant. This resulted in the reduction of his nett annual income from £96,000 in 1992 to £55,000. His capital assets were, however, in excess of a million pounds. The wife's nett annual income was less than £17,000. When mortgage and VHI contributions from her husband were taken into account, this figure rose to £20,000. Of this sum, £6,000 represented the maintenance devoted to her children, leaving her with a nett personal annual income of £14,000, in comparison to her husband's nett annual income after payment of his wife's (but not his children's) maintenance of £43,000.

The wife applied to the court under s. 5 of the 1976 Act seeking 'a review of maintenance'. She argued that s. 27 of the Act negated the effect of clause 29 of the separation agreement. She made not attempt to rely on clause 11 of the agreement as to a fundamental change of circumstances. The husband argued that the wife had been adequately provided for under the separation agreement and that this fact had been acknowledged by her in the agreement. He contended, moreover, that his changed financial circumstances since the deed had been executed amounted to a fundamental deterioration as envisaged by clause 11 and that in fairness there ought to be a *downward* revision of the maintenance provisions and that no increase in them should be authorised by the court.

Barr J, in the light of s. 27 and of *H.D. v P.D.*, held that the wife had a prima facie right to make a claim for revision of maintenance under the 1976 Act, notwithstanding clause 29. In an important passage, he said:

> It seems to me that if she can establish that her opinion as to the adequacy of maintenance provisions at the time when she executed the deed was not well founded, then it is open to the Court to review such terms in the light of all relevant circumstances prevailing at the time of the application. The test is whether the maintenance terms agreed were and remain fair and reasonable. It is the function of the Court to consider whether the husband has failed to provide such maintenance for the wife and the dependent children as is proper in the circumstances. In the vast majority of cases where marriages break down there is some inevitable decline in existing living standards for both spouses and the dependent children. Sadly this must be accepted as part of the harsh reality of marital breakdown. However, in circumstances where the husband's assets and annual income are substantial, in my opinion what is 'proper in the circumstances', as contemplated is section 5(1), is the continuance of a standard of living as near as reasonably practicable to that enjoyed by the wife and dependent children before the breakdown of the marriage, taking into account, as provided in subsection (4), all the relevant circumstances of both spouses and the dependent children, including capital payments made to the wife by the husband, and bearing in mind that the husband also is entitled to a reasonable post-breakdown standard of living.

Two points of particular significance may be noted. First, Barr J appears to require, as a pre-condition of entitlement to succeed in a s. 5 application subsequent to a maintenance agreement which contains an ouster clause defeated by s. 27, not merely that the failure of the respondent to provide maintenance is not proper at the time of the application, but also that the maintenance terms of the maintenance agreement, *when formulated*, were not fair and reasonable. This pre- requirement seems not to be warranted by either the words of s. 27 or the holding of the Supreme Court in *H.D. v P.D.* It would, moreover, present difficulties, as to issue estoppel and related evidential principles, in cases where the maintenance agreement was made a rule of court under s. 8 of the 1976. S. 8 obliges the court, before taking this step, to ensure that the agreement's provisions as to maintenance are fair as between both parties and their children.

Secondly, it is worth reflecting on Barr J's perception that, where the husband is rich, the court's obligation is to keep the standard of living of the wife and dependent children 'as near as reasonably practicable to that [which they] enjoyed . . . before the breakdown of the marriage. . . .' This reflects what was said several years ago by Barrington J, in *L.B. v H.B.* [1980] ILRM 257. In contrast, the wives and children of less well-off husbands may not obtain financial support that will keep them up to the standard of living that they had before the breakdown of marriage. If, with the introduction of divorce, a husband of moderate means who deserts and later divorces his wife is permitted to reduce further his maintenance obligations to her and the children in order to support a new wife, the prospect a further decline in their living standards seems inevitable. One may wonder how a court would respond to the claim by a deserting husband who has starting living with a new partner that he intends to divorce his wife and that accordingly, in the period before he is permitted to exercise his new constitutional freedom, his support obligation to his new partner requires the reduction in his maintenance obligations to his wife and children. Cf. *J.C. v C.C.*, High Court, November 23, 1995, discussed below, 312-3.

In the instant case, Barr J concluded that there was an unfair imbalance between the wife's nett annual income and that of her husband. She had not been in full-time employment since before her marriage and it had not been suggested that she had significant earning capacity. She had, moreover, the burden of providing a home of some of her children and her aged mother. Although she had a nett annual income which many would regard as comfortable, her quality of life in financial terms had probably deteriorated significantly and to a greater extent than that suffered by her husband, even allowing for his redundancy. Accordingly he increased the wife's monthly maintenance by £100 and that of each child by £50.

Assumption of new obligations In *J.C. v C.C.*, High Court, November 23, 1995, decided on the eve of the referendum on divorce, Kinlen J made an observation on which it may be useful to reflect. When raising the amount of an order for maintenance made against the husband by the Circuit Court from £30 per week to £40 per week in respect of the parties' ten year old son, Kinlen J noted that the husband was now living with a woman who had been twice divorced, with a child from each marriage, where the former husbands were not contributing any maintenance. The husband and the woman had a child from their relationship. Kinlen J observed that the husband had

> taken on the burden of providing for two children he did not father. It may concern the Circuit Court as to what efforts were made to make the respective fathers maintain their respective children. However, it is clear that the [husband] cannot avoid his liability to his son . . . because he has taken on other liabilities.

This case raises the question of what duty a spouse owes his or her child when the spouse moves on to a second relationship and what duty that spouse owes to the children of the second partner who are already on the scene. The tenor of Kinlen J's observation is that a spouse's obligation to his or her child cannot be shaken off by his or her voluntary assumption of new responsibilities to children who are not his or her own. Since the enactment of the Family Law (Maintenance of Spouses and Children) Act 1976, one spouse may assume a support obligation relative to the children of his or her spouse. The position is now covered by the Family Law Act 1995. It has not been suggested in earlier cases that it would be possible or desirable to distinguish between the entitlements of children to whom an obligation of support is owed. Kinlen J is correct in stating that the assumption of a maintenance responsibility to children who are not one's own should not permit a spouse to 'avoid his liability to his son', if that expression connotes a complete avoidance. The legislation does not, however, require in express terms that every child should receive the same amount. All the circumstances must be taken into account in determining their respective entitlements.

What Kinlen J was suggesting was surely that a spouse should not be entitled to repudiate or improperly reduce his or her responsibility to his children by entering into a new relationship and assuming extra responsibilities attendant upon that relationship (other than the responsibility directly flowing from parenthood). In other words, in a serial relationship structure, children of former relationships would look to their own parents, and not primarily to their stepparents, for support.

The modern system of no-fault divorce facilitates the establishment of second families and the generation of complex step-relationships. If, after a divorce, both spouses re-marry new partners who themselves are divorced parents, and in due course have more children, the children of the original marriage will have step-relationships with the children of their mother's second husband and his first wife, the children of their father's second wife and her first husband, the children of their father and his second wife and the children of their mother and her second husband.

It is a sad fact of modern life that many divorced fathers do not provide effective support for the children of their first marriage. There are many reasons for this deficiency. It is very hard for most people to support two families; fathers in second marriages can come to regard the claims of the first family as a millstone dragging them down; their loyalties may have transferred to their new wife and their new children (though not necessarily to the children of her previous marriage).

In *In re G.Y., an infant; M.Y. v A.Y.*, High Court, December 11, 1995, Budd J awarded a wife £500 *per* month for the maintenance for her son and such further sum as would provide her with £800 disposable income, under s. 14 of the 1989 Act. It appears that the basis of this order was s. 11 of the Guardianship of Infants Act 1964. Echoing Costello J's broad interpretation of the scope of the court's powers in relating to s. 11, in *E.D. v F. D.*, Hgh Court, October 23, 1980, Budd J was of opinion that the section empowered the court to make orders for the maintenance of the boy 'and also for his mother in whose custody he is.' It was, moreover, wide enough to empower the court to make orders in respect of lump sum provision for the purchase of a suitable house, which both parties agreed would be beneficial to their son. It appears that Budd J adopted this approach in the light of the fact that the husband, in breach of his undertaking, had converted an English divorce decree *nisi* into a decree absolute: see the Conflict of Laws Chapter above 113.

Legislative changes   Part VI of the Family Law Act 1995 includes several changes in the Family Law (Maintenance of Spouses and Children) Act 1976. We examine these later in the Chapter, below, 323.

LEGISLATION

The Family Law Act 1995 is a most important piece of legislation. Undoubtedly it was conceived and executed in the context of a wider debate about divorce. The irony is that, with the passage of the divorce referendum on 26 November 1995, many of the provisions of the Act are already looking slightly dated. For a comprehensive analysis of the legislation, see Claire Jackson's *Annotation*, ICLSA. The Act came into effect on August 1, 1996:

SI No. 46 of 1996.

The easiest way of analysing the changes brought about by the Act is to examine it on a Part by Part basis.

Part I: Preliminary and general   Part I contains four sections: the short title and commencement (s. 1), an interpretation section (s. 2), repeals (s. 3) and expenses (s. 4). We shall examine the crucial interpretations (notably of 'dependent member of the family' and 'relief order') in the specific contexts in later provisions of the Act, where these definitions impact strongly. Similarly we shall note the important repeals, effected by s. 3, in conjunction with the Schedule, in relation to themes occurring later in the Act. S. 4 simply provides that the expenses incurred by the Ministers for Equality and Law Reform, Health and Justice in the administration of the Act are to be paid out of moneys provided by the Oireachtas.

Part II: Preliminary and ancillary orders in or after proceedings for judicial separation   Part II largely re-enacts the provisions of Part II of the Judicial Separation and Family Law Reform Act 1989, which s. 3 of the 1995 Act repeals, save for s. 25: cf. the 1988 Review 229-42. Thus, s. 6 empowers the court to make preliminary orders in proceedings for judicial separation; this is similar to ss 11 and 12 of the 1988 Act: cf. the 1989 Review, 235. The preliminary orders are barring and protection orders, orders relating to the welfare of minors, under s. 11 of the Guardianship of Children Act 1964 and orders under s. 5 or s. 9 of the Family Home Protection Act 1976.

S. 7, providing for maintenance pending suit orders, is similar to s. 13 of the 1989 Act, but is novel in permitting interim *lump sum* payments. S. 8, providing for periodical payment orders, secured periodical payment orders, and lump sum orders on or after the court grants a decree of judicial separation, is similar to s. 14 of the 1989 Act but again includes a novel element. Whereas, under the 1989 Act, the attachment of earnings machinery could be applied only against a *defaulting* spouse, s. 8(6) now enables the court to make an attachment of earnings order *at the time it is making a periodical payments order*. Before deciding whether or not to do so, the court must give the spouse concerned an opportunity to make representations as to whether he (or she) would make the payments to which the attachment order relates. Presumably, if he (or she) produces a convincing case, it would be wrong for the court to make the attachment order, which carries a certain stigma. The subsection is silent on what type of evidence should stay the hand of the court, so it may be that an appellate court would be very slow to reverse the exercise of discretion by the trial judge save in the clearest of cases.

S. 9, largely echoing s. 15 of the 1989 Act (cf. the 1988 Review, 235) permits the court to make property adjustment orders on or after granting a decree of judicial separation. These may consist of orders for the *transfer* of property, the *settlement* of specific property, the *variation* of an ante-nuptial or post-nuptial settlement or the *extinguishment or reduction* of a spouse's interest under a settlement. Orders for transfer of property are not subject to variation. The other three types of orders may in principle be varied (according to the provisions of s. 18) but the court has the power under s. 9(2) when making an order of any of these three types to block the possibility of subsequent variation.

S. 9(5) eases the position where a person who has been directed to execute a deed in relation to land refuses or neglects to do so: rather than requiring the other party to invoke the cumbersome procedures of civil contempt, s. 9(5) empowers the court to order *another person* to execute the deed. During the Oireachtas debates, the Minister indicated that the County Registrar would be a likely candidate.

S. 9(7) gives priority to the second wife (or husband) after a divorce, in providing that s. 9:

> shall not apply in relation to a family home in which, following the grant of a decree of judicial separation, either of the spouses concerned, having remarried, ordinarily resides with his or her spouse.

This provision should be read in conjunction with the provisions of Part III of the Act (which we discuss below, 317-9), especially s. 23(2)(b)(ii). The failure to mention the intervening divorce is striking.

S. 10 echoes s. 16 of the 1989 Act in permitting the court to make a raft of ancillary orders when it has granted a decree of judicial separation, without requiring separate proceedings to be initiated. These relate to the exclusive occupation or sale of the family home, the determination of questions as to title or possession of any property (under s. 36), orders under s. 4, 5, 7 or 9 of the Family Home Protection Act 1976, barring or protection orders, orders for partition and orders relating to the custody and access of children under s. 11 of Guardianship of Infants Act 1964.

S. 11 is a new provision. It enables the court, on or after granting a decree of judicial separation, to make a *financial compensation order*, requiring a spouse:

> (i) to effect a policy of life insurance for the benefit of the other spouse or a dependent member of the family;
> (ii) to assign an interest in a life insurance policy;
> or
> (iii) to make payments on a life insurance policy.

S. 12 is one of the most important provisions of the Act. It reflects extensive consultation with the Pensions Board, the Irish Association of Pension Funds and other interested bodies. It enables the court, on granting a decree of judicial separation, to make a pension adjustment order, providing for the payment of a spouse's retirement benefit to persons (including the other spouse) specified in the order. S. 12 (5) permits pension splitting, on the application of the spouse in whose favour the court has made a pension adjustment order. For a comprehensive analysis of s. 12, see Kevin Finucane & Brian Buggy, *Irish Pensions Law and Practice* (1996), chapter 15 and Claire Jackson's *Annotation*, ICLSA, General Note of s. 12.

S. 13 empowers the court to direct trustees of a pension scheme to preserve the pension entitlements of a spouse after judicial separation. In this context, one should note s. 43, which applies s. 13 to situations where s. 8 of the Family Law (Maintenance of Spouses and Children) Act 1976 applies.

S. 14 enables the court, on or after granting a decree of judicial separation, to make an order extinguishing the share of either (or both) of the spouses that would otherwise arise as a legal right or an intestacy under the Succession Act 1965. This echoes s. 17 of the 1989 Act. See the 1988 Review, 237-8.

S. 15 is largely identical to s. 18 of the 1989 Act in empowering the court, when it has made a secured periodical payments order, a lump sum order or a property adjustment order, to make an order directing the sale of property in which a spouse has a beneficial interest. The court must listen to the representations of third parties before it makes any such order: s. 15 (5).

S. 16 sets out the criteria which the court should apply in deciding whether to make a preliminary order or ancillary order under Part II of the Act and in determining the provisions of the order. The basic test is to endeavour to ensure that such provision is made for both spouses and dependent members of the family as is 'adequate and reasonable having regard to all the circumstances of the case': s. 16(1).

Most of the specific criteria reflect the approach favoured in s. 20 of the 1989 Act: see the 1988 Review, 236-7. There is a weakening of the approach towards desertion, however. Under the 1989 Act, a deserting spouse would not be entitled to an array of orders for his or (much more usually) her support unless it would be 'repugnant to justice' not to make the order. Under the 1995 Act, a deserting spouse is denied this entitlement unless it would, in the opinion of the court, be 'unjust' not to make the order. There is no doubt that this is a substantive shift in value-judgment. It is easier for a court to hold that a particular decision would be 'unjust' than that it would be 'repugnant to justice'.

S. 17 gives the court power, in making a periodical payments order, to direct that the period in respect of which payments are to be made should be retrospective, that the amount retrospectively due should be paid in one sum and that credit should be given for any sums paid to the creditor spouse in the intervening period.

S. 18, echoing s. 22 of the 1989 Act, gives the court wide-ranging powers of variation and discharge of orders for maintenance, property transfer (subject to the limits imposed by s. 9, to which we have already referred) or occupation or sale of the family home, financial compensation orders, pension adjustment orders and orders relating to the preservation of pension entitlements.

Ss. 19 to 22 of the Act can be noted briefly. S. 19, echoing a policy that goes back to the Family Law (Maintenance of Spouses and Children) Act 1976, ensures that the sins of parents are not visited upon their children so far as orders for maintenance are concerned. S. 20 provides for the transmission of periodical maintenance payments through the District Court clerk. S. 21, echoing s. 27 of the 1989 Act, harmonises the provisions in the 1995 Act relating to maintenance pending suit, periodical payment orders and secured periodical payment orders with the reference in s. 98(1)(h) of the Defence Act 1954 to an order for the payment of alimony. This allows for deduction from the wages or salary of a member of the defence forces to satisfy a court order. Finally, s. 22 of the 1995 Act, echoing s. 28 of the 1989 Act, renders a defaulter in relation to a maintenance pending suit order or a periodical payments order liable to imprisonment or distraint under the Enforcement of Court Orders Act 1940.

Part III: Relief after divorce or separation outside the State Part III effects a most important change in the law. Previously, if a spouse obtained a divorce abroad which was recognised under the rules of private international law, that sounded the death knell to the maintenance entitlements of the other spouse under Irish law, save in cases where the spouse had already obtained a maintenance order under s. 5 of the Family Law (Maintenance of Spouses and Children) Act 1976: see *C.M. v T.M.* [1991] ILRM 268, noted in the 1988 Review 111-3, and *In re G.Y., an infant; M.Y. v A.Y.*, High Court, December 11, 1995, which we note in the Conflict of Laws Chapter, above 113, and earlier in this Chapter, above 313. Now s. 23 gives the Irish court power to make a relief order where a marriage has been dissolved abroad, or the spouses have been legally separated abroad, in circumstances where the foreign divorce or separation is recognised as valid in the State. The court may in essence make any order that it could have made under Part II of the Act (save a preliminary order under s. 7 or a maintenance pending suit order). S. 23(2)(b) prescribes the exceptions to this general rule. An important one, worthy of particular note, is that the court may not make an order under s. 15 in relation to a family home in which, following a foreign divorce, either spouse, having remarried, ordinarily resides with his or her spouse: s.

23(2)(b)(ii). cf. s. 9(7).

S. 24 provides for *maintenance pending relief orders* whereby the court can in effect, make interim maintenance orders — a power formally denied to it by s. 23(2)(c).

S. 25 enables a divorced spouse to seek an order for provision out of the estate of the other spouse. The court may make such provision for the applicant out of the estate as it considers appropriate, 'having regard to the rights of any other person having an interest in the matter', if satisfied that it was not possible to provide adequate and reasonable provision for the applicant during the lifetime of the deceased spouse under ss. 8 to 12 of the 1995 Act for any reason (other than the applicant's conduct): s. 25(1). The remarriage of the applicant kills a claim: s. 25(2).

The provision made for an applicant is not to exceed in total the share (if any) of the applicant in the estate of the deceased spouse to which the applicant was, or would have been, entitled under the Succession Act 1965 if the marriage had not been dissolved: s. 25(4). S. 25(5) allows for the application of s. 121 of the Succession Act 1995 to police dispositions designed to defeat or diminish the provision that the court would make for the applicant.

S. 26 prevents the court from making a relief order under s. 23 unless it is satisfied that in all circumstances it is appropriate to do so. It lists nine factors to which the court is in particular to have regard in determining this issue. They include the connection which the spouses have with the State and with the country where the divorce took place, any financial benefit which the applicant received in consequence of the divorce or legal separation, the financial relief given by a property transfer order in a foreign court and the entitlement of the applicant to apply for financial relief from the other spouse in a foreign jurisdiction. Once the court has decided that it is appropriate for it to make a relief order under s. 23, then it appears that the several factors listed in s. 26 lose their distinctive character and become some of the totality of circumstances to which the court is to have regard under s. 23.

S. 27(1) prescribes the jurisdiction of a court to make relief orders under s. 23. It is based on the domicile of either spouse in the State, the ordinary residence for one year within the State of either spouse or the fact that one or both of the spouses had a beneficial interest in land within the State. S. 27(2) excludes the application of s. 27(1) in relation to cases where the Jurisdiction of Courts and Enforcement of Judgments Acts 1988 and 1993 apply or to relief orders that are the subject of a request under s. 14 of the Maintenance Orders Act 1994: cf. the 1994 Review, 103.

S. 28(1) restricts the scope of the relief orders that a court may make where its jurisdiction is conferred by reason only of the fact that one or both of the spouses had a beneficial interest in land within the State. The court may make a lump sum order, certain categories of property adjustment order, an order extinguishing succession rights, an order for provision for a spouse (under s. 25) or an order directing the sale of one spouse's interest in the family home. S. 28(2) provides that the aggregate sum must not exceed the value of the interest of the spouse liable to make the payment in the family home concerned or the amount of the proceeds of the sale of the family home.

Part IV : Declarations as to marital status Part IV updates the law in relation to declarations as to marital status, which formerly had been subject to complex provisions in the Legitimacy Declaration Act (Ireland) 1868, which had been rendered more uncertain in their scope as a result of Ireland's acquisition of independence and the later promulgation of the Constitution: see W. Binchy, *Irish Conflicts of Law* (1988), 355-7. Jurisdiction is grounded on the domicile or ordinary residence of one year's duration of either of the spouses: s. 29(2). The court (which may be either the High Court or Circuit Court: s. 38) may make a declaration that a marriage was at its inception a valid marriage or that it subsisted (or did not subsist) on a specified date or that a foreign divorce, annulment or legal separation is (or is not) entitled to recognition: s.29(1). An application for any of these declarations may be made by or on behalf of either of the spouses concerned or by any other person who, in the opinion of the court, has a sufficient interest in the matter. Thus, for example, the Registrar General, if in doubt as to the validity of a foreign divorce, could apply under s. 29, although he is not obliged to do so: *P.L. v An tÁrd Chlaraithroir* [1995] 2 ILRM 241.

The court has power to order that notice of the proceedings be given to the Attorney General or any other person: s. 29(4). The Attorney General may in any event insist on being addressed as a party: s. 29(5). If a party to proceedings alleges that a marriage is or was void, or that it is voidable, and should be annulled, the court may treat the application under subs. (1) as an application for a decree of nullity of marriage and proceed to determine the matter accordingly and postpone the determination of the application under subs. (1).

S. 30(1) provides for the making of rules of court in relation to applications under s. 29(1). The court may require the other parties to the proceedings to pay the Attorney General's costs: s. 30(2). s. 30(3) provides that, without prejudice to the law governing the recognition of foreign divorces, a declaration under s. 29 conflicting with a previous final judgment or decree of a foreign court of competent jurisdiction may not be made unless the judgment or decree was obtained by fraud or collusion. This limitation is controversial. In respect of a foreign divorce obtained by duress, as occurred in *Gaffney v Gaffney* [1975] IR 133, this would require the Irish court, in effect, to uphold the validity of a foreign divorce even where there was coercive evidence that it had been obtained by duress. It is true that in *Gaffney v Gaffney*, Walsh J observed (at 153-4) that:

> it might well be that . . . it would be incumbent upon the plaintiff to have the decree of dissolution, made by the court having jurisdiction, set aside before she could successfully assert the status of wife.

A difficulty with this approach is that, if the law of the state where the divorce was obtained has only a limited entitlement (or indeed, no entitlement) to have the decree overturned on the grounds of duress, the spouse who is divorced as a result of duress may be seriously prejudiced. Prior to the introduction of divorce in November 1995, it might have been argued that it would be contrary to Article 41 for legislation to require the courts to uphold the validity of a foreign divorce decree obtained under duress. It is now less easy to do so, since it is possible to obtain a divorce within the State against the wishes of one's spouse, after the passage of the requisite period of time. From the standpoint of a spouse who wishes not to be divorced, the imposition of a divorced status against his or her will has an element of duress.

There is a further difficulty with s. 30(3). Courts in other jurisdictions are increasingly disposed to recognise the validity of a marriage entered into after a divorce the validity of which they did not recognise, provided the parties entering the second marriage have capacity to do so under the law of their domicile. If a party has obtained a declaration from a foreign court of the validity of the second marriage, which would not be capable of recognition under Irish law, it would seem wrong that the Irish court should in consequence of s. 30(3) be prevented from making a conflicting declaration.

A few matters of definitional uncertainty remain, but however they are resolved, the substance of the difficulties outlined abroad. They include the following questions. What is the scope of the concept of 'a previous final judgment or decree of a court of competent jurisdiction of a country or jurisdiction other than the State', in s. 30(3)? Clearly it embraces Northern Ireland, so we need not concern ourselves with the doubts expressed by Kenny J in this context in *Re Caffin deceased; Bank of Ireland v Caffin* [1971] IR 123, at 130: see Binchy, *op. cit.*, 278. Frankly, these doubts have long ago faded into complete obscurity, having been rendered obsolete by judicial and legislative initiatives. More substantively, we may ask whether the foreign court must have been one that granted the decree of divorce whose validity is in question or whether it could simply have made a *declaration* as to the validity of a decree of divorce in *another* state. To describe such a declaration as either a 'final judgment' or a 'decree' seems somewhat heavy language.

If such declarations do not fall within the scope of s. 30(3), we are saved some of the shackles that it imposes on Irish courts.

Part V: Marriage Part V of the Act makes two controversial changes to Irish marriage law. It raises the minimum age for marriage to eighteen years (s. 31) and introduces a three-month notification period as a prerequisite for marriage (s. 32). It also, uncontroversially, abolishes the right to petition for jactitation of marriage (s. 34). No proceedings for jactitation had been taken for many years. The Law Reform Commission recommended the abolition of the action in its *Report on the Restitution of Conjugal Rights, Jactitation of Marriage and Related Matters* (LRC 6 — 1983). In essence the jactitation remedy involved injunctive proceedings against a third party designed to obtain a judicial declaration as to the validity of one's marriage. This can be addressed now under s. 29 of the 1995 Act.

Minimum age for marriage Under the Marriages Act 1972 a marriage where at least one of the parties was under the age of sixteen was void unless the prior consent of the President of the High Court was obtained where this was 'justified by serious reasons' and was 'in the interests of the parties to the intended marriage'. Marriages where at least one of the parties was under the age of twenty one required parental consent or the authorisation of the President of the High Court if the parents refused or could not agree among themselves. Marriage in violation of the statutory requirements as to parental consent were not, however, void, these requirements being regarded as directory rather than mandatory.

Over the years successive agencies recommended an increase in the minimum age for marriage to sixteen years. These included the Law Reform Commission, in its *Report on the Age of Majority, the Age for Marriage and Some Connected Subjects* (LRC 5-1983), the the Oireachtas Joint Committee on Marital Breakdown in its Report, published in 1984, and the Second Commission on the Status of Women, in its Report. This recommendation sprang from concern for the instability of youthful marriages as well as a sense that young persons should be protected from exercising a freedom that is premised on an adult maturity.

S. 31(1)(a)(i) provides that a marriage solemnised after the commencement of the section, between persons either of whom is under the age of eighteen years 'shall not be valid in law'. This expression clearly renders the marriage void rather than voidable. The prohibition applies to any marriage solemnised in the State, irrespective of where the parties are ordinarily resident as well as to marriages solemnised outside the State, if, at the time at least one of the parties is ordinarily resident in the State: s. 31(1)(a)(ii). The minimum age requirement is a 'substantive requirement' for marriage:

s. 31(1)(a)(ii). This should minimise the potential problem of 'limping marriages' in private international law.

S. 33 enables the court, on application by both parties to an intended marriage, to make an order exempting the marriage from the minimum age requirement specified in s. 31. The court is not to make the order unless the applicants show that 'its grant is justified by serious reasons and is in the interests of the parties to the intended marriage': s. 33(2)(d). Since the proceedings must be heard 'otherwise than in public' (s. 33(2)(b)), the manner in which this judicial power is exercised in practice may not be widely known. One can confidently predict, however, that pregnancy, which was the unspoken primary rationale for the similar exemption process in the Marriages Act 1972, in relation to marriages under sixteen, will not be a reason that is likely to commend itself to judges in relation to marriages under eighteen.

Notification of intention to marry S. 32(1)(a) provides that a marriage solemnised in the State, after the commencement of the section (on August 1, 1996: SI No. 46 of 1996), between persons of any age is not valid in law unless either the parties have notified the local Registrar for Marriages in writing of their intention to marry at least three months previously or an exemption has been granted before the marriage, under s. 33. This requirement, like that relating to the minimum age for marriage, is declared to be a substantive requirement for marriage: s. 32(1)(b).

A three-month waiting period was recommended by the Joint Oireachtas Committee on Marriage Breakdown in its Report. It is designed to prevent spouses from rushing lightly into marriage. The notification requirement applies to all marriages, including Catholic marriages, which formerly were largely exempt from the detailed statutory regulations applying to other marriages.

The section, as originally drafted, required that all notifications should be available for public inspection at the Registrar's office. Concern for the privacy of the parties led to this element being dropped. In its place, s. 32(2) requires the Registrar to notify the parties in writing of the receipt by him or her of the notification of intention to marry. The Registrar's notification is not to be construed as indicating that the Registrar *approves* of the proposed marriage: s. 32(3). Thus, the Registrar is perfectly free to query the entitlement of the parties to marry on the basis of some impediment: cf. *P.L. v An tÁrd Chláraitheoir* [1995] 2 ILRM 241, noted above, 319.

The exemption procedure in relation to the prior notification requirement is contained in s. 33. It is identical in every respect to the minimum age requirement. An instance of a case where the exemption might be justified by serious reasons and be in the interests of the parties to the intended marriage may be where one of the parties is dying.

Part VI: Miscellaneous Part VI contains several important provisions.

S. 35 gives the court wide-ranging powers in relation to 'reviewable dispositions' intended to defeat or reduce a claim for financial relief made, or intended to be made, by a spouse under Part II or III of the Act. A similar power was created by s. 29 of the Judicial Separation and Family Law Reform Act 1989: see the 1988 Review, 239.

S. 35(4) provides that, in a case where neither of the jurisdictional conditions specified in s. 27(1)(a) or (b) relating to domicile or ordinary residence is satisfied, the court is not to make an order under s. 35(2) in respect of any property other than the family home.

S. 36 replaces s. 12 of the Married Women's Status Act 1957, which is repealed by s.3 and the Schedule. It goes further than s.12 in two respects. First it enables a spouse to follow money or property that represents an interest in property to which that spouse was beneficially entitled, if it is or was in the other spouse's possession or control: s.36(3) and (4). Secondly, following the recommendation of the Law Reform Commission in its *First Report on Family Law* (LRC 1–1981), s. 36 extends the entitlement to apply to the court to parties whose marriages have been annulled (under Irish or a foreign law) or dissolved under foreign law, provided the application is made within three years after the annulment or divorce: s. 36(7)(a). Moreover, where a marriage is void, but has not been so declared (either under Irish or a foreign law) the application may be made within three years after the parties have 'ceased to be ordinarily resident together': s. 36(7)(b). The concept of spouses ordinarily residing together is a novel one. Judicial precedents in Ireland and in other common law jurisdictions address the question of ordinary residence within a particular location (a province or state, for example) rather than in the context of an interpersonal relationship. One might have expected that the subsection would prescribe a test based on cohabitation or living together as man and wife. This would not have been an attractive connection in certain cases, such as, for example where a marriage is void on the ground of a prohibited degree of relationship.

S. 37 provides that payments of money pursuant to an order under the Act other than under s. 12, relating to pension adjustments is to be made without deduction of income tax. This reflects a policy that goes back to the Family Law (Maintenance of Spouses and Children) Act 1976.

S. 38 deals with questions of jurisdiction and venue. The Circuit Court, concurrently with the High Court, has jurisdiction to hear and determine proceedings under the Act and is to be known as the Circuit Family Court: s. 38(1). For the first time, it is given jurisdiction in relation to proceedings for a decree of nullity of marriage: s. 38(2). This jurisdiction harmonises with that under s. 29, in respect of declarations as to the validity of a marriage. We shall have to wait and see whether there will be savings in cost resulting from this change. Deputy Shatter criticised the change on the basis that the inexperience of Circuit Court judges in this area would lead to an increase in appeals, with consequent extra expense. One may doubt whether this is a real fear. At worst the problems would be a transitional one; moreover, the phenomenon of judicial inexperience can also affect the High Court bench.

In harmony with s. 31(3) of the 1989 Act, the Circuit Family Court must transfer proceedings to the High Court where the ratable valuation of land to which the proceedings relate exceeds £200, on the application of any person having an interest in the proceedings: s. 38(3). Thus, a mortgagee could normally insist on having the proceedings transferred to the High Court.

S. 38(b) preserves the distinct provisions contained in ss. 32 to 36 of the 1989 Act in relation to such matters as keeping family law proceedings separate from other cases, encouraging informality and dispensing with wigs and gowns.

Subs. (7) of s. 38 is an important provision. It requires each of the spouses and dependent members of the family, in all the crucial proceedings under Part II or Part III of the Act, to give each other 'such particulars of [their] property as may reasonably be required for the purposes of the proceedings'. Where a person fails or refuses to comply with subs. (7), the court, on application to it by a person having an interest in the matter, may direct the person to comply with the subsection: s. 38(8). The Act contains no express provision rendering failure to comply with this court order an offence. Certainly it is contempt of court, whether criminal or civil is not entirely clear. Perhaps the situation is sufficiently close to *Keegan v de Burca* [1973] IR 223 to render it criminal contempt.

S. 39 prescribes the rules for the exercise of jurisdiction by a court in relation to nullity of marriage. These are based exclusively on the domicile or ordinary residence within the State at least a year of either party on the date of the institution of the proceedings (or if a party is dead, up to the time of his or her death): s. 39(1).

The previous jurisdictional rules were a morass of confusion, compounded by the retrospective abolition of the domicile of dependency of marriage women in *W. v W.* [1993] ILRM 294: see Binchy, *op. cit.*, 250-5 and the 1992 Review, 115-26. S. 39 differs from what the Law Reform Commission had recommended in its *Report on Jurisdiction in Proceedings for Nullity of Marriage, Recognition of Foreign Nullity Decrees, and the Hague Convention on the Celebration and Recognition of the Validity of Marriages (1978)*, p. 33 (LRC 20–1985). The Commission had proposed that an Irish court should have jurisdiction (i) where, at the time of the proceedings, either party had his or her habitual residence in the State, (ii) where the marriage was celebrated in the State and a ground on which the marriage was alleged to be invalid was one to which the *lex loci celebrationis* applied or (iii) where, in the opinion of the court, either party had such substantial ties with the State as to make it appropriate to hear and determine the petition for nullity.

S. 39(2) enables a court having jurisdiction under subs. (1) to determine a pending application for the grant of a decree of nullity (or a court whose determination is being appealed) to determine an application for the grant of a decree of judicial separation in respect of the marriage concerned, notwithstanding the jurisdictional limitations of s. 31(4) of the Judicial Separation and Family Law Reform Act 1989.

S. 40 of the 1995 Act requires the person bringing proceedings under the Act to give notice of them to the other spouse or, as the case may be, both spouses and to any other person specified by the court.

Maintenance entitlements Ss. 41 to 45 introduce important changes, improving the position of maintenance creditors (usually wives). The Judicial Separation and Family Law Reform Act 1989 had introduced a wide range of financial orders in proceedings for judicial separation, but it left largely unaffected the position of those who went the route of the Family Law (Maintenance of Spouses and Children) Act 1976 or the Guardianship of Infants Act 1964.

S. 41 enables the court in maintenance proceedings under the 1964 or 1976 Acts any other legislation to make secured maintenance orders, by way of periodical payments for the support of the family.

S. 43 effects several changes. First, s. 43(a)(i) renders maintenance pending suit orders and periodical payments orders under the 1989 and 1995 Acts capable of falling within the attachment of earnings procedure established by the 1976 Act. Secondly, it raises the ages contained in the definition of 'dependent child of the family' in the 1976 Act, in harmony with the change brought about by the 1995 Act. Under the 1976 Act, the general maintenance obligation ended when the child reached sixteen; that is now raised by s. 43(a)(ii) to eighteen years. Where the child is, or would be, receiving full time education over that age, the 1976 Act extended the parental obligation to twenty-one. S. 43(b) raises it to twenty-three.

Thirdly, s. 43(c) amends s. 8 of the 1976 Act, which enables maintenance agreements to be made a rule of court, so as to include a provision, equivalent to that introduced by s. 13 of the 1995 Act, enabling the court to direct the trustees of a pension scheme to disregard the separation of the spouses by agreement as a ground for disqualifying either of them for the receipt of a benefit that would otherwise have been payable.

The final change relates to the attachment of earnings procedure. S. 43(d) enables the court to make an attachment of earnings order, on making an antecedent order for maintenance, without, as was previously the case, having to wait until the maintenance debtor *defaults* in making payments under the antecedent order. Before deciding whether to make an attachment of earnings order, the court must give the maintenance debtor an opportunity to make representations as to whether he (or she) would make the maintenance payments. S. 43(d) also extends the attachment of earnings procedure so that not only the *employer* of the maintenance debtor but also a *trustee of a pension scheme* under which the maintenance debtor is receiving periodical pension benefits may be required by the court to make the necessary deductions. S. 43(e), in harmony with the policy of s. 38(7)), requires the spouses and dependent members of the family to give each other such particulars of their property and income as may reasonably be required for the purposes of attachment of earnings proceedings.

S. 44 enables the court to discharge a maintenance order made under the 1976 Act where a spouse to whom the order relates applies to the court for an order granting a decree of judicial separation or an order under Part II or III of the Act.

S. 45 makes technical amendments to the Maintenance Act 1994 resulting from the enactment of the 1995 legislation. For consideration of the 1994 Act, which deals with international aspects of maintenance litigation, see the 1994 Review 102-6.

S. 46 enables a court, when granting a decree of nullity of marriage, to declare that either of the parties is unfit to have custody of any minor dependant member of the family. If it takes that course, that party will not be entitled as of right to the custody of the minor on the death of the other party. This provision is similar to s. 41 of the Judicial Separation and Family Law Reform Act 1989. (The guardianship entitlements generally of the fathers who have entered void or voidable marriages are dealt with by s. 9 of the Status of Children Act 1987, which we note in the 1987 Review, 181.)

S. 47 enables the court, in an array of family law proceedings, either of its own motion or on the application of any party to the proceedings, to procure a written report on any question affecting the welfare of any party to whom the proceedings relate, from the probation and welfare service or a health board nominee. S. 40 of the Judicial Separation and Family Law Reform Act 1989 introduced the process: see the 1988 Review, 242. The proceedings to which s. 47 applies are the Guardianship of Infants Act 1964, the Family Law (Maintenance of Spouses and Children) Act 1976, the Family Home Protection Act 1976, the Family Law (Protection of Spouses and Children) Act 1981, the Status of Children Act 1987, the Judicial Separation and Family Law Reform Act 1989, the Child Abduction and Enforcement of Custody Orders Act 1991, proceedings for nullity of marriage and proceedings under the 1995 Act.

S. 48 declares, for the avoidance of doubt, that the reference in s. 5(1) of the Family Law Act 1981 to the rules of law relating to the rights of spouses in relation to property in which either or both of them has or have a beneficial interest is to be deemed always to have related only to the rules of law for the determination of disputes between spouses, or a claim by one of them, in relation to the beneficial ownership of property in which either or both of them has or have a beneficial interest. The purpose of s. 48 is to make it clear, in particular, that s. 5(1) of the 1981 Act does not relate to the rules of law relating to the rights of spouses under the Succession Act 1965, the Family Home Protection Act 1976, the Judicial Separation and Family Law Reform Act 1989 or the 1995 Act itself.

S. 49 deals with the income tax position of spouses, resident in the State for tax purposes, who have been divorced abroad but have not remarried. The provisions of s. 4 of the Finance Act 1983 are to apply to them where a payment to which s. 3 of the 1983 Act applies is made in a year of assessment by one of the divorced spouses to the other. The effect of this change is to treat couples divorced abroad in the same way as separated couples; where one divorced spouse is paying maintenance for the benefit of the other, they thus will have the option of jointly electing to have their combined incomes aggregated for tax purposes. See Claire Jackson, *op. cit.*, General Note to s. 49.

Ss. 50 to 53 extend the tax exemptions previously applying in respect of financial and property transactions between married couples to similar transactions between couples divorced abroad. Thus the exemptions of certain transfers from stamp duty (s. 50) and capital acquisitions tax (s. 51) now apply to married spouses and spouses divorced abroad.

Under the Capital Gains Act 1975, disposals or transfers of assets between spouses living together are ignored for capital gains tax purposes. S. 52 of the 1995 Act extends this exemption to disposals by separated or divorced spouses where the particular disposal was by virtue or in consequence of (i) an order made under Part II of the 1995 Act, on or following the granting of a decree of judicial separation, (ii) a deed of separation, and (iii) a relief order made following a foreign divorce.

S. 53 ensures that, on the death of one of the parties to a marriage dissolved abroad, no probate tax will be payable in respect of any provision made by the court in favour of the surviving spouse out of the deceased spouse's estate, under s. 25 of the 1995 Act. The Minister explained that, if this provision consists of a life interest in property, the property tax on that property is postponed until the death of the surviving spouse. See Claire Jackson, *op. cit.*, General Note to s. 53.

The family home S. 54 makes important changes in relation to the scope of protection afforded by the Family Home Protection Act 1976. The first relates to the definition of 'dwelling' in s. 2 of the 1976 Act. S. 2, as originally drafted, had defined 'dwelling' as including any building or any structure, vehicle or vessel (whether mobile or not) or part thereof occupied as a separate dwelling and including any garden or portion of ground attached to and usually occupied with the dwelling or otherwise required for the amenity or convenience of the dwelling. S. 54(1)(a) now defines 'dwelling' as meaning:

> any building or part of a building occupied as a separate dwelling and includ[ing] any garden or other land usually occupied with the dwelling, being land that is subsidiary and ancillary to it, is required for amenity or convenience and is not being used or developed primarily for commercial purposes, and includ[ing] a structure that is not permanently attached to the ground and a vehicle, or vessel, whether mobile or not, occupied as a separate dwelling.

The effect of this change is to narrow the scope of protection so as to exclude from the definition of 'dwelling' premises and land used primarily for commercial purposes.

S. 54(1)(b) introduces a radical change, designed to establish a time limit of six years from the date of the conveyance for the institution of proceedings to have a conveyance declared void by reason of s. 3(1) of the 1976 Act. This time limit, contained in a new subs. (8) to s. 3 of the 1976 Act, is extended in relation to proceedings instituted by a spouse who has been in actual occupation of the land concerned from immediately before the expiration of six years from the date of the conveyance concerned until the institution of the proceedings. The time limit is declared to be without prejudice to the right of the other spouse referred to in s. 3(1) to seek redress for a contravention of s. 3(1) otherwise than by proceedings referred to in subs. 8(a)(i). In the 1989 Review, 302-3, we criticised the Law Reform Commission's Proposal, contained in its *Report on Land Law and Conveyancing Law: (1) General Proposals* (LRC 30–1989), that such a six-year limit should be introduced.

S. 54(1)(b) goes on to provide (by a newly created subs. 8(b) of s. 3 of the 1976 Act) that a conveyance is to be deemed not to be and never to have been void by reason of s. 3(1) unless either

> (i) it has been declared void by a court by reason of s. 3(1) in proceedings instituted before the passing of the 1995 Act or, if after its passing, in proceedings that comply with subs. 8(a),

(ii) subject to the rights of any other person concerned, it is void by reason of s. 3(1) and the parties to the conveyance or their successors in title so state in writing before the expiration of six years from the date of the conveyance.

A copy of this statement must be lodged in the Land Registry for registration pursuant to s. 69(1) of the Registration of Title Act 1964 or be registered in the Registry of Deeds, in either case before the expiration of the six-year period: s. 54(1)(b) of the 1995 Act, inserting subs. 8(c) into s. 3 of the 1976 Act).

Rules of court must provide that a person who institutes proceedings to have a conveyance declared void by reason of s. 3(1) should, as soon as may be, cause relevant particulars of the proceedings to be entered as a *lis pendens*: s. 54(1)(b), inserting s. 8(d) into s. 3 of the 1976 Act.

S. 54(1)(b) also deals with the subject of *general consents*, about which there had been some uncertainty. If, before or after the passing of the 1995 Act, a spouse gives a general consent in writing to any future conveyance or any interest in the family home and the deed for any such conveyance is executed after the date of that consent, the consent is deemed to be a prior consent in writing, for the purposes of s. 3(1): new subs. (9) of s. 3 of the 1976 Act. Presumably, *Bank of Ireland v Smyth* [1994] 1 ILRM 241, which we discuss above, 305, must have some implications in this context. It is hard to see how a general consent which was not a fully informed one could be efficacious when a specific consent would not.

Prior to the 1995 Act, the District Court had jurisdiction only in relation to s. 9 of the 1976 Act; its function was limited to preventing a spouse from disposing of household chattels whose value did not exceed £2,500. S. 54(1)(c) now confers on the District Court full jurisdiction under the 1976 Act where the rateable valuation of the land to which the proceedings related does not exceed £20. The Court's jurisdiction under s. 9 is extended to cases where the value of the household chattels does not exceed £5,000 or the chattels are (or were) in a family home whose rateable valuation does not exceed £20. The District Court is itself entitled to determine whether the rateable valuation of the family home would or would not exceed £20 in proceedings in relation to a family home that has not been given a rateable valuation or is the subject with other land of a rateable valuation.

S. 54(2) is a non-retrospective provision, making it plain that the change in the definition of 'dwelling' in the 1976 Act does not apply in relation to any conveyances referred to in s. 3 of the 1976 Act, the dates of which are before the commencement of s. 54, any proceedings under or referred to in the 1976 Act instituted before that commencement, anything referred to in s. 6 of the 1976 Act or done before that commencement and any transactions referred to in s. 14 of the 1976 Act occurring before that commencement.

S. 54(3) provides that, where a court granting a decree of judicial separation under the 1989 Act orders that ownership of the family home is to be vested in one of the spouses, it should order that s. 3(1) of the Family Home Protection Act 1976 is not to apply to any future conveyance by that spouse, unless it 'sees reason to the contrary'.

Child abduction S. 55 amends s. 2 of the Child Abduction an Enforcement of Custody Orders Act 1991, to take account of the transfer of functions under the 1991 Act from the Minister of Justice to the Minister for Equality and Law Reform. The latter Minister also has a role in relation to the Maintenance Orders Act 1994, which deals with international maintenance litigation: see the 1994 Review, 103.

Fisheries

FEEDINGSTUFFS

The European Communities (Feedingstuffs) (Tolerance Of Undesirable Substances And Products) (Amendment) Regulations 1995 (SI No. 73 of 1995) amended the European Communities (Feedingstuffs) (Tolerances of Undesirable Substances and Products) Regulations 1989 to 1994 (1994 Review, 20) and gave effect to Directive 94/15/EC (amending the principal Directive in this area, 74/63/EEC) which provided for amended maximum permitted levels of arsenic in complete feedingstuffs for fish. The 1995 Regulations came into effect on April 3, 1995.

FISH CULTURE AND FORESHORE LICENCES

In *Mulcahy v Minister for the Marine and Anor*, High Court, November 4, 1994, Keane J held that, where public rights were in jeopardy, the courts should adopt an interpretive approach to legislation which inclined to protect such rights.

The applicant owned a house on the shores of Lough Swilly in Co. Donegal. Having learned of a proposal to establish a salmon farm near the shore, he wrote to the first respondent to express his concern. A subsequent letter from the applicant's solicitors informed the Minister that proceedings would be instituted if licences were granted to the second respondent, a company. The applicant was informed in a letter written by the Principal Officer in the respondent's Department that no decision had been taken, but by letter of the same date by the Principal Officer to the second respondent, a director of that company was informed that the licences had been executed by the Minister and were attached.

A fish culture licence was granted by the Minister in purported exercise of his powers under s. 15 of the Fisheries (Consolidation) Act 1959 and a foreshore licence was similarly granted under s. 3(1) of the Foreshore Act 1933. S. 247 of the 1959 Act provides that the Minister is obliged to hold a public inquiry before making a decision on the grant of an oyster bed licence. No similar provision exists in relation to a decision on the grant of fish culture licences.

S. 54 of the Fisheries Act 1980 provides for a detailed procedure by which the Minister may by Order designate an area within which aquaculture can lawfully be carried on pursuant to an aquaculture licence. S. 54(4) of the 1980 Act provides for the holding of an inquiry with regard to a proposed order if the Minister sees fit to do so, having regard to any representations or objections made. S. 54(7) provides for an appeal to the High Court by any person aggrieved by the making of an order.

The applicant contended that the Minister had unlawfully granted the company licences enabling the company to establish a salmon farm and that the installations would seriously affect the area's public leisure amenities and ecosystem. He sought an order of *certiorari* quashing both licences and a permanent injunction restraining the operation of fish farming being carried on foot of the licences. Keane J granted the relief sought.

He observed that, if s. 15 of the 1959 Act was construed literally and in isolation from the 1980 Act, in particular s. 54 of the 1980 Act, the grant of the fish culture licence was a lawful exercise of the Minister's powers. Keane J was of the view that similar reasoning applied in relation to the foreshore licence under the 1933 Act. However, he went on to hold that it could not have been the intention of the Oireachtas that the Minister could render otiose the elaborate structure provided by s. 54 of the 1980 Act to protect the rights of the public merely by granting a series of fish culture licences and foreshore licences.

Elaborating on the correct interpretive approach to be applied, Keane J stated that, in the absence of a constitutional challenge, the Court was not entitled to tamper with the plain wording of an enactment in order to avoid unjust or anomalous consequences, but that the Court was not precluded from departing from a literal construction of an enactment and adopting in its place a teleological or purposive approach if this would better reflect the true legislative intention evident from the Act viewed as a whole. He accepted that this would mean attributing to the Oireachtas an intention in enacting s. 54 of the 1980 Act of providing for the exclusive machinery for the granting of aquaculture licences for public waters, and he concluded that this teleological or purposive approach should prevail. This expansive use of the teleological approach may be contrasted with Keane J's earlier reluctance to adopt this Civilian mode of interpretation: see Murphy v Bord Telecom Éireann [1989] ILRM 53, discussed in Byrne and McCutcheon, *The Irish Legal System*, 3rd ed. (Butterworths, 1996), pp.499-502.

Keane J went on that the principles enunciated by Johnson J in *Madden v. Minister for the Marine* [1993] 1 IR 567 (1993 Review, 377-9) should apply in the instant case. He noted that, in Madden, licences were also purportedly granted under s. 3 of the 1933 Act and s. 15 of the 1959 Act for fish farming activities at a site utilised for leisure activities. In the instant case, Keane J stated the use of s. 15 of the 1959 Act was inappropriate where public rights were officially being interfered with and the rights of other citizens were being interfered with by the granting of such a licence and that this should not occur without notice or access to the courts where the Oireachtas had so provided. Keane J concluded that in representing to the objectors that he was giving their objections consideration at a time when he had in fact granted the licence and had failed to make available to them the information on which he had based his decision, the Minister had not acted in accordance with the principles of constitutional justice, as adumbrated by Walsh J in *East Donegal Co-op Ltd v Attorney General* [1970] IR 317.

In any event, Keane J stated that the decision to grant the licences would have been set aside on the ground that the Minister had failed to act in accordance with the requirements of natural justice in not furnishing the applicant with the material on which the Minister had grounded his decision, including the environmental impact statement carried out on behalf of the respondent company. This failure had deprived the applicant of the opportunity to make comments on that material, in breach of the *audi alteram partem* principle of natural justice.

FRESH WATER LICENCES

In *Slevin v Shannon Regional Fisheries Board* [1995] 1 IR 460, Barron J granted an order of *mandamus* directing the respondent Board to grant the applicant an ordinary freshwater trout draft net fishing licence against the background that the applicant had obtained such a licence for the 25 years prior to the refusal giving rise to the instant proceedings. He held that the Board was obliged to grant the licence pursuant to s. 67(1) of the Fisheries (Consolidation) Act 1959. He concluded that there was nothing in any other sub- section of s. 67 which entitled the Board to refuse the licence in the circumstances which prevailed.

PROSECUTION OF OFFENCES

In *Kelly v Foyle Fisheries Commission and McMenamin*, High Court, April 24, 1995, Morris J rejected challenges to the validity of summonses applied for on behalf of the first respondent Commission and the North Regional Fisheries Board. The applicants had been summoned to appear before the second respondent, a judge of the District Court, on charges under the Foyle Fisheries Act 1952 and the Foyle Fisheries (Amendment) Act 1983, namely that they had in their possession prohibited nets and had assaulted a member of the Garda Smochana and a Foyle Fisheries Inspector, who were exercising power conferred on them by the 1952 Act. The summonses had been issued on foot of an application by the solicitor for the Commission and Board pursuant to the Courts (No. 3) Act 1986. The applicants submitted that, since the application for the issue of the summons had been made by the solicitor for the Commission and the Fisheries Board, respectively, they were invalid since the solicitor was engaged in prosecuting legal proceedings, which he was precluded from doing by virtue of s. 73 of the 1983 Act. The applicants also contended that the Commission and Board, being corporate bodies, were precluded from initiating criminal prosecutions since they were doing so in the capacity of common informers. As indicated, Morris J refused the relief sought.

We begin with a point discussed by Morris J towards the end of his judgment, in which he accepted that a body corporate does not have the right to prosecute without statutory authority in its capacity as common informer. In this respect, of course, Morris J followed the decision of the Supreme Court in *Cumann Luthchleas Gael Teo v Windle* [1994] 1 IR 525 (1993 Review, 476-9). However, he also noted that, in the instant case the Commission and Board, respectively, had not purported to act as common informers. Rather, he noted that since proceedings in the District Court for an offence under the 1952 Act, as amended by the 1983 Act, included the prosecution of an offence under the Act and specifically included the offences which were the subject-matter of these proceedings, the Commission and the Board had the necessary powers under the 1952 Act to initiate prosecutions against the applicants.

As to the procedure adopted, Morris J pointed out that the Courts (No. 3) Act 1986 provided that an application for the issue of a summons could be made by 'any person authorised by or under statute to prosecute the offence'. Since the Commission and Board were authorised to prosecute the offences, an application could be made for the issue of a summons on their behalf. As to the application having been made by the solicitor for the Commission and Board, he noted that the 1986 Act described the application for a summons as 'a matter of administrative procedure'. As the solicitor was clearly authorised to make the application, Morris J concluded that the issue of the summons in the circumstances was a proper exercise of this administrative act. In so applying for the issue of the summons, he considered that the solicitor had not purported to act as a common informer, as he was not proposing to prosecute the offence and the summons clearly stated that the prosecutor was to be the Commission and the Board, respectively. In those circumstances, he dismissed the applicants challenges to the summonses.

REGIONAL FISHERIES BOARDS

The Fisheries (Amendment) Act 1995 amended the Fisheries Acts 1959 to 1994 to provide that the Minister for the Marine may require a report from a Regional Fisheries Board and empowers the Minister to set up a commission to which specified functions may be delegated and to co-ordinate the functions of boards and commissions. The Act came into force on November 6, 1995.

Garda Síochána

DISCIPLINE

Reasonable request for assistance In *White v Glackin and Ors*, High Court, May 19, 1995, Costello P held that there had been no failure to comply with fair procedures in the disciplinary proceedings which had resulted in the dismissal of the applicant from the Garda Síochána. The applicant, a Garda, had instituted judicial review proceedings against the respondents following a sworn inquiry in which the applicant had been found guilty of breaches of the Garda Síochána (Discipline) Regulations 1989, arising from which his dismissal from the force was recommended.

The inquiry arose out of an incident in which the applicant had arrested two youths for the theft of a bicycle, one of whom gave a name, namely 'Derek Dunne', and address. It transpired that a person of that name lived at the address given and he was charged with the offence and, on his failure to appear to answer the charge, a warrant for his arrest was issued. Subsequently, one Derek Dunne and his mother visited the station where the applicant was serving and informed him that Derek Dunne was not the person who had been arrested by the applicant and that the arrested person had given a false name.

Derek Dunne made a statement to the effect that the applicant had accepted this and had agreed to cancel the warrant, but the warrant was not in fact cancelled. Derek Dunne was arrested on foot of the warrant and the applicant was informed by another Garda of this. Mr Dunne was remanded in custody by the District Court on two occasions, but on his second appearance the case against him was struck out with the acquiescence of the applicant. Mr Dunne's solicitors subsequently wrote to the Department of Justice claiming damages arising out of his arrest and this gave rise to the appointment of an investigating officer pursuant to the Garda Síochána (Discipline) Regulations 1989.

A form requesting a statement was sent to the applicant, to which he responded that he would make no statement before consulting a solicitor. In November 1993 the applicant notified the investigating officer that on counsel's advice he would make no comment on the allegations and the investigating officer duly completed his report. In January 1994 the names of witnesses intended to be called and each statement intended to be used at the inquiry was served on the applicant. In April 1994 a Board of Inquiry was appointed and the applicant was informed that the inquiry would be held on May 17, 1994. The applicant was charged with neglect of duty for, *inter alia*, failing to cancel the warrant issued against Derek Dunne and in failing to attend the District Court as a result of which Derek Dunne had been remanded in custody. On May 3, 1994, the applicant requested in writing that a number of statements and records which he listed be obtained and was informed that the inquiry would be going ahead as planned. On the day of the inquiry the applicant requested an adjournment and a direction that the statements he had referred to in the letter of May 3 be obtained, but these were refused. He made a second application for an adjournment so that he could contact the persons he had mentioned in the letter, which was also refused, whereupon he and his solicitor withdrew from the inquiry which continued in their absence. The applicant was subsequently informed that he had been found guilty of all the charges proffered against him. As already indicated, Costello P dismissed the applicant's challenge to the proceedings.

The applicant had argued that the respondents had failed to comply with the Gardaí's own booklet 'Notes on Disciplinary Procedures under the Garda Síochána (Discipline) Regulations 1989'. This included a requirement that those facing disciplinary proceedings be afforded assistance relating to reasonable requests. Costello P hold that this referred to requests made to the investigating officer during the period of his investigation rather than re-quests after the decision to charge had been taken. Thus, there had been no breach of the 'Notes' in failing to provide the assistance requested by the applicant at the opening of the actual hearing nor in the refusal to direct that assistance be given nor in the refusal of the application for an adjournment.

In this respect, Costello P noted that the applicant had consulted a solicitor by November 1993 and that he was aware of the charges and the evidence to be used against him in January 1994. In the absence of any explanation to justify the delay in making this request for assistance, he concluded that the request was not a reasonable one. Nor had there been a reasonable explanation forthcoming to show why the applicant himself could not have obtained the statements and records requested. Finally, the applicant had also argued that he had a legitimate expectation that the proceedings would be adjourned. However, Costello P considered that, even assuming the applicant had had an expectation that the hearing would be adjourned, it was not a legitimate one, as it was based on a misinterpretation of the 'Notes'.

Trainee: oral hearing In *McAuley v Garda Commissioner*, High Court, July 4, 1995 Barr J held that an oral hearing should have been conducted in the inquiry into whether the applicant, a trainee Garda, should be dismissed from the Garda Training College pursuant to the Garda Síochána (Admis-sions and Appointments) Regulations 1988. In holding that the procedures were quasi-judicial, Barr J did not appear to consider the effects of the Supreme Court decision in *Beirne v Garda Commissioner* [1993] ILRM 1 (see the 1992 Review, 382), which Barr J had himself applied in *Browne v Dundalk UDC* [1993] 2 IR 512; [1993] ILRM 328 (1993 Review, 15-16).

SUBSISTENCE ALLOWANCES

In *Kavanagh and Ors v Ireland*, Supreme Court, July 3, 1995, the Court rejected the plaintiffs' argument that they were entitled to a subsistence allowance under Article 5 of the Garda Síochána Allowances (Consolidation) Order 1965, which provides for the payment of a subsistence allowance to members of the Garda Síochána employed on duty away from their permanent stations. The appellants were either serving or retired members of the Garda Síochána attached to the mapping section of the Technical Bureau. In November 1983 the mapping section was moved from the Phoenix Park Depot to Harcourt Square. Since the mapping section remained a branch of the Technical Bureau its administrative headquarters remained at the Phoenix Park Depot. The appellants' claim that the Phoenix Park Depot was their permanent station and that they were entitled to subsistence allowances pursuant to the 1965 Order. As indicated, the Supreme Court rejected this argument, holding that since the 1965 Order was intended to provide subsistence allowances for members on duty removed from their regular place of work and since the plaintiffs' regular place of work was at Harcourt Square, they fell outside the terms of the 1965 Order.

Health Services

ABORTION INFORMATION

The decision of the Supreme Court in *In re the Regulation of Information (Services Outside the State for Termination of Pregnancies) Bill 1995* [1995] 1 IR 1; [1995] 2 ILRM 81 and the terms of the Regulation of Information (Services Outside the State for Termination of Pregnancies) Act 1995 are discussed in the Constitutional Law chapter, 145 *et seq.*, above.

DENTAL SERVICES

The Health (Dental Services for Children) Regulations 1995 (SI No. 21 of 1995), made under the Health (Amendment) Act 1994, extended the eligibility for children's dental services to the age of 14.

LICENSING OF HUMAN MEDICINES, BLOOD PRODUCTS AND CLINICAL TRIALS

The Irish Medicines Board Act 1995 provided for the establishment of the eponymous Irish Medicines Board, which replaces the National Drugs Advisory Board. The Act introduced a new regime for the regulation of the manufacture, production, preparation, importation, advertisement, sale and distribution of medicinal and cosmetic products. It also involved the transfer from the Minister for Health to the Irish Medicines Board of the power to grant permission to conduct clinical trials under the Control of Clinical Trials Acts 1987 and 1990 (1987 Review, 299-304 and 1990 Review, 332-36). In addition, the Board is responsible for the inspection of the collection, processing and distribution of blood, blood components, blood products and plasma derivatives. The 1995 Act confers significant new enforcement functions on the Irish Medicines Board, by comparison with the Advisory Board, and may thus be seen against the general background of attempts to ensure public confidence in the method by which pharmaceutical products intended for human use receive approval for being placed on the market. In relation to blood products, the 1995 Act must also be seen in the context of the contraction of Hepatitis-C by a large number of women who were given

an anti-D plasma during the 1970s through the Blood Transfusion Service
Board. This resulted in the establishment on a non-statutory basis of a
compensation tribunal for the affected women. Further developments during
1996 in this area precipitated the establishment of a tribunal of inquiry into
the matter, chaired by Mr Justice Thomas Finlay, former Chief Justice. We
will return to this matter in future Reviews. The 1995 Act came into force in
full between January 1, 1996 and February 1, 1996: Irish Medicines Board
Act 1995 (Commencement) Order 1995 (SI No. 345 of 1995), Irish Medicines Board Act 1995 (Establishment) Order 1995 (SI No. 345 of 1995) and
Irish Medicines Board Act 1995 (Commencement) Order 1996 (SI No. 40
of 1996).

MEDICAL PRACTITIONERS

Excessive visiting   In *Giblin and Ors v O'Connor*, Supreme Court, December 19, 1994, the Supreme Court upheld the conclusion of Lardner J in the
High Court, *sub nom. O'Connor v Giblin and Ors* [1989] IR 583 (1989
Review, 374-5) that the defendant Committee had acted erroneously in
reducing the plaintiff's remuneration from his health board for excessive
visiting. The statutory background was that Reg. 5(1)(a) of the Health
Services Regulations 1972, made pursuant to the Health Act 1970, provides
that health services shall be made available through agreements, so-called
'common contracts' with registered practitioners. By a 'common contract'
between the plaintiff and the Southern Health Board, the plaintiff agreed to
provide services in accordance with the terms and conditions of the agreement. Under the agreement, where a claim for remuneration submitted by
the medical practitioner appeared to indicate an excessive rate of attendance,
the circumstances were to be investigated by the Board and then referred to
an investigation group. Having regard to the claims for remuneration submitted by the plaintiff for the years 1983 and 1984 the Board made a reference
to the investigation group. The group considered that there was evidence of
over-visiting and a deduction was made to that effect. The decision was
upheld by the Appeal Committee who also approved the group's methodol-
ogy, that is, comparison of the plaintiff's rate of visiting with the average
visiting rates of other doctors.

    In the High Court, Lardner J had overturned this decision and he ordered
that the deduction be repaid. As indicated, the Supreme Court upheld Lardner
J's decision and dismissed the defendants' appeal. The Court pointed out that
the jurisdiction of the investigating group and of the Appeals Committee was
derived solely from the common contract for the supply of services. When a
claim appeared to indicate an excessive rate of attendance, the Court held

that any conclusion must be based exclusively on the investigation of the individual circumstances of the apparently excessive rate. The Court concluded that there was no basis in the agreement for a determination based on the average of other doctors' visiting. In adopting a standard not authorised by the contract, the Appeals Committee had thus acted in excess of jurisdiction.

As we noted in the 1989 Review, 375, the narrow holding in the case avoided the need to deal with a further issue raised in the case, namely whether the deduction of remuneration amounted to the imposition of a fine which might be contrary to the terms of Article 34 and 37 of the Constitution.

NURSING HOMES

In *O'Sullivan v Minister for Health* [1991] ILRM 744 (HC); Supreme Court, March 31, 1995, the Supreme Court upheld the decision of Barron J in the High Court (1991 Review, 264-5) that the Minister had not acted *ultra vires* the Health (Homes for Incapacitated Persons) Act 1964. The applicants had claimed that the Homes for Incapacitated Persons Regulations 1985 were ultra vires the 1964 Act in imposing a maximum limit to the number of persons who could be accommodated in homes registered under the 1964 Act. As indicated, Barron J had rejected that argument and his conclusion was upheld in the Supreme Court. As we indicated in the 1991 Review, 265, the 1964 Act has since been superseded by the Health (Nursing Homes) Act 1990, which has now been brought into effect along with detailed Regulations which replace those in issue in the *O'Sullivan* case: see the 1993 Review, 346-7.

REGISTRATION OF BIRTHS AND DEATHS

Amalgamation of Registrars' Districts In 1995, two further statutory instruments were made to amalgamate certain Superintendent Registrars' Districts and, where applicable, Registrars' Districts in Dublin so as to reduce the number of such districts in Dublin, continuing a process begun in 1993: see the 1993 Review, 348 and 1994 Review, 290. The relevant Orders were the Registration of Births and Deaths (Ireland) Act 1863 (Section 18) (Dublin) (No. 3) Order 1995 (SI No. 159 of 1995) and the Registration of Births and Deaths (Ireland) Act 1863 (Section 18) (Dublin) (No. 4) Order 1995 (SI No. 160 of 1995).

Labour Law

EMPLOYMENT EQUALITY

In *A Worker v Mid-Western Health Board* [1996] ELR 1, the claimant, a male psychiatric staff nurse, had been re-deployed from one area of work to another and replaced by a member of the opposite sex. He claimed that this amounted to less favourable treatment arising from an attribute of his sex. The Labour Court saw 'no logic' in this argument:

> He has to show that he has been treated less favourably. The treatment consists of re-deployment; it does not consist of the substitution. Unless that redeployment is less favourable than the treatment that would be accorded to a member of the opposite sex, and arises from an attribute of his sex, it is not discrimination within the meaning of the Act.

Neither could the Court find merit in the claimant's argument that the Act had been contravened if nurses were assigned to different tasks because of their gender. The Act would be contravened only if the assignments were less favourable treatment because of gender.

The Court was satisfied that the management of psychiatric hospitals required 'decisions to be made by management about the assignment of staff to varying tasks of responsibility at differing times'. The Court was also satisfied that, when psychiatric nurses took up employment in a psychiatric hospital, they assumed responsibility for a range of tasks involved in the care of mentally disturbed persons:

> Management must decide where to assign the particular staff at its disposition at any given time, and take into consideration the mix of skills of the particular staff. It must also take into consideration the safety and welfare of both patients and staff, and it may very well be that certain tasks at certain times are more appropriately handled by a nurse of one sex or the other. But the decision to assign a particular task to a nurse of a particular sex is not less favourable treatment if the task is within the range of responsibilities for which the nurse was employed. The equality legislation does not require that employees of both sexes be employed in exactly the same manner; it requires that they be not treated less favourably on account of being a male or a female.

In the instant case, there was no evidence that the redeployment of the complainant was less favourable treatment than would be accorded to a female member of staff. Accordingly the Labour Court, affirming the Equality Officer's recommendation, dismissed the claimant's appeal.

In *Kearney v Monkstown Park CBC* [1995] ELR 193, the claimant, a female, had been employed as a part-time temporary teacher by the respondent school. She unsuccessfully applied for one of two wholetime temporary teaching positions that became available. Two male applicants were appointed; some time later they were appointed as rugby coaches. The claimant alleged that her experience and the subjects she taught made her more suitable than the male appointees and that she had been discriminated against by being required to be able to coach rugby. The respondent claimed that the claimant had not been successful in her application because she had 'had a history of severe class disciplinary problems' in the senior school.

The Labour Court, endorsing the Equality Officer's findings, held that the respondent had discriminated against the plaintiff within the meaning of the Employment Equality Act 1977. On the issue of discipline, it found the evidence submitted by the school 'unsatisfactory' and was of the view that the claimant 'was no worse than other teachers in this matter'.

The Court was also satisfied that the claimant was more highly qualified for the advertised posts than the male teacher who was appointed. The fact that the formal assessment and weightings of the candidates' suitability were carried out by the principal subsequent to his decision on the appointment inclined the Court to disregard these weightings. The Court was satisfied that the decision of the school to appoint a less qualified male teacher to the post in question had been related to the sex of the applicants for the post.

In *Ryan v Braids Ltd* [1996] ELR 81, the Equality Officer referred the decisions of the Court of Justice, in *Barber v Guardian Royal Exchange Assurance Group* [1990] ELR I–1998, that pensions are pay within the meaning of the Article 119 of the Treaty of Rome, and *Ten Oever v Stichting Bedrifspensioenfonds voor het Glazenwassers en Schoonmaakbedriff* [1993] IRLR 501, that equality of treatment in the matter of occupational pensions might be claimed only in relation to benefits payable in respect of periods of employment subsequent to May 17, 1990, the date of the *Barber* judgment, save for those workers who had before that date initiated legal proceedings or raised an equivalent claim under applicable national law. In *Ryan* the claimant's employment had ceased in 1986 and her claim was not made until February 1992. She claimed that the takeover in 1991 of the company for which she had worked constituted a transfer of business and that her claim for equality of pension rights with male comparators has passed to the transferee. On the basis on the non-retrospective character of the *Barber* judgment, the Equality Officer dismissed her claim *in limine*.

In *An Employee v An Employer* [1996] ELR 139, the Equality Officer held that the claimant had been the victim of discrimination within the meaning of s. 2 the 1977 Act and contrary to s. 3 where the employer, when assessing her eligibility for a permanent position, had perceived her childcare responsibilities as interfering with her ability to commit herself to the position. The Equality Officer considered that 'the status of male candidates or female candidates who did not have the same childcare responsibilities would not have been similarly perceived by the employer as irreconcilable with a capacity to give a commitment to a permanent career position'.

In *Flynn v Commissioner of An Garda Síochána* [1995] ELR 129 the Equality officer held that the claimant, who was employed in a clerical capacity, was refused an appointment to a position for which she had applied because she was on maternity leave. The claimant alleged that the respondent discriminated against her within the meaning of ss. 2(A), (b) and (c) of the Act.

The Equality Officer noted that only women have cause to it had been established in the decisions of the Court of Justice in *Dekker v Stiching Vormings Centrum Voor Jorge Volwassenen* (ECJ Case No. 177/88) and *Handels-Og Kontorfunktionaerernes Forbund I Dankmark (acting for Hertz) v Dansk Arbejdsgiverforening* (ECJ Case No. 179/88) that pregnancy is a condition that is exclusive to women and a woman who suffers a detriment because of her pregnancy is subjected to direct discrimination because of her sex. It was not necessary to show that a man would have been treated more favourably. In view of these rulings of the European Court of Justice the fact that another woman had been appointed to the job in question was irrelevant.

The claimant had suffered a disadvantage because of her absence on maternity leave and, in applying the principle of equal treatment as defined in the European Court decisions, the Equality Officer found that the claimant, as a result of that disadvantage, suffered direct discrimination on the basis of her sex within the meaning of s. 2(a).

UNFAIR DISMISSAL

Who was the claimant's employer? In *Walsh v Oliver Freaney & Co. and Dunnes Stores Ltd* [1995] ELR 205, the claimant, a qualified accountant, had done his work exclusively on the premises of the second-named respondent, to whom he was solely accountable and by whom he had been soley given his instructions for the previous twelve years. He was required to perform his duties personally for the second-named respondent and was ultimately dismissed by the second-named respondent, though his P45 was issued in the name of the first-named respondent. He had received certain payments from the first-named respondent, who had given him a P60 annually. He had, however, received additional payments and benefits-in-kind, 'to a very considerable degree', directly from the second-named respondent.

In proceedings for unfair dismissal, the question arose to who was the claimant's employer. The Tribunal in its determination noted that the major test used to decide this issue in the past had been that of control. It observed that practitioners would be aware that this test had lost much of its significance over the years but it was still one of the major tests to be applied. Having addressed the five questions of where the claimant had worked, who paid him, who gave him his instructions, whether he had to perform the contract personally and who ultimately dismissed him, the Tribunal concluded that the *second-named* defendant had been the claimant's employer. The claimant had 'had only a tenuous connection with the first-named respondent which was used essentially as a paying agent by the second-named respondent'.

Contract 'of service' or 'for service'? In *Kane v McCann* [1995] ELR 175, the claimant took proceedings for unfair dismissal. The Tribunal's determination does not clearly indicate the nature of the work, but it appears to have involved the operation of a pilot boat by way of 'turn and turn about' between the claimant and the respondent, with the agreed percentage of the contract price going to the claimant. The agreement between the parties was expressed to be a partnership agreement.

In evidence the respondent confirmed that he would tell the claimant what to do and how to do it and that the claimant operated to his instructions. It appeared, however, that the claimant was not required to do the work himself and that in fact he often had sent someone else along to do it in his place.

This latter factor was decisive, in the view of the Tribunal, which held that the contract was one 'for service' and accordingly that it had no jurisdiction to hear the case. It noted that:

[a]ll the other factors adduced in evidence indicated the claimant to be an employee of the respondent, but this one overriding factor turned the issue around.

Misconduct In *Cavanagh v Dunnes Stores Ltd* [1995] ELR 164, the claimant, who had been employed by the respondent as group head of security since 1984, was asked to relocate from the group's head office to its store at the Ilac Centre. It was confirmed to him that his terms and conditions of employment, as well as his position within the group, would remain the same. He refused to relocate and was ultimately dismissed.

This bald summary of the facts does not capture the full story. The company was at the time undergoing a major restructuring which involved the dismissal of some of the most senior executives. The atmosphere in head office was 'tense and concerned' and people in the claimant's position were very likely to be anxious if any changes were suggested in their role or function. No attempt was made to secure proper office accommodation or facilities for the claimant at the Ilac Centre to enable him to continue to discharge his duties as group head of security: all that was available was a small area under a staircase which had insufficient space for the claimant, his assistant and files.

The claimant sought a written assurance that his conditions of employment would remain unchanged. When he received what purported to be such, it contained information that indicated a more reduced function. He requested a meeting with the managing director. One was arranged at least three times but on each occasion the managing director did not attend. Eventually a meeting took place, four months later. While the Tribunal was reluctant to hold that a managing director of a large company should be available at any time to her senior staff, it considered that, in view of the reporting structure which had existed previously for the claim and the fact that it had never been suggested to him that he was not entitled to see her, the delay was unreasonable.

It was clear from the evidence that, prior to the meeting, no one had ever informed the claimant that his job was at risk if he refused to go to the Ilac Centre or that the respondent would treat a refusal to go to the Ilac Centre as amounting to misconduct which could lead to dismissal. Nevertheless, in view of the claimant's wide experience, the Tribunal could not accept that he was completely unaware that he was refusing to obey the instructions of the respondent and that this could be viewed as misconduct. The Tribunal also took account of the fact that the respondent allowed the claimant to continue to discharge his functions and duties without change for a period of four months from the date he was first informed of the move to the date of the meeting with managing director. In these circumstances 'it would not have been unreasonable for the claimant to assume that the respondent placed little weight on his refusal to move'.

The Tribunal accepted that the claimant had been effectively dismissed at the meeting with the managing director.

S. 6(4) of the 1977 Act provides that the dismissal of the employee is to be deemed not to be an unfair dismissal if it results wholly or mainly from, among other matters, the conduct of the employee. S. 6(7), as inserted by the Unfair Dismissals (Amendment) Act 1993, provides that, without prejudice to the generality of subs (1), in determining if the dismissal is an unfair dismissal, regard may be had, if the Tribunal considers it appropriate to do so, to the reasonableness or otherwise of the conduct of the employer in relation to the dismissal. S. 7(2)(b) provides that, when determining the amount of compensation payable, regard must be had to the extent, if any, to which the financial loss was attributable to an action, omission or conduct by or on behalf of the employee.

The Tribunal noted that the effect of s. 6(7) was to give statutory recognition to the importance of fair procedures in the dismissal of an employee and to the need for an employer to act reasonably in all of the circumstances. The requirements of fair procedures had been stated by the Tribunal and the courts on numerous occasions.

The Tribunal was satisfied that in misconduct cases other than misconduct justifying summary dismissal there was an obligation on the employer to issue warnings to an employee where the employer felt that continuing misconduct of the nature alleged could lead to dismissal. This requirement appeared to be implied, at the very least, from the requirements of natural justice that a person be given notice or warning that dismissal was being contemplated and that the reasons for such an attitude be given. The Tribunal, in numerous cases involving alleged misconduct had required, that at the very, least, an employee must be given a warning that his or her conduct, if it continued was likely to lead to dismissal.

The Tribunal was satisfied that the claimant had been dismissed for alleged misconduct in refusing to obey an instruction from the respondent. In all of the circumstances the respondent had not satisfied the Tribunal that it had acted reasonably in and about the dismissal of the claimant.

Even if it had been established that the claimant's refusal to obey the instruction amounted to a refusal to obey a legitimate instruction justifying a dismissal, the dismissal would have been unfair by reason of the failure to accord to the claimant his right to fair procedures. The Tribunal was satisfied that the claimant had been entitled to be informed that his continuing refusal to relocate was being treated as misconduct and that if he persisted it was likely to lead to his dismissal, and that he was entitled to a fair hearing as to the reasons for his continuing refusal to relocate and have his concerns dealt with. Further, the claimant's right to be informed of the respondent's attitude to his continuing refusal to relocate required that the claimant be given clear and unequivocal notice or warning. He had never received such a notice.

The only possible opportunity the claimant had for an effective hearing of his grievances was at the meeting with the managing director. The managing director had been well aware of the nature of the claimant's grievances but she never sought to address them at that meeting, or to assure the claimant that his terms and conditions were unaffected and his status certain.

For those reasons the Tribunal considered that the claimant's right to fair procedures had been violated.

The Tribunal noted its entitlement to take the claimant's conduct into account to the extent to which such conduct contributed to the dismissal and to the resulting financial loss. The majority felt that while the claimant had contributed to his dismissal by reason of his conduct it was not substantial. Taking into account the substantial amount of financial loss resulting from the dismissal and the limit of 104 weeks' remuneration imposed on the Tribunal's award, no reduction in the award was merited.

Constructive dismissal In *Kennedy v Foxfield Inns Ltd t/a The Imperial Hotel* [1995] ELR 216, the claimant resigned from her position as waitress. She subsequently claimed that she had experienced difficulties with a manager shortly after her employment had commenced. He initially ignored her and then began to address disparaging remarks about her physical appearance to her supervisors. When working in the bar he would call her a 'slut' in front of customers. He regularly slapped her and pulled her hair when passing close to her. On one particular occasion when she was paying a bill at reception, the manager stood on her feet and slapped her on the back. She said that she decided to leave her employment after that incident.

This evidence was contested by several witnesses, including the manager, but the Tribunal was nonetheless satisfied that the claimant's evidence of verbal and physical abuse by the manager was correct.

The question for the Tribunal to decide was whether the claimant's decision to terminate her employment has been reasonable. It concluded on the evidence that 'by virtue of the type of conduct of which she had complained, coupled with the status of the perpetrator of that conduct, the claimant's situation in her employment became intolerable to the extent that she was left with no option but to terminate her employment'.

The Tribunal found therefore that the claimant had been constructively dismissed from her employment and that dismissal was unfair.

Redundancy

(a) *Selection criteria* In *Lynch v Baily* [1996] ELR 65, the Tribunal gave importance guidance on the question of unfair selection for redundancy. S. 6(2) of the Unfair Dismissals Act 1977 sets out a number of specific grounds, such as trade union membership or activities, religious or political opinions, pregnancy or age, which constitute an unfair reason for dismissal for redundancy. S. 6(3) provides as follows:

Without prejudice to the generality of subsection (1) of this section, if an employee was dismissed due to redundancy but the circumstances constituting the redundancy applied equally to one or more other employees in similar employment with the same employer who have not been dismissed, and either:

(a) the selection of that employee for dismissal resulted wholly or mainly from one or more of the matters specified in subsection (2) of this section or another matter that would not be a ground justifying dismissal, or
(b) he was selected for dismissal in contravention of a procedure (being a procedure that has been agreed upon by or on behalf of the employer and by the employee or a trade union, or an excepted body under the Trade Union Acts 1941 and 1971, representing him or has been established by the custom and practice of the employment concerned) relating to redundancy and there were no special reasons justifying a departure from that procedure.

then the dismissal shall be deemed, for the purposes of this Act, to be an unfair dismissal.

In *Lynch v Baily*, the claimant had worked in an accountancy firm for fourteen years as a secretary. The firm had undergone a couple of mergers with other firms, which had resulted in changes in work practices, leading to a diminution in the need for secretaries. A redundancy situation arose. Of the six full-time secretaries, the claimant was selected for redundancy in spite of the fact that she had worked in the position the longest.

The claimant unsuccessfully sought to establish that the 'last-in, first-out' (LIFO)) principle applied. The Tribunal noted that this principle had indeed been frequently enshrined in agreements between management and trade unions and had become the custom and practice in many forms of employment, but the practice, though widespread, had not become universal. It stressed that, under s. 6(3)(b), the Tribunal's function was not to impose the principle, but rather to recognise it where it existed. In the instant case the claimant had not proven that the principle was established by custom and practice either in the respondent firm or among the accountancy firms in general. The Tribunal was thus 'doubtful' that the case fell within paragraph (b).

The claimant nonetheless succeeded under paragraph (a). It transpired that, when the issue of selection had come before the partners, none of them had wished to give up his own secretary. The Tribunal, reasonably, characterised this as selection for redundancy 'by process of elimination'. The claimant, who was a secretary to a person who was no longer a partner, 'was therefore, so to speak, without a champion at the partner's table'.

The Tribunal referred to the phrase 'another matter that would not be a ground justifying dismissal', in paragraph (a). It noted that it had always taken the view that such other matter had to be something specific. In the instant case there *was* something specific: the fact that the claimant was no longer secretary to a partner. The question, therefore, was whether this was a 'ground justifying dismissal'.

The Tribunal reasoned as follows. In a partnership, unlike a limited company, each partner was individually answerable for the actions of the others, but partners are also collectively responsible. While there was evidence that the partners in the instant case had chosen their secretaries individually when they were first employed, their responsibility to the staff as a whole was collective. In making the redundancy selection the partners had been clearly influenced by personal preference and, personal loyalty. This was understandable, but the result was the selection of someone else for whom they were collectively responsible. The evidence showed that in addition to being personal secretaries, some at least of the secretaries had done other work, such as annual company returns and TMS, which related to the firm as a whole.

In this context seniority again arose, not under the LIFO principle but in general terms. Under the strict LIFO principle seniority of only a few days would be a factor. In the instant case the claimant had longer service than the other secretaries, much longer that most. She had worked in the firm for fourteen years, while all the others except two had been recruited in the previous six years. In choosing to retain their own secretaries, the partners, by elimination, had selected the claimant for redundancy in disregard of her long service. While the Tribunal understood their individual choices, in its view the collective effect had been to select and dismiss her for a 'matter that would not be a ground justifying dismissal'.

The Tribunal therefore found that the claimant had been unfairly selected within the meaning of section 6(3)(a).

(b) *Waiver and duress*   In *Short v Data Packaging Ltd* [1996] ELR 7, the Tribunal addressed two important legal issues: its jurisdiction to hear a claim where the claimant had signed a waiver of his entitlement to take proceedings for unfair dismissal and an assertion that the waiver had been obtained under duress.

As to the first issue, the Tribunal reserved its position until it had heard all the evidence. Having done so, it stated baldly that it determined that it did indeed have jurisdiction to deal with the case notwithstanding the signing of the waiver.

As to the second issue, the Tribunal made no express finding, contenting itself to state, in a single conclusory sentence, that, having considered all the evidence before it, it found that the employer had not successfully discharged the onus of proof to show that the claimant's dismissal was fair.

The claimant had alleged that he had been told by the employer that his position was being terminated by reason of redundancy and that, when he questioned the signing of the waiver form which the employer had proffered to accompany his payments on termination of employment, he had been advised that he would not receive his money (which involved as *ex gratia* payment) unless he signed the waiver. The claimant gave evidence that the following day he had indicated to the acting general manager of the company that he would sign the waiver without prejudice and that this had generated no response. The claimant attested that he had had no alternative but to sign the form on account of financial constraints.

The laconic quality of the Tribunal's determination makes it hard to fathom the precise conclusions on the evidence which it may have reached. This is unfortunate in view of the general significance of the issue involved.

Retirement   In *Tipperary (North Riding) County Council v Treacy* [1996] ELR 4, the claimant had been employed as a waterworks and sewage caretaker in 1976. As part of established, if not binding, practice, he was also offered, and he accepted, employment as a part-time fireman. At the time he took up the later role, the retirement age was sixty five for those engaged in both tasks so far as the element of firefighting was concerned. This contrasted with a retirement age of fifty five for part-time firemen who were not also employed as caretakers. In 1984, the County Council reduced the firefighting retirement age for those performing both functions to fifty five.

The Tribunal, upholding the decision of the Rights Commissioner, held that the case was governed by Flood J's decision in *Donegal County Council v Porter* [1993] ELR 101. Accordingly it held that the claimant had had a reasonable basis for looking forward to employment as a fireman until the age of sixty five and that his dismissal was thus unfair.

In *Kiernan v Iarnród Éireann* [1996] ELR 12, the Tribunal emphasised the need for an employer who relies on the normal retirement age provision of s. 2(1)(6) of the Unfair Dismissals Act 1977 (as amended) to give the precise age of normal retirement to the employee in writing. The claimant had been employed as a boy porter. His employer had not conveyed to him in writing that the retirement age was twenty. There was a conflict of evidence as to whether this fact had been mentioned orally at the interview. Without resolving this issue, the Tribunal found that the absence of written communication rendered the dismissal unfair.

Statutory apprenticeship   In *Boal v IMED Ireland Ltd* [1995] EKR 178, the respondent succeeded in convincing the Tribunal that the claimant, who had been working for six years for it, had been employed under a statutory

apprenticeship and that his employment had been properly and fairly terminated within a month after the completion of the apprenticeship. This was in
compliance with s. 4 of the 1977 Act and the matter was therefore beyond
the jurisdiction of the Tribunal.

Limitation period   In *Byrne v P.J. Quigley* [1995] ELR 205, the Tribune
had to interpret the meaning of s. 7(A)(2) of the Unfair Dismissals Act 1993,
which provides that a claim for redress must be instituted within six months
of the dismissal or, if the rights commissioner or the Tribunal is satisfied that
exceptional circumstances prevented the giving of notice within the six
month period, a period of twelve months from the date of the relevant
dismissal 'as the rights commissioner or the Tribunal, as the case may be,
considers reasonable': see the 1993 Review 369. In the instant case, the
claimant had been employed by the respondent for several years, his status
alternating between that of sub-contractor and that of employee. A Social
Welfare investigation into his insurability determined that he had been in
insurable employment from March 1992 to September 1993. The respondent
appealed this determination, the appeal being heard in September 1994. In
July, 1994, the claimant spoke to the social welfare officer who was investigating the appeal. This was his first involvement in the investigation. He
discovered that he might have had a full years' service as an employee and,
accordingly, be entitled to bring a claim for unfair dismissal against the
respondent. A subsequent appeal by the respondent resulted in a determination that the claimant had been self-employed during the relevant period.

The Tribunal, by a majority, rejected the claim. It reasoned as follows.
The words 'exceptional circumstances' were strong words, which should be
contrasted with the milder words 'reasonable cause' which permitted the
extension of time for lodging a redundancy claim under s. 12(2)(B) of the
Redundancy Payments Act, 1971. 'Exceptional' meant something out of the
ordinary. At least the circumstances had to be 'unusual, probably quite
unusual, but not necessarily highly unusual'.

In order to extend the time, the Tribunal had to be satisfied that the
exceptional circumstances 'prevented' lodging the claim within the general
time limit. It was not sufficient if the exceptional circumstances caused or
triggered the lodging of the claim. It followed that the exceptional circumstances involved had to arise within the first six months, 'the period aforesaid'. If they arose later, they could not be said to 'prevent' the claim is being
initiated within that period.

In the view of the majority the first element existed in the instant case.
The claimant had been working under a C45, which was widely recognised
in the construction industry as denoting subcontracting or self-employment
status. In July 1994 the claimant had learned that the Social Welfare officials

had ruled that his status was insurable as an employee. The result of the appeal, in September 1996, was to reverse this finding. This sequence of events was, by any standards, 'quite unusual, if not highly unusual, and would probably fit within the description "exceptional circumstances".'

The majority of the Tribunal considered, however, that the other elements did not exist. The Social Welfare enquiry had 'triggered' the lodging of the claim rather than hindered it:

> In other words, the exceptional circumstances caused the late lodging instead of preventing it. The claimant first became aware of the enquiry in July 1994, eight months after the dismissal. As far as he was concerned nothing of an exceptional nature happened within six months to 'prevent' him bringing a claim. During that six month period he seems to have believed that he had not been an employee when working under a C45. This system of working is very common in the construction industry and could not be described as exceptional.

For those reasons the majority held that the subsection did not apply and accordingly that the claim was out of time.

TRANSFER OF UNDERTAKINGS

In *Brett v Niall Collins Ltd (In Receivership)* [1996] ELR 69, the Tribunal recorded a strong doubt as to the constitutional validity of s. 15 of the Unfair Dismissals (Amendment) Act 1993, which we noted in the 1993 Review 371. S. 15 amends the First Schedule to the Minimum Notice and Terms of Employment Act 1973, which allows for a breach in continuity of service if the employee receives and retains a redundancy payment from the transferor. In the Tribunal's view, this was contrary to the Transfer of Undertakings Directive 187/77 EU (implemented in Ireland by SI No. 36 of 1980). The Tribunal noted that Regulation 5(1) of SI No 36 specifically prohibited the dismissal of employees by reason of the transfer of an undertaking:

> The effect of this prohibition is total although the force of this prohibition is blunted by insertion of the second sentence of the Regulation in allowing dismissals for economic, technical or organisational reasons which would entail changes in the workforce. The effect of this second sentence .... can have application only to the position of the workforce after the transfer and can have no application in this case. This in no way affects a receiver or manager while managing a company during the receivership and only comes into play where a transfer of undertak-

ing is the only option to the receiver. A worker cannot waive his/her rights in respect of the Directive. The Directive is mandatory and must be applied even if a worker purports to contract out of it. Therefore a worker cannot accept a diminution of his/her rights on a transfer. What can be done is that after the transfer a new form of rights can be agreed between the parties but not imposed by the employer as the Directive preserves the conditions of employment that existed prior to the transfer.

In the instant case, the receiver, appointed by a bank to the transferor company, had sold the premises, equipment and goodwill of the company to the transferee company, having first purportedly dismissed several of the staff by paying them redundancy. The Tribunal held that, under Regulation 5 of SI No. 36, the dismissal by reason of the transfer of the undertaking by the receiver was null and void and of no effect and, because redundancy required a dismissal, the payment could not be a 'redundancy payment' in the absence of any redundancy. Accordingly, assuming that s. 15 of the 1993 Act was constitutionally valid, it had no application. This meant that the Tribunal had jurisdiction to hear the claims for unfair dismissal made by those who had been thus purportedly dismissed.

In *Roche v Salthill Hotel Ltd* [1996] ELR 15, the Tribunal, applying the principles laid down in the High Court in *Bannon v Employment Appeals Tribunal and Drogheda Town Centre Ltd* [1993] 1 IR 500, which we noted in the 1992 Review, 401-2, held that there had been a transfer of part of the respondent's business within the Transfer of Undertakings Directive where the respondent hotel company transferred the function room restaurant and catering facilities by way of a leasing arrangement. The claimant, a chef, as well as the four other chefs, had been dismissed from his employment on the basis of redundancy in the context of the transfer. Two of the chefs were immediately thereafter employed by the lessee. The Tribunal held that the claimant had been unfairly dismissed, in the light of paragraph 5(1) of the European Communities (Safeguarding of Employees' Rights on Transfer of Undertakings) Regulations (SI No. 306 of 1980).

In *Cunningham v Oasis Stores Ltd* [1995] ELR 183, the Tribunal found that the respondent had established economic, technical or organisational reasons, as contemplated in the Directive, justifying the dismissal of the claimants from managerial positions in a retail clothes business. The transferee conducted the general management of the business, not from a Dublin head office (as had been the situation before the transfer), but from an area office in the north of England, which was already providing the overall management of several other shops. When the transfer took place, the transferee integrated the four shops which had been transferred into its own structure. There was no need for the managerial positions which the claimants had held because of this organisational change. The two claimants had in a sense become redundant in that the requirement in Dublin for employees in their kind of work no longer existed.

MATERNITY PROTECTION

The provisions of the Maternity Protection Act 1994, which repealed the Maternity Protection of Employees Act 1981, are discussed by Eilis Barry in (1995) 13 *ILT* 15, and in detail by Anthony Kerr in his Annotation of the 1994 Act in *ICLSA*.

Law Reform

In 1995 the Law Reform Commission published four reports: a *Report on the Hague Convention Abolishing the Requirement of Legislation for Foreign Public Documents* (LRC 48 – 1995), a *Report on Interests of Vendor and Purchaser in Land during the period between Contract and Completion* (LRC 49 – 1995), a report entitled *An Examination of the Law of Bail* (LRC 50 – 1995) and a *Report on Intoxication* (LRC 51 – 1995).

Legislation in 1995 gave effect to a number of recommendations made by the Commission in earlier reports. The Family Law Act 1995, which we discuss in the Family Law Chapter, above 313-30, is based in part of the Commission's *Report on the Age of Majority, the Age of Marriage and some Connected Subjects* (LRC5 – 1983), its *Report on Jurisdiction in Proceedings for Nullity Decrees and the Hague Convention on the Celebration and Recognition of the Validity of Marriages* (LRC 20 – 1985), its *Report on Jactication on Marriage and Related Matters* (LRC 6 – 1983) and its *Report on Land Law and Conveyancing Law: (1) General Proposals* (LRC 30 – 1989) (which we analysed in the 1989 Review 295-304). The Criminal Law (Incest Proceedings) (No. 2) Act 1995 contains provisions relating to anonymity and privacy for victims which are largely modelled on proposals in the Commission's *Report on Rape and Allied Offences* (LRC 24 – 1988).

The Occupiers' Liability Act 1995 implements many of the Commission's recommendations contained in its *Report on Occupiers' Liability* (LRC 46 – 1994), but goes further than what the Commission proposed in reducing the legal protection afforded to entrants onto property. We critically analyse the legislation in the Torts Chapter below, 493-518.

The Law Reform Commissions Report on Intoxication At present, intoxication is not a defence to a criminal charge in Irish law, though no Irish court has specifically departed from *Director of Public Prosecutions v Beard* [1920] AC 479, in which Birkenhead LC stated (at 501-2):

> Where a specific intent is an essential element in the offence, evidence of a state of drunkenness rendering the accused incapable of forming such an intent should be taken into consideration in order to determine whether he had in fact formed the intent necessary to constitute the particular crime. If he was so drunk that he was incapable of forming the intent required he could not be convicted of a crime which was

committed only if the intent was proved.

The concept of 'specific intent', as interpreted in later English decisions, has proved controversial. Courts there draw the distinction between offences of 'basic' intent and offences of 'specific' intent. Intoxication will not constitute a defence for offence's of basic intent, where criminal responsibility depends on proof of intent or recklessness. It will, however, afford a defence in respect of offences of specific intent, which involve an act or omission with the intent to achieve a particular objective, such as assaulting with intent to rob. If the accused was so intoxicated as to lack that intent, he or she will be acquitted.

This distinction has been subjected to criticism by leading authorities on the basis that it makes the intoxication defence depend on the particular drafting strategy that may have been adopted in the formulation of particular offences. The Commission observes that '. . . logic demands that intoxication should always be a possible defence or never a defence.'

The Commission proposes that self-induced intoxication should never afford a defence to a charge. Involuntary intoxication would, however, do so. A person's intoxication should be regarded as involuntary where, *inter alia*, he or she took an intoxicant solely for a medicinal purpose and either was not aware that taking it would give rise to aggressive or uncontrollable behaviour on his or her part or took it on medical advice and in accordance with directions.

There is something unsatisfactorily about the law's imposing criminal responsibility on the basis of an ascription of a mental disposition — intention or recklessness — to a person who did not in fact have this disposition. There are of course good reasons why the law should punish those who engage in hurtful conduct when voluntarily intoxicated but this does not have to be achieved by such a crude departure from the fundamental norms of criminal law. In *R. v Kinston* [1994] 3 All ER 353, Lord Mustill considered that voluntary intoxication 'estopped' the defendant from relying on the absence of the requisite mental element. This novel translation from the civil law is less than fully convincing. It is true that the defendant's lack of intent is attributable to his or her own prior acts and that the defendant may be considered culpable in thus removing his or her conduct from the scope of the necessary ingredients of criminal responsibility for certain offences. There is no objection in principle to punishing that culpable behaviour, but what legislators should not do, in frustration, is pretend that a fact has been established when it has not. Estoppel can work justly in the inter-party context of civil law but it should not be invoked by robust legislators to seal over the cracks. The strength of the criminal justice system lies in the acceptance of its own inherent boundaries, which derive from fidelity to deeply important and at times unpopular values.

There is an aura of pragmatism surrounding the Commission's analysis. Thus we find it stated that '[t]he public is injured by the criminal act whatever the state of 'the criminal mind'. Apart from the question-begging character of the reference to 'the criminal act', when its criminality is the matter at issue, the implicit suggestion that the legislator should abandon a fundamental principle to accommodate injury to the public runs contrary to the whole purpose of the criminal law. The Commission goes on to observe that:

> the traditional *mens rea* doctrine is an appropriate one for the sane and sober criminal, but to adhere to it in an unbending and inflexible fashion enables the offender himself, voluntarily, not just to 'move the "goalposts"' but to remove them altogether.

The perception of the 'offender' (again a question-begging description) cheating the prosecutor may be understandable from the standpoint of a frustrated prosecutor but it is not the best one for society to adopt. Principles that are sufficiently flexible to be bent when they come under pressure are not perhaps the most appropriate ones for constructing the criminal justice system.

Bail The Law Reform Commission's Report entitled *An Examination of the Law of Bail* (LRC 50 – 1995) contains a thorough analysis of the subject. It includes a consideration of empirical evidence, an examination of the law in Ireland and abroad and a discussion of possible approaches to the problem of offences committed while on bail which do not involve pre-trial preventive detention. We shall discuss aspects of this Report in some detail in the 1996 Review in the context of the referendum on bail, held in November 1996.

Licensing

INTOXICATING LIQUOR

Christmas arrangements The Intoxicating Liquor Act 1995 amended the Licensing Acts 1833 to 1994 to permit shops and supermarkets which are licensed to sell intoxicating liquor by retail and other licensed premises to remain open on Christmas Eve or December 23, in any year that either day falls on a Sunday, as if it were a weekday. This eventuality occurred in 1995 and since the 1995 Act came into effect on December 21, 1995 on its signature by the President its terms were applicable over the Christmas 1995 season.

Extinguishment In *O'Rourke and Flanagan v Grittar* [1990] ILRM 877 (HC); [1995] 1 ILRM 532 (SC), the Supreme Court held that two ordinary publican's on-licences could not be extinguished to acquire an off-licence since they were not 'of the same character' as the off-licence. In so holding, the Court upheld the conclusions of Gannon J in the High Court (1990 Review, 388).The applicant company, Grittar (an unlimited company), had applied in the District Court for a certificate for a new spirit retailer's off-licence and a new beer retailer's off-licence, pursuant to s. 13 of the Intoxicating Liquor Act 1960. The application related to a new supermarket premises in County Kildare. S. 13 of the 1960 Act provides that the applicant must show that he is the holder of two licences which will be extinguished upon the grant of the new licence or that he has procured the consent of the holder of two licences to the extinguishment of these licences if the new licence is granted. The applicant produced two contracts consenting to the extinguishment of two ordinary seven-day publican's on-licences. The objectors, O'Rourke and Flanagan, submitted that the applicant did not come within s. 13 since s. 13(2)(a) requires that the licence to be granted must be of the same character and be subject to the same conditions as the licence being extinguished. On a case stated to, the High Court, Gannon J held that the objectors were correct in law. On further appeal, the Supreme Court (Hamilton CJ and Blayney J; O'Flaherty J dissenting) upheld this view and dismissed the applicant's appeal.

Delivering the leading judgment, Hamilton CJ (with whom Blayney J concurred) noted that s. 13 of the 1960 Act expressly requires that the licence granted should be of the same character as that extinguished and that the legislative policy underlying the 1960 Act was to limit the number of licences for the sale of intoxicating liquor. Distinguishing the Court's decision in *Power Supermarkets Ltd v O'Shea* [1988] IR 206 (1988 Review, 288-90), Hamilton CJ stated that, although s. 62 of the Intoxicating Liquor Act 1927 provides for the conversion of an on-licence in a county borough into an off-licence and that a similar right probably also exists under s. 2 of the Licensing (Ireland) Act 1902, this did not assist the applicant in the instant case. Rather, he concluded that the High Court judge had been correct in concluding that s. 13 of the 1960 Act was to be construed according to the terms in which it was expressed, thus excluding the extinguishments proposed by the applicant.

In his dissenting judgment, O'Flaherty J took a different view of the purpose of the 1960 Act. He considered that the 'clear policy' of s. 13 of the 1960 Act was to encourage the extinguishment of as many redundant publican's licences that then existed in rural areas as possible. He considered that when it came to the extinguishment of one licence in favour of another, it was implicit in the legislative intention that the greater should include the lesser. Since, in his view, an on-licence had twin characters, namely that of an off-licence and that of an on-licence, it should be possible on the extinguishment of two on-licences to obtain an off-licence. However, as already indicated this view did not commend itself to the majority.

Prospective effect of licence In *DPP (O'Halloran) v Cronin*, High Court, February 10, 1995, Geoghegan J held that an intoxicating liquor licence could not be regarded as having been granted with retrospective effect. This holding was made in the following circumstances. The defendant was the holder of a wine retailers on-licence, which was due to expire in September 1992. On or before this date, he had applied to the Revenue Commissioners for a tax clearance certificate, the Finance Act 1992 having introduced the requirement that he be in possession of a valid certificate before there a renewal of a wine licence could occur. As a result of administrative problems, the tax certificate was not issued until January 1993 and a new licence was obtained two days later. The defendant was subsequently charged with offences contrary to the Intoxicating Liquor (General) Act 1924, which concerned dates during which the defendant had not had a licence, owing to the delay in obtaining the tax certificate from the Revenue Commissioners.

On a case stated from the District Court, the defendant conceded that there was no statutory provision granting either a licence, or an authority to trade, after the expiration of the existing licence and pending the outcome of an application for a tax clearance certificate. However, he argued that such a provision was implied in s. 156 of the Finance Act 1992. In the case where a licence had been issued for the previous year, the licence would be deemed to continue in force where an appeal had been lodged in the event of a refusal of a new tax certificate and the defendant contended that the use of the word 'continue' must necessarily imply continuation from the expiration of the old licence. Geoghegan J did not accept this argument.

He pointed out that an intoxicating liquor licence is dated the day it is issued and takes effect from that date and that there would appear to be no statutory support for any retrospective effect. He noted that the question of a licence being deemed to continue in force after the date of its expiration did not arise in the instant case as the tax certificate had been issued, albeit belatedly. Citing the views of the Supreme Court on statutory interpretation in *Howard v Commissioners for Public Works in Ireland* [1994] 1 IR 101; [1993] ILRM 665 (1993 Review, 430-2), he held that it would be wholly impermissible for the court to imply intentions into s. 156 of the 1992 Act which were not in any way to be found in the wording of the section, and indeed which would fly in the face of the wording. He also stated that it was a feature of the Licensing Acts that a person is not empowered to sell intoxicating liquor without either the appropriate excise licence or an express right under statute to trade.

While on this basis, Geoghegan J held against the defendant, he expressed the view that it was doubtful whether the Oireachtas would ever have intended the lacuna to arise which had been identified in the instant case. Indeed, he went further to express the hope that amending legislation, if necessary with retrospective effect, would be introduced to remedy the difficulty thus created.

Limitation of Actions

Dismissal for want of prosecution In *In re Southern Mineral Oil Ltd; Southern Mineral Oil Ltd v Cooney*, High Court, February 10, 1995, Murphy J was called on to determine the principles in relation to dismissal for want of prosecution in the context of proceedings taken by a liquidator against the respondents under ss. 297 and 298 of the Companies Act 1963. Six years had elapsed since the cause of action had arisen, but Murphy J considered that in the circumstances of the case the period of which complaint might be made was 'probably a maximum of six years but more realistically four'.

The delay was attributable in part to the fact that 'the proceedings were not instituted [in late 1990] because a series of counsel were unable or unwilling to draft the necessary documentation'.

The respondents contended that, since proceedings under these sections involved a punitive element, the Court should apply, or at least have regard to, the criteria set out in earlier decisions in determining whether in criminal proceedings should be dismissed or prohibited on the grounds of delay. The courts in *The State (O'Connell) v Fawsitt* [1986] IR 362 and *Director of Public Prosecutions v Byrne* [1994] 2 ILRM 91 had made it clear that a person charged with a criminal offence has the positive right to a trial with reasonable expedition.

Murphy J, following his own decision in *O'Keeffe v Ferris* [1994] 1 ILRM 425, had no doubt that the instant proceedings were not of a criminal character. He admitted to the possibility that the gravity of the proceedings was 'a factor to be taken into account in finding a balance between the rights of the parties' in an application such as the one before the court but, if so, it was a matter of lesser consideration. Indeed, insofar as it was relevant at all, it might be a factor to take into account as *against* a defendant, because he or she 'would be less likely to have overlooked or forgotten the details of a matter which was important in itself or serious in the consequences which it might have been expected to have for others'.

It was true that an application for liberty to bring the proceedings had to be made *ex parte*, under s. 231(A) of the 1963 Act. The Court dealing with the matter 'would properly have regard to any injustice which the proceedings might involve and indeed might set aside the order granting such permission if satisfied that the liberty granted would involve a probable breach of the constitutional rights of the intended defendant'.

In the instant case the period of time that had elapsed since the cause of action had arisen was very much less than the periods involved in *Ó Domhnaill v Merrick* [1984] IR 151 and *Toal v Duignan (Nos. 1 and 2)* [1991] ILRM 135, 140. It could not be said that the lapse of the period of four or six years was such that, in the circumstances of the case, it would be unjust to permit the proceedings to continue as against the respondents.

The respondents pointed to three particular factors which made it difficult for them to defend the case. These were the death in 1993 of a director, the illness of the former auditor of one of the companies and the winding up of another of the companies in 1991.

While not disputing that these factors existed, Murphy J was not swayed by them. The auditor, though ill, would be in a position to give evidence. Moreover, the evidence available to the liquidator could not be any more extensive than that available to the respondents. Murphy J observed that '[n]ecessarily it would seem to be less'. The liquidator's information was confined to the documents which he had received after his appointment in 1988 and such explanations as were given to him in respect of them. These documents would be available to the respondents. Insofar as the evidence related to discussions which had taken place or transactions which had been effected prior to the commencement to the liquidation, the recollection of the respondents might be inform in some respects but 'clearly they would have some advantage in this regard compared to the liquidator'.

In all of the circumstances, Murphy J reached the conclusion that, despite the regrettable lapse of time which had occurred and the events which had happened, the balance lay in favour of permitting the proceedings by the liquidator to continue on behalf of the creditors whose interests he was bound to protect.

European Community law In *Tate v Minister for Social Welfare* [1995] 1 ILRM 507, Carroll J provided an insightful analysis of the juridical nature of an action taken against the State for failure to implement a European Community law directive and of the consequences so far as the domestic law of limitation of actions is concerned. The substantive issues arising in *Tate* are examined in the chapters on Social Welfare law, below, 458-9 and Tort law, below, 541-2. Here we need only note that Carroll J characterised the State's failure to implement the directive on equal treatment between men and women regarding social security as 'a wrong arising from community law which has domestic effect and approximates to a breach of constitutional duty'. She did not accept that it was a breach of statutory duty.

Carroll J went on to observe that:

[w]hile the Supreme Court did speak separately of torts and breach of

constitutional rights in *Conway v INTO* [1991] 1 IR 305, it was not in
the context of the Statute of Limitations. I would be surprised if there
was no limitation period affecting breach of constitutional rights. Just
as the word 'tort' in the Statute of Limitations is sufficiently wide to
embrace breach of statutory duty even though not specifically mentioned, so also, in my opinion, the word 'tort' is sufficiently wide to
cover breaches of obligations of the State under community law. There
is nothing strange in describing the State's failure to fulfil its obligations
under the treaty as a tort.

Therefore I am satisfied that s. 11(2) of the Statute of Limitations does
apply to a breach of obligation to observe community law. This also
means that the plea of laches is no longer relevant.

It should be noted from this passage that Carroll J did not commit herself
to the proposition that an action for breach of constitutional rights is subject
to the Statute of Limitations. Whilst tentatively rejecting the notion that such
an action is subject to no limitation period (or periods), she left open the
possibility of the development of a distinctive limitation code for breaches
of constitutional rights. (She returned to this theme in *McDonnell v Ireland*,
High Court, January 16, 1996 and *Murphy v Ireland*, High Court, February
21, 1996. We shall examine these decisions in the 1996 Review.)

Carroll J went on to hold that the European Communities (Social Welfare) Regulations 1992, which retained an element of sex discrimination and
failed to give married women their full due, generated a fresh cause of action
but that their failure to include provisions for payment to women of the
equivalent of the transitional payments to which men were entitled was 'an
omission and not a positive act' and that accordingly there could not be a
fresh cause of action in that regard.

There are notorious problems of legal characterisation in relation to acts
and omissions. Whereas a complete failure to do anything even where
something is expected of one may legitimately be classified as an omission,
the failure to take a particular step when one is actually doing something
positive is less easy to describe as an omission. The failure to apply one's
brakes when the need arises should be regarded as a part of a wider chapter
of positive action. The defective formulation of the 1992 regulations could
on one view be seen as the predominant positive act from which it would be
wrong to subtract, and isolate, the failure to give married women their full
due.

Finally, Carroll J rejected the argument made by certain of the plaintiffs
that the State was estopped from relying on the Statute of Limitations to
defeat their claims. It was common cause that, if they had been misled by

unambiguous promises, the State could not rely on the Statute and that if they had therefore not issued proceedings in time, estoppel would apply but nothing like that had happened. The most that the State had done was to write saying that no further action was possible because the matter was before the court. There had been 'no words or conduct which could have misled any of these plaintiffs to infer liability would be admitted'.

Procedure In *Krops v Irish Forestry Board Ltd*, High Court, April 6, 1995, Keane J held that, where a plaintiff seeks to add a new cause of action arising out of the same, or substantially the same, facts as those originally pleaded, the court should not be precluded from permitting an amendment to the plaintiff's statement of claim. Thus, he extricated Irish law from what Edmund Davies LJ, in *Brickfield Properties Ltd v Newton* [1971] 3 All ER 328, at 341, had described as 'the deadening hand' of the English Court of Appeal's holding in *Weldon v Neal* (1887) 19 QBD 394. Whether *Weldon v Neal* went so far as subsequent English decisions had interpreted it is, as Keane J pointed out, uncertain.

In the instant case, the plaintiff had claimed that, while he and his wife were driving down a road in Wicklow, a tree had fallen on their car, killing his wife. His statement of claim, as originally delivered, averred that the tree had fallen as a result of the negligence, breach of duty and breach of statutory duty of the defendants in the felling of trees in that area. He later sought permission from the court to amend his statement of claim by the insertion of the words 'and nuisance' after the words 'breach of statutory duty'. The first-named defendants resisted this amendment on the grounds that it would deprive them of a defence that could otherwise be open to them under the relevant limitation period prescribed by s. 48(b) of the Civil Liability Act 1961, since the proceedings had not been instituted within three years of the death of Mrs Krops. It was common case that the proposed amendment did not involve the pleading of any new facts.

Keane J, granting the amendment, stated that:

> the pleadings which initiate an action in this Court carry with them from the time they are issued or delivered the potentiality of being amended by the Court in the exercise of its general jurisdiction to allow a party to amend his indorsement or pleadings 'in such manner and on such terms as may be just'. Where, as here, an amendment, if allowed, will not in any way prejudice or embarrass the defendant by new allegations of facts, no injustice is done to him by permitting the amendment In that sense, it is true to say that the amendment does not in truth deprive him of a defence under the Statute of Limitations: since the proceedings were always capable of amendment in such manner as might be just and in

order to allow the real question in controversy between the parties to be determined, it cannot be said that the defendant was at any stage in a position to rely on the Statute of Limitations.

One must welcome the holding in the case. The failure to have permitted an amendment would surely have frustrated rather than advanced the interests of justice. It would seem better to attempt to resolve the question of permitting an amendment with an eye on these interests rather than to adopt a definitional or formalistic solution. A defendant who resists an amendment on the basis that it would deprive him or her of a defence available under the Statute of Limitations is making a perfectly reasonable point. If an amendment is granted, it will indeed have that effect, though the deprivation will not necessarily be improper. The real question is whether or not, in the light of all the facts, it would be wrong to deprive the defendant of a defence that would otherwise have been available.

In the Chapter on Practice and Procedure, below, 383, Hilary Delany discusses *Palamos Properties Ltd v Brook*, High Court, January 11, 1995, where Flood J permitted the defendants, a firm of solicitors, who had been sued for negligence by the plaintiff, a former client, to amend their defence at a late stage so as to include (inter alia) the defence that the claim was barred by the Statute of Limitations. A factor that influenced Flood J was the understandable reluctance of the defendants to plead the statute against a former client:

It would hardly be an endearing basis upon which to hope to enter into any meaningful negotiation with a view to resolving the alleged claim for damages. . . . Such a course of conduct would be unlikely to appeal to any solicitor, save as an absolute last resort as it really amounts, in effect, to pleading the Gaming Act.

Unfair dismissal In the Labour Law chapter, above, 352-3, we discuss *Byrne v P.J. Quigley Ltd* [1995] ELR 205, where the Tribunal, by a majority, rejected the argument that exceptional circumstances existed which allowed for an extension of the time limit for initiating an unfair dismissal claim.

Local Government

ARTERIAL DRAINAGE

The Arterial Drainage Act 1995 extended the powers of the Commissioners for Public Works in Ireland (the Office of Public Works) to undertake drainage schemes under the Arterial Drainage Act 1945 in order to prevent or relieve localised flooding including flooding in urban and residential areas. The Act also provides a basis for computing compensation for the acquisition of or interference with lands or other rights and for vesting of lands. Penalties for offences under the 1945 Act were also increased. The Act came into effect on July 7, 1995 on its signature by the President.

FINANCE

The Securitisation (Proceeds of Certain Mortgages) Act 1995 provided for a scheme whereby income due from local authorities from housing loans they have made, with finance borrowed from the Exchequer through the Local Loans Fund, could be paid to a company established for this purpose. In return for the assignment of this income the company would pay to the Exchequer a lump sum, to be raised by issuing bonds, at the beginning of the transaction. Payments to the company would be treated as if they were payments to the Local Loans Funds and all rights and obligations would continue to apply. As can be seen, the Act provided for the raising of a large capital sum in connection with the annual income on interest available to local authorities from housing loans. The 1995 Act came into effect on November 30, 1995 on its signature by the President.

HOUSING

Sale of tenanted dwellings The Housing (Sale of Houses) Regulations 1995 (SI No. 188 of 1995), made under the Housing Act 1966, lay down the conditions governing the sale of tenanted dwellings to tenants of housing authorities under tenant purchase schemes. Such schemes must comply with the conditions laid out in the Regulations as to the determination of the purchase price, the conditions attaching to the sale and the terms of shared ownership leases. Where dwellings other than tenanted dwellings are being sold by housing authorities, the consent of the Minister to the sale must be obtained unless the sale is made at the best price reasonably available. The Regulations came into effect on July 18, 1995 and are applicable to sales under purchase schemes adopted with effect from May 1, 1995.

LOCAL GOVERNMENT REFORM

Bye-laws The Local Government Act 1994 (Commencement) (No. 4) Order 1995 (SI No. 362 of 1995) brought Part VII the Local Government Act 1994 (which concerns the making of bye-laws: 1994 Review, 346) into operation generally on January 1, 1996. The Local Government Act 1994 (Bye-Laws) Regulations 1995 (SI No. 360 of 1994) set out the principal procedural matters relating to the making of bye-laws by local authorities, also with effect from January 1, 1996.

Elections The Local Government Act 1994 (Commencement) Order 1995 (SI No. 245 of 1995) brought into effect on September 19, 1995 s. 22 of the 1994 Act, which provides for the making of Regulations for the conduct of local elections. The Local Elections Regulations 1995 (SI No. 297 of 1995), made under s. 22 of the 1994 Act, set out the detailed procedures for holding elections for local authorities and specify electoral offences and penalties in respect of such offences. They also empower all citizens of the European Union to vote in and stand as candidates in local elections, thus giving effect to Directive 94/80/EC, as envisaged by the Treaty on European Union (1992 Review, 326-31). The Regulations came into effect on November 13, 1995, thus applying to the local elections held later that month. The Local Government Act 1994 (Commencement) (No. 2) Order 1995 (SI No. 296 of 1995) brought into effect on 13 November 1995 the various provisions of the 1994 Act concerning local elections and local authority membership. On the 1994 Act generally, see the 1994 Review, 342-7.

Funding Two relatively minor but significant changes to local authority financing were effected by the Local Authorities (Traffic Wardens) Act 1975 (Disposal of Moneys) (Amendment) Regulations 1995 (SI No. 185 of 1995) and the Road Traffic (Parking Fees) (Amendment) Regulations 1995 (SI No. 186 of 1995). Both removed the need for the approval of the Minister for the Environment for the disposal by local authorities of moneys received by them from 'on the spot' fines and for parking fees, respectively. They came into effect on July 12, 1995. See also the Securitisation (Proceeds of Certain Mortgages) Act 1995, above.

Local authority associations The Local Government Act 1994 Commencement (No. 3) Order 1995 (SI No. 351 of 1995) brought s. 64 of the Local Government Act 1994 (which concerns local authority associations, in particular the General Council of County Councils) into effect generally on 1 January 1996.

PLANNING AND DEVELOPMENT

Access to information The Local Government (Planning and Development) (No. 2) Regulations 1995 (SI No. 75 of 1995), which came into effect on 6 April 1995, amended the Local Government (Planning and Development) Regulations 1994 to provide for access for public inspection of documents relating to planning appeals and other matters determined by An Bord Pleanála in any case received by it after April 10, 1995.

Compensation for refusal In *McKone Estates Ltd v Dublin County Council* [1995] 2 ILRM 283, the Supreme Court followed the decision of Costello J in *J. Wood & Co Ltd v Wicklow County Council* [1995] 1 ILRM 51 (1994 Review, 350) in holding that the Local Government (Planning and Development) Act 1990 (1990 Review, 414-5) had some retrospective effect in removing the extensive right of compensation for refusal of planning permission formerly contained in the Local Government (Planning and Development) Act 1963. The case arose against the following background.

In December 1989, the applicant company had applied to the respondent Council for planning permission to develop a site of land. In April 1990, the Council granted permission for the development, subject to a number of conditions imposed pursuant to s. 26 of the 1963 Act. In May 1990, the company appealed against the decision of the Council to An Bord Pleanála, as did a number of third parties. In June 1990, the 1990 Act came into force. S. 3 of the 1990 Act had repealed and replaced those provisions of the 1963 Act dealing with compensation for refusal of planning permission. In January 1991, the Board reversed the Council's decision to grant planning permission to the company. In July 1991, the company submitted a claim for compensation to under the 1990 Act in respect of the reduction in value of their site by reason of the decision of the Board. In May 1992, the company applied pursuant to s. 55 of the 1963 Act to the President of the Circuit Court for an extension of time within which to make a claim for compensation under the 1963 Act, and this was granted. The Council appealed against that order, arguing that since s. 55 of the 1963 act had been repealed by the 1990 Act, there was no jurisdiction to grant an extension under its terms. This matter was then referred by way of case stated to the Supreme Court.

The Court held that, while there were differences between the *Wood* case and the instant case, the essential factors in each were identical, namely, that there had been an application for planning permission before the passing of the 1990 Act, and a refusal by the Board after that Act had come into force. The Court considered that the manner in which Costello J had dealt with the legal position applied equally to the instant case, and adopted his statement of the law. In the instant case, since the company's right to claim compensation did not arise until January 1991, and since at that date the compensation provisions in the 1963 Act were no longer in force, they could no longer be relied on.

The company had also raised two points of European Community law not raised in the *Wood* case, namely, the doctrine of legitimate expectation and the doctrine of legitimate certainty which, as it pointed out, were of long standing in the jurisprudence of the Court of Justice of the European Communities. However, the Court came to the conclusion that those doctrines had no application to the interpretation of statutes in the domestic law of Ireland. At first sight, this is a rather surprising conclusion, given the acceptance of the concept of legitimate expectation in general terms in recent Irish law and indeed the notion that legal certainty is a fundamental aspect of the rule of law. It might be better to understand this rejection of the applicant's argument as being an adjunct to the Court's acceptance of the mode of interpretation adopted in *Wood* simply precluded the Court from holding that the right to compensation existed apart from the statutory provisions in question.

This would appear to be supported by the Court's emphasis immediately following the rejection of this argument on the application of the Interpretation Act 1937, as had occurred in the *Wood* case. The Court held that the planning procedures were part of the administrative system of the State rather than the judicial system. The Court considered that a planning authority was not a court and neither was An Bord Pleanála. Indeed, it noted that the company had not cited any authorities in support of its submission that an application for planning permission was a legal procedure within the meaning of s. 21(1)(c) of the 1937 Act. On this basis, the Court concluded that the President of the Circuit Court was not longer empowered to extend the time for submission of a claim for compensation under the 1963 Act since its provisions had been repealed by the 1990 Act.

Development plan: advertising alterations   The consequences of failure to advertise a proposed change to a development plan arose in unusual circumstances in *Keogh and Ors (Lower Salthill Residents Association) v Galway County Borough* [1995] 2 ILRM 312. The respondent Borough's 1991 development plan provided for the establishment of four halting sites in its functional area. The Borough then decided to vary the plan, in order to increase the number of proposed sites from four to 10. The Borough followed the procedures allowing for such alterations to the development plan, as laid down in s.21A of the Local Government (Planning and Development) Act 1963. Notices of the proposed alteration were published in *Iris Oifigiúil* and in newspapers circulating in the area to be affected. Under the 1991 development plan, the applicants would not have been affected, as their area of Salthill was not included. However under the proposed alterations, the Salthill area was to be considered. Prior to the meeting at which the alterations to the 1991 plan were to be considered, a report was received from the Borough's senior planning executive which indicated that there would be logistical difficulties in proceeding to develop three of the proposed 10 sites. On the basis of this report, the Borough adopted a resolution removing the three sites from the development plan. The applicants instituted judicial review proceedings seeking to quash this resolution on the ground that the removal of the three sites from the plan constituted a material change to the development plan and that, by not advertising notice of the proposed change, the Borough had failed to comply with the requirements of s. 21A of the 1963 Act. Morris J granted the relief sought.

He stated that the submissions made by the applicants to the Borough were made in connection with the proposal to increase the number of proposed sites from four to 10 and there was no reference in these submissions to the fact that certain sites might be excluded. Nor did he think that the Borough had considered any possible objections the applicants might have to the removal of three of the proposed sites when it passed its resolution.

Morris J pointed out that at no stage before the adoption of the resolution was consideration given by the Borough to the question whether the removal of three of the proposed sites constituted a material change to the development plan. He stated that, since no decision to that effect had been taken by the Borough, the Court was empowered to decide the issue *res integra*. He concluded that the decision to remove the three sites from the 10 originally contemplated constituted a material alteration to the 1991 development plan. As there had thus been a failure to publish a notice to this effect in *Iris Oifigiúil* and in one newspaper circulating in the area pursuant to s. 21A of the 1963 Act, he declared invalid the resolution made by the Borough and granted the applicants the relief sought.

Environmental impact assessment: piggery In *Shannon Regional Fisheries Board v. An Bord Pleanála and Ors.*, High Court, November 17, 1994, Barr J held that a pregnant pig, a gilt, constituted a 'sow' for the purposes of the European Communities (Environmental Impact Assessment) Regulations 1989. The case arose against the following background. The respondent Planning Board had upheld the granting of retention planning permission, subject to conditions, for a large piggery used primarily for breeding purposes. The piggery comprised 20 boars and 400 gilts. The applicant Fisheries Board, a statutory body responsible for the protection and development of fisheries, had objected to the granting of the permission, in particular on the ground that the piggery owner had failed to submit an Environmental Impact Statement (EIS) under the 1989 Regulations when submitting the application for retention permission. The 1989 Regulations requires an EIS for pig-rearing installations where their capacity exceeds 1,000 units, one pig constituting one unit and one sow constituting ten units. The question thus arose as to whether the 400 gilts constituted sows for the purposes of the 1989 Regulations. The Planning Board had concluded that a gilt was a pig which would not become a sow until it had had its first litter; thus during pregnancy one gilt was equivalent to one unit under the 1989 Regulations. On this basis, as Barr J noted, the piggery comprised 420 units pursuant to the 1989 Regulations, thus falling below the 1,000 units threshold for an EIS. As already indicated, Barr J held that each gilt constituted a sow, thus bringing the piggery well above the EIS threshold.

Addressing the issue of statutory interpretation, he held that in the absence of a statutory definition, the case turned on the appropriate meaning to be given to the word 'sow'. He considered that the meaning of 'sow' in the 1989 Regulations was not free from doubt and therefore was a matter for the court to determine. Applying the approach taken by the Supreme Court in *Howard v Commissioners of Public Works in Ireland* [1994] 1 IR 101; [1993] ILRM 665 (1993 Review, 430-34), he held that the 1989 Regulations should be construed according to their expressed intention. Noting that they had transposed into national law Directive 85/337/EEC, Barr J accepted that the 1985 Directive stemmed from a recognition that large-scale activities such as pig-rearing could cause substantial environmental damage and should be regulated to minimise that risk. He pointed out that the 1989 Regulations recognised that the pregnant breeding pig and her prospective litters would generate a greater effluent problem than her male counterpart, and it thus followed that there could be no practical distinction between a pregnant pig awaiting a first litter and a pig which had had more than one litter. Thus, each should have the same number of units allocated to them. Following from this, Barr J quashed the retention permission granted, directed the respondent Planning Board to exercise its power under Reg. 56(1) of the Local Government (Planning and Development) Regulations 1994 to require the piggery owner to furnish an EIS and to reconsider the application for retention permission in this light.

Exempted developments and application procedures The Local Government (Planning and Development) Regulations 1995 (SI No. 69 of 1995) amended the Local Government (Planning and Development) Regulations 1994 and introduced a number of changes concerning exempted developments and planning application procedures with effect from March 24, 1995.

Fair procedures In *McGoldrick v An Bord Pleanála*, High Court, May 26, 1995, Barron J held that the applicant was entitled to judicial review of a planning decision where he had not been made aware of the basis on which the decision was based. The applicant had purchased certain premises in August 1990, which at the time were let out in several holdings and which had been used in that way since the coming into force of the Local Government (Planning and Development) Act 1963 on October 1, 1964. Following the purchase, the applicant executed certain works, including the repair of a wall and the re-roofing of a single story annexe to the rear of the premises. The applicant believed that these works constituted exempted development as he was not increasing the floor area of the premises. In May 1991, the local Council, being the relevant planning authority, served a warning notice on the applicant requiring him to remove the annexe. He then applied for retention permission in relation to the new roof and wall of the annexe. The planning authority sought further information from the applicant, in reply to which he forwarded letters from his neighbours and from the previous owner of the premises verifying that the annexe had at the relevant times been in existence. He also offered to forward any further information to the planning authority should it be required. In November 1991, retention planning permission was refused. The applicant appealed against the refusal to the respondent Planning Board. For the appeal, he sought a reference pursuant to s. 5 of the 1963 Act, in which he submitted that the annexe had been in existence when the premises had been bought by him and as such was not a new extension. He again supplied all relevant documentation, as well as architectural plans of the annexe. The respondent Board refused the applicant's appeal on the ground that the retention of the roof and wall would be contrary to the proper planning and development of the area. It also held that the annexe did not constitute an exempted development. As indicated, Barron J granted the applicant judicial review of the Board's decision.

He began by stating a fundamental principle of judicial review, namely that it was no function of the court in such proceedings to determine the merits of the application. However, in the instant case, he noted that it had never been suggested to the applicant that the matter was being determined on the basis that his averments of fact were simply not accepted or that the real issue was the extent of the annexe and when it had been built. Thus, the applicant had not been put on notice of the real reason why permission was being refused. He stated that it had not been made clear to the applicant that what was being alleged against him was that he himself had built the annexe, and that he had not merely altered a roof and wall. Because of the approach taken by the planning authority and the respondent Board, Barron J held that the real issue between the parties had never been fully investigated and, as a result, the applicant had been deprived of the opportunity to prevent himself being found, in effect, guilty of dishonesty. In the circumstances, Barron J concluded that the applicant was entitled to have the particular issues of fact upon which his applications had been refused determined before the respondent Board and he granted relief on that basis.

Judicial review: leave to apply In *McNamara v An Bord Pleanála* [1995] 2 ILRM 125, Carroll J applied the principles laid down by the Supreme Court in *Scott v An Bord Pleanála* [1995] 1 ILRM 424 (1994 Review, 352) concerning the need to seek leave to apply for judicial review under the Local Government (Planning and Development) Act 1992 when challenging the granting of planning permission. She considered that the grounds put forward must be reasonable, arguable and weighty and must not be trivial or tenuous. In the instant case, Carroll J held that the applicant had made out 'substantial' grounds as required by the 1992 Act. The substantive grounds raised were rejected in the High Court by Barr J: see *McNamara v An Bord Pleanála (No 2)*, High Court, May 10, 1996 and *McNamara v An Bord Pleanála (No 3)*, High Court, July 31, 1996, which we will discuss in the 1996 Review. In *Keane v An Bord Pleanála*, High Court, June 20, 1995, Murphy J followed the approach taken by Carroll J in *McNamara*, holding that again substantial grounds had been made out. In this case, he later concluded that the applicants had made out their substantive case, a view upheld by the Supreme Court: *Keane v An Bord Pleanála (No. 2)*, High Court, October 4, 1995; Supreme Court, July 18, 1996: see the discussion below, 378.

Material change of user In *Lee and O'Flynn v O'Riordan and Ors*, High Court, February 10, 1995, O'Hanlon J held that a material change of user had occurred in the following circumstances.

The applicants sought an order restraining the respondents from using a quarry for the extraction of limestone rock. The respondents conceded that an application for planning permission had not been made at any time since the coming into operation of the Local Government (Planning and Development) Act 1963 but contended that the activity was an 'exempted development' within the meaning of the 1963 Act as quarrying had already commenced prior to the 'appointed day' under the Act, October 1, 1964. The quarry had been worked as a sand and gravel pit from the pre-1964 period to the late 1970s. Sand and gravel extraction process continued until the mid-1970s when the supply appeared to have been worked out. Thereafter a manufacturing process using imported materials was carried out but the operation closed down completely in 1979. The applicants claimed that the site then fell into disuse and that no material was quarried from the site for a period of over ten years until the respondents began to extract limestone from the quarry in March 1994. Expert evidence was adduced on the applicants' behalf to the effect that the extraction of limestone was in nature and form an entirely different exercise from the extraction of sand and gravel and involved a fundamental change in the nature of the use of the site which could not be regarded as a logical or natural extension of the previous use. Evidence was given on the respondents' behalf by a number of people who worked in the quarry to the effect that the nature of the work on the site in 1994 was essentially the same as that which had been carried out there previously but with bigger and more machines and that such activity had been carried out on the site over the previous 10 years. O'Hanlon J granted the injunction sought against the respondents.

He was of the view that there had been an abandonment of the quarry for a 12-year period from 1980 to 1992 with no real evidence of an intent on the part of the owners to make any further use of it. He took the view that the purchase price of the site seemed to be indicative of the sale of a worked out pit. He held that the quarrying of the limestone rock deposits which lay below the sand and gravel was undertaken for the first time on any scale when the sale of the property to the first respondent had been completed in 1992. In his view, the scale of quarrying operations which had taken place since 1992 had far exceeded any expectations of the magnitude and potential impact they might have had on the environment and the quality of life of those living in the neighbourhood.

In considering whether the activity was an exempted development, O'Hanlon J referred to the judgment of Costello J in *Patterson v Murphy* [1978] ILRM 85 and of Barron J in *Galway County Council v Lackagh Rock Ltd* [1985] IR 120 in stating that he could take into account whether or not the scale of operations had so intensified as to render contemporary operations materially different from those carried on before the appointed day. He went on to note that, where a previous use of land had ceased for a considerable time with no evidence of resuming it at any particular time, the Court was entitled to find that the previous use had been abandoned so that when it resumed the resumption constituted a material change of use. He cited in support the decisions in *Hartley v Minister for Housing and Local Government* [1970] 1 QB 413 and *Dublin County Council v Tallaght Block Co. Ltd* [1985] ILRM 512.

In the instant case, he concluded that the respondents had embarked upon an enterprise which was materially different from any previously carried out upon the lands in question. Indeed, he opined that even if some extraction of limestone could be shown to have taken place prior to the 'appointed day', he would still have been driven to the conclusion that the post-1992 operations constituted a new development requiring planning permission because of the abandonment of all quarrying activity over a 12-year period between 1980 and 1992. In addition, the intensification was of such a character that it represented a complete departure from the previous operation of the gravel pit.

A similar approach was taken a month later by O'Hanlon J in *Dublin Corporation v Aircold Refrigeration and Ors*, High Court, March 8, 1995, where he also held that a material change of user had occurred in the following circumstances. The respondents occupied premises in a small cul-de-sac, zoned for residential purposes. From 1988, they began a light industry for the storage, manufacture and repair of freezer units. They had not applied for planning permission, believing that since the previous user had carried on a sand and gravel business from the premises prior to the 'appointed date' under the Local Government (Planning and Development) Act 1963, that is October 1, 1964, the user was an exempted development. The applicant sought an order restraining the respondents from unauthorised user of the dwelling and requiring removal of all plant in the area and reinstating the holding to its original condition. As indicated, O'Hanlon J held that there had been a material change of user and granted the relief sought.

Although he accepted that there had been no intensification of user from the previous occupier, O'Hanlon J relied on the decision in *Galway County Council v Lackagh Rock Ltd* [1985] IR 120, as he had done in the *Lee* case in holding that a material change of use had occurred when the use made by the present occupier was compared with the previous occupier.

Music festival: whether constituting development   In *MCD Management Services Ltd v Kildare County Council* [1995] 2 ILRM 532, Laffoy J held that a music festival constituted a development requiring planning permission. The decision arose against rather involved circumstances. The applicant wished to hold a music festival, entitled "Féile '95", at the Mondello motor racing circuit in Kildare, and was of the view that specific planning permission for the festival was not required as such permission was implied in arrangements already put in place by the racing circuit's owner. The owner of the circuit had originally obtained planning permission for the motor race track in 1967. In February 1992, further to an application by the owner, the respondent Council, the relevant planning authority, had granted retention planning permission to the owner subject to a number of conditions. One of these was that any alternative uses to the site, including concerts, any retail sales, or markets of any kind should be the subject of prior planning permission being obtained in each case. The owner appealed to An Bord Pleanála against this condition. Their arguments were set out in an appeal letter, in which they contended that while the condition referred to the original 1967 planning permission, it was more restrictive in its wording, and they requested that wider definitions as contained in the 1967 permission be accepted as being applicable. They also asked that the condition be varied to allow a certain number of retail markets and concerts to be held subject to such conditions as may seem fair and reasonable. The Board directed in October 1994 that the Council remove the condition completely from the 1992 planning permission. The Board recited the fact that it had made this order in exercise of the powers conferred on it by s.15(1) of the Local Government (Planning and Development) Act 1992.

It was on the basis of the Planning Board's 1994 decision that the applicant believed that there was no planning law impediment to the holding of the music festival at the racing circuit. Having commenced preparations, the applicant appraised the Council of their intentions to hold the festival by letter in April 1994. The Council contended that the applicant required specific planning permission to stage the festival. In May 1995, the Council issued a warning notice pursuant to s.26 of the Local Government (Planning and Development) Act 1976 requiring that the applicant cease any preparations for a music festival. The applicant then obtained leave to seek judicial review of the Council's actions. The Council replied by seeking an order of prohibition. Laffoy J held in the Council's favour.

She held that the Council's 1992 decision continued to subsist subject to such variation of the conditions as the Planning Board had directed in October 1994. She also considered that the application on which the Board had adjudicated was that which had been made to the Council, and as such, the appeal document was not part of this application. However, she also stated that even if the letter of appeal could be called in aid in the interpretation of the determination of the Board, she was unable to reach the conclusion suggested by applicant as to the construction of the 1992 permission following the removal of the condition in October 1994.

She considered that reading the order of the Board by reference to the appeal letter alone did not raise any clear inference as to the intentions of the Board in deleting the condition, and that it certainly did not raise the inference suggested by the applicant or evince any intention on the part of the Board to authorise the use of the site for an event such as "Féile '95". In her view, the Board had intended to remove the condition imposed by the Council in 1992 but not the user limitation which existed prior to the imposition of the condition in the 1967 permission. In those circumstances, she felt it was unnecessary to comment on the submission by the Council that the Board would have been acting *ultra vires* had it purported to do what had been submitted by the applicant.

Ultimately, Laffoy J concluded that the staging of "Féile '95" at the motor racing circuit was not permitted by the 1992 permission and that it would constitute a development which was not exempt under the 1963 Act.

While the decision thus led to the cancellation of the festival at the racing track, we note here that permission was subsequently granted for the holding of the festival at an indoor venue in Dublin, the Point Depot.

Navigational aid system In *Keane v An Bord Pleanála (No. 2)*, High Court, October 4, 1995; Supreme Court, July 18, 1996, Murphy J held that the Commissioners of Irish Lights were not empowered to seek planning permission for the erection of a particular type of navigational aid system. The Commissioners had applied to Clare County Council for planning permission to erect a navigational aid, including a 750ft high radio mast, at Feeard Cross in County Clare. The navigational aid, known as the Loran-C system, uses electromagnetic impulses to allow positions to be fixed. The application was refused by the Council but, on appeal, the respondent Planning Board granted the permission sought. The High Court granted leave to the applicant to apply for judicial review of the decision to grant permission: of R2 to construct: *Keane v An Bord Pleanála*, High Court, June 20, 1995, referred to above, 374.

Ultimately, the case turned on whether the Loran-C system came within the powers granted to the Commissioners under the Merchant Shipping Act 1894. S.638 of the 1894 Act empowers the Commissioners to erect or place any 'lighthouse, buoy or beacon.' S. 742 of the 1894 Act provides that '"lighthouse" shall in addition to the ordinary meaning of the word include any floating and other light exhibited for the guidance of ships, and also any sirens and any other descriptions of fog signals, and also any addition to a lighthouse of any improved light, or any siren, or any description of fog signal' and that '"buoys and beacons" includes all other marks and signs of the sea'. Thus, the question was whether the Loran-C was a 'lighthouse, buoy or beacon' within the 1894 Act. Murphy J held that it did not, a view upheld by the Supreme Court.

Murphy J began his judgment by noting that the powers of a corporation created by a statute are limited and circumscribed by the statutes which regulate it, and extend no further than is expressly stated therein or is necessarily and properly required for carrying into effect the purposes of incorporation or may be fairly regarded as incidental to or consequential upon those things which the legislature has authorised. Thus, he pointed out, what the statute does not expressly or impliedly authorise is to be taken to be prohibited.

The issue in the instant case was whether the Loran-C system came within the express or implied ambit of the 1894 Act. Since the system had not been invented when the 1894 Act had been enacted, this raised a particular problem of statutory interpretation, namely whether the 1894 Act could be given an updated meaning. Murphy J referred to a number of cases in this area, including *Attorney General v Edison Telephone Co.* (1886) 6 QBD 244, *Grant v South Western & County Properties Ltd* [1975] Ch 185, *McCarthy v O'Flynn* [1979] IR 127, *Derby v Weldon* [1991] 1 WLR 652 and *Lake Macquarie Shire Council v. Aberdare County Council* (1969) 123 CLR 327. From these, he commented:

> I have no difficulty in accepting the desirability and, in general, the necessity for giving to legislation and 'updating construction'. Where terminology used in legislation is wide enough to capture a subsequent invention, there is no reason to exclude it from the ambit of the legislation. But a distinction must be made between giving an updated construction to the general scheme of the legislation and altering the meaning of particular words used therein.

In the case of the 1894 Act, he was of the view that it would have been possible to have defined 'lighthouse' in the 1894 Act as anticipating the use of electromagnetic impulses as a navigational aid system, but this had not been done in the instant case. Instead, the powers conferred by the 1894 Act were more narrow in scope. On this basis, he concluded that the general scheme of the Act and more particularly the range of powers and duties expressly or implicitly conferred on the Commissioners did not permit them to engage in the construction, maintenance or operation of the Loran-C system. As indicated, this view was ultimately upheld by the Supreme Court in 1996, and we will return to that decision in the 1996 Review.

Proper planning and development In *Child v Wicklow County Council and Wicklow County Manager*, High Court, January 20, 1995, the plaintiffs had applied for planning permission for the erection of a house. The elected members of the respondent Council directed the County Manager to grant permission, notwithstanding advice form various officials recommending that they refuse permission. The County Manager declined to grant the permission. Despite this, the plaintiffs went ahead with building the house and proceedings were then instituted by the Council in which the High Court (Lardner J) granted an injunction restraining the plaintiffs from continuing to erect the house. The plaintiffs then applied for retention planning permission, but were refused. The plaintiffs then instituted the instant proceedings, claiming that the County Manager's decision refusing permission was invalid as he had failed to carry out the instructions of the elected members and a declaration that the resolution of the elected members was valid. Costello J declined to grant the relief sought.

He dealt first of all with a preliminary issue concerning the application of the Local Government (Planning and Development) Act 1992, which introduced the requirement that planning decisions may only be challenged by way of judicial review (see the 1992 Review, 449). The Council had contended that the 1992 Act rendered the instant proceedings invalid. However, Costello J considered that to apply the 1992 Act in the instant case would operate to produce an unconstitutional result. He held that the plaintiffs had a proprietary right to challenge the Council's decision. As the decision in this case had been made before the coming into force of the 1992 Act, they would be deprived of their right to apply to the court by way of plenary summons if it was held to have such retrospective effect. Thus, he concluded that the 1992 Act should be construed as having prospective effect only. For further consideration of retrospection, see *McKone Estates Ltd v Dublin County Council* [1995] 2 ILRM 283, 369-70, above.

Turning to the substantive issues raised, Costello J applied the principles in *Flanagan v Galway City & County Manager* [1990] 2 IR 66 (1989 Review, 330-1), *Griffin v Galway City & County Manager*, High Court, October 31, 1990 (1990 Review, 417- 8) and *Kenny Homes Ltd v Galway City & County Manager*, High Court, April 3, 1992 (1992 Review, 458-9). He accepted that the elected members of the Council were not bound by the advice of the officials and they were free not to take such advice, but that there had to be some basis for refusing to accept it. In the instant case, the elected members had acted *ultra vires* since, by not following the advice given, they had failed to take into account the proper planning and development of their functional area, contrary to the Local Government (Planning and Development) Act 1963. In addition, they had acted unreasonably in failing to take into account the fact that previous applications for permission for the development of the site had been refused. He thus refused the relief sought by the plaintiffs. However, he granted a stay on the previous order restraining further work pending an application for permission to retain the structure if such application was brought within three months of his decision.

RATING (VALUATION)

Machinery   In *Irish Refining Plc v Commissioner of Valuation* [1995] 2 ILRM 223, Geoghegan J held that not all aspects of the processes of unloading to an oil refinery are exempt from rates. In the Circuit Court, it had been held that a continuing manufacturing process occurred at the applicant's refinery at Whitegate, Co Cork, from the moment crude oil was unloaded from oil tankers to the time it lay in the holding tanks so that, taken as a whole, all the relevant items involved in the process were 'machinery' within the meaning of s. 7 of the Annual Revision of Rateable Property (Ireland) Amendment Act 1860 and were therefore exempt from rating. The Commissioner of Valuation appealed by way of case stated from that decision and argued that the court should not give a strained interpretation to the wording of s. 7 of the 1860 Act to the extent that portions of the plant would be held to be machines which would not in ordinary parlance be so described. As indicated, Geoghegan J accepted this view.

He referred to a number of recent authorities on the point, including *Pfizer Chemical Corp v Commissioner of Valuation*, High Court, May 9, 1989; Supreme Court, April 7, 1992 (1992 Review 467-8) and *Siúicre Éireann Cpt v Commissioner of Valuation* [1992] ILRM 682 (1992 Review, 467-8). He stated that merely because the tanks or receptacles were fitted with equipment which enabled some activity to take place within them did not necessarily alter their character and convert them into machines. He accepted that, while the Circuit Court judge had been entitled to take the view that the plant could not be looked at in isolation, he had gone too far in including items as machines which should not have been included. Finally, Geoghegan J applied the view in the *Pfizer* case that the court had power to amend the Valuation List so as to have property included in the 'Miscellaneous' column provided for in the List.

REGIONAL AUTHORITIES

The Local Government Act 1991 (Regional Authorities) (Establishment Order) 1993 (Amendment) Order 1995 (SI No. 208 of 1995) amended the Local Government Act 1991 (Regional Authorities) (Establishment) Order 1993 (1993 Review, 435). The 1995 Order came into effect on July 28, 1995.

SERVICE CHARGES

Disconnection of water supply The Local Government (Delimitation of Water Supply Disconnection Powers) Act 1995 limits the powers of sanitary authorities to disconnect domestic water supplies for non-payment of service charges. It provides for the procedures to be adopted in demanding payment and provides that disconnection can only be authorised by order of the

District Court. It should be seen against the continuing public objections to certain aspects of local authority funding, including the imposition of such charges and was enacted as part of the programme of government agreed by the government formed in December 1994. The 1995 Act came into force on July 18, 1995 on its signature by the President.

Practice and Procedure

AMENDMENT OF PLEADINGS

Amendment of pleadings 'in such manner and on such terms as may be just' O.28, r.1 of the RSC 1986 provides that the court may, at any stage in the proceedings, allow either party to amend his pleading 'in such manner and on such terms as may be just'. The power to amend pleadings in accordance with this provision has been considered on a number of occasions this year. In *Palamos Properties Ltd v Brooks*, High Court, January 11, 1995 Flood J considered a number of relevant authorities and stated that in his view they supported the following proposition:

> That within the fact underlying the claim before the court there must be some evidence from which an inference can be reasonably be drawn as to why the plea which is sought to be introduced by way of amendment was not put in the original defence or express evidence given to explain the failure in a manner which renders the omission broadly excusable if not actually justifiable.

This statement was quoted with approval by Kinlen J in *Bell v Pederson* [1996] 1 ILRM 290 who stated that the main consideration in a case where an application is made to amend pleadings is to do justice between the parties and it was for this reason that O.28, r.1 was drafted in such wide terms. Further consideration was given to the rule by Keane J in *Krops v Irish Forestry Board* [1995] 2 ILRM 290. The plaintiff sought to amend his statement of claim which as originally delivered had pleaded that a tree which had fallen onto his car, killing his wife, had done so as a result of negligence, breach of duty and breach of statutory duty so as to include the words 'and nuisance'. Keane J allowed the amendment sought and considered the circumstances in which a court will permit amendments to be made under the terms of O.28, r.1 of the RSC by virtue of which he stated pleadings carry with them the potential of being amended by the court 'in such manner and on such terms as may be just'. Where as in the case before him, an amendment, if allowed, will not in any way prejudice or embarrass the defendant by making new allegations as to facts, no injustice will be done by permitting the amendment. Keane J added that where as in this case, the plaintiff sought to add a new cause of action arising out of the same, or substantially the same facts, there was no reason why the court should be precluded from permitting such an amendment. The Supreme Court subsequently upheld the findings of Keane J and dismissed the appeal.

CONSOLIDATION OF ACTIONS

Comerford v Greencore plc, High Court, January 24, 1995 involved a motion to consolidate four connected sets of High Court proceedings arising from the dismissal of the plaintiff as chief executive of the defendant State company, formerly Irish Sugar Ltd. The plaintiff in the first case was also plaintiff in the fourth and was one of the defendants in the second action. Owing to the similarity of the cases an application was made to the court to consolidate the first three actions, or else have them heard by the same judge at the same time and for the trial of the first three actions to commence after the fourth. Costello J granted the principal reliefs sought. He ordered that the first three actions would not be consolidated, but would be beard by the same judge simultaneously, or as the trial judge might direct. He also directed that the judge assigned to hear the first three actions should hear the fourth action. He considered that the parties would not suffer any prejudice if the fourth action was heard first as. Costello J fixed dates for the four actions and he granted liberty to the defendant company to bring a motion for directions with regard to the first three actions before the judge assigned to hear them. We note here that that the actions were subsequently settled.

COSTS

Complexity of case: personal injuries assessment   In *Best v Wellcome Foundation Ltd and Ors (No. 3)* [1996] 1 ILRM 34, Barron J reduced the fees agreed in connection with the hearing concerning the assessment of damages in this case, *Best v Wellcome Foundation Ltd and Ors* [1993] 3 IR 421; [1992] ILRM 609 (1992 Review, 610-11), in which the plaintiff had claimed damages for injuries received as a result of the negligence of the defendants. It will be recalled that, the claim had been dismissed in the High Court in 1991, but in 1992 the Supreme Court had reversed the High Court and held the first defendant liable, remitting the assessment of damages to the High Court. In *Best v Wellcome Foundation Ltd and Ors (No. 2)* [1995] 1 ILRM 554, Murphy J dealt with whether interest arose on the award of costs in the substantive proceedings: see below.

In the judgment delivered by Barron J in *Best (No. 3)*, the relevant facts were that the case had settled for £2.75 million plus costs on the third day of what was expected to have been a lengthy hearing in the High Court on the assessment of damages. The Bill of Costs for the damages hearing sought a solicitor's instructions fee of £440,000 for work since June 1992. For work before that date, that is for the hearings on liability in the High Court and Supreme Court, the previous Bill of Costs quoted an instruction fee of £400,000 which was reduced to £275,000 by agreement. On taxation, the Taxing Master reduced the instructions fee for the damages hearing to £400,000 while not accepting the defendant's submission that allowance should be made for work already done on the issue of damages before June 1992 or that the solicitor's task was eased in relation to the assessment of damages as he had acted in the main action. Counsel's fees for the damages hearing were allowed as marked, being £52,500 for each of two senior counsel and £35,000 for junior counsel. On appeal to the High Court, four aspects of the taxation were in contention: the plaintiff's solicitor's instruction fee, counsel's brief fee, professional fees for accommodation for the plaintiff, and the fee for a cost accountant for the preparation of the plaintiff's bill of costs.

On the general approach to the case, Barron J held that while the facts giving rise to the substantive action were unique and the case was one of extreme difficulty, the substance of the assessment of damages in a personal injuries action was the nature of the injury sustained. The real difficulty in this case was the presentation of the consequences of the injuries and to show what those meant in financial terms. In his view, the plaintiff's solicitor had over-emphasised the complexity and uniqueness of the matters with which he bad to deal and his input in these matters. He noted that there could be personal injury cases where the evidence on the question of damages would be more complex and more difficult to assess than the evidence relating to liability, thus meriting a higher fee. Where the issues of liability and damages were split, however, there was still only one action and this should not be overlooked on the taxation of the costs of the issue as to damages. The provisions of O.99, r.37(22)(ii) of the Rules of the Superior Courts 1986 set out the circumstances to which the Taxing Master had to have regard; Barron J considered that, ultimately, there were three criteria on which the fee was determined: any special expertise of the solicitor, the amount of work done and the degree of responsibility borne. In the instant case, the size of the settlement had over-influenced the costs accountants; there was no justification for adding a percentage of the basic fee for various elements in the case. He accepted that O.99 provided for the matters to be taken into account and while there could be cases where it can be assessed that the volume of work was increased by a particular proportion by virtue of some aspect of a case, generally, however, what had to be considered was the amount of work which the additional factor involved and the proper fee arrived at accordingly. He held that comparison with an appropriate case was ultimately the correct approach to assess the instructions fee, although the fee had to be one which took into account the differences between any two cases.

Barron J stated that the jurisdiction of the court was to determine the appropriate fee, and earlier cases in which it was laid down that the court's function was dependent upon an error in principle having been made by the Taxing Master were no longer authoritative. It was to be regretted, he said, that the court's view of the appropriate fee was at considerable variance with that determined by the Taxing Master. In the instant case, he felt that an instructions fee of £75,000 was appropriate.

As regards counsel's fee, what had to be considered was what the hypothetical counsel competent to do the case and not being in a position to expect a special or fashionable fee would be prepared to accept as his brief fee. In this respect, he followed the principles applied by Hamilton J (as he then was) in *Kelly v. Breen* [1978] ILRM 63. Barron J held that it was not the case that, once fees had been marked by agreement between solicitor and counsel, they had to be allowed by the Taxing Master or on appeal by the court. The fees sought should be allowed unless no solicitor acting reasonably carefully and reasonably prudently based on his experience in the course of his practice would have agreed to such fees, as discussed in *Crotty v An Taoiseach (No. 2)* [1990] ILRM 617 (1989 Review, 346-7) and *Smyth and Ors v Tunney and Ors* [1993] 1 IR 451 (1991 Review, 329-30). Barron J was of the view that no solicitor acting reasonably carefully and prudently based on his experience in the course of his practice would have agreed to counsel's fee here. He held that the appropriate fee would be 25,000 guineas for senior counsel and the same proportion of such fee as the proportion marked for junior counsel.

As to the fee sought by the cost accountant for drawing the bill of costs, since Appendix W, item 30 of the Rules of the Superior Courts 1986 provided for the drawing and engrossing of a bill of costs, the Taxing Master had been wrong to allow this under O.99, r.12(2)(a). If allowed at all, Barron J held that it should have been allowed under O.99, r.12(2)(b). In his view, there was nothing unusual in the employment of a cost accountant. A solicitor had an option between preparing his own bills, employing a cost accountant within his own office, or going to an outside cost accountant. Applying the approach in *O'Sullivan v Hughes* [1986] ILRM 555 and *In re Castle Brand Ltd* [1990] ILRM 97 (1989 Review, 64-5), Barron J held that the choice was the solicitor's own and the other party's liability could not be dependent on how he made that choice considered. However, in the instant case, since the costs of the cost accountant had already been given under the solicitor's scheduled fees it was not possible to give them again on a different basis. As there was no ground for allowing this item, Barron J ordered that it be deleted.

Complexity of case: personal injuries claim   In *Connolly v Kelly*, High Court, June 15, 1995, Costello P considered that the Taxing Master had erred in determining some aspects of the fees settled in a difficult personal injuries claim, while upholding others. The plaintiff had been employed by the defendant as a farm labourer between 1980 and 1986 and claimed that in the course of this employment he had inhaled toxic and poisonous chemical sprays which damaged his lungs. Although the defendant denied liability, the action was settled for £25,000. The plaintiff's legal costs amounted to £27,081.51. The Taxing Master had concluded that the senior brief fee claimed of £1,250 was too much and awarded £950 which he remarked was £200 more than he would usually allow for actions which settled for £25,000. This resulted in a junior counsel fee of £633.83. Both parties submitted that the wrong principle had been applied when assessing these fees at taxation. The Taxing Master also considered the instruction fee of £8,000 which the plaintiff's solicitor had charged should be reduced to £6,250. The defendant had submitted that the usual allowance for such a fee in a case settled for £25,000 would be £3,250. With regard to the engineer's fee the Taxing Master considered the initial claim of £9,032.23 to be excessive and reduced it to £4,292.23. On appeal, Costello P considered that the Taxing Master had erred in important respects in approach, but upheld the fees arrived at for the solicitor and counsel. However, he remitted the question of the fees charged by a chemical engineer retained by the plaintiff.

As to the general approach to counsel's fees, he took the view that the Taxing Master should have adopted the standard of the practising solicitor who was reasonably careful and reasonably prudent and that he should not purport to prescribe the standards which he required solicitors to adopt. Costello P followed the Supreme Court decision in *The State (Gallagher, Shatter & Co.) v de Valera* [1991] 2 IR 198 (1990 Review, 430-31) in this respect. Turning to the approach to a solicitor's fee, he held, in accordance with the decision of Murphy J in *Smyth and Ors v Tunney and Ors (No. 2)* [1993] 1 IR 541 (1991 Review, 329-30), that the basis for the taxation of an instructions fee was fundamentally different to that for counsel's fee in that the Taxing Master's task was to determine the appropriate fee in all the circumstances of the case.

As to the instant case, Costello P opined that, even if the Taxing Master did not err in principle when taxing a fee, the court still had a function to consider whether the fee determined by him was an appropriate one. He accepted the plaintiff's argument that this had been a particularly difficult case which involved a considerable amount of care and attention as well as professional knowledge and skill of a high order. Therefore the court confirmed the figure arrived at by the Taxing Master for the instructions fee.

As to the fee for the chemical engineer, he held that such a person was not qualified to express in court an opinion that the toxic nature of chemicals used caused lung damage. Unless it was shown that the witness had the necessary medical qualifications to express it, this opinion evidence would be inadmissible. Thus when taxing on a party and party basis, costs were to be allowed which were necessary and proper for the attainment of justice or for enforcing or defending the rights of the party whose costs were being taxed. This meant that the test to be applied was an objective one and whether a report was prepared on counsel's instructions or not was not conclusive. He held that the Taxing Master should determine what was a reasonable professional fee for the consultant engineer for describing the operations which the plaintiff was required to perform in his employment with the defendant and for expressing an opinion on the nature of the protection to be taken to avoid the inhalation of toxic sprays. He concluded that such a determination could be made by reference to what a prudent solicitor would pay for such professional services.

Constitutional case   In *T.F. v Ireland and Ors (No. 2)*, Supreme Court, 27 July 1995 the Court awarded the plaintiff the costs of his unsuccessful challenge to certain provisions of the Judicial Separation and Family Law Reform Act 1989: see *T.F. v Ireland and Ors* [1995] 2 ILRM 321 in the Family Law chapter, 286, above. The High Court had declined to make any order as to costs and the plaintiff had appealed to the Supreme Court against this order. The Attorney General argued that the plaintiff had failed in his challenge to the constitutionality of the relevant provisions and so the costs should be allowed to the successful party. The Court exercised its discretion by awarding the costs of the appeal to the plaintiff against the Attorney General.

The Court noted that the question of the costs of any proceedings before the court was a matter for the discretion of the judge hearing and determining such matter. In the instant case, the Court was satisfied that the trial judge had exercised his discretion in the matter judicially and in a proper manner and there were no grounds for interfering with the order made by him in respect of the proceedings before him. However, the Court had a similar discretion with regard to the costs of the proceedings before it. It acknowledged that there was no doubt but that the appeal before the Court involved issues of considerable public importance and that it was desirable that a decision on the issues involved be reached as early as possible. It was also clear that the Attorney General regarded this case as a test case and was anxious that the matter be disposed of as quickly as possible. While the Court accepted that the case was of considerable importance to the parties involved, it was also important to the parties involved in at least 3,000 cases in which orders had already been made under the 1989 Act. On that basis, the Court allowed the plaintiff his costs of the Supreme Court hearing.

Motion to set aside In *Voluntary Purchasing Groups Inc v Insurco Ltd and Anor* [1995] 2 ILRM 145, McCracken J awarded certain applicants the costs of their motion to set aside an order requiring them to be examined in the High Court in connection with proceedings in the United States against the following background. The plaintiff had obtained a judgment in default against the defendants in a United States court. In January 1994, the Irish High Court, on foot of an application by the United States court, made an *ex parte* order under the Foreign Tribunals Evidence Act 1856 requiring the defendants and KPMG Stokes Kennedy Crowley, a firm of accountants, to attend before the Examiner of the High Court to give evidence relating to the execution of the default judgment. The defendants and the firm applied to the High Court to have the examination orders set aside, arguing, *inter alia*, that an appeal against the default judgment was, at that time, pending before the United States court. In fact, the default judgment was set aside, thus rendering moot the examination of the parties by the Examiner.

McCracken J stated that once the examination order had been made, albeit at the request of the United States court, any examination carried out would have been by lawyers representing the plaintiff. Therefore, although in form the application had been made by the United States court, in reality it was an application by or for the benefit of the plaintiff. He was of the view that, quite apart from the provisions of any rule of court or of statute, there was an inherent jurisdiction in the courts, in the absence of an express statutory provision to the contrary, to set aside an order made *ex parte* on the application of any party affected by that such an order. In the interests of justice, he held that it was essential that an *ex parte* order be capable of being reviewed and an opportunity given to the parties affected by it to present their side of the case or to correct errors in the original evidence or submissions before the court. He also pointed that that the argument put forward by the plaintiff, namely that the defendants and the firm of accountants should have made their objections, if any, to the Examiner at the time of the examination, was one that had been rejected by Woolf LJ (as he then was), in *Boeing Co. v PPG Industries Inc* [1988] 3 All ER 839. Finally, McCracken J stated that, since the plaintiff had chosen to seek an order at a time when an appeal was pending before the United States court, it must suffer the consequences if that appeal proves to be successful. As indicated, he concluded that the Court's discretion to award costs should be exercised in favour of the defendants and the firm of accountants.

Security for costs The onus of proof under s. 390 of the Companies Act 1963 S. 390 of the Companies Act 1963 provides that where a limited company is a plaintiff in any action, and there is evidence that such company is unlikely to be able to pay the costs of a successful defendant, security may be required to be given for the costs and the proceedings may be stayed until this is given. This section was interpreted by Kingsmill Moore J in *Peppard & Co. Ltd v Bogoff* [1962] IR 180 to mean that it was not mandatory to order security in every case where the plaintiff company appeared to be unable to pay the costs of a successful defendant and that the court retained a discretion which might be exercised in special circumstances. However, as the Supreme Court made clear in its decision in *Jack O'Toole v MacEoin Kelly Associates* [1986] IR 277, the onus lies on the plaintiff to establish the special circumstances which would justify the refusal of such an order.

The manner in which the onus of proof shifts was well explained recently by Morris J in *Beauross v Kennedy*, High Court, October 18, 1995. In refusing the relief sought by the defendant under s. 390, Morris J stated that the onus lies on the party seeking security for costs to establish that he has a *prima facie* defence to the claim and that there is reason to believe that the plaintiff will not be able to pay his costs if the defence succeeds. If this is established the onus shifts to the plaintiff to show that there are special circumstances justifying the court in exercising its discretion not to make the order e.g. that the plaintiff's inability to pay the costs flows from the wrong of the party seeking the order — as was established in this instance — or that there has been delay on the part of that party.

Plaintiffs outside the jurisdiction Traditionally a order for security for costs was sought where the plaintiff resided outside the jurisdiction. As Murphy J recently acknowledged in *Proetta v Neil* [1996] 1 ILRM 457, while O.29, r.1 of the RSC 1986 does not express in positive terms that a foreign resident may be required to give security for costs it does proceed on the footing that such is the case. This point is reflected in the following principle laid down by Finlay P in *Collins v Doyle* [1982] ILRM 495, namely that: '*Prima facie* a defendant establishing a *prima facie* defence to a claim made by a plaintiff residing outside the jurisdiction has a right to an order for security for costs', although he acknowledged that this is not an absolute right and that the court must exercise a discretion based on the facts of each case. The question of whether an individual who is resident outside the jurisdiction but within the EU can be ordered to give security for costs on the basis of these principles has been considered in three recent High Court decisions.

In all likelihood this is largely due to the decision of the European Court of Justice in *Mund & Fester v Hatrex International Transport* (Case C-398/92) [1994] ECR-1467 in which the court re-appraised the question of whether such forms of indirect discrimination based on grounds of nationality could be justified in the light of current practice in relation to enforcement of judgments. The first opportunity for the High Court to re-assess the effect of O.29 on persons not resident within the jurisdiction in the light of the judgment of the European Court of Justice in *Mund & Fester* arose in *Maher v Phelan* [1996] 1 ILRM 359. The plaintiff, who was resident in England, argued that the defendant should not succeed in obtaining an order for security for costs, on the basis that the law in this area had 'radically changed' since the enactment of the Jurisdiction of Court and Enforcement of Judgments (European Communities) Act 1988. Carroll J considered the findings and conclusions of the European Court of Justice in *Mund & Fester* which she said 'put the matter beyond doubt' and held that as an individual litigant who is resident in Ireland cannot be ordered to provide security for costs, a plaintiff resident outside Ireland but within the EU should not be so ordered. Carroll J said that even if she were wrong in that view, she would not in any event grant an order as the rationale for granting one no longer exists as far as EU countries are concerned in which judgments are enforceable with comparative ease under the Brussels Convention and the Jurisdiction of Courts and Enforcement of Judgments (European Communities) Act 1988. She concluded that even without reference to the question of discrimination on grounds of nationality, the plaintiff was not impecunious and had assets within as well as outside the jurisdiction.

The decision of the European Court of Justice in *Mund & Fester* was also relied on by Murphy J in refusing an order for security for costs against a plaintiff, resident outside the jurisdiction, but within the EU in *Proetta v Neil* [1996] 1 ILRM 457. The proceedings between the parties arose out of a statement made by the defendant on a television programme broadcast by RTE which the plaintiff, who is a Spanish national residing in Gibraltar, claimed was defamatory of her. The plaintiff sought damages for libel and the defendant brought an application for security for costs on a full indemnity basis. Murphy J held that the conclusion reached in the *Mund & Fester* case was applicable to the facts before him although he added that were it not for the provisions of the Treaty of Rome, he would in the exercise of his discretion on the basis of the information before him have ordered the plaintiff to provide security for costs.

Taxation of costs: interest on award   In *Best v Wellcome Foundation Ltd and Ors (No. 2)* [1995] 1 ILRM 554 Murphy J considered the question whether interest arose on an order for costs from the time of the order made in the plaintiff's favour or only from the date when costs were ascet on award In *Best v Wellcome Foundation Ltd and Ors (No. 2)* [1995] 1 ILRM 554 Murphy J considered the question whether interest arose on an order for costs from the time of the order made in the plaintiff's favour or only from the date when costs were ascertained It will be recalled that, in *Best v Wellcome*

Foundation Ltd and Ors [1993] 3 IR 421; [1992] ILRM 609 (1992 Review, 610-11) the plaintiff had claimed damages for injuries received as a result of the negligence of the defendants. The claim had been dismissed in the High Court in 1991, but in 1992 the Supreme Court had reversed the High Court and held the first defendant liable. The Supreme Court order directed that the plaintiff recover against the defendant such sum for damages as would be assessed by the High Court. This matter was later settled when the parties agreed that damages of £2.75m would be paid to the plaintiff. As regards costs, the Supreme Court order provided that the plaintiff should recover his costs of the action in the High Court and of the appeal 'when taxed and ascertained.' The net amount of the plaintiff's High Court costs in the settled hearing for damages were the subject of a reference to the Taxing Master and the High Court: see *Best v Wellcome Foundation Ltd and Ors (No. 3)* [1996] 1 ILRM 34, discussed above.

The issue in the instant case before Murphy J was whether the sums claimed or agreed in respect of costs carried interest under the Courts Act 1981. The interest on the costs awarded concerning the High Court proceedings had been computed from January 1991, the date of the High Court decision, to the date of payment, January 1993. The interest on the costs awarded for the Supreme Court appeal was computed from June 1992, the date of the Court's decision to January 1993. The total amount claimed for interest was £172,148.92. The plaintiff claimed that interest was payable on the costs awarded pursuant to ss. 26 and 27 of the Debtors (Ireland) Act 1840 and O.42, r.15 of the Rules of the Superior Courts 1986 from the date of the High Court order and of the Supreme Court order respectively. The defendant argued that interest should only run from the date of taxation of the costs. Murphy J allowed the full amount claimed by the plaintiff.

Applying the principles laid down by the Supreme Court in *Cooke v Walsh (No. 2)* [1989] ILRM 322 (1988 Review, 322-3) and in his own judgment in *Hickey v Norwich Union Fire Insurance Ltd*, High Court, October 23, 1987 (1987 Review, xi), he held that where an order for costs was merely expressed as an order 'for costs', interest accrued from the date of the order and not from the date of the taxation, notwithstanding that the costs were of necessity unascertained until taxation. He did not consider that the addition of the words 'when taxed' or 'when taxed and ascertained' involved an element of futurity or imposed a condition precedent. In this respect, he distinguished the instant case from the circumstances in *K. v K.* [1977] 2 WLR 55 and those discussed by the Supreme Court in *Attorney General (McGarry) v Sligo County Council (No. 2)* [1989] ILRM 785 (1988 Review, 323).

Taxation of costs: re-submitted bill higher   In *Agritex Ltd v O'Driscoll* *and Ors* [1995] 2 ILRM 23, Lynch J held that the defendants, partners in a firm of solicitors, were precluded from submitting a higher bill of costs for taxation after they had initially submitted a bill of costs to the plaintiff. The defendants had initially furnished the plaintiff with a bill of costs in the sum of £15,730.28. After the plaintiff sought taxation, the High Court had ordered that the defendants furnish the plaintiff with a more particularised bill, suitable for submission to the taxing master. In compliance with this order, the defendants furnished the plaintiff with a new bill in the sum of £25,172.55. On reference to taxation, the plaintiff was granted an adjournment to apply to court for directions. As already indicated, Lynch J held that the defendants were precluded from presenting a bill in excess of the original.

Citing with approval the views of Budd J in *Whitney Moore & Keller v Shipping Finance Corp Ltd* [1964] IR 216 Lynch J emphasised that when dealing, as here, with mixed questions of law and fact, each case must be governed by its own facts. He accepted that the original bill had not been prepared in the manner required by O.99, r.29(5) of the Rules of the Superior Courts 1986. Nonetheless, he considered that it constituted a valid bill of costs in the sum of £15,730.28. In addition, he noted that the defendants had at no time suggested that further sums were due to them until they furnished the higher bill in 1993.

It is notable that Lynch J expressly described the right of a client to have a bill of costs taxed by the Taxing Master as an important protection of the public in a situation where almost invariably the client is in a dependent position *vis-à-vis* his solicitor. He commented that he was in no doubt that, if it were permissible for a solicitor to increase his fee upon being ordered to prepare a bill for submission to taxation, that would greatly inhibit the protection of citizens afforded by their entitlement to require taxation of costs.

COURTS AND COURT OFFICERS ACT 1995

The Courts and Court Officers Act 1995 was a long-awaited legislative response to calls for many years for substantial reform of the courts. Many elements of the 1995 Act may be traced to the 1990 *Report of the Fair Trade Commission on the Legal Profession* (1990 Review, 437-9). More immediately, however, the 1995 Act may owe its enactment to the political controversies surrounding the fall of the Fianna Fáil/Labour government in November 1994 and the formation of a Fine Gael/Labour/Democratic Left government in December 1994. Whatever the political background the 1995 Act contains welcome (in many cases overdue) reform. The many matters dealt with in the 1995 Act include: a significant increase in the number of

the judiciary in all the courts; an increase of three in the number of Supreme
Court judges and conferral on the Court of the power to sit in divisions; the
proposed transfer of the functions of the Court of Criminal Appeal to the
Supreme Court, with the consequent abolition of the Court of Criminal
Appeal; the establishment of a Judicial Appointments Advisory Board; the
first appointment of solicitors as judges of the Circuit Court; the introduction
of compulsory judicial training for new judicial appointees; the conferral of
additional powers on court officers, including the Master of the High Court
and the County Registrars; important changes in civil procedure aimed at
greater efficiency, including the exchange of reports in personal injuries
claims; and the abolition of the requirement that members of the Bar wear
wigs. All provisions of the 1995 Act, with one exception, came into effect
on December 15, 1995 on its signature by the President. The one exception
concerns the provisions of the Act providing for the abolition of the Court
of Criminal Appeal and the transfer of its functions to the Supreme Court.
This aspect of the Act requires a Commencement Order to come into effect.
It is anticipated that such an Order will be made only when the backlog of
civil claims in the Supreme Court existing at the time of the enactment of the
1995 Act has been dealt with. What follows is a discussion of the majority
of the provisions of the 1995 Act.

Increased judicial numbers   The 1995 Act provided for the appointment
of 18 additional judges in the different courts, the highest increase in a single
legislative sweep since the establishment of the present court system in 1924.
S. 6 of the 1995 Act (amending s. 1 of the Courts (Establishment and
Constitution) Act 1961) provided for three additional Supreme Court judges,
bringing the total to eight, including the Chief Justice. S. 9 provided for an
additional three High Court judges (initially two had been proposed, but a
third was added in the course of the Act's passage, based principally on the
unanimous recommendation of the Oireachtas Select Committee on Legislation and Security in this regard). This brought the total number of High
Court judges to 20, including the President of the High Court. S. 10 of the
Act provided for an additional seven Circuit Court judges, bringing the total
to 25, including the President of the Circuit Court. S. 11 provided for an
additional five judges of the District Court, bringing the total to 51, including
the President of the District Court. The 1995 Act thus brought the total
maximum complement of the judiciary to 104. We may note that three further
judicial positions in the Circuit Court were created by the Courts Act 1996,
bringing the total complement to 107. By contrast, the maximum permissible
number of permanent judges in the courts in 1924 was 50: see Byrne and
McCutcheon, *The Irish Legal System*, 3rd ed. (Butterworths, 1996), p.96.

Supreme Court sitting in divisions and Court of Criminal Appeal As already indicated, s. 7 of the 1995 Act (adding new sub-sections to s. 7 of the Courts (Supplemental Provisions) Act 1961) empowers the Supreme Court to sit in two or more divisions which may sit at the same time. Until the passage of the 1995 Act, the Supreme Court sat either in plenary session as a five-judge Court or else as a three-judge Court. The 1995 Act affirmed the existing arrangement that the Court must comprise five judges in cases involving the validity of any law having regard to the Constitution, but s. 7 of the 1995 Act changed the prior legislative arrangements for three-judge courts to read that, in any other case the Chief Justice, or in his or her absence the senior ordinary judge of the time being available, may direct that the Court will comprise a division of five or three judges only.

This significant innovation had two aims. First, it was intended to relieve the backlog of civil appeals in the Supreme Court list, the average waiting time in 1995 being over two years. Second, allied with the increased number of Supreme Court judges to eight, it reflected the proposed transfer to the Supreme Court of the functions of the Court of Criminal Appeal. The combination of these two measures replaced a previous proposal to retain the Court of Criminal Appeal and to create a Civil Court of Appeal which would have heard, for example, personal injuries appeals from the High Court, such cases comprising the bulk of cases which had led to the backlog of appeals to the Supreme Court. The proposal for a Civil Court of Appeal had been included in the ill-fated Courts and Court Officers Bill 1994, published in the dying days of the Fianna Fáil/Labour government. The proposal contained in the 1995 Act, namely, to combine the functions of the existing Court of Criminal Appeal with the suggested Civil Court of Appeal and to incorporate both within the jurisdiction of the Supreme Court apparently resulted from discussions between the Government and the judiciary during 1995 (458 *Dáil Debates*, col. 1756, 28 November 1995).

Abolition of Court of Criminal Appeal S. 4 of the 1995 provides for the abolition of the Court of Criminal Appeal and the transfer of its functions to the Supreme Court. S. 5 of the 1995 Act envisages a similar demise and transfer in respect of the Courts-Martial Appeal Court. When this change is effected (after the backlog of civil appeals to the Supreme Court has been dealt with), appeals against conviction or sentence from those courts conducted trials on indictment will lie 'directly' to the Supreme Court. Thus, s. 29 of the Courts of Justice Act 1924, by which an appeal from the Court of Criminal Appeal lies to the Supreme Court by leave on a point of law of exceptional public importance will be obsolete and provision is made in the 1995 Act for its repeal. A consequential provision is s. 44 of the 1995 Act, which replicates s. 11 of the Criminal Procedure Act 1993 (1993 Review,

213-4) by providing that no appeal shall lie to the Supreme Court from an acquittal in the Central Criminal Court.

Transfer to Dublin Circuit Criminal Court S. 32 of the 1995 Act provides that transfer of trials from outside Dublin to the Dublin Circuit Criminal Court will only occur where the Circuit Court judge considers that 'it would be manifestly unjust not to do so.' This restrictive provision replaced the marginally more extensive provision allowing for such transfers in s. 31 of the Courts Act 1981. The constitutionality of s. 31 of the 1981 Act (which had replaced the mandatory 'transfer on request' regime of s. 6 of the Courts Act 1964) had been upheld in *Tormey v Ireland* [1985] IR 289 and *The State (Boyle) v Neylon* [1986] IR 51.

Judicial Appointments Advisory Board S. 13 of the 1995 Act provides for the appointment of a Judicial Appointments Advisory Board for the purposes of 'identifying persons and informing the Government of the suitability of those persons for appointment to judicial office'. The establishment of such an Advisory Board had been recommended by the Fair Trade Commission in its 1990 Report on the Legal Profession, but the events surrounding the appointment of the President of the High Court in 1994 may have encouraged a political will to present such a proposal to the Oireachtas. S. 12 of the 1995 Act defines 'judicial office' as being: 'the office of ordinary judge of the Supreme Court, ordinary judge of the High Court, ordinary judge of the Circuit Court or judge of the District Court (other than the President of the High Court'. Thus, the remit of the Board excludes the offices of Chief Justice, President of the High Court, President of the Circuit Court and President of the District Court, though in relation to these offices, the Government is subject to some limitations in that it is required to 'have regard first' to the qualifications and suitability of existing judges (s. 23).

The Board comprises the following persons: the Chief Justice, who chairs the Board, the President of the High Court, the President of the Circuit Court, the President of the District Court, the Attorney General (who must withdraw from any deliberations of the Board concerning his or her suitability for judicial office (s. 18(3)), a practising barrister nominated by the Chair of the Council of the Bar of Ireland, a practising solicitor nominated by the President of the Law Society of Ireland and not more than three persons appointed by the Minister for Justice who are engaged in or have appropriate knowledge or experience of commerce, finance or administration or persons who have experience as consumers of the services provided by the courts.

S. 14 of the 1995 Act empowers the Board to adopt its own procedures, and in this respect it may: advertise for applications for judicial appointment, require applicants to complete application forms, consult persons concerning the suitability of applicants to the Board, invite persons, identified by the Board, to submit their names for consideration by the Board and arrange to interview applicants who wish to be considered for judicial appointment.

The Board thus has extensive powers to identify those persons suitable for appointment in accordance with its function under s. 13 of the 1995 Act. S. 21 of the 1995 Act also provides for staffing for the Board, while s. 22 is a standard provisions that the expenses incurred by the Board shall be paid out of moneys provided by the Oireachtas.

S. 16 of the 1995 Act specifies that a person who wishes to be considered for judicial appointment: 'shall so inform the Board in writing and shall provide the Board with such information as it may require to enable it to consider the suitability of that person for judicial office, including information relating to education, professional qualifications, experience and character'. S. 16 also provide that, where the Minister for Justice requests, the Board must submit to the Minister the name of each person who has informed the Board of his or her wish to be considered for judicial office. In general, the Board is required to recommend at least seven names from the list it submits, but this can be a lesser number where there are multiple vacancies for which there are less than the requisite multiple of seven who the Board considers it can recommend. As regards who the Board can recommend, any such person must comply with the relevant qualifications set out in the Courts (Supplemental Provisions) Act 1961, to which we return below. In addition, s. 16(7) and s. 19 provides that the Board must not recommend a person unless, in the Board's opinion, the person:

(a) has displayed in his or her practice as a barrister or solicitor, as the case may be, a degree of competence and a degree of probity appropriate to and consistent with the appointment concerned,
(b) is suitable on grounds of character and temperament,
(c) is otherwise suitable, and
(d) undertakes in writing to the Board his or her agreement, if appointed to judicial office, to take such course of training or education, or both, as may be required by the Chief Justice or the President of the court to which the person is appointed.

Clearly, this involves a new and elaborate procedure for judicial appointments. However, it must be remembered that, ultimately, the Constitution requires such appointments be made by the President acting on the advice of the Government. This is recognised in s. 16(6) of the 1995 Act, which provides: 'In advising the President in relation to the appointment of a person to judicial office the Government shall firstly consider for appointment those persons whose names have been recommended to the Minister pursuant to this section'.

Undoubtedly, the recommendations of the Board will undoubtedly be of considerable importance and s. 16(8) of the 1995 Act provides that appointments made under the procedure envisaged by the Act must be published in *Iris Oifigiúil*, and the notice must include a statement, if that is the case, that the name of the person was recommended by the Board to the Minister. This would appear to be an 'encouragement' to the Government to advise the appointment of recommended persons only. Nonetheless, the final decision rests with the Government. In addition, we have already noted that the functions of the Board do not extend to appointments to the offices of Chief Justice, President of the High Court, President of the Circuit Court and President of the District Court. One other limitation is that the Board's recommendation function does not apply where the Government proposes to 'promote' a sitting judge (s. 17). However, aside form these limitations, the changes effected by the 1995 Act created a degree of openness in the appointments procedure, though we note that s. 20 of the 1995 Act provides that the proceedings of the Board and all communications to it are confidential and shall not be disclosed except for the purposes of the Act.

Judicial training and Judicial Studies Institute   S. 16 of the Courts and Court Officers Act 1995 introduced for the first time a mandatory requirement that candidates for judicial appointment undertake to agree to take any course of training or education as may be required by the Chief Justice or the President of the court to which the person is appointed. While such training and continuing education is not mandatory for those appointed prior to 1996, a Judicial Studies Institute has been established with a view to providing continuing education for all judges (458 *Dáil Debates*, col. 1765, November 28, 1995). S. 48 of the 1995 Act provides that such training and education may be funded by the Minister for Justice.

Appointments of solicitors as judges   Prior to the 1995 Act, solicitors were eligible for appointment as judges of the District Court: s. 29(2) of the Courts (Supplemental Provisions) Act 1961. However, s. 17(2) of the 1961 Act confined to practising barristers of ten years standing appointment to the Circuit Court, while s. 5(2) confined appointment to the High Court and Supreme Court to barristers of 12 years standing. Solicitors had pressed for an amendment to the 1961 Act so that they could be eligible for appointment to the Circuit Court as well the High Court and Supreme Court. Indeed, the 1990 Fair Trade Commission Report had accepted there were grounds for acceding to this, at least in relation to the Circuit Court and with indirect appointment through promotion to the superior courts. Although the 1995 Act, when published as a Bill, contained no provision in this regard, the Act as passed involved a significant change in the status quo ante. S. 30 of the 1995 Act amended s. 17(2) of the 1961 Act to provide that, in addition to a practising barrister of ten years' standing, a practising solicitor of ten years' standing is now eligible for appointment as a judge of the Circuit Court. As to appointment to the High Court and Supreme Court, s. 28 of the 1995 Act amended s. 5(2) of the 1961 Act to provide that a judge of the Circuit Court of four years' standing is qualified for appointment as a judge of the High Court or Supreme Court. Thus, although solicitors are not qualified for 'direct' appointment to the High Court or Supreme Court, the 1995 Act has opened up at least the possibility that a former solicitor, having been appointed as a judge of the Circuit Court, might become a judge of the High Court or Supreme Court. The first appointments of solicitors to the Circuit Court bench (three from the seven provided for in the 1995 Act) occurred in July 1996.

European courts Another significant amendment effected by s. 28 of the 1995 Act was that service as a judge of the Court of Justice of the European Communities, as a judge of the Court of First Instance attached thereto or as an Advocate- General of the Court of Justice are to be deemed practice at the Bar for the purposes of appointment. This apparently facilitated the appointment of Barrington J, who had been the first Irish judge of the Court of First Instance, to be appointed to the Supreme Court. Although Barrington J had been a judge of the High Court prior to being appointed a judge of the Court of First Instance, there had been some doubt as to whether the 1961 Act required a person to have been in practice and/or have been a judge of the Irish courts immediately prior to being appointed to the Bench. It is notable that the Divisional High Court in *The State (Walshe) v Murphy* [1981] IR 275 had not so interpreted the comparable provisions in s. 51(1) of the Courts of Justice Act 1936 concerning the appointment of temporary judges of the District Court.

Retirement ages S. 47 reduced the retirement age of High Court and Supreme Court judges from 72 to 70, but this does not apply to judges appointed to judicial office prior to the 1995 Act. The retirement age for a Circuit Court judge remains at 70, while although a District Court judge's normal retirement age is 65, he or she may be continued on from year to year until the age of 70. Thus, the 1995 Act has introduced, at least prospectively, a certain element of uniformity in retirement ages.

Master of High Court Prior to the 1995 Act, the Master of the High Court was largely confined to exercising powers conferred by rules of court: see Barron and Ford, *Practice and Procedure in The Master's Court* (Round

Hall Press, 1994). The Master continues to exercise these functions, but the 1995 Act added significantly to them. S. 24 of the 1995 Act provides that the Master is empowered to exercise limited functions of a judicial nature within the scope of Article 37 of the Constitution (thus giving belated effect to the principal recommendations in the *16th Interim Report of the Committee on Court Practice and Procedure* (Prl. 2350, 1972). In addition, the Master may exercise all the powers of a High Court judge in ex parte applications or applications on notice and in applications for judgment by consent or in default of appearance or defence: in effect, the Master may enter final judgment in these cases, whereas up to the passing of the 1995 Act, a decision by a High Court judge was required. Another significant increase in the Master's power is contained in s. 50, by which the Master is empowered to award interest in a case for a debt or a liquidated sum where an application is made for judgment in default of defence. In *Mellowhide Products Ltd v Barry Agencies Ltd* [1983] ILRM 152, Finlay P (as he then was) held that s. 22 of the Courts Act 1981 did not confer on the Master any power to award interest, though he added that he saw no logical reason why the Master should not be given such power. S. 50 of the 1995 Act gave effect to this recommendation. Finally, s. 25(2) also contains a list of matters excluded from the Master's jurisdiction, such as any matter of a criminal nature and certain civil matters such as judicial review proceedings or any matter relating to the custody of children.

Taxing Master, County Registrars and Costs　A number of provisions of the 1995 Act were intended to assist in the reduction of court costs. S. 27 of the 1995 Act confers additional powers on the Taxing Masters and County Registrars concerning taxation of costs. Significantly, the 1995 Act places taxation of fees presented by both solicitors and barristers on an equal footing. S. 25 provides that the test to be applied in both instances is whether the fees are 'fair and reasonable in the circumstances'. Prior to the 1995 Act, O.99 of the Rules of the Superior Courts 1986 specified a 'fair and reasonable test' for solicitors only; but barristers fees were to be taxed on the basis of what a 'reasonable and prudent' solicitor would agree. The 1995 Act was intended to introduce a more objective element in the assessment of fees marked by counsel. It remains to be seen whether this will produce the intended result. As a 'fall back' position, s. 46 of the 1995 Act envisages the possibility of introducing statutory levels of both solicitors' and counsel's fees.

County Registrars　In addition to the powers conferred by the 1995 Act on County Registrars concerning taxation of costs, s. 34 of and the Second

Schedule to the 1995 Act conferred additional powers on County Registrars comparable to those conferred on the Master of the High Court.

Civil procedure: personal injuries actions S. 45 of the 1995 Act provides that rules of court may be made to provide that in civil proceedings concerning personal injuries certain documents, such as medical reports, may be exchanged prior to court hearings rather than requiring both sides to call medical consultants in court to confirm the information contained in their reports. It is expressly provided that this was to avoid the restrictions imposed by the rule against hearsay. On the general area, see the Law Reform Commission *Report on the Rule Against Hearsay* (LRC 25-1988), discussed in the 1988 Review, 340-43.

Court dress While the prohibition of the wearing of wigs had been proposed in the Courts and Court Officers Bill 1995, ultimately, s. 49 of the Courts and Court Officers Act 1995 provides only that the wearing of wigs by members of the Bar 'shall not be required' and thus is a matter for their own discretion and is no longer mandatory. As this discretionary rule only became effective in December 1995, it is difficult to measure its full impact, but it would appear that, for the present, the majority of members of the Bar continue to wear wigs, those appearing 'wigless' remaining the notable exceptions.

DELAY — DISMISSAL FOR WANT OF PROSECUTION

The general principles to be applied It is well established that the courts have the power to dismiss an action for want of prosecution on the basis that there has been inordinate and inexcusable delay on the part of the plaintiff which has resulted in such prejudice to the defendant that a fair trial would no longer be possible. However, in making any such decision the court is required to strike a balance between the rights of both parties and the conduct of both plaintiff and defendant may be relevant and this balancing process has recently been examined and clarified by the Supreme Court in *Primor plc v Stokes Kennedy Crowley*, Supreme Court, December 19, 1995. One important issue considered by the court was whether conduct on the part of the defendant which might induce a plaintiff to incur further expense in pursuing the action should constitute an absolute bar to relief or merely amount to a relevant factor which might influence the manner in which the court's discretion is exercised. The actions concerned claims brought by the plaintiff company which was under administration alleging negligence, breach of duty and breach of statutory duty against two firms of accountants which had acted as auditors for it. The Master of the High Court had granted applications brought pursuant to O.63, r.1(8) of the RSC 1986 to dismiss the plaintiff's claims against both defendants for want of prosecution and in both cases the Master's order was set aside on appeal to the High Court. The Supreme Court heard both appeals together and were unanimous in overturning the decisions of the High Court. Hamilton CJ undertook a detailed review of the relevant decisions in this area and set out the following principles which it is useful to reproduce in full:

> (a) the courts have an inherent jurisdiction to control their own procedure and to dismiss a claim when the interests of justice require them to do so;
>
> (b) it must, in the first instance, be established by the party seeking a dismissal of proceedings for want of prosecution on the ground of delay in the prosecution thereof, that the delay was inordinate and inexcusable;
>
> (c) even where the delay has been both inordinate and inexcusable the court must exercise a judgment on whether, in its discretion, on the facts the balance of justice is in favour of or against the proceeding of the case;
>
> (d) in considering this latter obligation the court is entitled to take into consideration and have regard to:
>
>> (i) the implied constitutional principles of basic fairnes of procedures,
>>
>> (ii) whether the delay and consequent prejudice in the special facts of the case are such as to make it unfair to the defendant to allow the action to proceed and to make it just to strike out the plaintiff's action,
>>
>> (iii) any delay on the part of the defendant because litigation is a two party operation the conduct of both parties should be looked at,
>>
>> (iv) whether any delay or conduct of the defendant amount to acquiescence on the part of the defendant in the plaintiff's delay,
>>
>> (v) the fact that conduct by the defendant which induces the plaintiff to incur further expense in pursuing the action does not, in law, constitute an absolute bar preventing the defendant from obtaining a striking out order but is a relevant factor to be taken into account by the judge in exercising his discretion whether or not to strike out the claim, the weight to be attached to such conduct depending upon all the circumstances of the particular case,
>>
>> (vi) whether the delay gives rise to a substantial risk that it is not be possible to have a fair trial or is likely to cause or have caused serious prejudice to the defendant,

(vii) the fact that the prejudice to the defendant referred to in (vi) may arise in many ways and be other than that merely caused by the delay, including damage to a defendant's reputation and business.

Hamilton CJ concluded that the learned trial judge in the *Stokes Kennedy Crowley* case would have been entitled to regard the defendant's conduct as relevant in exercising his discretion but instead he had treated it as being fatal to its claim and in so holding, in his view, he had erred in law. As a result of applying such an approach, neither trial judge had properly considered the effect of the prejudice which the defendants had undoubtedly suffered by reason of the plaintiff's delay. In the view of the Chief Justice, prejudice caused to a defendant by inordinate and inexcusable delay on the part of a plaintiff is a 'fundamental ingredient which may and should be taken into account' in an application to dismiss proceedings for want of prosecution and if the prejudice is such that a fair trial could not be held at that stage, the proceedings should be dismissed. Hamilton CJ was satisfied that there had been inordinate and inexcusable delay on the plaintiff's part and went on to consider whether the balance of justice was in favour of or against the case proceeding. He found that the defendants' conduct was not such as would amount to a countervailing circumstance as would negative or provide an answer to the inordinate and inexcusable delay on the part of the plaintiff. He concluded that the prejudice caused to the defendants by the plaintiff's delay was such as to place an inexcusable and unfair burden on the defendants in defending the proceedings and was such as to make it impossible that a fair trial between the parties could now proceed. O'Flaherty J agreed that there had been inordinate and inexcusable delay on the part of the plaintiff and that the prejudice chronicled by the defendants was 'total and insurmountable'.

As Hamilton CJ made clear in *Primor*, even where the delay has been both inordinate and inexcusable the court must exercise a judgment on whether, in its discretion, on the facts the balance of justice is in favour of or against the proceeding of the case. Amongst the issues which may affect where this balance of justice lies in a particular case is prejudice e.g. in the form of non-availability of an essential witness, as was the case in *Byrne v ITGWU*, High Court, November 30, 1995. The plaintiff had been dismissed from his employment in 1981 and claimed that he had instructed a representative of the defendant union to proceed with his appeal to the Employment Appeals Tribunal but no appeal was lodged within the six week limitation period. The tribunal found that it had no jurisdiction to hear the appeal and the plaintiff claimed that the failure to lodge the appeal amounted to negligence on the part of the union. The first two firms of solicitors which the plaintiff approached did little to further the case and in 1992 he consulted a third firm which proceeded with the claim. The defendant brought a motion to have the claim dismissed for want of prosecution and claimed that it had been prejudiced by the delay as the person who had been handling the case had died in the meantime. Morris J dismissed the claim for want of prosecution finding that the delay had been inordinate, and as no excuse had been offered, also inexcusable, and as a result of the delay the defendant had been prejudiced in that an essential witness had died.

DISCOVERY OF DOCUMENTS

Affidavit: deponent's belief referable to anonymous informant In *Bridgeman v Kilcock Transport Ltd (St. Vincent's Hospital, Fairview, Dublin, Notice Party)*, High Court, January 27, 1995, Keane J declined to order discovery in the following circumstances. The plaintiff had instituted an action in negligence against the defendant company for personal injuries. In its defence, the defendant claimed that the plaintiff had deliberately caused the accident which resulted in his injuries. The defendant then sought third party discovery from the notice party, a hospital, seeking in particular details as to whether the plaintiff suffered from any psychiatric problems. The defendant grounded its application on an affidavit in which it averred that it had been informed of the plaintiff's condition by an acquaintance who did not wish to be identified. The Master of the High Court refused the order sought and the defendant appealed to the High Court, but Keane J upheld the Master's decision and refused third party discovery.

He pointed out that an affidavit grounding such an application must comply with the requirements of O.40, r.4 of the Rules of the Superior Courts 1986, which requires that the grounds of the deponent's belief that the material sought is relevant to the proceedings must be set out. As to the instant case, Keane J considered that the deponent would be depriving the court of the opportunity to determine whether such a belief was well founded by assuring an acquaintance that his identity will not be disclosed. However, Keane J gave liberty to the defendant to renew its application at some future date, but he indicated clearly that any such application would meet with a similar fate if the defendant renewed the non-disclosure assurance.

NOTICE FOR PARTICULARS

The consequences of failure to comply with a notice for particulars O.19, r.7 of the RSC 1986 provides that a further and better statement of the nature of the claim or defence or further and better particulars of any matter stated in any pleading, notice or written proceeding requiring particulars may be ordered on such terms as to costs or otherwise as may be just. The provisions of this rule were considered by the Supreme Court in *Church and General Insurance plc v Moore* [1996] 1 ILRM 203. Hamilton CJ stated that while O.19, r.7 — unlike O.31 r.21 which deals with failure to comply with an order for discovery or interrogatories — does not specifically provide for the striking out of a defence for failure to comply with an order for further and better particulars, the courts have an inherent jurisdiction to enforce an order made by it and if there is a failure to comply with an order, then in certain circumstances a claim can be dismissed for want of prosecution or a defence struck out. He considered what had been said by Lord Esher MR in relation to the equivalent English provision in *Davey v Bentinck* [1893] 1 QB 185, 188 namely that the rule gives the court the power 'to add as a consequence that if the order is not complied with within a certain time the action shall be dismissed'. He concluded that the terms of the rule and the statement of Lord Esher envisaged an order requiring that further and better particulars be provided on terms and that if the order were not complied with within a certain time, then the action should be dismissed or the defence struck out.

The High Court had ordered the defendant to deliver to the plaintiff particulars requested and when this was not complied with it directed that these should be delivered on or before a certain date and that in default thereof, the defendant's defence should be struck out. The replies were not forthcoming and the High Court ordered that the defence be struck out and further ordered that execution should be stayed for two weeks and in the event of compliance with the order requiring replies and the paying into court of the sum of £50,000 during that time, execution would be stayed pending the trial. The defendant complied with the part of the order requiring replies within the two week period but successfully appealed to the Supreme Court against the part of the order requiring the payment into court. Hamilton CJ stressed that the inherent jurisdiction of the court and the power given to it by r.7 was for the purpose of ensuring compliance with any orders made by the court and the requirement to pay the money was not necessary to ensure compliance with the orders for further and better particulars. It could only be regarded as a penalty and the High Court had no power to impose such a penalty.

DISCOVERY

O.31, r.12 and the interpretation of the phrase 'relating to any matter in question' O.31, r.12 of the Rules of the Superior Courts 1986 provides that any party may apply to the court for an order directing any other party to a cause or matter to make discovery on oath of documents 'which are or have been in his possession or power relating to any matter in question'. The meaning of this latter phrase was considered by Kenny in *Sterling-Winthrop v Farbenfabriken Bayer AG* [1967] IR 97 in which he quoted with approval from the judgment of Brett LJ in *Compagnie Financiere du Pacifique v Peruvian Guano Co.*, 11 QBD 55, 62 as follows:

> Every document relates to the matters in question in the action, which not only would be evidence upon any issue, but also which, it is reasonable to suppose, contains information which *may* — not which *must* — either directly or indirectly enable the party requiring the affidavit either to advance his own case or to damage the case of his adversary.

This principle was followed recently by Flood J in *Woodfab Ltd v Coillte Teoranta*, High Court, August 11, 1995. The plaintiff brought proceedings against the defendant claiming declarations in relation to the defendant's alleged abuse of a dominant position in the raw timber market in Ireland and sought an order seeking further and better discovery or an order striking out the defence in default of such discovery. The High Court was required to consider which documents related to 'any matter in question' and were discoverable. Flood J agreed that a broad interpretation should be given to this phrase and said that the documents to be produced were not confined to those which would be evidence to prove or disprove any matter in question but should include those which it was reasonable to suppose contained information which might enable the party requiring the affidavit either to advance his own case or damage that of his adversary. In the case before him, Flood J concluded that documents which went to show the manner in which the defendant conducted its business with customers were relevant.

Further consideration was given to the meaning of O.31, r.12 by Morris J in *McKenna v Best Travel Ltd* [1995] 1 IR 577. The plaintiff sought damages for personal injuries sustained while on holiday in the Holy Land. The first named defendant went into voluntary liquidation and the plaintiff sought details of the insurance company which indemnified this defendant. The Master of the High Court made an order directing the first named defendant to disclose the identity of the insurance company and it success-fully appealed against the order. Morris J stressed that it is only documents which would support or defeat an issue which arises in an existing action which are required to be discovered. As O.31, r.12(1) made clear that discovery could only be directed of documents 'relating to any matter in question'. Unless documents enable the plaintiff to advance his case or to damage that of his opponent, they will not be discoverable. Morris J stated that none of the issues identified in the pleadings related to the first named defendant's indemnifiers and he concluded that documents which went outside these issues should not be required to be discovered.

Striking out a defence for failure to comply with an order for discovery O.31, r.21 provides that if any party fails to comply with an order for discovery or for interrogatories, he shall be liable to attachment, and also if a plaintiff, to have his action dismissed for want of prosecution, or if a defendant, to have his defence struck out. This latter aspect of the rule was considered by the Supreme Court in *Mercantile Credit Co. of Ireland v Heelan*, Supreme Court, February 14, 1995. Hamilton CJ stated that the power given to the court to strike out a defence for failure to comply with an order of discovery was discretionary and should only be made where there was wilful default or negligence on the part of a defendant and said that die court's powers should not be exercised so as to punish a party for failure to comply with a discovery order within the time limited by the order. In this case while the second named defendant had delayed in complying with various orders for discovery and had prolonged proceedings, the interests of justice required that he be afforded an opportunity of controverting the plaintiff's claim. In the circumstances, the court was satisfied that the order striking out the second named defendant's defence should not have been made.

LEGAL AID AND ADVICE

The Civil Legal Aid Act 1995 consolidated in statutory form the 1979 non-statutory Scheme of Civil Legal Aid and Advice (Prl.8543, 1979), as amended, and also took account of the international obligations on the State concerning civil legal aid. The 1995 Act came into effect on October 11, 1996: Civil Legal Aid Act 1995 (Commencement) Order 1996 (SI No. 272 of 1996).

Legal Aid Board The 1995 Act made provision for the replacement of the existing Legal Aid Board by the establishment of the Legal Aid Board as a separate legal entity. The Board, comprising a chairperson and 12 other members, is appointed by the Minister for Equality and Law Reform. S. 4 of the Act provides that two members of the Board must be barristers, two must be solicitors and two must be members of the staff of the Board. S. 5 states that the principal functions of the Board are, *inter alia*, to provide, within its resources, legal aid and advice in civil cases to persons who satisfy the eligibility criteria of the 1995 Act, and to disseminate information concerning its services. The Board must publish an Annual Report of its activities (s. 9), continuing a practice of the non-statutory Board. The Board has a chief executive, who is also a civil servant (s. 10), and the Board is also empowered to appoint full-time staff to carry out its functions. These full-time staff are located in Law Centres (s. 30). A proportion of the staff are solicitors, who may be designated as civil servants, but the 1995 Act provides that this designation shall not occur unless staff representatives are consulted (s. 11). This preserves the position prior to the 1995 Act, namely that administrative staff were designated as civil servants, but that solicitors were not; such solicitors thus enjoyed the full standing of solicitors under the Solicitors Acts 1954 to 1994. In addition, the Board is empowered to establish a panel of solicitors and barristers in private practice who are willing to provide legal aid and advice under the Act (s. 30). During the passage of the Act, the Minister for Equality and Law Reform provided some information on the growing cost of civil legal aid and advice (see 455 *Dáil Debates*, col. 763, 29 June 1995). Between 1993 and 1995, the administrative staff of the non-statutory Legal Aid Board had risen from 60 to 129, while the number of solicitors had risen from 39 to 75. In addition, the number of full-time Law Centres had risen from 16 to 26 in the same period. The overall cost of the Legal Aid Scheme has risen from £2.7m in 1992, to £4.97m in 1994 and £6.2m in 1995. It is clear that this increase in funding was absolutely necessary if the Scheme, whether statutory or otherwise, was to cope with the massive increase in the calls on its resources.

Legal advice and legal aid The 1995 Act covers both legal advice and legal aid. Legal advice is defined in wide terms in s. 25 to include any oral or written advice given to a person by a solicitor or barrister on the application of the law of the State. It is worthy of note that s. 26(4) also authorises the Board to grant advice concerning the law of another State if it deems this appropriate. Legal aid is defined in s. 27 of the Act as representation by a solicitor or barrister in the categories of civil proceedings covered by s. 28 of the Act as well as relevant preparatory work.

Eligibility for legal aid and advice The 1995 Act sets out two basic tests of eligibility for legal aid: a 'merits' test and a 'means' test. For legal advice, the means test only applies. The merits test is laid down in s. 24, which provides that a person shall not be granted legal aid unless, in the Board's opinion, a reasonably prudent person who could afford to engage such services would be likely to do so and where a solicitor or barrister would be likely to advise such a person to obtain such services at his or her own expense. The means test is contained in s. 29, which provides that a person cannot receive legal aid or advice unless (a) he or she satisfies the requirements concerning financial eligibility specified in the Act and in any Regulations made under the Act; and (b) pays a contribution to the Board towards the cost of any legal aid or advice, the level of contribution to be laid down in Regulations made under the Act. The key financial eligibility question is the level of disposable income of the applicant (that is, gross income, less items such as income tax, mortgage repayments, rent, social insurance, health insurance contributions and other items to take account of, for example, dependent children) and, where applicable, disposable capital (excluding the value of any home). The Civil Legal Aid Regulations 1996 (SI No. 273 of 1996) specify the current net disposable income limit at £7,350. This was the figure set under the non-statutory scheme in 1995, which the Minister noted represented an 18.5% increase on the previous level (455 *Dáil Debates*, col. 766). The 1996 Regulations also set a minimum contribution for legal advice of £4, plus an additional £19 where the applicant needs to take or defend court proceedings. The maximum contribution for legal aid under the 1996 Regulations could be £583. However, s. 29(2) of the 1995 Act also provides that Regulations may give the Board the power to grant legal aid or advice without reference to the means of an applicant and may also empower the Board to waive any contribution and this discretion was conferred on the Board by the 1996 Regulations.

Criteria for obtaining legal advice S. 26 of the 1995 Act empowers the Board to provide that legal advice if the applicant satisfies the means test in s. 29 of the Act and any Regulations made under the Act. S. 26(2) confirms that legal advice cannot deal with a criminal law matter, unless it concerns how legal aid can be obtained under by the Criminal Justice (Legal Aid) Act 1962. In addition, s. 25(3) provides that a complainant in a sexual assault case is entitled to legal advice from the Legal Aid Board 'free of any contribution'. This provision continues the arrangement in place under the non- statutory scheme by Ministerial Policy Directive No. 1 of 1991 (Pl.7936). This was introduced after the enactment of the Criminal Law (Rape) (Amendment) Act 1990, and comprised the limited response to calls for a right of audience for an adviser to complainants. It was considered that a right of audience was incompatible with the adversarial nature of the criminal trial. At the time of writing (November 1996), the extension to complainants of a right to legal representation is under consideration. We will return to this matter in a future Review if such is enacted into law. Legal advice cannot be provided by the Board in respect of the excluded categories of civil matters referred to in s. 28(9) of the Act, which we discuss below. Subject to that proviso, legal advice may be given in respect of virtually any legal matter. This includes advice to a person who has a case pending before a tribunal. As we will see, the 1995 Act prevents the Board from giving legal aid to such a person, but it is not precluded from giving legal advice.

Criteria for obtaining legal aid   S. 28(2) of the 1995 Act lays down the essential criteria under which the Board grants legal aid, by means of a legal aid certificate. Such a certificate must be granted if, in the Board's opinion:

(a) the applicant satisfies the financial eligibility criteria in s. 29 of the Act;

(b) the applicant has as a matter of law reasonable grounds for instituting, defending or being a party to the proceedings for which legal aid is sought;

(c) the applicant is 'reasonably likely to be successful in the proceedings';

(d) the proceedings for which legal aid is sought are the most satisfactory means of achieving the result sought by the applicant; and

(e) having regard to all the circumstances (including the probable cost to the Board, measured against the likely benefit to the applicant), it is reasonable to grant the application.

S. 28(3) provides that factors (c) and (e) will not apply where the proceedings in question concern the welfare of a child, including custody or access. This was inserted to give effect to the decision of the Supreme Court in *M.F. v Legal Aid Board* [1993] ILRM 797 (1993 Review, 334-5) in which the Court held that the test of reasonable likelihood of success in the equivalent of s. 28(2) in the non-statutory scheme was appropriate only in disputes *inter partes*. S. 28(5) further provides that legal aid shall be provided by the Board where the State is obliged by international obligations to do so. In this respect, it refers expressly to international child abduction and custody cases (within the Child Abduction and Enforcement of Custody Orders 1991: 1991 Review, 81-6) and those involving international enforcement of maintenance orders (within the Maintenance Act 1994: 1994 Review, 102).

Legal aid in courts and prescribed tribunals   S. 27 of the 1995 Act provides that legal aid may be given in connection with any civil proceedings (save those excluded by s. 28(9) of the Act) in any court, from the District Court to the Supreme Court. Proceedings brought to the European Court of Justice under Article 177 of the EC Treaty may also be legally aided. In general, the Board will grant legal aid in the lowest court having jurisdiction in the matter (s. 28(8)). In addition, the Board may be authorised by Ministerial Order to provide legal aid for proceedings in any prescribed court or tribunal. During the passage of the Act, it was proposed that it apply immediately to hearings in the Employment Appeals Tribunal, but this was resisted on the grounds of excessive costs. However, a commitment was given that the required Ministerial Order would be made if the budgetary situation so allowed (see Select Committee on Legislation and Security, L5, No. 4, cols. 269-72 (12 July 1995)).

Excluded matters S. 28(9) of the 1995 Act prohibits the Board from providing legal aid (and legal advice) in the following categories of cases:

(a) defamation claims;
(b) disputes concerning rights and interests in or over land (but family law proceedings concerning land and landlord and tenant disputes concerning residential property are not excluded: s. 28(9)(c));
(c) civil matters covered by the District Court small claims procedure (1993 Review, 466);
(d) licensing (but where hardship may arise, licensing disputes are not excluded: s. 28(9)(c));
(d) conveyancing;
(e) election petitions;
(f) claims made in a representative, fiduciary or official capacity;
(g) claims brought by a person on behalf of a group of persons to establish a precedent on a particular point of law (so-called 'test cases');
(h) any other group or representative action.

These exclusions largely replicated the excluded categories in the non-statutory scheme, with the exception that it had originally been proposed to exclude claims concerning debt collection also. This exclusion was removed during the debate on the Act in the Oireachtas (458 *Dáil Debates*, cols. 451-2). Another divergence from the non-statutory scheme is that the Minister for Equality and Law Reform is authorised by s. 28(10), subject to the consent of the Minister for Finance, to remove by Order any of the excluded categories. As with the possible extension of the Act to claims before the Employment Appeals Tribunal, any removal of the excluded categories would depend on the general Government budgetary position (455 *Dáil Debates*, col. 770). In the meantime, test cases and defamation actions contemplated by those of limited means will continue to require the goodwill of members of the legal profession to proceed to court. For an extended critique of these exclusions, see Phelan, 'The Civil Legal Aid Bill 1995: A Critique' (1995) 13 *ILT* 109. Although this article deals with the Bill, many of the 1995 Act's provisions reflect the text of the Bill as there described.

Recovery of costs Ss. 33-36 of the 1995 Act describe the circumstances in which the Board is required to seek to recover costs in successful and unsuccessful actions involving legally-aided persons.

RES JUDICATA

In *Clare County Council v Mahon and Quinn* [1996] 1 ILRM 521, Carroll J rejected the suggestion that the doctrine of *res judicata* could arise to estop a party raising an issue of statutory interpretation. In the instant case, the Council sought a declaration that the defendants were required to pay water charges pursuant to the Local Government (Financial Provisions) Act 1983. The defendants had raised as a preliminary question of law whether they were entitled to a supply of water free of charge as provided in an indenture of lease dated February 1, 1877 made between a person and the Council's predecessor in title. The defendants also pointed to previous litigation in the Circuit Court in which the Council had sought unsuccessfully to recover alleged arrears of water charges from a person. It had been held in that case that under the same lease of 1877 that the defendants now relied on, a public charitable trust had been established which entitled the party in the 1989 proceedings to his supply of water free of charge. However, the Circuit Court judge had stated that the matter was to be regarded as limited to a specific District Court appeal between the parties and had no further effect. He also indicated that the matter might be better litigated in a declaratory action in the High Court. Nonetheless, the defendants submitted that they were claiming identical rights to those at issue in the previous case and that therefore, there existed a privity of title and interest between them. As indicated, Carroll J rejected this argument.

She noted that the defendants were not bound by the result of the 1989 case since they had no part in the conduct of that defence. Citing *Lawless v Bus Éireann* [1994] 1 IR 474 and *Reamsbottom v. Raftery* [1991] 1 IR 531 (1990 Review, 449), she held, therefore, that there could be no mutuality between the cases. She also noted that, since the Council was required by statute to charge for water supplies, a finding that the matter was *res judicata* would have the effect of repealing the statute She continued that the question of whether statutory provisions overrode a charitable trust was a matter of statutory interpretation and could not be res judicata. In this respect, she applied the decision in *Kildare County Council and Brady v Keogh* [1971] IR 880. She also referred with approval to three English authorities, *Marginson v Blackburn Borough Council* [1939] 2 KB 426, *Carl Zeiss Stiftung v Rayner & Keller Ltd (No. 2)* [1967] 1 AC 853, and *North-West Water Ltd v Binnie & Partners* [1990] 3 All ER 547, in support of her conclusion that there could be no estoppel which would preclude the Council from pursuing its statutory duty or from arguing the interpretation of a statute.

RULES OF COURT

District Court: child care The District Court (Child Care) Rules 1995 (SI No. 338 of 1995) prescribe the procedures to be followed and forms to be used in applications to the District Court under the Child Care Act 1991. The Rules came into effect on December 7, 1995.

District Court: small claims procedure The District Court (Small Claims Procedure) Rules 1995 (SI No. 377 of 1995) increased the monetary limit on claims initiated under the District Court (Small Claims Procedure) Rules 1993 (1993 Review, 466) from £500 to £600, with effect from January 22, 1996. It is anticipated that further increases to £1,000 will be phased in the medium term.

District Court: summonses The District Court (Service of Summonses) Rules 1995 (SI No. 305 of 1995) provide that a summons may be served by delivery by hand by any member of an Garda Síochána other than the person on whose behalf the summons purports to be issued, as envisaged in s. 22(1)(c) of the Courts Act 1991. The Rules came into effect on November 30, 1995.

Circuit Court: lodgments and defences The Circuit Court Rules (No. 2) 1995 (SI No. 216 of 1995) provided for (a) the issuing of Civil Bills or other originating documents prior to service and for renewal of Civil Bills, (b) the amendment of procedures in relation to the payment into court of and payment out of lodgments in satisfaction of claims and (c) the delivery of defences without the necessity of lodging these in the Circuit Court Office with consequent changes in applications for judgment in default of defence and summary judgment. The Rules came into effect on October 1, 1995.

Circuit Court: planning The Circuit Court Rules (No. 1) 1995 (SI No. 215 of 1995) concern applications to the Circuit Court for injunctive relief under s. 27 the Local Government (Planning and Development) Act 1976. The Rules came into effect on October 1, 1995.

High Court: foreign arbitral awards The Rules Of The Superior Courts (No. 1) 1995 (SI No. 243 of 1995) inserted a new O.11, r.l(q) into the Rules of the Superior Courts 1986 to allow for proceedings to enforce foreign arbitral awards. The Rules came into effect on October 2, 1995.

SERVICE OF SUMMONS

Service out of the jurisdiction O.11, r.1 of the RSC 1986 provides that service out of the jurisdiction of an originating summons may be allowed in specified circumstances, and r.1(e)(ii) refers to an action brought in relation to a contract made by an agent within the jurisdiction on behalf of a principal outside the jurisdiction. R.1(e)(iii) confers jurisdiction where a breach of a contract occurs within the jurisdiction, irrespective of where the contract was made. Where it is sought to bring an application to serve a summons out of the jurisdiction, it is important to identify the correct rule under which to apply. This point was made clear by by Carroll J in the course of her judgment in *United Meat Packers v Nordstern* [1996] 2 ILRM 260. In this case the plaintiff applied under r.1(e)(iii) and was granted leave to serve a summons outside the jurisdiction. Some of the defendants applied to set aside service of the notice on the grounds that the contract was not made within the jurisdiction by their agent. Carroll J granted the relief sought and said it could not be assumed that another judge would grant service outside the jurisdiction pursuant to subparagraph (iii) on the evidence which had been before the court. However, she pointed out that the plaintiff was free to make another application under O.11, r.1(e)(iii).

O.11, r.1(h) provides that service out of the jurisdiction may be allowed where any person out of the jurisdiction 'is a necessary or proper party' to an action brought against another duly served within the jurisdiction. The meaning of this phrase was considered by O'Hanlon J in *Short v Ireland*, High Court, March 30, 1995 in the context of proceedings brought by the plaintiffs in an attempt to prevent the further development of the Thorp nuclear reprocessing plant in Cumbria. The plaintiffs claimed that the action was founded on a tort committed within the jurisdiction and that British Nuclear Fuels — the third named defendant — was a necessary and proper party to an action properly brought within the jurisdiction. He concluded that the link between the proceedings brought against the first two named defendants and the claim against the third named defendant was sufficiently close and that r.1(h) could be invoked.

THIRD PARTY NOTICE

Setting aside a third party notice S. 27(1)(b) of the Civil Liability Act 1961 provides that any party who wishes to make a claim for contribution under the Act shall, if the person from whom he wishes to claim contribution is not already a party to the action, serve a third party notice 'as soon as is reasonably possible' and having done so is not entitled to claim contribution except under the third party procedure. In addition, O.16 of the RSC which sets out the procedure for joining third parties provides at r.8(3) that third party proceedings may be set aside at any time by the court. By far the most common reason for bringing an application under O.16, r.8(3) is that a defendant has not sought to issue third party proceedings 'as soon as is reasonably possible'. A further question which must be addressed is whether a court will set aside a third party order once a third party has participated in the proceedings. These issues were considered by Morris J in *Carroll v Fulflex International Co.*, High Court, 18 October 1995 in which he stressed that a motion to set aside a third party order should only be brought before the third party has taken an active role in the proceedings, and it would appear that such a motion will not be successful where the third party has entered a defence in the third party proceedings.

In *Carroll*, a third party sought an order setting aside third party proceedings against it on the basis that the defendant had not applied for liberty to serve the proceedings as soon as was reasonably possible within the meaning of s. 27(1)(b) of the 1961 Act. The statement of claim had been delivered in March 1992 and liberty to issue and serve a third party notice was only sought in December 1993 and granted in March 1994. The court rejected the justification offered for the delay and found that it was impossible to accept that it had taken nearly two years to identify the person responsible for the condition of the container which had collapsed when the plaintiff was driving a fork lift truck into it. Morris J said that in normal circumstances the third party order would have been set aside because of the defendant's failure to act with the required expedition, but in this instance, the third party had delivered a full defence. He held that a motion to set aside a third party order should only be brought before the third party has taken an active role in the proceedings and that it was implied in the 1961 Act that anyone making such an application would move with reasonable speed and certainly before significant costs had been incurred in the third party procedure.

An almost identical set of circumstances arose in *Tierney v Sweeney*, High Court (Morris J), October 18, 1995 which concerned a claim in relation to injuries suffered by the plaintiff while using a lawn-mower purchased from the first named defendant and manufactured by the proposed third party. The statement of claim had been delivered in July 1991 and the defendant applied for and was granted liberty to serve a third party notice in January 1994. The third party entered a defence to the third party action in October 1994 in which he complained of the delay in instituting the third party procedure. However, the motion to set aside the third party notice was not issued until June 1995 when the action between the plaintiff and defendant had reached a conclusion. Morris J held that under normal circumstances the delay would have led to the third party notice being set aside, but in this case the third party had also been guilty of delay and had entered a defence and the application to set it aside had not been brought within the time scale envisaged by the Act, which was as soon as reasonably possible.

Prisons

ACCESS TO LAWYER

In *Walsh v Governor of Limerick Prison* [1995] 2 ILRM 158, the Supreme Court rejected arguments that the applicant's detention was rendered unlawful by virtue of his complaint that he could not have a proper consultation with his legal advisers out of the hearing of the prison staff, and that this interfered with his right of access to the courts. The applicant was serving a sentence of imprisonment in Limerick Prison and it was arguable that he had a statutory entitlement to such access to his lawyers by virtue of the Rules for the Government of Prisons 1947. The High Court refused the applicant's *ex parte* application for an inquiry into the legality of his detention under Article 40.4 of the Constitution. This was affirmed by the Supreme Court. The Court accepted that convicted prisoners had rights under the Constitution, which included the right of access to the courts. However, where a person had been detained to serve a sentence after conviction on indictment, he was *prima facie* detained in accordance with the law. It cited its decision in *The State (McDonagh) v Frawley* [1978] IR 131, in which O'Higgins CJ had quoted with approval the view expressed in *The State (Cannon) v Kavanagh* [1937] IR 428 that it would require the most exceptional circumstances for the court to grant even a conditional order of *habeas corpus*, which the Court continues to equate with the procedure under Article 40.4.

The Court described as 'startling' the applicant's proposition that a breach of the Prison Rules 1947 could in some way render unconstitutional his imprisonment and entitle him to release. The Court stated that this was a proposition never contemplated by the Constitution or case law, though the Court did not dissent from the view expressed by Barrington J as a High Court judge in *The State (Richardson) v. Governor of Mountjoy Prison* [1980] ILRM 82 that breach of prison rules could reflect constitutional obligations. However, in the instant case, the Court stated that, to take the applicant's case at its height and assuming he were able to make out that case, this would not constitute exceptional circumstances entitling him to be released from custody. In those circumstances, as already indicated, the Court affirmed the High Court refusal of relief.

TRANSFER FROM FOREIGN PRISONS

The Transfer of Sentenced Persons Act 1995 enabled the State to ratify the Council of Europe Convention on the Transfer of Sentenced Persons (1983). It will be recalled that, in *Hutchinson v Minister for Justice* [1993] ILRM 602 (1992 Review, 148-9) Blayney J had rejected the proposition that the government was in any way bound by its signature of the Convention. The 1995 Act facilitates the transfer of sentenced persons from foreign states to the State and vice versa so that they may serve their sentence or the balance of their sentence in their home country. The principal conditions specified in the Convention and the 1995 Act are that the person is a national of the administering State (the State where the sentence will be completed), the judgment is final, the sentence has at least six months to run (save in exceptional circumstances), the offence would constitute an offence in the administering State and the sentenced person, the sentencing State and administering State all agree to the transfer. The 1995 Act sets out the procedure for the transfer of the persons including continued enforcement of the nature and duration of the sentence by way of warrant issued by the High Court on the application of the Minister for Justice. It is believed that the majority of prisoners seeking to be transferred to this State would be serving sentences in prisons in the United Kingdom; similarly, that applications to be transferred from Irish prisons would involve completion of sentences in prisons in the United Kingdom. The effect of the 1995 Act would appear to require a marginal increase in prison spaces in the State. The Act came fully into operation on July 17, 1995 on its signature by the President.

TRANSFER FROM ST PATRICKS INSTITUTION TO PRISON

S. 7 of the Prisons Act 1970 empowers the authorities in St Patrick's Institution (the detention centre for convicted male juveniles between the ages of 17 and 19, formerly borstal) to transfer any excess population to prison. The Prisons Act 1970 (Section 7) Order 1995 (SI No. 167 of 1995) continued s.7 of the 1970 Act in operation for a two year period from June 28, 1995. The previous 1991 and 1993 Orders had also involved a two year period (1991 Review, 356 and 1993 Review, 469), though prior extensions (see the 1990 Review, 457; the 1989 Review, 364; and the 1988 Review, 353) had involved periods of one year only.

Revenue Law

Dermot P. Kelly, Barrister-at-law

CASE LAW

Constitution — farm tax *Purcell v Attorney General, Ireland and the Minister for the Environment* [1995] 3 IR 287. The plaintiff was the owner of a farm of approximately 650 acres. In 1986, he was assessed for farm tax. The plaintiff refused to pay this and proceedings were instituted in the District Court seeking to recover the sum from him. Thereupon, the plaintiff issued proceedings claiming that the Farm Tax Acts 1985 and the regulations made thereunder were null and void, of no effect and repugnant [*sic*] to the Confutation, together with other reliefs.

Before Farm Tax could be charged on any farm, it had to be included in a classification list. This meant that it had to have a adjusted acreage determined by the Farm Tax Commissioner ('the Commissioner'). It was the intention of the Oireachtas that The Commissioner would determine the adjusted acreage of taxable farms gradually over a period of approximately five years. The effect of the Farm Tax Regulations 1986, and the Farm Tax (Adjusted Acreage) Regulations 1986, was that for the year 1986, a taxable farm meant a farm of more than 150 adjusted acres and the tax was imposed on this category of farm only, to the exclusion of all other farms of more than 20 adjusted acres.

In 1987, the Minister for Finance stated in his budget speech that the Act was to be repealed and that the farm tax due for 1987 would not be collected. In separate proceedings brought by officials in the office of the Commissioner claiming that the termination of their employment was in breach of the terms by which they had been appointed, the High Court held that the action of the Government had been unlawful.

In the instant case, the High Court held that as the legislation had been interfered with unlawfully, what remained was not the will of the Oireachtas and ceased to be enforceable both for the future and for the past. The plaintiff, therefore, was not liable to pay any farm tax. The defendant appealed to the Supreme Court.

It was held by the Supreme Court in a judgment (deferred) by Blayney J and concurred in by Hamilton CJ and Denham J, that the correct construction of the Farm Tax Act 1985 was that it was not intended by the Oireachtas that farm tax should be imposed until the Commissioner had completed his determination of the unadjusted acreage of all the farms in excess of 20 adjusted acres. The cotrary construction of the Act would have the effect of unfairly discriminating against owners of farms whose farms were taxed prior to the completion of the classification lists. The Farm Tax Regulations 1986, had the effect of bringing the Farm Tax Act 1985, into operation prior to the Commissioner having completed the compilation of the classification lists. The effect of this was to discriminate unfairly against owners of farms in excess of 150 acres because the tax was imposed on them alone and did not affect the owners of other farms within the ambit of the Act, 1985. This was not in accordance with the intention of the Oireachtas and accordingly the Farm Tax Regulations 1986, were invalid.

Blayney J summarised the position as follows at p. 294:

> I am satisfied that the correct construction of the Act is that it was not intended by the Oireachtas that the Farm Tax should be imposed until the Commissioner had completed his determination of the unadjusted acreage of all farms in excess of 20 adjusted acres. What caused it to be imposed before this was not the provisions of the Act itself but the statutory instrument made by the Minister for the Environment bringing the farm tax into operation in the year 1986. There was no need for the Minister to prescribe 1986. He could have waited until the Farm Tax Commissioner had completed compiling the classification lists. If he had done this he would have given effect to the intention of the Oireachtas. In the particular circumstances, the effect of the statutory instrument making the tax begin in 1986 was to bring about a state of affairs which was not in accordance with the intention of the Oireachtas and accordingly was invalid. The effect of the statutory instrument was to discriminate unfairly against the owners of farms in excess of 150 adjusted acres because the tax was imposed on them alone and did not effect the owners of other farms within the ambit of the Act.

Capital Gains Tax — tax avoidance scheme — revenue or capital transaction *McCabe v South City and County Investment Co. Ltd*, unreported, High Court, January 11, 1995. On May 26, 1983, the respondent company agreed to accept an offer of an annuity from its parent company, Crosspan Developments Ltd. Under the terms of the annuity contract, the respondent would pay Crosspan Developments Ltd a capital sum in the amount of £1,290,000 and the right to receive an annuity equal to £500 plus 95% of the profits of Crosspan Ltd for each of the three following periods being the 11th month period to April 30, 1983 and for the years ending April 30, 1984 and April 30, 1985. The respondent paid the capital sum of

£1,290,000 to Crosspan Developments Ltd on May 27, 1983 and Crosspan Developments Ltd paid an annuity sum of £1,140,000 on May 30, 1983 to the respondent. The said receipt of £1,140,000 was treated in the accounts of the respondent:

(i) As to £1,105,000 as capital (retained profit in the balance sheet);
(ii) As to £35,500 as income (interest receivable in the Profit and Loss Account).

The only issue on the appeal was whether the receipt of the particular annuity should be treated as income assessable to Corporation Tax in the hands of the respondent or that part of that annuity should be considered as receipt of capital and therefore not accessible to Corporation Tax.

Judge Martin in the Circuit Court determined the appeal in favour of the appellant and held that part of the annuity receipt represented a Capital Receipt and was not chargeable to Corporation Tax.

A case was stated for the Opinion of the High Court. Carney J held that the Circuit Court judge was correct in law in his determination of the appeal.

The case provides little insight into the principals to be applied in approaching a tax avoidance of the nature involved in the case, but perhaps since subsequent legislation has closed off this particular route for avoiding tax the missed opportunity is of little moment.

Corporation Tax – revenue or capital transaction *Brosnan v Mutual Enterprises Ltd* [1995] 2 ILRM 304. On September 3, 1979 the respondent purchased for £300,000 a leasehold interest in premises which were to be used for carrying on its business. In January 1980 the respondent obtained a loan of stg£280,000 for the specific purpose of financing the acquisition of the leasehold interest. The terms of the loan provided that it would be repayable on demand, but went on to indicate that it was the lenders intention that fixed proportions of the loan should be repaid on specific dates between 1981 and 1985. From time to time the sterling indebtedness was converted into various European currencies so that the best possible rate of interest would be achieved. During the period of the loan the respondent incurred losses on foreign currency and sought to include these losses in computing trading profits and allowable losses for the purposes of Corporation Tax. The appellant refused to allow this to be done.

An appeal was brought before the Circuit Court which held that the losses were not capital withdrawn from or sums employed or intended to be employed as capital in the respondent's trade and that the losses were connected with the trade and thus allowable under s. 61(e) of the Income Tax Act 1967.

The Circuit Court judge stated a case to the High Court for the opinion of the High Court of whether he had been correct in law in holding that the respondent was entitled to include the losses on currency transactions when computing trading profits and allowable losses.

It was held by Murphy J in the High Court that the test to be applied in determining whether borrowing constitutes a revenue transaction is whether the loan is a means of fluctuating and temporary accommodation. A loan which is not by way of fluctuating and temporary accommodation constitutes an accretion to capital. Whether accommodation is fluctuating or temporary is a question of fact to be determined in the light of all relevant circumstances of the case.

The principle reason why the appeal was brought in this case would appear to be that the Revenue were seeking to rely on a curious decision of the House of Lords in *Beauchamp v F.W. Woolworth plc* [1989] 1 WLR 50 in that case, Lord Templeman in delivering the unanimous decision of the House of Lords propounded the novel proposition that whether transactions were of revenue or capital nature was to be decided by whether or not the loans were by way of fluctuating and temporary accommodation was a question of law to be determined in the light of the facts found by the Commissioner. This decision was diametrically opposed to the judgment of Lord Justice Nourse in the Court of Appeal who decided that the question whether loans were revenue transactions or accretions to capital was 'obviously one of fact' and that the basic principle in regard to loans is that they are means of fluctuating and temporary accommodation, they are be to regarded as revenue transactions and not accretions to capital.

Murphy J decided at pp. 310-311 that:

> the test to be applied was whether the loans were a means of fluctuating and temporary accommodation. If one then goes on to enquire whether compliance with that test is a matter of law, the answer, in my view, must be in the negative. Whether accommodation is 'fluctuating' or 'temporary' is to my mind demonstrably a question of fact to be determined by all the relevant circumstances of the case.

As has been indicated in many decisions arising on cases stated to the High Court, the fact that the High Court judge may disagree with the conclusions reached by the Circuit Court judge, does not mean in fact the decision of the Circuit judge must be overturned. The question is whether there were grounds on which it was reasonable for a Circuit Court judge to reach the conclusion he did.

It is clear in the instant case that Murphy J would have reached a different conclusion from the Circuit Court judge, but he refused to overturn the

Circuit Court judge's decisions stating:

> To my mind the fact that the purpose of the borrowing was clearly
> identified and that that purpose was the acquisition of a capital asset and
> that it was implemented was a factor of very considerable importance.
> These relevant facts were obvious to the trial judge. It may be that he
> attached less weight to them than I would have done or that he attached
> greater significance to other factors, such as, the fact that the borrowing
> was repayable 'on demand'. All one can say is that there were a number
> of factors to be taken into account and I cannot say that no reasonable
> judge of first instance could have concluded on the facts as a whole that
> the loans were a means of fluctuating and temporary accommodation.
> In the circumstances there are no grounds on which I would be justified
> in interfering with the decision which he reached.

It should, however, be noted that this case is under appeal to the Supreme
Court.

It is not for this author to comment except that it would appear that in
order for the appellant to succeed the Supreme Court would have to adopt
the unorthodox approach to Revenue cases which has been characteristic of
the House of Lords in recent years.

Corporation tax — plant   *Ó Cúlacháin v McMullen Brothers Ltd* [1995]
2 IR 217. The respondent company claimed that canopies in the forecourts
of its petrol filling stations constituted 'plant' for the purposes of corporation
tax, and that, therefore, their cost was a permissible deduction in assessing
its liability to tax. It cannot be were in the respondent's individual colours
with the respondent's trading name visible from a distance or of greater
height than was necessary simply to provide shelter from wind and rain.

The issue came before the Circuit Court on appeal and the Circuit Court
judge stated the applicable test to be whether the canopies were 'a part of the
means by which the trade is carried out in an appropriately prepared setting',
and he further stated that 'settings' and 'plant' were not mutually exclusive
concepts. He found as a fact that the purpose of the canopies was to provide
an attractive setting for the sale of the respondent's products, to advertise and
promote the respondent's products and to create an overall impression of
efficiency and financial solidity and most important of all to attract customers. He concluded, therefore, that the canopies constituted 'plant'. On a case
stated the High Court (Lardner J) found that the Circuit Court judge had been
correct in so holding. The matter was appealed to the Supreme Court where
it was held that where a court had before it a case seeking its opinion as to
whether a particular decision by a judge (or any other party) was correct in

law, the following principles applied:

(a) Findings of primary fact should not be disturbed unless there was no evidence to support them;
(b) Inferences from primary facts were mixed questions of fact and law;
(c) If the conclusions of the judge showed that he had adopted a wrong view of the law, they should be set aside;
(d) If the conclusions were not based on a mistaken view of the law they should not be set aside unless the inferences which he had drawn were ones which no reasonable judge could draw;
(e) Some evidence might point to one conclusion, other evidence to the opposite: these were essential matters of degree and the judge's conclusions should not be disturbed (even if the Court did not agree with them, for it is not retrying the case) unless they were such that a reasonable judge could not have arrived at them or they were based on a mistaken view of the law. It has further held that if the canopies were part of the apparatus used for the carrying on of the respondent's business then they constituted part; but if they were simply the building or part of the building or the setting in which the business was carried on, and served no other purpose, they were not part; and that the fact that something was a building or structure was not decisive.

As the Circuit Court judge's finding as to the functions fulfilled by the canopies had not been unsupported by the evidence his conclusion that the canopies constituted plant could not be set aside. The Supreme Court therefore, upheld the decision of the Circuit Court judge that the forecourt canopy qualified as 'plant' within the meaning of s. 241(1) of the Income Tax Act 1967, as amended.

Circuit Court — jurisdiction — costs on appeal *Inspector of Taxes v Arida Ltd* [1995] 2 IR 230. The respondent successfully appealed a determination by the Appeal Commissioners pursuant to s. 429(1) of the Income Tax Act 1967, and applied for and was awarded its costs of the proceedings in the Circuit Court. On the application of the appellant the Circuit Court judge stated a case pursuant to ss. 428 and 430 of the Income Tax Act 1967, as applied to Corporation Tax by s. 146 of the Corporation Tax Act 1976 for the Opinion of the High Court as to whether a Circuit Court judge hearing an Appeal pursuant to s. 429 of the 1967 Act had jurisdiction to make an award of costs.

At the hearing of the case stated in the High Court it was submitted on behalf of the appellant that as the Appeal Commissioners had no power to award costs it followed accordingly, that a judge of the Circuit Court hearing an appeal from a determination of the Appeal Commissioners could have no such power, having regard to the provisions of s. 429(2) of the Act of 1967.

S. 27(1) of the Courts (Supplemental Provisions) Act 1961, provided:

> The jurisdiction which is by virtue of this Act vested in or exercisable by the Circuit Court . . . shall be exercised so far as regards pleading, practice and procedure generally, including liability to costs, in the manner provided by the Rules of Court. . . .

O. 58, r.1 of the Circuit Court Rules 1950 provides:

> Save as otherwise provided by statute, or by these rules, the granting of or withholding of the costs of any party to any proceeding in the Court shall be in the discretion of the judge.

Murphy J in the High Court answered the case stated in the affirmative holding, *inter alia*, that an appeal from the Appeal Commissioners to the Circuit Court was a 'proceeding' within the meaning of O. 58, r.1 of the Circuit Court Rules 1950 (see 1992 Annual Review).

The appellant appealed to the Supreme Court. It was held by the Supreme Court in an unanimous decision, that, it was inconceivable that the Oireachtas intended that the procedural rules provided by the Circuit Court Rules 1950, should not apply in any case in which the jurisdiction of the Court arose otherwise than by virtue of the Court's Acts. It was further held that where additional jurisdiction was conferred by statute upon the Circuit Court, it would be necessary for that statute expressly to provide that the Circuit Court Rules 1950 did not apply to the exercise of such jurisdiction before a Court could hold that the Rules to be inapplicable. Nothing in s. 27(1) of the Courts (Supplemental Provisions) Act 1961, precluded the possibility of applying the Circuit Court Rules to any jurisdiction that might be conferred by statute on the Circuit Court.

Egan J in delivering the decision of the Court, stated, at p. 236:

> It is inconceivable, in the absence of any indication to the contrary that the Oireachtas intended that the whole paraphernalia of procedural regulation provided for by the Circuit Court Rules 1950 should be disapplied merely because a particular jurisdiction is conferred upon the Circuit Court by legislation other than the Courts Acts.

The Supreme Court affirmed the decision of Murphy J.

Income Tax — husband and wife — right of election *Fennessy v McConnellogue* [1995] 1 IR 500. The respondent resided in Northern Ireland with his wife. His entire earnings accrued, and were chargeable to tax, within the State. The respondent's wife had earnings which were not chargeable to tax within the State, but the respondent sought to be assessed to tax in respect of his wife's earnings, pursuant to s. 194 of the Income Tax Act 1967, with a view to claiming her Tax Free Allowances.

S. 194 of the 1967 Act, as inserted by s. 18 of the Finance Act 1980, provides that a husband and wife living together may elect to be assessed for tax in accordance with the provisions of s. 194 of the Act of 1967, as inserted by s. 18 of the Act of 1980, which provides that where a husband and wife have so elected:

> the husband shall be assessed and charged to tax not only in respect of his total income (if any) for that year, but also in respect of his wife's total income (if any). . . .

A case was stated by the Appeal Commissioner at the request of the Inspector of Taxes against a finding to the effect that the respondent was entitled to be jointly assessed with his wife and get full married allowance and double band rates under s. 194 of the Income Tax Act 1967, by virtue of s. 195(4) of the Income Tax Act 1967.

At the hearing of the case stated the respondent did not appear.

It was held by Carroll J that since the respondent's wife was not capable of being assessed and charged to tax, the respondent was not capable of being assessed to tax in respect of her income either. It followed that since s. 194 was not capable of applying to the respondent, there could be no election under s. 195 to be assessed pursuant to s. 194.

Income Tax — payments made 'on account of injury to or disability of holder of office' *O'Shea v Mulqueen* [1995] 1 IR 505. The respondent's doctor and cardiologist in May 1991, diagnosed the respondent as suffering from job related stress and recommended immediate retirement; his employer's doctor agreed with that recommendation. The respondent submitted his resignation and his employer notified him that it agreed to his early retirement and had decided to make an *ex gratia* payment of £325,000 on his resignation on health grounds. The respondent had had no agreement with his employer entitling him to any lump sum on retirement, nor did the employer have any standard practice for making any payment to personnel who retired on grounds of ill health. In January, 1991 the employer had been offering a voluntary severance programme featuring severance payments to employees under the age of 60. By that time the respondent had already passed 60 and had not applied. It was contended by the appellant that the payment made to the respondent did not come within s. 115(1)(a) of the Income Tax Act 1967 which provided that tax should not be charged in respect of 'any payment made on account of injury to or disability of' the holder of an office or employment, and that the payment had been made on account of the respondent's retirement and not on account of injury or disability.

The Appeal Commissioner concluded that the payment did come within the terms of s. 115(1)(a) and stated a case for the opinion of the High Court as to whether he had been correct.

Carroll J identified the issue for determination as being whether a lump sum payment of £325,000 to the respondent on his retirement is exempt from income tax and whether, on the facts of the case, the respondent received the gratuity (a) on account of his illness or (b) by way of redundancy package on offer just before his retirement in recognition of past service.

Carroll J concluded, at p. 508:

> There is clear evidence to support the finding of fact by the Appeal Commissioner. He found that the payment was made because of early retirement due to ill health. It is not a retirement package which happened to be paid to a person who was injured or disabled as in *Cahill v Harding* [1990] ITR 233. The company did not give the package to the respondent because of his retirement *simpliciter*. It was because he had to retire on health grounds that it was given. To my mind that falls squarely within s. 115(1)(a) of the Income Tax Act 1967.

Revenue powers — discovery *Quigley v Burke* [1995] 3 IR 278. The appellant employed an accountant to prepare and furnish his books and records in support of an Income Tax Appeal. The accountant prepared the accounts from the accounting records, information and explanations supplied to him by the appellant. In dealing with the appeal the respondent sought additional information and accounting records. These were furnished except for the nominal ledger. The appellant's accountant maintained that the nominal ledger was not part of the appellants primary books and records, but had been made up by him as part of his working papers and was his property and not in the power or possession of the appellant. The respondent claimed that the accountant was merely the tax payers agent and so the nominal ledger was owned by the appellant.

On appeal to the Circuit Court it was accepted by the Court that the appellant kept correct records and accounts of his business and the Circuit Court judge held that the nominal ledger was the property of the accountant. The respondent was held not to be entitled to view the nominal ledger or insist that it be put in evidence.

S. 174(1) of the Income Tax Act 1967, as amended derives that an authorised officer of the Revenue Commissioners may in certain circumstances, serve on a person a notice requiring him:

> (a) To deliver to an Inspector copies of such accounts (including balance sheets) relating to the trade or profession as may be specified or described in the notice within such a period as may be therein specified including, where the accounts had been audited, a copy of the auditor's certificates.
> (b) To make available . . . all such books, accounts and documents in his possession or power as may be specified or described in the notice.
> . . .

A case was stated to the High Court which answered the questions in the negative and remitted the matters to the Circuit Court the appellant appealed to the Supreme Court.

It was held by the Supreme Court that the fundamental issue was whether the accountant was acting as a Tax Agent of the appellant and whether the ledger prepared by him was in the power and possession of the appellant or whether it was part of the accountant's working papers and outside the power of possession of the appellant. The test to be applied in determining this issue was whether the appellant had a legal right to obtain the nominal ledger. If he did, it was in his power and possession and he was obliged to produce it. Where an agent brings into existence certain documents while in the employment of his principal, they are the principals property and he can claim production of them.

It was further held by the Supreme Court that the accountant was not engaged to conduct an audit of the appellant's business but as a tax agent to prepare and submit accounts and documents to enable the proper assessment of his income tax liability to be made. As the nominal ledger was prepared in the course of this duty, the appellant was entitled to obtain the ledger from his agent, the accountant. Consequently the ledger was in the possession of power of the appellant within the meaning of the Income Tax Act 1967.

Stamp Duty — deed of release *Cherry Court v Revenue Commissioners* [1995] 2 IR 212. By the first Schedule to the Stamp Act, 1891, *ad valorem* stamp duty is payable on a 'release or renunciation of any property, or interest in any property upon a sale'.

An option was granted over a certain lands. The appellant subsequently acquired a superior interest. A deed made between the appellant and the optionees provided, *inter alia*:

The optionees, as beneficial owners, in consideration of the allotment by Cherry Court to the said optionees of 800,000 redeemable preference shares of £1 in the capital of Cherry Court credited as fully paid up the allotment of which to the optionees credited as fully paid up is hereby acknowledged and of the several warranties on the part of Cherry Court hereinafter contained in Clauses 3 and 4 hereof hereby jointly and separately grant and release under Cherry Court all that the option herein above firstly receded . . . to hold the same on to Cherry Court to the intent that the same shall be merged into the subject property and extinguished, and that the same shall be released and forever discharged therefrom. and from all claims or demands in respect thereof.

The respondents contended that the transaction amounted to 'a release of property . . . upon a sale' within the meaning of the first schedule of the Act of 1891. The appellant contended that there had been no sale, so that the deed was liable only to a fixed duty of £10. A case was stated by the respondents for the opinion of the High Court as to whether *ad valorem* stamp duty was payable.

It was held by McCracken J, that the Court must look to the legal effect of the document and the legal rights of the parties thereunder.

It further held that to constitute a valid sale, there must be a concurrence of the following elements:

(a) Parties competent to contract;
(b) Mutual assent;
(c) A thing, the absolute or general property in which was transferred from the seller to the buyer;
(d) A price in money, or measured in money though not necessarily payable in cash, paid or promised.

McCracken J held that in the instant case, the nett issue was whether the deed had effected a transfer or properties. He held that the wording of the deed was open only to the interpretation that there had been a transfer of property, in that (a) the words 'as beneficial owner' had the effect of implying the covenant set out in s. 7 of the Conveyancing Act 1881, including a covenant that the grantor had full power to convey the subject matter; (b) the word 'grant' could only arise on a transfer, although the word 'release' on its own might not imply a transfer; (c) the words 'to hold the same onto Cherry Court' meant that the appellant was to hold the option, which it could not do unless the option was transferred; (d) 'to the intent that it shall merge into the subject property and be extinguished' — for a merger to occur two interests in the same property must vest in the same person, the intention of the parties being that the lesser interest merge with the greater, for this to happen there must be a transfer.

McCracken J in reaching his decision stated at p. 216:

> I should say that I accept the appellants contention that the parties intention was simply to remove an impediment, but the manner in which they chose to remove that impediment was to sell the option to the appellant. I do not think the release can be construed in any other way. Accordingly, *ad valorem* stamp duty is payable on the release.

Withholding tax — Constitution *Daly v Revenue Commissioners Ireland and the Attorney General* [1995] 3 IR 1. By s. 14 of the Finance Act 1987, a sum equal to Income Tax at standard rate must be withheld from fees payable to professionals by certain persons, for remittal to the Revenue Commissioners. The sums so withheld is assessed on the gross amount of fees without any allowance for deductible expenses. S. 18(2) of the Act of 1987 as originally enacted provided the amount of tax so withheld in one accounting period could be set off against the tax payable for the same accounting period. By s. 14 of the Finance Act 1990 income tax under cases I and II of schedule D became chargeable on the profits and gains of the year of assessment itself rather than on the year preceding the year of assessment as had previously been the case. This change applied with effect from the year 1990/91 onwards. To prevent a windfall gain for those tax payers who had had tax withheld under s. 14 of the Act of 1987 in the period 1990/91. S. 18 of the Act of 1987 was amended by s. 26(1) of the Act of 1990 so that tax withheld in any accounting period from 1990/91 onwards could henceforth only be set off against tax payable for the next accounting period.

In the period from March 31, 1989 to March 31, 1994 almost £69,000 had been withheld pursuant to s. 14 of the Act of 1987 from fees payable to the applicant, whereas his total liability to tax for the period was only £42,500. Unable to set off monies withheld under s. 14 of the Act of 1987 against his tax liabilities for the same accounting period, the applicant had been forced to borrow from his bank to fund those tax liabilities. Due to strain arising from this financial hardship he had been forced to take a lengthy break from his practice as a doctor in the year 1990/91 and to employ a locum. His application for a hardship interim relief was refused in respect of the year 1992/93. The applicant sought a declaration that by depriving him of the ability to set off tax deducted pursuant to s. 14 of the Act of 1987 in a particular period against his tax liabilities for the same period, s. 26(1) of the Act of 1990 was an unjust attack on his property rights contrary to Article 40.3.2° of the Constitution.

It was held by Costello J in declaring the impugned section to be invalid having regard to the provisions of the Constitution that the operation of the withholding tax regime as amended by s. 26(1) of the Act of 1990 produced the following results:

(a) Since tax withheld was calculated on the gross fees, without any deduction of expenses, the amount of tax withheld from the fees was greater than the tax held directly payable thereon;

(b) The effect of withholding tax was to reduce the funds available to the taxpayer to discharge his liabilities;

(c) The result of withholding tax by not permitting the sums withheld to be set off against the tax payable on the fees meant that the tax payer was required by law to suffer a double payment of tax on the same income;

(d) S. 19 had failed adequately to mitigate the above hardship.

Further it was common case that the system of tax collection which proceedings related constituted an interference with the applicant's property rights and fees from which tax had been withheld and that the applicant could show that this interference was an unjust attack on those rights if the law which restricted it or otherwise infringed them failed to past the test of proportionality. That test of proportionality could be stated as follows:

(a) The objective of the impugned provision must be of sufficient importance to warrant overriding a constitutionally protected right, and must relate to concerns pressing and substantial in a free and democratic society;

(b) The means chosen must be rationally connected to the objective and not the arbitrary, unfair or based on a rational considerations; they must impair the right as little as possible and must be such that their effect on the right was proportional to the objectives.

S. 26(1) failed the test of proportionality for the following reasons:

(a) It produced results which were manifestly unfair in that the withholding of tax reduced the ability of the tax payer to pay the tax the sums had been withheld to discharge, and require double payment of tax. This unfairness was not adequately mitigated by s. 19 of the Act of 1987 and the hardship was exacerbated by the fact that the sums withheld in a particular period might ultimately exceed the taxpayers liability for that period.

(b) The subsection was designed to deal with the transition of such a situation but was a permanent measure which involved a permanently unfair method of collecting tax and the effect was not confined to those taxpayers who would otherwise have enjoyed a windfall in respect of the period 1990/91, but was also suffered by those who had sub-sequently entered the withholding regime.

FINANCE ACT 1995

As usual with the Finance Act, the 1995 Act contains a great many provisions making minor alterations to the wording of the provisions in earlier Acts and, of course, the usual adjustments in the rates of tax and balances. It is not within the scope of this work to list all of those minor adjustments but rather to concentrate on new provisions of major alterations in existing provisions.

Reliefs The 1995 Act made a number of provisions relating to new cate-gories in tax relief.

(1) S. 6 provides that fees paid for undergraduate courses in a College approved by the Minister for Education and which is an accordance with standards set by the Minister for Education with the approval of the Minister for Finance shall be deductible at the standard rate of tax but such that the relief may reduce the income tax to nil but that no rebate may be claimed if the amount paid exceeds the tax payable. The relief may be claimed by a person paying fees on his own behalf or on behalf of his dependant.

(2) S. 7 of the Act introduced a new relief in respect of Service Charges. Where an individual can show that he has in any financial year paid in full and on time the Service Charge imposed by any local authority up to a limit of one hundred and fifty pounds, the individual concerned is entitled to relief on the standard rate on the sum paid or on one hundred and fifty pounds whichever is the lesser. Again no rebate is payable if the amount paid should exceed the amount of income tax payable by the taxpayer.

(3) Another new feature is the tax relief for designated charities. A charity (be it a body of persons or a trust) which has as its sole object the relief and development in a country or countries which is or are for the time being on the list of aid recipients produced by the organisation for Economic Co-operation and Development, is a designated charity for the purposes of the Act. A designated charity may claim the tax paid by the donor on a donation of a sum which is not less than two hundred pounds or more than seven hundred and fifty pounds in any tax year. The donation, to qualify, must:

(a) Take the form of the payment of a sum or sums of money;
(b) Not be subject to a condition as to repayment;
(c) Not involve any benefit to the donor or any person connected to the

donor;

(d) Not be conditional on or associated with or part of an arrangement involving the acquisition of property by the designated charity, otherwise given by way of gift, from the donor or by a person connected to the donor;

(e) The donor must be resident in the State in the relevant year of assessment. The donation must be made by an individual, donations by companies would not qualify, the donor must have given an appropriate certificate in relation to the donation to the designated charity and must have paid the tax referred to in the appropriate certificate and the donor is not entitled to claim a repayment of that tax or any part of it.

Covenants　The 1995 Act has, to all intents and purposes, abolished the tax benefits attaching to income covenants which were widely used to pay School and University fees.

The tax benefits may still be claimed in relation to dispositions by covenant to an individual who is permanently incapacitated by reason of mental or physical insanity or who is aged sixty five years or over.

Payments may also be made to any University or College in the State for the purpose of enabling that University or College to carry on research, provided that the disposition is payable for a period which is or may be three years or longer.

A payment may also be made to any body of persons to which the provisions of s. 20 of the Finance Act 1973 apply (that is a body having consultive status with the United Nations or the Council of Europe) and the disposition is payable for a period which is or may be three years or longer.

In order to attract the tax relief the payment made must not be in excess of 5% of the total income of the disponer for the year of assessment (s. 12 and s. 13).

Heritage items and significant buildings　The Finance Act 1982 made provision that expenditure incurred on the repair and maintenance or restoration of a building determined by the Commissioners of Public Works in Ireland to be a building which is intrinsically of significant scientific, historical, architectural or aesthetic interest may be set off against the income of the person owning the said building and incurring the said expenditure as if it were a loss sustained by the taxpayer in a trade carried on by him.

Expenditure incurred on the maintenance or restoration of any land occupied or enjoyed with an approved building as part of its gardens or grounds of an ornamental nature may also be set off against tax as aforesaid.

In order to qualify for tax relief the building has to be one in respect of which the Revenue Commissioners made a determination that reasonable access was afforded to the public.

The categories of qualifying buildings have now been extended to include buildings which are in use as a Tourist Accommodation Facility for at least six months in any calendar year including not less than four months in the period commencing on 1 May and ending on 30 September in any year. To qualify as 'Tourist Accommodation Facility' the accommodation must be registered in the Register of Guest Houses maintained and kept by Bord Fáilte Éireann or listed in the list published or caused to be published by Bord Fáilte Éireann under s. 9 of the Tourist Traffic Act 1957: s. 20 1995 Act amending s. 19 (as amended by the Finance Act 1994) of the Finance Act 1982.

The 1995 Act has also extended the relief in relation to heritage property contained in s. 55 of the Capital Acquisitions Tax Act 1976.

'The relevant heritage property' is defined by s. 166 of the 1995 Act as any one or more of the following:

(a) Objects to which s. 55 of the Principal Act applies;

(b) A house or garden referred to in s. 39 of the Finance Act 1978.

The objects to which the section applies are defined as any pictures, prints, books, manuscripts, works of art, jewellery, scientific collections or other things not held for the purposes of trading which the Revenue Commissioners deem to be of national, scientific, historic or artistic interest. The house or garden referred to is of a kind referred to in s. 20 of the 1995 Act and referred to above.

The exemption from tax applies where a person received a gift or inheritance of such heritage property. S. 166 of the 1995 Act extends that exemption to a gift or inheritance of one or more shares in a private company which is controlled by the donee or his successor to the extent that its market value for tax purposes is attributable to relevant heritage property.

If the share in the private company which is exempted in whole or in part from tax is sold within six years after the valuation date and before the death of the donee or successor the exemption ceases to apply to such a share. Similarly if any item of the heritage property is sold within six years after the valuation date and before the death of the donee or successor the exemption from tax shall cease to apply to the extent that the market value is attributable to such item of heritage property. A gift of the heritage item to the National Gallery, the National Museum or any other similar national institution, any University in the State or any constituent College thereof, local authority or the Friends of the National Collections of Ireland within six years of the valuation date shall not lead to the termination of the exemption.

S. 176 of the 1995 Act provides for tax relief on the donation or gift to the State or one of its agencies of heritage items. The gift to an approved body, i.e. the National Archives, the National Gallery of Ireland, the National

Library of Ireland, the National Museum of Ireland, the Irish Museum of Modern Art or any other body which may be approved by the Minister for Arts Culture and the Gaeltacht, with the consent of the Minister for Finance, of any 'heritage item'.

A 'heritage item' is defined as any archaeological item archive, book, state record, manuscript or painting determined by a selection committee consisting of the Chairman of the Heritage Council and the Directors of the Arts Council, the National Archives, the National Gallery, the National Library, the National Museum and the Irish Museum of Modern Art to be an item which is an outstanding example of the type of item involved, pre-eminent in its class, whose export from the State would constitute a diminution of the accumulated culture of heritage of Ireland, and is suitable for acquisition by an approved body. Before making a determination the selection committee shall request the Revenue Commissioners in writing to value the item or collection of items. The selection committee shall not make a determination in respect of any heritage item or items where the market value of the item or collection of items is determined by the Revenue Commissioners, less than seventy five thousand pounds or greater than five hundred thousand pounds or such lesser sums calculated by the formula five hundred thousand pounds minus the amount equal to the market value (which may be nil) at the valuation date of the heritage item or the aggregate of the market values of all the heritage items in respect of which its termination or determination has or have been made by the selection committee in any one calendar year and revoked in that year. This provision contained at s. 176(2)(c) is somewhat insolicitously drafted. In that it states that the selection committee shall not make a determination under paragraph (a) where the market value of the item or collection of items (as the case may be), as determined by the Revenue Commissioners in accordance with subsection (3), at the valuation date:

(i) If less than seventy five thousand pounds, or
(ii) It exceeds an amount (which shall not be less than seventy five thousand pounds) determined by the formula —

five hundred thousand pounds minus m

Where m is an amount (which may be nil) equal to the market value at the valuation date of the heritage item (if any) or the aggregate of the market values with the respective valuation dates of all the heritage items (if any) or as the case may be, in respect of which a determination or determinations, as the case may be, under this subsection has been made by the selection committee in any one calendar year and not revoked in that year.

The determination to be made by the selection committee is for the item or items is or are an outstanding example of the type of item involved, as already indicated and whether such item or items is or are or suitable for acquisition by an approved body. This determination shall not be made unless the item or items, as determined by the opinion of the Revenue Commissioners, are valued at not less than seventy five thousand pounds or greater than five hundred thousand pounds less a sum (which may be nil) equal to the market value of the heritage item or aggregate market values of all the heritage items in respect of which a determination or determinations under this subsection has been made by the selection committee in any one calendar year.

This would appear to limit to a maximum value of five hundred thousand pounds the heritage items which may be received from all sources in the course of any one calendar year.

A gift of an heritage item to an approved body may be credited against any outstanding or present liability to tax. Any such gift shall be credited firstly against any arrears of tax due for payment and only when all arrears have been cleared against any current liability of the person making the gift.

Capital Acquisitions Tax S. 140 of the 1995 Act made amendments to the definition of agricultural value such that 'agricultural value' means:

(a) in the case of farm machinery, livestock and bloodstock 50% of the market value of such property,
(b) in the case of gift of agricultural property, other than farm machinery, livestock and bloodstock, 50% of the market value of the agricultural property comprised in the gift reduced by 30% of that market value or by the sum of ninety thousand pounds, whichever is the lesser and in the case of an inheritance of agricultural property other than farm machinery, livestock and bloodstock, 50% of the market value of the agricultural property comprised in the inheritance reduced by 15% of that market value or by a sum of forty five thousand pounds whichever is the lesser.

S. 159 of the 1995 Act amended the Finance Act 1994 by the substitution of a new s. 126 which provided, *inter alia*, that where the whole or any part of the taxable value of a taxable gift or inheritance is attributable to the value of any relevant business property, the whole or that part of the taxable value shall be treated as being reduced by 50%. This provision is to bring business inheritance somewhat into line with agricultural inheritance.

An important new provision in the 1995 Act is that as and from 12 April 1995 an inheritance taken by a parent of a disponer on the death of that disponer shall be exempt from tax and shall not be taken into account in computing tax if the deceased disponer took a non-exempt gift or inheritance from either or both of that disponer's parents within the period of five years immediately prior to the date of death of that disponer.

Appeals against assessment of excise duly Chapter five of Part two of the 1995 Act makes provision that where an assessment to excise duty has been made a taxpayer may appeal against liability or amount of such assessment to the Revenue Commissioners who must determine the appeal within thirty days. If, no determination is made within thirty days the appeal is deemed to have been rejected. An appeal lies from a determination by the Revenue Commissioners to the Appeal Commissioners whose decision is final and conclusive and if the Appeal Commissioners state a case on a point of law for the determination of the High Court.

Safety and Health

CHEMICAL SAFETY

Aerosols dispensers The European Communities (Aerosol Dispensers) (Amendment) Regulations 1995 (SI No. 127 of 1995) amended the European Communities (Aerosol Dispensers) Regulations 1977 in order to implement Directive 94/1/EC (the 1994 Directive had amended the 1975 Directive 75/324/EEC, which had been implemented by the 1977 Regulations). The 1995 Regulations imposed additional technical specifications and labelling requirements in relation to the manufacture, filling, marketing and labelling of aerosol dispensers with effect from May 17, 1995.

Chemicals (mixtures) The European Communities (Classification, Packaging and Labelling of Dangerous Preparations) Regulations 1995 (SI No. 272 of 1995) replaced and revoked the European Communities (Classification, Packaging and Labelling of Dangerous Preparations) Regulations 1993 (1993 Review, 526-7). The 1993 Regulations had implemented the 1988 Directive on the Classification, Packaging and Labelling (CPL) of Dangerous Preparations, 88/379/EEC. The 1995 Regulations update the implementation process to take account of Directives 93/18/EEC, 93/21/EEC and 93/112/EC, which involved additional requirements associated with the 1988 Directive. The 1995 Regulations came into effect on October 16, 1995.

Explosives The European Communities (Placing On The Market And Supervision Of Explosives For Civil Uses) Regulations 1995 (SI No. 115 of 1995) gave effect to Directive 93/15/EEC, with the exception of Articles 10 and 11 which had already been implemented by the European Communities (Acquisition and Possession of Weapons and Ammunition) Regulations 1993 (1993 Review, 232-3). The 1995 Regulations prohibit any person from placing explosives on the market unless they satisfy the essential safety requirements laid down in the Directive, have been subject to conformity assessment and have had a 'CE' mark affixed to them. The Regulations also establish a system for the supervision of transfers by way of export, import or in-State transfer of explosives, which essentially requires an authorising document issued by the relevant 'recipient competent authority'. For the purposes of importation into the State, the Minister for Justice is the relevant authority, while for in-State transfers the relevant Garda Superintendent is the relevant authority. The Conveyance Of Explosives (Amendment) Byelaws 1995 (SI No. 251 of 1995), made under the Explosives Act 1875, are referred to in the Transport chapter, 551, below. These requirements should be seen in conjunction with connected statutory Regulations and Orders made in 1994 under the Explosives Act 1875: see the 1994 Review, 394.

Packaging: ADR The Dangerous Substances (Amendment) Regulations 1995 (SI No. 103 of 1995), made under the Dangerous Substances Act 1972, amended the Dangerous Substances (Retail and Private Petroleum Stores) Regulations 1979, the Dangerous Substances (Oil Jetties) Regulations 1979, the Dangerous Substances (Petroleum Bulk Stores) Regulations 1979 and the Dangerous Substances (Conveyance of Petroleum by Road) Regulations 1979. The purpose of the amendments was to authorise the use of certain types of packaging for containers containing dangerous substances referred to in the amended version of the 1957 European Agreement Concerning the International Carriage of Dangerous Goods by Road (the ADR Agreement), as published by the United Nations in 1995. The 1995 Regulations came into effect on May 2, 1995.

Pesticides The European Communities (Export and Import of Certain Dangerous Chemicals) (Pesticides) (Enforcement) Regulations 1995 (SI No. 135 of 1995 and SI No. 183 of 1995) lay down certain administrative arrangements required to give effect to the 1992 Regulation (EEC) 2455/92, as amended by Regulation (EC) 3135/94, in so far as the 1992 Regulation concerns pesticides exported to and imported from 'third countries'. The 1992 EEC Regulation, as amended, is, of course, directly applicable, and contains a listing of chemicals which are either banned or whose use is severely restricted owing to their effects on health and the environment. The 1995 Regulations provide that, in so far as such chemicals are used as pesticides, the relevant Competent Authority for the purposes of the 1992 Regulation is the Pesticide Control Service of the Department of Agriculture and Food.

Transport by sea of dangerous or polluting goods The European Communities (Minimum Requirements For Vessels Carrying Dangerous Or Polluting Goods) Regulations 1995 (SI No. 229 of 1995), which gave effect to Directive 93/75/EEC, are referred to in the Transport chapter, 547, below.

ENVIRONMENTAL SAFETY

Access to information   The Environmental Protection Agency (Licensing) (Amendment) (No. 2) Regulations 1995 (SI No. 76 of 1995) amended the Environmental Protection Agency (Licensing) Regulations 1994 (1994 Review, 397) to enable access for inspection or purchase of documents relating to applications for licences or revised licences or review licences or written reports for the Agency for the purposes of licence determination. The Regulations, which came into effect on May 2, 1995, have some retrospective effect in that they apply in relation to applications received after April 2, 1995.

Energy efficiency 'eco-label': household electrical refrigerators and freezers   The European Communities (Energy Labelling Of Household Electric Refrigerators And Freezers) Regulations 1995 (SI No. 122 of 1995), which gave effect to Directive 94/2/EC, prohibits the placing on the market for sale, hire or reward of household electrical refrigerators and freezers unless accompanied by information relating to their electric energy consumption, that is, an 'eco-label'. The Regulations do not apply to appliances in respect of which production ceased before January 1, 1995. The Regulations place the onus of the accuracy of such information on the suppliers. They came into effect on May 17, 1995.

EPA Act 1992: commencement   The Environmental Protection Agency Act 1992 (Commencement) Order 1995 (SI No. 56 of 1995) brought into effect certain aspects of the 1992 Act concerning Integrated Pollution Control (IPC) licenses: see below. The Environmental Protection Agency Act 1992 (Commencement) (No. 2) Order 1995 (SI No. 337 of 1995) brought into effect ss. 43 and 105 of the 1992 Act with effect from December 11, 1995. S. 43 concerns regional environmental units, while s. 105 concerns the power to hold a formal inquiry.

EPA: Integrated Pollution Control (IPC)   The Environmental Protection Agency Act 1992 (Established Activities) Order 1995 (SI No. 58 of 1995), the Environmental Protection Agency (Licensing) (Amendment) Regulations 1995 (SI No. 59 of 1995) and the Environmental Protection Agency Act 1992 (Established Activities) (No. 2) Order 1995 (SI No. 204 of 1995), specify dates on or after which the established activities concerned must have applied for an integrated pollution control (IPC) licence from the EPA. See further the 1994 Review, 396.

Motor vehicles   Emission controls for motor vehicles are specified in the

European Communities (Mechanically Propelled Vehicle Emission Control) Regulations 1995 (SI No. 192 of 1995): see the Transport chapter, 550, below.

FOOD SAFETY

Additives   The European Communities (General Provisions on the Control of Additives and in Particular Colours and Sweeteners for use in Foodstuffs) Regulations 1995 (SI No. 344 of 1995) gave effect to Directives 89/107/EEC, 94/35/EC, 95/31/EC and 95/45/EC. They consolidate and replace existing provisions concerning all food additives, colours and sweeteners, which are generally signified by 'E' numbers. The Regulations came into effect on December 31, 1995.

Extraction solvents   The Health (Extraction Solvents in Foodstuffs) Regulations 1995 (SI No. 283 of 1995) further implemented Directives 88/344/EEC, as amended by Directives 94/52/EC and 94/115/EC. They specify by name all the substances which may be used as extraction solvents and their conditions of use. They came into effect on December 7, 1995.

Food Safety Advisory Board   The Food Safety Advisory Board (Establishment) Order 1995 (SI No. 155 of 1995), made under the Health (Corporate Bodies) Act 1961, established the Food Safety Advisory Board whose functions are to obtain and assess information regarding the safety of food and zoonetic diseases, advise the Minister for Health of developments in domestic and European law relating to food and on food with particular reference to nutrition, to co-ordinate scientific research and undertake other tasks as requested by the Minister. The Board was established on June 22, 1995. At the time of writing (November 1996), the Advisory Board had been superseded by a Food Safety Board, which is intended to take up an enforcement role in this area under legislation which will be discussed in a future Review.

Labelling, presentation and advertising   The European Communities (Labelling, Presentation and Advertising) (Amendment) Regulations 1995 (SI No. 379 of 1995) further amended the European Communities (Labelling, Presentation and Advertising) Regulations 1982 and gave effect to Directives 94/54/EC and 95/42/EC, which had in turn updated Directive 93/102/EC. In addition, products whose durability has been extended by use of packaging gas must be so indicate by labelling. Trade in products not complying with the updated requirements if the 1994 and 1995 Directives is prohibited under the 1995 Regulations from June 30, 1996. The Regulations came into effect on December 22, 1995.

Quick-frozen foods: temperature European Communities (Monitoring Of Temperature in the Means of Transport, Warehousing and Storage of Quick-Frozen Foodstuffs and Sampling Procedure and Methods of Analysis for Control of the Temperatures of Quick-Frozen Foods Intended for Human Consumption) Regulations 1995 (SI No. 370 of 1995) gave effect to Directives 92/1/EC and 92/2/EC. They provide for monitoring of temperatures and sampling and analysis procedures in respect of quick-frozen foods intended for human consumption and create offences for failure to comply with the provisions of the 1992 Directives. They came into effect on December 15, 1995. The title of the Regulations would be unlikely to claim first prize for providing a succinct statement of their subject-matter.

MANUFACTURING STANDARDS

In previous Reviews, we have noted the increased number of EC 'New Approach' or 'Approximation' Directives which establish minimum safety and health criteria for various products and which are linked to detailed technical standards, or European Norms (EN), developed by the European Standards bodies such as CEN and CENELEC. In 1995, a number of Regulations gave effect to further 'New Approach' Directives. We also refer to a statutory Order concerning furniture safety owing its origin to national standards-setting.

Appliances burning gaseous fuels The European Communities (Appliances Burning Gaseous Fuels) (Amendment) Regulations 1995 (SI No. 150 of 1995) amended the European Communities (Appliances Burning Gaseous Fuels) Regulations 1992 (1992 Review, 538) to give effect to Directive 93/68/EEC on the 'CE' marking Directive (1994 Review, 402) in so far as it related to Directive 90/396/EEC, which had been implemented by the 1992 Regulations. The 1995 Regulations came into effect on June 12, 1995.

Boilers The European Communities (Efficiency Requirements For New Hot-Water Boilers Fired With Liquid Or Gaseous Fuels) (Amendment) Regulations 1995 (SI No. 72 of 1995) amended the European Communities (Efficiency Requirements For New Hot-Water Boilers Fired With Liquid Or Gaseous Fuels) Regulations 1994 in order to give effect to Directive 93/68/EEC, the 'CE' marking Directive (1994 Review, 402) in so far as it related to Directive 92/42/EEC, which had been implemented by the 1994 Regulations. The 1995 Regulations came into effect on March 23, 1995.

Explosives The European Communities (Placing On The Market And Supervision Of Explosives For Civil Uses) Regulations 1995 (SI No. 115 of 1995) are discussed above, 437.

Furniture: fire safety The Industrial Research and Standards (Fire Safety) (Domestic Furniture) Order 1995 (SI No. 316 of 1995) was made pursuant to s. 44 of the Industrial Research and Standards Act 1961. It provides that new and second- hand furniture is designed, manufactured and constructed to a particular standard so as not to endanger persons or property. Furniture will be accepted as complying with the order if it is to IS 419: 1988 or equivalent standard. The Order came into force on January 1, 1996 and replaces the Industrial Research and Standards (Fire Safety) (Domestic Furniture) Order 1988 (1988 Review, 375), which was revoked.

Machinery The European Communities (Machinery) (Amendment) Regulations 1995 (SI No. 372 of 1995) amended the European Communities (Machinery) Regulations 1994 (1994 Review, 403) and gave further effect to Directive 89/392/EEC, as amended by Directives 91/368/EEC, 93/44/EEC and 93/68/EEC. In particular, they expand and clarify provisions in relation to roll over and falling object protective structures (ROPS and FOPS), which are particularly important in the construction sector. The 1995 Regulations came into effect on December 21, 1995.

OCCUPATIONAL SAFETY

Repeal and revocation of obsolete legislation In the 1993 Review, 486, we referred briefly to the terms of the Safety, Health and Welfare at Work Act 1989 (Repeals and Revocations) Order 1995 (SI No. 357 of 1995). In brief, the 1995 Order effected the repeal of much well-established primary and secondary legislation, with effect from December 21, 1995. The Order was made pursuant to the powers of repeal and revocation conferred by ss. 1 and 4 of the Safety, Health and Welfare at Work act 1989 by which virtually all pre-1989 legislation in this area may be repealed by Order. The 1995 Order is the most radical such Order to date and may be seen against the background of the Safety, Health and Welfare at Work (General Application) Regulations 1993 (1993 Review, 483-503) which, along with other Regulations, had made redundant existing legislation. The opportunity was also taken to repeal and revoke otherwise obsolete legislative provisions. While not principally heralded as a 'deregulation' provision, the 1995 Order may be seen as having removed much legislative 'dead wood', albeit provisions with which practitioners had become familiar.

Office premises The 1995 Order repealed in toto the Office Premises Act 1958 and all Regulations made under the Act; premises which were previously regulated by the 1958 Act (as well as smaller offices not covered by the 1958 Act) are now, of course subject to the 1989 Act and the many Regulations made under the 1989 Act.

Factories and industrial premises The 1995 Order also repealed a great deal of the Factories Act 1955, as amended by the Safety in Industry Act 1980 and revoked many Regulations made under these Acts and their predecessors. In connection with the 1955 Act, all or portions of 53 sections (out of a total of 126 in the original Act) were repealed, leaving only 60 sections in force, either in whole or in part (the 1989 Act had itself repealed certain provisions of the 1955 Act). A similar pruning is evident in connection with the 1980 Act. It is evident that the 1955 Act is ultimately destined to be repealed in full, leaving factories and other industrial premises to be governed by the 1989 Act and the Regulations made under it. To underline the scope of the pruning effected, the 1995 Order also revoked 51 separate statutory instruments made under the 1955 and 1980 Acts or their predecessors, most involving complete rather than partial revocations. These revocations included the Manufacture of Felt Hats Regulations 1902 (the 'mad hatter' Regulations), the Factories (Electricity) Regulations 1972 and 1979, the Factories Act 1955 (Manual Labour) (Maximum Weights and Transport) Regulations 1972 and the Factories (Protection of Eyes) Regulations 1979. As with the provisions of the 1955 and 1980 Acts, these were either obsolete or had otherwise been superseded by Regulations made under the 1989 Act, notably the Safety, Health and Welfare at Work (General Application) Regulations 1993.

Other provisions A number of provisions of the Mines and Quarries Act 1965, the Dangerous Substances Act 1972 and the Safety, Health and Welfare (Offshore Installations) Act 1987, as well as Regulations under the 1965 and 1972 Acts, were also repealed and revoked by the 1995 Order.

Effect of 1995 Order The 1995 Order clearly effected substantial pruning of pre-1989 legislative provisions, as envisaged by the 1989 Act. Similar pruning has been effected in relation to equivalent provisions in British legislation, such as the Factories Act 1961. In the Irish context, the 1989 Act and the Regulations made under it must now be seen as the new generation of legislative provisions in this area. It is important to bear in mind that not only does the 1989 Act involve the modernisation of factory and office legislation, its terms also apply to virtually all places of work, whether factory, office, shop, school, university or motor vehicle. In that respect, the transformation of the legislative landscape has been more radical than a mere 'tidying up' of pre-1989 legislation.

Construction and civil engineering The Safety, Health and Welfare at Work (Construction) Regulations 1995 (SI No. 138 of 1995), made under the Safety, Health and Welfare at Work Act 1989 (1989 Review, 379-93) implemented Directive 92/57/EEC. The 1995 Regulations are more wide-ranging than their title might indicate. The Regulations apply, of course, to building sites, but they also include many civil engineering projects as well as maintenance activities connected with existing buildings, such as painting, cleaning and other decorating. They also revoked and replaced the Construction (Safety, Health and Welfare) Regulations 1975, as amended (thus effecting further updating in this area, though not as radical as the Repeals and Revocations Order 1995 discussed above). While the 1995 Regulations involved some welcome updating of the 1975 Regulations, Part II (Regs. 3 to 7) also introduced for the first time important new obligations on those involved in the preparation and design of building and civil engineering projects which commence on or after March 1996.

Design and management duties The 1995 Regulations impose significant design and management duties on the following: the client (the person who commissions a project); the project supervisor for the design stage (who must be appointed by the client at the pre-tender stage of a project, or its equivalent in the case of project not placed to tender); designers other than project supervisors; and the project supervisor for the construction stage (who must also be appointed by the client at the post-tender stage of a project, or its equivalent).

It is not possible in the present context to outline the extent of the duties imposed on the different parties by the 1995 Regulations. We note, however, that they are wide-ranging and have caused considerable controversy within the building trade and associated professions such as architects, particularly having regard to the potential for increased civil liability for accidents occurring in the course of a projects even where such accidents are incurred by persons employed or under the control of sub-contractors. Such vicarious liability was a matter of fact under the previous Regulations in this area, but the 1995 Regulations may have further extended the scope of such claims. This may be seen from the type of documentation which the 1995 Regulations requires of those involved in the management of construction projects.

Safety and Health Plan; Safety File Two documents feature in the design and management of projects covered by the terms of the 1995 Regulations, the Safety and Health Plan and the Safety File. Both documents are the principal responsibility of the project supervisors appointed by the client. The Safety and Health plan is not defined with precision in the 1995 Regulations, but Reg.4 requires that the project supervisors take account of the requirements of s. 12 of the Safety, Health and Welfare at Work Act 1989, which involves the need to engage in risk assessments and organisational measures to implement safety policy. This would appear to include the risks involved for all persons in a project. Indeed, the Regulations require the project supervisor to co-ordinate the activities of all contractors involved in a project to ensure the consistent application of safe working practices; failure to do so could clearly have implications in civil liability. Reg.4(2) specifies that a Safety and Health Plan is required either: (a) where notification of the construction site is required under Regulation 7 (that is, work will last longer than 30 working days or the volume of work will exceed 500 person-days); or (b) where the work involves particular risks, including those specified in the Second Schedule to the Regulations. Thus, a Safety and Health Plan is not required for all the construction projects covered by the 1995 Regulations. However, where required it appears to impose wide-ranging responsibilities on those appointed as Project Supervisors.

By contrast with the Safety and Health Plan, the 1995 Regulations expressly provide that the Safety File is intended to provide information for use during any subsequent construction work following completion of the project; that is it is a type of Maintenance Manual and would include, for example, electrical plans, pipe-work and similar matters. The Safety File is therefore intended to have an almost indefinite life span. Reg.6(2) specifies that a safety file must be prepared by the Project Supervisors where more than one contractor is engaged in a construction project. and it must be given to the client at the end of the project. Reg.3 requires the client to keep the Safety File available for inspection.

Duties of contractors in construction work As was the case with the Construction (Safety, Health and Welfare) Regulations 1975, the primary responsibility for ensuring the safety, health and welfare of people at work on a construction site rests on their direct employer. This is, of course, entirely consistent with the general principles contained in the Safety, Health and Welfare at Work Act 1989. While the 1995 Regulations have imposed additional obligations on those involved in the design and overall management of a project, these are in the nature of supervisory and co-ordinating functions. It remains the case that the employer/contractor retains a great deal of responsibility. This may be seen in the retention in Reg.9 of the 1995 Regulations of the obligation on the contractor/employer to appoint a Safety Officer where 20 or more persons are under the contractor's control.

Detailed requirements for safety, health and welfare The contractor is required by the 1995 Regulations to comply with the detailed provisions contained in Parts IV to XVIII of the Regulations (Regulations 14 to 128) as well as the appropriate requirements of the Fourth and Fifth Schedules as regards any place of work under the contractor's control (another 29 major headings). We do not discuss these provisions in detail here, but it may be of some use to list the various headings involved, which include the traditional topics of scaffolding as well as some additional provisions, such as working in a compressed air atmosphere. The following is a listing based on the headings in the 1995 Regulations.

1. Access to places where facilities are provided (Fourth Schedule, point 15).

2. Accommodation areas (Fourth Schedule, point 14).

3. Atmospheric influences (Fourth Schedule, point 5).

4. Carriage of persons and secureness of loads (Part XVII, Regulations 119 to 123).

5. Chains, ropes and lifting gear (Part XV, Regulations 105 to 113).

6. Cofferdams and caissons (Part VI, Regulations 26 to 29).

7. Compressed air (Part VII, Regulations 30 to 33).

8. Dangerous or unhealthy atmospheres (Part IX, Regulations 35 to 38).

9. Demolition (Part XII, Regulations 47 to 50).

10. Disabled (handicapped) workers (Fourth Schedule, point 17).

11. Doors and gates (Fourth Schedule, point 9 and Fifth Schedule, point 8).

12. Emergency routes and exits (Fourth Schedule, point 3 and Fifth Schedule, point 2).

13. Energy distribution installations (Fourth Schedule, point 2).

14. Escalators and travelators (Fifth Schedule, point 10).

15. Excavations, shafts, earthworks, underground works and tunnels (Part V, Regulations 20 to 25).

16. Explosives (Part VIII, Regulation 34).

17. Fire fighting and detecting (Fourth Schedule, point 4).

18. Floors, walls, ceilings and roofs of rooms (Fifth Schedule, point 6).

19. Freedom of movement at workstations (Fourth Schedule, point 12 and Fifth Schedule, point 11).

20. General safety of workplaces (Part IV, Regulations 14 to 19).

21. Heights (including scaffolds)(Part XIII, Regulations 51 to 79).

22. Hoists (Part XVI, Regulations 114 to 118).

23. Lifting appliances (Part XIV, Regulations 80 to 104).

24. Lighting (Fourth Schedule, point 8 and Fifth Schedule, point 5).

25. Loading bays and ramps (Fourth Schedule, point 11).

26. Miscellaneous (Part XVIII, Regulations 124 to 128).

27. Perimeter (Fourth Schedule, point 18).

28. Pregnant women and nursing mothers (Fourth Schedule, point 16).

29. Stability and solidity (Fourth Schedule, point 1 and Fifth Schedule, point 1).

30. Temperature (Fourth Schedule, point 7 and Fifth Schedule, point 4).

31. Traffic routes — danger areas (Fourth Schedule, point 10 and Fifth Schedule, point 9).

32. Transport, earthmoving and materials-handling machinery and locomotives (Part XI, Regulations 41 to 46).

33. Ventilation (Fourth Schedule, point 6 and Fifth Schedule, point 3).

34. Water (work on or near) (Part X, Regulations 39 and 40).

35. Welfare facilities (Fourth Schedule, point 13).

36. Windows and skylights (Fifth Schedule, point 7).

It is clear from this listing that the 1995 Regulations contain considerable prescriptive detail in line with their 1975 predecessor.

Safety signs and signals The Safety, Health and Welfare at Work (Signs) Regulations 1995 (SI No. 132 of 1995) implemented Directive 92/58/EEC. Unlike the Construction Regulations 1995 discussed above, the 1995 Regulations apply to virtually all places of work; indeed they apply to construction projects as well as factories, offices, shops and schools. The 1995 Regulations revoked and replaced the European Communities (Safety Signs at Places of Work) Regulations 1980, which applied to a limited number of places of work (thus effecting yet more reform of previous legislative provisions, though on a more modest scale than that contained in the Repeals and Revocations Order 1995, discussed above).

General duty Reg.4 of the 1995 Regulations requires all employers to provide safety or health signs and ensure that they are in place where hazards cannot be avoided or adequately reduced by either techniques for collective protection or measures, methods or procedures used in the organisation of work.

Signs and signals Although the 1995 Regulations use the simple word 'signs' in their title, they in fact apply to a very wide range of methods for providing information or instructions about safety or health. These include:

— colours, based on an internationally recognised colour coding system

— pictograms, that is signs providing pictorial rather than textual information

— illuminated signs, including 'Emergency Exit' and similar signs

— labels required for pipes and other containers of dangerous substances and preparations

— signals, including acoustic, verbal and hand signals; and

— signboards, including the 'no smoking' sign.

This indicates that the scope of the 1995 Regulations are much wider in scope than the 1980 Regulations they replace: the 1995 Regulations apply to a much greater range of places of work and they require employers to provide signage and signals across a much greater range of matters (the 1980 Regulations being confined primarily to signboards only).

New and existing signs Reg.7 of the 1995 Regulations specifies that signs used for the first time after the Regulations came into force, on June 1, 1995, must comply with the Regulations immediately. However, signs already in use on June 1, 1995 were given until December 1, 1996 to comply with the 1995 Regulations, assuming any adjustment or modification was required.

Welfare provisions The Safety, Health and Welfare at Work (Miscellaneous Welfare Provisions) Regulations 1995 (SI No. 358 of 1995) apply to most 'indoor' places of work (thus, construction projects, covered by the Construction Regulations 1995, discussed above are excluded from the requirements of the Regulations). They require employers to ensure that appropriate arrangements are in place to remove accumulations of rubbish on a daily basis and that appropriate facilities for providing drinking water and accommodation for meals are in place. The Regulations also impose an obligation to provide seating to employees where work may be done seated. A previous statutory arrangement for seating, contained in the Shops (Conditions of Employment) Act 1938, suffered from the dual defect that it applied only to shops and applied only for the benefit of female employees; the 1995 Regulations are gender neutral. The 1995 Regulations, which came into effect on 21 December 1995, are 'miscellaneous' in that many matters which may be thought to fall under the heading of 'welfare' had been dealt with in Part III of the Safety, Health and Welfare at Work (General Application) Regulations 1993 (1993 Review, 492-4). The 1995 Regulations have extended to many places of work provisions that formerly applied to factories and larger offices only. They may also be seen against the background of the Safety, Health and Welfare at Work (Repeals and Revocations) Order 1995 (SI No. 357 of 1995), discussed above, which were also signed into law on the same date.

TOBACCO

Smoking restrictions in public areas   The Tobacco (Health Promotion and Protection) Regulations 1995 (SI No. 359 of 1995), made under the Tobacco (Health Promotion and Protection) Act 1988 (1988 Review, 377) revoked and replaced the Tobacco (Health Promotion and Protection) Regulations 1990 (1990 Review, 476). The 1995 Regulations extended the range of public places and facilities (such as bus and train stations, cinemas, food preparation areas, restaurants, theatres and places of public assembly) in respect of which the consumption of tobacco products is either prohibited or restricted. The Regulations came into effect in the main on January 1, 1996. However, new provisions concerning the provision of a minimum proportion of non-smoking seating in restaurants, cafes and snack bars came into effect on May 1, 1996.

WATER POLLUTION

Sea pollution: contracting States   The Prevention Of Pollution From Ships (Marpol 73/78) (Countries Of Acceptance) Order 1995 (SI No. 116 of 1995), made under the Sea Pollution Act 1991 (1991 Review, 366) provided that the governments of the countries specified in the Schedule have accepted the 1973 International Convention for the Prevention of Pollution from Ships as amended by the 1978 Protocol thereto (commonly known as Marpol 73/78) and that the Convention extends to the territories specified in Part II of the Schedule. The Sea Pollution Act 1991 (Intervention Convention) (Countries Of Acceptance) Order 1995 (SI No. 117 of 1995), also made under the 1991 Act, declared the countries specified in the Schedule to have accepted the 1969 International Convention relating to Intervention on the High Seas in Cases of Oil Pollution Casualties and that the Convention extends to the territories specified in Part II of the Schedule. The Sea Pollution Act 1991 (Intervention Protocol) (Countries Of Acceptance) Order 1995 (SI No. 118 of 1995), also made under the 1991 Act, declared the countries specified in the Schedule to have accepted the 1973 Protocol relating to Intervention on the High Seas in Cases of Pollution by Substances other than Oil and that the Protocol extends to the territories specified in Part II of the Schedule. The three Orders came into effect on May 15, 1995.

Social Welfare

Gerry Whyte, Law School, Trinity College Dublin

SOCIAL WELFARE ACTS

Two Social Welfare Acts were passed during 1995. The Social Welfare Act 1995 provides for the annual budgetary increases in welfare payments. In addition, it also provides for the introduction of an Adoptive Benefit Scheme and for an extension of the Carer's Allowance Scheme to carers of incapacitated people age 66 or over who are not in receipt of a social welfare payment. The Act also effects some changes in the rates of PRSI contributions and other miscellaneous changes to the social welfare code.

The Social Welfare (No. 2) Act 1995 was enacted in anticipation of the removal of the constitutional ban on divorce and it seeks to ensure that no spouse will be disadvantaged in terms of his or her social welfare entitlements as a result of being divorced. Thus, in particular, entitlement to Survivor's Pension is extended to divorced persons on the death of their former spouse, provided that they have not remarried or are not cohabiting.

REGULATIONS

Twenty one regulations pertaining to income maintenance schemes were passed during 1995. They were as follows:

European Communities (Social Welfare) Regulations 1995 [SI No. 25 of 1995] — These regulations provide for the payment of Health and Safety Benefit to a woman who (a) is pregnant or has recently given birth (up to 14 weeks after giving birth) or is breastfeeding (up to 26 weeks after giving birth); (b) has been awarded health and safety leave under s. 18 of the Maternity Protection Act 1994 and c) satisfies the appropriate contribution conditions.

Social Welfare (Consolidated Payments Provisions) (Amendment) Regulations 1995 [SI No. 26 of 1995] — These regulations prescribe the amount of reckonable weekly earnings a claimant must have to qualify for Health and Safety Benefit. They also provide for the payment of reduced rates of benefit to claimants whose reckonable weekly earnings are below this prescribed amount, the making of claims and payments and the determination of the amount of welfare payable where a person is entitled to both Health and Safety Benefit and another social welfare payment at the same time.

Social Welfare (Modifications of Insurance) (Amendment) Regulations 1995 [SI No. 77 of 1995] — These regulations provide for the extension of full PRSI to new employees in the public sector from April 6, 1995 and for the modification of the amount of PRSI payable in a number of miscellaneous employments.

Social Welfare (Optional Contributions) (Amendment) Regulations 1995 [SI No. 79 of 1995] — These regulations reduce the minimum social insurance contribution payable by share fishermen who apply to become optional contributors in the contribution year in which they first became insured as self-employed contributors from £250 to £230.

Social Welfare (Subsidiary Employments) Regulations 1995 [SI No. 80 of 1995] — These regulations specify certain categories of employment as being of subsidiary nature.

Social Welfare Act 1995 (Section 11) (Commencement) Order 1995 [SI No. 93 of 1995] — This order brings s. 11 of the 1995 Act, which provides for the payment of Adoptive Benefit, into effect from April 19, 1995.

Social Welfare (Consolidated Payments Provisions) (Amendment) (No. 2) Regulations 1995 [SI No. 94 of 1995] — These regulations provide for the maximum and minimum rates of Adoptive Benefit and also regulate a number of miscellaneous matters pertaining to that benefit.

Social Welfare Act 1995 (Section 14) (Commencement) Order 1995 [SI No. 112 of 1995] — This order brings s. 14 of the 1995 Act, which extends the definition of a qualified child for the purpose of paying child dependant increases, into effect on different specified dates for different payments between April 27 and May 3, 1995.

Social Welfare (Understanding with Quebec on Social Security) Order 1995 [SI No. 120 of 1995] — This order gives effect to a bilateral understanding between Ireland and Quebec allowing for, *inter alia*, recognition of insurance contributions paid in Ireland and periods of residence/insurance in Quebec to count towards eligibility for specific welfare payments in the other jurisdiction.

Social Welfare (Occupational Injuries) (Amendment) Regulations 1995 [SI No. 137 of 1995] — These regulations provide for increases in the reduced rates of certain occupational injuries benefits.

Infectious Diseases (Maintenance Allowances) Regulations 1995 [SI No. 140 of 1995] — These regulations provide for the annual increase in this payment.

Disabled Persons Maintenance Allowances Regulations 1995 [SI No. 141 of 1995] — These regulations consolidate earlier regulations relating to this scheme and provide for the annual increase in payment.

Social Welfare (Rent Allowance) (Amendment) Regulations 1995 [SI No.

143 of 1995] — These regulations provide for increases in the amount of means disregarded for the purposes of the means test for rent allowance and also prescribe the minimum rent for the purpose of the scheme. They also extend the definition of child in relation to certain aspects of the scheme.

Social Welfare (Consolidated Payments Provisions) (Amendment) (No. 3) Regulations 1995 [SI No. 146 of 1995] — These regulations provide for increases in the reduced rates of certain specified benefits and for increases in the minimum and maximum weekly rates of Maternity Benefit and Adoptive Benefit. They also provide that a woman will not be entitled to Disability Benefit in respect of any day for which she is paid by her employer in respect of health and safety leave.

Social Welfare (No. 2) Act 1995 (Section 11) (Commencement) Order 1995 [SI No. 241 of 1995] — This order brings s. 11 of the Social Welfare (No. 2) Act 1995, which amends the means test for Unemployment Assistance purposes in the case of persons engaged in seasonal work, into effect from September 7, 1995.

Social Welfare (Consolidated Payments Provisions) (Amendment) (No. 4) Regulations 1995 [SI No. 242 of 1995] — These regulations exempt from the assessment of means for social assistance purposes the capital value of a person's home where they vacate the home on a temporary basis or indefinitely due to old age or incapacity. In addition, where the property has been put on the market, the property will not be assessed during a period of not more than two years from the date it was offered for sale while it remains unsold. The regulations also prescribe the method of assessing the weekly earnings of a person derived from seasonal work for the the the purposes of Unemployment Assistance.

Social Welfare (Temporary Provisions) Regulations 1995 [SI No. 302 of 1995] — These regulations provide for the payment of the annual Christmas bonus.

Social Welfare (Consolidated Payments Provisions) (Amendment) (No. 5) Regulations 1995 [SI No. 303 of 1995] — These regulations provide for the payment of child dependant increases to recipients of long term welfare payments in respect of children up to the age of 22 in full-time education. They also amend SI No. 242 of 1995 (see above) so as to confirm that the exemption from the assessment of means of a person's home which s/he has vacated due to old age or infirmity only applies where the home has not been put to profitable use.

Social Welfare (School Meals (National Schools)) Regulations 1995 [SI No. 307 of 1995] — These regulations provide for the continuation of the Urban School Meals Scheme in the Dun Laoghaire Borough area.

Social Welfare (Consolidation) Act 1993 (Sixth Schedule (Paragraph 3))

Commencement Order 1995 [SI No. 381 of 1995] — This order brings into effect paragraph 3 of the sixth Schedule to the 1993 Act with effect from January 1, 1996. This paragraph provides for the payment of supplements under the Supplementary Welfare Allowance scheme.

Social Welfare (Consolidated Supplementary Welfare Allowance) Regulations 1995 [SI No. 382 of 1995] — These regulations continue the important process of consolidation of social welfare regulations initiated by the Department of Social Welfare in 1993. On this occasion, the regulations relating to Supplementary Welfare Allowance are consolidated.

The new regulations also provide that the disqualification of people in full-time education will not apply to participants in educational initiatives for the unemployed and that the disqualification of people in full-time employments will not apply to participants in special schemes for the unemployed.

EQUAL TREATMENT

During 1995, Directive 79/7/EEC on the progressive implementation of the principle of equal treatment of men and women in matters of social security continued to be the focus of a number of Court of Justice decisions and of one important High Court case. (Readers are referred back to the 1993 Review, pp. 512-25, for an overview of the impact of this Directive.)

Scope of the Directive: Ratione materiae In *Bestuur van het Algemeen burgerlijk pensioenfonds v G.A. Beune*, Case 7/93, 28 September 1994, the Court of Justice was asked to determine the dividing line between Art. 119 of the Treaty of Rome, which guarantees equal pay, and Directive 79/7/EEC in relation to a statutory scheme of pensions for civil servants. The Court ruled that the fact that the scheme was directly governed by statute was not sufficient to exclude it from the scope of Art. 119 and that the decisive criterion was whether the pension was paid to the worker by reason of the employment relationship between the worker and his former employment. It followed that the civil service pension scheme in the instant case fell within the scope of Art. 119 rather than Directive 79/7/EEC.

In *R. v Secretary of State for Health, e.p. Richardson*, Case C-137/94, October 19, 1995, the Court of Justice held that a statutory system of exemptions from prescription charges fell within Art.4(1).

Direct discrimination The prohibition of direct discrimination provided for by Directive 79/7/EEC is not absolute. Article 7(1) allows member States to exclude certain matters from the scope of the Directive, namely:

> the determination of pensionable age for the purposes of granting old age and retirement pensions and the possible consequences thereof for other benefits; advantages in respect of old age pension schemes granted to persons who have brought up children and the acquisition of benefit entitlements following periods of interruption of employment due to the bringing up of children; the granting of old age or invalidity entitlements by virtue of the derived entitlements of a wife;
> the granting of increases of long-term invalidity, old age, accidents at work and occupational disease benefits for a dependent wife;
> the consequences of the exercise, before the adoption of this directive, of a right of option not to acquire or incur obligations under a statutory scheme.

Prior to the promulgation of the Social Welfare (Old Age (Contributory) Pension) Regulations 1994 [SI No. 235 of 1994], the Irish welfare code had not had to rely on any of these derogations. However those regulations provide that contribution years spent working in the home while caring on a full-time basis for a child up to the age of 6 or an incapacitated person will be disregarded in calculating a person's yearly average number of contributions for the purposes of certain social insurance entitlements. Such a provision clearly constitutes indirect discrimination in favour of women who constitute the majority of carers and therefore needs to come within the scope of Art.7(1) or be objectively justified if it is to avoid challenge under the 1979 Directive. While Art.7(1) clearly permits special arrangements to be made in relation to persons who were engaged in full-time child-care, unfortunately it makes no comparable provision for persons engaged in full-time care of an incapacitated person. However a policy of providing adequate care for incapacitated persons arguably provides objective justification for this latter aspect of the 1994 Regulations.

In the light of this reliance, for the first time, by the Irish welfare code on Art.7(1), it is perhaps worth summarising briefly the jurisprudence of the Court of Justice on the derogations permitted to Directive 79/7/EEC.

The first derogation referred to in Art.7(1) was considered by the Court of Justice in *R. v Secretary of State for Social Security, ex parte the Equal Opportunities Commission*, Case 9/91. Here the Court held that though Art.7(1) did not refer expressly to discrimination in respect of the extent of the obligation to contribute for the purposes of the pension, such a discrimination would be permissible if it was found necessary in order to achieve the objective of that article, in this context, permitting member states to retain different pensionable ages for men and women. According to the Court, '[i]n a system such as the one concerned in the main proceedings, whose financial equilibrium is based on men contributing for a longer period than women, a different pensionable age for men and women cannot be maintained without altering the existing financial equilibrium, unless such inequality with respect to the length of contribution periods is also maintained'. In the subsequent case of *Thomas v Secretary of State for Social Security*, Case 328/91, 30 March 1993, the Court held that Art.7(1) did not entitle the British authorities to maintain different qualifying ages for severe disablement allowance and invalid care allowance as these forms of discrimination were not necessarily and objectively linked to differences in retirement age. More recently again, in *Van Cant v Rijksdienst voor Pensioenen*, Case 154/92, July 1, 1993, the Court of Justice held that Arts. 4(1) and 7(1) precluded national legislation which permits men and women to retire at identical ages but which maintains in the method of calculating the pension a difference depending on sex, such difference being linked to differences in retirement age which existed under previous legislation.

In a subsequent case, *Bramhill v Chief Adjudication Officer*, Case 420/92, 7 July 1994, the Court of Justice departed from its previous strict approach to the interpretation of Art.7(1). At issue here was whether Art.7(1)(d), which permits a departure from the principle of equal treatment in respect of the granting of increases of long-term invalidity, old age, accidents at work and occupational disease benefits for a dependent wife, protected a system of dependency allowances which provided increases for both husbands and wives but on different conditions. The claimant's main contention was that Art.7(1)(d) only protected a system of such allowances payable exclusively to husbands. However this argument was rejected by the Court of Justice on the ground that it would impede the *progressive implementation* of the principle of equal treatment and accordingly it held that the discrimination in question fell within the scope of the derogation. In *van Munster v. Rijksdienst voor pensioenen*, Case 165/91, October 5, 1994, the Court of Justice held that Art.7(1)(c) allowed a member State to refuse to pay the houshold rate of pension (applicable to claimants with dependent spouses) to a claimant whose spouse is entitled in his/her own right to a pension. The Court also held, in *Secretary of State for Social Security v Graham*, Case C-92/94, August 11, 1995, that member States are entitled to provide that the rate of invalidity pension payable to persons becoming incapacitated before pensionable age is to be limited to the actual rate of retirement pension from the age of 60 in the case of women and 65 in the case of men and to reserve entitlement to invalidity allowance, payable in addition to invalidity pension, to those persons who are aged under 55, in the case of women, and under 60, in the case of men, at the time when they first become incapacitated for work. However, in *R. v Secretary of State for Health, e.p. Richardson*, Case C- 137/94, October 19, 1995, the Court held that Art.7(1)(a) did not allow a member State to use different qualifying ages, based on the differing pensionable ages, in a statutory scheme of exemptions from prescription charges.

Indirect discrimination In the 1993 Review, it was suggested that the exclusion of many part-time workers from social insurance prior to 1992 (and the continued exclusion of a small number of such workers since that time) might constitute unlawful indirect discrimination, contrary to the 1979 Directive — see the 1993 Review, p. 518. However two decisions of the Court of Justice in 1995 indicate that this may not, in fact, be the case. In Case C-317/1993, *Nolte v Landesversicherungsanstalt Hannover*, December 14, 1995, the Court held that the exclusion of some minimal employment (regularly consisting of fewer than 15 hours' work a week and regularly attracting remuneration of up to one-seventh of the average monthly salary) from old age insurance corresponded to 'a structural principle of the German social security scheme' and so was not contrary to Directive 79/7/EEC. A similar decision was reached in Case C-444/1993, *Megner v Innungs-kranken-Kasse Vorderpfalz*, December 14, 1995, concerning the exclusion of minor or short-term employment from certain insurance schemes.

In the earlier case of *MA Roks v Bestuur van de Bedrijsvereniging voor de Gezondheid*, Case 343/92, February 24, 1994, the Court of Justice placed certain limits on the defence of objective justification under Directive 79/7/EEC when it ruled that budgetary considerations could not justify indirect discrimination. The Court reasoned that to accept such a justification would be to accept that the application and scope of as fundamental a rule of Community law as that of equal treatment between men and women might vary in time and place according to the state of the public finances of the Member States.

Reception of the Directive in Ireland It will be recalled that implemen-tation of Directive 79/7/EEC in Ireland took place in three different stages and that the promulgation of the European Communities (Social Welfare) Regulations 1992 [SI No. 152 of 1992] in the last of these three stages still left many doubts about whether Ireland had complied sufficiently with its obligations under the 1979 Directive — see the 1993 Review, p. 520. In *Tate v Minister for Social Welfare* [1995] ILRM 507; [1995] 1 IR 418, Carroll J clarified many aspects of the law governing entitlement to arrears under Directive 79/7/EEC. First, she confirmed that the payment of transitional payments between November 1986 and July 1992 constituted a breach of the Directive and that, having regard to *Marshall v Southampton and South West*

Hampshire Area Health Authority (No. 2), Case 271/91, August 2, 1993, the amount of arrears payable to any claimant would have to be adjusted in line with the Consumer Price Index in order fully to compensate for delay. She also held that the failure of the State to comply fully with the Directive was neither a breach of constitutional rights, a breach of statutory duty nor a breach of duty of care but was rather a wrong under Community law which approximated to a breach of constitutional duty. The word 'tort' in the Statute of Limitations was sufficiently wide to cover this breach of the State's obligations under Community law so that the limitation period of six years in s. 11(2) of the Statute was applicable. The 1992 Regulations created a new cause of action insofar as they failed fully to implement the Directive with regard to entitlement to dependency allowances and arrears of unemployment assistance so that, with regard to these claims, the time limit started to run from June 1992. However, insofar as the Regulations never addressed the issue of transitional payments at all, there was no new cause of action here. Moreover, having regard to the effect, in practice, of s. 11(2) in cases of continuing breach of duty (i.e. it limited the amount of arrears payable but did not preclude the initiation of any action), that section could be relied on by the State in the light of Case 338/91, *Steenhorst-Neerings v Bestuur van de Bedrijfsveriniging voor Detailhandel, Ambachten en Huisvrouwen*, October 27, 1993. (For discussion of this case, see the 1993 Review, pp. 516, 523) The judge also found that there was no evidence to support the claim that the State was estopped from relying on the Statute of Limitations. Finally, she held that it was not necessary to declare the 1992 Regulations to be null and void but that the State could not rely on any portion thereof which had the effect of not fully recognising the plaintiffs' rights under the Directive.

In the aftermath of this decision, the Minister for Social Welfare, Proinsias de Rossa, TD announced that compensation of up to £265m would be paid to 70,000 married women, thereby effectively bringing the long-drawn saga over the implementation of Directive 79/7/EEC in Ireland to a close.

TRADE DISPUTE DISQUALIFICATION

One of the by-products of the industrial dispute at the Irish Press companies was the resurrection of the Social Welfare Tribunal (SWT) which has been inactive for much of this decade. In *O'Connor v Irish Press Newspapers Ltd*, A1/95, [1995] ELR 152, the Tribunal was asked to determine, pursuant to s. 275 of the Social Welfare (Consolidation) Act 1993, whether the applicants had been unreasonably been deprived of their employment such that they could qualify for receipt of unemployment benefit and unemployment assistance, notwithstanding their participation in industrial action.

Operating pursuant to ss. 274-6 of the 1993 Act, the Social Welfare Tribunal is empowered to award unemployment benefit and/or unemployment assistance to workers who are unemployed as a result of a trade dispute where it is determined that they have been unreasonably been deprived of their employment. The Tribunal is thus authorised to moderate the impact of ss. 47(1) and 125(3) which disqualify such workers for receipt of unemployment benefit and assistance respectively. The Tribunal does not hear appeals from the decision of the deciding and appeals officers on the application of ss. 47(1) and 125(3) — indeed it can only proceed where an appeals officer has confirmed the decision of a deciding officer to apply the trade dispute disqualification. Those officials have to decide whether the conditions for the application of the disqualification apply and their findings are not open to challenge before the Tribunal. Instead the Tribunal has to address an entirely new issue, namely, whether the claimant was unreasonably deprived of employment. S. 275 apparently envisages that the Tribunal should approach this task in two stages, though it must be said that on this point the intention of the legislators is not very clear. S. 275(a) directs the Tribunal, before deciding this issue, to have regard to all the circumstances of the stoppage of work and of the dispute which led to the stoppage. In particular, it must consider whether the claimant was deprived of employment through some act or omission on the part of the employer which amounted to unfair treatment of the claimant; whether the claimant was prevented by the employer from attending for work without any reasonable or adequate consultation by the employer with the applicant or his trade union or without the use by the employer of the services normally availed of by employers in the interests of good industrial relations; whether any action or decision by the employer, amounting to a worsening of the terms or conditions of employment of the applicant and taken without adequate consultation or notice, was a material cause of the stoppage of work or of the trade dispute; and whether the conduct of the applicant or of his trade union was reasonable. S. 275(b) then directs the Tribunal to decide whether the applicant was unreasonably deprived of his employment after having considered, inter alia, whether the conduct of the applicant or of a union acting on his behalf was reasonable and whether the employer or a body acting on his behalf was willing to avail of the services normally availed of in the interests of good industrial relations. In reaching its ultimate conclusion under s. 275(b), it would appear that the Tribunal has to weigh in the balance its various findings under s. 275(a).

The almost invariable tendency of the Tribunal when consulted with these considerations is to focus on the procedures used (or not used) by the parties to the dispute, rather than on the merits of the issue. So it was in the

O'Connor case. The facts of this case, briefly, were that following the summary dismissal of a senior journalist by the company on May 25, 1995, the NUJ employees of the company went into mandatory session. Attempts to arrange a meeting that day under the auspices of the Labour Relations Commission failed because management would not agree to meet unless there was a return to work and the union was not willing to return to work unless the dismissal was suspended, a step which the company was not willing to take. On the same day, and in an entirely unrelated matter, the Supreme Court handed down a decision which exacerbated the already difficult financial situation faced by the company. When the *Irish Press* did not appear the following day, all other staff at the company were laid off. The NUJ members vacated the company's premises on May 30 and a Labour Court hearing on May 31 failed to resolve the dispute. On June 1, the company indicating its intention to go into liquidation though before this process was completed, the workers succeeded in having an examiner appointed to the company. That examinership was still in existence when the case came before the SWT.

On these facts, the Tribunal found, pursuant to s. 275(a)(i), that the applicants were only available for work and willing to work after May 26 but that even then, the employer had not done anything which amounted to unfair or unjust treatment of the applicants. The Tribunal did accept that, after May 26, the applicants could be said to have been prevented from attending for work without reasonable or adequate consultation in the sense of s. 275(a)(ii). However it also took the view that the importance of both of these considerations was significantly diminished by virtue of the financial crisis faced by the company. The Tribunal tersely dismissed the claim that the summary dismissal of the journalist and its surrounding circumstances amounted to a worsening of the terms and conditions of the employment of the applicants under s. 275(a)(iii) before moving on to consider its decision under s. 275(b).

In relation to the behaviour of the union, the Tribunal disapproved of the mandatory meeting being extended into a situation of unofficial industrial action but noted that the union had made reasonable and genuine efforts to resolve the dispute which were not reciprocated by the company. This led on to the Tribunal's further holding that the company did not fully meet the requirement of being willing to avail of the services normally availed of in the interests of good industrial relations. Accordingly the Tribunal concluded that the applicants had been unreasonably deprived of their employment from May 29 and therefore were entitled to receive unemployment benefit or assistance, as the case may be, with effect from that date. (The workers had been laid off on May 26 and so May 29 would have been the earliest date in respect of which unemployment benefit or assistance would ordinarily be payable, given that one cannot claim either payment in respect of the first three days of unemployment — see ss. 42(3) and 120(2)(a) of the 1993 Act.)

This case throws some light on the relationship between paragraphs (a) and (b) of s. 275 insofar as it appears to suggest that a finding in favour of the applicant under any of the headings in paragraph (a) may be vitiated by external factors — in this case, the financial crisis experienced by the company — and so need not automatically lead to a ruling in favour of the applicant under paragraph (b).

SOCIAL WELFARE APPEALS

In *O'Sullivan v Minister for Social Welfare*, High Court, May 9, 1995, Barron J held that, in deciding whether to award costs under s. 298(11) of the former Social Welfare (Consolidation) Act 1981, an appeals officer could not fetter his discretion by deciding to award instead the standard fee of £30 agreed between the Appeals Office and the Law Society as expenses for a solicitor's attendance at a welfare appeal. Section 261(1) of the Social Welfare (Consolidation) Act 1993, which re-enacted s. 298(11), was subsequently amended by s. 34 of the Social Welfare Act 1996 to restrict the appeals officer's discretion to the award of expenses only where expenses mean, *inter alia*, 'an amount only in respect of [the] actual attendance [at a hearing of the appellant's representative]'.

SCOPE OF SOCIAL INSURANCE

The period under review witnessed two decisions on the scope of social insurance cover. In *Denny & Sons Ltd v Minister for Social Welfare*, High Court, October 18, 1995; [1996] 1 ILRM 418; [1996] ELR 43, Carroll J held that an appeals officer's decision that a demonstrator in supermarket outlets was an employee and not an independent contractor was not unreasonable or based on a mistaken view of the law. The appeals officer had based his conclusion on the fact that the elements of control, direction and dismissal which apply in the normal employer/employee relationship were present in the instant case.

In the earlier case of *Foras Áiseanna Saothair v Abbott*, Supreme Court, May 23, 1995, Egan J, delivering the judgment of the Court, drew an important distinction between contracts of employment which are illegal, and therefore not covered by social insurance, and those which are merely *ultra vires* and therefore possibly covered. The contracts in the instant case had infringed a statutory prohibition against *FÁS* entering into contracts for the appointment of staff without the consent of the Ministers for Labour and

Finance. According to the Supreme Court, the relevant statutory provisions — s. 7(1)(a) of the Labour Services Act 1987 and s. 12(3) of the Industrial Training Act 1967 — were intended only to allow the Ministers to exercise an element of control over the expenditure of FAS and did not render any contract entered into in contravention of their terms illegal. Moreover the Court held that the legislation here did not impose a mandatory requirement on *FÁS* and that consequently the contracts were not *ultra vires*.

DISABLED PERSON'S MAINTENANCE ALLOW-ANCE

In *O'Connell v Ireland*, High Court, 31 July 1995; [1996] 1 ILRM 187, the plaintiff, a personal litigant, successfully challenged the validity of Art.6 of the Disabled Person's Maintenance Allowance Regulations 1991 [SI No. 200 of 19911. This provision purported to restrict the amount of Disabled Person's Maintenance Allowance (DPMA) payable to two people married to each other to the amount which would have been payable if one of the spouses was treated as the adult dependant of the other. The effect of this provision would have been to reduce the amount of DPMA payable to the plaintiff s household by approximately 20 per cent. Following *Cooke v. Walshe* [1984] IR 710, Barron J. held that s. 72 of the Health Act 1970, pursuant to which the 1991 regulations had been made, did not empower the Minister to remove, reduce or otherwise alter the obligations imposed on the Health Boards by the 1970 Act and that insofar as the 1991 regulations purported to modify the plaintiff s right to DPMA under s. 69 of that Act, they were *ultra vires* the Minister.

PUBLICATIONS

Finally, attention should be drawn to a number of interesting books and reports which were published during 1995. Professor Robert Clark's *Annotated Guide to Social Welfare Law* is an annotated guide to the Social Welfare Acts 1993 to 1995 while *The Irish Social Welfare System: Law and Social Policy* by Mel Cousins provides an analysis of the social welfare system from both a social and legal perspective. February 1995 witnessed the publication of both the *Interim Report of the Task Force on Long-Term Unemployment* (Pn. 1476) and the Sixth Report of the National Economic and Social Forum, entitled *Quality Delivery of Social Services* (Pn. 1389). The *Report of the Task Force on the Travelling Community* (Pn. 1726) was also published during the year, as was that of the Departmental Review Group on the *Role of Supplementary Welfare Allowance in relation to Housing* (Pn. 2235).

Solicitors

EXEMPTIONS FROM PROFESSIONAL EXAMINATIONS

Prior to 1995, pursuant to Reg.15 of the Solicitors Acts 1954 and 1960 (Apprenticeship and Education) Regulations 1991, the Law Society had granted exemptions from FE-1, the 'entrance examination' to their professional course, to law graduates from the universities of the State provided they had successfully completed the relevant 'core' subjects in their law degrees. In *Bloomer and Ors v Incorporated Law Society of Ireland* [1995] 3 IR 14 (HC); Supreme Court, 6 February 1996, Laffoy J held in the High Court that the exemption in Reg.15 of the 1991 Regulations for law graduates from the universities in the State was invalid because it was in conflict with the prohibition of discrimination on grounds of nationality in Article 6 of the EC Treaty. The plaintiffs, law graduates of Northern Ireland universities, had sought parity with their counterparts from the State. In light of the High Court decision, the Law Society stated that it would henceforth require all persons to sit the FE-1 Examination rather than extend the prior exemption. However, pursuant to Reg.30 of the 1991 Regulations, which empowers it to modify any requirement of the Regulations 'in exceptional circumstances', it decided that the plaintiffs in Bloomer be granted an exemption from FE-1. The effect of this was that the plaintiffs in *Bloomer* had achieved the objective of their proceedings, namely, exemption from FE-1. The plaintiffs had already appealed the High Court decision to the Supreme Court, but the Law Society's decision rendered this moot. Consequently the Supreme Court *ex tempore* judgment in *Bloomer* was concerned primarily with the question of costs, though the Court's formal order confirmed the High Court decision that Reg.15 of the 1991 Regulations was invalid. We will return to the *Bloomer* case in the 1996 Review to discuss it with the subsequent decision of McCracken J in *Abrahamson and Ors v Law Society of Ireland*, High Court, 15 July 1996, in which over 800 undergraduate law students in the State's universities successfully argued that they should also be granted exemptions from FE-1 under Reg.30 of the 1991 Regulations.

JUDICIAL APPOINTMENTS

The effect of the Courts and Court Officers Act 1995 on the appointment of solicitors to the Bench is discussed in the Practice and Procedure chapter, 398, above.

INSTRUCTIONS

In *Mackie v Wilde and Longin* [1995] 1 ILRM 468, the question as to whether a solicitor had been fully instructed in proceedings arose against the following background. The plaintiff and first defendant in the action were joint owners of a fishery. The plaintiff had issued proceedings alleging breach by the first defendant of an oral agreement which restricted the amount of fishing the parties could allow on their respective sides of the river and seeking an injunction against the first defendant. At all material times the first defendant was represented by a solicitor. Before the matter was heard, the plaintiff became aware that the second defendant had acquired a 35% interest in the first defendant's property and a 35% interest in the fishing rights which were the subject of the proceedings. When the matter came to hearing, the plaintiff applied to join the second defendant in the proceedings. The solicitor acting for the first defendant believed he also acted for the second defendant and had indicated to his counsel several days before that the second defendant might have to be joined as a party.

An order was made, by consent, joining the second defendant in the proceedings. The plaintiff was granted the reliefs sought together with an order for costs. The second defendant subsequently applied to have the judgment set aside on the grounds that it had been obtained by mistake and that he was unaware he had been joined as a party. Although both the plaintiff and the solicitor who had acted for the first defendant (he no longer acted for the first defendant by this time) were notice parties to this motion, they did not attend the hearing and accordingly the judgment in so far as it affected the second defendant was set aside. The solicitor then applied for a stay on the order setting aside the judgment in favour of the second defendant. A motion was then set down as to whether the solicitor had, in fact, instructions to represent the second defendant in the action and authority to consent to his being joined as a party.

The defendant stated that while acting for the first defendant, he became concerned that his client would not be in a position to finance the action but was assured that the second defendant, who had acquired the 35% interest in the fishing rights, would pay whatever costs were necessary. The solicitor gave evidence of two meetings he had had with both defendants. At the first, he said every aspect of the case was discussed and he was retained by the second defendant with clear instructions that he had full authority to take whatever steps were necessary. At the second meeting he said his instructions were confirmed including joining the second defendant should this prove necessary. However, the second defendant claimed that he had originally acquired fishing rights when he had given the first defendant a gift of £2,000 and that he later acquired a share in the first defendant's estate when he helped the first defendant out of financial difficulties with the bank. He stated that he had agreed to finance the defence of the action but only to help out the first defendant. He stated that he at no time expected the solicitor to represent him as he bad his own solicitor whom he used regularly and he did not expect to be joined as a party to the action. The first defendant agreed with the second defendant's description of the meeting and stated that although the second defendant was prepared to pay the costs, he viewed this as a loan which had to be repaid.

It was argued that as the solicitor had not obtained a written retainer, the court should prefer the second defendant's version of events. However, Morris J rejected the proposition suggested by *Allen v Bone* (1841) Ch 493 and *Griffiths v Evans* [1953] 1 WLR 1424 to the effect that, if a solicitor fails to get a retainer in writing from a client and that client subsequently disputes the terms of the retainer, the client's evidence must be preferred by the court. Morris J considered that this would conflict with the guarantee of equality in Article 40.1 of the Constitution, in that it failed to treat all persons equally before the law. He held that such a proposition was offensive in that it presupposed that the evidence of the client, no matter who, was to be accepted by the court in preference to any solicitor or officer of the court. He considered that, in many circumstance a written retainer would be impossible to obtain.

As to the conflicting accounts, Morris J preferred the solicitor's evidence and accepted that he had authority from the second defendant to consent to his being joined as a defendant. He went on to state that the challenge to the rights enjoyed by the first defendant was also a challenge to the rights enjoyed by the second defendant by virtue of his interest in the estate. He noted that the second defendant had seen the necessity in defending those rights and that separate representation would duplicate the costs. Morris J concluded that the second defendant had decided that the solicitor should represent his interests also and so instructed him. He held that these instructions extended to giving the solicitor authority to consent to being joined as a co-defendant in the action.

MISREPRESENTING BUSINESS AS SOLICITOR

Incorporated Law Society of Ireland v Carroll and Ors [1995] 3 IR 145 was a, largely unsuccessful, action by the Law Society seeking relief against the five defendants who, it was claimed, misrepresented themselves as solicitors, contrary to s. 56 of the Solicitors Act 1954. The background was as follows.

The first and third defendants were the directors and shareholders of a company, Associated Consultants Compensation Services Limited (ACS), which processed claims for the purpose of obtaining compensation. The second defendant, a brother of the first and third defendants, was apprenticed to the fifth defendant, Ryan, who was at all material times a practising solicitor. The fourth defendant was employed as secretary to ACS. The Law Society initiated proceedings against the defendants claiming declaratory relief that they were in breach of the Solicitors Act 1954 and injunctions restraining them from carrying out these breaches. It was claimed that the first four defendants were in breach of ss. 55 and 56 of the 1954 Act in that they individually represented themselves to members of the public to be solicitors and held themselves out as practising in association with each other under the style of ACS and/or in association with the fifth defendant trading under the name and style of 'Chris Ryan and Company'. It was also claimed that the first four defendants had furnished members of the public and other third parties with documents purporting to emanate from the solicitor's practice of Chris Ryan and Company. It was claimed that the fifth defendant was in breach of s. 59 of the 1954 Act in that he permitted the other defendants to act and be remunerated as qualified solicitors and allowed them to utilise his name, letterhead, business cards and premises.

The fifth defendant had qualified as a solicitor in 1982 and had been carrying on a practice in Dublin. The second defendant had been taken on by him as an apprentice for nine months. The second defendant then informed the fifth defendant that the first and third defendants had purchased a premises in Rialto for their insurance assessor business. The second defendant stated that they no longer required this premises and he persuaded the fifth defendant to open a branch office there on the basis that he would enjoy the premises rent free if he provided for staff, heating and other outgoings. The fifth defendant took a lease of office equipment in his own name and engaged secretarial staff and a qualified solicitor to assist in the working of the branch office. However the second defendant was permitted to have complete control of the business carried on at that branch. Finance for the branch office was negotiated out of an overdraft on the second defendant's bank account and he received no salary as such. The evidence adduced by the Law Society established that many of the claims which were originally processed in the ACS premises matured into litigation. The legal documents in relation to these proceedings were settled by junior counsel who believed they were being briefed by the Rialto branch of the fifth defendant's firm. Correspondence was sent to clients after a visit to the ACS premises on notepaper headed 'Chris Ryan & Co. Solicitors' and a number of clients had been given the second defendant's business card showing his name and academic qualifications below the title 'Chris Ryan & Co. Solicitors'.

The fifth defendant maintained he was unaware of the large lodgments and withdrawals taking place on the branch account and had no idea as to the magnitude of business taking place at that office, nor had he benefited from it in any way. He denied that he had authorised the preparation of stationary bearing the Rialto branch address and also denied he was aware of payments out of the Rialto. branch bank account to ACS.

In the High Court, Murphy J concluded that the first two defendants had represented themselves as solicitors but he dismissed the case against the third and fourth defendants. He also concluded that while the fifth defendant was not aware of the details or extent of the operations at the Rialto branch, he did have some knowledge of what was being carried out. He then went on to considered whether the extent of the fifth defendant's knowledge came within the terms of s. 59 of the Solicitors Act 1954, which provided that a solicitor should not 'wilfully permit' his name to be made use of for the profit of an unqualified person.

Applying the principles laid down in *Grays Haulage Co. Ltd v Arnold* [1966] 1 WLR 534 and *Green v Burnett* [1955] 1 QB 78, Murphy J concluded that it was the essence of the offence to permit someone to do something that there should be either actual knowledge or knowledge which arises from shutting one's eyes to the obvious or allowing something to go on, not caring whether or not an offence is committed or not. In the context of s. 59 of the 1954 Act, he held that the use of the word 'wilfully' in conjunction with 'permit' did not significantly change the need for knowledge or the nature of the knowledge required. In this respect, he referred approvingly to the approach taken in *Maguire v Shannon Regional Fisheries Board* [1994] 2 ILRM 253 (1994 Review, 398).

In the instant case, he considered that what he described as the 'extraordinary' facts in relation to the Rialto branch of the fifth defendant's firm established that at the very least he had such knowledge of the circumstances that it could be said he closed his eyes to the obvious and allowed matters to proceed not caring whether his name was used upon account or for the profit of an unqualified person.

Turning to the relief sought by the Law Society against the first four defendants, Murphy J noted that the claims made against the first four defendants were that they had committed criminal acts and that the Law Society had sought a declaration to that effect. Murphy J referred to the relevant case law concerning the dangers of using civil remedies to enforce the criminal law. In concluding that the instant case was not appropriate for the relief sought, he relied in particular on *Attorney General v Paperlink Ltd* [1984] ILRM 373, *Attorney General v Chaudry* [1971] 1 WLR 1614 and *Gouriet v Union of Post Office Workers* [1978] AC 435. While he acknowledged that in *Parsons v Kavanagh* [1990] ILRM 560 (1988 Review, xv) and *Lovett v Gogan* [1995] 1 ILRM 12 (1994 Review, 445), the High Court had accepted it had a reserved power to enforce the law by way of injunction. Murphy J considered that this should only be exercised in exceptional circumstances where, as here, a statute makes provision for other remedies including criminal sanction. He held that nothing had been shown that would demonstrate that this was a case of an exceptional nature as would warrant granting a civil remedy in respect of a criminal wrong.

However, Murphy J went on to note that the nature of the proceedings against the fifth defendant was different in that s. 59 of the Solicitors Act 1954 does not describe the acts it prohibits as constituting an offence, nor does it seem that these acts constitute a civil wrong. Nonetheless, this distinction was to prove of little avail to the Law Society. Murphy J noted that one of the purposes of the 1954 Act was to control solicitors and the Act established the Disciplinary Committee of the Law Society for that purpose. Thus, he concluded that the appropriate remedy in the case was an adjudication in the first instance by that Committee. As there was a more appropriate remedy available, it was thus open to the High Court to decline jurisdiction, in accordance with the view he had himself taken in *O'R. v O'R.* [1985] IR 367.

All the parties to the High Court proceedings appealed to the Supreme Court, but the Court unanimously dismissed the appeal.

The Court held that there was credible evidence from which the High Court was entitled to infer that the first and second defendants had represented themselves and allowed themselves to be represented to be solicitors; thus this inference could not be disturbed on appeal.

As to the standing of the Law Society to seek declaratory or injunctive relief, the Supreme Court agreed with Murphy J that, since the purpose of s. 56 of the 1954 Act was to protect the public and not to protect any private right, the only party with sufficient standing to bring civil proceedings to enforce a public right was the Attorney General. In this respect, the Court referred to the leading authority on the role of the Attorney general, *Moore and Ors v Attorney General* [1930] IR 471. The Court also referred to the judgment of McCarthy J in *Society for the Protection of Unborn Children Ltd v Coogan* [1989] IR 734; [1990] ILRM 70 (1989 Review, 106-7) and the views expressed in *Goodman International v Hamilton* [1992] 2 IR 542; [1992] ILRM 145 (1991 Review, 109-11) as to the role of the Attorney in cases concerning the vindication of public rights.

The Supreme Court also agreed with Murphy J that the issue concerning the fifth defendant was essentially a question of alleged misconduct on the part of a solicitor and that he had been correct in holding that the appropriate remedy was an application for an inquiry to the Disciplinary Committee pursuant to s. 7 of the Solicitors (Amendment) Act 1960. In this respect, the Supreme Court considered that Murphy J had erred in making any findings of fact with regard to the Law Society's allegations against the fifth defendant. The Supreme Court noted that the findings of fact served no useful purpose, since Murphy J had declined to make any declaration based on them, and the Disciplinary Committee would have to undertake a wholly separate investigation uninfluenced by such findings.

NEGLIGENCE

Cases involving solicitors' liability in negligence are discussed in the Torts chapter, 474-6, below.

REGULATIONS

The following Regulations were promulgated in 1995.

Education and training   The Solicitors Acts 1954 to 1994 (Apprenticeship and Education) (Amendment) Regulations 1995 (SI No. 102 of 1995) amended the Solicitors Acts 1954 and 1960 (Apprenticeship and Education) Regulations 1991 in order to alter the term of service under indentures of apprenticeship or persons or specified categories of persons seeking to be admitted as solicitors and the requirements for becoming bound by indentures of apprenticeship as well as the required courses of education or training and the required examinations for persons seeking to be admitted as solicitors, as provided for in the Solicitors (Amendment) Act 1994 (1994 Review, 417). The 1995 Regulations came into effect on May 1, 1995. The Solicitors Acts 1954 to 1994 (Apprentices Fees) Regulations 1995 (SI No. 380 of 1995) set out the revised fees to be paid to the Law Society in respect of courses and examinations, with effect from January 1, 1996. See also the discussion of the *Bloomer* case, above.

Interest payments to clients   The Solicitors (Interest On Clients' Moneys) Regulations 1995 (SI No. 108 of 1995), made under s. 73 of the Solicitors (Amendment) Act 1994 (1994 Review, 432) provide that where a solicitor holds money on account for a client the solicitor must account to the client for interest thereon unless the interest involved would be less than £75. The 1995 Regulations came into effect on May 3, 1995.

Practising certificates and Compensation Fund The Solicitors (Practising Certificate 1995/1996) Regulations 1995 (SI No. 1 of 1995) prescribed the form of practising certificate for 1995 to 1996. The Solicitors (Practising Certificate 1995/1996 Fees) Regulations 1995 (SI No. 2 of 1995) set out the relevant fees for a practising certificate for 1995 to 1996 and the appropriate contribution to the Compensation Fund. The Solicitors (Practising Certificates) Regulations 1995 (SI No. 349 of 1995) prescribed the form of practising certificate required by the Solicitors (Amendment) Act 1994 from 1996 onwards. The Solicitors (Practising Certificates 1996 Fees) Regulations 1995 (SI No. 350 of 1995) set out the relevant fees for a practising certificate for 1996 and the appropriate contribution to the Compensation Fund. On the changes effected by the Solicitors (Amendment) Act 1994, see the 1994 Review, 417.

Professional indemnity insurance The Solicitors Acts 1954 to 1994 (Professional Indemnity Insurance) Regulations 1995 (SI No. 312 of 1995), made pursuant to s. 26 of the Solicitors (Amendment) Act 1994 (1994 Review, 422) established a Professional Indemnity Insurance Committee of the Law Society of Ireland. They also provide that solicitors applying for a practising certificate must have a minimum level of professional indemnity insurance. They provide for an Assigned Risks Pool and the maintenance by the Law Society of an insurance record. The Regulations came into effect on December 1, 1995.

Statutory Interpretation

Revenue legislation: tax avoidance In *McCabe v South City and County Investment Co.*, High Court, January 11, 1995 (discussed in the Revenue chapter, 420-1, above), Carney J held that the courts were precluded from condemning tax avoidance schemes which have not been prohibited by statute.

Teleological or schematic approach In *Mulcahy v Minister for the Marine and Anor*, High Court, November 4, 1994 (discussed in the Fisheries chapter, 331-3, above) Keane J held that, where public rights were in jeopardy, the courts should adopt a teleological or schematic approach to the interpretation of relevant legislation which affected such rights.

Updated meaning In *Keane v An Bord Pleanála (No. 2)*, High Court, October 4, 1995; Supreme Court, July 18, 1996, Murphy J considered the circumstances in which an updated meaning may be given to legislative provisions: see the discussion in the Local Government chapter, 378-9, above.

Tort

DUTY OF CARE

In *Wrenn v Bus Átha Cliath/Dublin Bus*, Supreme Court, March 31, 1995, the scope of a bus conductor's duty to protect passengers fell for consideration. The plaintiff, aged 19, had boarded the last bus on a Saturday night on the route from Eden Quay to Artane, in the company of a group of young men and women. He had sat at the back seat with a few of his friends. The plaintiff was wearing all black clothes; his hair was back-combed and (in his own words) 'all over the place.' Another young man, who was known to one of his friends, sat near the plaintiff and started to 'slag' him. He then stood up and started to push the plaintiff, who tried to push him back. The scuffling and pushing developed into a fracas. One of the plaintiff's friends tried to break up the altercation. All three were shouting.

The conductor witnessed the occurrence and spoke to the group, saying: 'Leave it out lads, give me a break'. This had the effect of calming the group and the conductor moved a few seats up the bus. He then left the upstairs area of the bus. Within a very short period, however, the original aggressor moved back to the plaintiff, cut the left side of his cheek with a razor blade and punched him in the face.

Morris J imposed liability on the bus company. He considered that, once the earlier fight had developed, it was 'readily foreseeable' that a similar fight would occur if the group was permitted to remain together at the back of the bus. He held that, given the circumstances, the conductor should either have called the gardaí after the original fracas or required the troublemaker to leave the bus. It was agreed in evidence that at the time problems of violence at week-ends on late buses were well known to the defendants and Morris J held that, when the conductor had left a potentially violent group and gone downstairs, he had failed to take reasonable care of the plaintiff.

The defendants appealed unsuccessfully to the Supreme Court. Hamilton CJ (O'Flaherty J concurring) reiterated Morris J's analysis. Whilst the defendants could not be expected 'to ensure that travelling on buses is safe', they had been under an obligation to take reasonable precautions to ensure the safety of passengers, including the plaintiff, and this they had not done.

Egan J dissented. He noted that all the evidence in the case had been to the effect that the original incident had appeared to have diffused itself and that order had been restored after the conductor's intervention. The troublemaker had actually moved up in the bus to another seat. No reasonable person would in the circumstances have anticipated that within a minute he would have produced a razor and slashed the plaintiff's face.

It must be said that Egan J's dissent is more convincing. The reality of late travel in Dublin at weekends is that most passengers are, to a greater or less degree, intoxicated. The journey home will be a slow process if the gardaí are constantly being called to deal with what are petty assaults and breaches of the peace; if conductors choose the other option of attempting to evict passengers who display propensities for violence, the prospect of unnecessary escalation is a real one.

It should be noted that, in *Wrenn*, Morris J invoked Regulation 44 of the Road Traffic (Public Services Vehicles) Regulations 1963, which requires that carriers 'take all reasonable, precautions to ensure the safety of passengers.' He was satisfied that this regulation, which was for the benefit of passengers rather than the common good, generated a civil claim for breach of statutory duty at the instance of the passenger: cf. B. McMahon & W. Binchy, *Irish Law of Torts* (2nd ed., 1990) chapter 21. The Supreme Court appeal proceeded on the basis that this duty was in essence the same as that imposed by the common law tort of negligence. No distinction was drawn between the requirement of reasonable care at common law and the regulation's requirement that the carrier take all reasonable precautions to ensure the passengers' safety.

PROFESSIONAL NEGLIGENCE

Legal malpractice   In *Hussey v Dillon*, High Court, June 23, 1995, the defendant, who was the plaintiff's solicitor, of the plaintiff had not carried out a search in the Companies Office to ascertain whether the documents that the petitioning creditor in bankruptcy proceedings against the plaintiff was obliged to file established that a procedural irregularity had occurred in the initiation of the bankruptcy proceedings. The plaintiff argued that, if such irregularity had been discovered, it would have led to the annulment of the bankruptcy. It had not occurred to the defendant to carry out this search. His knowledge of the law of bankruptcy had led him to the conclusion that since a motion to show cause against the validity of the adjudication had already failed, the court would not entertain a second application to annul the adjudication and he had advised the plaintiff that he should bend his efforts to effecting a composition with his creditors. Costello J considered that the defendant's view of the law was correct; it was not open to a bankrupt to succeed in a second application to annul the adjudication if the point relied on was one which could have been raised in an earlier application.

Costello P regarded the Supreme Court decision of *Roche v Peilow* [1985] IR 232 as irrelevant to the issues that arose in *Hussey v Dillon*. Roche had been concerned with the liability of a solicitor for negligence who had sought to rely on a universal practice in his profession as a defence to an allegation that he had acted negligently: see McMahon & Binchy, *op. cit.*, 259-60. In the instant case, the defendant had not sought to invoke a universal practice: his justification was based on a view of the law of bankruptcy relating to the circumstances in which an adjudication would be discharged. The Supreme Court decision in *Roche v Peilow* had related to a duty to search in circumstances 'entirely different' from those in the instant case and was not an authority for any general principle applicable in bankruptcy matters. Though Costello P did not in this context specifically say so, the essential difference between the two cases rested on the practical utility of carrying out a search in terms of its probable efficacy in protecting the interests of the client.

In *Doran v Delaney* [1996] 1 ILRM 490, some important issues relating to due care in conveyancing fall for consideration. Vendors of property sold to the plaintiffs some land to which a certain history attached. They had unwittingly encroached on their neighbour's property to a small extent. This had precipitated a strong response, with the threat of litigation. The map they had shown the plaintiffs was the one which had been used when the vendors applied for planning permission for the construction of a house on their land. The map was inaccurate: it represented some small part of the neighbour's property as part of the vendors' property.

The plaintiffs sought to have the boundaries of the property staked out. Their solicitors advised them that this would be unnecessary and that the matter could be dealt with by inserting a clause in the contract requiring the production of an ordinance survey map with the boundaries clearly marked on it. The vendors' solicitor responded to this approach by stating that:

> this is not necessary as we are selling the entire of the property which we are entitled to be registered with and which was formerly comprised in both folios. Accordingly the certified copy file plan attaching to the folios should be sufficient. Accordingly, we cannot accept same.

The plaintiff's solicitors did not insist on the inclusion of the requirement as to the ordinance survey map. The conveyance was completed and in due course the plaintiffs discovered that they owned less than they had thought and that they were, in effect, landlocked.

The plaintiffs' action for misrepresentation against the vendors was successful. They had misrepresented the area of the subject matter of the sale and they had wrongly claimed that there was no dispute with regard to this area and that no adverse claim had been made in regard to it.

The plaintiffs' claim against their own solicitors in negligence was also successful. Hamilton P stressed the fact that a clear delineation of the boundaries was of particular importance in the case because of the restricted nature of the access to the land for the purpose of erecting a dwelling house there. A 'particular duty' had thus fallen on the plaintiffs' solicitors to ensure before the execution of the agreement for sale that it contained conditions which would clearly establish the extent of the boundaries of the land being acquired by the plaintiffs, that the land shown on the map presented to the plaintiffs and that there was access to the lands for the purpose of building on them. The plaintiffs' solicitors could have discharged this duty by having the boundaries staked out or by insisting on the provision of an ordinance survey map, with the boundaries delineated on it.

Hamilton P relied on the evidence of two experienced conveyancing solicitors to the effect that the deletion of the condition regarding the ordinance survey map and good practice of conveyancing solicitors.

Hamilton P held that the vendors' solicitors had not been negligent. No evidence had been adduced which established that they were aware of the existence of the map that had been shown to the plaintiffs. Hamilton P was satisfied from the evidence that the first they knew about the map was when it was discovered in the course of the litigation. 'In the ordinary way', a vendors' solicitor did not owe a duty of care to the purchaser but, as Lord Jauncey had made plain in *Midland Bank plc v Cameron, Tong, Peterkin and Duncans* (1988) SLT 611 at 616, a duty could arise where the solicitor assumed responsibility for the advice or information given. Lord Jauncey had gone on to observe (at 617) that the solicitor must have 'been converted from someone merely transmitting that information on the client's instructions to someone who has assumed responsibility for and thus the role of principal in relation to that information so far as the third party is concerned.'

It was clear from the nature of their replies to the requisition on title that the vendors' solicitors were merely transmitting their clients' instructions and not assuming responsibility for them. The plaintiff's solicitor, who had been 'completely free' to insist on the insertion of the condition as to the ordinance survey map, had agreed to its deletion.

Hamilton P, in imposing liability on the plaintiffs' solicitors, made it clear that they were entitled to be indemnified by the vendors.

Medical malpractice

Diagnosis What duty is owed to a patient who is less than fully frank about the provenance and nature of his symptoms? The question arose in *Caffrey v North Eastern Health Board*, High Court, February 10, 1995. The plaintiff had received injuries to his throat in a traffic accident. He was admitted to the casualty department of the defendant's hospital in a country town at 7.50 am on a Saturday. He initially said that he could not remember anything. He complained of suffering from asthma and maintained that position until the following Monday. His symptoms included difficulty in swallowing, stridor, breathlessness, pain in the area of the neck and inability to speak.

There was no ear, nose and throat surgeon on duty in the hospital that weekend. The following Monday, the plaintiff told the hospital staff that he had suffered an injury to the larynx. He explained that he had said that he could remember nothing because he thought he was in trouble as the car which crashed was not his own. A correct diagnosis was then made and the plaintiff was moved to a Dublin hospital where he was operated upon. This 'left him with a permanent flap in his throat for the purpose of assisting him in breathing', as well as some other disabilities not identified in Johnson J's judgment.

The plaintiff sued the surgeon into whose care he had been placed in the first hospital. He claimed that the doctor ought to have diagnosed his condition earlier than the Monday. With 'a great deal of doubt', Johnson J held that the defendant could be criticised for having failed to examine the exterior or the interior of the throat before Monday, having regard to the symptoms that were present. He balanced this finding with a very severe criticism of the plaintiff for his lack of candour.

On the issue of causation, Johnson J was bemused and apparently angry at the failure of either party to have called as a witness the surgeon who had operated on the plaintiff in the Dublin hospital. Johnson J recorded in his judgment that it had been left to him 'to force the parties' to call this witness; he observed that if they had failed to do so, he would have been obliged to do so himself, in view of the surgeon's crucial role. The evidence of this surgeon was to the effect that the delay in diagnosis had no effect on the outcome. Accordingly, Johnson J held that the defendants were not liable to the plaintiff for his injury.

Obstetric practice In *Russell v Walsh and the Mid-Western Health Board,* High Court, April 3, 1995, Johnson J dismissed the plaintiff's action for negligence against a gynecologist obstetrician who had performed a hyster-ectomy on her. The plaintiff had suffered ischaemia to the ureter as a result of the operation.

An expert witness for the plaintiff, a former Master of Holles Street Hospital, contended that the defendant should have palpated the ureter; an expert witness for the defendant, another former Master of Holles Street Hospital, said that he would under no circumstances take this course. In the light of this difference of opinion, it was not, perhaps, surprising that Johnson J, applying the principles laid down in *Dunne v National Maternity Hospital*

[1989] ILRM 735; [1989] IR 91 (cf. The 1989 Review, 421-5), found that the technique used by the defendant was an acceptable one.

Johnson J addressed the question of the burden of proof in the case. He noted that in *Lindsay v Mid-Western Health Board* [1993] 2 IR 147, at 184, O'Flaherty J had quoted Andrews J in *Girard v Royal Columbian Hospital* (1976) 66 DLR (3d) 676, at 691, to the effect that:

> The human body is not a container filled with material whose performance can be predictably charted and analysed. It cannot be equated with a box of chewing tobacco or a soft drink. . . . Thus, while permissible inferences may be drawn as to the normal behaviour of these types of commodities, the same kind of reasoning does not necessarily apply to a human being. Because of this medical science has not yet reached the stage where the law ought to presume that a patient must come out of an operation as well as or better than he went into it. From my interpretation of the medical evidence the kind of injury suffered by the plaintiff could have occurred without negligence on anyone's part. Since I cannot infer that there was negligence on the part of the defendant doctors, the maxim of *res ipsa loquitur* does not apply.

The medical evidence in the instant case had indicated the general acceptance that there was an inherent danger in all operations and that the particular damage of which the plaintiff complained could have occurred without negligence on the part of the defendant. Johnson J adopted in particular O'Flaherty J's statement in *Lindsay* that 'each case must of course be dealt with in accordance with its own particular facts'. In the instant case Johnson J believed that the defendant had 'met the *prima facia* case made against him as fully as could be expected' and he therefore dismissed the plaintiff's case.

Johnson J did not refer explicitly to the *res ipsa loquitur* doctrine, which was central to *Lindsay*: cf. the 1992 Review 592-8. One may wonder whether *Russell* was a case in which that doctrine was relevant. The plaintiff had sought to impugn the operating strategy which the defendant had admittedly adopted — namely, one that neglected to include a particular technique which the plaintiff argued was essential to due care. Once Johnson J took the view (in the light of the defence evidence on this issue) that the defendant's operating strategy had not been negligent, then the plaintiff's case collapsed.

What Johnson J might with benefit have done was to point out that Andrews J's observations amount to the argument that the *res ipsa loquitur* doctrine should *not* be applied to medical operations that have an unhappy outcome, yet in *Lindsay* the Supreme Court interpreted those observations as *supporting* the application of the res ipsa loquitur doctrine. In this context it should be noted that in *O'Reilly Brothers (Quarries) Ltd v Irish Industrial Explosives Ltd*, Supreme Court, February 27, 1995, O'Flaherty J characterised *Lindsay* as involving 'an expansion to the applicability of the doctrine of *res ipsa loquitur*', 'to take account of the special position of patients *vis-à-vis* hospital personnel'. We analyse the decision below 525-27.

Nurses In *Allen v Ó Súilleabháin and the Mid-Western Health Board*, High Court, July 28, 1995, Kinlen J gave important guidance on the respective roles of the obstetrician in charge, the hospital management and the nursing team in the discharge of a hospital duty of care to the nurses. The plaintiff, a student midwife, aged twenty five, received a very serious back injury when holding the leg of a patient who was in the process of giving birth by caesarean section. She had been holding the leg for more than fifteen minutes. The other leg was draped over the shoulders of a doctor. The plaintiff signalled her pain with her eyes but one of the staff nurses, who saw her eyes rolling, 'assumed it was just tiredness as [the plaintiff] had been on shift for twelve hours.' The obstetrician in charge, who was senior obstetrician at the maternity hospital, had made it clear that he did not require stirrups to be used.

The evidence in the case indicated that the midwives were in the process of developing a policy which required the use of stirrups, but this had not been communicated to the obstetrician. Several obstetricians gave evidence, which tended to support the use of stirrups in all cases, save possibly in exceptional circumstances.

Kinlen J observed that '[t]he obstetrician owes a very real duty, not merely to the patient and unborn baby, and to the staff assisting.' The obstetrician was not the plaintiff's employer. Nonetheless, Kinlen J considered that, 'under the principles of 'the good neighbour' [in *Donoghue v Stevenson* [1932] AC 562] he certainly owed a duty to the plaintiff.'

The obstetrician had been under a clear duty to make sure that the system he established was correct and to work out what should happen if the procedure took longer than anticipated. While his primary duty was to the mother and child, he also had a duty towards his 'team'. Kinlen J stated:

He can, of course, depend on the staff as being efficient and trained but he is the captain of the team and it was both foreseeable and, in my opinion, reckless not to establish a proper regime from the one he used. This is not a case of medical negligence. This is a case of utter failure to establish and maintain a team response to a foreseeable event.

Once the process started taking longer than anticipated, something should have been done to reduce the strain on the plaintiff.

protested. Kinlen J observed that 'awe of consultants should be consigned to the dustbin of history'. Consultants:

> certainly deserve respect and their status and skill entitle them to some authority but they are relying on other professionals who should, at least where appropriate, protest while carrying out the procedure directed. In the current case neither of the trained midwives there saw fit to establish a proper system of work and at least have the legs balanced, nor did they protest. It is quite clear that the obstetrician owed a duty to the plaintiff and certainly her employers did and in particular the two midwives on duty did. It is sincerely hoped that as a result of this case there will be respectful and immediate discussions between the various professionals and that the health and safety of everyone in the delivery ward and in the operating theatre should be of primary concern particularly since the [Safety, Health and Welfare at Work] Act [1989] and also on the basis of the duty owed by each professional, one to the other, as well as their duty to the patient.

Kinlen J held that the obstetrician and the defendant Health Board were liable in negligence, equally, to the plaintiff. He observed that:

> [t]here was great talk about team work. The obstetrician is the overall captain with overall responsibility. However, the senior midwife in the theatre or delivery ward is in charge of the midwifery services. The midwives are now treated, as indeed they should always have been, as a highly skilled and important group of professional people. However, there was a clear break down in communications. The midwives apparently decided they would not take any orders from consultants requiring them to endanger themselves. However, the plaintiff here knew nothing of these rules, nor did the obstetrician. Also, the senior midwives who gave evidence stated that, if they were directed by the doctor to do so, they would — but 'under protest'. It is for the management to see that the various professions understand, not merely their own duties, but also their inter-relationship with other participants in the labour ward and in the operating theatre. It is not for the Court to lay down what these should be. It is purely a matter for management. The nurses and midwives are not there merely to facilitate the consultant.

These passages provoke three comments. First, Kinlen J is willing to characterise the work of nurses as a *professional* activity. In *Kelly v St. Laurence's Hospital* [1989] ILRM 437, noted in the 1988 Review 417, the Supreme Court was of the view that nursing care should not be subject to the distinctive principles that apply to professionals when determining whether or not they are guilty of negligence. The increasing sophistication of nursing practice, with the expansion and improvement of the process of education for nurses, may lead to a re-assessment of the *Kelly* holding. It would be wrong to place too much emphasis on Kinlen J's use of the word 'professional'. He was speaking in the context of what was essentially a claim for employers' liability rather than for professional negligence.

Secondly, Kinlen J's emphasis on the duty of *management* to address the strategy of providing a safe working environment for its employees strongly reflects the policy of the Safety, Health and Welfare at Work Act 1989: see the 1989 Review, 379-393, especially 380-1, 388-9. *Pace* Kinlen J, the development of policy in this area is not 'purely a matter of management', since the courts are entitled to stigmatise as negligent at common law a particular policy adopted by management even after much careful consideration. Careful consideration does not guarantee that the choice of policy will necessarily be a prudent one. Nonetheless, the 1989 Act lays great emphasis on the process of deliberation by which management reaches its decisions, so one can envisage situations where liability may arise under common law negligence but not the 1989 Act. It is also true that, even under common law, some Irish judges in recent years, possibly influenced by the growth of judicial review applications, have placed an emphasis on the process of management deliberation in the development of safety policies rather than assessing the adequacy of the decision ultimately reached. In this context, Barron J's decision in *Mullen v Vernal Investments Ltd*, High Court, December 15, 1995, which we analyse later in the chapter, below, 490-2, is of some interest.

Finally, Kinlen J's judgment rightly stresses the need for hospitals to replace traditional hierarchical structures with a more democratic teamwork approach. From the standpoint of the patient, who increasingly perceives himself or herself as a consumer of a service, the internal hierarchy is a matter of indifference. From the standpoint of the law, the trend is to regard the hospital as potentially liable, not just on the basis of vicarious liability but also on the basis of a non-delegable duty of care.

Kinlen J held that the plaintiff was not guilty of any contributory negligence. Although she was 'a highly intelligent, well-schooled, trained nurse' aged twenty five, Kinlen J thought, as one witness had stated, that:

> it would be extremely cheeky for a student midwife to interrupt the obstetrician or the other fully trained midwives. She stood grimacing, doing the best she could, and she is not to be faulted for doing that.

It has to be said that a system of work with an ethos that coerces a worker

It has to be said that a system of work with an ethos that coerces a worker into silence when undergoing pain severe enough to render her unemployable for the rest of her life is one that would benefit from review. It should be noted that the defendants' liability was not based on this fact; rather the plaintiff was considered not to have acted unreasonably in deciding not to defy the ethos. If one envisages a case where the source of a nurse's pain was not attributable to prior negligence on the part of the hospital but the ethos of silence forced the nurse to suffer without protest, thus rendering the injury more severe, it is hard to see why this should not be an independent basis of liability on the part of the hospital for the enhancement of the injury.

In *Murphy v South Eastern Health Board*, High Court, February 6, 1995, Flood J rejected an action for negligence against the nursing staff of the defendant's hospital. The outcome of the case depended essentially on matters of evidence. Flood J, 'exercising all the charity at [his] command', thought that there could be 'no doubt that at the very minimum the plaintiff is not a reliable historian.'

The plaintiff's case was that, after surgery for varicose veins, she was in bed in a ward, with both her legs bandaged. The following morning she indicated to a nurse that she wished to go to the toilet, although she was feeling somewhat dizzy. The nurse, she said in evidence, gave her a commode and then left her unattended. She felt faint, fainted and must have fallen on the floor. Her next recollection was lying across the bed with two nurses in attendance. She claimed that she received a shoulder injury when she fell.

The story told by the two nurses was quite different. They said that at all times one of the nurses remained in attendance beside the plaintiff. She noticed that the plaintiff was becoming pale and she called her colleague. Both of them moved the commode parallel to the bed, holding the plaintiff across the chest, and they then lifted her on to the bed. One of the nurses said that, during a conversation at another time, the plaintiff had complained of a long-standing pain in her neck.

Flood J was satisfied that the two nurses had told 'the absolute truth' and that the plaintiff had not fallen. The plaintiff had never known what had happened to her after she lost consciousness. In the succeeding months she had developed a very painful and disabling condition in her shoulder which, on the medical evidence, could have been spontaneous or could have been caused by trauma. If the latter was the explanation, Flood J was 'absolutely satisfied as a matter of fact' that the trauma had not occurred while the plaintiff was in the care of the defendants' staff at the hospital.

EMPLOYERS' LIABILITY

Existence of Employment Relationship between the Parties In *Mulligan v Holland Dredging (Ireland) Ltd*, High Court, January 23, 1995, plaintiff, a construction worker, was recruited by the defendant company to work as a deck-hand on a dredger operating in the port of Haifa in Israel. The defendant company was a subsidiary company of a Dutch company. The dredging work in Haifa was being carried out by another subsidiary of the Dutch parent company.

The parent company accepted responsibility for payment of the plaintiff's wages while he was working in Haifa, and also the cost of transport of the plaintiff between his home in Ireland and Israel. The inter-company arrangement was that the defendant company initially made the necessary payments to the plaintiff, having made the appropriate deductions in respect of a person whose domicile was in Ireland, and was later recouped for this expenditure by the Dutch parent company. While on board the dredger, the plaintiff was under the command of an employee of the parent company.

The plaintiff was injured when he fell from a vertical ladder linking the deck of the vessel to a stores area beneath. He took proceedings for employer's liability against the defendant company.

O'Hanlon J held that the relationship of employer and employee had not existed between the plaintiff and the defendant company on the date of the accident. All powers of control over his attendance for duty and the discharge of his duties in relation to the work being done in Haifa were exercised by those in charge of the vessel and 'no element of control of the work-place or of the plaintiff's involvement therein was vested in the defendant company at any time while the vessel was in Israel.' Since the plaintiff was not in the employment of the defendant company at the time of the accident, it 'therefore' had not been established that the defendant company owed him any duty of care in relation to the safety of his place of work in Haifa.

The decision seems an entirely reasonable one. Nonetheless, it is worth noting that, in the general context of employment activities, it may be possible for a person who is not actually the employer of the plaintiff nonetheless to owe him or her a duty of care in negligence which is closely akin to that of an employer. See, e.g., *Allen v Ó Súilleabháin*, High Court, July 28, 1995, which we discuss earlier in the chapter, above, 479-82.

Safe system of work and safe premises *Boyle v Marathon Petroleum Ireland Ltd*, High Court, November 1, 1995, is an important case in the area of employers' liability and its relationship with the action for breach of statutory duty. The plaintiff, an operative working on an offshore gas platform, took proceedings for negligence and breach of statutory duty against his employer arising from injuries he sustained when he hit his head against a girder at the bottom floor of the platform while cleaning the floor. He alleged that the defendant had negligently failed to provide a safe place or system of work and was in violation of s. 10(5) of the Safety, Health and Welfare (Offshore Installations) Act 1987, which imposes a duty on the installation manager to ensure that every workplace on the offshore installation 'is, so far as is reasonably practicable, made and kept safe.'

It seemed to McCracken J that the use of the words 'so far as is reasonably practicable' 'recognised that offshore installations do have practical problems which differ from onshore factories or other workplaces.' The test of reasonable practicability had to be one 'based on the actual circumstances of each individual offshore installation.' This approach may be somewhat lenient to employers of workers on offshore installations. The test of reasonable practicability is not limited to offshore installations but applies widely throughout industry. Cf. John White, *Civil Liability for Industrial Accidents* (1993), volume 1, paras. 13.4.01ff.

In the instant case, the platform had originally been constructed with two floors, twenty two feet apart. This had involved employees climbing ladders to reach valves as high as eight feet from the bottom floor, where congestion resulting from piping in connection with fire fighting equipment and electrical wiring made it difficult to use the ladder. The employees had complained to the defendant about these (and other) dangers. The solution adopted was to add an extra floor between the two original floors.

The drawback to this solution was that employees had to stoop when working on the bottom floor, where seven large structures (known as target blocks) housed the valve system controlling the wells. The accident had taken place because the plaintiff, using a helmet of standard design with a visor, had found it difficult to see where he was going, resulting in his head striking one of the girders.

When assessing the necessity of the insertion of the middle floor, McCracken J considered that he had to balance the benefits and additional safety to people working on the blocks on the middle floor against the possible dangers to people working on the bottom floor. There was no doubt that working on the bottom floor was 'now difficult, inconvenient and to some degree hazardous, and certainly it requires the operative to exercise considerable care.' However, very little work was carried out on the bottom floor — the plaintiff worked there about six times a year — whereas the middle floor was used a number of times every day.

Expert engineering evidence was adduced by both sides. McCracken J was also influenced by the fact that the middle floor had been inserted following complaints by operatives as to the danger of the system as it had previously existed. No such complaints appeared ever to have been made in relation to the addition of the extra floor, which had operated for over ten years without an accident of the kind the plaintiff sustained. On balance, therefore, McCracken J considered that the insertion of the middle floor 'was providing a workplace which was as safe as was reasonably practicable.'

McCracken J rejected three possible other solutions which the plaintiff's engineer suggested might have avoided the accident.

The first was that, instead of a whole middle floor, catwalks could have been constructed around the blocks. In McCracken J's view, the type of accident that had occurred might happen just as frequently if there were catwalks, because there still would be parts of the bottom floor which would only be four feet three inches high. In addition, a catwalk would probably have to be supported by a number of pillars from the bottom floor, thus creating more obstruction on that floor.

Secondly, the plaintiff's engineer had suggested that the helmets should not have a visor, thus enabling the operative to see straight ahead more easily. This again, in McCracken J's view, raised the question of balancing risks. The purpose of a visor was to protect the face of the wearer of the helmet. Part of the surface of the middle floor was a form of grill, through which small obstacles could fall or liquid such as oil could drip onto the bottom floor. A visor was a necessary protection to people working underneath the grill, and the risk of not having a visor would outweigh any advantages such as had been suggested on behalf of the plaintiff.

Finally, McCracken J rejected the argument that the girders should have been highlighted in some way so that they would stand out. The outer perimeter of the middle floor was in fact highlighted in that it was painted yellow. The girders under the middle floor were painted white, they were at two foot intervals, and anybody working in the area 'could not fail to be aware of them.' McCracken J did not think there would be any appreciable difference if they were painted some other colour.

McCracken J concluded that this was an area in which it was not reasonably practicable to have any system of work which would not have the inherent dangers of low ceilings and obstructions. Undoubtedly operatives working in this area were required to take extra care, but they would be well aware of the difficulties, McCracken J commented that 'similar areas exist of necessity in other workplaces such as engine rooms of ships and parts of certain types of factories.' Accordingly, the defendants had not been in breach of any of their obligations, statutory or otherwise, to the plaintiff.

In *Mulligan v Holland Dredging (Ireland) Ltd*, High Court, January 23, 1995, O'Hanlon J dismissed the plaintiff's claim for negligence resulting from injuries he sustained when he fell off a ladder while working on a dredger in Haifa. O'Hanlon J held that the defendant was not in fact the plaintiff's employer: see above 483. Even if that issue of law had not told against the plaintiff, his action would still have failed as he did not prove as a matter of probability that the ladder and hatch arrangement had presented 'any real or significant danger to crew members of access to and from the stores area, if taking reasonable care for their own safety'.

This articulation of the duty of an employer seems unduly narrow. Carelessness by employees is endemic in the employment environment but contributory negligence is treated somewhat gently by the courts in this context: see McMahon & Binchy, *op. cit.*, 334-6. Moreover, an employer's duty is not necessarily defined so narrowly as to be limited to those employees who are using due care for their own safety. There are, however, some work environments where, of necessity, the work activity can safely be contemplated only where the employee can be relied on to take the appropriate level of care. Descending a ladder from a hatch in a vessel is one such situation.

Nonetheless, the plaintiff's evidence indicated that what was required of employees was a high standard, not only of caution, but also of dexterity. He claimed that, when making his way from the hatch opening at deck level onto the ladder beneath, it was necessary for him to put one leg down until his foot rested on a narrow bracket linking the top of the ladder to the structure of the vessel and then bring the other leg down to the top rung of the ladder and begin the descent in that manner. He said that on the day of the accident he had just reached a position with one foot on the bracket or top of the stile of the ladder and the other on the top rung, when he slipped and fell over twelve feet to the floor beneath, striking his back against a freezer which was located beside the ladder.

Expert witnesses giving evidence on behalf of the plaintiff expressed the view that the procedure was unsafe because of the danger of the foot resting on the bracket or stile of the ladder slipping at some stage due to the inadequacy of the foothold, and also because of what they regarded as an inadequate handhold around the rim of the hatch.

The expert witness who gave evidence on behalf of the defendant demonstrated that the hatch gave just sufficient space to admit a person of normal build, and that the arms and hands would have to be brought in close to the body when they were passing through the opening. The feet could go down a couple of steps of the ladder while the upper body was still projecting out through the hatch superstructure at deck level, and the hands and arms could then be brought in. He said the bracket should not be used as a step and that it was unnecessary to do so. He testified he was regularly on small vessels with such an arrangement and did not experience any difficulty using the ladders.

The skipper of the dredger, who had been associated with the vessel from the time it was in the course of construction in 1983, gave evidence that he had gone up and down the ladder many times without difficulty, and no complaints had been received from any crew members. There could be some difficulty if coming up the ladder while carrying cans of paint or similar loads and the system adopted was to haul them up from below by rope.

O'Hanlon J was of the view that the accident had not happened in the manner described by the plaintiff. Two persons with whom the plaintiff had been in contact at the time had carried away the firm impression that he had fallen when engaged in coming up the ladder with a supply of paint. He had allowed almost three years to elapse before making any claim; during that period he took photographs of the ladder in question, but of sections which were irrelevant in the context of the claim as ultimately presented by him. He had explained the absence of photographs of the hatch area by saying they were taken into the light and failed to come out.

A secure working environment Employers must take reasonable care to provide a secure working environment for their employees. No employer is obliged to ensure that the employees are totally secure: it is a sad fact of modern life that total security can be guaranteed to noone.

There have been a few cases in recent years where the issue of employee security was raised. In *Ryan v Ireland* [1989] IR 177, a soldier who had not had enough sandbags on his hut in the Lebanon when working as part of the United Nations peace-keeping force convinced the Supreme Court that this was an issue of employer's liability which would warrant the Court in imposing on the Army the duty of taking reasonable care to protect soldiers from the risk of injury or death in the course of active combat. Finlay CJ went so far as to express the opinion that:

> [t]here could . . . be no objective in a master and servant relationship which would justify exposing the servant to a risk of serious injury or death other than the saving of life itself.

In *McCann and Cummins v Brinks Allied Ltd and Ulster Bank Ltd*, High Court, May 12, 1995, the plaintiffs were security men who were employed by Brinks Allied Ltd. They were injured when delivering a cash payment of £1,000,000 to the Rochestown Avenue branch of the Ulster Bank, in south County Dublin in 1990. They were assaulted by bank raiders who shot the first plaintiff in the leg.

The branch in question was a relatively modern purpose-built bank set back from the public road with a paved or slabbed forecourt and a service road running up beside the bank and around the rear of the building. Because bollards had been erected on the road side of the slabbed forecourt and because the bank objected to the van driving over the slabs, which it said were not intended to support the weight of the van, it was necessary to park the van on the service road. This meant that the closest the van could get to the hall door was forty-seven feet. While the plaintiffs were traversing the forty-seven feet to the door of the bank they were set upon by two armed and masked men and they were kicked and beaten and ultimately the first plaintiff was shot in the leg.

The plaintiffs argued first that their *employer* had been negligent. They contended that the location of the branch of the bank made it a peculiarly acceptable target for bank raiders because it was situated close to a shopping centre car park, from which the raiders could survey the scene and lie in wait and also because it was adjacent to a roundabout which provided a satisfactory escape route. The branch had been raided on three previous occasions; two of the raids involved the theft, or attempted theft, of money from security officers in the process of making deliveries to the bank. It was fundamental to the safe delivery of cash to a bank that provision should be made for the van to drive as close as possible to the bank. To require the security personnel to traverse forty-seven feet exposed them to such a high risk that Brinks were, they said, negligent in requiring them to work in these circumstances. Brinks should have ensured that arrangements were put in place to enable the delivery van to be brought close to the bank door or alternatively provide for a chute or 'bank-link' facility which would enable the funds to be transferred from the van to the bank without exposing the men to risk.

As regards their claim of negligence against the *bank*, the plaintiffs pointed out that discovered documents showed that as a result of the previous bank raids, the bank was aware of the fact that the distance which was to be traversed by the delivery men gave rise to a significant danger. They argued that this could have been avoided by reinforcing the slabbed forecourt area of the bank and, if necessary, the removal of the bollards. All of this could have been achieved without unreasonable expense. Moreover, the provision of a cash-link facility was something which could have been done without unreasonable expense and the only reason that it had been done was a reluctance on the part of the bank to co-operate.

Morris J, fortified by expert evidence from a former Detective Chief Superintendent, accepted the plaintiffs' argument about the foreseeability of a raid. He believed that it was 'a self-evident fact that the shorter the distance that the money is exposed to potential raiders then the safer the delivery would be.'

He also accepted the evidence of the expert witness that cash-link units had been on the market for some years prior to the date of the incident and could, without undue expense, have been fitted to the side wall of the bank. This would have negated the necessity to expose the security men to the dangers associated with the walk to the front door of the bank. While Morris

J was prepared to accept that it had not been the practice in banking circles at the relevant time to use the cash-link units, he was of the view that, given the fact that the branch had already been singled out for two previous raids on the delivery security men and given that the cost of erecting these units and making them compatible with a corresponding unit on the side of the van was small, this work should have been carried out by Brinks if they chose to take on the contract of delivering the money to this bank.

It was impossible to prove as a mathematical certainty that, had the appropriate steps been taken, the bank would not have been raided on the fateful day. The plaintiff had, however, established on the balance of probabilities that, if the relevant steps had been taken to shorten the walk or install a cash-link unit, the injuries of which they complained would not have occurred.

Therefore Brinks, as the employers of the plaintiffs, were liable in negligence for their failure to provide the plaintiffs with a safe system of work and to take all proper and reasonable precautions for their safety.

Morris J dismissed the plaintiffs' claim against the bank. He reasoned as follows. At the time it entered the contract with the bank to provide security services, Brinks knew, or must be taken to have known, that this was a branch at which problems existed. In a memorandum from the Ulster Bank's security adviser, some months before the contract was completed, it was recited that the operations executive of Brinks had 'expressed concern that the carrier vehicle, due to bollards, is unable to get closer to the bank door and this factor increases security risk for their security guards and gives the criminals more space to make snatch attempts'.

The attitude of the bank was that, for their own reasons, they did not wish to have the Brinks vans travel over the forecourt area of the bank. In Morris J's view, the options open to Brinks at this stage were clear. It could have declined to enter into the contract or alternatively it could have entered into the contract, in which case it would be obliged to devise a method of carrying out the contract which both incorporated the appropriate safety features and met with the bank's approval. It could not, for commercial and financial reasons, accept the contract encumbered with its unsatisfactory safety features, of which it was well aware, and at the same time seek to blame the bank if loss was suffered by its security men by reason of that problem.

In practical terms Morris J saw no reason why Brinks could not, if the contract was sufficiently valuable to it, have obtained the permission of the bank to erect within the side wall of the bank a bank-link machine.

In Morris J's view, the bank had discharged its obligation to the plaintiffs by drawing attention, at the outset, to a fact which Brinks itself must already have known, namely, the potential danger that the distance of the long walk from the vehicle involved. The bank was not required to remedy the problem.

The bank had been 'perfectly at liberty to decline the invitation of Brinks to alter the paved area, albeit that the cost of so doing would be small.'

It has to be said that this conclusion is surprising. Morris J's reluctance to impose any obligation on the bank, and his decision to place the full burden on the security company, is controversial. It is unlikely to encourage proper security standards and it protects large enterprises from developing a responsibility which would seem properly theirs as well as that of security companies.

The Supreme Court nevertheless affirmed Morris J, on November 4, 1996. We shall analyse the appeal in the 1996 Review.

Relationship with Statutory Duty In *Mullen v Vernal Investments Ltd*, High Court, December 15, 1995, the relationship between breach of statutory duty and common law negligence was addressed but, by reason of the particular facts of the case, left in an unclarified state. The plaintiff was employed as the manageress of the drapery and household section of the defendant's retail premises in Carlow. Once every month she went to Dublin to buy goods for sale in her section of the store. She used to buy from five wholesalers in the city centre and carry or, if needs be, drag what she had bought, in plastic sacks, to a car-park nearby. On the occasion in question, she injured her back when using the staircase in the car-park while half carrying, half dragging four sacks containing the purchases for the day, which were too heavy for her.

The plaintiff claimed that the defendant had failed to take any steps to prevent the danger to her because of the weight of the purchases. She relied on the statutory duties imposed on employers by Part II of the Safety, Health and Welfare at Works Act 1989, with special emphasis upon the provisions of s. 12, which requires the preparation of a safety statement to deal with the identification of the hazards and an assessment of the risks to safety and health at the place of work to which the statement relates. Evidence was adduced on her behalf that the weight of the sacks — twenty one kilograms — exceeded the weight which should reasonably have been required of a female employee.

The defendant sought unsuccessfully to resist liability on the basis that the accident that befell the plaintiff was one that was likely to occur in a non-work environment. Barron J stated:

> The whole tenor of . . . the 1989 Act is to ensure that thought is given to work situations so that dangers from carelessness or from failure to give any thought to a particular danger may be eliminated. Even though the provisions contained in sections 6 to 11 of Part II of the Act do not by virtue of section 60 confer any right of action in civil proceedings

an employer cannot escape liability for failure to consider possible dangers merely because the employee can meet the same problems or dangers in her ordinary life where she must deal with them herself.

Barron J was went on to express the view that, although there had been no safety statement, none had been required by the section in the circumstances of the case. Such a statement would relate to the place of work, not to places where an employee might be in the course of his or her work. Thus, s. 12 would not require safety statements for employees who travelled throughout the State or abroad on the business of their employers. This did not, however absolve employers from a *common law* duty to give consideration to the health and safety of employees who in the course of their employment had to leave their main place of work to carry out their duties elsewhere.

In the instant case, the employer had not given any consideration to what problems might arise during a buying trip, regarding the plaintiff's safety or health. The question to be answered was whether, if he had done so, he would have anticipated the need to give the plaintiff any advice or to formulate a particular system of work which would have avoided the injury. He was aware that, following these buying trips, the plaintiff arrived into work bringing with her goods carried in black plastic sacks; but there was no evidence to suggest that he was aware that the plaintiff carried the sacks with her in the course of her trip, regardless of how many there were, or that to do so caused her any physical problems.

The system whereby the manager of the drapery section had made a monthly visit to Dublin for the purpose of buying had existed for many years. During the entirety of this period and during the several months during which this work had been carried out by the plaintiff, there had never been any question of any problems involved in it other than one remark made by the plaintiff in relation to whether or not a helper might be provided. That remark had 'not [been] made in the context of any particular problem.'

Barron J concluded:

> Where [the plaintiff] bought the goods and how she got them back to the shop was a matter for [her]. She alone knew what was involved. There was nothing in those facts which should have led the defendant to anticipate the need to give any particular advice to the plaintiff nor to formulate any particular system of work. In the circumstances, the plaintiff's claim fails.

The decision provokes a couple of observations. First it is clearly the case that employers have a common law duty to take reasonable care towards their employees in relation to premises they visit in the course of their employment: see, e.g., *Mulcare v Southern Health Board* [1988] ILRM 689, which we analyse in the 1988 Review, 422-4. The scope of that duty is not too onerous. Thus Pearce LJ in *Wilson v Tyneside Window Cleaning Co.* [1958] 2 QB 110, at 121 could observe (in language that betrays the passage of time):

> If a master sends his plumber to mend a leak in a respectable private house, no one could hold him negligent for not visiting the house himself to see if the carpet in the hall creates a trap.

It is also true that an employer owes a common law duty of care to employees who peregrinate in the course of their employment. This duty is usually expressed in terms of the duty to take reasonable care to provide a safe system of work: see, e.g., *Murtagh v Lawlor*, Supreme Court, December 4, 1959; cf. *Coyle v An Post* [1993] ILRM 508, which we analyse in the 1992 Review, 573-6.

Secondly, Barron J's emphasis on the obligation of employers to give *consideration* to the health and safety of their employees reflects an approach, apparent in earlier decisions of the same judge, which is evocative of judicial review proceedings. It is unusual in negligence litigation for courts to concentrate on processes and procedures; instead the reasonableness or otherwise of any decisions ultimately reached is assessed. A defendant who has adhered to an excellent, elaborate procedure, addressing all the right questions, will be held liable if the decision he or she has made is not a reasonable one. Conversely a defendant who makes reasonable decisions intuitively, backed by no trail of sound procedures, is not guilty of negligence. The 1989 Act does, however, place a strong emphasis on management procedures. In this context, it may be useful to refer to Kinlen J's decision in *Allen v Ó Súilleabháin and the Mid-Western Health Board*, High Court, July 28, 1995, which we analyse above, 479-82.

RESTAURATEUR

In *Fagan v Wong, High Court*, July 6, 1995, Flood J imposed liability on restauranteurs where they permitted a coat-hanger to become so overloaded that it fell upon a patron dining in the restaurant.

OCCUPIERS' LIABILITY

Legislation The Occupiers' Liability Act 1995 represents an important legislative intervention in the law of torts, a subject that very largely depends on common law principles developed by the courts. Apart from the Civil Liability Acts 1961 and 1964, there has been little by way of legislation on torts and most of what has emerged is either a substantial copy of English initiatives or flows from our European obligations. The legislation has generated much analysis. Barry Doherty has written an incisive *Annotation* in the *Irish Current Law Series Annotated* and Dr Eamonn Hall has written a very helpful article, 'The Occupiers' Liability Act 1995, Codification of Occupiers' Duty to Entrants', in 89 *Incorp. L. Soc. of Ireland Gazette* (1995) 189. The most recent useful discussion is by Edward Walsh in chapter 9 of the text edited by him, *Agriculture and the Law* (1996).

The 1995 Act marginally improves the position of some entrants, essentially by stating in legislative terms what was generally presumed to be the existing law but without a definitive judicial authority putting the matter beyond doubt. But the more distinctive feature of the legislation is that it reduces the extent of occupiers' obligations to trespassers and (a new concept) 'recreational users' of the premises.

The Act is the product of a strong lobby by farming organisations, supported by organisations, such as hunting and fishing groups, who are concerned with the recreational use of agricultural property. The voice of the trespasser, notably the adventurous urban child, was not heard. Where politicians are responding to a lobby from one side of an argument, there is always the danger of lopsided legislation. Undoubtedly there are important social and economic reasons for taking steps to ensure that agricultural land will remain open to hikers and other recreational users: tourism would not be well served by farmers turning their holdings into fortresses. One may nonetheless wonder whether a coherent case, from the standpoint of justice, was made out in favour of releasing occupiers from the duty of care to trespassers, especially in crowded urban environments where the trespasser is a child. The concerns of the members of the Law Reform Commission on this matter, in their Consultation Paper on the subject in 1993 and their Final Report in 1994, suggest that the legislation may have gone too far in aid of the occupier. For perceptive analysis of the policy issues, see Eoin O'Dell, 'Reform of Occupiers' Liability? — Part 2', 86 *Incorp. L. Soc. of Ireland Gazette* (1992) 359, at 361-3.

The former law Let us examine very briefly the former law on the subject. It will be recalled that courts used to categorise entrants as either *contractual entrants, invitees, licensees or trespassers*. To the contractual entrant, in the absence of express contractual provisions on the issue, the occupier owed an implied duty of reasonable care that the premises were in a safe state. To the invitee, the occupier was obliged to take reasonable care to afford protection from unusual dangers of which the occupier was actually aware or ought to have been aware. Licensees were a good deal less privileged. The occupier had merely to warn them of hidden dangers of which the occupier was actually aware. Trespassers were originally owed no duty of care in negligence. The occupier was obliged not to injure them intentionally nor to act with reckless disregard for their presence on the premises.

The law relating to the position of trespassers was radically changed by two decisions of the Supreme Court: *Purtill v Athlone Urban District Council* [1968] IR 205 and *McNamara v Electricity Supply Board* [1975] IR 1. The effect of these decisions, stated without embellishment, was that the immunity from the duty of care towards trespassers was removed from occupiers. If in any case the trespasser was in a sufficiently proximate relationship with the occupier and his or her presence was reasonably foreseeable by the occupier, then (and only then) the occupier would fall under a duty to take reasonable care relative to the trespasser.

It was plain that this important change in the law did not mean that trespassers were inevitably successful in litigation against occupiers. The courts proved themselves perfectly able to say no to these claims where there was not sufficient proximity or foreseeabilty. See, *e.g.*, *Keane v Electricity Supply Board* [1981] I.R. 44, *Smith v Córas Iompair Éireann* [1991] 1 IR 314. See further the 1990 Review 508-13.

After *Purtill* and *McNamara*, there was uncertainty as to whether the principles underlying those decisions permeated into the law relating to invitees and licensees, which (especially in regard to licensees) fell short of the negligence standard embraced in *Purtill* and *McNamara*. Some decisions, notably *Foley v Musgrave Cash and Carry Ltd*, Supreme Court, December 20, 1985 and *Daly v Avonmore Creameries Ltd* [1984] IR 131, indicated that the courts would take this step; others, notably *Rooney v Connolly* [1986] IR 572, displayed a surprising judicial hesitation at the brink.

The lobby is marshalled The present inadequacies of tort law have been widely canvassed. The insurance dimension has blunted the fault-based philosophy of negligence in two principal ways. Insurance companies will settle cases, even where the liability issue is seriously in question, where this will save costs overall. This practice leaves disgruntled defendants, with no day in court to vindicate their name, facing higher premiums the following year. There is also the phenomenon of 'doubtful' litigation against large, faceless, institutions, such as local authorities, who have responsibility for substantial areas of land, where the alleged accident occurs at a place and time where the institution has no witness but the plaintiff by good fortune has. Judges have done their best to control abuses but no one would suggest that the problem has disappeared. It must also be mentioned that some judges, in all courts, find it more difficult than others to dismiss a negligence claim where the plaintiff has suffered a serious injury.

Against this background, a fear arose in the agricultural community when it became plain that no lawyer could give an assurance that a claim brought by a trespasser or recreational user of a farmer's lands, arising from injuries sustained on the lands, would inevitably fail. The right legal advice was surely that, in the light of *Purtill* and *McNamara*, a farmer is in principle capable of falling under a duty of care to either of these entrants but that the requirements of proximity and foreseeability would ensure that an undue burden of care would not be placed on the farmer — unless the court was affected by sympathy for the injured plaintiff or the insurance company decided, on cost considerations, to settle. Two further points could be made to ease the farmer's anxiety. First, there is no volume of cases in which courts have shown themselves hostile to farmers in relation to negligence claims; indeed, for a country where agriculture has such an important role, there is a surprising dearth of reported litigation on the subject. Secondly, the cost of insurance in this area is very small indeed, so small that the issue for farmers was apparently one of principle rather than of practical economics.

Nevertheless, the fear, once planted, grew to awesome dimensions and became the basis of a strong political lobby. The farmers' organisations were less than fully happy with the Law Reform Commission's recommendations on the subject. They kept up the pressure and the legislation that ultimately went onto the statute book represents a victory for those interests.

The main features of the Act   The Act has two main goals. First, it creates the category of visitor, to whom the occupier owes 'the common duty of care' — in essence, the same standard as that applied in negligence cases at common law. The category of visitor, broadly speaking, encompasses entrants who formerly would have been categorised as contractual entrants, invitees and licensees, but with one important exception. A new concept of *'recreational user'* is introduced. This is an entrant who, with or without the occupier's permission, enters premises without a charge, to engage in a recreational activity, such as hiking or hunting or exploring caves or visiting buildings of historical or scientific interest. Clearly, under the former law, a recreational user would normally be categorised as a licensee; courts were disposed to take a broad view of what amounted to implied permission to be on the occupier's lands.

Under the new dispensation, the occupier does *not* owe any duty of care in negligence to recreational users or trespassers with regard to dangers due to the state of the premises. All that the occupier must do is ensure that he or she does not injure the recreational user or trespasser intentionally or act with reckless disregard for the recreational user or trespasser. This change represents the overturning of *Purtill* and *McNamara*, not just in the agricultural context but in respect of *all* premises, urban and rural. The trespassing child in Dublin or Cork city is no longer owed a duty of care by the occupier *qua* occupier.

Other important features of the legislation include the restriction of duty owed to criminal entrants — in regard to whom occupiers are now free to act recklessly; the introduction of an entitlement on the part of the occupier to restrict the scope of his or her duty to visitors under the legislation, by express agreement or by reasonable notice; and the preservation by the Act of special defences (such as self-defence and defence of property) and special duties (notably the duty of an employer to his or her employees).

We will now turn to examine the provisions of the legislation in detail.

The scope of liability A crucial limitation in the legislation is that it relates only to dangers *due to the state of the premises*: s.1(1). Thus, what are known as 'activity' duties remain unaffected by the Act. If, for example, an occupier fells a tree or knocks down a wall on his or her land or drives a vehicle there, the activity will be judged by the negligence standard, regardless of the status of the entrant. That proposition can be hazarded with a reasonable degree of confidence. It represents the universal trend in common law jurisdictions (cf. J. Fleming, *The Law of Torts* (8th ed., 1992), 455-456), including our own: see McMahon & Binchy, *op. cit.* 209-10.

The problem here is that, for the past two decades and more, Irish courts have not been required to make the conceptual distinction between 'activity' and 'occupancy' duties because frankly the outcome of the case would not be affected by it. A trespasser who was owed the duty of care could invoke the negligence standard however the facts were characterised.

Now that the legislation draws this crucial distinction between 'activity' and occupancy duties, courts will be obliged to address the issue. Clearly it will be in the interests of a trespasser or recreational user to rest the case on an 'activity' rationale since then the occupier can be held to a standard of negligence, assuming, of course, that the plaintiff is considered by the court to have sufficient proximity and foreseeability to generate a duty of care on the part of the 'active' occupier.

Who is to say when the facts of the case should be characterised one way or the other? Very often the plaintiff's story will include elements of passive 'occupancy' default coupled with an activity on the part of the defendant. Neither element of the whole picture can easily be identified as predominant.

In *Smith v Córas Iompair Éireann* [1991] 1 IR 314, the plaintiff, who came onto the defendant's railway line by means of a wall that had not been kept fully repaired, could point to either the train (active) or the wall (passive occupancy) as the basis of liability. In truth, his case depended on a complex intermingling of both elements. The plaintiff's case was defeated by insufficient proximity and lack of foreseeability: see the 1990 Review, 508-13.

It is worth noting on this context that, in respect of a danger existing on premises, s. 4(1)(b) imposes on the occupier the obligation 'not to act with reckless disregard' for the person or property of the recreational user or trespasser. Of course it is quite possible to envisage acts by an occupier that are distinctively centred upon dangers due to the state of the premises. For example, an occupier might excavate ground near a building thereby rendering the building unsafe. There are, however, other cases where the act of the occupier has *some* connection with the state of the premises but that connection does not feature centrally in the manner in which the recreational user or trespasser is injured. For example, a farmer spraying a crop with material that is injurious to inhale might carelessly turn the hose in the direction of the recreational user or trespasser. The activity of spraying seems undoubtedly one that creates a danger 'due to the state of the premises', but could not the injured recreational user or trespasser claim that the injury from the misdirected hose had such a close nexus with the careless activity that, in spite of the fact that the activity generated a danger in respect of the premises, it should nonetheless be capable of being characterised as negligent activity rendering the farmer liable in a straightforward negligence action taken by the recreational user or trespasser?

Would the position be different if, ten minutes after the farmer had stopped spraying the crop, another recreational user or trespasser entered the field, inhaled the spray and was injured? The notion of a danger 'due to the state of the premises' connotes some element of continuity over time. But for how long?

Who are occupiers? Formerly, 'occupation', for the purposes of occupiers' liability, was identified with the right to exclude. Gradually the element of *control* became crucial. Courts came to accept that the concept of control is a relative rather than absolute one and that it is possible for more than one person to be an occupier in this sense: cf. *Wheat v Lacon* [1966] AC 552.

Section 1(1) of the Act provides that an 'occupier', in relation to any premises, means:

> a person exercising such control over the state of the premises that it is reasonable to impose upon that person a duty towards an entrant in respect of a particular danger thereon and, where there is more than one occupier of the same premises, the extent of the duty of each occupier

towards an entrant depends on the degree of control each of them has over the state of the premises and the particular danger thereon and whether, as respects each of them, the entrant concerned is a visitor, recreational user or trespasser.

This amalgam of questions of responsibility and control is a source of potential confusion, since the court, in determining whether or not a particular defendant is an Ooccupier' — a threshold characterisation issue — is in some sense engaging, even inchoately, in an assessment of the liability issue: cf. David Howarth, *Textbook on Tort* (1995), 371.

The concept of 'premises'   Under the Act 'premises' include not only land, water and any fixed or moveable structures on land or water but also vessels, vehicles, trains, aircraft and other means of transport: s. 1(1). This breadth of definition reflects the former common law: cf. McMahon & Binchy, *op. cit.*, 208. When it is recalled that one may sue only in relation to a danger 'due to the state of the premises' (s. 1(1)) it becomes clear that there is no prospect of running-down cases off the highway succeeding under the Act. A passenger who was burned by defective electrical fittings in a vehicle would, however, have a right of action under s. 3, if a visitor, or s.4 otherwise, regardless of whether the vehicle is on private property or on the highway at the time. 'Activity' duties are still dealt with under the common law principles.

Who are visitors?   A 'visitor' for the purposes of the Act, is:

(1) an entrant as of right (such as a member of the Garda Síochána or a fire fighter, for example);
(2) an entrant, other than a recreational user (of which more anon), who is present on premises by virtue of an express or implied term in a contract (such as a patron of the local cinema, for example);
(3) an entrant (other than a recreational user) who is present on premises at the invitation , or with the permission, of the occupier (such as a shop customer or a social guest, for example, or a person permitted to be on the premises for his or her own purposes); and(4) an entrant present on premises on which 'recreational activities' are capable of taking place, without a charge being imposed for the purpose of engaging in a recreational activity, where the entrant is:

(a) a member of the occupier's family who is ordinarily resident on the premises;
(b) an entrant who is present at the express invitation of the occupier

(or family member of the occupier); *or*

(c) an entrant who is present with the permission of the occupier (or member of his or her family) for social reasons connected with the occupier (or family member).

Broadly speaking, therefore, visitors are those entrants who would formerly have been categorised as contractual entrants, entrants as of right, invitees and licensees, save for those licensees who fall within the definition of 'recreational user.' One is a visitor while he or she is present on the premises for the purpose for which he or she is invited or permitted to be there, for the purpose of the performance of the contract or for the purpose of the exercise of the right. So if a person invited onto premises engages in conduct inconsistent with that purpose he or she loses the status of visitor and becomes a trespasser. The legislation has removed any uncertainty that might formerly have attached to the status of a shoplifter, for example. Cf. *Purtill v Athlone UDC* [1968] IR 205, at 210 (Supreme Court, *per* Walsh J).

The occupier's duty to visitors An occupier owes what is called 'the common duty of care' towards a visitor: s. 3(1). This is a duty to take such care as is reasonable in all the circumstances to ensure that a visitor does not suffer injury or damage by reason of any danger existing on the property: s. 3(2). In essence the test is that of reasonable care; in other words, the same as the negligence criterion of common law.

Some points about this duty may be noted. *First*, in determining what care is reasonable in the circumstances, the court must have regard to the care which a visitor may reasonably be expected to take for his or her own safety and, if the visitor is on the premises in the company of another person, the extent of the supervision and control the latter person may reasonably be expected to exercise over the visitor's activities: s. 3(2). Thus, an occupier is entitled to take into account that an adult normally can look after his or her own welfare; but this general expectation may, of course, have to be modified where the occupier is or ought to be aware that an adult visitor is more vulnerable, on account of mental incapacity, for example. Similarly, when a child comes onto the premises in the company of an adult, the occupier may normally place some reliance on the likelihood that the adult will take reasonable care of the child, (cf. *White v Primark* [1996] Ir Log Weekly 18, discussed below, 518-9), but again circumstances may alter the strength of this reliance and in no case may an occupier contend that, merely because the adult was in charge of the child, the occupier was relieved of any duty of care towards the child.

Secondly, the common duty of care towards visitors applies in all cases save where it is extended, restricted, modified or excluded in accordance with

s. 5. We shall see, when considering s. 5, that the occupier is not permitted
to reduce the level of his or her duty below that owed to recreational users
and trespassers, which requires the occupier not to injure these entrants
intentionally or act with reckless disregard for them: cf. s. 4.

What are recreational activities?   The legislation defines 'recreational
activity' as meaning:

> any recreational activity conducted, whether alone or with others, in the
> open air (including any sporting activity), scientific research and nature
> study so conducted, exploring caves and visiting sites and buildings of
> historical, architectural, traditional, artistic, archeological or scientific
> importance.

Thus, most obviously, such activities as hunting, shooting, fishing, hiking
and picnicking will come within the earlier part of the definition. A few points
should be noted. First, the reference to scientific research is limited to cases
where it takes place *in the open air*, but visiting a building of scientific
importance also comes within the scope of the definition. Secondly, the only
indoor activities envisaged by the definition, apart from exploring caves,
consist of 'visiting sites and buildings of historical, architectural, traditional,
artistic, archeological or scientific importance.' Obviously a visit to an
ancient tower or castle to examine it from an historical, architectural, traditional, artistic, archeological or scientific standpoint will fall within the scope
of the definition, but what about the case where a person enters a building of
this kind with no such lofty purpose? Take, for example, a person who goes
to a three-hundred-year old house to canvass for a political party. Is he or she
engaging in a 'recreational activity', for the purposes of the Act, because, as
a matter of definition, the house is admittedly of scientific importance? The
'right' answer, from the standpoint of the policy of the Act, is of course in
the negative; but the drafting is not as clear as one might have wished. As
we shall see presently, the legislation excludes three categories of entrant
from the definition of 'recreational user', but the political canvasser does not
fall within any of these categories.

Perhaps the courts would interpret the expression 'visiting' in a narrow
way as being limited to cases where the motivation for entry springs from a
concern for the historical (or other definitionally-relevant) aspect of the
building.

Who are recreational users?   The legislation defines a 'recreational user'
as:

an entrant who, with or without the occupier's permission or at the occupier's implied invitation, is present on premises without a charge (other than a reasonable charge in respect of the cost of providing vehicle parking facilities) being imposed for the purpose of engaging in a recreational activity, including an entrant admitted without charge to a national monument pursuant to section 16(1) of the National Monuments Act 1930, but not including an entrant who is present and is —

(a) a member of the occupier's family who is ordinarily resident on the premises,
(b) an entrant who is present at the express invitation of the occupier or such a member, or
(c) an entrant who is present with the permission of the occupier or such a member for social reasons connected with the occupier or such member.

Several points about this definition are worth noting. *First*, as is plain, to be a recreational user, one must not have paid for the privilege of entry (other than for parking one's car). Thus, owners of ancestral homes who charge members of the public to see around the building are required to discharge the 'common duty of care' to the entrants, who are *visitors* rather than recreational users.

Secondly, the three exclusions are obviously necessary to ensure that those who are not in truth recreational users should retain their entitlement to hold the occupier to the common duty of care. We have suggested already that the political canvasser (or other entrant who has no interest in the recreational potential of the premises) should also be entitled to the common duty of care. It is unfortunate that so much has to depend on the scope of the term 'visiting' in the definition of 'recreational activity'.

Thirdly, it is worth reflecting on the implications of the exclusion from the definition of 'recreational user' of an entrant who is present at the *express* invitation of the occupier or a member of the occupier's family. If the occupier (or family member) meets a would-be recreational user and welcomes him or her onto the land, there is a danger that this will raise the entrant's status to that visitor. At what point does casual civility give way to an 'express invitation'? If there is a doubt on the matter, should solicitors be advising occupiers of agricultural land or of historical sites to shun conversations with would-be recreational users lest they transform them into visitors?

It appears clear that, to fall within the definition of 'recreational user', the entrant must be present on the premises for the *purpose of engaging in a recreational activity*. It might be thought that the reference to such a purpose should be read as part of the phrase 'without a charge . . . being imposed for the purpose of engaging in a recreational activity', and that therefore, if no such charge is imposed, the entrant's purpose is of no further relevance to the definition. Such an interpretation cannot be right, since it would mean that all entrants on the premises would have to be characterised as recreational users if present at the occupier's implied invitation or with or without the occupier's permission *unless* either a charge was imposed for engaging in a recreational activity or they fell within one of the three exceptions specified in paragraphs (a), (b) and (c) of the definition. Manifestly that was not the intent of the Oireachtas. The more plausible interpretation, therefore, is that, to be a recreational user, the entrant must be present for the purpose of engaging in a recreational activity. Note that the definition does not require that the recreational user should have *entered* the premises with this purpose: all that is necessary is that he or she be 'present' there with this purpose. It would seem, therefore, that a person who came onto the premises without this purpose, either as a visitor or as a trespasser, could in certain circumstances *change* his or her status by forming the purpose of engaging in a recreational activity. It is not necessary that the occupier be aware of the purpose. Thus, an entrant's status can depend on a state of mind that may or may not be known, or knowable, to the occupier.

We are indebted to Dr Clive Symmons, Research Associate of the Law School of Trinity College, for raising the following uncertainties relating to the definition of 'recreational user'. S. 1(1) defines a recreational user as an entrant who, 'with or without the occupier's permission or at the occupier's implied invitation', is present on the premises, in the circumstances prescribed by the subsection. The absence of the occupier's permission, prior to the legislation, rendered an entrant a trespasser. The effect of the definition is thus to remove from certain trespassers this stigmatic character and to place them into a different, new, category.

Since the Act imposes on the occupier the *same* duty in relation to both trespassers and recreational users in all circumstances save those falling within the scope of s. 5(4), this transformation of status for unpermitted entrants may seem to be a matter of no importance, but it does raise a question about the occupier's entitlement to prevent such entrants from coming on to the premises or to exclude or them once they have entered the premises, as well as the implications for the traditional rules of law in this context. An occupier was under common law entitled to use reasonable force to prevent a trespasser from coming onto the property or to expel the trespasser. S. 8 of the legislation provides that nothing in the Act is to be construed as affecting any enactment or rule of the law relating, *inter alia*, to 'the defence of property'. If the traditional rule of law relating to the entitlement to exclude trespassers is unaffected by the legislation, does this mean that the occupier is not permitted to prevent entry by, or to expel, a recreational user who wishes to be, or is, on the premises without the occupier's permission? The answer must surely be that an occupier is still entitled to prevent entry or to expel any entrant on the premises without the occupier's consent. The fact that some entrants without consent are not characterised as trespassers under the Act does not change the fundamental basis of the entitlement to exclude, which is the absence of consent for that person to be on one's premises rather than the particular label attached by particular legislation to particular entrants. The idea that an occupier would be obliged to tolerate without redress the unpermitted presence of entrants on his or her property seems quite unconvincing.

In this context it is useful to consider the position of children. The definitions of 'recreational activity' and 'recreational user' are capable of embracing children. Certainly children are not excluded from them, thought it is fair to say that the definition of 'recreational activity' connotes a degree of purposeful maturity that is not easy to ascribe to the carefree activities of childhood. If some children go into a neighbour's garden and play tig there, this can no doubt be designated a 'recreational activity . . . in the open air', but the children may be oblivious of the location of the game and certainly pay no attention to whether it is indoors or in the open air. They fall within the definition accidentally, as it were.

The point is of crucial importance because of the distinction in duties owed to a visitor and a recreational user. Under the legislation, an entrant who is present with the permission of the occupier will be a visitor, and will be owed a high level of care, even though he or she confers no economic benefit on the occupier, *unless* the entrant is a recreational user. There thus are many entrants who would formerly have been characterised as licensees who are now designated visitors. They will be reduced to the lower category of recreational user only if they are present for the purpose of engaging in a recreational activity. When children come onto a neighbour's premises, they may intend to have a game of tig; often, they will have no particular game plan. Mooching is part of the condition of being young; it is a collaborative exercise. Yet the legislation makes a crucial distinction in relation to their status, and the level of care owed to them, on the basis of whether or not they formed a sufficiently focused intention to warrant characterising their purpose as being to engage in a recreational activity.

So alien is this line of enquiry from the reality of childhood experience that one is forced to look again at the definition of 'recreational activity'. It is at least worth arguing that the courts should construe the concept narrowly, so as to embrace only activities that are of greater focus and organisation than mooching, even if the moochers kick a stone or a ball (a 'sporting activity') as they progress somewhat aimlessly through their neighbour's property. This is not to suggest that the concept requires any particular *formality*: an *ad hoc* game of football, with three a side, is surely a sporting activity for the purpose of the definition. It may well turn out that the courts will disdain any attempt to distinguish between activities on the basis suggested above and will characterise as recreational users all children engaging in open-air activities who do not fall within the exceptions specified in the definition.

Who are trespassers?   A trespasser, for the purposes of the legislation, is an entrant other than a recreational user or visitor: s. 1(1). Thus, one can be a 'good' or 'bad' trespasser, a mischievous child or a burglar. Later in the Act, distinctions are made between different types of trespasser. The purpose of committing (or attempting to commit) an offence, or the commission of an offence on the premises, radically reduces the scope of the duty owed to the entrant: s. 4(3).

Duty owed to recreational users and trespassers   An occupier, in respect of a danger existing on premises, owes recreational users and trespassers on the premises only the limited duty *not to injure them or damage their property intentionally* and *not to act with reckless disregard for them or their property*: s. 4(1). The occupier is *not* required to discharge the standard of reasonable care (the 'common duty of care'), which *visitors* can insist upon by virtue of s. 3. The owner is, of course, free to *extend* this duty, by express agreement or notice in accordance with s. 5(1).

In determining whether or not an occupier has acted with reckless disregard for a recreational user or trespasser (or his or her property), the court must have regard to *all the circumstances* of the case, including nine factors specified in s. 4(2). It may be useful to identify these nine factors and comment briefly on some of them.

Whether the occupier knew or had reasonable grounds for believing that a danger existed on the premises Under the law, prior to the legislation, an occupier would be held liable to an invitee for failure to protect an invitee from an unusual danger of which the occupier was, or ought to have been aware. *Indermaur v Dames* (1866) LR 1 CP 274. The duty to a licensee was far more restricted: it arose only where the danger was a hidden one, of which the occupier was actually aware. Thus a failure — even if culpable — to be aware of a danger immunised the occupier against liability to a licensee. Factor (a) might at first sight seem to apply to recreational users and trespassers the level of duty formerly appropriate to invitees but this is not so. The court is required to have regard to this factor among nine specified factors, which in turn are but elements of the entirety of the circumstances of the case. S. 4(2) does not give any indication or guidance as to what should be the implications of a finding that the occupier had knowledge of the danger or that he or she had reasonable grounds for believing that it existed. Nothing crucial attaches to thisr finding; it is but part of the tapestry of facts in relation to which the court is to form a view as to the issue of reckless disregard.

Whether the occupier knew or had reasonable grounds for believing that the person and, in the case of damage, property of the person, was or was likely to be on the premises

and

Whether the occupier knew or had reasonable grounds for believing that the person or property of the person was in, or was likely to be in, the vicinity of the place where the danger existed We can consider these two factors together. Even under the progressive principles of *Purtill* and *McNamara*, the courts required a high degree of foreseeability of a *trespasser's* presence on the property in the danger area. This is evident from such Supreme Court decisions as *Keane v ESB* [1981] IR 44, *O'Keeffe v Irish Motor Inns Ltd* [1978] IR 85. and *Smith v Córas Iompair Éireann* [1991] 1 IR 314, for example. Again there is no express requirement under s. 4(2) to dismiss a case taken by a trespasser (or recreational user) whose presence was not highly foreseeable. This factor is part of the picture; the court must have regard to it; but it is not in itself a reason for dismissing a case where other factors, in the totality of circumstances, weigh in favour of the plaintiff.

Whether the danger was one against which, in all the circumstances, the occupier might reasonably be expected to provide protection for the person and property of the person This provision echoes s. 1(1)(c) of England's Occupiers' Liability Act 1984, which was the legislature's response to the House of Lords decision in *British Railways Board v Herrington* [1972] AC 877. It is singularly devoid of factual specificity and frankly, in view of the inclusion of the eight other factors, adds almost nothing to the quality of the judicial assessment of the recklessness issue.

The burden on the occupier of eliminating the danger or of protecting the person and property of the person from the danger, taking into account the difficulty expense or impracticability, having regard to the character of the premises and the degree of the danger of doing so This factor is inherent in all assessments of whether or not the defendant in a negligence action should be held to have breached the duty of care. For example, in *Callaghan v Killarney Race Co.* [1958] IR 366, at 375 (Supreme Court, 1956), Kingsmill Moore J stated:

> In judging what a reasonable and prudent man would think necessary,
> more than one element has to be considered. The rarity of the occurrence
> must be balanced against the gravity of the injury which is likely to
> ensue if the occurrence comes about, and some consideration must be
> paid to the practicality of precautions suggested.

In that case, the defendants, who were race-course proprietors, were held
not to have been negligent in failing to provide a double fence at a hurdle
sufficiently durable to prevent a horse from crashing through it. Kingsmill
Moore J observed that, if there was to be an obligation to double fence the
whole perimeter or to surround it with an unbreakable fence, 'the expense
might well put an end to many of the smaller race-courses or involve a higher
price for admission.' A similar balancing process is apparent in *Boyle v
Marathon Petroleum Ireland Ltd*, High Court, 1 November 1995, which we
discuss above, 483-5.

In the context of the Act, this calculation of the balance of advantage will
take place at the level of recklessness rather than of negligence but the
calculus is similar.

*The character of the premises including, in relation to premises of such a
character as to be likely to be used for recreational activity, the desirability
of maintaining the tradition of open access to premises of such a character
for such an activity* This factor reminds the court of the policy considerations
that inspired the enactment of the legislation. If the law lays too heavy a
burden on occupiers, they will withdraw the permission they gave to recreational users to come on their lands.

*The conduct of the person, and the care which he or she may reasonably be
expected to take for his or her own safety, while on the premises, having
regard to the extent of his or her knowledge thereof* The inclusion of conduct
as a factor to be considered by the court ensures that a distinction may be
made between 'innocent' trespassers, such as young children, for example,
and 'guilty' trespassers, such as burglars, thieves and entrants who will not
leave when asked. We shall see presently, that there is a specific additional
provision (s. 4(3)) dealing expressly with entrants who commit an offence
or enter the premises for that purpose.

*The nature of any warning given by the occupier or another person of the
danger* This factor, in contrast to s. 5(5), relating to warnings to *visitors*,
makes the nature of every warning given to the recreational user or trespasser
an element to be assessed in conjunction with all the other circumstances of
the case. There is no rule of law *requiring* an occupier to give the recreational
user or trespasser a warning in every, or any specific, case. It may be, of

course, that in a particular case the court will conclude that the failure to have given a warning renders the occupier liable, having regard to all the circumstances or that a particular warning was so deficient that the occupier should be held to have been reckless.

Whether or not the person was on the premises in the company of another person and, if so, the extent of the supervision and control the latter person might reasonably be expected to exercise over the other's activities An occupier might reasonably expect that an adult in charge of children will take proper care of them when on the occupier's premises. This is not an inflexible rule, however. There will be some cases where it is clear the adult is *not* exercising proper care: many people have had the experience of wondering whether to intervene in situations of danger to children where their parents seem blithely unaware of the risk. Of course it is possible for an injured child to sue parents for negligence: see McMahon & Binchy *op. cit.*, pp. 294-8, Binchy, 74 *Incorp. L. Soc. Gazette of Ireland* 35 (1980), and the Law Reform Commission's *Report on the Liability in Tort of Minors and the Liability of Parents for Damage Caused by Minors*, chapter 3 (LRC 17–1985). This does not happen in practice for several reasons, not least the fact that parents are rarely insured for this type of liability. A theoretical right of joinder of the parents is of little comfort to the occupier.

The nature of 'recklessness' It is clear from consideration of the several factors prescribed in the legislation that recklessness connotes *objective* default rather than necessarily requiring any subjective advertence on the part of the occupier to the risk of injury. An occupier who culpably failed to discover, or who forgot about, a particular danger will not on that account be relieved of liability. In favouring the objective test of recklessness, the legislation is merely echoing the approach formerly adopted by the Irish courts, in relation to the occupier's duty to trespassers, before the *Purtill/McNamara* reform: cf. McMahon & Binchy, *op. cit.*, (1st ed., 1981), 225-6. One can only speculate about the extent to which the courts are in practice going to set the standard at a lower level than the (equally objective) standard of reasonable care. The Act gives no guidance as to how much lower the level should be. The nine factors specified in s. 4(2) contain no such yardstick; indeed, they might constitute a trap to an unwary judge who could easily seek to apply them without adverting to the fact that, although they are similar to criteria applicable for determining the issue of negligence, they have to be pitched at a level more indulgent to the defendant.

Criminal entrants The spectre of liability to a burglar or other law-breaker haunted the Oireachtas Debates. Non-lawyers have great difficulty in contemplating that an occupier could ever owe such unpleasant entrants *any* duty of care. The solution adopted by s. 4(3)(a) of the legislation is that the occupier should be relieved of the obligation not to act with reckless disregard of a person *who enters onto premises for the purpose of committing an offence or a person who, while present on premises, commits an offence there.* An 'offence', either intended or actually committed, embraces an *attempted* offence: section 4(3)(b).

A few points about s. 4(3) should be noted. *First*, the immunity is not absolute: it does not apply in a case where a court determines otherwise 'in the interests of justice'. It is impossible to predict with any degree of certainty how the court will exercise this function. One may anticipate that it would be disposed to hold occupiers to the recklessness standard where the offender was very young or the offence was trivial — such as picking a flower.

Secondly, it seems that it is not necessary that the person should have entered the premises where the injury occurs for the purpose of committing an offence *there*. A would-be thief who enters one premises as a means of access to another, where he intends to steal, falls within the section. Conversely, a person who goes into a cafe to pass the time before a bank robbery has not entered the cafe 'for the purpose of' committing an offence, but merely with the intention of doing so afterwards, there being no connection between the cafe and the bank.

Thirdly, the occupier is relieved only of the duty not to act with reckless disregard for the entrant; he or she is still under the duty not to *injure* the entrant (or damage the entrant's property) *intentionally*. In some cases, of course, that obligation will in turn be 'trumped' by the occupier's entitlement to use proportionate force for his or her self-defence, the defence of others or the defence of property: cf. s. 8(a).

Structures on premises   An occupier owes a duty to take *reasonable* care to recreational users in one situation : this is where a structure on premises is provided for use primarily by recreational users. The occupier must take reasonable care to maintain it is a safe condition: s. 4(4). A few points about this requirement should be noted.

First, the kinds of structure here envisaged include such equipment as playground slides, benches in public parks and viewing points in scenic areas.

Secondly, it is not necessary that the *occupier* should have provided the structure: a duty of reasonable care with respect to its maintenance attaches to the occupier even where someone else provided it. As a result, as Barry Doherty notes, 'if the Office of Public Works has built a stairway or gate to allow access to a national monument on private land, it is the landowner who is responsible if it becomes dangerous': *Annotation*, ICLSA, General Note to s. 4. Certainly, the landowner has a duty of care, by virtue of s. 4(4). The subsection does not purport to exclude the duty of care resting on the Office of Public Works. Whether such a duty of care arises and, if so, has been discharged will of course depend on the particular circumstances of the case. It is possible that, in the particular circumstances, the Office of Public Works could have retained sufficient control over the stairway or gate or fall within the definition of 'occupier' in s. 1(1).

Thirdly, s. 4(4) contains a proviso to the effect that:

> where a stile, gate, footbridge or other similar structure on premises is or has been provided not for use primarily by recreational users, the occupier's duty towards a recreational user thereof in respect of such structure shall not be extended by virtue of this subsection.

This proviso appears to be otiose, since the duty of reasonable care arises in the first place only where the structure 'is or has been provided for use primarily by recreational users'.

Fourthly, it is worth considering the position of a recreational user who is present on the premises *without the occupier's permission*. As we have seen, s. 1(1) characterises this entrant as a recreational user in spite of the absence of permission. Can it be that s. 4(4) imposes a duty of reasonable care on the occupier to maintain the structure in a safe condition for such an unpermitted entrant? The point is one of some practical significance. It is easy to envisage premises that are subject to frequent unpermitted incursion by people who fall within the definition of recreational user. Can it be that s. 4(4) imposes on the occupier a full duty of care in relation to them?

Against this interpretation, the following argument may be considered. S. 4(4) states that where a structure is or has been provided 'for use primarily by recreational users', the occupier owes a duty of care 'towards such users'. Manifestly the occupier has not provided the structure for use by *unpermitted* recreational users; the only objects of the occupier's beneficence are recreational users permitted by the occupier to come onto the premises. This being so, the reference to 'such users' should be interpreted as being limited to permitted recreational users. This argument can no doubt be attacked on the basis that the reference to Ouse primarily by recreational users' embraces the entire class of recreational users, permitted and unpermitted.

We can assume that the occupier, when providing the structure primarily for the use of recreational visitors, did not thereby intend to provide it for the use of unpermitted recreational users, but as long as it can correctly be said that the occupier provided the structure 'for use primarily by recreational users', the language of s. 4(4), and in particular its reference to 'such users', requires the conclusion that all members of the class of recreational users were intended by the Oireachtas to receive the benefit of the duty of care

imposed on the occupier by s. 4(4). This interpretation is probably strengthened by the fact that the subsection, as we have seen, is not concerned with
who actually provided the structure for this purpose. Since the occupier is
not necessarily the person who did so, the particular attitude of the occupier
towards certain recreational users should scarcely be decisive in determining
the duty of care owed to them under the subsection.

Modification of occupiers' duty to entrants   S. 5 of the Act deals with
modification of the occupier's duty towards entrants. It enables an occupier,
by express agreement or notice, to *extend* his or her duty towards any
category of entrant: subs. (1). This of course does not happen often in
practice. It also enables an occupier, again by express agreement or notice,
to *restrict, modify* or *exclude* his or her duty towards *visitors* (subs. (2)(a)),
subject to certain qualifications. The visitor will not be bound unless the
restriction, modification or exclusion is *reasonable in all the circumstances*:
subs. 2(b)(ii). Moreover, where the occupier seeks to accomplish his or her
goal by *notice* rather than by obtaining the visitor's express agreement, the
occupier must take reasonable steps to bring the notice to the attention of the
visitor: subs. 2(b)(ii). The occupier will be presumed unless the contrary is
shown, to have taken such reasonable steps if the notice is *prominently
displayed at the normal means of access to the premises*: subs. 5(2)(c).

There is a minimum level of obligation to visitors below which the
occupier is not permitted to venture: the occupier may not exclude liability
to injure a visitor or damage the visitor's property intentionally or to act with
reckless disregard for a visitor or the property of a visitor: s. 5(3). So the
minimum level that the occupier can engineer by agreement or notice is
identical to the duty an occupier owes under the legislation to recreational
users and trespassers: cf. s. 4(1). The Act does not permit the occupier to
reduce that level of obligation to recreational users by agreement or notice.
This seems clear from the drafting of s. 5, which does not expressly permit
such a reduction, and more particularly by the drafting of s. 4, which
prescribes the duty to recreational users and trespassers and goes on to
provide that this duty is owed 'except in so far as the occupier extends the
duty in accordance with s. 5'. That exception, thus expressly limited, does
not allow the occupier to restrict or exclude his or her duty to these entrants.

It may be useful to consider how the court would respond to a situation
where an occupier puts up a notice at 'the normal means of access to the
premises', which states:

> No liability shall attach to the occupier of these lands in respect of any
> injury sustained on these lands by any visitor, recreational user or
> trespasser, howsoever caused.

Recreational users and trespassers are unaffected by it, because, being *restrictive* of the occupier's duty, it has potential application only to *visitors*. Should the notice be interpreted, in relation to them, as having no legal validity because it professes to exclude liability which the occupier is not permitted to exclude by virtue of s. 5(3)? We consider that the answer is no, and that instead the notice should be interpreted *as restricting the occupier's liability as far as s. 5(3) permits, but no further*. S. 5(3) provides that a restriction, modification or exclusion 'shall not be taken as allowing' an occupier to injure the visitor intentionally or to act in reckless disregard for the visitor. That expression strongly suggests that the court, in interpreting the scope of the notice, should artificially restrict it to the permitted level of reduction of obligation. Nevertheless, courts do not like rewriting contractual terms and it may be that, although the notice is not such a term, the court would adopt the traditional 'blue pencil' rule. The moral is clear. Notices should not overreach; they should be drafted in terms that go no further than the law permits. 'therwise confusion will result.

It may be worth considering briefly the question of when a restriction, modification or exclusion is 'reasonable in all the circumstances'. This is a matter of considerable practical importance but far from easy to resolve. Why should it ever be unreasonable for an occupier to restrict his or her liability? Clearly s. 5(2) is premised on the acceptance of the judgment that there are cases where a restriction of liability is unreasonable. Perhaps the courts will have regard to social factors, including the necessity of people to go on certain premises, such as social welfare offices or hospitals. One suspects that the courts would not look with favour on a notice purporting to restrict liability to 'entrants as of right', such as the Gardaí, bailiffs or fire fighters for example. The courts may even engage in an 'enterprise theory' approach, echoing that with which McCarthy J briefly flirted (cf. The 1990 Review, 518-21), to the effect that supermarkets, which generate large profits through a system that exposes customers to an inevitable risk of slip-and-fall injuries, should not be entitled to restrict their liability under this subsection.

The adequacy of a warning to a visitor Let us turn to another, related but separate, matter covered by s. 5. Where injury or damage is caused to a visitor (or the visitor's property) by a danger of which the visitor had been warned by the occupier or another person, the warning is not, without more, to be treated as absolving the occupier from liability unless, in all the circumstances, it was enough to enable the visitor, by having regard to warning, to avoid the injury or damage so caused: s. 5(5).

This extends the scope of liability from what had formerly been the position. In England, the House of Lords had taken the view that a warning to an invitee would disentitle the invitee to sue for injury resulting from the

risk that had thus been brought to his or her attention: *London Graving Dock
v Horton* [1951] AC 737. The Irish courts took a more nuanced approach:
only if the warning was such as to 'enabl[e] the careful invitee to perform
his task without danger' would it render the occupier immune from liability.
O'Donoghue v Greene [1967] IR 40, at 46. See also *Long v Saorstát and
Continental Steamship Co. Ltd* 93 ILTR 137 (1953), *Morley v Eye, Ear &
Throat Hospital Incorporated* [1967] IR 143 and *Power v Crowley and
Reddy Enterprises Ltd*, Blayney J, October 29, 1992; cf. The 1992 Review
591-2. The present legislation extends potential liability in this context to all
visitors, not just invitees. There are many entrants who are characterised as
visitors who were not invitees at common law. Social guests are one group;
also those permitted by the occupier to use the premises as a short-cut or
even, for example, the neighbouring boy who comes over the wall to retrieve
his ball.

Under the former approach, the rationale was that, if a person is coming
onto your property to confer an economic benefit upon you, it is only fair
that your warning should have the effect of making it possible for him or her
to confer that benefit upon you in safety. Where there is no such benefit
flowing to the occupier, it is more debatable whether an occupier should be
required, by the warning, to render the premises safe for the visitor. If, for
example, the ball that has been kicked over the wall lands in an area where
weedkiller has been placed, and the neighbour who wants it back is a twelve
year old boy, a warning will not suffice unless it is enough to enable the youth
to avoid injury from the weedkiller. Merely apprising him of the danger is
not necessarily enough. Contrast this with a situation where the danger is of
the same level but the occupier is out when the boy comes over the wall and
thus no question of a warning arises. Here there is no rule of law which
imposes liability on the occupier unless a certain specified level of care is
delivered by the occupier; the case is reduced to the opaque standard of 'the
common duty of care' to visitors under s. 3. The result may in some cases be
the same but it will not necessarily be so.

Duty of occupiers to strangers to contracts   There are many situations
where an occupier who is in a contractual relationship with one person — a
builder or repairer, for example — permits other persons — the employees
of the builder or repairer, or independent contractors engaged by the builder
or repairer — to come on the premises. The occupier will not normally be in
a contractual relationship with these other persons though the contract
between the occupier and builder or repairer may envisage, and sometimes
specifically prescribe, that they are to come onto the property. What should
the occupier's position be relative to these persons? They are undoubtedly
visitors. Under s. 1, the term 'visitor' includes an entrant present with the

occupier's permission or one present 'by virtue of an express or implied term is a contract'. (Note that the contract need not necessarily be with the occupier.) The 'stranger to the contract' comes within both of these criteria. Should the occupier be permitted, by a term in the contract between him or her and the builder or repairer, to exclude or modify the liability that would otherwise arise under section 3 to these visitors?

S. 6 of the Act makes it plain that the answer is no. Under subs. (1), the duty that an occupier owes an entrant under the Act is not capable of being modified or excluded by a contract to which the entrant is a stranger, whether or not the occupier is bound by the contract to permit the entrant to enter or use the premises. S. 6(2) provides that an entrant is deemed a stranger to a contract if he or she is not for the time being entitled to the benefit of the contract as a party to it or as the successor by assignment or otherwise of a party to it; accordingly, a party to the contract who has ceased to be so entitled is deemed a stranger to the contract.

Two points may here be noted. First, s. 6 merely prevents the occupier from using a contract with *one* person (for example, the builder or repairer) to reduce or remove his or her liability to *other* persons (the builder's or repairer's employees or independent contractors). It does not prevent the occupier from using s. 5 of the Act to achieve the same purpose. This could be done by express agreement with the employees or independent contractors or by the *notice* procedure prescribed by subs. (2).

A question of policy arises as to whether s. 5(2)(b)(i) has the *inevitable* effect of defeating this strategy. That clause renders ineffective any express agreement or notice seeking to restrict, modify or exclude the occupier's liability towards visitors unless it is 'reasonable in all the circumstances'. No doubt the employees and independent contractors would argue that, in the light of s. 6, an employer should not be permitted to achieve directly what he or she is not permitted to achieve indirectly by means of a provision in the contract with the employer or engager of these visitors. As against this, it can credibly be replied that the policy underlying s. 6 is to ensure that entrants do not lose their statutory protection by virtue of a provision in a contract *to which they are not parties and from which they derive no benefit*. It is not intended to go further than this and prevent an occupier from entering into a contract with these entrants which contains such a restriction, modification or exclusion of liability.

This brings us to the second point, which relates to the present law relating to *privity of contract* and *consideration*. The traditional view was that only parties to a contract who provided consideration should be able to enforce the contract. Specific exceptions were conceded, notably that of the contractual trust. The accepted wisdom for many years was that the privity doctrine had sufficient vitality to resist third party beneficiary claims and that the contractual trust doctrine was in decline. Recently, courts throughout the common law world, notably in Canada (*London Drugs v Kuehne & Nagle International* (1992) 97 DLR (4th) 261) and Australia (*Trident General Insurance v McNeice* (1988) 165 CLR 107), have been willing to countenance an assault on the privity doctrine. Irish courts have yet to confront the issue squarely: cf. *Bula Ltd v Tara Mines Ltd* [1988] ILRM 157, noted in the 1987 Review, 113-4 and *McManus v Cable Management*, High Court, Morris J, July 8, 1994. If they follow the example of other common law jurisdictions, they may well extend the scope of entitlement to enforce a term of a contract to which one is not privy.

For practical purposes, this change would have little effect under s. 6. S. 6(2) defines a 'stranger to a contract' in such a way that, even if the entrant who is not a party to the contract is entitled to the benefit of the contract, and to enforce that entitlement, he or she remains a stranger because he or she is not so entitled *as a party* to the contract. If the law develops in the future in such a way that parties to the contract who do not provide consideration have the right to sue to enforce the benefit prescribed to them under the contract, they will clearly not be 'strangers'. One cannot be definitive about parties to a contract which contains a term conferring benefit on them where they do not provide consideration. Are they 'entitled to the benefit as a party to it' because (let us assume) some *other* party, who has provided consideration, could enforce the term as to their benefit? Or does 'entitlement' necessarily encompass a *personal* right of action on the part of the person so entitled? It may be predicted (tentatively) that the latter approach is the one the court would favour.

Liability of occupiers for the negligence of independent contractors
Under s. 7 of the legislation, an occupier is not liable to an entrant for injury or damage caused to the entrant (or his or her property) by reason of a danger existing on the premises due to the negligence of an independent contractor employed by the occupier if the occupier has taken all reasonable care in the circumstances, unless the occupier has or ought to have had knowledge of 'the fact that the work was not properly done.' Taking reasonable care in this context includes taking such steps as the occupier ought reasonably have taken to satisfy himself or herself that the independent contractor was competent to do the work concerned.

S. 7 avoids the uncertainties created by a similarly drafted provision in English law (Occupiers' Liability Act 1957, s. 2(40)) which limited the occupier's immunity to cases where the damage was caused by a danger 'due to the faulty execution of any work of construction, maintenance or repair' by the independent contractor. This forced the English courts to provide 'a broad and purposeful interpretation' of this limitation (*Ferguson v Welsh*

[1987] 1 WLR 1553, at 156 (H.L. (Eng.), *per* Lord Keith)) so as to include demolition or a builder's failure to take adequate precautions against flooding, for example: cf. *AMF International v Magnet Bowling Ltd* [1988] 1 WLR 1028, at 1043 (Mocatta J). The Law Reform Commission rightly recommended that the provision should be drafted in a manner that was free of these unnecessary confusions.

Barry Doherty points out (*Annotation*, ICLSA, General Note to s. 7) of the Act that an independent contractor can sometimes be an occupier, as, for example, where a builder takes over a site long enough to falls within the definition of 'occupier' under s. 1 of the Act. Of course the injured person will always have a right of action against the independent contractor for negligence, regardless of whether the independent contractor falls within that definition. The Act has nothing to say on the nature and extent of the duty of care of an independent contractor to trespassers (or other entrants). The philosophical and policy basis of *Purtill* and *McNamara* suggests that the courts should be slow to deny a foreseeable trespasser a right of action against the independent contractor by reason of the fact that he or she is a low-prestige entrant. The passage of the Occupiers' Liability Act 1995 should not have altered this position. There may (or may not) be good reasons for reducing the duty owed by occupiers to recreational users or trespassers. These reasons relate to the encouragement of tourism and of access to rural areas and the removal of a potentially oppressive level of liability from occupiers. They do not impact to any similar extent in relation to independent contractors who choose to do work for occupiers and have no long-term stake in the property.

An important point to note here, which we shall consider in more detail when we consider s. 8, is that paragraph (c) makes it plain that nothing in the Act is to be construed as affecting any enactment or rule of law relating to (*inter alia*) the liability imposed on a occupier for a tort committed by another person in circumstances where the duty imposed on the occupier is of such a nature that its performance may not be delegated to another person. It is well established under common law that the occupier has a non-delegable duty with regard to 'ultra-hazardous activities': cf. McMahon & Binchy, *op. cit.*, 761-3. In *Crowe v Merrion Shopping Centre Ltd* (1995) 15 ILT (ns) 302, which we note below, 518-9, Judge Spain held that an occupier may not avoid liability by delegating to an independent contractor menial tasks that are within the occupier's competence to perform. This notion of a non-delegable duty is extending deeply into the realm of employers' liability : see *Connolly v Dundalk Urban District Council* [1990] 2 IR 1, analysed in the 1992 Review, 568-9. In practice, the concept of a non-delegable duty means that the court will hold the occupier liable for the negligence of an independent contractor on the basis of what amounts to vicarious liability.

Preservation of higher duties   S. 8 of the Act makes it plain that nothing in the Act is to be construed as affecting any enactment or rule of law relating to *three* specific areas.

Self-defence, defence of others and defence of property   This is an area where the law allows a fairly robust response by the occupier. It is fair to say that the courts have not injected many legal refinements into what ultimately is a somewhat primitive value judgment about the limits of protection of the rights to life, bodily integrity and property, all of which are endowed with constitutional status. The cases tend to be decided 'on the facts', with little precedential worth for later cases. The law requires reasonable proportionality between the threat to these values and the response by the occupier. Where the line is to be drawn depends on 'all the circumstances' but one or two principles at least are clear. In the defence of his or her property an occupier is not permitted to subject a trespasser to the imposition of retributive force. Thus for two centuries the use of spring guns or other engines of retribution have rendered the occupier liable to compensate the unwelcome entrant. Moreover, there is recent authority that commercial enterprises should seek injunction proceedings rather than have recourse to 'private violence' in protection of their property interests. *MacKnight v Xtravision*, Circuit Court, Caroll J, July 5, 1991, analysed in the 1991 Review, 417-9, and extracted in McMahon & Binchy's *Casebook on the Irish Law of Torts* (2nd ed., 1991), 407.

Liability imposed on an occupier as a member of a particular class of persons
The second situation which is unaffected by the Occupiers' Liability Act 1995 is that relating to any liability imposed on an occupier as a member of a particular class of persons. S. 8(b) of the Act gives *three* examples in a non-exclusive list:

> (1) persons by virtue of a contract for the hire of, or for the carriage for reward of persons or property in, any vessel, vehicle, train, aircraft or other means of transport;
> (2) persons by virtue of a contract of bailment;
> and
> (3) employers in respect of their duties towards their employees.

A few words about these three classes may be of assistance. Carriers and bailees have for centuries been subjected to onerous duties, in excess of that of the common law duty of care, in certain circumstances. This is because those who place themselves or their goods in their charge are sometimes in a vulnerable situation. Five hundred years ago, it was always possible for carriers to conspire with highway men and for bailees to facilitate the theft of goods in their care. Human nature has not changed markedly over the years. Carriers are mentioned by s. 8 because of the broad definition of 'premises' in s. 1, which, as we have seen, embraces vessels, vehicles, trains, aircraft and other means of transport.

Hotel proprietors are not mentioned in s. 8. The Hotel Proprietors Act 1963 prescribes the duties owed by hotel proprietors to guests. For either of two reasons, this legislation is unaffected by the 1995 Act. Either s. 2(1) does not reach it because it is limited to replacing the duties Oheretofore attached by the *common law*' (emphasis added) or, if the 1963 Act nonetheless is putatively affected by the 1995 Act, s. 8 makes it plain that nothing in the 1995 legislation is to be construed as affecting 'any *enactment* or rule of law' (emphasis added) relating to any liability imposed on an occupier 'as a member of a particular class of persons. . .': s. 8(b).

In this context it is worth considering the present status of s. 21(3) of the Control of Dogs Act 1986, which provides that:

[a] person is liable in damages for any damage caused by a dog kept on any premises or structure to a person trespassing thereon only in accordance with the rules of law relating to liability for negligence.

Could this provision be characterised as imposing a liability on an occupier as a member of a particular class of persons? It is true that it prescribes a liability but in truth the provision is essentially subtractive rather than impositional since it relieves the owner of the dog of strict liability which would otherwise attach: see McMahon & Binchy, *op. cit.*, 513-5. The most convincing interpretation of s. 21(3) is that it makes the liability for damage caused to trespassers by dogs one that does *not* rest on the fact that the occupier is a member of a particular class of persons but rather subsumes that liability into the vast generic category of liability for negligence.

Perhaps the entire question of liability for dogs has no present relevance, since, if an aggressive dog does not constitute a danger *due to the state of the premises*, as s. 1(1) requires, the 1995 Act will simply not apply. Once more, the troublesome question of how to distinguish between passive conditions and activities on the premises falls for consideration. Is it possible to distinguish between the teeth of a spring gun, when activated, and the teeth of a dog recently roused from his slumber?

Non-delegable duties We have already mentioned the tendency of the courts in recent years to expand the scope of employers' liability under the characterisation of the non-delegable duties. S. 8(c) of the 1995 Act removes from its scope non-delegable duties. Thus, a non-delegable duty, whether relating to an employer's liability to an employee or otherwise will be capable of rendering the person on whom that duty is imposed liable for the tortious acts or omissions of an independent contractor. In our discussion of s. 7, we have referred to Judge Spain's holding in *Crowe v Merrion Shopping Centre Ltd* (1995) 15 ILT (n.s.) 302 (Circuit Court (Dublin), which characterises an occupier's menial duties relating to the safety of the premises as non-delegable: see below 518-9.

Commencement of the legislation   The legislation came into operation on 17 July 1995, one month after the date of its passing: s. 9(2).

Common law liability   The courts have not shown great warmth to supermarkets in occupiers' liability cases. In *Mullen v Quinnsworth Ltd (No. 1)* [1990] 1 IR 59, McCarthy J was willing to go so far as to impose absolute liability on large supermarkets for slip-and-fall injuries. See the 1990 Review, 518-2. It is true that he later retreated from these ruminations, in *Mullen v Quinnsworth Ltd (No. 2)* [1991] ILRM 439, noted in the 1991 Review, 393-5, but there remains a sense that courts view the injuries that befall customers of supermarkets as the inevitable outcome of the system of open shelf selling of thousands of products in relatively confined spaces.

In *White v Primark* [1996] Ir. Law Log Weekly 18 (Circuit Court (Dublin)), Carroll J, November 10, 1995), the plaintiff, aged two, accompanied her mother on a shopping trip to the defendant's supermarket. She wandered off and tripped over a protruding foot of a free standing body-length mirror in an aisle. Her face hit the floor.

Judge Carroll observed that there was no question that the defendant had discouraged the presence of young children with their parents on the premises. The owners of such premises by advertisement invited the public to come with their children and the fact that a crèche was provided was not the answer. Those who ran these emporia must realise that, if they attracted the average person there, the average person would behave as such. A parent was entitled to inspect something which he or she had been carefully invited to inspect and if, as a result, a child engaged in mischief, then the onus on those who managed these places was very high. The momentary lapse of parental attention had to be expected and provision made, as far as possible, that it should not end in mischief.

Judge Carroll accordingly imposed liability on the defendant. In the instant case it appears that there was no question of parental negligence. It should be noted that Judge Carroll's reasoning as to why a shop might be liable is not inconsistent with the possibility of there being parental negligence in certain cases. Tort law accepts that one party's negligence may consist in inducing another party to be negligent to a third party.

In *Crowe v Merrion Shopping Centre Ltd and Southside Contract Cleaners Ltd* (1995) 15 Ir L Times (ns) 302 (Circuit Court (Dublin), Spain

J, the plaintiff, a patron of a shopping centre, was injured when she fell on a slippy floor surface which had been created by the carelessness of an employee of contract cleaners who had been engaged by the shopping centre to clean its floor surfaces. Undoubtedly the contract cleaners were vicariously liable for the negligence of their employee; it was also clear that they were independent contractors. The crucial question was whether the shopping centre should be held vicariously liable for the negligence of its independent contractors.

On one line of authority, the occupier of premises is liable only where he or she has been negligent in the selection or supervision of an incompetent independent contractor. Another line of authority imposes on the occupier a 'non-delegable' duty, 'at least with respect to non-technical jobs that he could have performed himself, like cleaning stairs or clearing walkways': J. Fleming, *The Law of Torts* (8th ed., 1992), 460. (It is worth noting that Fleming's preference is for the first approach.)

In *Crowe*, Judge Spain preferred the second approach. The work for which the independent contractors had been engaged could have been done by the shopping centre itself. The fact that it had contracted out this work did not absolve it of its Oprimary responsibility' to ensure that its premises were reasonably safe for those who had been invited to come in as customers. Accordingly Judge Spain held both defendants liable, with a complete indemnity against the contract cleaners in favour of the shopping centre.

PURE ECONOMIC LOSS

In *Kennedy v AIB Public Ltd and AIB Finance Ltd*, High Court, May 18, 1995, Kinlen J, on the evidence, rejected the plaintiff's claim that the defendants were guilty of breach of contract and negligence, as bankers, in the provision of loan and overdraft facilities. Murphy J quoted a passage from Gannon J's judgment in *Tulsk Co-Operative Livestock Mart Ltd v Ulster Bank Ltd*, High Court, May 13, 1983, to the effect that:

> [a]lthough the relation of customer and banker between the parties warrants the founding of a claim in part on contract and the alleged breach of contract, the essential issues in dispute are subject to the law relating to negligence. The plaintiff's claim is founded more upon alleged failures on the defendant's part to measure up to the duties and standards of care appropriate to the purported performance of the contractual obligations rather than on alleged failure to perform in accordance with the express or implied contractual terms. The nature of the duties which the law imposes depends upon the circumstances of

the relationships between the parties and the harm, loss or detriment to either party which would reasonably be foreseeable from such circumstances and relationships.

This bold assertion that the law of negligence can generate liability in the context of performance of contractual obligations may be called in aid by a plaintiff in an Irish court when, as will surely occur, in the short to medium term, a defendant invites the court to apply the approach favoured by the House of Lords in *Murphy v Brentwood DC* [1991] 1 AC 398 and resile from the position adopted by Costello J in *Ward v McMaster* [1986] ILRM 43; [1985] IR 29, affirmed by the Supreme Court [1988] IR 337.

NEGLIGENTLY INFLICTED EMOTIONAL SUFFERING

In the 1993 Review 549-50, we noted Lavan J's decision in *Kelly v Hennessy* [1993] ILRM 530. The case arose from a traffic accident in which the plaintiff's husband and two daughters had received severe injuries. The plaintiff, who was at home at the time, was telephoned shortly afterwards by her niece who told her of the tragedy. The plaintiff immediately went into shock, became upset and began vomiting. She was taken to the hospital where her family had been removed. She saw each of them. They were all in an appalling condition. The plaintiff's husband and one of her daughters remained in hospital for nearly four months. Her other daughter did not leave hospital for a year. The plaintiff's husband and one daughter were left brain damaged. This involved major problems for the plaintiff in managing the home.

There was conflicting medical evidence in the case. Lavan J preferred the evidence adduced on the plaintiff's behalf. He was satisfied that the plaintiff had suffered 'immediate nervous shock resulting in vomiting' on receiving the fateful telephone call from her niece and that this condition had been 'gravely aggravated' by the scenes she had immediately thereafter witnessed at the hospital. He considered that she had suffered from post-traumatic stress disorder for at least four years after the accident and that she continued to suffer a serious depression from which she would probably never fully recover. He awarded her £35,000 for pain and suffering prior to judgment and £40,000 for future pain and suffering.

The defendant appealed unsuccessfully to the Supreme Court. Two judgments were delivered: by Hamilton CJ and Denham J.

Hamilton CJ considered that 'the cases' (not specifically identified, although he later referred to several) established that, to succeed in an action for damages for nervous shock, the plaintiff had to establish:

> 1. that he or she had actually suffered a recognisable psychiatric illness;
> 2. that this illness was 'shock-induced' (echoing Brennan J in *Jaensch v Coffey* (1984) 155 CLR 540);
> 3. that the nervous shock was caused by the defendant's act or omission;
> 4. that the nervous shock sustained by the plaintiff was 'by reason of actual or apprehended physical injury to the plaintiff or a person other than the plaintiff'. (The Chief Justice here echoed Deane J's remarks in *Jaensch v Coffey*);
> 5. that the defendant owed the plaintiff a duty of care not to cause him or her a reasonably foreseeable injury in the form of nervous shock. (The Chief Justice again followed the lead of Deane J who had stated that 'a duty of care will not arise unless risk of injury in that particular form (i.e. psychiatric injury unassociated with conventional physical injury) was reasonably foreseeable.')

It has to be said that these five propositions scarcely advance the law much further than it had been declared in *Bell v Great Northern Railway Company of Ireland* (1896) 26 LR Ir 428. What is striking about Hamilton CJ's further analysis is its reluctance to take a definitive position on the four crucial questions that have dominated judicial analysis over the past three decades. These are, *first*, whether the courts should on policy grounds prescribe specific limitations on liability, narrower than the parameters of reasonable foreseeability of the injury; *secondly*, (and, on one view, contingent upon an affirmative answer to the first question), whether only a restrictive class of plaintiffs, based on their personal relationship with the primary victim, should be entitled to compensation; *thirdly*, whether it is a condition of liability that the plaintiff should have suffered the injury as a result of directly witnessing the accident involving the primary victim or its immediate aftermath; and *finally* (and clearly related to the third of these questions), whether a plaintiff who suffered injury on being told of the accident involving the primary victim should be entitled to compensation.

In the instant case, the plaintiff would be entitled to succeed, even if a restrictive approach were adopted towards all of these questions. The worst that could have happened would be that some diminution in her damages might have been prescribed to take account of the fact that she had begun to experience shock on being told of the accident.

It seems a futile exercise to parse Hamilton CJ's observations in an attempt to derive some guidance on the crucial questions. His statement that the relationship between the plaintiff and the person injured in the accident Omust be close' could suggest some notion of a policy limitation in relation to the first of the four questions such as Lord Wilberforce proposed in *McLoughlin v O'Brian* [1983] AC 410. This inference is strengthened by the Chief Justice's apparently approving quotation from Lord Wilberforce's speech on this precise question. Yet later in his judgment the Chief Justice, observing that there 'is no public policy that the [plaintiff]'s claim, if substantiated, should be excluded', goes on to quote with apparent approval from Lord Russell's observations in *McLoughlin* to the effect that fear of opening the floodgates should not deny a deserving plaintiff compensation.

The final issue addressed by the Chief Justice was whether the plaintiff's depression should be attributed to the post-traumatic stress disorder she had undoubtedly suffered or to the grief and strain caused by having to assume and maintain such a burden of care for her husband and daughter after their discharge from hospital. He invoked the formula expressed by McCarthy J in *Hay v O'Grady* [1992] 1 IR 210, at 217 on the role of an appellate court where there was credible testimony before the trial judge to justify his or her findings of fact or inferences therefrom.

Denham J's judgment reflects the approach she adopted in *Mullally v Bus Éireann* [1992] ILRM 722 (cf. the 1992 Review, 401-4) to the extent that she identified the two main approaches to the subject apparent in *McLoughlin v O'Brian*: Lord Bridge's endorsement of reasonable foreseeability as the basis of liability and Lord Wilberforce's preference for policy-based restrictions cutting down on the potential liability generated by reasonable foresight, which would remain a necessary, but not a sufficient, basis of liability. In *Mullally*, while acknowledging that the facts of the case would have yielded a verdict for the plaintiff on the application of either test, Denham J expressed a preference for Lord Bridge's approach. In *Kelly v Hennessy*, Denham J took a more neutral position, commenting that it was 'not necessary in this case to choose between either the general or the more restricted approach in common law.' She noted that she had 'used the cases to isolate the factors which are relevant in law and applied these factors to the facts of this case.' The factors Denham J identified and the lexicon of proximity of relationship which she adopted savoured more of Lord Wilberforce's approach.

ACCIDENTS ON THE HIGHWAY

McCormack v McCabe Transport Ltd, Supreme Court, January 26, 1995 is an example of how difficult it is to appeal successfully against findings of fact. The case was a simple one: the plaintiff's van had collided with the defendant's trailer and truck unit. The trial judge had held in favour of the plaintiff, holding that the defendant's vehicle must have been partially over on the plaintiff's side of the road, not giving the plaintiff room to pass in safety. The defendant sought to convince the Supreme Court that there was evidence in the case, apart from that of the driver, which pointed against a finding of liability. Egan J (Hamilton CJ and O'Flaherty J concurring) was not impressed by this evidence, which related to skid marks, photographs taken by a director of the defendant company of the scene of the accident and evidence of the investigating guard. He considered that none of this evidence advanced the defendant's case. He concluded:

> Even though the learned judge stated that the case turned in the credibility of the two drivers it does not necessarily follow that he ignored all other evidence. On matters of credibility he had all the advantages which this court does not enjoy and there would require to be objective matters of a compelling nature and leading to contrary conclusions before his findings could be upset. I have been unable to find such matters.

Accordingly the appeal was dismissed.

In *Kinsella v Doran*, High Court, July 27, 1995, Barron J was faced with an accident where neither party had any recollection as to what had transpired. On the basis of conflicting evidence from motor engineers called by both sides, he concluded that the defendant had negligently driven into the path of the plaintiff and that the plaintiff had been too slow in responding to the danger. He imposed liability on the defendant, reducing the plaintiff's damages by 20% on the basis of his failure to keep a proper look-out.

The paucity of evidence in the case is striking. The vehicles, following the collision, were found in the plaintiff's side of the road, the camber of which sloped somewhat towards the plaintiff. One may wonder what would have been the position if the doctrine of *res ipsa loquitur* (never mentioned in the judgment) had been applied. It is hard to see how the defendant could have escaped liability, on the basis that the doctrine shifted onto him the onus of showing that he was not negligent or at least the obligation to offer some plausible explanation as to why he might not have been negligent. Since the defendant was completely unaware of what had happened, there is no way in which he could have avoided liability if the *res ipsa loquitur* doctrine had been applied, with such potent effect.

In *Skinner v Harnett and Cork Corporation*, High Court, February 3, 1995, which we discuss in the section on Causation, later in the chapter, below, 528, O'Hanlon J imposed 50% liability on the driver of a car, with the lights in his favour, who collided with a cyclist who had broken the lights. The defendant claimed that he had been travelling at 25 m.p.h. This did not assist his case. At such a slow speed the defendant should have been able to stop earlier than he had done. He might, however, have been travelling 'at a good deal higher speed than his estimate' or he might have simply reacted in an inexpert manner by sounding his horn in the hope of warning the cyclist to keep out of the way and only applying his brakes when a collision was well-nigh inevitable.

It was true that the plaintiff had been guilty of 'carelessness of a very high order' but the defendant had had 'a very heavy responsibility . . . to exercise constant care in the manner in which he drove a motor vehicle on the public highway by reason of the potentially fatal consequences for other users of the highway if he neglected to do so.' It has to be said that a 50% — 50% allocation of fault seems very harsh on the defendant.

CONTRIBUTORY NEGLIGENCE

In *Wrenn v Bus Átha Cliath/Dublin Bus*, Supreme Court, March 31, 1995, which we discuss earlier in the chapter, above, 473-5, the plaintiff passenger was injured when attacked by another passenger. Morris J imposed liability on the bus company for negligence in failing to protect the plaintiff from the attack but reduced the award by 50% to take account of the plaintiff's contributory negligence. The Supreme Court reversed the finding of con- tributory negligence as the issue had not been pleaded and no evidence had been adduced in its regard.

In *Crosbie v Boland National Car Ltd t/a Euro dollar Rent-A-Car*, High Court, July 7, 1995, the plaintiff, a pedestrian, was injured by the defendants' vehicle when he was crossing a dual-carriageway slip road, close to Dublin Airport, at noon in the summertime. Morris J imposed liability on the defendant for negligently having failed to avoid coming in contact with the plaintiff. He reduced the damages by 50% on the basis of the plaintiff's contributory negligence. The plaintiff had crossed the road at a time that was 'improper and potentially dangerous.' Given that he was crossing a dual carriageway, he should reasonably have expected that cars would travel fast on this stretch of the road and he should have delayed crossing until he was sure that it was safe to do so rather than attempt the venture when a car was approaching.

Earlier in the chapter, in the section on Accidents on the Highway, above, 523, we critically analyse O'Hanlon J's allocation of 50% contributory negligence, in *Skinner v Harnett and Cork Corporation*, High Court, Febru- ary 3, 1995, to a cyclist who broke the lights where she collided with the defendant's car. We consider that this holding was unduly harsh on the defendant in the circumstances.

Earlier in the chapter, 479-82, we analyse *Allen v Ó Súilleabháin and the*

Mid-Western Health Board, High Court, July 28, 1995, where Kinlen J held that a 25-year-old student midwife had not been guilty of contributory negligence in failing to communicate verbally to the obstetrician and mid-wives that she was in great pain and resulting from holding the leg of a patient during childbirth. To have interrupted the obstetrician and midwives 'would be extremely cheeky for a student midwife'. We criticise the ethos that underlies this holding and examine the possibility that it may involve negligence on the part of those who employ nurses.

In *Kinsella v Doran*, High Court, July 27, 1995, an interesting question about the relationship between negligence and contributory negligence does not appear to have been resolved. The parties were involved in a head-on collision. Neither party had any recollection of the accident. Each had been alone in his car. There were no witnesses. Reconstructing from the circum-stantial evidence how the accident probably occurred, Barron J concluded that, 'for whatever reason, the defendant's car came across to its wrong side of the road and that the accident in the main was caused because of this.' He also was of the view that the plaintiff had not been keeping a proper look out. He held that 'the relative degrees of fault should be 80% on the defendant and 20% on the plaintiff.'

It would appear from the judgment that Barron J was adjudicating both a claim and a counterclaim; it is hard to see why he would otherwise have assessed the defendant's damages. If this is so, there were in essence two separate claims, in respect of which it was necessary in each case to determine the *negligence* of the party against whom negligence was alleged. But what about the question of contributory negligence? It is quite possible to conceive of cases where the quantum of a driver's contributory negligence would not be the same as that of his or her negligence. If, for example, the plaintiff had been travelling too fast and was not wearing a seat belt, then the quantum of reduction of damages to take account of the plaintiff's contributory negli-gence would be likely to be greater than the quantum of negligence that would be ascribed to him in the defendant's counterclaim. In practice, the failure to keep a proper look to may often be as serious an act of *contributory* negligence, which involves carelessness about *one's own* safety, as it is *negligence*, which involves carelessness about *another's* safety, but there is no necessary identity.

Res Ipsa Loquitur In *O'Reilly Brothers (Quarries Ltd v. Irish Industrial Explosives Ltd*, Supreme Court, February 27, 1995, a relatively straightfor-ward issue arose. If a blasting operation in a quarry causes unintended damage, should the *res ipsa loquitur* doctrine apply? In the classic recitation of the doctrine in *Scott v London and St. Catherine Docks Co.* (1865) 3 H & C 596, at 601, 159 ER 665, at 667, Erle CJ stated:

There must be reasonable evidence of negligence but where the thing is shown to be under the management of the defendant or his servants and the accident is such as in the ordinary course does not happen if those who have the management use proper care, it affords reasonable evidence, in the absence of explanation by the defendants, that the accident arose from want of care.

In the instant case, the plaintiff, who owned a quarry, engaged the defendants to use explosives to free certain parts of the rock in the quarry to enable the rock to be crushed. The plaintiff decided where the blasting operations would take place and bored holes in the rock face. The defendants inspected the holes and decided on the quantity of explosives required to execute the blasting operation and the order in which the explosives would be detonated. They then supplied the explosives and detonators and had the task of supervising the filling of the holes with the proper amount of explosives in the proper sequence.

On the fateful day, blasting took place in an area quite close to the crusher area and the crusher. The risk of damage to the crusher was discussed between the parties and it was agreed that two of the bore holes nearest the crusher would not be filled with explosives and that three of the holes would be filled with a reduced charge.

When the blasting took place, it caused serious damage to the crusher. The crucial question was whether the damage was caused by a fissure or defect in the rock or was, on the contrary, the result of the negligence of the defendants in the manner in which the timing sequence had been laid. An expert witness called by the plaintiff gave evidence to the effect that the only explanation that he could come up with was that the blasting sequence had been reversed from what it should have been. This was denied by the person who had responsibility for this function. If it had occurred it would have amounted to serious negligence on his part.

The trial judge dismissed the case, on the basis that '[i]t really stagger belief' that this could have occurred, in view of the extraordinary lapse of judgment that it would involve, the fact that the person in question had denied that he had done it and the fact that his colleagues thought it incomprehensible. The plaintiff appealed to the Supreme Court. One ground was that the doctrine of *res ipsa loquitur* should have been applied to shift the onus onto the defendants to disprove negligence.

The Supreme Court dismissed the appeal. Hamilton CJ (O'Flaherty and Blayney JJ concurring) quoted the passage from Erle CJ's judgment in *Scott*, and stated that:

[h]aving regard to the nature of the work to be carried out in this case

— a blasting operation — it is obvious that there was an inherent risk of damage without negligence on the part of anyone.

This had been accepted by the parties themselves, who had discussed the question of the risk beforehand and who had agreed that the plaintiff should sign an indemnity against liability for any damage to plant or structures in the quarry. Whilst the indemnity would not have afforded the defendants any protection against liability from their negligence, it was of relevance 'as indicating that there was a risk or danger of damage in the blasting operation'.

In a very brief concurring judgment, O'Flaherty J observed:

> While there was an expansion to the applicability of the doctrine of *res ipsa loquitur* in the case which was cited to us: *Lindsay v Mid-Western Health Board* [1993] 2 IR 147, this was to take account of the special position of patients *vis-à-vis* hospital personnel. I am satisfied that the well established purview of the doctrine applies in this case which requires that a circumstance of negligence must be apparent in the first instance before the doctrine can be invoked.

The decision in *O'Reilly Brothers (Quarries) Ltd v Irish Industrial Explosives Ltd* provokes a number of comments.

First, it is noteworthy that Hamilton CJ quoted with apparent approval Henchy J's restatement of the *res ipsa loquitur* doctrine in *Hanrahan v Merck Sharp & Dohme (Ireland) Ltd* [1988] ILRM 629, at 634-5. We have already criticised this restatement on the basis that it wrongfully dispenses with the requirement for the plaintiff to establish that the 'thing' that caused the injury (to use Erle CJ's expression) was under the management of the defendant: see the 1988 Review, 448-9. Henchy J's approach cannot be reconciled with Erle CJ's formula in *Scott v London and St. Catherine Docks Co.*, which the Chief Justice quoted with approval and applied. It is true that Griffin J, in *Mullen v Quinnsworth Ltd* [1990] 1 IR 59, at 62 had also cited Erle CJ's formula with approval but Griffin J did not cite *Hanrahan's* case even though it was a judgment of the Supreme Court delivered only two years previously. It is noteworthy that in *O'Shea v Tilman Anhold and Horse Holiday Farm Ltd*, Supreme Court, October 23, 1996, Keane J observed that Henchy J's approach in Hanrahan had been criticised and might 'need to be reconsidered at some stage'. Hamilton CJ reserved his positiion on the question.

Secondly, there was a good reason for rejecting the application of the *res ipsa loquitur* doctrine apart from the fact that blasting operations have an inherent risk of damage without negligence on the part of anyone. This is that the plaintiff was not resting its case on unfocused inferences of circumstantial evidence but rather had a definite theory of the case, which was that the blasting sequence had been reversed.

Thirdly, O'Flaherty J's observations are a little difficult to discern. Nothing was stated in *Lindsay v Mid-Western Health Board*, either by Morris J at trial or by the Supreme Court itself which would suggest that the doctrine of *res ipsa loquitur* was being *extended* to take account of the special position of patients *vis-à-vis* hospital personnel. See our comments in the 1992 Review 592-8. It is true that there are ways in which the doctrine can with benefit be extended to take account of the special position of dependency of hospital patients. California did as much, nearly half a century ago, in *Ybarra v Spangard* (1944) 25 Cal 2d 486, 154 P 2d 687. S. 11(3) of the Civil Liability Act 1961 has achieved a somewhat similar, but not identical, reform: see McMahon & Binchy, *op. cit.*, 58.

CAUSATION

In *Skinner v Hartnett and Cork Corporation*, High Court, February 3, 1995 a nett issue of causation arose. The plaintiff cyclist was injured in a crossroads collision with the defendant's vehicle. O'Hanlon J upheld the allegation that the traffic lights did not allow a cyclist starting off from a stationary position and cycling at a normal speed to reach the far side of the junction in safety before the lights turned against him or her. In the circumstances of the case, however, this was not sufficient to impose liability on the Corporation because the cyclist had in fact broken a red light rather than waiting for it to turn to green. Although the Corporation had been negligent in its traffic light system, that negligence had not causally contributed to the accident.

REMOTENESS OF DAMAGE

Difficult questions of causation, physical and legal, can arise in relation to successive injuries. If the victim of a particular injury on a previous occasion is then involved in an accident caused by the defendant's negligence and later his or her physical condition worsens, in what circumstances should the defendant have to compensate the plaintiff for this worsened state? The answer is simple in theory but less easy to apply in practice. If the worsened condition is attributable entirely to the progress of the injury sustained previously, the defendant will not be liable to pay damages in relation to it. If, however, it is attributable exclusively to the accident caused by the defendant, then the defendant will be obliged to compensate the plaintiff for it. This will be so even where, as a result of the earlier injury, the plaintiff has been rendered particularly vulnerable to the new injury. Thus the 'eggshell skull' plaintiff can recover fully against the negligent defendant.

In *McKinney v Brinks Allied Ltd*, High Court, February 23, 1995, the plaintiff, a soldier, had previously endured a severe condition of stress when on duty in the Lebanon as a result of witnessing 'a very violent incident' (not further described in the judgment). Some years later he was involved in an accident, in which liability was admitted. Thereafter he suffered panic attacks and other symptoms.

After a review of the evidence, O'Hanlon J concluded that these later injuries were a recurrence of his earlier condition rather than attributable to the accident in relation to which he had taken legal proceedings. O'Hanlon J considered that the plaintiff's case had been exaggerated; he felt that 'if the plaintiff were living in a less sheltered environment than the Army, he would have shaken off all effects of the accident at a much earlier stage than actually happened and got on with the ordinary business of holding down a job and looking after a family.' (One suspects that these words are unlikely to appear on Army recruitment posters.)

DEFAMATION

Report of court proceedings What are the respective roles of judge and jury in defamation proceedings? On the question whether the words of which the plaintiff complains are defamatory, the Supreme Court has no doubt: in *Barrett v. Independent Newspapers* [1986] ILRM 601, at 607, Henchy J stated:

> Because the community standard represented by the jury may differ radically from the individual standard of the judge in determining what is defamatory, it would be a usurpation of the jury's function in the matter if the judge where to take upon himself to rule conclusively that the words were defamatory.

Few would disagree with this approach.

But what is the position in relation to the defence of qualified privilege and specifically the statutory defence under s. 24 of the Defamation Act 1961 protecting 'fair and accurate' reports of court proceedings when made out with malice? The issue arose in *Murphy v. Dow Jones Publishing Company (Europe) Inc*, High Court, January 11, 1995, where the plaintiff claimed damages for defamation and injurious falsehood in an article in the European edition of the Wall Street Journal and the defendant invoked s. 24. The defendants sought an order under O. 25, s.1 of the Rules of the Superior Courts 1986 directing that the question of qualified privilege be determined as a preliminary issue by a judge without a jury.

Flood J refused to grant this order. He referred to Lord Finlay LC's observations in *Allen v Ward* [1917] AC 309, at 318 that:

[i]t is for the judge, and the judge alone, to determine as a matter of law whether the occasion is privileged, unless the circumstances attending it are in dispute, in which case the facts necessary to raise the question of law should be found by the jury.

Flood J commented:

Put another way the privilege is dependent upon the report being fair and accurate, but it is the province of the jury and not of the judge to determine whether the language used exceeds the proper limits of the privilege which the section affords.

Flood J considered that:

[t]he essence of the statutory protection of privilege is that the report is 'a fair and accurate report'. In principle the fairness and accuracy of anything concerned with defamation are factual matters and have been held to be eminently suitable for decision by a jury. What is fair and accurate is a matter of opinion. Matters of opinion and matters of fact have always been the preserve of the jury.

He was of the view that the *Barrett* approach to the issue of the defamatory character of a defendant's words applied with equal force to the question whether a report was 'fair and accurate'. Flood J accepted that, if a court was convinced that it would be perverse on the part of the jury to hold that the report was not a fair and accurate one, the court had jurisdiction to try a preliminary issue in such circumstances. One instance of this would arise where a newspaper reported a judgment verbatim. He considered that the instant case did not come within this exceptional category.

The case provokes a number of comments. First, there is a world of difference between the question whether a statement is defamatory, where the courts rightly concede the importance of community values, and the question whether a newspaper report in fair and accurate. In the latter instance, there is far less likelihood of community values being relevant. Accuracy is a matter of fact; fairness does involve a value judgment, but one in which community standards will normally be of little relevance.

Secondly, Flood J accepts that it is possible, in certain instances, for a court with propriety to make the determination sought by the defendants in the instant case. He requires of the court, however, that it make this determination as a matter preliminary to the exercise of its jurisdiction to try the preliminary issue. It may be hard to do this before the evidence has been adduced.

Capacity of words to bear a defamatory meaning In *Conlon v Times Newspapers Ltd* [1995] 2 ILRM 76, Murphy J gave important guidance on the approach that a court should adopt when there has been a motion in defamation proceedings to strike out the plaintiff's claim as disclosing no reasonable cause of action or on the ground that it is clearly unsustainable and bound to fail. The plaintiff had been wrongly convicted and unjustly imprisoned in Britain. He wrote a book on his experiences, which Murphy J said he had no reason to doubt was an accurate account. A film, *In the Name of the Father*, was made on the basis of the book. It was not disputed that the film did not purport to be an accurate account of historical events. It was common case that for artistic reasons the facts which were the subject matter of the book were varied in the making of the film.

The film critic for the Sunday Times, Julie Birchall, when commenting on the film, made two observations which the plaintiff alleged were libellous. In the first she stated that the plaintiff's 'awe inspiring pacifist father never forgave him for implicating him in his forced confession which Gerard doesn't do here, and he died before there was a reconciliation'.

The second passage was as follows:

> 'I could never do anything right for you' moans Gerry after Guiseppe was thrown into jail on his churlish son's account, before going on to justify his life of crime by claiming that his old Dad 'never cheered him loudly enough at football'.

Murphy J considered that on the face of it, these two statements appeared to be defamatory:

> I would have thought that it was at least arguable that these words were capable of a meaning which would reduce the plaintiff in the eyes of right thinking people. To implicate an innocent in a serious crime — or to say of somebody that they implicated somebody of a serious crime of which they were innocent — would surely be defamatory. To describe somebody as churlish in the context that they permitted their own father to be thrown into jail must at lest be capable of a defamatory meaning. I doubt that anyone would suggest that the position was otherwise and the defendant is not attempting to make such an unreal argument.

The defendant contended that, reading the article as a whole and recognising the state of facts known to the public generally at the time when it was written, no right thinking person could think the less of the plaintiff for what he in fact had done, having regard to the circumstances in which the action occurred. It conceded that the statements were wrong but argued that they could not have caused damage.

Murphy J refused the defendant's motion for a dismissal of the proceedings. The appropriate test was not whether the words were *capable* of bearing a particular meaning but rather the *arguability* as to whether they were capable of a particular meaning. It was the trial judge's function at trial to determine whether the words had that capability. On a motion to dismiss, however, it was sufficient if the plaintiff could show that there was at least an argument that the words were capable of the meaning for which he contended. Murphy J had no doubt that the plaintiff had shown this:

> It seems to me the words themselves are capable of certain meanings and that the concern of the defendant and the argument adduced by the defendant is essentially the context in which those words should be construed and interpreted and understood either by the trial judge, or in the event of the matter going to a jury, by the jury itself. To my mind it has not been established that the plaintiff's case is clearly unsustainable or that it is bound to fail. I do not think it is suggested, or could be seriously suggested, that the statement of claim does not disclose a cause of action. Manifestly it discloses a cause of action. . . .
>
> Without myself in any way expressing any view as to what the probable outcome would be, I do not accept, on the argument or on the evidence, that it has been established to the satisfaction of this Court that the plaintiff's claim is clearly unsustainable or that it is bound to fail. It does seem to me that the preference in every case should be that, unless these matters are clearly established, . . . a plaintiff in every case should be afforded the opportunity of having his case fully heard by a judge, and more particularly, a jury, where that is an appropriate remedy.

Proposed legislative changes On February 9, 1995, the Defamation Bill 1995 was presented to the Dáil, as a private member's measure, by Deputy Michael McDowell. It is largely modelled on the proposals contained in the Law Reform Commission's Report on the *Civil Law of Defamation* (LRC 38–1991), which we analysed in the 1991 Review, 453-9. It goes further than the Commission in a number of respects, perhaps most importantly in prescribing a defence of qualified privilege to the media for matters published concerning issues 'of legitimate public concern', where the publisher and author intended the publication to be 'for the public benefit', 'took every reasonable care to establish the truth of the matter published and to avoid defaming the plaintiff' and believed on reasonable grounds that the matter published was true: s. 21. This would in certain instances give the media a defence which would not be available to them under the principles stated by the United States Supreme Court in *New York Times v Sullivan* (1964) 376 US 245.

Another major departure from the Commission's recommendations is in relation to the reputation rights of deceased persons. The Commission had proposed that there should be a moratorium on defamatory publications for three years after the defamed person had died; the Bill favours an open season commencing with the death, on the basis that the Commission's proposal would be 'anomalous and unworkable' and that 'it might have serious repercussions in so far as it could inhibit the recording and discussion of recent history' (*Explanatory Memorandum to the Bill*, p. 1 (Feabhra, 1995)). It has to be said that, whatever merits there may be in giving licence to taking away the good name of a person, posthumously, by the dissemination of false accusations, those who oppose a three-year moratorium on the basis that the recording and discussion of recent history will be inhibited have a hard case to make.

PUBLIC NUISANCE

In the 1996 Review, we shall analyse the important decision of *Convery v County Council of the County of Dublin*, Supreme Court, November 12, 1996, reversing High Court, October 13, 1995. Carroll J had held that the defendant was guilty of public nuisance, arising from negligence in the discharge of its statutory duty, in relation to the large volumes of traffic using the road where the plaintiff resided as a 'rat run'. The Supreme Court that the action for public nuisance should fail because the traffic had not originated in any premises owned or occupied by the County Council and had not been generated as a result of any activities carried on by it on land in the area. O'Hanlon J's decision in *Kelly v Dublin County Council*, High Court, February 21, 1981 (discussed in McMahon & Binchy, *op. cit.*, 472-3) was thus distinguishable. The claim in negligence foundered because the plaintiff had failed to establish that there was a relationship between her and the County Council which generated a common law duty on the part of the County Council to take reasonable care arising from its public duty under statute.

THE RULE IN *RYLANDS v FLETCHER*

In *Dockeray v Manor Park Homebuilders Ltd*, High Court, April 10, 1995, O'Hanlon J held that the defendant builders were liable, under the rule in *Rylands v Fletcher* (1868) LR 3HL 330, for flooding of the plaintiff's lands as a result of building operations in which the defendants were engaged, which were not able to cope with a concentrated very heavy, but by no means unprecedented, rainfall. O'Hanlon J quoted from McMahon & Binchy's *Irish Law of Torts* (2nd ed., 1990) 492, to the effect that it appears that:

> only the most extreme of natural phenomena will afford a good defence. Thus, gales in this country, heavy rainfalls in Wales and Scotland and heavy snowfalls in England have been held on the evidence not to have been Acts of God.

In the instant case, whilst the rainfall at the fateful moment had been 'of extraordinarily high proportions', it had 'not been of such phenomenal nature as to justify the description of Act of God.' O'Hanlon J noted that some of the expert witnesses had indicated that such events might be expected to recur on a twenty-year cycle and other expert evidence had indicated clearly that 'it was a wise precaution when developing a building site not to leave the entire sewage and draining system wide open to the ingress of stormwaters at any time.'

No reference was made in the judgment to the House of Lords decision of *Cambridge Water Co. Ltd v Eastern Counties Leather plc* [1994] 2 AC 264, which holds that foreseeability of damage of the type that occurred is a prerequisite of liability under the rule in *Rylands v Fletcher*. This would not have assisted the defendants in the instant case, since the damage was undoubtedly of a type that was foreseeable, the debate relating rather to the likelihood of its occurence.

In *Iarnród Éireann/Irish Rail v Ireland* [1995] 2 ILRM 161, at 203, Keane J, in wide-ranging examination of the historical development of tort law, leading ultimately to a consideration of the constitutional validity of the provisions in the Civil Liability Act 1961 relating to contribution and indemnity, had this to say about the tort system which was retained after the promulgation of the Constitution:

> [It] allowed for liability where it could not be said that the injury or damage had been the result of any blameworthy conduct, let alone intentional wrongdoing. The rule in *Rylands v Fletcher*, the doctrine of vicarious liability and the law as to animals *ferae naturae* are obvious examples. But its characteristic manifestation, most clearly demon-

strated in the ever-developing tort of negligence, was the action based on fault.

It is interesting to consider this description of the rule in *Rylands v Fletcher* in the light of developments in other common law jurisdictions in 1994, not just in the *Cambridge Water Company* case but also in the decision of the High Court of Australia in *Burnie Port Authority v General Jones Pty* (1994) 120 ALR 42. For analysis of these cases, see Heuston, (1994) 110 *LQ Rev* 185, Heuston & Buckley (1994), 110 *LQ Rev* 506, Wilkinson (1994) 57 *Modern L Rev* 799, Weir [1994] *Camb LJ* 216, Dziobon & Mullander [1995] *Camb LJ* 23.

WRONGFUL INTERFERENCE WITH CHATTELS

Conversion   Sir John Salmond observed over ninety years ago that the law relating to wrongful interference with chattels was:

> a region still darkened with the mists of legal formalism, through which no man will find his way by the light of nature or with any other guide save the old learning of writs and forms of action and the mysteries of pleading: 'Observations on Trover and Conversion' (1905) 21 *LQ Rev* 43, at 43.

In *Hanley v ICC Finance Ltd* [1996] 1 ILRM 463, analysed by Eoin O'Dell, 'Restitution Law Review' (forthcoming). Kinlen J called for legislative clarification. The facts were relatively straightforward. The defendant finance company had seized a car which the plaintiff had bought from a motor sales company which had gone into liquidation subsequent to the purchase. The motor sales company had had no legal title to the car, which was the defendant's at the time of the sale but, by virtue of s. 25 of the Sale of Goods Act 1893 and s. 2(1) of the Factors Act 1889, the plaintiff had acquired a good title to it. Judge Lynch so held in the Circuit Court and Kinlen J, on appeal, agreed.

The plaintiff had sought a mandatory injunction directing the defendant to deliver up possession of the vehicle to him, as well as somewhat baldly making a claim for 'damages', without indicating whether it rested on negligence, conversion or detinue. In view of the assertion in the plaintiff's endorsement of claim that the defendant had converted the vehicle to its own use, Kinlen J considered that the case should be decided on the basis solely of a claim for conversion.

Judge Lynch had ordered the return of the car to the plaintiff. In relation to the issue of damages, a separate action by the plaintiff for defamation arising from the seizure of the car (near his place of work, the Embassy of the United States of America) was settled in terms that included the issue of damages arising in the instant case. Kinlen J's observations on this issue are nonetheless worth recording. He was impressed by Denning's LJ's ruminations in *Strand Electric Co. v Brisford Entertainments* [1952] 2 QB 246, at 255 that the action for conversion resembles one for restitution rather than tort because the defendant has had the benefit of the goods. Kinlen J interpreted Denning LJ's remarks as 'subsuming th[e] two distinctive torts [of detinue and conversion] into a claim for restitution. Kinlen J found such a proposition:

> very attractive. It seems to me that the trial judge should look at all aspects of the case and decide the relevant periods and nature of damage having regard to all the particular circumstances of each individual case. The matter should be clarified by statute.

When it comes to formulating such a statute, we would do better than to adopt thoughtlessly Britain's Torts (Interference with Goods) Act 1977 which, while abolishing detinue, 'is only a piecemeal attempt to deal with certain deficiencies in the common law and is in no way a code governing interference with goods': *Winfield & Jolowicz on Tort* (14th ed., by W.V.H. Rogers, 1994), 485.

Eoin O'Dell (*op. cit.*) submits that Kinlen J's *dictum* 'should be read only as endorsing the availability of a claim for damages in the restitution measure . . . for the tort of conversion, but should not be seen as precluding a claim for damages in the compensation measure . . . for the tort of conversion where that is appropriate'. This is surely correct. One of the attractions of the torts of detinue and conversion is the breadth of the available remedies. A restitutionary entitlement should supplement, rather than replace, this range of options.'

In *Shield Life Insurance Co. Ltd v. Ulster Bank Ltd*, High Court, December 5, 1995, Costello J held the defendant bank liable for having converted a cheque for £30,000 of which the plaintiffs were payees, which an insurance broker who was a fraudster had lodged in a branch of the bank for collection, having either endorsed the cheque himself or having had it endorsed on his direction, in an ambiguous fashion which could have been an endorsement executed by him, as broker, on behalf of the payee or an endorsement by him, as broker, claiming to be its holder in favour of the bank. The broker asked the bank to pay the proceeds of the cheque into his client's account and to transfer £5,000 to his office account. His office account had been continuously overdrawn for the previous fifteen months and the bank had refused to honour a number of cheques.

S. 4 of the Cheques Act 1959 gives a substantial element of protection to collecting banks, provided they have acted 'in good faith and without negligence'. In *Harfani & Co. Ltd v. Midland Bank Ltd* [1968] 2 All ER 573, at [579], Diplock LJ observed in respect of s. 4 of England's Cheques Act 1957 (which was the model for the Irish provision) that '[t]he only respect in which this substituted statutory duty differs from a common law cause of action in negligence is that, since it takes the form of a qualified immunity from a strict liability at common law, the onus of showing that he did take such reasonable care lies on the defendant banker'.

In the instant case, Costello P stated that the plaintiffs were entitled to damages for conversion unless the defendants could establish that they had failed to take reasonable care that their customer's title to the cheque was not defective. What facts were sufficient to cause a bank reasonably to suspect that its customer was not the true owner of the cheque depended on current banking practice. All the circumstances surrounding the transaction might be relevant.

S. 4(3) of the 1959 Act made it clear that a banker was not to be treated as having been negligent by reason only of his failure to concern himself with an irregularity in the indorsement of a cheque but, if there were other circumstances either antecedent to the transaction in suit or part of that transaction which, taken in conjunction with the irregularity of the indorsement and the failure of the banker to concern himself with the irregularity, these might be considered by the court in considering whether the banker had been guilty of breach of duty to the cheque's true owner.

Costello J observed:

> Each case must ultimately depend on its own facts. But there may be special circumstances in a case which affect the banker's duty of care to which the banker should pay particular regard. Those special circumstances may include, as in this case, a situation in which a customer maintains two accounts, an office account and a clients' account, and in which it is clear that the customer is holding money in an account as a trustee. Previous movements in and out of that account by the customer which may suggest that it is not being operated in a manner consistent with the customer's duty as a trustee may be relevant in considering the bank's duty in relation to the payment into a client's account of a cheque which has been irregularly indorsed.

In the instant case the endorsement was ambiguous. The bank could have inferred from the fact that the broker asked the bank to pay the proceeds of the cheque into his client's account that the proceeds did not belong to him.

The broker's instruction to the bank to transfer £5,000 to his office account amounted to an instruction to pay to himself a substantial sum out of the proceeds of a cheque which the payee had not endorsed. Bearing in mind the inference as to the possible impropriety of the transfers from the customer to the client's account, the nature of the irregularity of the endorsement and the circumstances surrounding its lodgment, Costello J came to the conclusion that a prudent banker would have made enquiries about the cheque before accepting it for collection. The bank had been negligent in the manner it discharged its duty to the plaintiffs and the plaintiffs' claim for damages for conversion had to succeed.

Trespass to goods   Irish courts in recent years have contributed much to the development of the law of negligence but relatively little to the law of trespass. This is in contrast with the position in other common law jurisdictions, where the law of trespass, whether to the person, goods or lands, is gradually, albeit with some resistance, giving way to a generic tort of intentional wrongdoing.

The traditional two hallmarks of the action for trespass are the requirement of proof of directness between the defendant's act and the contact with the plaintiff's person, goods or land, and the absence of any requirement for the plaintiff to establish intention or negligence on the part of the defendant. As to the second of these, originally the tort had at least the appearance of strict liability but over the centuries courts came to acknowledge that a defendant who could establish the absence of any intentional or negligent wrongdoing on his or her part should be entitled to avoid liability.

This is as far as the Irish courts have so far gone. Courts in England (*Fowler v Lanning* [1959] 1 QB 426, *Letang v Cooper* [1965] 1 QB 232, *Wilson v Pringle* [1987] QB 237), New Zealand (*Beals v Hayward* [1960] NZ LR 131) and in some Canadian provinces have taken the further step of abolishing the concept of negligent trespass and of requiring the plaintiff to plead and prove all the ingredients of a negligence action in such a case. Courts in the United States have shifted the onus of proof onto the plaintiff even where the defendant has acted intentionally.

The requirement of directness has proven more difficult to dislodge though there is now evidence that the courts may be willing to interpret it more broadly than formerly. Thus in *Farrell v Minister for Agriculture and Food*, High Court, October 11, 1995, Carroll J held that there had been a direct interference with the plaintiff's right to possession of his cattle when the Minister, 'with the mantle of statutory regulations assumed to be valid around him', constrained the plaintiff to bring his herd to be slaughtered purportedly in compliance with the provisions of the Diseases of Animals Act 1966. Carroll J observed:

The Minister did it knowingly and intended the consequences, though he did not act [with] *mala fides* because he did not know the Regulations were *ultra vires*. To my mind that is a direct interference with the plaintiff's right to possession of his animals and therefore the tort of trespass to chattels was committed. . . .

We consider the issue regarding the legality of the regulations in the Agriculture Chapter, above, 7. In the present it seems clear that Carroll J had no great enthusiasm for a narrow interpretation of the requirement of direct interference. She responded to the invocation by counsel for the Minister of Blayney J's decision in *McDonagh v West of Ireland Fisheries Ltd*, High Court, December 19, 1986, where the directness requirement had not been fulfilled, by referring to McMahon & Binchy's statement (*op. cit.*, 523-3) that the law relating to wrongful interference with chattels lacks clarity and consistency and that it is not easy to say where the line is to be drawn between direct and indirect interference.

In the context of trespass to goods, it is hard to see why an intentional interference with another's goods which falls short of conversion and is not detinue should remain uncompensated by reason solely of the fact that the wrongdoer accomplished the purpose by indirect means. In the instant case there is a credible argument that there was a direct interference even though neither the Minister nor any of his agents laid a hand on any of the plaintiff's beasts. If I by waving a gun at you force you to drive your cattle over a cliff, I can not credibly argue that my interference was not direct, any more than could the malefactor in *Scott v Shepherd* (1773) 2 W Bl 829, 96 ER 525.

PASSING OFF

In *Mitchelstown Co-Operative Agricultural Society Ltd v Goldenvale Food Products Ltd*, High Court, December 12, 1985, Costello J regarded it as 'axiomatic' that in most passing off actions damages would be an inadequate remedy for a successful plaintiff. Thus, plaintiffs who establish a serious question to be tried will normally expect that an interlocutory injunction application will go their way.

B. & S. Ltd v Irish Auto Trader Ltd [1995] 2 ILRM 152 is what McCracken J described as 'one of these unusual cases where the balance of convenience lies in favour of refusing an interlocutory injunction, notwithstanding the fact that this is altering the *status quo*'. The plaintiff published a magazine entitled 'Buy and Sell', which consisted of advertisements placed by persons wishing to buy anything 'from a bantam hen to a wedding dress'. Advertisements relating to motor vehicles and accessories were a very important part of the business. Since December 1993 the section of the magazine dealing with motor vehicles was headed 'Autotrader' at the top of each page. The cover page, from February 1994, was headed 'Buy and Sell Ireland's Free Ads Paper' and carried the words 'including Autotrader'. From February 1995, the back page was used to promote 'Autotrader'.

The defendant had published a magazine in Britain since 1985 under the title 'Auto Trader'. In late 1994 its Scottish edition was put on sale in Northern Ireland and in February 1995 it launched an Irish edition; on its front page it stated: 'Ireland's Own Auto Trader Serving Northern Ireland and the Republic.'

The plaintiff sought an interlocutory injunction against passing off. In McCracken J's view, it established a serious issue to be tried, on the basis of Lord Diplock's identification of the characteristics of passing off in *Erven Warnink BV v J. Townsend and Sons (Hull) Ltd* [1979] AC 731, at 742.

On the issue of the balance of convenience, McCracken J concluded that this lay against granting an injunction. The defendant had clearly acted in a totally *bona fide* manner, and had not chosen its name with a view to taking advantage of the plaintiff's business, but simply as an extension of its own business. The possible loss to the defendant would considerably exceed the possible loss to the plaintiff. It would clearly be quite unrealistic for the defendant to produce a magazine with a different name for the Republic of Ireland, and it was 'almost equally unrealistic' to expect it to produce a magazine for the whole of Ireland under a different name from that used by it in Britain. It was highly unlikely that any traders would be confused. Finally, in the short term it was quite clear that the defendant's magazine was largely going to be based in Northern Ireland and, while purchasers might buy the magazine believing it to be the plaintiff's magazine, the probability was that they would make this mistake only once, as they would very quickly find out it was not the same magazine.

In *Private Research Ltd v Brosnan and Network Financial Services Ltd*, High Court, June 1, 1995, the plaintiff company, which produced a monthly publication containing financial information about certain Irish companies, sought an interlocutory injunction to prevent breach of copyright, passing off and misuse of confidential information allegedly resulting from the defendants' proposed publication, which would operate from a different office in the same building and was intended to produce similar information to that produced in the plaintiff's publication. The first defendant had worked as marketing manager for over two years with the plaintiff but had resigned and shortly afterwards, with others, established the second defendant, aimed at the same market. A point of difference was that, unlike the plaintiff, it intended to provide on-line computer services.

On the issue of passing off, McCracken J noted that the defendants' proposed publication bore 'no resemblance whatever' to that of the plaintiff and that the circular sent out by the defendants had been clearly headed with the name of the second defendant, which could not be confused with that of the plaintiff. Notwithstanding this, there was evidence of some incidents of confusion, probably generated in part by the fact that the defendants operated from the same address as the plaintiff. Nevertheless, isolated incidents of confusion would not in themselves amount to passing off, as the essence of the action was that there had to be a misrepresentation which would lead a third party to believe that the defendant's business was that of the plaintiff. In the circumstances, McCracken J did not think that there was a serious issue as to whether the defendants were passing off. The defendants were carrying on business in quite a distinctive manner and any confusion which might have occurred would be 'very short-lived' because it would quickly have become known that the first defendant was no longer connected with the plaintiff.

On the issues of breach of copyright and breach of confidential information, McCracken J held that the plaintiff had established a statable case but that the balance of convenience lay against granting an injunction.

EURO-TORT

In the Chapter on Limitation of Actions, above 363-5, we discuss *Tate v Minister for Social Welfare* [1995] 1 ILRM 507, where Carroll J held that the plaintiffs' claims for damages resulting from the State's failure to implement Directive 79/7/EEC, which established the principle of equal treatment between men and women as regards social security, should be characterised as a tort, to which the Statute of Limitations 1957 applied. Here we seek to analyse the process by which Carroll J reached her conclusion.

Carroll J accepted that the Supreme Court in *Conway v Irish National Teachers' Organisation* [1991] 1 IR 305, at 316 and *Hanrahan v Merck Sharp & Dohme (Ireland) Ltd* [1988] ILRM 629, at 636 had made a distinction between torts and breaches of constitutional rights. Counsel for the plaintiffs was, moreover, correct in saying that tort and the action for breach of a duty imposed by the European law were two distinct causes of action but, in a crucial passage, Carroll J stated that she did:

> not agree that the relief sought is a separate question. I think the relief sought indicates which cause of action is being pursued.

A cause of action based on direct effect entitled the victims of discrimination to sue for the entitlement that was being withheld. If this were the cause of action being pursued, the plaintiffs would have to claim the actual benefits awarded by the social welfare code to men in a similar situation on the basis that the same rules should be applied to them. Since limitation of actions was a rule that applied to men where a cause of action arose more than six years previously, then, '[o]n the basis that what is sauce for the gander is sauce for the goose', the same rule should have to apply to women making this type of claim.

In the instant case, however, the plaintiffs' claim was for damages rather than for an account; their cause of action was based, not on direct effect, but on the State's failure to implement the directive. Carroll J did not accept that the State's failure was a breach of statutory duty:

> It is . . . a wrong arising from community law which has domestic effect and approximates to a breach of constitutional duty. While the Supreme Court did speak separately of torts and breach of constitutional rights in *Conway v INTO*, it was not in the context of the Statute of Limitations. I would be surprised if there was no limitation period affecting breach of constitutional rights. Just as the word 'tort' in the Statute of Limitations is sufficiently wide to embrace breach of statutory duty even though not specifically mentioned, so also, in my opinion, the word 'tort' is sufficiently wide to cover breaches of obligations of the State under community law. There is nothing strange in describing the State's failure to fulfil its obligations under the Treaty as a tort.

> Therefore I am satisfied that s. 11(2) of the Statute of Limitations does apply to a breach of obligation to observe a community law. This also means that the plea of laches is no longer relevant.

Carroll J's conclusion that it was best to characterise the State's conduct as tortious was no doubt a sensible one since tort law seems well capable of adapting itself to new State liabilities under European law. For example, the Liability for Defective Products Act 1991, belatedly implementing the European Product Liability Directive, in s. 2(1) characterises liability thereunder as tortious: see the 1991 Review, 421. One may, however, wonder whether there should be an inexorable tortious characterisation of every violation by the State of a duty arising under European law. Some duties are of a public nature which does not easily translate into a private right of action. That is why the courts make precisely this distinction in their assessment of whether there should be a civil right of action for breach of statutory duty: se McMahon & Binchy, *op. cit.*, 377-80. There are, moreover, situations where courts consider it preferable not to impose a duty of care in negligence, even though there may have been wrongdoing by public agencies. Thus, for example, the House of Lords has thought it inappropriate to impose an enforceable duty of care on police officers in the detection of crime: *Hill v Chief Constable of West Yorkshire* [1989] AC 53.

If a European directive imposes an obligation on member states to investigate drugs offences or terrorist offences, for example, and one member state fails to implement the directive effectively, with the result that a particular citizen of that state is injured, Carroll J's judgment in *Tate* would appear to imply that there should be a remedy in damages, since the state will be guilty of an innominate tort, without the restrictions that apply to the torts of negligence or breach of statutory duty. It may well be the position, of course, that a court in such a new case would engraft qualifications onto the Euro-tort, reflecting the public policy considerations that underlie the limitations to the torts of negligence and breach of statutory duty.

UNINCORPORATED ASSOCIATIONS

The strict rule that members of unincorporated associations, such as clubs, may not sue their association in tort because this would involve them, in effect, in suing themselves was applied in *Murphy v Roche (No. 2)* [1987] IR 656: see the 1987 Review, 337. In *Kirwan v Mackey*, High Court, January 18, 1995, Carney J invoked the *Murphy* decision when holding, as a preliminary issue, that the plaintiff's claim for negligence against the officer board of a gun club of which he was a member was not maintainable in law against it. The plaintiff, a member of the club, had been injured in the eye by a pellet fired by a former member. He sued the officers, committee and trustees of the gun club, alleging that the former member's membership had lapsed and that accordingly he was not insured or indemnified by the game hunting compensation fund of the National Association of Regional Game Councils.

In holding that the proceedings were not maintainable against the officer board of the club, Carney J ventured to state that he did not accept that there had been a duty resting on it to notify the plaintiff as to whose membership was live and whose had lapsed 'and that a failure to so notify him could make the officer board of the club liable to the plaintiff in damages'. If this holding goes no further than articulating the general proposition that a member of the club may not sue the officers of the club in their representative capacity and that accordingly no duty has been breached, it is unexceptionable. If, however, Carney J was addressing a wider duty issue, centred in the scope of the duty of care under the 'neighbour' principle articulated by Lord Atkin in *Donoghue v Stevenson* [1932] AC 562, at 580, then he was touching on some large policy issues similar to those that have come before Irish and English courts in recent years. Thus, for example, in *Sweeney v Duggan* [1991] 2 IR

274, which we analysed in the 1991 Review 386-7, Barron J rejected the argument that an employer of people working in a quarry had a duty of care to the employees to secure a policy of liability insurance and in *Van Oppen v Trustees of the Bedford Charity* [1989] 3 All ER 389, the English Court of Appeal held that a school was not under a duty to take out personal accident insurance for pupils playing rugby or to advise their parents that it had not done so.

CONTRIBUTION AND INDEMNITY

In *Iarnród Éireann/Irish Rail v Ireland* [1995] 2 ILRM 161, Keane J upheld the constitutional validity of ss. 12 and 14 of the Civil Liability Act 1961, which enable a plaintiff to enforce a judgment against any concurrent wrongdoer, regardless of the proportion of fault of that wrongdoer, leaving him or her with the theoretical possibility of seeking from an impecunious concurrent wrongdoer the share of the impecunious wrongdoer, which may, of course, be of a significantly higher proportion than that of the pecunious wrongdoer against whom judgment in full has been executed.

The pith of Keane J's judgment is in the following passage:

> If the arguments of [those challenging the constitutional validity of ss. 12 and 14] are well-founded, it means that the defendant whose conduct has been blameworthy in this sense will escape liability for a significant part of the damage which he has brought about, solely because another person was also to blame and is impecunious. The effect of the Constitution will thus have been to exonerate to that extent the blameworthy at the expense of the blameless. I am satisfied that it cannot have been the intention of the framers of the Constitution, in providing protection for the property rights of the citizen, that the Constitution should be the source of a significantly greater injustice than is involved in the abridgment of those rights which was the necessary consequence of a civilised and humane system of tortious liability.

The Supreme Court affirmed Keane J: [1996] 2 ILRM 500. We shall examine the Supreme Court appeal in the 1996 Review. We need note here merely that Keane J's judgment ranges widely over several of the central features of tort law, in a way that is unusual in the Irish courts. Since his elevation to the Supreme Court, Keane J has shown a continuing willingness to develop the analytic framework of Irish tort law. This is apparent in such decisions as *Convery v Dublin County Council*, Supreme Court, November 12, 1996 and *O'Shea v Tilman Anhold and the Horse Holiday Farm Ltd*, Supreme Court, October 23, 1996.

DAMAGES

Pain and Suffering   The problems that may result for plaintiffs in waiting for the final outcome of personal injuries litigation were mentioned by O'Hanlon J in *Behan v Brinks Allied Ltd*, High Court, February 23, 1995. In both *Behan* and in a related case, *McKinney v Brinks Allied Ltd*, High Court, February 23, 1995, O'Hanlon J awarded the fairly modest sum of £12,000 for general damages. He thought that the plaintiffs had become 'somewhat preoccupied with their claims for damages, which were launched not long after the occurrence of the accident and in which they seemed certain to receive an award of damages'. O'Hanlon J thought it was this circumstance that prevented each of the plaintiffs from shaking off the effects of their injuries.

In *Russell v Dublin Corporation*, High Court, July 11, 1995, the plaintiff had been the victim of seven accidents, two of which occurred in the employment of the defendant. He suffered neck and back injuries. Kinlen J awarded £3,000 damages for pain and suffering in respect of the first accident and £9,000 damages for pain and suffering in respect of the second. He considered that the plaintiff 'ha[d] been, to put it mildly, exaggerating his claim' in regard to the first accident. Kinlen J added that, '[i]n reality, he may have got his various accidents mixed in his mind'.

Loss of Income   In *Smith v Rhone Poulenc Ireland Ltd*, High Court, January 11, 1995, the plaintiff, the sole operator of a beautician's salon, was injured in a traffic accident caused by the defendant when the plaintiff was 27 years old. She was totally disabled from gainful employment. Flood J awarded her compensation on the basis that she would have retired at the age of sixty five. Taking into account the principles articulated in *Reddy v Bates* [1984] ILRM 197 (discussed in McMahon & Binchy, *op. cit.*, 784-5) and assuming that there were a number of variables which could affect her future income, Flood J thought it not unreasonable to discount the sum awarded by 25%. He identified these variables as:

ill-health, changes in fashion, competition from more luxurious establishments, cyclical depression in the economy and other factors which affect luxury trades such as beauticians. . . .

Transport

AIR TRANSPORT

Chicago Convention   The Irish Aviation Authority Act 1993 (Amendment Of Schedule) Order 1995 (SI No. 171 of 1995), made under the Irish Aviation Authority Act 1993 (1993 Review, 584), provides that the Minister for Transport, Energy and Communications is to be the authority for exercising powers under Annex 12 of the Chicago Convention, other than powers relating to Rescue Co-ordination Centres and Sub-Centres, in this State. The Order came into effect on July 28, 1995.

Designated areas: Defence Forces   The Air Navigation (Designated Areas) Order 1995 (SI No. 170 of 1995), made under the Irish Aviation Authority Act 1993 (1993 Review, 584), designated certain additional areas of airspace for use by the Defence Forces, with effect from September 14, 1995.

Licence fees   The Air Navigation (Fees) Order 1995 (SI No. 74 of 1995), made under the Irish Aviation Authority Act 1993 revoked and replaced the Air Navigation (Fees) Order 1990 (1990 Review, 585) and gave effect to increases in fees for aeronautical licences, certificates and permits and provided for the introduction of new fees with effect from March 31, 1995.

Pilot licensing   The Air Navigation (Personnel Licensing) (Amendment) Order 1995 (SI No. 222 of 1995) was made under the Irish Aviation Authority Act 1993. It removes the aircraft weight limitations from the pilot in command, the privileges of Airline Transport Pilot licences for licence holders over 60 years of age and restricts the exercise of all professional pilot privileges to pilots under 65 years of age. Where a public transport aircraft is operated outside Irish airspace, the holder of a professional pilot licence over the age of 60 years may act as a member of a multi-pilot crew provided that such holder is the only pilot in the flight crew who has attained the age of 60 years. Where a public transport aircraft is operated solely within Irish airspace, the holder of a professional pilot licence up to the age of 65 years may act as pilot in command. The 1995 Order came into force on August 25, 1995.

MERCHANT SHIPPING

As in previous Reviews, we note a number of Regulations which give effect to amendments to the 1974 IMO Convention for the Safety of Lives at Sea (SOLAS). The essential requirements of SOLAS were incorporated into Irish law by the Merchant Shipping Act 1981 and many Regulations have been made since 1981 to give effect to detailed requirements of, and amendments to, SOLAS. S.3 of the 1981 Act also empowers the Minister for the Marine to amend any provision of the Merchant Shipping Acts 1894 to 1994 in order to give effect to SOLAS requirements.

Certification of officers and shipping operations The Merchant Shipping (Recognition of British Certificates of Competency) Order 1995 (SI No. 228 of 1995) provides for the recognition of British certificates of competency for the categories listed therein, with effect from August 25, 1995.

Dangerous or polluting goods The European Communities (Minimum Requirements For Vessels Carrying Dangerous Or Polluting Goods) Regulations 1995 (SI No. 229 of 1995) gave effect to Directive 93/75/EEC. They set out additional requirements for vessels carrying dangerous or polluting goods to or from Community ports, designate Competent Authorities to be notified of intended arrivals and/or departures of vessels carrying dangerous goods and provided with certain information concerning such goods. They also provide for the collation and dissemination of information on the movement of dangerous or polluting goods and incidents involving such goods. The Regulations came into effect on September 13, 1995.

Light dues The Merchant Shipping (Light Dues) Order 1995 (SI No. 71 of 1995), made under the Merchant Shipping (Light Dues) Act 1983, removed the surcharge applicable to passenger (Ro-Ro) ferries in respect of vessels which hold a valid International Tonnage Certificate. The Order came into effect on April 1, 1995.

Maritime casualty: State liability In *ACT Shipping (PTE) Ltd v Minister for the Marine and Ors; The MV 'Toledo'* [1995] 2 ILRM 30 Barr J considered the issue of State liability for maritime casualties against the following background. In February 1990 the hull of the MV 'Toledo' had been damaged at sea en route from Canada to Denmark. The captain altered course for Bantry Bay, Cork, the nearest anchorage of refuge. At a point 270 miles south west of Bantry, the captain decided that the condition of the vessel constituted an unreasonable risk to the lives of the crew and they were airlifted to safety. On the following day the ship was abandoned. On receiving a 'mayday' signal the Irish State's naval vessel LE 'Deirdre' put to sea. Having inspected the casualty, it appeared clear that the vessel was at risk of sinking. On the advice of the Deputy Chief Surveyor in the Department of the Marine it was decided that the vessel should not be allowed to enter Irish territorial waters. The ship's owners arranged for a salvage tug, owned and operated by the plaintiff company, to tow the vessel to Falmouth, England. Soon after towing commenced the Minister informed the plaintiff company not to enter Irish territorial waters. Shortly after this, the vessel began to sink and was eventually beached at a beach three miles from Falmouth. The ship's cargo was discharged but the vessel was later declared to be a constructive total loss and was scuttled in deep water. The plaintiff instituted these proceedings claiming that the vessel had become a 'maritime casualty' within the meaning of the Oil Pollution of the Sea (Amendment) Act 1977 and claimed damages from the defendants, representing the State, arising from the Minister's refusal to allow the vessel to enter Irish waters and obtain safe anchorage. Barr J dismissed the claim.

He accepted that customary international law recognises that foreign vessels in serious distress have a *prima facie* right to the benefit of a port or anchorage of refuge in the nearest maritime State with available facilities. Citing the leading decision of the Supreme Court in *In re Ó Laighéis* [1960] IR 93, Barr J also accepted that Article 15.2 of the Constitution of Ireland 1937 does not inhibit the use of the principles of international customary law in Irish domestic law, provided that they are not contrary to the provisions of the Constitution, statute law or the common law. In this respect, he concluded that the international custom in maritime law that a ship in distress is entitled to safe refuge was so long established that it must be deemed to have been absorbed into Irish domestic law before the enactment of the Constitution.

However, Barr J went on to point out that the right of a foreign vessel to seek safe refuge in the waters of a foreign state was not an absolute right. If safety of life was not a factor, he considered that the State may lawfully refuse refuge if there were reasonable grounds for believing that there was a significant risk of substantial harm to the State or its citizens. On this basis, he held that the Minister had a right as a matter of customary international law to refuse on reasonable grounds a haven of refuge to a foreign ship which was in serious distress.

Barr J then turned to what was, in effect, an issue of administrative law, that is, whether the Minister had acted reasonably in the circumstances which had arisen. He adopted the well established 'hands-off' approach of the courts in such instances, as evidenced by the Supreme Court decisions which he cited in support, *The State (Keegan) v Stardust Victims Compensation Tribunal* [1986] IR 642, and *O'Keeffe v An Bord Pleanála* [1993] 1 IR 39;

[1992] ILRM 237 (1991 Review, 17-19). He stated that the courts should be loath to interfere with what appeared to be an *intra vires* administrative decision on the merits, particularly where, as here, the decision maker is acting within his own area of professional expertise and a court should only interfere with the decision if it is established that it flies in the face of reason and common sense. In the instant case, he held that the advice to the Minister was not at variance with reason and common sense and the plaintiff thus had no claim against the Minister arising out of his refusal to allow the MV 'Toledo' to enter Irish waters.

As to the relevance or otherwise of the Oil Pollution of the Sea (Amendment) Act 1977, Barr J noted that the Minister had no power under the 1977 Act to direct that a casualty should not enter Irish territorial waters. Since in the instance case, the Minister had not purported to give any such direction, Barr J conclude that the Act was irrelevant to the circumstances of the case. We may note here that the 1977 Act had since been replaced by the Sea Pollution Act 1991: see the 1991 Review, 366.

Ro-Ro passenger ships: survivability: EEA States The Merchant Shipping (Ro-Ro Passenger Ship Survivability) (Amendment) Rules 1995 (SI No. 40 of 1995) extended to the States of the European Economic Area (EEA) the requirements of Reg.7 of the Merchant Shipping (Ro-Ro Passenger Ship Survivability) Rules 1994 (1994 Review, 468) with effect from February 14, 1995.

ROAD TRAFFIC

Road Traffic Act 1995 The Road Traffic Act 1995 replaced the disqualification penalties introduced by the Road Traffic Act 1994 (1994 Review, 468) for convictions under the Road Traffic Act 1961. 'Sliding scale' periods of consequential disqualification arising from convictions for drink driving offences under the 1961 Act were provided for, dependent on the level of alcohol in blood or urine samples of drivers. These replaced the controversial 'flat scale' disqualifications under the 1994 Act. However, the reduction in the 1994 Act of the permitted level of alcohol remained in place, in spite of considerable agitation that it too be increased to the previous level. The requirement in the 1994 Act that a driving test be taken by a person convicted under the 1961 Act was restricted by the 1995 Act to convictions under ss. 53 and 106 of the 1961 Act, which concern dangerous driving causing death and leaving the scene of an accident involving personal injury ('hit and run'). S. 3 of the 1995 Act contained transitional provisions for persons convicted of relevant offences between the date of the coming into force of the Road

Traffic Act 1994 and the coming into force of the 1995 Act, whereby they may apply to the court which imposed a disqualification order for a review of that order. The 1995 Act came into effect on May 25, 1995.

Compulsory insurance The European Communities (Road Traffic) (Compulsory Insurance) (Amendment) Regulations 1995 (SI No. 353 of 1995) gave further effect to Directives 72/166/EEC, 84/5/EEC and 90/232/EEC. They increased the statutory minimum coverage for property damage arising out of one accident to £90,000 and revise the geographic coverage of motor insurance policies to take account of the new members of the European Union. They came into effect on January 1, 1996.

Construction Standards The European Communities (Motor Vehicles Type Approval) (Amendment) Regulations 1995 (SI No. 151 of 1995), which came into effect on June 14, 1995, further amended the European Communities (Motor Vehicles Type Approval) Regulations 1978 to take account of a number of Directives, all of which lay down technical specifications for the construction of motor vehicles. The 1995 Regulations now contain the most updated listing of the Directives to which manufacturers must comply. The result is that the list of Directives in the European Communities (Motor Vehicles Type Approval) (Amendment) Regulations 1994 (1994 Review, 469) became obsolete.

Declaration and designation of public roads The Roads Act 1993 (Declaration of National Roads) Order 1995 (SI No. 49 of 1995) declared a proposed Dublin Northern Port Access Route as a national primary. See generally the Roads Act 1993 (Declaration of National Roads) Order 1994 (1994 Review, 470).

Detention of vehicles The Road Traffic Act 1994 (Section 41) Regulations 1995 (SI No. 89 of 1995), give effect to s. 41 of the Road Traffic Act 1994 and describe the procedures governing the detention, removal, storage and subsequent release or disposal of vehicles detained under s. 41 of the 1994 Act, and came into effect on April 19, 1995.

Emission levels The European Communities (Mechanically Propelled Vehicle Emission Control) Regulations 1995 (SI No. 192 of 1995) prohibit the issue of first licences for certain new vehicles from January 1, 1997, unless they comply with the air pollutant emission control requirements specified in Directives 93/81/EEC and 94/12/EC. Certain limited exemptions are specified for end of series vehicles as well as penalties for non-compliance. The Regulations came into effect on September 1, 1995. The European

Communities (Mechanically Propelled Vehicle Emission Control) (Amendment) Regulations 1995 (SI No. 334 of 1995) give effect to further controls required under Directive 94/12/EC with effect from December 7, 1995.

Explosives The Conveyance Of Explosives (Amendment) Byelaws 1995 (SI No. 251 of 1995), made under the Explosives Act 1875, amended the Conveyance of Explosives Byelaws 1955 and provide that the engine of a freight vehicle carrying explosives shall not be run while the doors of the freight compartment are open or during refuelling. They came into effect on October 1, 1995.

International carriage of goods: Austria The Road Transport (International Carriage of Goods by Road) Order 1995 (SI No. 35 of 1995) gave effect to an agreement between the State and Austria authorising the Austrian authorities to issue permits allowing access by Austrian hauliers to the State, with effect from February 7, 1995.

International carriage of goods: Latvia The Road Transport Act 1978 (Section 5) (No. 2) Order 1995 (SI No. 201 of 1995) gave effect to an agreement between the State and Latvia and exempts certain types of road transport operations performed in Ireland by Latvian carriers of passengers and hauliers of goods from the requirements to be authorised by licence or permit, with effect from July 13, 1995.

International carriage of goods and persons: Russian Federation The Road Transport Act 1978 (Section 5) Order 1995 (SI No. 84 of 1995) gave effect to an agreement between the State and the Russian Federation and exempts certain types of road transport operations performed in Ireland by Russian carriers of passengers and freight from the requirements to be authorised by licence or permit, with effect from April 4, 1995. The Road Transport (International Carriage Of Goods By Road) (No. 2) Order 1995 (SI No. 85 of 1995) gave effect to an agreement between the State and the Russian Federation and allows the Russian transport authorities to issue permits on Ireland's behalf for access by Russian hauliers to Ireland, also with effect from April 4, 1995.

Licensing of drivers The Road Traffic (Licensing Of Drivers) (Amendment) Regulations 1995 (SI No. 217 of 1995) revised the arrangements for the fees payable for driving tests, with effect from August 8, 1995.

'On-the-spot' offences The Road Traffic Act 1961 (Section 103) (Offences) Regulations 1995 (SI No. 87 of 1995) list those road traffic offences to which s. 103 of the Road Traffic Act 1961 applies, which provides for 'on-the-spot' fines to be imposed for certain offences, for example parking a vehicle in a prohibited area such as a clearway. The Regulations also prescribe the form of notice to be affixed to vehicles, to be given to persons alleging offences to have been committed and the amount of the 'on-the-spot' fine which a person may pay as an alternative to the institution of a prosecution. The 1995 Regulations, which came into effect on June 1, 1995, revoked and replaced the Road Traffic Act 1961 (Section 103) (Offences) Regulations 1976 to 1990. Similarly, the Local Authorities (Traffic Wardens) Act 1975 (Section 3) (Offences) Regulations 1995 (SI No. 88 of 1995) list those offences to which s. 3 of the Local Authorities (Traffic Wardens) Act 1975 applies and prescribe the form of notice to be affixed to vehicles, to be given to persons alleging offences to have been committed and the amount which a person may pay as an alternative to the institution of a prosecution. These Regulations, which also came into effect on June 1, 1995, revoked and replaced the Local Authorities (Traffic Wardens) Act 1975 (Section 3) (Offences) Regulations 1975 to 1990.

Registration and licensing The Road Vehicles (Registration and Licensing) (Amendment) Regulations 1995 (SI No. 125 of 1995) amended the procedures relating to notification of ownership changes where vehicles registered on or after January 1, 1993 are sold to motor dealers and the issue of Vehicle Licensing Certificates in such cases. The Regulations came into effect on July 1, 1995.

Road freight licences The Road Transport (Road Freight Carrier's Licence Application Form) Regulations 1995 (SI No. 66 of 1995), made pursuant to the Road Transport Act 1933, altered the prescribed form for an application for a road freight carrier's licence. The European Communities (Merchandise Road Transport) (Amendment) Regulations 1995 (SI No. 67 of 1995) amended the format of certain affidavits which must be submitted with an application for a road freight carrier's licence while the European Communities (Road Passenger Transport) (Amendment) Regulations 1995 (SI No. 68 of 1995)amended the format of affidavits which must be submitted with an application for a road transport operator's licence. These three sets of Regulations came into effect on March 24, 1995 and implemented further amendment to Directives 74/561/EEC, 77/796/EEC, 84/647/EEC, 89/438/ EEC and 90/398/EEC.

Taxis and hackneys The Road Traffic (Public Service Vehicles) (Amendment) Regulations 1995 (SI No. 136 of 1995) assigned to local authorities certain powers relating to the licencing, of taxis and hackneys. They empowered local authorities, *inter alia*, to declare areas to be taximeter areas, alter boundaries of taximeter areas, grant and renew taxi licences, wheelchair accessible taxi licences and hackney licences and to determine the number of taxis to be licensed in the area and determine the fare structures applicable. They came into effect on September 1, 1995.

TOUR OPERATORS AND TRAVEL AGENTS

The Tour Operators (Licensing) (Amendment) Regulations 1995 (SI No. 212 of 1995) amended the Tour Operators (Licensing) Regulations 1993 (1993 Review, 593) by revising the fees payable for granting these licences. Similarly, the Travel Agents (Licensing) (Amendment) Regulations 1995 (SI No. 213 of 1995) amended the Travel Agents (Licensing) Regulations 1993 (1993 Review, 593) concerning fees payable for such licences. The 1993 Regulations were made under the Transport (Tour Operators and Travel Agents) Act 1982. On the 1982 Act, see the 1987 Review, 242. See also the Package Holidays and Travel Trade Act 1995, discussed in the Commercial Law chapter, 49-53, above.

Index